CANADA'S WINE COUNTRY COOKBOOK

Shari Darling
&
Michelle Ramsay

Macmillan Canada
Toronto

Canadian Cataloguing in Publication Data

Darling, Shari, date.
    Canada's wine country cookbook

Includes index.
ISBN 0-7715-9195-0

I. Cookery (Wine). I. Ramsay, Michelle, date.
II. Title.

TX726.D37 1993   641.6'22   C93-093000-2

  3 4 5 6 MIL 98 97 96 95

Cover and text design by David Montle

Cover illustration by Linda Montgomery

Interior illustrations by Agnes Aru

Macmillan Canada wishes to thank the Canada Council and the Ontario Ministry of Culture and Communications for supporting its publishing program.

Macmillan Canada
A Division of Canada Publishing Corporation
Toronto, Ontario, Canada

Printed in Canada

CONTENTS

～

*I*NTRODUCTION
ᔊ

*I*N THE PAST TWO DECADES Canadians have become more educated about wine, and the
demand for quality has noticeably increased. In our own search for excellence, we discovered
that fine wines were being produced right here in our own country. Some of the most noble
grape varieties in the world — Chardonnay, Riesling, Gewürztraminer, Pinot Noir and
Cabernet Sauvignon — are flourishing in British Columbia, Ontario, Quebec and Nova Scotia.

And why not? We have the climate. The Niagara Peninsula, at 43° North latitude, is more
southerly than all of the wine areas of France. In British Columbia, the Okanagan Valley is at
the same latitude as the Rhine Valley in Germany and the Champagne region of France.

European grape varieties can thrive in specific viticultural areas of Canada because each
experiences a special microclimate created by the surrounding geological features.

The Niagara Peninsula, for example, is bordered on the north by Lake Ontario and protected on the south by the Niagara Escarpment. Throughout the year the lake moderates the
climate, while the escarpment acts as a natural barrier against continental trade winds. This
cool climate allows grapes to ripen slowly, thus gaining complex chemical compounds and firm
acidity — perfect elements for quality wines with concentrated flavours and good ageing
potential.

British Columbia's Okanagan Valley benefits from mild microclimates as well. Stretching
for 80 miles north to south, Okanagan Lake moderates temperatures throughout the year.
Intense sunlight and minimal rainfall allow grapes to ripen properly, while cool nights help
them retain high acidity. As a result, Okanagan wines are full bodied and highly flavoured,
with good acidity.

Yet there is a lot more to producing quality wine than growing grapes in ideal environmen-
tal conditions. Our winegrowers have spent many years travelling in search of the best grape
clones the world has to offer, while constantly perfecting their vine training and cultivating
methods at home.

Those passionate winemakers have contributed to the quality of Canadian wine by increasing their technical competence and by making huge financial investments in their winemaking

facilities. A few years ago, Château des Charmes, in Niagara-on-the-Lake, made one of the largest purchases of wine barrels in Canadian history. Their 135 oak barrels were hand-crafted from French Allier oak by the firms Radoux and Mercier, two of France's most renowned barrel-makers.

More proof of quality is the VQA label you will find on Ontario and British Columbia wines. The Wine Council of Ontario and the British Columbia Wine Institute explain the system this way: "The Vintners Quality Alliance is an 'Appellation of Origin' system by which consumers can identify wines of Ontario and British Columbia based on the origin of the grapes from which they are produced. The new VQA medallion is awarded to wines of the highest distinction, as selected by a panel of experts.

"With the VQA system, Canada joins other leading wine-producing countries in developing a body of regulations and high standards for its finest wines. In 1935, for example, France introduced its Appellation d'Origine Controllée (AOC) system that remains in effect today. Italy introduced its Denominazione di Origine Controllata e Garantita (DOCG) designation in 1963. Germany's QmP [Qualitätswein mit Prädikat] system was finalized in 1971, and the U.S. system in 1978."

Just how good are Canadian wines? The fact is, our winemakers have been entering their wines in many renowned international wine competitions (such as the annual InterVin and VinExpo) and bringing home gold and silver medals. This is an enormous accomplishment, especially when you consider that some of our European competitors have been producing wine for many generations.

Consequently, it is these fine Canadian wines that are the perfect accompaniment to Canada's multicultural cuisines, which you will find in this cookbook. We have gathered recipes and wine tasting notes from Canada's winemakers, chefs who work at outstanding restaurants that specialize in Canadian cuisines and the most prominent wine authorities in the country. Being passionate about this project, we couldn't help adding a few suggestions of our own.

In most cases, the winemakers' tasting notes recommend a varietal wine. This means that at least 75 per cent of one grape variety was used to produce the wine, thus giving it characteristics typical of that grape variety. For example, even though the Gewürztraminer grape can grow in various climatic and soil conditions and can be vinified in different styles by different winemakers, the wines it produces should share a typical Gewürztraminer character — floral, spicy and exotic aromas and flavours. It is these primary characteristics, along with style, body and texture, that have been considered when marrying wines to specific recipes.

On the recommendation of a few winemakers and chefs, we excluded vintages (years) from the tasting notes; this restricts you less when you are purchasing wine. However, in doing so we had to exclude mentioning the VQA trademark in the tasting notes, since this medallion is awarded to specific vintages. So keep in mind that, although you will not see VQA in the tasting notes, many of the wines mentioned do reach — indeed surpass — VQA status each year.

We have also included tasting notes for a few dessert wines that are not produced every year. If you cannot locate the exact dessert wine mentioned, choose one made by another Canadian producer. You will also find blended wines in the tasting notes. If this blend is not available where you shop, try our suggested varietal wine.

This brings us to another point. Most provincial wines are not available outside their province. Therefore, if you cannot find the wine named in the recipe, ask your wine merchant to recommend a similar varietal. Just make sure it's Canadian.

In closing, we would like to pay tribute to the many Canadian wineries that produce wine from berries, other fruits and honey. Although we did not include these products in the book, they are splendid aperitifs, great companions for dishes containing the same fruit and delicious as dessert wines.

So, plunge into this cookbook. A myriad of mouth-watering recipes awaits your imagination and magic touch.

CHAPTER ONE

THE *Food* AND *Wine* *Marriage*

WINE IS MORE THAN JUST A BEVERAGE. It's a slice of our history and culture, an expression of our hospitality and friendship and a way of celebrating life.

Wine is also becoming a staple in the Canadian meal. In fact, nearly half of Canadian adults drink wine with their meals, according to a national study conducted for the Ontario Wine Marketing Program.

The fact is, however, that more Canadians would marry wine with their meals, if it wasn't for the sometimes intimidating etiquette concerning this union. It can be hard enough to differentiate between vines, grapes and wines, let alone understand what wines work with specific flavours. And worse, wine experts themselves differ in opinion. Some believe there are stringent rules when it comes to combining food and wine; others liberally claim there are no such rules.

Take heart: combining food and wine may seem like an elaborate skill, but it is rather simple if you follow a few general guidelines.

Basically, there is a natural sequence to serving wine with food. Always serve a dry wine before a sweet one, an average vintage before a great one, a white before a red, and a young wine before an aged one. More importantly, a wine should always *complement* the dish, not overpower it.

There are definitely marriages made in heaven, such as the pairing of light-bodied whites with delicate foods (such as oysters and mussels) and full-bodied reds with red meat. Nowadays, however, light-bodied, fruity reds (among them Pinot Noir and Gamay Noir) are being served with seafood and poultry, especially if these dishes have sauces or contain meat. (Light, fruity reds are at their best when slightly chilled; refrigerate for half an hour.)

When choosing a wine to accompany your meal, always consider too the primary spices used to enhance the dish. Cayenne pepper adds considerable spice, while tarragon is herbal and sweet. Here are some safe guidelines.

LOBSTER AND CRAB:
The fattiness of lobster and crab should be matched to full-bodied whites and those with oak

ageing. Sparkling wine is always a safe bet because its fizzle cuts through the fatness in these meats.

DELICATE WHITE MEATS:

Quail, squab and guinea hen, being delicate birds, go well with a delicate red wine like Pinot Noir.

PASTA, RICE AND NOODLE DISHES:

Pair the wine with the sauce. Cream-based sauces require full-bodied whites; tomato-based sauces work with light-bodied, fruity reds.

CHEESE:

Cheese has always raised controversy among food and wine authorities. The distinctive aroma, taste and texture of the cheese must be carefully considered. The safest approach is to match mild cheeses with mild wines and sharp cheeses with heavier wines. An aged Maréchal Foch, with its powerfully earthy aromas, is an ideal companion for old Cheddar and its strong, earthy flavours. By the same token, this red would overpower a milder cheese like Colby.

FOODS TO AVOID:

Taboos do exist in the food and wine union. Many soups and salads, eggs, lemons, artichokes, spinach and asparagus can make a perfectly good bottle of wine taste offensive and vice versa. If you want to serve a wine with salad use a mild vinegar dressing and add substantial elements such as nuts. Marry this salad with a light-bodied white with high acid (for example, Sauvignon Blanc). The acidity in the wine will stand up to the acidity in the vinaigrette. As for eggs and soup — if these dishes are heavy in flavour, you can serve them with wine. Otherwise, accompany them with dry sherry.

DESSERTS:

Desserts are tricky, too. Cream, butter and chocolate are usually enemies of wine. If you minimize these ingredients and use fruit or nuts, or both, you can serve wine with your sweets.

Keep in mind that certain wines *are* dessert. Icewine, an exotic dessert wine made from frozen grapes harvested in below-freezing temperatures, is splendid on its own. Botrytis-affected (B.A.) wines, those made from grapes affected by a fungus called noble rot, are great with desserts and after-dinner cheeses. Riesling B.A. is an example. In addition, ports and sherries have always served as the perfect ending to a delicious meal.

CANADIAN WINE AND FOOD

The chart (on page 6) lists suggestions only. The profile of a wine depends not only on the climate and soil conditions under which the grape variety grows from year to year but also on the winemaker's techniques and style. Therefore, when choosing a wine to accompany a meal — sample before you buy!

Hors d'Oeuvres	sparkling wine, Canadian Champagne
Soup	dry sherry
Vegetarian Dishes	Aligoté, Chasselas, Scheurebe
Salad: VINAIGRETTE	Sauvignon Blanc, very dry acidic Riesling
CREAM DRESSING	Seyval Blanc, Grüner Veltliner, Ehrenfelser
Pasta/Noodles/Rice: CREAM-BASED SAUCE	Chardonnay, Auxerrois, Bacchus, oaky Sauvignon Blanc
TOMATO-BASED SAUCE	Gamay Noir, Pinot Noir, de Chaunac, Chelois
SPICY TOMATO SAUCE	Maréchal Foch
Chicken	Chardonnay, Auxerrois, Bacchus, oaky Sauvignon Blanc
Game Birds	Pinot Noir
Light Meats: VEAL	Gamay Noir, Pinot Noir, de Chaunac, Chelois
PORK	off-dry Gewürztraminer, off-dry Riesling, off-dry Vidal, Ehrenfelser
HAM	Villard Noir, Chancellor, off-dry Chenin Blanc, Rosé
Heavier Meats: BEEF/LAMB/GAME DUCK/GOOSE	Baco Noir, Cabernet Franc, Michurinetz, Merlot, Cabernet Sauvignon, Chancellor, Chambourcin
Fish: GRILLED	Aligoté, Chasselas, Scheurebe, Chardonnay
LEMON SEASONING	Sauvignon Blanc, dry Riesling
CREAM-BASED SAUCE	off-dry Riesling, Ehrenfelser
SMOKED	dry Riesling
Shellfish: LOBSTER/CRAB	Chardonnay, Auxerrois, Bacchus, oaky Sauvignon Blanc, sparkling wine
OYSTERS/MUSSELS	Aligoté, Chasselas, Scheurebe, dry Vidal, Chenin Blanc
SHRIMP/SCALLOPS	Seyval Blanc, Gruner Veltliner, Aurore, dry Gewürztraminer, dry Riesling
Desserts	sparkling wine, Canadian Champagne, port, sherry, Icewine, Riesling B.A., Late harvest wines

CHAPTER TWO

CHEESE & WINE

Perfect Companions

*C*HEESE AND WINE WERE MADE FOR ONE ANOTHER. If you've ever sipped a full-bodied Canadian Cabernet Sauvignon and followed it with a taste of well-aged Canadian Brie, you'll understand why this is a perfect marriage.

There's more to this pairing than taste. Cheese and wine both have strong colour, texture, aroma and taste characteristics, which demand to be considered. For instance, light, fresh cheeses can be overpowered by full-bodied wines, so marry them with light-bodied, delicate whites. A goat's milk cheese is superb with dry, fruity reds. Pair soft, blue cheeses with robust, full-bodied reds or fortified wines such as sherry and port. A word of caution about soft cheeses in ripe crusts (Brie and Camembert): the fullness of these cheeses can easily clash with the fruitiness of a wine. To avoid this problem, serve them with well-balanced, vigorous reds. A soft cheese with a light crust is best with a light, fruity red, while pressed hard cheeses work with a wide range of reds.

The ritual fondue is a wonderful way of combining the pleasures of cheese and wine. In the classic Neuchâtel fondue, Gruyère and Emmenthal cheeses are combined with a dry white wine with some acidity and a hint of Kirsch (cherry brandy). Lemon juice, nutmeg and pepper add extra body to the fondue. Although the Swiss traditionally drink a Neuchâtel wine with the fondue and sip brandy halfway through, the North American way is to have wine throughout the meal. A good choice is a white wine such as Sauvignon Blanc or a light, fruity red like Gamay Beaujolais.

CHEESE AND WINE PRINCIPLES
As applied at *Say Cheese Restaurant* in London, Ontario

BASICS FOR THE BEGINNER:
- Fruity, medium-bodied whites, such as Chardonnay or Riesling, complement most cheeses.
- Light-bodied, fruity reds, such as Pinot Noir, complement most cheeses.

PRINCIPLES FOR THE ADVENTURER:

Although reading will provide you with insight into the principles involved in marrying cheese and wine, experimenting is more enjoyable and educational. Our sense of smell, taste and feel are the best learning tools available. In fact, you'll soon discover that, once you are familiar with the basic characteristics of certain wines and cheeses, choosing a great combination is almost instinctive.

But remember, certain variables play an important and often misunderstood role in our enjoyment and appreciation of cheese and wine.

• Ripeness or freshness of the cheese
As cheese ripens it moves through several stages, from mild to strong or from crumbly to soft and sensuous. One particular cheese may be best paired with a different wine at each stage. So explore and experiment with a cheese and wine.

• Context in which you're eating and drinking
Consider the occasion and the time of day. A slice of Cheddar accompanied by a rich port is an exquisite combination if served after dinner. On a picnic, however, this same marriage is too heavy and therefore unsuitable. A chilled, easy-drinking white is a better choice in this case.

• Your temperament
Your temperament is really the key to your enjoyment of cheese and wine. While you are under stress, your body chemistry will be profoundly different than when you are relaxed and content. Likewise, your appreciation of cheese and wine will be significantly different. For example, while on holiday you might sip a fairly rough wine and nibble a slice of earthy cheese and find the pair utterly magical. Recreate this same marriage at home after a stress-filled day when your gastrointestinal system is aggravated with high acid levels, and what will you discover? Whoops! An estrangement of taste.

Above all, have fun! Cheese and wine were created to please. Besides, you can never be wrong. Combining food and wine is as subjective as enjoying art, music and literature.

Here is a basic guideline for cheese and wine combinations:

PAIRING CANADIAN-MADE CHEESES AND DOMESTIC WINES

CHEESE	WINE
young Brie	Vidal, Scheurebe
aged Brie	Merlot, Cabernet Sauvignon
young Camembert	Vidal, Scheurebe
aged Camembert	Merlot, Cabernet Sauvignon
Double Cream, Triple Cream	Chardonnay
bocconcini, Caciotta, Fior di Latte, mozzarella Scamorza, Suris, Trecce	young Cabernet Franc
Alpine, Burrini, Casata, Havarti, Monterey Jack, Muenster, Saint Paulin, Tomme	Aligoté
cow's milk feta	Vidal, Scheurebe
Limburger	young Cabernet Franc
Oka	young Cabernet Franc
Serra	Vidal, Scheurebe
brick	Vidal, Pinot Blanc, Aligoté, Scheurebe
Caciocavallo	Pinot Noir, Gamay Noir, de Chaunac
mild Cheddar	Vidal, Scheurebe
medium Cheddar	Pinot Noir, Gamay Noir, de Chaunac
old Cheddar	Baco Noir
Elbo, Emmenthal, farmer's, Fontina, Friulano, Gouda, marble, Montasio, New Bra	WHITES: Vidal, Pinot Blanc, Aligoté, Scheurebe REDS: Pinot Noir, Gamay Noir, de Chaunac
provolone, raclette, Saint André, skim-milk Swiss, Tenero	Pinot Blanc
Tilsit	Pinot Noir, Gamay Noir, de Chaunac
Bra, Kefalotyri, Parmesan, Romano	de Chaunac, Maréchal Foch
blue-veined (blue cheese) at lunch	Cabernet Sauvignon
blue-veined (blue cheese) after dinner	port, Riesling B.A., Icewine
goat cheese	Gamay Noir, de Chaunac
semi-soft to hard goat cheese	off-dry Riesling

CHAPTER THREE

Cooking With Wine

WINE CAN TRANSFORM AN AVERAGE MEAL into an exciting gourmet affair. Just as garlic, salt and pepper add flavours and aromas to most cuisines, so too does wine. It is the ideal medium for marinating, simmering, basting, baking, saucing, glazing, deglazing, dressing a salad or flaming an exotic dessert.

Only one principle really applies to cooking with wine: a wine's quality, taste and aroma will come through in the meal. So it's time to throw out that old bottle of cooking wine and purchase something respectable. It doesn't have to be an expensive vintage. In fact, it's silly to open an extravagant wine and use only a little in the recipe, unless you will enjoy the remainder with dinner. Blended wines and table wines suffice, as long as they possess body and flavour. Inferior wines, thin wines, cooking wines containing salt, preservatives and chemicals, or wines long past their prime will only leave you and your guests disappointed.

When do you add wine to your dish? If using wine as a blending ingredient, a tenderizer or a marinade, add it at the beginning of meal preparation. If you want the wine's flavour and aroma to predominate in the dish, add it at the end. Be sure to cook the wine sufficiently so the alcohol evaporates and the aromas and flavours can come through. And remember, it's better to add too little than too much.

There are no rules concerning the type of wines that enhance specific dishes. Your imagination is your best guide; don't be shy about experimenting. Reds and whites are interchangeable, with the exception of fish and seafood dishes, which require whites. Use dry, young, full-bodied reds and whites with a hint of sweetness. If the white is acidic, this may overpower other elements in the dish. Also, it's best to add wine to only one dish in the menu, otherwise the effect will be lost.

Here is a list of products you will use most often when cooking with wine.

- dry red wine (young, robust, full-bodied)
- dry sherry
- port
- white wine
- medium-dry sherry
- brandy

GUIDE TO COOKING WITH WINE

Soup	medium-dry sherry, white wine
Meat: BEEF	red, sherry
LAMB/VEAL	white, rosé
PORK	red, white, sherry
HAM	port, rosé
LIVER	red, white
VENISON	red
RABBIT	white
Poultry/Game: CHICKEN	port, red, white
TURKEY	red, white
CORNISH HENS	white
DUCK	red
GOOSE	red
PHEASANT	port, red, white
QUAIL	port, red, white
Seafood and Fish	white
Cheese Dishes	white
Egg Dishes	white
Pasta/Noodles/Rice: CREAM-BASED SAUCE	white, sherry
TOMATO SAUCE	red, sherry
CHEESE SAUCE	white, sherry
Dessert: FRUIT-BASED	port, sherry, sweet white
SORBETS/ICES	sherry, brandy, port
HOT SOUFFLÉS	sherry, brandy, port

CHAPTER FOUR

SERVING WINE

*B*EFORE YOU UNCORK THAT BOTTLE of wine at your next dinner party — or to savour on your own with dinner — keep in mind that there are ways to enhance the pleasures of the grape.

STORAGE:

You've just selected a fine vintage that's not quite ready to drink. If you plan to savour this wine at a later date, proper storage is a must. Wine must be stored on its side, so the cork is in contact with the wine. If the cork dries out, the wine will spoil. Store your wine in a cool, undisturbed place where the temperature remains even, and keep the bottles away from direct heat or light.

A wine rack is ideal for storage if you have only a few bottles. The ideal temperature for wine is 55 to 58°F (13 to 14°C), but a fairly constant house temperature of 68 to 72°F (20 to 22°C) won't harm your bottles.

If you plan to collect wines, a wine cellar is essential. A proper cellar is temperature-controlled with a special cooling unit and humidity monitor. Prices range from $1,200 for a basic model to $5,000 or more for a deluxe storage area. Do-it-yourselfers can contact their provincial wine council for free easy-to-follow instructions on building a cellar.

TEMPERATURES:

Full-bodied and medium-bodied red wines should be served at room temperature (60 to 68°F/16 to 22°C) in order to enjoy their full flavour.

Light-bodied reds such as Gamay Noir and Pinot Noir should be served slightly chilled. Half an hour in the refrigerator is usually sufficient.

White wines, sparkling wines and rosés all require chilling for one to two hours. Any longer and the taste and bouquet could be affected. The rule here is, the sweeter the wine, the cooler the temperature. The range for chilling is 40 to 52°F (4 to 11°C).

UNCORKING:

The first thing you'll need is a *good* corkscrew. Anyone who has come out on the losing end of a fight with a bad corkscrew understands this premise. Straining a good bottle of wine for bits of cork does not make for a pleasurable experience. There are several models of corkscrews, the most popular home one being the butterfly, where the wings rise when the helix is inserted into the cork. It is fairly easy to use but has a tendency to wear out quickly if you open a lot of bottles. The lever model is used in most restaurants, and once you become accustomed to it, it's fairly easy to use. Another trouble-free corkscrew is the screwpull. This one is three to four times more expensive than the other two types, but is the simplest to use.

Before uncorking a bottle of wine, cut around the foil below the lip of the bottle. Next, wipe the top of the cork with a clean cloth. Insert the corkscrew and follow directions for your particular model. When the cork has been removed, wipe the lip of the bottle with a clean cloth.

Feel the cork. If it is moist, the wine should be fine. If it has dried out, this may be a sign that air has seeped into the bottle, thus oxidizing — and spoiling — the wine.

Champagne and sparkling wines require a different tack. Don't be melodramatic and spray precious bubbly around the room for effect. Save your Champagne for drinking. Remove the foil and put your thumb over the cork while you untwist the wire. To properly open the bottle, hold it at a 45-degree angle with a kitchen towel held over the end. Firmly hold the cork with one hand and gently twist the bottle with the other to ease out the cork and slowly release the pressure. At all times keep your thumb on the cork; the pressure in a bottle is about 90 lbs per square inch.

DECANTING:

Only certain red wines need decanting. Generally this procedure is necessary only if you're drinking an extremely fine vintage or unfiltered wine. Decanting involves gently pouring the wine from its bottle into a decanter; in doing so, you leave the unwanted sediment behind in the bottle and you aerate the wine (allow it to breathe).

To decant, uncork the wine and let it stand so it settles. Light a candle and begin to pour the wine gently into the decanter. Position the candle behind the shoulder of the bottle, so you can see when the sediment gets close to the neck. Don't pour too quickly or you will disturb the sediment and cloud the wine. As soon as you notice the first bits of sediment appearing in the neck of the bottle, stop pouring. There should be less than an inch of wine left in the bottle.

GLASSES:

You don't need expensive glasses, but they should be large and clear. A good wine glass is also narrower at the lip than in the bowl to contain the bouquet of the wine. The best all-round glass has a tulip shape. Use it for red, white and rosé wines. The classic red wine glass has a larger bowl than the tulip glass. White wine glasses are slimmer, while fortified wine glasses are smaller with a narrower rim than bowl. For Champagne, always use a flute rather than a saucer-type glass, which causes the bubbles to quickly disappear.

TASTING WINE:

You can enhance your enjoyment of a bottle of wine by using your senses. First, look at the wine for colour and clarity. It should be bright and without sediment. Swirl your glass to bring out the aroma, also called the nose or bouquet. Think of words to describe the wine, such as fruity, vegetative, floral, spicy, nutty, earthy or woody or chemical smells. (If the wine smells of vinegar, it's too old.) Then taste the wine, noting fruitiness, acidity, tannins and alcohol. Swirl it slowly around your mouth before swallowing. Your tongue has four different taste areas and is able to taste sweetness at the tip, sour (acidity) on the upper edges, bitterness at the back and texture (body and astringency) down the centre and on the sides of the cheeks. A good wine will have a balance of these elements. Finally, pay attention to the finish. There should be a lingering taste that reaffirms the quality of the wine.

$\mathcal{M}$ANGO AND LOBSTER SALAD | Serves two

$\mathcal{A}$PPETIZERS

Lotus, Toronto, Ontario

LOTUS, A GASTRONOMIC TEMPLE for adventurous food lovers, pairs fresh exotic and local ingredients in an eye-catching presentation. Chef-owner Susur Lee has captured Canadian palates by combining his classical training at the famed Peninsula Hotel in Hong Kong with the Asian principles of yin and yang. The result is a cuisine of complementary opposites that is truly unique in Canada. Located on a quiet corner not far from the bustle of trendy Queen Street West, the restaurant takes a minimalist approach with its decor, saving the fanfare for Susur Lee's designer plates. This delicate, tropical salad is one of his favourite summer appetizers.

I	lobster (2 lb/I kg), steamed and cooled	I
I	large mango	I
4 tsp	mayonnaise	20 mL
2 tsp	lemon juice	10 mL
½ tsp	Dijon mustard	2 mL
Pinch	salt	Pinch
½ cup	fresh basil, finely chopped	125 mL
⅓ cup	whipping cream	75 mL
	Basil leaves (for garnish)	

1 Sever lobster head from body. Cut head in half lengthwise and reserve for garnish. Remove lobster meat from shell; cut meat into cubes and place in a mixing bowl. **2** Cut mango in half lengthwise. Remove pit and scoop out flesh, taking care not to tear the skin, which will be used to hold the salad. Cube mango and add to lobster meat. **3** In a blender or food processor, purée mayonnaise, lemon juice, mustard, salt and basil. Transfer to separate bowl. **4** Whip cream and fold into basil purée. **5** Fold dressing into lobster mixture. Divide between mango cups. Garnish with basil leaves and halved lobster heads.

Cave Spring Cellars Off-Dry Riesling

JORDAN, ONTARIO

The hint of sweetness, tropical fruit flavours of pineapple and grapefruit and a nose of pineapple and apricot complement this exotic combination of mango and lobster. Intensely aromatic, this wine's off-dry style gives weight to spicy Asian dishes.

WINEMAKER'S TASTING NOTES

BRIE AND ROSEMARY
BRUSCHETTA | Makes four slices

Say Cheese, London, Ontario

HILARY ALDERSON has been educating southern Ontarians about the pleasures of cheese since opening her cheese shop/restaurant in 1969. The popularity of her tiny eatery and her burgeoning selection of cheeses from around the world soon necessitated a move to larger quarters. The current Dundas Street location is always a hive of activity with customers looking for the latest cheese finds in the downstairs shop. Upstairs, the restaurant offers two menus—the traditional, featuring the original Say Cheese recipes, and the innovative seasonal menu, both using only the freshest and healthiest of local ingredients. The restaurant has been the site of many wine-tasting events, often highlighting Ontario's finest vintages. Hilary Alderson's commitment to promoting local wines began in 1982 when she declared March "all-Canadian wine month." The tradition continues to this day.

Stoney Ridge Cellars Auxerrois

(SWENKER VINEYARD), WINONA, ONTARIO

This dry, flavourful wine is robust enough against the olive oil and garlic in this dish. Clean and somewhat like Chardonnay, but without the complexity.

I	clove garlic, crushed	I
I cup	olive oil	250 mL
4	slices olive sourdough bread, ½-inch (I-cm) thick	4
12 oz	Canadian Brie, thinly sliced	375 g
I½ cups	sliced mushrooms button, oyster OR shiitake	375 mL
2 tbsp	butter OR olive oil	25 mL
I tbsp	fresh rosemary, finely chopped	15 mL
	Salt and pepper	

1 Add garlic to olive oil, mixing well. **2** Toast sourdough bread. **3** Brush one side of each slice with olive oil. (Remaining oil will keep, refrigerated, and can be used for cooking or in salad dressing.) Lay Brie slices over toast. **4** Lightly sauté mushrooms in butter; add rosemary, salt and pepper **5** Grill bruschetta slices until Brie is soft and begins to run. **6** Place toast on warmed plates and smother with mushrooms. Serve immediately.

*B*ISHOP'S CRAB CAKES | Makes six cakes

Bishop's, Vancouver, British Columbia

A JEWEL OF A BISTRO in the heart of the upscale Kitsilano neighbourhood of Vancouver, Bishop's offers a cornucopia of British Columbia's best ingredients and wines. Dramatic paintings pay homage to local artists who number among proprietor John Bishop's loyal customers. The food and art at Bishop's reflect the flavour of coastal British Columbia. A consummate host and wine aficionado, John Bishop suggests perfect pairings of local wines with the restaurant's impeccably executed dishes. Chef Adam Busby has an eclectic style, often adding Asian touches to his dishes. This spicy crab cake is a popular appetizer at the bistro.

½ lb	fresh shelled crab meat	250 g
½ lb	baby shrimp, peeled and deveined	250 g
½ bunch	coriander leaves, chopped	½ bunch
3	green onions, finely chopped	3
I	hot red pepper, cored, seeded and chopped	I
I	egg	I
3 tbsp	mayonnaise	50 mL
I cup	soft bread crumbs	250 mL
	Salt and white pepper to taste	

1 Drain crab meat thoroughly. In a large bowl, mix with shrimp, coriander, green onions, red pepper, egg, mayonnaise and bread crumbs. Season with salt and white pepper.
2 Divide crab mixture into six balls and press into patties 2 inches (5 cm) across, ½ inch (I cm) thick. Refrigerate patties, covered, until ready to use. **3** In a dry nonstick skillet over medium heat, brown patties on both sides. Transfer to baking sheet and bake at 350°F (180°C) for about 5 minutes to heat through. Patties should be crisp on both sides and piping hot. Serve with a chilled fruit salsa or a hot and spicy sauce.

Mission Hill Vineyards Private Reserve Sauvignon Blanc (Barrel-Aged)

WESTBANK, BRITISH COLUMBIA

Complex, with an attractive herbaceous bouquet and subtle oak overtones that accent the spiciness of this dish. Full fruit and weight, yet not overly assertive. Crisp acid balance of the wine is a pleasant astringent to the mayonnaise.

WINEMAKER'S · TASTING NOTES

CAMEMBERT SPRING ROLLS WITH
BLUEBERRY-PEAR CHUTNEY | Makes six spring rolls

Queenston Heights Restaurant,
Niagara Falls, Ontario

OPERATED BY THE NIAGARA PARKS COMMISSION, this restaurant offers a picturesque view of the Niagara River. From May through December, chef Barry Burton's innovative menu is complemented by a complete list of Ontario wines. The restaurant features the products of one Niagara winery each month, and a display case of Ontario wines boosts awareness of Niagara labels with customers.

Reif Estate Winery Chardonnay Reserve

NIAGARA-ON-THE-LAKE, ONTARIO

The full, rich butter flavour and a fruity apple-lemon nose accentuate the smooth cheese and zesty fruit of this popular Queenston Heights appetizer. This wine marries well with dishes that have a richness of flavours of their own.

Wild blueberries must be used in this recipe, as cultivated varieties contain too much water. You will find spring roll wrappers in Asian markets or in the frozen food or produce sections of supermarkets.

CHUTNEY:

8 oz	wild blueberries (fresh or frozen)	250 g
2	Anjou pears, peeled, cored and diced	2
¼ cup	brown sugar	50 mL
¼ cup	blueberry vinegar	50 mL
2 tbsp	red wine vinegar	25 mL
	Finely chopped zest and juice of ½ orange	
	Juice of ½ lemon	
¼ tsp	ginger	1 mL
Pinch	nutmeg	Pinch
Pinch	salt	Pinch
¼ cup	red currant jelly	50 mL

1 In a medium saucepan, combine all chutney ingredients, except currant jelly. Bring to a boil and reduce heat. Simmer 40 minutes, uncovered, stirring occasionally. Remove from heat, stir in jelly, and refrigerate until needed. Reheat before using.

SPRING ROLLS:

2	rounds (4½ oz/125 g) Canadian Camembert	2
24	sun-dried cherries	24
6	spring roll wrappers (9 inches/23 cm square)	6
I	egg, beaten with 2 tbsp (25 mL) cold water	I
3 cups (approx)	peanut oil for deep frying	750 mL
	Fresh seasonal fruit (for garnish)	

1 Cut each Camembert round lengthwise into three pieces. Stuff four cherries into the soft part of each piece of cheese. **2** Separate wrappers and keep covered with damp cloth. Working with one wrapper at a time, lay out wrapper in diamond formation. Place one cheese piece about I inch (2.5 cm) from top corner. Fold in sides and roll up. Moisten ends well with eggwash and press to seal. Keep prepared spring rolls under damp cloth. **3** In a deep saucepan over medium-high heat, heat oil to 325°F (160°C). Fry spring rolls 2 minutes or until they float to top. Drain on paper towels. **4** Arrange on plate with reheated blueberry-pear chutney and garnish with fresh fruit.

Steamed Vine Leaves with Chardonnay Cream | Serves six

Bishop's, Vancouver, British Columbia

CHEF ADAM BUSBY has updated the classic Greek vine leaf recipe with seafood and a creamy Chardonnay sauce.

Mission Hill Vineyards Private Reserve Chardonnay

WESTBANK, BRITISH COLUMBIA

Fermented in oak barrels and allowed to sit in contact with the lees to further bring out the complex flavours of the wine, this Chardonnay is distinctive and rich, well paired with this creamy sauce.

1 lb	prawns, peeled and deveined	500 g
1 tsp	each finely chopped garlic, shallot, gingerroot, parsley, coriander, fresh tarragon	5 mL
2	red peppers, peeled, seeded and finely diced	2
	Salt, white pepper, lemon juice to taste	
12	large marinated vine leaves	12

CHARDONNAY CREAM SAUCE:

1 tbsp	butter	15 mL
1 tbsp	chopped shallots	15 mL
1 tbsp	chopped garlic	15 mL
¼ cup	tarragon vinegar	50 mL
2 cups	Mission Hill Vineyards Private Reserve Chardonnay (white wine)	500 mL
1 cup	whipping cream	250 mL
½ lb	unsalted butter	250 g
	Salt and white pepper to taste	

1 In a bowl mix together prawns, garlic, shallot, gingerroot, parsley, coriander, tarragon and red peppers; season with salt, pepper and lemon juice. **2** Lay flat each of the vine leaves. Divide the prawn mixture evenly between them. Roll each leaf around the stuffing, forming a tube. Pinch ends and fold under. **3** Steam vine leaves over rapidly boiling water for 5 to 8 minutes, or until tender. Keep warm.

4 While vine leaves are steaming, melt 1 tbsp (15 mL) butter in a saucepan over low heat. Sweat shallots and garlic until soft, about 2 minutes. **5** Pour in vinegar. Simmer, uncovered, stirring occasionally until vinegar has evaporated. **6** Stir in wine and reduce by two-thirds. **7** Stir in cream and simmer very slowly until reduced by half. **8** Whisk in butter 1 tbsp (15 mL) at a time, stirring constantly. Remove sauce from heat and season with salt and white pepper. **9** Serve vine leaves on a bed of Chardonnay sauce.

GRILLED MUSHROOMS | Serves four

Culotta Wines, Oakville, Ontario

ONLY 20 MINUTES WEST OF TORONTO, midway to the Niagara Peninsula, lies a small family-operated wine centre. With the aid of their winemaster, Robert Claremont, more than 30,000 cases of wine are shipped from the Oakville winery annually, ranging from an impressive selection of Ontario varietals, international blends, Limited Edition and VQA wines to such specialty wines as their Premium Champagne and Vidal Icewine. Many Culotta wines have been awarded medals at InterVin International Wine Competitions. Although Culotta Wines is proud of these achievements, the first priority remains the judgement of their customers.

Culotta Wines Cabernet Sauvignon

A delicate balance of austere flavours, reminiscent of currants and herbs, make this the ideal partner for vegetables and salads with vinaigrette. Aged in French oak, this very dry, full-bodied wine with its herbal finish marries quite nicely with this herb mixture.

WINEMAKER'S · TASTING NOTES

This appetizer also makes a fine side dish with chicken or pork.

2 tbsp	thyme	25 mL
2 tbsp	oregano	25 mL
I tbsp	tarragon	15 mL
I tbsp	rosemary	15 mL
I tbsp	mint	15 mL
¼ cup	Culotta Wines Cabernet Sauvignon (red wine)	50 mL
I tbsp	each olive oil and lemon juice	15 mL
I tsp	Worcestershire sauce	5 mL
I	clove garlic, minced	I
	Salt and pepper to taste	
½ lb	medium mushrooms	250 g

1 In a bowl combine dried herbs. Stir in wine, oil, lemon juice, Worcestershire sauce, garlic and salt and pepper. Add mushrooms, mixing well, and marinate 15 minutes.
2 Grill mushrooms on High setting for 4 minutes; turn and grill an additional 4 minutes.

MENNONITE SUMMER SAUSAGE PANCAKES | Makes 10 pancakes

Metropolis Restaurant / Grill, Toronto, Ontario

BEFORE CANADIAN CUISINE became much sought after in Toronto, Metropolis was creating homey yet au courant food that was quintessentially Canadian. Founded in 1987, Metropolis is still producing exciting Canadian cuisine under the direction of chef Terry Kennedy. Ontario-raised rabbit, duck and lamb all have a prominent place on the Metropolis menu.

I tbsp	unsalted butter	15 mL
I	green onion, chopped	I
2 oz	summer sausage, finely diced	50 g
I cup	all-purpose flour	250 mL
I cup	milk	250 mL
2	eggs	2
I tbsp	lemon juice	15 mL
I tsp	Worcestershire sauce	5 mL
I tsp	baking powder	5 mL
½ tsp	each salt and black pepper	2 mL
½ lb	Oka cheese, shredded	250 g

1 In a large nonstick skillet over medium heat, sauté green onion in butter until slightly transparent. **2** In a bowl, combine sautéed green onion, sausage, flour, milk, eggs, lemon juice, Worcestershire sauce, baking powder, salt and pepper. Stir until smooth. **3** Into same nonstick skillet over medium heat, spoon 3 tbsp (50 mL) of batter for each pancake. Cook pancakes for 2 to 3 minutes or until tiny air bubbles form. Flip pancakes over and brown on other side for I minute or until golden. **4** Transfer cooked pancakes to heatproof baking sheet. Sprinkle each pancake with Oka cheese and grill until cheese is slightly melted.

Inniskillin Wines Pinot Noir Reserve

NIAGARA-ON-THE-LAKE, ONTARIO

This selection has the perfect acid-to-sugar content, in addition to berry-like aromas and cherry-like flavours. French oak ageing has contributed to the complexity and smooth texture of this wine, allowing it to cleanse the palate of the strong, robust sausage flavour.

WINEMAKER'S TASTING NOTES

*T*EA-SMOKED HALIBUT CARPACCIO | Serves four

The Raintree Restaurant, Vancouver, British Columbia

MANY TIMES AN AWARD WINNER for its fine selection of Pacific Northwest wines and innovative regional cooking, The Raintree remains one of the culinary leaders of the West Coast. Founding chef Rebecca Dawson put The Raintree on the map with her skillful blending of rustic and natural ingredients, creating an authentic West Coast cuisine. With the exception of a few cheeses from Oregon, California olive oil and some West Coast American wines, everything here is produced in British Columbia. Dawson has left The Raintree to teach her special brand of cooking, and chef Anthony Hodda continues the tradition of promoting the best products British Columbia has to offer. In 1992, The Raintree won the British Columbia Wine Institute's VQA Gold Award of Distinction. The restaurant also won a silver medal in the 1992 Vancouver Playhouse International Wine Festival for its West Coast wine list.

CedarCreek Estate Winery Gewürztraminer

KELOWNA, BRITISH COLUMBIA

Well-balanced with plenty of flavour to combine well with the strong flavours in this appetizer, this wine is clear and intense. It contains soft and spicy fruit aromas and clean, lightly-spiced peach and lemon flavours, which work with the slight sweetness of the pickled carrot mixture.

WINEMAKER'S TASTING NOTES

1 tbsp	chopped parsley	15 mL
½ tsp	Dijon mustard	2 mL
1 tsp	Worcestershire sauce	5 mL
½ tsp	salt	2 mL
¼ tsp	freshly cracked pepper	1 mL
1 lb	fresh halibut loin	500 g

PICKLED CARROT:

¾ cup	julienne carrot	175 mL
2 tsp	clear honey	10 mL
1 tbsp	cider vinegar	15 mL
1	red chili, finely chopped	1
2 tbsp	finely chopped peanuts	25 mL
2 tsp	finely chopped red onion	10 mL
2 tsp	finely chopped fresh coriander	10 mL
2 tsp	finely chopped fresh mint	10 mL

TEA SMOKE MIX:

I cup	Earl Grey tea leaves	250 mL
¼ cup	brown sugar	50 mL
¼ cup	salt	50 mL

Black and white sesame seeds (for garnish)	

1 Combine parsley, mustard, Worcestershire sauce, salt and pepper. Baste halibut loin with mix and marinate at least 2 hours. **2** Combine ingredients for Pickled Carrot and let stand at least 30 minutes. **3** Combine ingredients for Tea Smoke Mix. Smoke halibut according to smoker instructions until flesh starts to sweat (approximately 30 minutes). Let halibut cool. Cut thinly and arrange on top of Pickled Carrot. Sprinkle with sesame seeds.

JOE FORTES' CAJUN OYSTERS | Serves four

Joe Fortes',
Vancouver, British Columbia

FRESH LOCAL OYSTERS and a vast selection of wines (by the glass as well as the bottle) take centre stage at this always crowded midtown eatery. Owner Bud Kanke has the same high-quality standards over ingredients as at his two other establishments, The Cannery, and The Fish House at Stanley Park. Joe Fortes' is an ideal place to experiment with local wines. Order a glass of B.C. Chardonnay and half a dozen fresh beach oysters and taste the West Coast.

Gray Monk Cellars Pinot Auxerrois

OKANAGAN CENTRE,
BRITISH COLUMBIA

A refresher, this cousin to Pinot Gris is crisp with a fruity bouquet. Full on the palate with a lovely peach flavour that glows to a lingering finish. The full fruit flavours react well with the spiciness of this dish.

2 tbsp + I tsp	Cajun Magic (recipe follows)	30 mL
4 oz	dried bread crumbs	125 g
	All-purpose flour for dredging	
2	eggs, beaten with 2 tbsp (25 mL) milk	2
12	oysters, shucked	12
2 tbsp	peanut oil	25 mL
3 tbsp	butter	50 mL
	Salt and pepper to taste	
¼ cup	whipping cream	50 mL

1 Blend 2 tbsp (25 mL) of Cajun Magic with bread crumbs. Arrange separate dishes of flour, beaten eggs and milk, and seasoned bread crumbs. **2** In skillet or sauté pan heat peanut oil. **3** Dredge oysters in flour, dip in egg mixture and roll in bread crumbs. Add oysters and 1 tbsp (15 mL) butter to hot oil. Sauté oysters until golden brown on all sides. Drain on paper towels. Sprinkle with salt and pepper. **4** In a saucepan over medium heat, melt remaining 2 tbsp (25 mL) butter. Add cream. Add 1 tsp Cajun Magic. Bring to a boil, whisking, until desired consistency. (If sauce is too thin, add butter. If sauce has overboiled and begins to separate, add a dash of cream.) Season with salt and pepper. **5** Spoon sauce onto four plates. Arrange sautéed oysters on sauce and serve immediately.

CAJUN MAGIC:

3 tbsp	paprika	50 mL
1 tsp	cayenne	5 mL
1 tsp	crumbled oregano	5 mL
1 tsp	basil	5 mL
1 tsp	thyme	5 mL
1 tsp	cumin	5 mL
1 tsp	garlic powder	5 mL
	Salt and pepper to taste	

1 Combine dried herbs and spices. Mixture keeps up to six months in an airtight container.

BAKED MARINATED SHRIMPS AND SCALLOPS IN ORANGE AND GINGER CREAM | Serves four

The Victorian, Ocean Pointe Resort
Victoria, British Columbia

LOCATED ON VICTORIA'S FAMOUS INNER HARBOUR, this spectacular resort offers nourishment for the body and the soul. A spa provides an array of treatments and therapies while the three restaurants span a gastronomic spectrum. Executive chef Craig Stoneman and chef Ray Henry have made The Victorian a dining experience to be savoured with the eyes as well as the palate. Healthy food is very much in evidence here, with sumptuous low-fat and low-sodium dishes on the menu. The cheerful Boardwalk Deli serves casual fare in a fun atmosphere, while the Boardwalk Brasserie has a distinctly European style. In true British Columbian form, local wines are proudly served to complement this West Coast style of cooking.

16	scallops	16
8	medium shrimp, peeled	8

MARINADE:

⅓ cup	olive oil	75 mL
½ tsp	crushed garlic	2 mL
I tsp	chopped ginger	5 mL
I tbsp	orange zest, finely chopped	15 mL
2 tsp	each chopped coriander and parsley	10 mL

ORANGE AND GINGER CREAM:

2	medium shallots, sliced	2
I tsp	chopped gingerroot	5 mL
½ tsp	crushed garlic	2 mL
¾ cup	CedarCreek Dry Riesling (white wine)	175 mL
1½ cups	whipping cream	375 mL

I tbsp	orange juice concentrate	15 mL
¼ tsp	salt	I mL
	zest of ½ orange, blanched	
I tbsp	chopped chives	15 mL
	Salt and freshly cracked pepper	
4	4-inch (10-cm) circles of puff pastry	4
I	egg, beaten with 2 tbsp (25 mL) water	I

GARNISHES:

I	tomato, peeled, seeded and diced	I
24	small mizuna leaves*	24
8	long chives	8

1 Mix marinade ingredients together. Marinate scallops and shrimp several hours, covered, in the refrigerator. **2** In a saucepan heat I tsp (5 mL) olive oil over low heat and sweat shallots, ginger and garlic. Add wine; reduce by half. Add cream; reduce by half. Do not let sauce boil. **3** Stir in orange juice concentrate and salt. Strain sauce. Return to heat and stir in orange zest and chopped chives. Over low heat cook sauce for 3 to 4 minutes. Cover and keep warm. **4** Drain shrimp and scallops. Season with salt and cracked pepper. Heat I tsp (5 mL) oil over medium heat. Lightly sauté shrimp and scallops, enough to seal them and to give some colour. They should be no more than half cooked. **5** Place puff pastry circles on parchment paper spread on a baking sheet. Arrange 4 scallops and 2 shrimps on each circle. **6** Brush exposed part of pastry with egg-wash. Bake at 375°F (190°C) for 5 to 7 minutes, until golden. **7** Place each pastry in the centre of a plate and pour a little orange sauce over and around it. Garnish with diced tomato, mizuna leaves and chives.

CedarCreek Estate Winery Dry Riesling

KELOWNA, BRITISH COLUMBIA

Uncompromisingly dry and crisp, with aromas of orange blossoms, jasmine and green apples that complement the orange and ginger in this creamy sauce. In the mouth these aromas meld with crisp, juicy flavours of apricot and lemon for a firm-textured wine that sets a benchmark for the Okanagan. The dry style of this Riesling brings out the grape's natural crispness and bouquet, making it the perfect food wine. It is a wonderful complement to the delicate scallops in this recipe.

WINEMAKER'S TASTING NOTES

Available at specialty markets or substitute oak leaf lettuce or dandelion greens.

GRILLED OYSTERS AND NASTURTIUM BUTTER SAUCE | Serves two

Sooke Harbour House, Sooke, British Columbia

SINCLAIR AND FREDRICA PHILIP's famed country inn needs little introduction among lovers of fine cuisine. One of the earliest establishments in Canada to wholeheartedly embrace indigenous ingredients, Sooke Harbour House has led the way for the growing movement towards regional cuisine. Only the highest-quality and freshest ingredients make it to the kitchen, where a progressive team of chefs turns out such imaginative dishes as this appetizer. The House has been featured in leading newspapers and food magazines around the world, and has won numerous awards for its food, wine and hospitality.

Mission Hill Private Reserve Pinot Blanc (Barrel-Aged)

WESTBANK, BRITISH COLUMBIA

Delicate enough so as not to overpower the nasturtium flowers, this oak-aged wine is full bodied enough to stand up to the peppery nasturtium leaves and is an excellent match for the oysters. It has a distinctive apple-orchard aroma.

WINEMAKER'S TASTING NOTES

8	large oysters, shucked	8
1½ cups	cups fish stock	375 mL
¼ cup	Mission Hill Private Reserve Pinot Blanc (white wine)	50 mL
2 tsp	nasturtium vinegar (recipe follows) OR cider vinegar	10 mL
4	large nasturtium leaves and 8 flowers, coarsely chopped	4
¾ cup	unsalted butter	175 mL
2 or 4	small nasturtium flowers and leaves (for garnish)	2 or 4

1 Grill oysters on both sides until brown. Keep warm. **2** In a sauté pan, blend fish stock, wine and vinegar. Reduce over high heat to ¼ cup (50 mL). Add nasturtium leaves and flowers. Remove from heat and whisk in butter until melted. **3** Pour sauce on plates, arrange oysters on sauce and garnish with small leaves and flowers.

NASTURTIUM VINEGAR:

Fill a stainless steel container with nasturtium flowers, leaves and seed pods. Pour in enough apple cider vinegar to cover. Cover with plastic wrap, leaving a small opening for breathing. Store in a cool, dry place for a few weeks before using.

OYSTERS ON HORSEBACK | Makes 36 to 48 pieces

Michelle Ramsay / Vignoble Dietrich-Jooss, Iberville, Quebec

VICTOR DIETRICH AND CHRISTIANE Jooss founded Vignoble Dietrich-Jooss in Iberville, Quebec, in 1986 with Maréchal Foch, de Chaunac and Seyval as the main varieties vinified. A testing field of 30 grape varieties from around the world was also added. So far they produce Maréchal Foch, de Chaunac, Seyval and a few blends.

½ lb	bacon	250 g
2	cans (3½ oz/100 g each) smoked oysters	2
I	pkg (8 oz/250 g) cream cheese	I

1 Cut each bacon slice into three. Place one oyster on each bacon piece. Place a dollop of cream cheese on each oyster. Roll up and secure with a toothpick. **2** Bake in the middle of a 400°F (200°C) oven for 10 minutes. Turn and cook another 8 to 10 minutes or until bacon is crisp. Drain on paper towels and serve hot.

Vignoble Dietrich-Jooss Storikengold

A blend of Seyval, Cayuga white, Geisenheim and Vidal. This dry, fruity wine was aged in American oak for six months, giving it a hint of oak that marries well with the smoked flavour of oysters. Being light bodied, this wine is perfect with most appetizers.

Suggested Varietal: oaky Sauvignon Blanc

WINEMAKER'S · TASTING NOTES

Softshell Crab with Chunky Mango-Basil Sauce | Serves four

Michelle Ramsay

INSPIRED BY A CRAB APPETIZER at Susur Lee's Lotus restaurant, Michelle created this dish.

Pelee Island Winery Scheurebe

KINGSVILLE, ONTARIO

This wine is exotic enough with its cardamom-orange flavours and touch of sweetness to complement spicy Asian and Mexican dishes. The spicy mango and hint of curry in this dish mesh well with this wine. Although not as high in acidity as Riesling, this variety possesses enough to cut through the richness of crab.

2	mangoes, peeled, pitted and diced	2
1	cayenne chili, seeded and minced	1
⅓ cup	fresh basil, minced	75 mL
	Juice of 1 lime	
¾ cup	all-purpose flour	175 mL
¾ cup	cornmeal	175 mL
1 tsp	Jamaican curry powder	5 mL
Pinch	cumin	Pinch
	Salt and pepper to taste	
4	softshell crabs, cleaned	4
1 cup	peanut oil	250 mL
½ cup	buttermilk	125 mL
	Fresh basil and 1 lime, quartered (for garnish)	

1 In bowl of a food processor, combine mango, chili, basil and lime juice. Pulse five times. **2** Blend flour, cornmeal, curry powder, cumin, salt and pepper. **3** In a saucepan, heat peanut oil over medium-high heat. **4** Dip crabs in buttermilk. Dredge in flour-cornmeal mixture. Sauté crabs until golden brown, about 6 minutes each side. **5** Divide mango sauce on plates. Arrange crabs on sauce. Garnish with fresh basil leaves and lime quarters.

CAVIAR CHIPS | Serves four

Hillebrand Estates Winery, Niagara-on-the-Lake, Ontario

HAVING BECOME A LEADING PRODUCER of quality varietal wines, Hillebrand is now establishing a notable reputation in versatility. Recent achievements include the creation of Mounier and the Trius wine series. Located on the same premises, but considered a separate company, Mounier produces sparkling wine through the traditional méthode champenoise. The Trius wine series, for which Hillebrand has won awards, consists of three distinctly different Chardonnays, a dry Riesling and a blend called Trius red. To achieve such versatility in their wines, Hillebrand purchases grapes from 45 Niagara growers and conducts experiments in their 15-acre estate vineyard.

3	large white potatoes, peeled	3
12	green onions (green part only)	12
1¼ cups	vegetable oil	300 mL
	Salt to taste	
¼ cup	sour cream	50 mL
1	jar (3½ oz/100 g) Malossol or Sevruga caviar*	1

1 Slice potatoes ⅛ inch (3 mm) thick. Rinse potato slices under cold water until water runs clean. Pat dry. **2** Cut green onions into 2-inch (5-cm) pieces. **3** Make two 2½-inch (6-cm) cuts, ½ inch (1 cm) apart, in centre of each potato slice. Weave a green onion piece into each potato slice. (Reserve remaining green onions for garnish.) **4** In a skillet or sauté pan over moderately high heat, heat oil to almost smoking point. Fry potato slices on both sides for 2 to 3 minutes or until crisp and golden brown. Drain on paper towels. Salt lightly. **5** Spoon ½ tsp (2 mL) sour cream on each slice and top with caviar. Garnish with sticks of green onion.

Mounier Brut Champagne

The Mounier cuvée is made from Chardonnay and Pinot Noir grapes grown in vineyards along Lake Ontario's shoreline in the Niagara Peninsula. This area produces berries with high acid, low brix (sugar) and rich varietal character. As a result, Mounier Brut Champagne is straw yellow with fine bubbles and a long mousseux. Not overly toasty and yeasty, this bubbly is clean, crisp and refreshing, making it the consummate beverage to clean the palate between bites.

WINEMAKER'S TASTING NOTES

*Salmon or lumpfish caviar may be substituted.

$\mathcal{P}$ACIFIC HALIBUT WITH MAPLE BUTTER SAUCE | Serves four

Chartwell, Four Seasons Hotel, Vancouver, British Columbia

THE DAYS OF MEDIOCRE HOTEL FOOD are becoming a relic as chains like the Four Seasons continue to dazzle palates around the world. Winner of the 14 Distinguished Restaurants of North America awards in 1992, the Four Seasons chain has truly elevated hotel cuisine. Chartwell, winner of one of the 14 honours, is testimony to the fine and innovative cuisine being created in Four Seasons establishments. This recipe from executive chef Wolfgang von Wieser teams local halibut with maple syrup. What could be more Canadian?

CedarCreek Estate Winery Chardonnay

KELOWNA, BRITISH COLUMBIA

Barrel-fermented, this wine has beautifully balanced aromas of apple, lemon and oak, which are followed by apple flavours with accents of citrus and spicy oak. This wine is an exciting enhancement to this dish, with the citrus balancing the fried fish and the oak complementing the creamy butter sauce.

WINEMAKER'S TASTING NOTES

	Juice of 1 lemon	
1	bay leaf	1
1	clove	1
1 tbsp	CedarCreek Chardonnay (white wine)	15 mL
3 tbsp	maple syrup	50 mL
2 tbsp	whipping cream	25 mL
3 tbsp	cold butter	50 mL
2 tbsp	olive oil	25 mL
	Sea salt and freshly ground white pepper	
4	fresh Pacific halibut (about ¼ lb/100 g each)	4

1 In a saucepan, combine lemon juice, bay leaf, clove, wine and maple syrup. Over moderately high heat, reduce to one-quarter. Add cream and reduce by half. **2** Remove from heat and whisk in butter. Discard clove and bay leaf. Keep sauce warm. **3** In a skillet, heat oil over medium heat. Season halibut with salt and pepper. Cook, one side only, for 6 minutes or until bottom of fish is crispy and top is opaque. **4** Drain halibut on paper towels. Arrange halibut on plates, drizzle with warm sauce and serve immediately.

$\mathcal{H}$ALIBUT PÂTÉ | Serves six

Shari Darling / Vignoble Le Cep d'Argent, Magog, Quebec

VIGNOBLE LE CEP D'ARGENT (the silver vine-stock) is operated by four owners—François and Jean-Paul Scieur, Jacques Daniel and Denis Drouin. More than six years old, the 25-acre vineyard is flourishing with Seyval Blanc, Maréchal Foch and de Chaunac grapes. They make eight products from these varieties.

I lb	halibut fillets	500 g
¼ cup	olive oil	50 mL
2	thick slices whole wheat bread	2
	Juice of ½ lemon	
I	clove garlic, crushed	I
½ cup	mayonnaise	125 mL
I tbsp	butter	15 mL
I tbsp	Vignoble Le Cep d'Argent Sélection des Mousquetaires (sparkling wine)	15 mL
	Salt	
½ tsp	crushed black peppercorns	2 mL
	Capers and whole black peppercorns (for garnish)	

Vignoble Le Cep d'Argent Sélection des Mousquetaires Blanc de Blancs

Made from the Seyval Blanc grape, this bubbly was done in the méthode champenoise. It is lightly fruited with a very small hint of apple. The crisp, clean taste refreshes the palate between bites.

WINEMAKER'S · TASTING NOTES

1 Wrap halibut in aluminum foil and bake at 350°F (180°C) for 10 minutes or until flaky. **2** In a bowl combine oil and 2 tbsp (25 mL) water. Cut crusts from bread and soak in oil. Squeeze bread dry. **3** In bowl of a food processor, combine halibut, bread, lemon juice, garlic, mayonnaise, butter, wine, salt and crushed peppercorns. Process until smooth, adding 3 tbsp (50 mL) olive oil to moisten mixture if too dry. Taste; if fish flavour is too strong, add garlic and lemon juice. **4** Serve pâté in a crock with thin slices of rye bread with capers and peppercorns for garnish.

CHAPTER SIX

SALADS

TOMATO-AVOCADO-PEPPER SALAD | Serves four

Michelle Ramsay

Brights Wines Late Harvest Baco Noir

NIAGARA FALLS,

ONTARIO

Firm body weight. Long oak ageing smooths out the wine's tannins. Smoky, toasted oak flavour brings out the balsamic vinegar taste in this dish. The wine's dryness is a perfect contrast to the sweetness of the peppers.

I	red bell pepper	I
I	yellow bell pepper	I
I tbsp	olive oil	15 mL
I	small clove garlic, finely minced	I
¼ tsp	crushed hot pepper flakes	I mL
I tbsp	balsamic vinegar	15 mL
½ tsp	Dijon mustard	2 mL
¾ cup plus 2 tbsp	extra virgin olive oil	100 mL
	Salt and pepper	
2	large tomatoes	2
2	avocados	2
¼ cup	fresh basil, cut into ribbons	50 mL

1 Roast peppers on barbecue or under broiler until skins are black. Let cool, and peel away skins. Seed peppers and slice. Toss with I tbsp (15 mL) olive oil, garlic and pepper flakes. **2** To make vinaigrette, combine vinegar and mustard. Slowly whisk in extra virgin olive oil until well blended. Season with salt and pepper to taste. **3** Slice tomatoes and avocados. In a large bowl, combine tomatoes, avocados, peppers and basil. Pour vinaigrette to taste over salad and toss well.

GRASSBERRY SALAD | Serves eight

*The Cellar Bench Restaurant Wine Bar,
St. Catharines, Ontario*

CHEF GREGORY WILLIS is a Niagara native who grew up with a strong curiosity about the local vineyards. Now owner of The Cellar Bench and a certified sommelier, he focuses on healthy regional cuisine, complementing it with a vast stock of Niagara wines. Housed in the historic District Courthouse, The Cellar Bench features monthly promotions of regional wineries that include an evening with the winemaker.

I cup	Henry of Pelham Gewürztraminer (white wine)	250 mL
I½ cups	olive oil	375 mL
2 tbsp	finely chopped fresh chervil	25 mL
I tbsp	finely chopped fresh basil	I5 mL
I½ tsp	finely chopped fresh tarragon	7 mL
I½ tsp	finely chopped fresh marjoram	7 mL
2	green onions, finely chopped	2
	Salt and pepper to taste	
2 lb	asparagus, blanched, cut on diagonal	I kg
2 lb	strawberries, hulled and quartered	I kg

Henry of Pelham Gewürztraminer

ST. CATHARINES, ONTARIO

This medium-bodied wine, full of fruit (melons and peaches) and spice, marries well with the asparagus while the acid in the strawberries balances well with the acid level of the wine.

1 In a saucepan over medium-high heat, reduce wine to ½ cup (125 mL). Blend in olive oil to create an emulsion. Stir in fresh herbs, onions, salt and pepper; let stand overnight. (This is enough dressing for two salads. Remainder keeps in refrigerator for several weeks.)

2 Toss asparagus and strawberries with half of dressing and serve immediately.

THAI GREEN MANGO SALAD | Serves two to three

Michelle Ramsay

Vineland Estates St. Urban Semi-Dry Riesling

VINELAND, ONTARIO

This wine has a hint of sweetness. Pale gold with an apricot aroma and apricot/peach on the palate, this wine brings out the fruit in the salad. With refreshing acidity, it is a perfect companion for salad.

WINEMAKER'S TASTING NOTES

I	small clove garlic, minced	I
I tsp	coarsely chopped shallot	5 mL
½	hot red chili, minced	½
2 tbsp	fish sauce*	25 mL
3 tbsp	fresh lime juice	50 mL
I tbsp	palm sugar*	15 mL
2	small green mangoes, peeled and grated	2
	Bibb lettuce cups	

GARNISHES:

I tbsp	dried shrimp, pounded to powder	15 mL
I tbsp	coarsely chopped roasted peanuts	15 mL
I tbsp	diced red bell pepper	15 mL

1 With a mortar and pestle, pound minced garlic, shallots and chilies. Gradually work in fish sauce, lime juice and sugar. Pour over grated mangoes. **2** Spoon salad into lettuce cups. Garnish with dried shrimp, peanuts and red pepper.

*Fish sauce and palm sugar are available in Asian markets. Brown sugar can be substituted for palm sugar.

LOBSTER POTATO SALAD | Serves six

Michelle Ramsay

2 cups	coarsely chopped cooked lobster meat (fresh or frozen)	500 mL
4 cups	diced cooked potatoes	1 L
¼ cup	thinly sliced green onions	50 mL
1 tsp	salt	5 mL
½ tsp	pepper	2 mL
⅔ cup	mayonnaise	150 mL
2 tsp	lemon juice	10 mL
2 tsp	horseradish	10 mL
1 tsp	dry mustard	5 mL
½ tsp	cayenne	2 mL
	Romaine leaves	

GARNISHES:

Hard-boiled egg wedges
Red and yellow cherry tomatoes, halved

1 If using fresh lobster, reserve claws for garnish.
2 In a large bowl, lightly toss together lobster meat, potatoes, onions, salt and pepper. **3** Mix mayonnaise with lemon juice, horseradish, dry mustard and cayenne. Pour over potato mixture; toss lightly. Adjust salt, pepper and cayenne to taste. Refrigerate at least 1 hour before serving. **4** Just before serving, fan out romaine leaves on a platter or in a large salad bowl. Pile salad on top and garnish with hard-boiled egg wedges, halved cherry tomatoes and lobster claws.

Hillebrand Estates Canadian Champagne

NIAGARA-ON-THE-LAKE, ONTARIO

A crisp Charmat method bubbly with a touch of residual sugar to contrast the heat of the salad dressing. The wine's fruity characteristics marry well with the sweetness of the lobster.

WINEMAKER'S TASTING NOTES

SALADE DU SOLEIL (SUNSHINE SALAD) | Serves four to six

Andrew Sharp

ANDREW SHARP is a leading wine educator in Canada and founder of InterVin, the highly respected international wine competition. His books include the *1989-90 Guide to Award-Winning Wines, Vineland 1000, A Canadian View of Wine* and *Winetaster's Secrets.* Sharp also hosts a syndicated wine program on WWKB-TV in Buffalo and a weekly wine show on CHFI radio in Toronto.

Konzelmann Estate Winery Gewuerztraminer

NIAGARA-ON-THE-LAKE, ONTARIO

Done in a Germanic style, this white wine shows floral on the nose with spiciness and a hint of sweetness on the palate— elements that accent the salad's sweet-sour dressing. The wine's fine acidity is also a nice contrast to the grilled vegetables and soft fruit.

WINEMAKER'S TASTING NOTES

DRESSING:

I	clove garlic	I
I	small mango, peeled and sliced	I
2 tbsp	rice vinegar	25 mL
I	each orange, nectarine and peach	I
½	head radicchio	½
½	turnip, peeled	½
½ cup	yellow bell pepper, peeled and seeded	125 mL
½ cup	waxed beans, stem and ends cut off	125 mL
I	head leaf lettuce	I

1 To make dressing, roast garlic in skin at 350°F (180°C) for 45 minutes. Press clove out of skin and mash. Place mango with garlic in blender. Add rice vinegar. Blend until smooth. Set aside. **2** Peel and segment orange and nectarine. Slice peach. Cut radicchio, turnip and yellow bell pepper into julienne strips. **3** Place turnip, pepper and beans on baking sheet and grill at 350°F (180°C) for about 15 minutes or until tender. **4** Lay lettuce leaves on individual places. Sprinkle with radicchio strips. Arrange grilled vegetables and fruit slices on plate. Pour dressing over salad.

$\mathcal{T}$ROPICAL SALAD | Serves four

Shari Darling / Summerhill Estate Winery, Kelowna, British Columbia

SUMMERHILL ESTATE WINERY is owned by Stephen and Wendy Cipes and winemaker Eric Von Krosigk, a graduate in beverage engineering from Geisenheim Viticultural Institute in Germany. This winery is the first in British Columbia to specialize in méthode champenoise sparkling wines. They also produce varietal wines, a few of these being Ehrenfelser, Riesling and Late Harvest Riesling.

½ cup	vegetable oil	125 mL
½ cup	raspberry vinegar	125 mL
½ cup	pineapple juice	125 mL
I oz	pine nuts	25 g
	Freshly ground pepper to taste	
2	avocados	2
2	papayas	2
½	sweet red onion, diced	½
	Red leaf lettuce	

GARNISHES:

I cup	raspberries	250 mL
	Mint leaves and macadamia nuts	

Summerhill Estate Cipes Brut Champagne

This bubbly was made from the grape variety Johannisberg Riesling. Aged for one year in bottles, it is crisp and clean with enough acidity to work with the raspberry vinaigrette. Honey, violet and green apple dominate the nose while citrus, peach and pear linger on the palate—excellent characteristics to marry with this tropical fruit salad.

WINEMAKER'S · TASTING NOTES

1 To make dressing, blend together well oil, vinegar, pineapple juice, pine nuts and pepper. **2** Peel avocado and papaya and cut into small cubes. Place in a bowl. Add red onion. Pour dressing over and marinate for about I hour. **3** Drain avocado and papaya, reserving dressing for another use. Arrange on a bed of red leaf lettuce and garnish with raspberries, mint leaves and macadamia nuts.

*I*NDIAN SUMMER QUAIL SALAD | Serves six

Scaramouche, Toronto, Ontario

THE SPECTACULAR VIEW of the city is one drawing card here, but executive chef Keith Froggett's impeccable cooking and dazzling presentation have made Scaramouche a perennial favourite. The French-inspired menu changes weekly, and the wines—local as well as imported—pay proper homage to the food. Quality and fresh ingredients are the cornerstone of the culinary philosophy here.

Cave Spring Cellars Indian Summer Riesling

JORDAN, ONTARIO

Characteristic pear and lichee fruit predominate. Acidic enough to balance residual sugar and cut through the oiliness of the quails.

WINEMAKER'S TASTING NOTES

6	plump quails, cut in half, bones removed and reserved	6
2 cups	Cave Spring Indian Summer Riesling (white wine)	500 mL
¼ cup	vegetable oil	50 mL
I	small carrot, coarsely chopped	I
I	small onion, coarsely chopped	I
2	stalks celery, coarsely chopped	2
I tsp	tomato paste	5 mL
4 cups	chicken stock	I L
	Thyme sprigs	
2	large potatoes, peeled and shredded	2
⅓ cup	chilled cubed butter	75 mL
	Salt and freshly ground pepper	
	Vinaigrette (recipe follows)	
	Various salad leaves	

GARNISHES:

Chopped fresh thyme
Chopped Chinese parsley

1 Place quail halves in a nonmetallic dish. Add I½ cups (375 mL) wine, cover, and marinate for at least 2 hours.

2 In a saucepan with a heavy bottom, heat vegetable oil.

Gently brown quail bones, carrots, onion and celery. Drain off oil. **3** Stir in tomato paste and cook a few minutes more. Add chicken stock and thyme sprigs. Bring to a boil. Reduce heat and simmer until liquid is reduced to about 1 cup (250 mL). **4** Strain stock through cheesecloth into a small saucepan. Add remaining ½ cup (125 mL) wine and reduce liquid to ½ cup (125 mL). **5** Meanwhile, cook shredded potatoes in a large, lightly oiled skillet to make a thin golden pancake. Drain on paper towels. **6** When sauce has reduced, whisk in butter to thicken and enrich the sauce. Remove from heat and whisk in 3 tbsp (50 mL) vinaigrette. **7** Remove quails from marinade and pat dry. Season with salt and pepper. **8** In a heavy skillet over medium heat, cook quails skin side down in a little vegetable oil. When the skin is a rich mahogany colour, turn quails and sear the flesh side. The insides should remain pink and moist. **9** Toss salad leaves in some of the remaining vinaigrette and arrange on a serving plate. Break the potato pancake into large pieces and stand them up randomly in the salad. Arrange quails on the plate. Drizzle sauce over the entire dish. Garnish with fresh thyme and parsley. Serve immediately.

VINAIGRETTE:

¾ cup	extra virgin olive oil	175 mL
¼ cup	white wine vinegar	50 mL
Pinch	sugar	Pinch
Pinch	prepared mustard	Pinch
	Salt and pepper to taste	

1 Whisk all ingredients together.

MEDITERRANEAN CHICKEN SALAD | Serves four to six

Shari Darling / Vignoble Angell

RUSTIC, QUAINT AND INFORMAL, Vignoble Angell is one of five farm wineries in the Haut-Richelieu region of Quebec. The winery produces 2,000 gallons annually of three blends—red, white and rosé. Proprietor/winemaker Jean-Guy Angell began as an amateur, vinifying Californian grapes. In 1971 he purchased a farm and planted 16 acres to vines. Fourteen years later he opened Vignoble Angell. Since then he has brought in vinifera root stocks from Kelowna, British Columbia, and Niagara-on-the-Lake, Ontario, in order to produce a wider selection of wines. To introduce new customers to his products and to keep faithful patrons returning, Jean-Guy hosts barbecues for groups of 35 or more, where he cooks lamb and pig and serves them with cheese and salads.

Vignoble Angell Rosé

SAINT-BERNARD DE LACOLLE, QUEBEC

This rosé combines 50 per cent Seyval Blanc and 50 per cent Gamay Noir grapes. With light pink robe and a hint of sweetness, this wine has a fresh acidity that works with the acid in tomatoes and lemon juice. Its citrus fragrance and fruity palate complement the salad's orange slices.

WINEMAKER'S TASTING NOTES

I	medium yellow onion, quartered	I
2	carrots, peeled and chopped	2
I	leek (white part only), sliced	I
I tsp	dried thyme	5 mL
I	bay leaf	I
6	sprigs parsley	6
12	black peppercorns	12
4	cloves	4
3 lb	whole chicken breasts	1.5 kg
⅓ cup	olive oil	75 mL
1½ tsp	oregano	7 mL
	Juice of I lemon	
¾ cup	black olives, pitted	175 mL
2 tbsp	capers	25 mL
8	medium tomatoes, cut into wedges	8
I	tangerine, peeled, and segments cut in half	I
¼ lb	green beans, cooked	125 g
	Salt and freshly ground black pepper to taste	

1 Measure 4 quarts (4 L) water in large pot. Add onion, carrots, leek, thyme, bay leaf, parsley, peppercorns and cloves. Bring to a boil, reduce heat, and simmer, uncovered, for 15 minutes. **2** Add chicken breasts and return to a boil. Reduce heat and simmer, uncovered, until chicken is cooked. Remove from heat and let cool. **3** Once broth has cooled, remove chicken. Discard skin and bones. Tear chicken into large pieces and toss in a bowl with olive oil and oregano. Cover and refrigerate for 1 hour. **4** Toss remaining ingredients with chicken and marinade. Serve immediately.

Note: If making this salad ahead for a picnic or barbecue, reserve green beans and add them to salad just before serving to avoid discolouration.

SALADE COMPOSÉE AUX GÉSIERS DE CANARDS CONFIT (WARM SALAD WITH DUCK-GIZZARD CONFIT) | Serves four

*Hostellerie les Trois Tilleuls,
Saint-Marc-sur-Richelieu, Quebec*

TWENTY MINUTES FROM MONTREAL, in a country setting on the magnificent Richelieu, sits this charming hostellerie. Operated by Michel Aubriot and Bernard Môme, this award-winning Relais & Chateaux establishment offers fine Quebec cuisine and a selection of 600 wines. Local game birds, lamb, fish and produce figure prominently on chef Roger Robin's menus. This unusual warm salad is typical of the creativity in the hostellerie's kitchen.

L'Orpailleur elevé en fût de Chêne (aged in oak barrels) of Vignoble de l'Orpailleur

DUNHAM, QUEBEC

Seyval Blanc grapes were vinified to make this white. Woody, smoky nose and hints of vanilla on the palate, this wine has enough body to stand up to the duck confit and Roquefort cheese. It is supple and well balanced, with a soft mouth and long finish.

WINEMAKER'S TASTING NOTES

CONFIT:

7 oz	duck gizzards	200 g
	Coarse salt	
1 tbsp	duck fat	15 mL
1	large clove garlic	1
1	sprig thyme	1
1	bay leaf	1

VINAIGRETTE:

2 tbsp	red wine vinegar	25 mL
1 tsp	Dijon mustard	5 mL
3 oz	walnut oil	90 mL
	Salt and pepper	

	A mixture of salad greens (mâche, arugula, oak leaf lettuce, curly endive, etc.)	
¼ cup	crumbled Roquefort cheese	50 mL
4	toasted walnuts, halved	4
1 tbsp	duck fat	15 mL
2 tbsp	red wine vinegar	25 mL

1 Rub duck gizzards with coarse salt and let stand 2 to 3 hours, refrigerated. Wipe off excess salt. **2** Melt duck fat in a heavy heatproof casserole; add duck gizzards, garlic, thyme and bay leaf. Cook, covered, in 250°F (120°C) oven about 4 hours or until meat is tender and all fat has come off it. Discard garlic, thyme and bay leaf.

3 Pack gizzards in a terrine with the rendered duck fat. Cover and set aside. **4** To make vinaigrette, whisk together well red wine vinegar and Dijon mustard. Gradually whisk in walnut oil. Season with salt and pepper to taste.

5 Place greens in a large salad bowl and toss well with vinaigrette. Sprinkle with Roquefort and arrange walnuts on top. **6** Just before serving, unmould duck gizzards. In 1 tbsp (15 mL) duck fat over medium-high heat, quickly sauté gizzards until warmed through, about 1 minute. Add red wine vinegar to pan, reducing to half. Arrange gizzards over salad and pour on reduced sauce. Serve immediately.

WINE-MARINATED SUMMER VEGETABLE SALAD | Serves six

*Cartier Wines and Beverages,
Niagara Falls, Ontario*

No OTHER WINERY could be more committed to service and excellence than Cartier Wines. One person who lives by these principles daily is Mira Ananicz, the only woman in Ontario to hold the position of chief winemaker. For 18 years Mira has been supervising such innovative creations as reduced-alcohol wine coolers, juice coolers, carbonated juices, sparkling wines, table wines and dairy-based refreshments. Using a hands-on approach, she also produces six varietal wines, all of high enough quality to be VQA-listed.

Cartier Wines L'Ambiance

A blend of Seyval and Vidal grapes. Pale straw in colour, L'Ambiance is clean, crisp and easy drinking with a pear-like nose and fruity palate. It is medium bodied, making it a great mate for most salads, fish and chicken, and it is great on its own.

Suggested Varietal: Vidal

WINEMAKER'S · TASTING NOTES ·

MARINADE:

¾ cup	L'Ambiance (white wine)	175 mL
¼ cup	vegetable oil	50 mL
2 tbsp	lemon juice	25 mL
2 tbsp	Dijon mustard	25 mL
1½ tsp	chopped fresh tarragon	7 mL
¼ tsp	each salt and pepper	1 mL
½ lb	mushrooms, halved	250 g
2	green onions, sliced	2
1	medium zucchini, sliced	1
1 cup	slivered red and green bell peppers	250 mL
1	can (19 oz/540 mL) chick-peas, drained and rinsed	1
	Spinach leaves	
1 cup	mild Cheddar, cut into strips	250 mL

1 In a nonmetallic shallow dish whisk together all marinade ingredients. **2** Add mushrooms, green onions, zucchini, peppers and chick-peas. Cover and chill several hours or overnight. **3** To serve, arrange spinach in salad bowl. Pour marinade and vegetables over spinach. Top with cheese strips.

SPICY SWEET POTATO SOUP | Serves six

Michelle Ramsay

2	large sweet potatoes, quartered	2
4	lemongrass bulbs	4
6 cups	vegetable stock	1.5 L
4	cloves garlic, minced	4
1 or 2	whole dried chili peppers	1 or 2
¾ cup	fresh coconut milk (recipe follows), OR canned	175 mL
⅓ cup	lime juice	75 mL
	Salt to taste	
	Fresh coriander leaves (for garnish)	

1 Boil sweet potatoes until soft. Peel and mash. **2** Remove tough outer layer of lemongrass bulbs. Grate bulbs by hand or in food processor. **3** In a large pot, combine potatoes, grated lemongrass, vegetable stock, garlic, chilies, coconut milk, lime juice and salt. (Note: Reduce salt if you use a powdered vegetable stock.) Bring to a boil and simmer, partially covered, for 20 minutes, stirring occasionally. **4** Purée soup in batches in food processor or blender. Strain or run through a food mill to remove woody bits of lemongrass. **5** Reheat soup. Spoon a few dollops of coconut milk over top and swirl lightly. Transfer to soup bowls and garnish with coriander leaves.

COCONUT MILK:

Grate fresh coconut meat, or grind in batches in blender or food processor. In a mortar and pestle, or with processor motor running, pour in 2 cups (500 mL) boiling water. Blend 1 minute. Let cool at least 5 minutes. Press pulp through a fine sieve lined with moistened cheesecloth.

Reif Estate Winery Medium-Dry Gewürztraminer

NIAGARA-ON-THE-LAKE, ONTARIO

Generally, soups and wine are enemies. However, this recipe has enough substance to stand up to a wine. With lots of spice, and two parts residual sugar, this wine accents the sweet ingredients in the soup and blends well with the spices.

WINEMAKER'S TASTING NOTES

CHILLED CHERRY SOUP
WITH SOUR CREAM AND THYME | Serves four

*Chartwell, Four Seasons Hotel,
Vancouver, British Columbia*

CHARTWELL IS AN AWARD-WINNER for both its elegant, exciting cuisine and its extensive wine list. One of the first to fuse Eastern and Western cooking, executive chef Wolfgang von Wieser and his team of chefs have created their own delectable version of West Coast cuisine. Local sweet Okanagan cherries are used to create this sumptuous delight.

Sumac Ridge Estate Winery Johannisberg Riesling

SUMMERLAND, BRITISH COLUMBIA

Vinted off-dry, this wine is highlighted by a green apple nose and is light and fresh to the palate with a clean, crisp finish that offsets the creaminess of the soup while emphasizing its full sweet cherry taste.

WINEMAKER'S · TASTING NOTES

2 tsp	butter	10 mL
I tbsp	minced shallots	15 mL
2 tbsp	fresh thyme	25 mL
I lb	sweet cherries, pitted	500 g
I cup	chicken stock	250 mL
½ cup	sour cream	125 mL
¼ cup	Sumac Ridge Riesling (white wine)	50 mL
	Juice of ½ lemon	

1 In a skillet, melt butter and sauté shallots and thyme until shallots are soft. Cool. **2** Add cherries and chicken stock. In a blender or food processor, purée the mixture. Strain soup. Chill. **3** Just before serving, blend in sour cream, wine and lemon juice.

Cucumber and Dill Soup | Serves six

Miestro Restaurant, London, Ontario

ECLECTIC IS THE BEST DESCRIPTION of the cooking of chef/owner Mies Bervoets. An interest in Indonesian and Asian cooking shows up on her always innovative menus. A focus on fresh local ingredients and Ontario wines adds to the calibre of the menu in this tiny bistro.

2 English cucumbers, peeled, cut in 1-inch (2.5-cm) lengths		2
3 cups	plain yogurt	750 mL
1 cup	chicken stock	250 mL
¼ cup	liquid honey	50 mL
1 tbsp	dried dillweed	15 mL
	Salt and pepper to taste	
	Finely chopped smoked salmon (optional for garnish)	

1 In a food processor, process half the cucumber pieces. **2** Add half the yogurt, half the chicken stock, half the honey and half the dillweed; process until very smooth. Transfer to a bowl. **3** Process remaining yogurt, stock, honey and dillweed; add to first half, mixing well. Season to taste. Refrigerate for at least 3 hours. **4** Garnish with smoked salmon, if using.

Stoney Ridge Cellars Chardonnay

(EASTMAN VINEYARD), WINONA, ONTARIO

Fermented and aged in three types of oak, this wine is full bodied with rich buttery and nut flavours that complement the creaminess of the soup and the salty smoked salmon; a long, satisfying finish.

WINEMAKER'S TASTING NOTES

APPLE SOUP | Serves four to six

*Hainle Vineyards Estate Winery,
Peachland, British Columbia*

SMALL BUT MIGHTY, HAINLE VINEYARDS produces 10,000 gallons of wine yearly. Walter Hainle and daughter-in-law Sandra manage the vineyards and winery, leaving the winemaking up to Walter's son, Tilman, a trainee from the Weinsberg Technical School in Germany. Purity is Tilman's priority; insecticides and herbicides are forbidden in the vineyard. While vinifying, he refrains from using sulphites before fermentation, which he says places most of his wines within organic standards. With the exception of their Riesling Icewine, all Hainle wines are completely dry and show intense varietal character, having been fermented and aged in stainless steel without the addition of sweet reserves. This approach to winemaking has brought critical acclaim to the Hainle clan. Among their many awards, the family has won four gold medals for their 1987 Riesling Icewine from international wine competitions.

Hainle Vineyards Traminer Dry, Estate Bottled

Light straw in colour, this white has a bold aroma suggesting cloves and exotic fruit. It is full bodied, dry and has a pepper/bitter almond finish. These spicy characteristics coincide with the smoky flavours of cumin and coriander found in the Apple Soup.

WINEMAKER'S TASTING NOTES

SOUP:

3 tbsp	butter	50 mL
½ tsp	minced gingerroot	2 mL
2	cloves garlic, minced, skins reserved for stock	2
1½ cups	chopped onion, skins reserved for stock	375 mL
4 cups	chopped apples (McIntosh or Spartan), peels and cores reserved for stock	1 L
1 tsp	salt	5 mL
	Juice of 1 lemon	

FLOUR-SPICE MIXTURE:

3 tbsp	all-purpose flour	50 mL
1 tsp	dry mustard	5 mL
1 tsp	turmeric	5 mL
1 tsp	cumin	5 mL
1 tsp	coriander	5 mL
Pinch	each cardamom and cayenne	Pinch

STOCK:

	Peels and cores from the apples	
2½ cups	unsweetened apple juice	625 mL
	Cleaned skins from onions and garlic	
2	cinnamon sticks	2
½ cup	Hainle Traminer (white wine)	125 mL
2 cups	yogurt (room temperature)	500 mL
	Toasted slivered almonds (for garnish)	

1 In a large heavy skillet or Dutch oven over moderate heat, melt butter. Add gingerroot and garlic; cook, stirring, for about 1 minute. Add onions and cook 5 minutes. Stir in apples, salt and lemon juice. **2** Stir together all flour-spice mixture ingredients. Sprinkle onto apple-onion mixture, stirring constantly to blend smoothly. Cover and cook about 10 minutes over low heat, stirring occasionally. Let cool to room temperature. **3** Combine all stock ingredients in a large pot. Add 2 cups (500 mL) water. Boil gently, partially covered, for 45 minutes, stirring occasionally. Remove from heat and let stand for 1 hour. Strain through a fine sieve to remove solids. **4** In batches in a blender or food processor, purée stock and apple-onion mixture until smooth. Whisk in yogurt. Chill until serving time. Serve cold, topped with almonds.

TRAPPER'S GREEN PEA AND PEPPERCORN SOUP | Serves four to six

Trapper's, Toronto, Ontario

HOME-GROWN INGREDIENTS and Canadian wines abound at Trapper's. One of the city's first restaurants to offer a vast selection of local wines by the glass as well as the bottle, Trapper's features market-fresh cuisine that provides an ideal complement to the food. Owners Chris and Larkin Boland take pride in all things Canadian and graciously educate their customers about local wines and foods.

Cave Spring Cellars Dry Riesling

JORDAN, ONTARIO

The wine's clean, crisp citrus flavours with apple, pear and citrus nose work well with the spice and weight of the soup.

¼ cup	butter	50 mL
I	medium onion, chopped	I
I	large potato, cubed	I
2 cups	frozen green peas	500 mL
I tbsp	green peppercorns	15 mL
5 cups	chicken stock	1.25 L
½ tsp	each onion salt, celery salt and garlic salt	2 mL
2 tbsp	chicken bouillon powder	25 mL
¼ cup	soy sauce	50 mL
¾ cup	whipping cream	175 mL

Bacon bits and freshly grated Parmesan cheese (for garnish)

1 In a large pot, melt butter and sauté onions until translucent. Add potato, peas and peppercorns; cook for about 3 minutes. Add chicken stock, onion salt, celery salt, garlic salt, bouillon powder and soy sauce. Bring to a boil and simmer, uncovered, over medium heat for 15 to 20 minutes or until potatoes are soft. **2** In a blender or food processor, purée the soup until smooth. Return to pot, add cream and simmer for 5 minutes or until heated through. Do not boil. Pour into soup bowls and garnish with bacon and Parmesan.

Spicy Tomato Soup with Orange Cream | Serves four

Michelle Ramsay

¾ cup	plain low-fat yogurt	175 mL
2 tbsp	orange juice	25 mL
I tsp	orange zest	5 mL
2 tbsp	extra virgin olive oil	25 mL
2	cloves garlic, minced	2
I	large onion, thinly sliced	I
5 lb	tomatoes, peeled, seeded and chopped	2.2 kg
I tsp	sugar	5 mL
I	bay leaf	I
2	jalapeño peppers, seeded and chopped	2
I quart	chicken OR vegetable stock	I L
	Salt, pepper and cayenne to taste	
	Fresh basil, sliced into ribbons (for garnish)	

Stoney Ridge Cellars Cabernet Franc

WINONA, ONTARIO

A full-bodied wine, Cabernet Franc has enough of a raspberry-like aroma that it will work with the tomatoes, but won't break down the orange in the recipe. The wine's spicy finish also works with jalapeños.

WINEMAKER'S TASTING NOTES

1 Place yogurt in a paper coffee filter or sieve lined with cheesecloth and allow to drain several hours in the fridge. When yogurt is very thick, stir in orange juice and zest. Refrigerate until needed. **2** In a large saucepan, heat oil over medium heat and sauté garlic and onion until fragrant, taking care not to burn. Add tomatoes, sugar, bay leaf and jalapeños; cook over medium-low heat for 10 minutes. Add stock and simmer, uncovered, for 20 to 30 minutes, stirring occasionally. **3** Pass soup through a food mill or sieve. Season with salt, pepper and cayenne. Pour into soup bowls and garnish with a dollop of orange cream and basil ribbons.

Spicy Corn Soup | Serves four

Michelle Ramsay

ANCHO CHILIES, which are dried poblano chilies, have a mild fruit flavour with tones of dried plum, raisins, coffee, licorice and tobacco. They are available in the produce section of most supermarkets and specialty markets.

Hillebrand Estates Trius Chardonnay

(SHOEMAKER VINEYARD)
NIAGARA-ON-THE-LAKE,
ONTARIO

Oaky from barrel fermenting, this wine can handle the smoky tones of the soup. Medium to full-bodied, this wine is well balanced with toasty caramel tones that match well with the sweetness of the roasted garlic and corn.

WINEMAKER'S · TASTING NOTES

3	cloves garlic, unpeeled	3
4 tsp	olive oil	20 mL
6	cobs corn, husked	6
¾ cup	finely chopped leeks	175 mL
I	large carrot, finely chopped	I
3	coriander roots	3
I	jalapeño pepper	I
I	medium dried ancho chili	I
3 tbsp	sour cream	50 mL
I cup	whipping cream	250 mL
	Salt and white pepper to taste	
¼ cup	finely chopped fresh coriander	50 mL

1 Brush garlic cloves with olive oil. Roast at 300°F (150°C) for 15 minutes. Cool and peel. **2** Barbecue corn over medium fire or set under broiler for 8 to 10 minutes, turning frequently so it doesn't burn. Cool. Slice kernels from cob. **3** In a medium pot, combine leeks, carrot, coriander roots and jalapeño with 2½ cups (625 mL) water. Bring to a boil and simmer 10 minutes. Add corn kernels and simmer another 10 minutes. **4** Meanwhile, roast ancho chili in 450°F (230°C) oven for 30 seconds. Cover with 3 tbsp (50 mL) hot water for 15 minutes or until soft. Pour chili and hot water into food processor or blender, and blend to a paste. Push paste through a sieve to remove seeds. Stir in sour cream. **5** Remove coriander roots from soup mixture and discard. In a food processor or blender purée mixture in batches. Strain through a sieve or food mill and return to pot. Stir in whipping cream and set over low heat until heated through. Season with salt and pepper. Pour into soup bowls and garnish with ancho cream and chopped coriander.

CHICKEN, COCONUT AND GALANGAL SOUP (TOM KHA GAI) | Serves four

Michelle Ramsay

6 cups	chicken stock	1.5 L
I tsp	salt	5 mL
3	kaffir lime leaves*	3
I	stalk lemongrass, bruised and minced	I
I inch	galangal root, thinly sliced*	2.5 cm
2	fresh small green chilies, minced	2
4	coriander roots, washed well and bruised	4
I tbsp	fish sauce*	15 mL
2	boneless chicken breasts, cubed	2
1½ cups	fresh unsweetened coconut milk (recipe on page 49), OR canned	375 mL
	Fresh lime juice to taste	
	Freshly chopped coriander (for garnish)	

Cave Spring Cellars Gewürztraminer

JORDAN, ONTARIO

This dry, crisp white wine has tart acidity and a light lichee aroma that is characteristic of this grape variety. The pear fruit and a grapefruity-herbal bitterness give the wine enough character to stand up to this hot, spicy soup.

1 In a large pot, bring to a boil chicken stock, salt, lime leaves, lemongrass, galangal, chilies, coriander roots and fish sauce. **2** Reduce heat and add chicken. Simmer 10 to 15 minutes, covered, until chicken is cooked. Add coconut milk and lime juice; simmer 2 minutes. Remove coriander roots. Garnish with fresh coriander.

Galangal, a strong relative of gingerroot, kaffir lime leaves and fish sauce can be bought at Asian markets.

SOUP PROVENÇALE | Serves four

Anthony's Seafood Bistro,
London, Ontario

DAVID CHAPMAN, chef/owner of this unpretentious little bistro, is a seafood magician. His ability to transform a piece of fish into an edible work of art is legend in southern Ontario. Whether it is a simple piece of grilled tuna or a fanciful rendition of softshell crab, Chapman manages to hit just the right note with his customers. An appreciation of local foods and wines is evident on the menu and the wine list. But one of the main attractions of Anthony's is the creation of impromptu dishes for customers.

Inniskillin Wines Gewürztraminer

NIAGARA-ON-THE-LAKE, ONTARIO

This dry, full-bodied and spicy wine is able to hold its own with this garlicky, aromatic soup. Rich in flavour and with tropical fruit aromas, the wine is vinified in the tradition of Alsatian Gewürztraminers.

WINEMAKER'S TASTING NOTES

I tbsp	olive oil	15 mL
I	small leek, sliced	I
2	cloves garlic, chopped	2
	Oregano flakes	
Pinch	saffron	Pinch
2 cups	fish stock	500 mL
I	large potato, thinly sliced	I
2 tbsp	olive oil	25 mL
8	large shrimp, peeled	8
8	sea scallops	8
12	mussels	12
I½ lb	firm fish (e.g., halibut, swordfish), cut in pieces	750 g
12	toasted croutons	12
	Rouille (recipe follows)	

1 In a medium saucepan, fry leeks in I tbsp (15 mL) olive oil until leeks are soft but not browned. Stir in garlic, oregano, saffron, stock and potatoes. Bring to boil. Adjust seasoning and reduce heat to a simmer. **2** In a large saucepan, heat 2 tbsp (25 mL) olive oil. Add fish pieces and gently toss. Add seasoned stock. Bring to boil and simmer for no more than 3 minutes. **3** Brush toasted croutons with rouille and pour over soup. Serve soup in cooking pot.

ROUILLE:

1 cup	mayonnaise	250 mL
1	clove garlic, chopped	1
¼ cup	canned pimiento, drained	50 mL
Dash	Pernod	Dash

1 In a food processor or blender, purée until well blended.

JOSEPH LASSAGA'S BOUILLABAISSE | Serves six

Andres Wines,
Port Moody, British Columbia

WITH LOCATIONS IN FIVE PROVINCES (British Columbia, Alberta, Ontario, Quebec and Nova Scotia) and distribution extending to the United States, Europe and Japan, Andres Wines is Canada's second-largest winery. They produce a broad spectrum of products, from the generic labels of Hochtaler and Domaine D'Or to wine-based liqueurs and now the more reputed vinifera varietal wines. Recently, Andres released the Peller Estate wines. The 1990 Peller Estate Pinot Blanc won the People's Choice Award Gold Medal at the 1991 Pacific National Exhibition Wine Festival. Ron Taylor is winemaster at Andres in Port Moody. He has 22 years of winemaking experience behind him, which helped him immensely when he was select- ed to be part of the original VQA tasting panel set up in British Columbia in 1990. This bouillabaisse recipe was recommended to Ron Taylor by chef Joseph Lassaga of Andersons Restaurant in Vancouver.

Andres Peller Estates Vintage Pinot Blanc

Using Jost Vineyards grapes, Andres produced this Pinot Blanc. It exhibits hints of lemon, toast and vanilla on the nose and palate and has a clean finish. Normally, soup and wine do not work together, but this bouillabaisse is filled with flavoured seafood, giving it enough substance to match this light-bodied white.

WINEMAKER'S TASTING NOTES

3	lobsters (I lb/500 g each), steamed and cooled	3
½ cup	olive oil	125 mL
I lb	fish bones	500 g
I	onion, diced	I
I	leek, diced	I
I	carrot, sliced	I
2	stalks celery, sliced	2
I	bay leaf	I
½	bunch parsley, chopped	½
¼ tsp	thyme leaves	I mL
¼ tsp	aniseed	I mL
¼ tsp	oregano	I mL
2	cloves garlic, minced	2
Pinch	saffron	Pinch
	Salt and pepper to taste	
2 tsp	tomato paste	10 mL

½ cup	Andres Wines Pinot Blanc (white wine)	125 mL
Dash	Pernod	Dash
I	can (10 oz/284 mL) plum tomatoes, chopped	I
6	salmon, cod, halibut or snapper fillets (2 oz/50 g each)	6
12	mussels	12
12	clams	12
12	prawns	12
6	scallops in shell	6
I	Dungeness crab, steamed and cooled	I
	Garlic croutons (for garnish)	

1 Sever lobster head from body. Cut head in half lengthwise and reserve for garnish. Remove lobster meat from shell and cube. **2** Over a sink, split crab in half lengthwise. Remove gills, stomach and coral. Remove meat from shell and cube. **3** In a large pot, heat olive oil. Sauté fish bones and lobster meat. Add onion, leek, carrot, celery, bay leaf, parsley, thyme, aniseed, oregano, garlic, saffron, salt and pepper, and tomato paste. Stir in wine, Pernod, tomatoes and 6 cups (1.5 L) water. Simmer for 30 minutes. Strain broth into a large pot. **4** Bring broth to a boil. Add fish and shellfish. Simmer for 6 to 7 minutes until crab is heated through and prawns are opaque. Discard any mussels and clams that do not open. Add croutons. Transfer to soup bowls and garnish with lobster heads.

DUNGENESS CRAB AND HUBBARD SQUASH CONSOMMÉ | Serves four

Sooke Harbour House, Sooke, British Columbia

AN EARLY INNOVATOR OF West Coast cuisine, Sooke Harbour House is legendary for its spectacular use of local ingredients as well as its accommodations. Owners Fredrica and Sinclair Philip offer sumptuous rooms furnished with antiques and native art and a dining room that attracts food lovers from across the continent. This soup is an adaptation of the classic consommé, using vegetables and herbs grown in the Sooke Harbour House garden.

Mission Hill Vineyards Private Reserve Sherry (non-vintage)

WESTBANK,

BRITISH COLUMBIA

Made mainly from 1974 wine, this sherry was fortified and stored in heavily charred whiskey barrels for 10 years in the traditional Spanish manner. It has a golden colour and nutty taste with a dry finish that works well with this consommé.

6 cups	clear rabbit OR chicken stock	1.5 L
2	live Dungeness or Red Rock crabs	2
I cup	finely chopped carrot	250 mL
I cup	finely chopped onion	250 mL
I cup	finely chopped celery	250 mL
I cup	finely chopped flesh of Hubbard squash	250 mL
I cup	finely chopped fennel bulb	250 mL
½ cup	mixed fresh savoury herbs (rosemary, sage, Chinese parsley, fennel), finely chopped	125 mL
3	juniper berries, crushed	3
6	peppercorns, crushed	6
I tsp	caraway seeds	5 mL
5	egg whites	5
	Low-sodium tamari sauce (optional)	

GARNISHES:

4	pincer claws from crab	4
I tsp	finely chopped shallots	5 mL
⅓ cup	Mission Hill white wine OR dry vermouth	75 mL

1 In a 2-quart (2-L) saucepan, bring rabbit stock to a boil. Set aside. **2** Over a sink, split crabs in half lengthwise to kill. Remove gills, stomach and coral. Remove pincer claws and reserve, refrigerated, for garnish. Wrap crab bodies in a lint-free towel and crush with a mallet or hammer. **3** In a mixing bowl, combine crushed crabs with carrot, onion, celery, squash, fennel, herbs, juniper berries, peppercorns, caraway seeds and egg whites. Stir well to mix evenly. **4** Place vegetable-crab mixture in a 4-quart (4-L) saucepan and set over high heat. Gradually add rabbit stock, stirring constantly. **5** Reduce heat to medium and carefully stir occasionally to prevent sticking. When a raft (coagulated vegetable, egg and crab mixture) starts to form, stop stirring and reduce heat. (The process will take approximately 15 minutes.) **6** Simmer slowly for 45 minutes to 1 hour. Do not stir. Do not boil rapidly or the raft will separate. The raft should feel firm to the touch, not soft and mushy. **7** Meanwhile, prepare garnish. In an oven-safe saucepan over medium heat, bring wine to a boil. Add crab claws and shallots; cover. Transfer lidded saucepan to oven. Steam at 375°F (190°C) for 4 minutes. **8** Slowly strain consommé through a strainer lined with cheesecloth. Adjust for seasoning with tamari, if using. (Consommé may be prepared to here, cooled and chilled. Reheat before serving.) Ladle consommé into heated bowls and garnish with freshly steamed crab claws.

CHAPTER EIGHT

PASTA

MICHELLE'S SPICY LINGUINE | Serves four

Michelle Ramsay

¾ lb	linguine	375 g
8 oz	cold Brie	250 g
⅓ cup	extra virgin olive oil	75 mL
3 or 4	large cloves garlic, minced	3 or 4
2	large shallots, minced	2
1	habanero (Scotch bonnet) pepper (fresh or bottled), cut in half	1
4	red bell peppers, peeled, seeded and cut into ½-inch (1-cm) wide strips	4
1 cup	sliced fresh mushrooms	250 mL
½ cup	chopped fresh basil OR coriander	125 mL
	Salt and pepper to taste	

1 In a large pot of boiling salted water, cook linguine until al dente. **2** Meanwhile, using a wet knife, remove peel from Brie. Cut Brie into 1-inch (2.5-cm) chunks. **3** Just before pasta is ready, in medium saucepan over medium-low heat, heat olive oil and sauté garlic, shallots and habanero pepper until garlic is fragrant, about 1 minute. Do not let garlic burn. **4** Add bell peppers and cook about 5 minutes. Add mushrooms and sauté another 2 minutes. Remove habanero pepper. **5** Toss drained cooked pasta with vegetable mixture. Add Brie pieces and toss again. Add basil and mix well. Season with salt and pepper. Garnish with additional basil.

*F*ETTUCCINE GIULIANA | Serves four

C a v e   S p r i n g   C e l l a r s ,
J o r d a n ,   O n t a r i o

DISTINCTIVENESS IS THE KEY TO Cave Spring Cellars' success. Winemaker Angelo Pavan purchases only those grapes grown on the Beamsville Bench in Niagara. On this first "shelf" of the Niagara Escarpment, a mild microclimate and clay-loam soils prevail, giving the grapes and therefore Cave Spring Cellars' varietal wines aromas reminiscent of peaches and flavours similar to citrus fruit (grapefruit and lime). This distinctiveness has put Cave Spring Cellars in the forefront of Ontario's wine industry. Recently, company president Leonard Pennachetti received the prestigious Prix du Jury (top Canadian wine award) for his 1990 Chardonnay Barrel-Fermented, from the 1992 Sélections Mondiales Wine Competition, in Montreal.

2 tbsp	butter	25 mL
6 oz	prosciutto, cut into ribbons	150 g
2 tbsp	all-purpose flour	25 mL
2 cups	whipping cream	500 mL
1 cup	cooked peas	250 mL
2 tbsp	freshly grated Parmesan cheese	25 mL
	Salt and pepper to taste	
1 lb	fettuccine	500 g

1 In a skillet or sauté pan, melt butter. Sauté prosciutto until well coated with butter. **2** Sprinkle on flour and cook for a few minutes. Add cream while stirring with a wire whisk. Cook until sauce thickens. Do not boil. **3** Stir in peas, Parmesan and salt and pepper. Remove from heat and keep warm. **4** In a large pot of boiling salted water, cook fettuccine until al dente. Drain well. **5** Toss fettuccine with sauce. Serve immediately with additional Parmesan cheese.

Cave Spring Cellars Chardonnay

(BEAMSVILLE BENCH SERIES)

This white varietal was made in the lean, crisp style often associated with Chablis, France. A long, cool fermentation has preserved its classic fruit character while adding complexity through partial malolactic fermentation. This Chardonnay works with Fettucine Giuliana in two ways. While the acid contrasts with the richness of cream, the wine's diverse fruit flavours mirror the diversity of cream, peas, prosciutto and fettuccine.

WINEMAKER'S · TASTING NOTES

ARND'S VEGETARIAN LASAGNA | Serves eight

Arnd Jüergensen

FREELANCE VANCOUVER CHEF Arnd Jüergensen created this healthy, 1990s-style lasagna. The former New Yorker is a vegetarian who often incorporates Thai and South American touches into his dishes.

Inniskillin Wines Cabernet Sauvignon/ Cabernet Franc

NIAGARA-ON-THE-LAKE, ONTARIO

Robust tannins from the Cabernet Sauvignon lend backbone to the wine and allow it to stand up to the chilies in the dish. The Cabernet Franc provides the fruity aromas and softer, sweeter-tasting tannins that enhance the creamy cheeses.

Suggested Varietal: Cabernet Sauvignon

WINEMAKER'S · TASTING NOTES

3 tbsp	olive oil	50 mL
I to 2	chilies, minced	I to 2
2	cloves garlic, minced	2
I	large onion, chopped	I
I cup	textured vegetable protein (TVP)	250 mL
2 tbsp	soy sauce	25 mL
2 cups	sliced mushrooms	500 mL
I	bunch broccoli, chopped	I
3 cups	tomato sauce	750 mL
¾	block tofu	¾
½ lb	ricotta cheese	250 g
2	eggs, slightly beaten	2
	Salt and pepper to taste	
12	lasagna strips, cooked	12
2	medium zucchini, thinly sliced	2
I cup	cashews	250 mL
I½ cups	freshly grated Parmesan cheese	375 mL
2 cups	shredded mozzarella cheese	500 mL

1 Heat oil in saucepan and sauté chilies and garlic for I minute. Add onion and sauté until slightly translucent. Mix TVP with soy sauce and add to saucepan; cook I minute, stirring occasionally. Add mushrooms, broccoli

and tomato sauce; simmer 5 minutes. **2** In a bowl, mash tofu. Mix with ricotta and eggs. Season with salt and pepper. **3** Spread one-third of vegetable sauce in a 13- x 9-inch (3.5-L) lasagna dish. Top with layer of lasagna noodles (about 3 noodles), then one-third of sauce, one-third of tofu, one-third of zucchini and one-third of the cashews. Sprinkle with one-third of the Parmesan and one-third of the mozzarella. Top with 3 noodles. Create two more layers the same way, ending with sauce, tofu, zucchini, cashews, Parmesan and mozzarella.
4 In centre of oven, bake at 350°F (180°C), uncovered, about 35 minutes, until hot and bubbly.

CURRIED RICE NOODLES WITH CASHEWS AND BASIL | Serves four

Shari Darling / LeComte Estate Winery, Okanagan Falls, British Columbia

JUST THREE MILES south of Okanagan Falls, between Penticton and Oliver, LeComte Estate Winery has been creating delicious wines since 1986. Albert LeComte is owner and wine-maker. He produces more than 23,000 gallons of wine each year and can boast several awards for his work. At the 1992 Pacific National Exhibition Wine Festival, for instance, LeComte won a silver medal for his 1987 Gewürztraminer, followed by another silver for his 1990 Bacchus at the 1992 International Eastern Wine Competition. Riesling, Pinot Blanc, Chardonnay, Bacchus and Gewürztraminer are but a few of the many vines planted on the 50-acre estate vineyard.

LeComte Estate Winery Gewürztraminer Dry

Stainless steel fermented and aged, Gewürztraminer Dry has lots of spice on the nose with a hint of melon and faint grape-fruit flavours on the mouth. Known for its spiciness, this white is great with all Asian dishes.

WINEMAKER'S · TASTING NOTES

1½ tsp	vegetable oil	7 mL
½ tsp	salt	2 mL
12 oz	rice noodles	350 g
3 tbsp	olive oil	50 mL
2 tbsp	finely chopped red onion	25 mL
I	clove garlic, minced	I
I tbsp	curry paste	15 mL
I cup	fresh coconut milk (recipe on page 49), OR canned	250 mL
2 tbsp	fish sauce	25 mL
2 tsp	paprika	10 mL
½ cup	whipping cream	125 mL
⅔ cup	sliced snow peas	150 mL
½ cup	thinly sliced red bell pepper	125 mL
2 tbsp	finely chopped toasted cashews	25 mL
2 tbsp	finely chopped fresh basil	25 mL

◼ In a large pot bring 8 cups (2 L) water to a boil. Add vegetable oil, salt and rice noodles. Boil until noodles are

cooked, about 2 to 3 minutes. Drain, rinse and set aside.
2 In a large skillet over medium heat, heat olive oil. Sauté onion and garlic until lightly browned. Add curry paste and stir for 1 minute. Add coconut milk, fish sauce and paprika; return to a boil. Pour in cream; return to a boil, stirring constantly, and cook 2 minutes. Reduce heat and simmer 5 minutes. **3** Add snow peas, bell pepper, cashews, basil and cooked noodles; toss until noodles are well coated. Serve immediately.

SPAGHETTI WITH BLACK OLIVES AND ORANGE | Serves four

Michelle Ramsay

¾ lb	spaghetti	375 g
¼ cup	extra virgin olive oil	50 mL
1	large red onion, thinly sliced	1
	Finely grated rind of 2 large oranges	
2	large cloves garlic, minced	2
20	cured black olives, coarsely chopped	20
	Salt and pepper to taste	
	Freshly grated Parmesan cheese (optional)	
	Fresh basil leaves (for garnish)	

1 In a large pot of boiling salted water, cook spaghetti until al dente. **2** While pasta is cooking, in a skillet heat olive oil over medium heat and sauté onion for 2 minutes. Add orange rind, garlic and olives; sauté 1 minute. **3** Toss onion with drained cooked pasta. Season with salt and pepper. Add Parmesan, if using, and toss again. Garnish with fresh basil leaves.

Cave Spring Cellars Riesling Off-Dry

JORDAN, ONTARIO

Fermented in stainless steel at cool temperatures, this wine retains the freshness and aromatics of the Riesling grape. The forward green and grapefruit aromas enhance the citrus orange and basil flavours of this pasta. The tart acidity of Riesling lifts the dish.

WINEMAKER'S TASTING NOTES

Spring Risotto | Serves four to six

Michelle Ramsay

USE A MIXTURE OF domestic and exotic mushrooms (oyster, chanterelle, porcini, shiitake) to accentuate the flavours.

Henry of Pelham Gamay Noir

ST. CATHARINES, ONTARIO

This light, creamy-textured wine works well with the creaminess of the risotto. Excellent ruby colour, fresh raspberry aromas and flavours with a lasting peppery finish.

2	large red bell peppers	2
½ lb	asparagus	250 g
¼ cup	butter	50 mL
¼ cup	olive oil	50 mL
I	small onion, finely chopped	I
2 cups	sliced fresh mushrooms	500 mL
¼ cup	brandy	50 mL
2 cups	arborio rice	500 mL
5 cups	(approx) hot vegetable OR chicken stock	1.25 L
I cup	freshly grated Parmesan cheese	250 mL
	Salt and freshly cracked pepper to taste	
	Fresh basil leaves (for garnish)	

1 Grill peppers until skins are charred; cool. Peel, seed and finely dice peppers. **2** Blanch asparagus in salted water for I minute, drain and refresh under cold water. Chop into I-inch (2.5-cm) segments. **3** In a medium saucepan over medium heat, heat butter and oil. Sauté onion until golden and fragrant. Add mushrooms and sauté until soft. Add brandy and bring to a simmer. **4** Add rice and sauté about 5 minutes, stirring often to ensure that each grain is glossy. **5** Add stock I cup (250 mL) at a time, stirring frequently until stock is completely absorbed each time. (The risotto will be cooked in about

25 minutes.) When rice reaches a creamy consistency, remove from heat and stir in peppers, asparagus and half the Parmesan. Mix well and let stand about 5 minutes, keeping warm. **6** Serve risotto in individual dishes. Garnish with remaining Parmesan and fresh basil leaves.

SPAGHETTI SQUASH ALFREDO | Serves two

Shari Darling / Vignoble Grenier Martel, Waterloo, Quebec

VIGNOBLE GRENIER MARTEL's sole proprietor Claude Grenier produces three wines from the main varieties Chancellor and V50-20I, both grown on his 50-acre vineyard.

I tbsp	butter	I5 mL
I	clove garlic, minced	I
2 tbsp	finely chopped fresh parsley	25 mL
	Salt and pepper to taste	
I cup	ricotta cheese	250 mL
¼ cup	freshly grated Parmesan cheese	50 mL
2 cups	cooked spaghetti squash	500 mL

Vignoble Grenier Les Grapillons

Grapillons translates as "little grapes." Winemaker Claude Grenier vinified only the smallest Seyval grapes on the vines to produce this white. Fresh, fruity and low in acid, it is a suitable companion for the delicate tastes of ricotta and spaghetti squash.

1 To cook squash, cut in half and scoop out seeds. Pour ¼ inch (5 mm) water in microwave-safe baking dish. Place half of squash in baking dish, cut side down. Cover with plastic wrap. Microwave at High for I0 minutes, or until squash is tender. Cook other half of squash same way. Remove skin. Measure 2 cups (500 mL) squash and set aside. (Keep remainder for another use.) **2** In a large nonstick skillet over medium-low heat, melt butter. Add garlic, parsley, salt and pepper, ricotta cheese and Parmesan cheese; cook until mixture is hot, about 2 to 3 minutes. **3** Add cooked spaghetti squash. Heat, stirring gently, until squash is hot. Transfer to serving dish and sprinkle with freshly ground pepper.

RISOTTO CON ASPARAGI (RICE WITH ASPARAGUS) | Serves two

Divino Estate Winery and Busnardo Vineyard, Oliver, British Columbia

SNUGGLED IN THE OKANAGAN HILLS south of Oliver, British Columbia, Divino Estate Winery makes 40,000 gallons of wine each year. Although owners Joe and Barbara Busnardo established the winery in 1982, their 71-acre vineyard is planted with 15-year-old vines. Some of the varieties to be found here are Merlot, Cabernet Franc and Chardonnay, as well as Malvasia and Trebbiano, white varieties of Italian origin. Winemaker Joe Busnardo vinifies these grapes into Italian-styled wines. The wines have won many awards in international wine competitions.

Divino Estate Winery Pinot Bianco

Stainless steel fermenting and ageing produced this white. Made from Pinot Blanc grapes, the wine is full bodied and dry, with floral aromas and a hint of fruit on the palate. A wine less full bodied would be lost as an accompaniment to this vegetarian dish.

¼ cup	olive oil	50 mL
2	celery sticks, finely chopped	2
½	large onion, finely chopped	½
I	clove garlic, minced	I
	Salt and pepper to taste	
¼ cup	Divino Estates Pinot Bianco (white wine)	50 mL
1½ cups	arborio rice	375 mL
5 cups	vegetable stock	1.25 L
2 cups	chopped cooked asparagus OR I can (14 oz/398 mL) asparagus, drained	500 mL
I tbsp	unsalted butter	15 mL
¼ cup	grated Parmesan cheese	50 mL

1 In a saucepan over medium heat, heat oil. Sauté celery and onions for 2 to 3 minutes. Add garlic, salt and pepper. **2** Pour in wine, stirring well to deglaze pan. Add rice and sauté until glossy, about I minute. **3** Add ¾ cup (175 mL) stock at a time, stirring frequently, until stock is completely absorbed each time. When rice reaches a creamy consistency, remove from heat. Stir in asparagus, butter and Parmesan cheese. Serve immediately.

CAPPELLETTI WITH GORGONZOLA CREAM AND MÜLLER-THURGAU | Serves six

Shari Darling / Okanagan Vineyards, Oliver, British Columbia

WITH BUSINESS EVER INCREASING, Okanagan Vineyards has made a few positive changes over the past couple of years. Once considered an estate winery, they have now gone commercial, making more than 100,000 gallons of wine annually. They have also replanted their 22-acre vineyard to the more desirable vinifera vines and have hired winemaker Sandor Mayer to vinify the grapes.

1 cup	Okanagan Vineyards Müller-Thurgau (white wine)	250 mL
2½ cups	whipping cream	625 mL
	Freshly ground black pepper to taste	
Pinch	nutmeg	Pinch
1½ lb	fresh cappelletti	750 g
¾ lb	gorgonzola cheese, crumbled	375 g
4 tsp	grated Parmesan (preferably Reggiano) cheese	20 mL

1 In a heavy saucepan, bring wine to a boil and reduce by half. **2** Add cream. Bring to a boil and lower heat. Stir in pepper and nutmeg. Simmer, uncovered, for about 15 minutes or until sauce is reduced by one-third. **3** In a large pot of boiling salted water, cook cappelletti until al dente. Drain and return to pot. **4** Remove cream sauce from heat, stir in half the gorgonzola and all the Parmesan. Pour over cappelletti. Set pasta over medium heat and cook gently, stirring constantly, for 5 minutes or until cream and cheese mixture has thickened. **5** Serve on heated plates. Sprinkle with remaining gorgonzola.

Okanagan Vineyards Müller-Thurgau

A cross between the Riesling and Sylvaner grape varieties, Müller-Thurgau produces a light-bodied white with soft texture and low acidity—ideal elements to marry with the creamy texture of gorgonzola, while allowing the strong flavours to predominate.

WINEMAKER'S • TASTING NOTES

*T*AGLIATELLE WITH SALMON AND LEMON | Serves four

Le Mitoyen, Sainte-Dorothée, Quebec

ARTISTIC FOOD IS PRESENTED IN A charming house in this Montreal suburb. Popular with discerning food-lovers, this restaurant has won numerous awards, including the prestigious *Guide Zagat's* 1990 award for best cuisine and service for Montreal and region. This modern twist on pasta is a favourite of Le Mitoyen's customers.

Vignoble Les Arpents de Neige Vendange Sélectionné

DUNHAM, QUEBEC

Oak-aged, this clear yellowish wine has a slight oaky flavour and a vegetal aroma, so it is strong enough to stand up to the salmon and lemon in this pasta. The body of this wine is mainly ripe Seyval with a pineapple aftertaste. It's acidic enough to cut through the cream.

Suggested Varietal: Sauvignon Blanc

3 tbsp	olive oil	50 mL
2	shallots, minced	2
I	clove garlic, minced	I
¼ tsp	minced gingerroot	I mL
¼ cup	lemon vinegar	50 mL
I½ cups	whipping cream	375 mL
I lb	tagliatelle noodles	500 g
7 oz	fresh Atlantic salmon, cubed	200 g
	Zest of I lemon, blanched and finely chopped	
I cup	finely chopped fresh parsley	250 mL
	Salt and freshly cracked pepper to taste	

1 In a medium saucepan over medium heat, sauté the shallots, garlic and ginger in 2 tbsp (25 mL) olive oil. **2** Add lemon vinegar and reduce until liquid has evaporated. Pour in cream and reduce to one-third. **3** Meanwhile, in a large pot of boiling salted water, cook tagliatelle until al dente. **4** While pasta is cooking, in a large skillet heat remaining 2 tbsp (25 mL) olive oil. Sauté salmon pieces 2 to 3 minutes. **5** Combine drained cooked noodles with ginger-shallot sauce, lemon zest and parsley. Season with salt and pepper, mixing well. Arrange pasta on plates and garnish with salmon and additional freshly cracked pepper.

LINGUINE OF THE SEA | Serves four

Shari Darling / Vignoble Des Pins, Sabrevois, Quebec

VIGNOBLE DES PINS is nestled in the Haut-Richelieu region of Quebec. Here, proprietor/ winemaker Gilles Benoit grows French hybrid grapes on five acres of vineyard and makes 600 gallons of wine each year. His white blend combines Seyval Blanc and Aurore grapes; the red blends are made from Maréchal Foch and de Chaunac.

2 tbsp	olive oil	25 mL
½ cup	finely chopped red onion	125 mL
I can (28 oz/798 mL) plum tomatoes, drained and chopped		I
2 tsp	tarragon	10 mL
Salt and freshly ground black pepper to taste		
I cup	whipping cream	250 mL
I	lobster (about 3 lb/1.5 kg), steamed and cooled	I
Pinch	cayenne	Pinch
I lb	linguine	500 g
4 sprigs parsley (for garnish)		

Vignoble Des Pins Mousseux Méthode Champenoise

SABREVOIS, QUEBEC

Made in the traditional méthode champenoise, this bubbly is a cuvée of Seyval Blanc and Aurore grapes. Crisp, light and refreshing, Mousseux Méthode Champenoise effervesces, so it lessens the rich taste of lobster and cream.

1 In a saucepan over medium heat, heat oil. Cook onion until golden. **2** Add tomatoes, tarragon, salt and pepper. Bring mixture to a boil; simmer, uncovered, for 30 minutes, stirring occasionally. Remove from heat and cool. **3** Purée cooled mixture in blender or food processor. **4** Return purée to saucepan and stir in cream. Simmer 15 minutes, stirring constantly. Add lobster and cayenne. Simmer 3 to 5 minutes, until lobster is heated through. **5** In a pot of boiling salted water, cook linguine until al dente. Drain well and arrange on warm serving plates. Spoon sauce evenly over top. Garnish with sprigs of parsley and lobster claws.

WINEMAKER'S · TASTING NOTES

Spaghetti Piccante con Gamberi Freschi | Serves four to six

Corsi Trattoria, North Vancouver, British Columbia

MARIO CORSI'S NORTH SHORE RESTAURANT, just across from Lonsdale Quay, sets the standard for Italian food in the area. His sunny dishes bear the Corsi trademarks of tender homemade pasta, extra virgin olive oil, fresh basil, sun-dried tomatoes and balsamic vinegar. The Corsi Italian magic and hospitality is also worked at two other venues—Café Roma, which Mario runs with his brother Antonio, and the Park Royal Hotel in Vancouver.

Gray Monk Cellars Pinot Auxerrois

OKANAGAN CENTRE, BRITISH COLUMBIA

A refreshing, crisp, light-bodied wine that is full on the palate with a peach flavour that flows into a lingering finish. A fruity bouquet. This wine is ideal with lightly spiced dishes like this pasta.

WINEMAKER'S TASTING NOTES

20 to 24	large fresh prawns OR scampi	20 to 24
6	cloves garlic, finely chopped	6
Dash	cayenne	Dash
	Salt and freshly cracked black pepper	
2 lb	spaghetti	1 kg
¼ cup	extra virgin olive oil	50 mL
1	red onion, thinly sliced	1
1	each green, yellow and red bell pepper, thinly sliced	1
4	jalapeño peppers, seeded and chopped	4
3 oz	Gray Monk Cellars Pinot Auxerrois (white wine)	90 mL
1	large tomato, peeled, seeded and chopped	1
8	sun-dried tomatoes, thinly sliced	8
4	artichoke hearts, cut into eighths	4
1 tsp	crushed hot pepper flakes	5 mL
1½ cups	tomato sauce	375 mL
16	fresh basil leaves, cut into ribbons	16
3	sprigs coriander, chopped	3
2 oz	pecorino cheese, grated	50 g
	Chopped parsley (for garnish)	

■ Peel prawns, leaving the tails and heads on. In a bowl, blend half the garlic with cayenne, salt and pepper.

Marinate prawns, refrigerated, for at least 1 hour.
2 In a large pot of boiling salted water, cook spaghetti until al dente. **3** Meanwhile, heat olive oil in a large skillet until not quite smoking. Add drained prawns, turning once. **4** Stir in onion. Add bell peppers, jalapeños and remaining garlic; cook for 1 minute. Add wine and reduce by half. **5** Stir in tomato, sun-dried tomatoes, artichoke hearts and pepper flakes. Stir in tomato sauce and cook 1 minute. **6** Remove prawns to a heated bowl and toss with basil and coriander. **7** Pour sauce over drained cooked spaghetti and toss with half the pecorino cheese.
8 Pour the spaghetti onto a heated platter and arrange prawns around the perimeter. Sprinkle with remaining grated pecorino and chopped parsley.

PASTA À LA BOERKAMP (CHEF JOHN BOERKAMP'S PASTA) | Serves four

Vignoble de l'Orpailleur, Dunham, Quebec

Founded in 1982, Vignoble de l'Orpailleur saw its first harvest in 1985. That year they made 15,000 bottles of a white wine called L'Orpailleur (searcher of gold). Today the winery produces four wines—two whites, a bubbly and an aperitif—all from Seyval Blanc grapes. They have three estate vineyards totalling 25 acres, two of these planted to Seyval Blanc and one experimentational vineyard planted with 36 types of vines. The four proprietors—Hervé Durand, Frank Furtado, Charles-Henri de Coussergues and Pierre Rodrigues—all work together to run the company. Charles-Henri is responsible for the production of the wine. The son of viticulturists, he is qualified to teach viticulture and oenology and spent four years in Guard, France, learning to vinify grapes. Vignoble de l'Orpailleur sees more than 50,000 visitors each year.

L'Orpailleur from Vignoble de l'Orpailleur

L'Orpailleur is made from Seyval Blanc grapes. Dry and fruity, this white has a clear robe with aromas resembling bananas, green apples and white flowers. The flavours are similar to green apples with a hint of violets. Being medium bodied, l'Orpailleur can match the richness of cream and the strong flavour of clams.

2 tbsp	butter	25 mL
3	shallots, minced	3
24	fresh baby clams	24
½ cup	L'Orpailleur (white wine)	125 mL
¼ cup	Pernod	50 mL
3 cups	whipping cream	750 mL
	Salt and pepper to taste	
I	can (5 oz/142 g) baby clams, drained and rinsed	I
I lb	fettuccine	500 g

1 In a large saucepan over medium heat, melt butter. Cook shallots until juice starts to run, about 2 minutes. Add fresh clams and wine. Cover immediately and steam clams, shaking pot from time to time, about 5 to 10 minutes. Once clams begin to open, remove cover and evaporate juice. Discard any clams that do not open. **2** Pour Pernod into metal ladle. Flame Pernod and pour over clams. Cook I to 2 minutes, or until liquid has evaporated.

3 Add cream; bring to a boil and reduce to desired consistency. Season with salt and pepper. Add canned clams and cook gently until heated through. Keep warm. **4** In a large pot of boiling salted water, cook fettuccine until al dente. **5** Pour clam sauce over drained cooked pasta and serve immediately.

MEDITERRANEAN ROTINI | Serves four

*Wellington Court Café,
St. Catharines, Ontario*

THE MENU AT Wellington Court Café is filled with culinary delights, such as gourmet pizza, grilled veal chops and beef tenderloin. The wine list emphasizes wines produced in the Niagara Peninsula.

4	boneless skinless chicken breasts, diced	4
I cup	olive oil	250 mL
¾ lb	rotini	375 g
I	clove garlic, finely chopped	I
I cup	diced tomatoes	250 mL
I	bunch green onions, chopped	I
½ cup	chopped olives	125 mL
2 tbsp	capers	25 mL
I cup	crumbled feta cheese	250 mL

1 In a large skillet over medium heat, heat 2 tbsp (25 mL) oil. Cook diced chicken for 10 minutes or until pieces are white and tender. Remove chicken and keep warm.
2 Meanwhile, in a pot of boiling salted water, cook rotini until al dente. **3** Add remaining oil to skillet. Sauté garlic until golden brown. Add tomatoes and green onions; cook until tomatoes are tender. Reduce heat to medium-low. Add olives and capers; cook 5 minutes. **4** Pour sauce over drained cooked rotini and toss. Add chicken. Sprinkle with feta cheese and serve immediately.

Marynissen Estates Chardonnay

NIAGARA-ON-THE-LAKE, ONTARIO

Barrel-fermented in Allier, Troncais and Nevers oak for six weeks, this wine is full bodied and shows some tropical bananas, melons and apples on the nose with smoky, butter character on the palate. This wine has enough substance to marry well with this heavy, oil-based dish.

WINEMAKER'S TASTING NOTES

CHAPTER NINE

SAVOURIES

PARMESAN AND BASIL GÂTEAU | Serves six

$L o o n s , \quad T o r o n t o , \quad O n t a r i o$

OWNERS CHARLES PART AND JENNIFER WARREN-PART have carved out a tiny gastronomic enclave in Toronto's Beach neighbourhood with their delicious market-fresh cuisine. The combination of local ingredients with worldly recipes (a blend of Italian and French in this gâteau) makes for an exciting culinary adventure. As members of the Knives and Forks Club, an alliance of chefs and organic growers concerned about the environment, the Parts place a premium on excellence in ingredients. In addition to their extensive use of local products, the Parts have peppered their wine list with some of Ontario's finest vintages.

Cave Spring Cellars Chardonnay Musqué

JORDAN, ONTARIO

Fermented entirely in stainless steel, this wine is called Musqué for its spicy, muscat-like attributes. Floral, citrus and honey flavours predominate. Clean with a crisp, long finish, it has a light creamy texture that works well with the cheeses in this dish.

WINEMAKER'S · TASTING NOTES

6 oz	cream cheese	175 g
8 oz	ricotta cheese	250 g
8 oz	Parmesan cheese (preferably Reggiano), grated	250 g
4	eggs	4
3 cups	fresh basil	750 mL
2	cloves garlic	2
	Juice of 2 lemons	
I tbsp	all-purpose flour	15 mL
2 tbsp	melted butter	25 mL
	Salt, pepper, grated nutmeg to taste	
¾ cup	sour cream	175 mL
	Sliced tomatoes	
	Extra virgin olive oil and pine nuts (for garnish)	

1 In a food processor, process cream cheese, ricotta and Parmesan for 2 minutes. **2** Add eggs, basil, garlic, lemon juice, flour, butter, salt, pepper and nutmeg. Process until well blended. **3** Add sour cream and pulse until just mixed. **4** Pour mixture into a well-greased 8-inch (2-L) springform pan. Bake at 325°F (160°C) for 50 minutes.

Test for doneness by inserting wooden skewer into gâteau. Skewer should come out clean. Cool on rack and remove gâteau from pan. **5** To serve, slice with a hot knife and arrange over tomato slices. Drizzle with olive oil and pine nuts.

Cœur au Chèvre Frais | Serves five to six

Say Cheese, London, Ontario

OWNER HILARY ALDERSON and chef Ruth Klassen developed this little bit of heaven in the restaurant's kitchen one balmy spring afternoon.

The cœur can be made in six individual heart-shaped moulds with drainage holes or in the standard 7-inch (18-cm) mould.

8 oz	goat cheese	250 g
8 oz	Quark cheese	250 g
½ cup	half-and-half cream OR whipping cream	125 mL
¼ tsp	salt	1 mL
4	egg whites	4
6	small sprigs fresh herb of choice	6

1 In a bowl, thoroughly mix goat cheese, Quark, cream and salt. **2** Beat egg whites until stiff. Gently fold into cheese mixture, one-third at a time. **3** Line each mould with rinsed and squeezed cheesecloth. Place one sprig of fresh herb in each mould. Gently fill each mould with cheese mixture. **4** Drape cheesecloth over top to cover completely, cover lightly with plastic wrap and place on plate. Allow to drain 8 hours in refrigerator. **5** To serve, unfold cheesecloth and unmould cœur onto individual plates.

Cave Spring Cellars Riesling Dry

JORDAN, ONTARIO

Fermented in stainless steel at cool temperatures, this wine has a ripe apple, pear and citrus nose. On the palate, it is well balanced, with crisp acidity that provides a good counterpoint to the creaminess of this dish.

WINEMAKER'S TASTING NOTES

FIDDLEHEAD AND GOAT CHEESE FLAN | Serves six

The Britton House, Gananoque, Ontario

MARK BUSSIÈRES BEGAN HIS LOVE AFFAIR with Canadian cuisine when he opened Toronto's Metropolis Restaurant. In 1989, he and his wife, Nicole LaPrairie, bought The Britton House, a big old comfortable bed and breakfast. Antiques combine with contemporary furnishings and the walls are adorned with the works of Canadian artists. And the cooking is true to form: it's a blend of modern with old-fashioned Canadian. Wild, organic and garden-fresh herbs and vegetables, farm-raised game and local meats and fish all work towards creating a new style of Canadian cuisine that is lighter, fresher and healthier.

Henry of Pelham Barrel-Fermented Chardonnay

ST. CATHARINES, ONTARIO

This wine has a big mouth feel, lots of toast and butter with subtle undertones of oak. Intense apple, clover and sweet citrus are found in the aroma. The earthiness of fresh fiddleheads and the slightly gamey flavour of goat cheese compete admirably with this big Chardonnay.

1 cup	fresh fiddleheads	250 mL
½ cup	whipping cream	125 mL
½ cup	chicken stock	125 mL
3	eggs	3
½ tsp	salt	2 mL
½ tsp	grated lemon rind	2 mL
1 tsp	honey mustard	5 mL
Pinch	nutmeg	Pinch
¼ tsp	curry powder	1 mL
¼ tsp	black pepper	1 mL
1 tsp	finely minced garlic	5 mL
2 tbsp	finely chopped chives	25 mL
¼ lb	goat cheese	125 g
1	unbaked 9-inch (23-cm) single-crust pie shell	1

1 Plunge fiddleheads into boiling water and cook briefly until bright green and tender-crisp. Immediately refresh fiddleheads under cold water and drain. **2** In a large bowl whisk together all ingredients except fiddleheads and goat cheese. **3** Press pastry into a 9-inch (23-cm) flan pan

with removable bottom. **4** Evenly distribute the fiddleheads
and goat cheese in the flan shell. Pour egg mixture evenly into
shell. **5** Bake at 325°F (160°C) for 30 minutes or until
firm. **6** Allow flan to rest for 10 minutes before serving.

*Note: Other flavour options to add to the basic egg mixture are smoked
salmon, fresh herbs, asparagus, sun-dried tomatoes, sweet peppers or old
Cheddar cheese.*

SMOKED SALMON AND DILL
CHESECAKE | Serves six to eight

*Shari Darling / Andres Wines,
Winona, Ontario*

ANDRES WINES HAS BEEN satisfying Canadians since 1961. Founded by Andrew Peller, the company is now run by his son Joseph and grandson John. They offer an expanded line of products that includes several nonvintage table wines, most notably Hochtaler and Domaine D'Or. Their latest success story? The Peller Estates French Cross and Peller Estates varietal wines (Cabernet Sauvignon, Chardonnay, Chambourcin and two Rieslings), all produced from Niagara grapes.

Peller Estates Riesling (Off-Dry)

WINONA, ONTARIO

This is a delicate, light Riesling with pale straw colour, floral-apricot aromas and citrus flavours. These fruit-like characteristics ideally suit cream cheese. Although showing a hint of sweetness, this wine has enough acidity to cut through the fattiness in smoked salmon, while complementing the saltiness of this fish and caviar.

SOUFFLÉ LAYERS:

2 tbsp plus	butter	35 mL
⅓ cup	flour	75 mL
Pinch	each salt and pepper	Pinch
1¾ cups	skim milk	425 mL
2 tsp	lemon juice	10 mL
3	eggs, separated, plus 1 egg white	3

SALMON FILLING:

⅔ lb	sliced smoked salmon	350 g
1¼ lb	cream cheese	625 g
1 tbsp	lemon juice	15 mL
1 tsp	tomato paste	5 mL

GREEN HERB FILLING:

9 oz	cream cheese	300 g
¼ cup	finely snipped fresh dill	50 mL
¼ cup	finely snipped fresh chives	50 mL
1 tsp	lemon juice	5 mL
1	small clove garlic, crushed	1

GREEN PEPPERCORN COATING:

½ lb	cream cheese	250 g
I tbsp	green peppercorns	15 mL

GARNISHES:

3½ oz	smoked salmon 'extra'	100 g
I	small jar black caviar	I
	Large sprig fresh dill	
I	lemon, sliced thinly	I
3	Lebanese cucumbers, sliced thinly	3

1 To make soufflé layers, grease three shallow 8-inch (1.2-L) round cake tins and line with waxed paper. Make a white sauce by combining in a saucepan butter, flour, salt, pepper and milk; boil for 30 seconds. Stir in lemon juice. Remove from heat, cool slightly and beat in yolks. Beat egg whites until soft peaks form; fold into mixture. Spread mixture evenly in the three tins. **2** Tap tins to expel air bubbles. Bake at 350°F (180°C) for 25 minutes or until golden and firm to touch. Cool on a rack and turn on to plastic wrap. **3** To make smoked salmon filling, in a food processor or blender, blend all salmon filling ingredients until smooth. Chill. **4** To make green herb filling, in a food processor or blender, blend all herb filling ingredients until smooth. Chill. **5** To make peppercorn coating, combine cream cheese and green peppercorns in large bowl and beat by hand to avoid crushing the corns. **6** To assemble the cheesecake, place a soufflé layer on a serving dish. Spread with half the salmon filling. Top with second soufflé layer and spread with the green herb filling. Top with last soufflé layer and spread with remaining salmon filling. Chill to set. **7** When firm, spread top and sides of cheesecake with green peppercorn mixture. Decorate top with small rolls of smoked salmon, black caviar, dill, lemon slices and cucumber.

Salmon Boats in a Sea of Spinach | Serves twelve

Shari Darling / David Lawrason

David Lawrason is wine columnist for the *Globe and Mail* and publisher of the independently written *Wine Access*. As founder of the Wine Tutor wine appreciation program and wine consultant to the hospitality industry, he has helped many Canadians discover the joys of wine and food. For a subscription to *Wine Access*, write 189 Floyd Avenue, Toronto, Ontario M4J 2H9, or call (416) 423-3487.

TERRINE:

I	salmon fillet (10 oz/300 g)	I
½ cup	whipping cream	125 mL
Pinch	each dillweed, salt, freshly ground pepper	Pinch
7 oz	smoked salmon, thinly sliced	200 g
¼ cup	butter, whipped	50 mL
2 tbsp	cream cheese, whipped	25 mL
½ cup	whipping cream, whipped	125 mL
2 tbsp	lemon juice	25 mL
Pinch	parsley	Pinch

SPINACH LAYER:

I	bag (10 oz/284 g) fresh spinach, 2 oz (60 g) reserved for spinach sauce	I
	Salt and pepper	
¼ tsp	unflavoured gelatin	I mL

SPINACH SAUCE:

2 oz	fresh spinach	60 g
I cup	whipping cream	250 mL
I tbsp	vinegar	15 mL
I tbsp	lemon juice	15 mL
	Salt and freshly ground pepper to taste	

1 In a saucepan over medium-low heat, poach salmon in ½ cup (125 mL) cream. Season to taste with dill, salt and pepper. Let cool. **2** Mince poached salmon and half the smoked salmon; combine with butter, cream cheese, whipped cream, lemon juice and parsley. Set aside. **3** To make spinach layer, blanch 8 oz (225 g) spinach for I minute; season to taste with salt and pepper. Dissolve gelatin in 4 tsp (20 mL) water. In blender or food processor, blend gelatin with spinach. Transfer to bowl and cool until gelatin has set. **4** On a sheet of plastic wrap, spread thin layer of remaining smoked salmon. Top with thicker layer of salmon-cream mixture. Spread spinach layer on top and carefully roll, peeling back the plastic wrap as necessary. Cover with plastic wrap and refrigerate for at least 30 minutes. **5** To make spinach sauce, lightly blanch 2 oz (60 g) spinach. In blender or food processor, blend spinach, cream, vinegar, lemon juice, salt and pepper. Serve sauce with sliced salmon roll.

Cave Spring Cellars Reserve Chardonnay

JORDAN, ONTARIO

David Lawrason notes: The 1990 Reserve Chardonnay was technically one of the best Ontario Chardonnays I've encountered, which means it also tasted good. Forward butterscotch and oak aromas dominated, but good apple and grapefruit flavours lurked behind, and finished with some authority. The balance was very good, tight with some creaminess too. Finished a bit tart, with good length. All Reserve Chardonnay vintages will complement this dish on two levels: oak aromas will work with the smoked salmon flavours, while the wine's creaminess will parallel the creamy texture of the rolls.

WINEMAKER'S TASTING NOTES

STEAK, OYSTER AND GUINNESS PIE | Serves four

The Angel Inn,
Niagara-on-the-Lake, Ontario

ONE OF ONTARIO'S OLDEST INNS, this circa 1816 building has seen plenty of history in the making. The action of the War of 1812 swirled around the inn. When nearby Fort George was captured the next year, retreating American soldiers set fire to the town and the Harmonious Coach House—as the inn was known back then—was badly burned. After the war it was rebuilt and named The Angel Inn. Owner Peter Ling continues to serve traditional pub fare as well as a wide selection of ales, draft beers and local wines.

Marynissen Estates Merlot Barrel Select

NIAGARA-ON THE-LAKE, ONTARIO

This light-bodied Merlot has good acid balance and was barrel-aged in French oak to achieve its beautifully balanced finish. Plum and blackberry flavours are evoked, and the wine has a peppery tobacco character reminiscent of some of the finest wines of Burgundy. It makes a perfect foil for this traditional pub pie.

WINEMAKER'S · TASTING NOTES

I cup	Guinness beer	250 mL
I	large onion, chopped	I
2	bay leaves	2
I	sprig thyme	I
I tbsp	tomato purée	15 mL
I lb	lean beef steak, cubed	500 g
I	veal kidney, trimmed of fat and cubed	I
I tbsp	flour	15 mL
12	oysters, shucked	12
8 oz	puff pastry	250 g
I	egg, beaten with 2 tbsp (25 mL) water	I

1 In a large bowl, combine Guinness, onion, bay leaves, thyme and tomato purée. Add beef and kidney; marinate, refrigerated, for several hours. **2** Drain meat, reserving marinade. In a saucepan stir together meat and flour. Pour in marinade and simmer, uncovered, over medium heat 30 to 40 minutes. Let cool. Refrigerate overnight to improve flavour. **3** Discard bay leaf and sprig of thyme. Drain meat and place in four individual pie dishes. Add oysters. **4** Roll out puff pastry and cut to fit each pie. Brush with eggwash. Bake at 425°F (220°C) for 25 minutes or until crust is golden brown.

*B*EEF MARROW TARTLETS | Serves four to eight

*Shari Darling / Marynissen Estates Winery,
Niagara-on-the-Lake, Ontario*

ONCE A PRIZE-WINNING AMATEUR WINEMAKER, John Marynissen is now a prize-winning professional. He has several awards to his credit, including the Best of Show Award for his 1989 Chardonnay from the American Wine Society Competition. John was the first to produce Cabernet Sauvignon from Niagara vines, a decision that has led many others to follow suit.

½ lb	puff pastry	250 g

CABERNET SAUVIGNON SAUCE:

6 tbsp	butter	75 mL
I tbsp	chopped shallots	15 mL
3 cups	Marynissen Estate Cabernet Sauvignon (red wine)	750 mL
I¾ cups	veal stock	425 mL
I lb	beef marrow, diced	500 g
I tbsp	chopped fresh parsley (optional)	15 mL
	Salt and pepper to taste	
	Fried parsley sprigs (for garnish)	

Marynissen Estates Cabernet Sauvignon

With its Cabernet Sauvignon sauce and beef marrow filling, this entree is the appropriate match for Marynissen Estate Cabernet Sauvignon. Aged in French Allier and Nevers oak barrels for eight months, the wine is medium bodied with a plum-blackberry bouquet and a peppery-tobacco taste.

WINEMAKER'S · TASTING NOTES

1 Roll out pastry and cut to fit eight 5-inch (12-cm) oval tartlet tins. Bake at 400°F (200°C) until almost baked, about 15 minutes. Cool on a rack. **2** To make Cabernet Sauvignon sauce, in a saucepan over medium-high heat, melt 2 tbsp (25 mL) butter. Sauté shallots about 2 minutes. Pour in wine and reduce to one-quarter. Add veal stock and simmer, uncovered, I hour. Strain sauce through a fine sieve; blend in remaining butter. **3** In the saucepan, lightly poach beef marrow in water. Add to the sauce. Add chopped parsley, if using. Season with salt and pepper. **4** Fill tartlet shells with marrow mixture. Bake at 400°F (200°C) until tartlets are golden, about 5 minutes. Serve immediately.

CHAPTER TEN

FISH

BAKED SALMON À LA SIMPLE | Serves four

Wine Tidings

PUBLISHED IN CANADA eight times a year, *Wine Tidings* features recipes, gourmet menus and wine serving suggestions in each issue. Tips and techniques on buying and appreciating wine are also included. For subscription information on this first-class magazine, call (514) 481-5892 or fax (514) 481-9688.

Nichol Vineyard Pinot Blanc

(IRVINE VINEYARD), NARAMATA, BRITISH COLUMBIA

Wine Tiding's publisher Judy Rochester notes that the wine has a pale straw colour and a fresh, clean, lemony nose, followed by a good acidic attack and a mouthful of fat, round, fruit flavours with a hint of herbs and almonds. Excellent balance of acidity and fruit with its hint of residual sugar. The wine's lemon nose works with the lemon juice and dill seasoning, while its fat, round flavours are able to stand up to this meaty fish.

WINEMAKER'S TASTING NOTES

3 tbsp	butter	50 mL
2 tsp	lemon juice	10 mL
Pinch	chopped parsley	Pinch
I	filleted salmon (about 2 lb/I kg)	I
	Fresh dill and lemon wedges (for garnish)	

1 Spread butter on sheet of aluminum foil, sprinkle with lemon juice and parsley. **2** Lay salmon on foil and wrap tightly. Put ½ inch (I cm) water in roasting pan and lay wrapped salmon on it. **3** Bake at 350°F (180°C) for 2 hours. If water evaporates, add more to keep oven steamy. Unwrap salmon onto platter and garnish with fresh dill and lemon wedges.

SALMON WITH RED WINE SAUCE | Serves two

*Anthony's Seafood Bistro,
London, Ontario*

CHEF/OWNER DAVID CHAPMAN pairs salmon with red wine in this unusual and delicious recipe. In line with the chef's philosophy of giving customers the ultimate dining experience, Anthony's wine list provides a guide for marrying various wines with seafood and fish.

2	Atlantic salmon fillets (6 oz/150 g each)	2
	Flour seasoned with salt and pepper	
2 tbsp	unsalted butter	25 mL
2 tsp	diced red onion	10 mL
1 tbsp	diced seeded tomato	15 mL
¼ cup	Inniskillin Wines Pinot Noir (red wine)	50 mL
¾ cup	whipping cream	175 mL
	Salt and pepper	
Pinch	chopped parsley	Pinch

Inniskillin Wines Pinot Noir

NIAGARA-ON-THE-LAKE, ONTARIO

Berry-like aromas, mild cherry fruit and light oak can be found in this varietal. This wine is able to meet the acidity of the tomatoes and still hold its own.

WINEMAKER'S TASTING NOTES

1 Dip salmon fillets in seasoned flour. Melt butter in an oven-safe skillet and brown fillets lightly on both sides.
2 Transfer skillet to oven and bake at 375°F (190°C) for 4 minutes or until salmon fillets are firm. Remove from skillet and keep warm. **3** Set skillet over high heat. Add onion and tomato. Deglaze with wine. Add cream. Reduce until sauce thickens. Season to taste and stir in parsley.
4 Pour sauce on each plate and arrange salmon on top. Serve immediately.

ZESTY PACIFIC SALMON STEAKS | Serves four

Sumac Ridge Estate Winery, Summerland, British Columbia

SUMAC RIDGE ESTATE WINERY was the brainchild of the creative entrepreneurs Harry McWatters and Lloyd Schmidt. These adventurous fellows purchased a nine-hole golf course on Highway 97 in Summerland and transformed some of the property into a vineyard and winery.

Today, we can still play golf and dine in the original Club House Restaurant, which now overlooks the winery's barrel and fermenting cellar. In 1990 Bob Wareham, a longtime associate of McWatters, purchased Schmidt's interest in the winery and joined Harry in managing Sumac Ridge Estate Winery.

Sumac Ridge is renowned throughout British Columbia for their white varietals—their Chardonnay, Pinot Blanc, Gewürztraminer and Riesling. They also produce a Blanc de Blanc and a Blanc de Noir, two bubblies made in the traditional méthode champenoise. Recent awards include: First Place with the 1992 Gewürztraminer Private Reserve in both the People's Choice and Consumers Award during the Okanagan Wine Festival; Restaurants Gold Choice at the 1992 VQA Awards of Distinction for their 1990 Gewürztraminer Private Reserve; and a bronze medal for their 1990 Pinot Blanc and 1990 Verdelet at the 1992 National Orange Show in San Bernardino, California.

Sumac Ridge Estate Winery Gewürztraminer Private Reserve

Sumac Ridge's Gewürztraminer Private Reserve has spicy aromas and grapefruit flavours with a tinge of sweetness—elements that harmonize with the spicy taste of cayenne, the slight sweetness of garlic and the wine flavours found in the pan sauce.

4	Pacific salmon steaks, 1 inch (2.5 cm) thick	4
Pinch	cayenne	Pinch
2 tbsp	olive oil	25 mL
2	cloves garlic, crushed	2
⅓ cup	chopped fresh parsley	75 mL
2 tsp	capers	10 mL
½ tsp	grated lemon rind	2 mL
½ cup	Sumac Ridge Gewürztraminer Private Reserve (white wine)	125 mL
	Juice of ½ lemon	

1 Sprinkle salmon steaks lightly with cayenne. **2** In a skillet, heat oil over medium heat. Sauté one clove garlic until golden. Discard garlic. **3** Increase heat to medium-high. Sauté salmon steaks for 4 minutes on each side. Add remaining garlic, parsley, capers, lemon rind and wine. Sprinkle lemon juice over each steak. **4** Cook 1 to 2 minutes longer. Arrange salmon steaks on a serving platter. Stir pan juices and drizzle over salmon.

GRILLED SALMON FILLETS WITH CREAM SHERRY | Serves six

Brian Bannon

SINCE 1979 BRIAN BANNON has been wine columnist for the Windsor *Star* and organizer of Le Bec Fin Wine and Food Club.

6	fresh salmon fillets (½ lb/250 g each)	6
¼ cup	each soy sauce and cream sherry	50 mL
2 tsp	sugar	10 mL
2 tbsp	grated gingerroot	25 mL
3	cloves garlic, finely chopped	3
	Oil	
	Lemon wedges	

1 Slice salmon fillets crosswise into 2-inch (5-cm) wide strips. Arrange in a shallow glass dish. **2** In a small saucepan, combine soy sauce, sherry and sugar. Heat only until sugar is dissolved. Stir in ginger and garlic; pour over salmon. Marinate salmon, covered, at room temperature for 30 minutes. **3** Transfer salmon to a rack on a broiler pan; reserve marinade. Brush oil on both sides. **4** Grill salmon flesh side down for 4 to 5 minutes, basting with marinade. Turn and grill another 4 to 5 minutes, basting, until salmon is pink. Garnish with lemon wedges.

D'Angelo Vineyards Vidal

AMHERSTBURG, ONTARIO

Fermented and aged in stainless steel, this varietal has a fruity nose and palate. Being a light-bodied white, it is the perfect partner for this delicate fish.

WINEMAKER'S · TASTING NOTES

POACHED ATLANTIC SALMON WITH COLD CUCUMBER DILL SAUCE | Serves four

McKelvie's, Halifax, Nova Scotia

PERCHED ON THE WATERWAY in downtown Halifax, this seafood eatery transforms local fish into dishes of note. The nautical decor gives the restaurant an air of adventure, which is carried through in the cuisine. The recipe here is one of the most popular dishes.

Jost Vineyards Habitant Blanc

MALAGASH, NOVA SCOTIA

Crisp, clean and fruity, with a slight vanilla and full grape finish, this wine complements both the salmon and the cucumber flavours of the dish. The 1990 vintage won a silver medal at the Atlantic Wine Summit in Atlanta, Georgia.

WINEMAKER'S TASTING NOTES

SAUCE:

I	medium cucumber, peeled, seeded and puréed	I
I tbsp	fresh dill	15 mL
2 tsp	Dijon mustard	10 mL
I tsp	lemon juice	5 mL
I	clove garlic	I
I tsp	chopped parsley	5 mL
¾ cup	mayonnaise	175 mL

POACHING LIQUID:

I	clove garlic, crushed	I
2 to 3	whole peppercorns	2 to 3
I	bay leaf	I
2	lemon quarters	2
¼ cup	Jost Winery Habitant Blanc (white wine)	50 mL

4	salmon fillets (6 oz/150 g each)	4

1 To make sauce, place cucumber purée in strainer over a bowl and press down to remove excess water. Reserve liquid. **2** In a food processor or blender, combine dill, mustard, lemon juice, garlic and parsley; chop finely. Combine with cucumber purée and mayonnaise, adding some of the reserved cucumber water to thin if necessary. Refrigerate I hour. **3** To make poaching liquid, in a shallow pan large enough to hold fillets, combine garlic, peppercorns, bay leaf, lemon quarters, wine and 4 cups (I L) water. Simmer, uncovered, 25 to 30 minutes, taking care not to boil. Add salmon fillets and poach 9 to 12 minutes or until fish is firm to the touch. **4** Arrange salmon on serving plates and pour cucumber sauce over top. Serve immediately.

Steamed Pickerel with Asian Mustard Sauce | Serves four

Michelle Ramsay

½ cup	Dijon mustard	125 mL
½ cup	sesame oil	125 mL
2 tbsp	rice vinegar	25 mL
I tbsp	rice wine	15 mL
	Salt and pepper to taste	
⅓ cup	chopped fresh coriander	75 mL
4	pickerel fillets (5 oz/125 g each)	4

1 In a blender, combine mustard, sesame oil, rice vinegar, rice wine, salt and pepper; blend well and set aside.
2 Steam pickerel about 10 minutes or until opaque.
3 Stir chopped coriander into sauce and serve with pickerel.

Château des Charmes Estate Chardonnay

NIAGARA-ON-THE-LAKE, ONTARIO

This rich, creamy dish requires a rich Chardonnay to stand up to the lemony cream sauce and moderate the high fat content of the salmon. Buttery, with rich vanilla flavours, this elegant wine is overlaid with oak. It is intense with subtle complexities.

WINEMAKER'S TASTING NOTES

SALMON IN POTATO CRUST WITH MADEIRA-MUSHROOM ESSENCE | Serves four

The Old Prune, Stratford, Ontario

SET IN AN EDWARDIAN HOME and run by Eleanor Kane and Marion Isherwood, this favourite of festival-goers serves fresh, creative cuisine using the best foodstuffs the region has to offer. Chef Bryan Steele takes a light approach with his creations, combining the healthier flavours and cooking techniques of the 1990s with classic European cuisine. The result is an elegant market-fresh style.

Cave Spring Cellars Merlot

JORDAN, ONTARIO

Medium-bodied with a sweet, oaky finish to match the woodsy mushroom flavours, this wine has a slightly tart acidity that cuts through the oil in salmon.

WINEMAKER'S TASTING NOTES

4	potatoes (preferably Yukon Gold), peeled	4
4	boneless skinless Atlantic salmon fillets (6 oz/150 g each)	4
	Salt and pepper	
½ cup	unsalted butter, melted	125 mL

MUSHROOM ESSENCE:

¼ cup	oil	50 mL
3 cups	mushrooms (we use a mixture of field, oyster and enoki)	750 mL
I tbsp	oil	15 mL
I	small onion, diced	I
½ cup	dry white wine	125 mL
I	small sprig fresh thyme	I
½	clove garlic	½
I tbsp	Madeira	15 mL
	Salt and black pepper	
2 tbsp	unsalted OR clarified butter	25 mL

1 Trim potatoes lengthwise to form perfect cylinders. Cut cylinders into thin slices. In a pot of simmering water, cook potato slices 3 to 4 minutes or until tender. Drain and allow to cool slightly. **2** Season one side of the salmon with salt and pepper. Arrange salmon in a shallow baking dish large enough to hold the fillets, and top with potato slices, overlapping each slightly (like the scales of a fish). Pour melted butter over top. Chill the potato-topped salmon until butter has solidified. (The salmon can be prepared up to this stage and kept refrigerated for a couple of hours before cooking.) **3** To make mushroom essence, in a large skillet over high heat, heat ¼ cup (50 mL) oil and sauté mushrooms until browned. Meanwhile, in another pan heat 1 tbsp (15 mL) oil over moderate heat and sauté onion until caramelized. **4** In a nonaluminum saucepan, combine mushrooms, onion, wine, thyme and garlic. Add enough cold water to cover and bring to a boil. Gently simmer, covered, for 1 hour or until mushrooms have yielded all their flavour. **5** Pass mushroom essence through a fine mesh strainer and continue to simmer essence over low heat, skimming occasionally, until reduced to 1 cup (250 mL). Add Madeira and salt and pepper to taste. Set aside. **6** To serve, melt 2 tbsp (25 mL) butter in a nonstick skillet over moderate heat. Season salmon-potato fillets lightly. Fry salmon fillets, potato side down, for 3 to 4 minutes or until potatoes are golden brown and crispy. Reduce heat to low, turn the salmon and cook 1 to 2 minutes. Serve immediately with mushroom essence.

Steamed Skate Wing with Cranberry Vinegar Butter Sauce | Serves two

*Sooke Harbour House,
Sooke, British Columbia*

Co-chef Pia Caroll combines a classic French fish with Canadian ingredients in this inspired recipe.

Wild Goose Vineyards Pinot Blanc

**OKANAGAN FALLS,
BRITISH COLUMBIA**

Awarded VQA Gold in the summer of 1991, this limited-production wine is dry and full bodied with a delicate bouquet of peaches and pears. It is full bodied enough to handle the tart cranberry butter, while the fruitiness blends well with the dish.

WINEMAKER'S TASTING NOTES

2	skate wings (6 oz/150 g each), skin and bone removed	2

CRANBERRY VINEGAR BUTTER SAUCE:

1 cup	fish stock	250 mL
½ cup	Wild Goose Vineyards Pinot Blanc (white wine)	125 mL
1	clove garlic, minced	1
1	shallot, minced	1
⅓ cup	cranberry vinegar (recipe follows)	75 mL
⅓ cup	unsalted butter, cubed	75 mL

GARNISHES:

2	sprigs anise-hyssop	2
2	bunches chickweed	2

1 To make sauce, in a heavy-bottomed medium saucepan, bring fish stock, white wine, garlic and shallot to a boil. Reduce until sauce is a syrupy consistency, 3 to 4 minutes. Stir in cranberry vinegar and cook for 1 minute. Remove from heat and slowly whisk in butter, one cube at a time, until well blended. Set aside, keeping warm. **2** In a steamer over medium-high heat, steam fish fillets, covered, for 6 to 7 minutes or until firm. Drain fish on paper towels.
3 Spoon sauce onto plates and arrange skate wing on top. Garnish with anise-hyssop flowers and leaves and chickweed.

CRANBERRY VINEGAR:

Place 1 cup (250 mL) cranberries in a ceramic or glass bowl.

Cover with 2 cups (500 mL) white wine vinegar. Cover bowl, leaving a small opening to let vinegar "breathe," and store in a cool place for 1 to 2 weeks. Strain and bottle.

GRILLED SWORDFISH STEAKS | Serves two

Bill Munnelly

BILL MUNNELLY writes a monthly newsletter called *Best Bottles*, which is well known to wine-lovers throughout western Ontario. Recommendations from this newsletter appear regularly in the *London Free Press*. For a subscription write to: *Best Bottles*, Box 503, Stratford, Ontario N5A 6J7.

¼ cup	red wine (same wine served with dinner)	50 mL
1 tsp	dried basil	5 mL
1 tsp	tarragon	5 mL
1½ tsp	salt	7 mL
1 tsp	freshly ground pepper	5 mL
⅓ cup	olive oil	75 mL
2	swordfish steaks, 1 inch (2.5 cm) thick	2
	Boiled then lightly grilled zucchini, broccoli and potatoes (for garnish)	

1 Combine wine, basil, tarragon, salt and pepper. Gradually whisk in olive oil. Set aside. **2** Place swordfish steaks on well-oiled rack and grill 5 minutes on each side or until meat is white. **3** In a large saucepan, heat marinade until lukewarm. Remove from heat and add steaks. Marinate steaks for a few minutes. Arrange steaks on plates and garnish with grilled vegetables.

Hillebrand Estates Cabernet/Merlot Collector's Choice

NIAGARA-ON-THE-LAKE, ONTARIO

This blend combines 60 per cent Cabernet Sauvignon, 30 per cent Merlot and 10 per cent Cabernet Franc. Dark burgundy in colour, the wine has a nose reminiscent of grass, oak and fruit, while the palate reveals black currant, pepper and a vanilla-like finish. Having been produced in a Burgundian style, this blend works with grilled, meaty fish.

Suggested Varietal: medium-bodied Merlot

Morue en Ecaille de Pommes de Terre (Salt Cod in a Potato Crust) | Serves six

La Pinsonnière, Charlevoix, Quebec

A member of Relais & Chateaux and a four-diamond hotel and restaurant award-winner (CAA Quebec), this imposing inn is set deep in the lush Charlevoix countryside overlooking the St. Lawrence River. Owned and operated by Janine and Jean Authier, the inn has 28 individually decorated rooms with fireplaces and whirlpool baths. Chef Christophe Geffray of Brittany, a former student of Michelin three-star chef Bernard Loiseau, champions simple, light cuisine that makes use of the freshest local ingredients. An extensive wine cellar complements the innovative cuisine.

L'Orpailleur from Vignoble de L'Orpailleur

DUNHAM, QUEBEC

L'Orpailleur is made from Seyval Blanc grapes. Dry, medium-bodied and fruity, this white has a clear robe with aromas resembling bananas, green apples and white flowers. The flavours are similar to green apples with a hint of violets. Not overpowering, this wine is an ideal partner for the delicate potato-crusted cod.

WINEMAKER'S TASTING NOTES

2 lb	salt cod	1 kg
6	potatoes, peeled and thinly sliced	6
2 tsp	butter, melted	10 mL
	Pepper to taste	
2 tbsp	olive oil	25 mL
1	clove garlic, minced	1
2	bay leaves	2
1	sprig fresh thyme	1
2	red bell peppers, diced	2
1	zucchini, diced	1
1	onion, chopped	1
2	shallots, minced	2
6	sprigs parsley, minced	6
	Fish stock	
	Salt and pepper to taste	

1 Soak salt cod 24 hours or overnight, changing water several times. Remove bones and skin. Make 1 cup (250 mL) of fish stock with the bones. **2** Divide salt cod into six portions and arrange in a buttered heatproof baking dish.

3 Toss potato slices with melted butter. Lay potato slices over fish pieces, overlapping each slightly. Season with pepper. **4** In a skillet over medium heat, heat olive oil. Sauté garlic, bay leaves and thyme 30 seconds, stirring frequently. Add red peppers, zucchini, onion and shallots, combining well. Cover and cook 10 minutes. **5** Mix parsley with just enough hot fish stock to make a smooth paste. Add more hot fish stock to create a jus (light broth). Season with salt and pepper. Set aside. **6** Bake fish pieces at 350°F (180°C) for 10 minutes or until golden. **7** Transfer fish to plates. Arrange cooked vegetables around fish. Nap with parsley jus.

Rare Roasted Tuna with Sherry Soy Butter Sauce, Smoked Onion Confit and Chive Flower Fritters | Serves four

Cheyna Restaurant and Bistro, Vancouver, British Columbia

The East-West combinations of this dish work marvellously well.

Gray Monk Cellars Pinot Chardonnay

OKANAGAN CENTRE, BRITISH COLUMBIA

Apple and lemon flavours and a lingering aftertaste, this rich, well-balanced wine complements the butter sauce and the tuna. Although it has not undergone oak-ageing, it is distinctive enough to pair with this dish.

WINEMAKER'S TASTING NOTES

Mirin, a sweet Japanese rice wine, is available at liquor stores and specialty markets.

SMOKED ONION CONFIT:

4	large sweet onions (preferably Walla Walla), peeled	4
I	pkg (400 g) smoker chips (alderwood)	I
½ cup	unsalted butter	125 mL
7 oz	Mission Hill Organic Maréchal Foch (red wine)	200 mL
¼ cup	honey	50 mL
	Salt and pepper to taste	

BATTER FOR CHIVE FLOWER FRITTERS:

½ cup	cornstarch	125 mL
½ cup	flour	125 mL
I tsp	baking powder	5 mL
	Oil for deep-frying	

SAUCE:

¾ cup	Gray Monk Cellars Chardonnay (white wine)	75 mL
¼ cup	dry sherry	50 mL
I tsp	mirin*	5 mL
I tsp	balsamic OR sherry vinegar	5 mL
I tsp	chopped shallots	5 mL
½ cup	fish OR chicken stock	125 mL
¼ cup	whipping cream	50 mL
4 oz	cold unsalted butter, cubed	125 g
2 tsp	julienne pickled ginger	5 mL
2 tsp	low-sodium soy sauce	5 mL

1½ lb	tuna loin (ahiu or yellowfin), cut in 4 pieces	750 g
20	chive flowers with 1 inch (2.5 cm) stem	20
2 tsp	chopped chives	10 mL
½ cup	deep-fried shoestring potatoes (optional)	125 mL

1 Smoke onions on a barbecue or in a smoker following manufacturer's directions. Or place smoker chips in a roasting pan and fit a cooling rack on top. Heat over medium heat until smoke is just achieved; reduce heat to low. Place onions on rack and cover with aluminum foil; let smoke about 90 minutes. **2** Julienne onions. In a saucepan, sweat onions in butter until soft but not caramelized. Add red wine and simmer until most of the wine is reduced and absorbed by the onions. Stir in honey, salt and pepper. Set aside confit. **3** To make batter for fritters, in a bowl combine cornstarch, flour and baking powder. Slowly stir in water until a thick paste is formed. (Paste should cover the back of a spoon.) **4** In a deep saucepan, heat oil to 325°F (160°C). Coat chive flowers with batter and deep-fry until crisp and golden. Drain on paper towels; keep warm. **5** To prepare sauce, in a large saucepan combine wine, sherry, mirin, vinegar and shallots. Reduce over medium heat to 1 tbsp (15 mL) liquid. Add fish stock and cream; reduce to one-third. Remove from heat and whisk in butter, one cube at a time, to form an emulsion. Stir in pickled ginger and soy sauce. Set aside, keeping warm. **6** Sear tuna over high heat on barbecue, or grill until browned on all sides. Bake at 375°F (190°C) for 3 to 4 minutes. Allow fish to rest for 5 minutes. **7** Spoon onion confit into the centre of each warm plate. Spoon sauce around the confit. Cut the tuna in half to display the rosy centre and arrange tuna on the confit. Arrange chive flower fritters around the plate. Sprinkle with chopped chives. Garnish with shoestring potatoes, if using.

Mission Hill Vineyards Maréchal Foch Organic

WESTBANK, BRITISH COLUMBIA

This fruity wine, with its caramel-like aromas and slight plum, raspberry flavours, is an ideal red accompaniment to this dish. Oak-ageing has led to a complexity of flavours strong enough to stand up to the sauce.

WINEMAKER'S TASTING NOTES

At the entrance to historic Gastown, Steven Wong's Cheyna bistro was an instant hit when it opened in May 1992. Specializing in Pacific Rim cuisine, the menu offers such tantalizing East-West combinations as salmon dumplings with sake cream sauce, Dungeness crab ravioli with saffron coconut sweetpea sauce, and wok-seared halibut with lime-coconut rice and black bean sweet plum sauce. The dishes are complemented by an inspired wine list of local and regional wines. To top it all off, the restaurant affords a spectacular view of the mountains and sea.

SHORT HILLS RAINBOW TROUT WITH CHARDONNAY SAUCE | Serves four to six

Henry of Pelham Family Estate Winery, St. Catharines, Ontario

IN THE SOUTHWEST CORNER OF St. Catharines at the crossroads of Pelham and Effingham is the Henry of Pelham Family Estate Winery. In 1842 Henry Smith, known in the archives as Henry of Pelham, built this structure to serve as a tavern and inn and later as a tollgate. The rustic building has been restored to its original condition and now functions as a wine store, cooperage and wine school run by Henry's descendants Paul and Bobbi Speck and their sons. The winery's 175 acres of vineyard are on the north end of the Short Hills on the Beamsville Bench, where the climate, clay-loam soil and natural air flow is suitable for French hybrid and vitis vinifera grapes. While the Speck family concentrates on tending the vineyards and running the winery, winemaker and microbiologist Ron Giesbrecht transforms the grapes into quality varietal wines. Chardonnay, Cabernet Sauvignon, Riesling, Seyval Blanc and Baco Noir are but a few of the many wines of Henry of Pelham.

Henry of Pelham Chardonnay

This Chardonnay was stainless steel fermented, with 30 per cent being aged in French Allier oak for two months. The wine has intense apple, clover and sweet citrus aromas with a palate showing full fruit flavours and crisp acidity. All these flavours harmonize with the delicate nature of trout.

WINEMAKER'S TASTING NOTES

CHARDONNAY SAUCE:

1 tbsp	butter	15 mL
¼ cup	chopped chives	50 mL
½ cup	Henry of Pelham Chardonnay (white wine)	125 mL
1 tbsp	lemon juice	15 mL
2 tbsp	butter	25 mL
¼ cup	flour	50 mL
1½ cups	fish OR chicken stock	375 mL
⅓ cup	mushroom, finely sliced	75 mL
2 tbsp	sour cream	25 mL
1 cup	chopped celery	250 mL
¼ cup	chopped onions	50 mL
2 tbsp	each chopped chives and fresh dill	25 mL
1 tbsp	chopped parsley	15 mL
½ cup	mayonnaise	125 mL

6 fresh whole rainbow trout, about 10 inches (25 cm) long	6
Toasted sliced almonds and lemon wedges (for garnish)	

1 Melt 1 tbsp (15 mL) butter in saucepan over medium heat and cook chives until tender. Add wine and lemon juice; cook until reduced by half. **2** In a second saucepan over low heat, melt 2 tbsp (25 mL) butter. Stir in flour and cook 1 minute. Gradually add fish stock, stirring until thickened. Add mushrooms; simmer for 30 minutes, uncovered, stirring occasionally. **3** Pour wine-chive mixture into thickened fish stock. Simmer 10 minutes. Stir in sour cream. Keep sauce warm, but do not boil. **4** Mix together celery, onions, chives, dill, parsley and mayonnaise. Stuff trout with mixture. **5** Grill trout over high heat for about 5 minutes each side or until golden and crispy. **6** Arrange grilled trout on heated platter and spoon wine sauce over top. Garnish with freshly toasted sliced almonds and lemon wedges.

Eric's Amazing Wild Berry-Butter Sauce for Fish | Serves twelve to sixteen

April Point Lodge,
Quadra Island, British Columbia

Eric Peterson of April Point Lodge offers this wonderfully fruity, buttery sauce, which is a perfect complement to grilled salmon or rockfish barbecued over alderwood chips, or to seared oysters. It's ideal for a crowd, and can be cut in half for smaller numbers. Try it at your next big barbecue.

Quails' Gate Estate Winery Late Harvest Optima B.A.

WESTBANK,
BRITISH COLUMBIA

Aged in small French oak barrels for 15 months, this wine has layers of apricot, peach and nectarine that blend well with the berries in this sauce. The nutty taste and toasty bouquet complement grilled fish or shellfish.

¾ to I lb	cold unsalted butter, cubed	375 to 500 g
½ cup	minced shallots OR green onions	125 mL
2 cups	Quails' Gate Chasselas (white wine)	500 mL
2 cups	fish OR chicken stock	500 mL
3 tbsp	minced gingerroot (optional)	50 mL
	Salt (if stock is unsalted)	
	Freshly ground pepper	
2 to 3 cups	fresh berries (such as huckleberries, blackberries, raspberries, cranberries, Oregon grapes), divided	500 to 750 mL
2 tsp	liquid honey OR maple syrup	10 mL
2 tbsp	apple cider vinegar OR white wine vinegar	25 mL
	Fresh berries and mixed greens (for garnish)	

1 Melt 2 tbsp (25 mL) unsalted butter in a large sauté pan. Cook shallots until tender, about 3 to 5 minutes.
2 Add wine, stock, ginger (if using), salt and pepper to taste, 1½ cups (375 mL) berries, honey and vinegar. Cook, stirring, over high heat until reduced to one-quarter and almost syrupy. Pass through fine strainer; discard pulp.
3 Return sauce essence to sauté pan. Bring to a rapid boil. Remove from heat. Stir in additional fresh berries. Gradually whisk in butter, one cube at a time, until well

blended. Correct seasoning. (Sauce may be rewarmed in warm water bath, but must be whisked constantly.)

4 On plates, arrange mixed greens and fresh berries around the fish. Top fish with sauce. Serve immediately.

$\mathcal{M}$ONKFISH IN DRY MUSCAT BLANC | Serves four

Shari Darling/Hillside Cellars Vineyards and Farm Winery, Penticton, British Columbia

WINEMAKER VERA KLOCKOCKA, born in Prague, Czechoslovakia, produces five estate wines (Johannisberg Riesling, Pinot Auxerrois, Gamay Noir, Muscat Ottonel and Cabernet Sauvignon). All are produced according to VQA standards. Founded in 1990, British Columbia's smallest winery is housed in a century-old farmhouse overlooking five acres of estate vineyard and Okanagan Lake; it produces only 3,000 gallons of wine a year. In 1992 Vera and her husband, Bohumir, completed a new tasting room decorated with wine crates and ceramic tile.

4	½-lb (250-g) monkfish tails	4
8	shallots, finely chopped	8
⅔ cup	fresh mushrooms, thinly sliced	150 mL
	Salt and freshly ground pepper to taste	
	Few sprigs parsley	
½ lb	butter, cubed	250 g
1 cup	Hillside Cellars Dry Muscat Blanc (white wine)	250 mL
½ cup	dried bread crumbs	125 mL

1 Remove skin and gelatinous part from monkfish. Wash fish and slice thinly. **2** Arrange most of the shallots and mushrooms in a heatproof baking dish. Lay monkfish on top; season with salt and pepper. Top with remaining shallots and mushrooms, parsley and butter cubes. Pour wine over fish. Cover with bread crumbs. **3** Bake at 375°F (190°C) for 10 to 20 minutes or until top is slightly browned and sauce is reduced to a light syrup.

Hillside Cellars Dry Muscat Blanc

A light-bodied white. With a floral bouquet and hints of apricot and champagne-like effervescence on the palate, Dry Muscat Blanc is great with delicate, flavourful foods, such as white fish and shellfish. Serve chilled like Champagne.

*T*HRESHER SHARK ESCALOPES WITH BERRY COMPOTE | Serves six

Oceanwood Country Inn, Mayne Island, British Columbia

IN 1990 MARILYN AND JOHNATHAN CHILVERS opened their casual country inn with its picturesque view. The daily menu focuses on fresh, seasonal foods, and the wine list features the best from British Columbia and the Pacific Northwest. The inn has received awards for its food and wine, including an honourable mention in the West Coast wine list category at the Vancouver Playhouse International Wine Festival in 1992.

Gray Monk Cellars Pinot Chardonnay

OKANAGAN CENTRE, BRITISH COLUMBIA

Made in the French white Burgundy style, since winemaker George Heiss refuses to use oak, this Chardonnay has lemony fruit flavours that mesh well with the berry compote in this dish. Increased malolactic fermentation gives the wine a buttery, smooth roundness that matches the delicacy of the shark slices. A rich, well-balanced wine with a distinctive aroma and a superb lingering aftertaste.

WINEMAKER'S TASTING NOTES

	Olive oil	
¼ cup	chopped thyme, lemon thyme OR silver thyme	50 mL
	Crushed mixed peppercorns and salt to taste	
12	thresher shark slices (3 oz/75 g each), cut in ½-inch (1-cm) strips on a slight angle across the grain	12
2 cups	blueberries, raspberries OR red currants	500 mL
	Mixed greens (such as mixed lettuces, watercress, kale)	
	Steamed carrots, green beans, bell peppers and potatoes	

1 Brush olive oil on baking sheet. Sprinkle with one third of the thyme, one half of the peppercorns and salt. **2** Lay the shark slices on the baking sheet, without overlapping. Brush with olive oil and sprinkle with one third of the thyme, remaining peppercorns and salt. Marinate for up to 1 hour. **3** In a large dry nonstick skillet over moderately high heat, sauté shark slices for 2½ minutes each side. Remove from pan and keep warm. **4** To make the berry compote, put berries into a 1-quart (1-L) saucepan over medium heat, bring to a boil, and simmer over low heat for 20 minutes. **5** Lightly steam mixed greens. Season with remaining thyme. Arrange greens on plates. Top with fish. Arrange steamed vegetables and potatoes around the fish. Drizzle berry compote over the fish.

$\mathcal{H}$ALIBUT CHEEKS | Serves four

John Schreiner

A JOURNALIST SINCE 1958, John Schreiner became seriously interested in wine after hand-crushing some California Cabernet Sauvignon in 1974. An award-winning home winemaker since then, he has written extensively about wine in *Vancouver* magazine, *The Financial Post* and other publications. He has judged wine both in Canada and in Europe and has travelled to all the major wine regions. He is the author of the comprehensive 1984 book *The World of Canadian Wine*. He is a member of five wine societies in Vancouver, where he lives, and is an editor of the *Western Wine Review*, a wine newsletter.

John Schreiner recommends a simple family favourite: halibut cheeks. These can be found in the better fish shops, always priced at a discount to halibut steaks. Don't be put off: the cheeks are good-sized rounds of richly textured flesh that tastes somewhat like lobster.

I lb	fresh halibut cheeks	500 g
	Flour for dusting fish	
¼ cup	butter	50 mL
	Salt and pepper to taste	
I tbsp	lemon juice	I5 mL
	Lemon wedges (for garnish)	

1 Dust fish lightly with flour. In a skillet, heat 2 tbsp (25 mL) butter over medium heat and sauté halibut cheeks about 5 minutes each side. Add more butter to skillet if needed. Transfer cooked halibut cheeks to warm platter.

2 Add remaining butter, salt, pepper and lemon juice to skillet. Bring to a boil, scraping up solids. Pour over halibut just before serving. Garnish with lemon wedges.

Gray Monk Cellars Pinot Gris

OKANAGAN CENTRE, BRITISH COLUMBIA

John Schreiner notes that this is the trademark wine of one of the Okanagan Valley's most consistent wineries. It shows a lovely bronze blush in the glass and an aroma of lichees and peaches. It is packed with fruit—stewed rhubarb and strawberries—with a racy acidity that gives the wine a vivacious freshness and the ability to complement the richness of this food.

WINEMAKER'S · TASTING NOTES

ORANGE ROUGHY WITH TRI-CITRUS BEURRE BLANC | Serves four

D ' A n g e l o   V i n e y a r d s ,   A m h e r s t b u r g ,   O n t a r i o

AFTER 16 YEARS OF AMATEUR WINEMAKING and several awards, Sal D'Angelo decided to turn professional and transformed his farm into a winery. Business is flourishing, allowing him to produce such varietal wines as Chardonnay, Riesling, Gamay Noir, Merlot, Cabernet Sauvignon, Pinot Blanc and Vidal. His most recent achievement was a gold medal for his Icewine in the 1992 All Canada Wine Championship.

This is a delicious recipe developed by chef Normand Riel of the Horse and Hound Restaurant in London, Ontario.

D'Angelo Vineyards Vidal

Fermented and aged in stainless steel, this varietal is light bodied and has distinctive fruity aromas and flavours that do not overpower the orange roughy while enhancing the citrus flavours in the cream sauce.

2 tbsp	vegetable oil	25 mL
4	pieces orange roughy (5 oz/100 g each)	4

SAUCE:

2 tbsp	butter	25 mL
1 tbsp	each grapefruit juice and lime juice	15 mL
1 tsp	orange juice	5 mL
3 tbsp	fish stock	50 mL
½ cup	D'Angelo Vineyards Vidal (white wine)	125 mL
1 tbsp	chopped shallots	15 mL
1	clove garlic, minced	1
1 tbsp	whipping cream	15 mL
¼ lb	cold butter, cubed	125 g

GARNISHES:

12	pink grapefruit segments	12
	Pink peppercorns and orange rind	

■ To make Tri-Citrus Sauce, in a heavy saucepan over medium heat, combine 2 tbsp (25 mL) butter, grapefruit juice, lime juice, orange juice, fish stock, wine, shallots and garlic. Reduce to one-quarter; add cream. Cook, stirring,

4 minutes or until sauce thickens. **2** Remove from heat and whisk in butter, one cube at a time, until well blended. Cool sauce to room temperature. **3** In a large oven-safe skillet, heat oil over medium heat. Fry orange roughy until golden on both sides. Transfer to oven and bake at 350°F (180°C) for 7 minutes or until tender. **4** Arrange fish on plates; pour sauce over fish. Garnish fish with three grapefruit segments, a few pink peppercorns and a few strands of orange rind.

GRILLED RED SNAPPER WITH SWEET AND SPICY GLAZE | Serves four

Shari Darling / Konzelmann Estate Winery, Niagara-on-the-Lake, Ontario

LIKE ALL CONSCIENTIOUS WINEMAKERS, Herbert Konzelmann believes fine wines begin with the grape, which is why he tends the 40-acre vineyard himself. Unlike other growers in Ontario, however, Konzelmann uses an untraditional vine-training method called Vertico. Among its many advantages, Vertico training permits the sun's rays and wind to circulate through the vines, drying off morning dew and rain. This method has proved successful for Konzelmann. He has not only won several gold and silver medals for his wines but has acquired a steadfast clientele. This winery offers 21 products, ranging in style from a dry Chardonnay to a delicious Vidal Icewine. All are estate-bottled and most obtain VQA status every year.

Konzelmann Estate Winery Gewuerztraminer

Konzelmann's Gewuerztraminer is the perfect partner for this dish. The wine's floral and spice aromas, tropical fruit flavours and hint of sweetness complement the Thai spices and sweetness of garlic and honey in the glaze.

4	whole fresh red snapper (gutted)	4
4	large cloves garlic, thinly sliced	4
4	small sprigs fresh rosemary	4
	Vegetable oil	

THAI SEASONING:

2 tsp	cayenne	10 mL
¾ tsp	ground caraway	4 mL
1 tsp	coriander	5 mL
½ tsp	freshly ground black pepper	2 mL
½ tsp	ground ginger	2 mL

GLAZE:

1 cup	olive oil	250 mL
2 tbsp	chopped garlic	25 mL
1 tsp	chopped serrano chili	5 mL
1 tsp	white pepper	5 mL
½ cup	honey	125 mL
¼ cup	lemon juice	50 mL
2 tbsp	rice vinegar	25 mL

2 tbsp	finely chopped rosemary (fresh or dried)	25 mL
4 tsp	fish sauce	20 mL

GARNISHES:

4	sprigs fresh rosemary	4
16	2-inch (5-cm) slices red bell pepper	16

1 To make Thai seasoning, in a small bowl combine cayenne, caraway, coriander, pepper and ginger.

2 To make glaze, heat olive oil in skillet over medium heat. Add garlic and stir until lightly browned. Add serrano chili and white pepper; stir for 1 minute. Add honey, lemon juice, vinegar, rosemary and fish sauce; bring to a boil, stirring constantly, and cook until sauce is thickened to glaze consistency, about 3 minutes. Keep warm. **3** Trim fins from fish. Rinse fish under cold water and pat dry. Arrange garlic slices and rosemary sprigs inside each fish. Coat fish with vegetable oil and sprinkle with Thai seasoning. Grill at 400°F (200°C) 7 to 9 minutes on each side or until fish is flaky. **4** Arrange fish on a warm platter and pour glaze over it. Garnish with rosemary sprigs and bell pepper slices.

PIQUANT PERCH | Serves two

London Winery,
London, Ontario

LONDON WINERY has a lineage that dates back to 1927, when their products first went on sale in liquor stores across Ontario. Since this time the company has remained a pacesetter in Ontario's wine industry. They were the first to use the Flor process in sherry-making, the first to introduce a hollow glass stopper for wine decanters and the first to produce Ancient Mead from fermented honey. Winemaker Jim Patience has earned a notable reputation for his sherries, ports, vermouth, Ancient Mead, fruit wines and Icewine.

London Winery's Cedar Springs Proprietors Reserve Riesling

Fermented and aged in stainless steel, Cedar Springs Proprietors Reserve Riesling has retained its typical varietal character. It has a golden robe, fruity aromas and a dry, flinty mouth. Being light bodied, this Riesling matches a delicate fish like perch, while adding a refreshing lift to the meal.

WINEMAKER'S · TASTING NOTES

2	Lake Erie perch	2
⅓ cup	butter	75 mL
2 tbsp	olive oil	25 mL
2 tbsp	flour	25 mL
I tsp	paprika	5 mL
Pinch	each salt and pepper	Pinch
I	egg, beaten	I
½ cup	cracker crumbs	125 mL
I tsp	grated onion	5 mL
½ cup	chicken stock	125 mL
I tbsp	chopped parsley	15 mL
3 tbsp	London Winery Golden Cream Sherry	50 mL
2 tsp	thyme	10 mL
	Pepper to taste	
I cup	sour cream	250 mL

1 Rinse perch and pat dry. In a skillet, heat butter and oil over medium heat. **2** In a shallow dish, mix together flour, paprika, salt and pepper. Dip fish in seasoned flour, then in egg and then in cracker crumbs. Fry fish until golden brown. Transfer to warm plates. **3** To same pan add onion, stock, parsley, sherry, thyme and pepper. Bring to a boil and reduce heat. Add sour cream and stir until hot. Do not boil. Serve sauce over perch.

GRILLED HALIBUT WITH MANGO GINGER SAUCE | Serves four

Anthony Gismondi

ANTHONY GISMONDI is the wine columnist for the Vancouver *Sun* and considered by many to be Western Canada's most influential wine writer. Known throughout the wine community for his no-nonsense, straightforward opinions, his popular "Wine of the Week" selections as profiled in the *Sun* are constant sellouts in provincial liquor stores. The former associate editor of *The Wine Consumer—A Wine Buyer's Guide for Canadians* is also a regular contributor to several West Coast publications.

As chairman of the Selections Committee for the annual Vancouver Playhouse International Wine Festival, Anthony Gismondi is in charge of selecting the 110 wineries featured at North America's largest and most successful consumer wine show.

4	halibut steaks, ¾ inch (2 cm) thick	4
Pinch	each freshly ground pepper, seasoning salt, cayenne	Pinch

MANGO GINGER SAUCE:

2	mangoes, peeled and pitted	2
I tbsp	lemon juice	15 mL
2	cloves garlic, minced	2
I tbsp	Dijon mustard	15 mL
I tsp	chopped gingerroot	5 mL
Dash	Worcestershire sauce	Dash
	Salt and freshly ground pepper to taste	

CedarCreek Estate Winery Pinot Blanc

KELOWNA, BRITISH COLUMBIA

Anthony Gismondi notes that the CedarCreek Pinot Blanc is the creation of winemaker Ann Sperling. The wine, which features the addition of 15 per cent Auxerrois to the blend, is part of an exciting new lineup coming out of this tiny winery that clings to the bluffs above Okanagan Lake.

1 Rinse halibut in cold water and pat dry. (Leave the skins on to hold fish together on grill.) Season steaks with pepper, seasoning salt and cayenne. **2** Grill steaks at

All of the Auxerrois and 17 per cent of the Pinot Blanc was clean fermented in stainless steel tanks.

The remaining 67 per cent of Pinot Blanc was barrel fermented (in older French oak) and put through a secondary malolactic fermentation. Maturation of 80 per cent of the wine took place in barrels for a further eight to 10 months before bottling.

The wine has an intriguing mix of fresh-cut pears (Pinot Blanc) and green apples (Auxerrois) on the nose with just a hint of spice from the oak. Its creamy, buttery, waxy texture is set off by just the right amount of acidity in the finish. Good intensity and weight only add to its appeal. A perfect foil for the halibut-mango combination.

WINEMAKER'S TASTING NOTES

400°F (200°C) for 15 minutes on each side or until flesh is flaky. **3** Meanwhile, make sauce. In a blender or food processor combine mango flesh, lemon juice, garlic, mustard, ginger, Worcestershire sauce, salt and pepper. Purée until smooth. **4** Pour purée into saucepan and heat. Do not boil. **5** Arrange fish on plates and pour purée over fish just before serving.

CHAPTER ELEVEN

SEAFOOD

SHRIMP WITH LIME CHILI BEURRE BLANC | Serves four

Michelle Ramsay

I tbsp	finely chopped shallots	15 mL
⅓ cup	lime juice	75 mL
¼ cup	Cave Spring Cellars Gewürztraminer (white wine)	50 mL
¼ to ¾ tsp	crushed hot pepper flakes	I to 4 mL
I cup	unsalted butter, cubed	250 mL
I	tomato, peeled, seeded and coarsely chopped	I
2 tbsp	chopped fresh coriander	25 mL
I lb	large shrimp, peeled and deveined	500 g
	Vegetable oil	
	Fresh coriander (for garnish)	

LeComte Estate Winery Gewürztraminer

OKANAGAN FALLS, BRITISH COLUMBIA

This Gewürztraminer shows true varietal character with forward red pepper and lichee aromas. The spicy grapefruit mouth enables this wine to stand up to the chilies in the sauce. Rich and soft with a long finish.

WINEMAKER'S TASTING NOTES

1 In a small saucepan, combine shallots, lime juice, wine and pepper flakes. Over high heat, reduce to about 2 tbsp (25 mL). **2** Remove from heat, immediately reducing heat to low. After I minute return pan to heat and whisk in butter, one cube at a time, until all butter is absorbed and sauce emulsifies. **3** Whisk in tomato and coriander. Keep sauce warm over a pan of lukewarm water. **4** Brush shrimp with vegetable oil and grill 3 inches (8 cm) from a medium-high element for about 3 minutes each side. If barbecuing, grill 4 inches (10 cm) from coals for 4 to 5 minutes each side. **5** Arrange shrimp on a plate or over a bed of noodles and pour sauce over top. Garnish with coriander leaves.

$\mathcal{K}$ILLER PRAWNS | Serves six

The Fish House in Stanley Park, Vancouver, British Columbia

RESTAURATEUR BUD KANKE opened this monument to fresh local seafood in 1991. The emphasis here is on casual, down-home food in a picturesque setting in Stanley Park overlooking English Bay. The Fish House offers one of the city's widest selections of fresh oysters, both local and regional. Heart Smart dishes appeal to the health-conscious, and there is always a touch of the exotic with such menu items as ginger hot pot with salmon and seafood paella. British Columbia wines are given a prominent place on the wine list.

Domaine de Chaberton Madeleine Sylvaner

LANGLEY, BRITISH COLUMBIA

From one of British Columbia's newest estate wineries, opened by ninth-generation French winemaker Claude Violet in 1991, the Sylvaner is an off-dry German-style wine. Its fairly low acidity and peachy flavours blend perfectly with the spicy tomato sauce surrounding the prawns. This mellow-tasting wine is more full bodied than the Chaberton Blanc and can be used with stronger-flavoured seafoods.

WINEMAKER'S · TASTING NOTES ·

1 tbsp	olive oil	15 mL
1 tsp	minced shallots	5 mL
1 tsp	finely minced garlic	5 mL
1 tbsp	chopped fresh rosemary	15 mL
1 tbsp	chopped fresh basil	15 mL
1 tsp	coarse black pepper	5 mL
1 tbsp	tomato paste	15 mL
2 tbsp	crushed tomatoes	25 mL
1 tbsp	horseradish	15 mL
2 tbsp	chili sauce	25 mL
½ tsp	hot pepper sauce	2 mL
1 tbsp	Worcestershire sauce	15 mL
4 cups	fish stock	1 L
3 oz	Domaine de Chaberton Sylvaner (white wine)	90 mL
48	fresh prawns, headed, peeled and deveined	48
6	mini baguettes, heated or freshly baked	6

1 In a small saucepan, heat olive oil over medium heat. Lightly sauté shallots, garlic, rosemary, basil and black pepper. Stir in tomato paste and cook for 1 minute, stirring occasionally. **2** Blend in crushed tomatoes, horseradish, chili sauce, hot pepper sauce and Worcestershire sauce. Cook for 2 minutes, stirring occasionally. **3** Add fish stock and bring to a boil over high heat. Reduce heat to low and simmer, uncovered, 45 minutes or until sauce is reduced to 2 cups (500 mL). Adjust seasonings to taste. (Mixture can be prepared to here, cooled and refrigerated. Flavours will improve overnight.) **4** Add wine to sauce. Bring to a boil over high heat and add prawns. Cook 30 seconds or until prawns are pink. Divide among six bowls and serve with mini baguettes.

VINOTECA SHRIMP | Serves four to six

Vinoteca, Woodbridge, Ontario

VINOTECA PRODUCES two substantially different groups of wine. The first group includes Pinot Noir, Cabernet Sauvignon, Chardonnay and Riesling. These wines have obtained VQA status and are made with 100 per cent Ontario grapes. The second group of wines are obtained by blending Ontario grapes with California grapes and juices from Italy. All the wines show intense varietal fruit character and natural sweetness, having been produced in stainless steel and complemented with limited editions of Oak-Fermented and Oak-Aged Reserve wines. In total, winemaker Giovanni Follegot produces a Riesling, Chardonnay, Pinot Noir, Cabernet Sauvignon, Albino, Gaio and two table wines.

Vinoteca Riesling

Vinoteca's Riesling has a delicate fruity bouquet and varietal fruit flavours that complement the delicate taste of shrimp. The wine's high acidity also works with the acidity found in tomatoes.

WINEMAKER'S · TASTING NOTES

¼ cup	oil	50 mL
I	green bell pepper, diced	I
2	stalks celery, sliced	2
2	medium onions, diced	2
2	cloves garlic, crushed	2
2	cans (14 oz/398 mL) crushed tomatoes, undrained	2
2	bay leaves	2
I tsp	hot pepper sauce	5 mL
Pinch	each salt, pepper, thyme	Pinch
2 tbsp	cornstarch	25 mL
¼ cup	Vinoteca Riesling (white wine)	50 mL
I½ lb	peeled shrimp, uncooked	750 g

1 Heat oil in saucepan over low heat. Add green pepper, celery and onions; cook for 5 minutes. Add garlic; cook I minute. Add tomatoes, bay leaves, hot pepper sauce, salt, pepper and thyme. Bring to a boil and simmer 5 minutes, uncovered. **2** In a small bowl, whisk together a few spoonfuls of hot tomato liquid with cornstarch and wine.

Stir into saucepan. Bring to a boil, stirring constantly until thickened. Add shrimp and simmer, covered, for 10 to 15 minutes. Discard bay leaves. Serve over rice.

CHARDONNAY SHRIMP | Serves four

Southbrook Farms Winery, Maple, Ontario

ESTABLISHED IN 1939, Southbrook Farms, with its 285 acres of agricultural land, specializes in growing fruit, pumpkins and sweet corn. The Redelmeier family operates the farm with a roadside market that sells fresh produce, preserves and homemade pies, cookies and muffins. In 1992, Bill Redelmeier opened the winery, which is located in two of the oldest dairy barns. They use 100 per cent Niagara grapes to make nine of their wines. His first vintage consisted of an oaked and non-oaked Chardonnay, dry and off-dry Riesling, two blends, a white house wine, a Vin gris and a blush.

⅓ cup	Southbrook Farms Winery Chardonnay (white wine)	75 mL
2	cloves garlic, minced	2
4 tbsp	olive oil	50 mL
2 lb	fresh shrimp, peeled	1 kg
1 cup	coarse dry bread crumbs	250 mL
2 tsp	fresh thyme	10 mL
6 oz	feta cheese	150 g
	Freshly ground pepper to taste	

Southbrook Farms Winery Chardonnay

Fermented and aged in stainless steel, Southbrook's Chardonnay is crisp and clean and has good body and length. With apple and quince on the nose and palate, this wine complements the tang of feta and spiciness of thyme.

WINEMAKER'S · TASTING NOTES

1 In a glass bowl, combine wine, half the garlic and 2 tbsp (25 mL) oil. Add shrimp and marinate at least 2 hours in refrigerator. **2** In remaining 2 tbsp (25 mL) oil, sauté remaining garlic, bread crumbs, thyme, feta cheese and pepper. **3** Drain shrimp and arrange them in a heat proof baking dish. **4** Spread bread-crumb topping evenly over the shrimp. Bake, uncovered, at 450°F (230°C) for 15 to 20 minutes. Test shrimp to make sure they are tender. Serve immediately.

Shrimp with Snow Peas, Apples and Walnuts | Serves four

Shari Darling / Quails' Gate Estate Winery, Westbank, British Columbia

A PROVINCIAL CHARM PREVAILS at Quails' Gate Vineyards and Estate Winery. Its wine and gift shop is housed in the restored log home of John and Susan Allison, settlers to the Okanagan Valley in 1873. Ben and Ruth Stewart opened the winery in 1990, and although the business may be new, the Stewarts' 70-acre estate vineyard has been undergoing renovation for more than 12 years. It is planted to the varieties Chasselas, Chardonnay, Pinot Noir, Optima, Chenin Blanc, Gewürztraminer and Riesling. Winemaker Elias Phiniotis, who trained at the University of Budapest, produces 23,000 gallons a year of Chasselas, Chardonnay, Pinot Noir and an Optima dessert wine. The Stewarts sell their Gewürztraminer, Chenin Blanc and Riesling grapes to local wineries.

Although new to the wine industry, the Stewarts have proven to be proficient wine-growers. This capability, along with Elias Phiniotis's talent and expertise, has already brought the Stewarts critical acclaim. They won a silver medal for their Optima dessert wine in the 1992 Los Angeles County Fair. Fourteen other Canadian and international awards have been earned by Quails' Gate products. All wines have also earned the prestigious VQA emblem.

1 lb	snow peas, trimmed and stringed	500 g
6 tbsp	unsalted butter	90 mL
2	large firm tart apples, peeled, cored and thickly sliced	2
2 tbsp	sugar	25 mL
½ cup	finely minced yellow onion	125 mL
2 lb	medium shrimp, peeled and deveined	1 kg
¾ cup	Quails' Gate Chasselas (white wine)	175 mL
⅔ cup	Dijon mustard	150 mL
¾ cup	whipping cream	175 mL
½ cup	walnuts	125 mL

1 Boil snow peas until tender-crisp, about 3 minutes. Drain peas and plunge immediately into cold water. Set aside. **2** In a large lidded skillet, melt 2 tbsp (25 mL) butter over medium heat. Sauté apple slices for 5 minutes or until tender. Sprinkle slices with sugar; increase heat and rapidly turn slices until brown and lightly caramelized. Remove slices from pan and set aside. **3** In same skillet melt remaining butter over medium heat. Add onion and cook, covered, 25 minutes or until onions are golden. **4** Increase heat to high. Stir in shrimp and toss rapidly for 3 minutes or until firm and pink. Remove shrimp and set aside. **5** Pour wine into skillet and boil until reduced by two-thirds. Lower heat and stir in mustard. Pour in cream and simmer for 15 minutes, stirring occasionally, until sauce is reduced slightly. **6** Drain snow peas and pat dry. Stir peas, apples, walnuts and shrimp into cream sauce; simmer for 1 minute. Serve immediately over rice.

Quails' Gate Vineyards Chasselas

Chasselas is the most widely planted variety at Quails' Gate. It delivers a wine with golden yellow colour and typical varietal aromas resembling apple and citrus with a hint of black pepper. With sufficient acidity, the wine is crisp and smooth. Delicate in nature, it should be married with delicate foods such as salad, fruit, white meats and shellfish. This recipe is a suitable partner, as its apple flavours complement the wine's aromas.

WINEMAKER'S TASTING NOTES

PAN-SEARED SCALLOPS WITH RED PLUMS, ROASTED SHALLOTS AND NASTURTIUMS

Horizons Restaurant, Burnaby, British Columbia | Serves eight

LOCATED HIGH ATOP Burnaby Mountain, this restaurant offers a panoramic view of Burrard Inlet, the North Shore mountains and Stanley Park. The restaurant provides a warm, relaxed atmosphere created by the cherrywood, natural slate, wrought iron and earth tones. The cuisine is just as wonderful. Chef Deborah Connors has created a traditional menu offering favourites such as braised duck with wild honey, chilies and basmati rice, and barbecued B.C. salmon.

Gray Monk Cellars Pinot Gris

WINFIELD,

BRITISH COLUMBIA

This white wine has a hint of pink in its colour. The spicy-floral flavours contrast nicely with the intensely flavoured red plum shallot sauce. A very well balanced wine, one of Gray Monk's best.

WINEMAKER'S · TASTING NOTES

¼ cup	small shallots, peeled	50 mL
2 tbsp	honey	25 mL
6	red plums	6
¼ cup	red wine	50 mL
½ tsp	freshly ground black pepper	2 mL
I tbsp	butter	15 mL
32	medium scallops	32
	Black pepper to taste	

Nasturtium leaves OR other peppery salad greens (for garnish)

1 In a small baking dish, roast shallots in melted honey at 350°F (180°C) for 10 minutes or until shallots are slightly translucent. Drain honey into a small saucepan; set shallots aside. **2** Cut four of the plums into quarters; remove pits. Add to honey in saucepan. Stir in red wine and black pepper. Bring to a boil; simmer gently, uncovered, for 15 minutes, stirring occasionally. In a blender or food processor, purée mixture; set aside. **3** Finely chop remaining two plums; set aside. **4** In a small saucepan over high heat, melt butter. Add scallops and season with black pepper. Sear scallops I minute each side. Add shallots and fresh plum pieces; toss. Remove from heat. **5** Pour sauce on eight small plates. Arrange scallops, shallots and plums on plates. Garnish with fresh nasturtium leaves.

*H*ONEY AND GARLIC SCALLOPS AND PRAWNS | Serves six

Herons Restaurant, Waterfront Centre Hotel, Vancouver, British Columbia

AWARD-WINNING EXECUTIVE CHEF Thomas Dietzel combines his classical training with an interest in Asian and Mediterranean foods to offer a unique brand of cuisine at the Waterfront Centre. The emphasis is on dishes that are light, healthy, fresh and fun. Local fish, meats and organic produce are used to create meals that have a world-beat flavour but are still unmistakably British Columbian. This dish was inspired while Dietzel was working in Hong Kong.

6 tbsp	olive oil	100 mL
30	scallops	30
30	prawns, peeled and deveined	30
½ cup	unpasteurized honey	125 mL
2 tsp	chopped garlic	10 mL
	Salt and cayenne to taste	
4 tbsp	unsalted butter	50 mL
I cup	julienne leeks (white part only)	250 mL
½ cup	Domaine de Chaberton Blanc (white wine)	125 mL
½ cup	whipping cream	125 mL

1 In a sauté pan over medium-high heat, heat 3 tbsp (50 mL) olive oil. Sauté scallops until half-cooked. Remove from pan and set aside. **2** In same pan heat remaining 3 tbsp (50 mL) olive oil over medium-high heat. Sauté prawns until half-cooked. Add honey, garlic, salt and cayenne. Toss in shrimp. Do not overcook. **3** In a saucepan, melt butter over medium heat. Sauté leeks for I minute. Add wine and cook leeks until all liquid is evaporated. Add cream and reduce, stirring, to desired thickness. **4** Serve scallop and prawn mixture on a bed of creamed leeks.

Domaine de Chaberton Blanc

LANGLEY, BRITISH COLUMBIA

A premium house blend, made with the highest quality of vitis vinifera grapes, this clean wine has a subtle, fragrant, yet light fruity aroma and dry, crisp refreshing taste that complements the seafood in this recipe. Fruitiness is subtle enough that it does not take away from the flavours in the sauce.

WINEMAKER'S · TASTING NOTES

STEAMED PENDER HARBOUR SPOT PRAWNS WITH GINGER LEMON DRESSING | Serves four to five

Gehringer Brothers,
Oliver, British Columbia

SINCE 1985 GEHRINGER BROTHERS has produced Germanic-style varietals such as Verdelet, Johannisberg Riesling, Pinot Auxerrois, Ehrenfelser and Müller-Thurgau. Their winemaking approach is unequivocal but distinctive. After the grapes are pressed, a portion of the fresh juice is stored while the remainder is fermented into dry wine. Before bottling, the unfermented juice is blended back into the wine, giving the wines a concentrated varietal flavour and a hint of natural sweetness.

The winery's success can be attributed to the two generations of Gehringer brothers. Helmut and brother Karl concentrate on managing the vineyard, while Helmut's sons, Walter and Gordon, operate the business and make the wine. Walter trained at the University of Geisenheim in Germany, graduating with an engineering degree in viticulture and oenology, followed by an apprenticeship at a winery near Stuttgart and five years' employment as winemaker for Andres Wines in British Columbia. Gordon also trained in West Germany, where he obtained a winemaking degree from Weinsberg.

DRESSING:

	Juice and rind of 2 lemons	
1 tbsp	honey	15 mL
1 tbsp	fish sauce	15 mL
3 tbsp	peanut oil	50 mL
1 tbsp	grated gingerroot	15 mL
1 tbsp	shredded kaffir lime leaves OR lemon balm	15 mL
1 tbsp	finely sliced red chili	15 mL

PRAWNS:

1 tbsp	sugar	15 mL
1 tbsp	soy sauce	15 mL
1 tbsp	virgin olive oil	15 mL
20	prawns, headed and peeled	20

1 To make dressing, whisk together lemon juice, honey and fish sauce. While whisking, pour in oil in a thin stream. Stir in lemon rind, ginger, kaffir lime leaves and chili. **2** To prepare prawns, in a glass bowl blend sugar, soy sauce and olive oil; marinate prawns for 20 minutes. **3** Steam prawns in a bamboo basket over boiling water for about 2 minutes or until firm and pink. Serve prawns in the basket with dressing as a dip.

Gehringer Brothers Pinot Auxerrois

Pinot Auxerrois, also called Auxerrois Blanc or simply Auxerrois, is grown widely in Alsace and southern German districts. Gehringer Brothers' Pinot Auxerrois exhibits tropical fruit and earthy aromas with peach undertones on the palate and a hint of natural sweetness. These characteristics enhance the ginger-lemon-honey flavours in the dressing. Being light bodied, the wine complements this delicate meat.

WINEMAKER'S TASTING NOTES

PRAWNS WITH YELLOW PEPPER AND GINGER CREAM | Serves two

Mission Hill Vineyards, Westbank, British Columbia

LOCATED IN THE OKANAGAN VALLEY south of Kelowna, Mission Hill Vineyards is one of Canada's most attractive wineries. Set on the crown of Mission Hill above the town of Westbank, it enjoys a fantastic view of vineyards, orchards and Okanagan Lake. The winery is also impressive, done in a mission style with stained-glass windows, antiques, stucco walls and ceramic tile. This spectacular setting and attractive building are not the only attributes of Mission Hill, however. Their wines are delicious. Swiss-born winemaker Daniel Lagnaz produces a wide spectrum of products, ranging from award-winning varietals (Chardonnay, Chasselas, Chenin Blanc, Johannisberg Riesling, Gewürztraminer, Cabernet Sauvignon, Merlot and Pinot Noir) to eaux-de-vie and brandy. Among their 300 awards, Mission Hill has a gold medal for their 1989 Private Reserve Cabernet Sauvignon/Merlot from the International Eastern Wine Competition held in Watkin's Glen, New York.

8 to 10	jumbo prawns	8 to 10
	Juice of ½ lemon	

YELLOW PEPPER AND GINGER CREAM:

2 tsp	butter	10 mL
½	bay leaf	½
2	shallots, diced	2
I	small yellow pepper, diced	I
I	sprig fresh thyme	I
2 tsp	grated gingerroot	10 mL
⅓ cup	Mission Hill Johannisberg Riesling Private Reserve (white wine)	75 mL
⅓ cup	fish stock	75 mL
¼ cup	whipping cream	50 mL
	Salt and pepper to taste	
2	sprigs fresh watercress (for garnish)	2

1 In a saucepan over medium heat, melt butter. Add bay leaf, shallots, yellow pepper, thyme and ginger. Cook slowly for 3 minutes. Increase heat to high. Add wine and reduce by half. Add fish stock and reduce by half. Remove from heat. Discard thyme and bay leaf. **2** In a blender or food processor, purée pepper mixture. Strain purée, return to saucepan and set aside. **3** In a pot of boiling salted water, add lemon juice. Boil prawns, covered, for 2 to 3 minutes. Drain prawns; peel and devein. Keep warm. **4** Bring pepper purée to a boil. Remove from heat and gently stir in cream; season with salt and pepper. **5** Pour purée onto each plate. Arrange warm prawns on top. Garnish with sprigs of watercress.

Mission Hill Vineyards Johannisberg Riesling Private Reserve

Johannisberg Riesling is the most widely planted old world grape variety in British Columbia. Mission Hill Johannisberg Riesling Private Reserve is made in the off-dry style, which allows the gentle apple and honey flavours of the wine to fully open. These flavours are a pleasant counterpoint to the pepper and ginger flavours of the purée and provide an unobtrusive background to the delicate prawn meat. The wine's crisp finish is especially refreshing when accompanying creamy sauces.

WINEMAKER'S TASTING NOTES

Mussels and Scallops in Orange Cumin Sauce | Serves four

Silver Spoon Restaurant and Café, Halifax, Nova Scotia

DEANNA SILVER became known for her desserts when she opened a small café in Halifax more than a decade ago. Since then, the talented entrepreneur has expanded to a large, restored nineteenth-century downtown building and has opened another Silver Spoon in the city's trendy Park Lane Mall. The creativity of these kitchens has resulted in Silver being featured in a CNN cooking series, awards and rave reviews by both the Canadian and American food media.

Jost Vineyards Habitant Blanc

MALAGASH, NOVA SCOTIA

Named after the village and vineyard in the Annapolis Valley where this grape variety is grown, this dry wine has a fruity, clean finish with a touch of vanilla. The balanced fruit and acid work well with the flavourful sauce in this dish.

WINEMAKER'S TASTING NOTES

24	mussels, scrubbed and debearded	24
½ cup	unsalted butter at room temperature	125 mL
I lb	scallops	500 g
I	clove garlic, minced	I
3	shallots, finely chopped	3
⅓ cup	orange juice concentrate	75 mL
¼ cup	dry vermouth	50 mL
1¼ tsp	cumin	6 mL
2 tbsp	fresh thyme (or ¾ tsp/4 mL dried)	25 mL
½ cup	whipping cream	125 mL
	Salt and pepper to taste	

1 In a large pot, bring to a boil 1½ inches (4 cm) water. Steam mussels, covered, about 5 minutes or until mussels open. Discard unopened mussels. Remove mussels from shells and set aside. **2** To make sauce, in a large skillet melt 2 tbsp (25 mL) butter and sauté scallops until slightly translucent inside and golden outside. Transfer to warm bowl. **3** In same pan, melt 2 tbsp (25 mL) butter. Sauté garlic and shallots 2 to 3 minutes or until shallots are translucent. Combine orange concentrate with 3 tbsp (50 mL) water; add to shallots. Stir in vermouth and simmer

2 minutes or until reduced slightly. Blend in cumin, thyme and cream; simmer until reduced by one-third. **4** Over low heat, whisk in remaining butter, I tbsp (15 mL) at a time, until well blended. When mixture is sauce consistency, season with salt and pepper. **5** Add mussels and scallops to sauce. Reheat gently and serve in a porcelain scallop shell accompanied by fresh seasonal vegetables.

COZE AL ROSSO | Serves four

La Perla Dining Room, Dartmouth, Nova Scotia

PEARL McDOUGALL's popular eatery is renowned for its superb northern Italian food, with at least a dozen fresh pastas daily, fresh East Coast seafood and such local specialty meats as rabbit, quail and lamb. Since McDougall opened La Perla in 1984, the restaurant has been consistently rated one of Canada's best by *enRoute* and *Where to Eat in Canada*.

2½ tbsp	garlic butter	35 mL
2 lb	mussels, scrubbed and debearded	I kg
½ cup	Sainte Famille Wines Chardonnay (white wine)	125 mL
2 tbsp	chopped fresh basil	25 mL
I tsp	chopped fresh oregano	5 mL
¼ tsp	salt	I mL
½ tsp	freshly cracked black pepper	2 mL
I½ cups	tomato sauce	375 mL

1 In a large lidded skillet, brown garlic butter over medium heat, about 2 minutes. **2** Add mussels and toss to coat. Add wine, basil, oregano, salt and pepper. Cover and steam 3 minutes or until shells open. Discard unopened mussels. **3** Add tomato sauce and cook until sauce thickens slightly, another 3 to 4 minutes. Serve with crusty bread.

Sainte Famille Wines Chardonnay

FALMOUTH, NOVA SCOTIA

This well-balanced, crisp dry white is vinted in the nouveau California style with no oak. The flavour and bouquet are a slightly fruity green apple-pear that work well with robust seafood and the herbs in this dish.

WINEMAKER'S TASTING NOTES

SCALLOPS IN WINE SAUCE | Serves two

*Jost Vineyards,
Malagash, Nova Scotia*

PROTECTED BY THE WARM WATERS of the Northumberland Strait on the shores of the Malagash Peninsula, Jost Vineyards grows premium French hybrid and vinifera vines. Since its inception in 1984, the winery has won more than 27 awards in international competitions. Winemaker Hans Christian Jost makes 16 products, including varietals such as Maréchal Foch and Chardonnay.

Jost Vineyards Riesling/Vidal

Jost Vineyards Riesling/Vidal won a bronze medal at the International Eastern Wine Competition in New York State. Riesling (60 per cent) adds body and floral aromas to this wine, while Vidal (40 per cent) provides intense fruit flavours. This combination gives the wine an excellent fruit-acid balance, which enhances, without overpowering, the mellow taste of fresh scallops and light cream.

Suggested Varietal:
dry Riesling

1 cup	Jost Vineyards Riesling/Vidal (white wine)	250 mL
1	bay leaf	1
	Peppercorns to taste	
1 lb	scallops	500 g
2 tbsp	each butter and flour	25 mL
½ cup	shredded Gruyère OR Cheddar cheese	125 mL
1½ cups	whipping cream	375 mL
2	egg yolks, beaten	2
	Lemon pepper to taste	
½ cup	buttered bread crumbs	125 mL

1 In a saucepan over medium heat, heat wine with bay leaf and peppercorns. Poach scallops until they begin to turn opaque. Do not overcook. Transfer scallops to warm bowl. Reduce wine stock to ½ cup (125 mL). **2** Meanwhile in a separate saucepan melt butter over medium heat. Add flour and stir for 2 minutes. Add cheese and cream; stir for 2 to 3 minutes. Beat a couple of spoonfuls of sauce into beaten egg yolks. Stir into cream sauce. Add reduced stock, scallops and lemon pepper. Heat gently, stirring frequently. Do not boil. **3** Pour into 4-cup (1-L) casserole and top with buttered bread crumbs. Put under broiler until top is lightly browned.

CREAMY GRILLED LOBSTER | Serves four

Shari Darling / Domaine des Côtes d'Ardoise, Dunham, Quebec

A FARM WINERY with European appeal, Domaine des Côtes d'Ardoise is owned by Jacques Papillon. The winemaker is Patrick Barrelet, a graduate in winemaking from the University of Dijon. His creations include both varietal and blended wines, all vinified from European and French hybrid grapes grown on the 17-acre estate vineyard. A few of the grape varieties planted here are Chardonnay, Gamay Noir, Riesling, de Chaunac, Maréchal Foch and Vidal.

4	live lobsters (1¼ lb/625 g each)	4
	Salt and freshly ground pepper to taste	
½ cup	virgin olive oil	125 mL
2 tbsp	chopped shallots	25 mL
I cup	port	250 mL
I cup	whipping cream	250 mL
6	egg yolks, slightly beaten	6
	Salt and cayenne to taste	

1 Cut lobsters in half lengthwise, splitting the head first to kill. Remove internal organs and sack of grit from head. Sprinkle meat with salt and pepper and brush lightly with olive oil. Place under broiler and grill, first shell side down for 15 minutes, then meat side down for 15 minutes.
2 In a saucepan over moderately high heat, combine shallots and port; boil until reduced by half. In another saucepan reduce cream slightly; mix in egg yolks and sprinkle with salt and cayenne. Blend cream mixture and reduced port; strain through a sieve. **3** Arrange lobsters on a serving dish, shell side down, and coat meat with sauce. Serve remaining sauce in a separate bowl.

Domaine des Côtes d'Ardoise Carte d'Or Seyval

Produced entirely from Seyval Blanc grapes, this white was mostly stainless steel aged with only a portion aged for three months in American oak. Pears and a hint of olive dominate the nose, while apples and pears come through on the palate. Full-bodied and flavourful, Carte d'Or Seyval stands up to the rich taste of cream and lobster.

WINEMAKER'S TASTING NOTES

OCTOPUS IN PINOT BLANC | Serves four

Shari Darling / Gray Monk Cellars, Okanagan Centre, British Columbia

GRAY MONK CELLARS is blessed with one of the most breathtaking settings in British Columbia's wine country. Encircled by vineyards, the winery overlooks Okanagan Lake and its backdrop of mountains. The winery was established in 1982 by the Heiss family. George makes the wine, while wife Trudy promotes the business. Son George Jr., who graduated as a winemaker from Weinsberg, Germany, is cellar master. Recent awards include a gold medal for their 1990 Chardonnay at the Pacific National Exhibition Wine Festival. Although George Jr. makes a few reds, he is renowned for his whites; Pinot Gris, Pinot Blanc and Chardonnay.

Gray Monk Cellars Pinot Blanc

Gray Monk Cellars Pinot Blanc is crisp and clean with medium body and a hint of natural sweetness. It is apricot and nutty on the nose and shows varietal fruit on the palate. Given its delicate nature, this wine goes best with lightly textured, flavourful foods, such as octopus and other shellfish.

I	octopus (about 5 lb/2.2 kg)	I
2 tbsp	olive oil	25 mL
4	green onions, thinly sliced	4
I	clove garlic	I
Pinch	rosemary	Pinch
¼ tsp	thyme	I mL
I tbsp	minced fresh parsley	15 mL
2	medium tomatoes, peeled and diced	2
¾ cup	Gray Monk Cellars Pinot Blanc (white wine)	175 mL
	Salt to taste	

1 If octopus is whole, slit open head cavity and discard interior. Cut away and discard beak (between legs); wash thoroughly. Separate legs from head. **2** In a large pot of boiling salted water, simmer legs and head, covered, until skin can be peeled or stripped from the flesh, about 30 minutes. Let octopus cool in cooking water. Remove and discard skin. Dice octopus and set aside. **3** In a large saucepan, heat olive oil over medium heat. Sauté onions, garlic, rosemary, thyme, parsley and tomatoes until soft. Stir in octopus and wine. Pour all into a shallow 1½-quart

(1.5-L) casserole and bake, uncovered, at 325°F (160°C)
for 2 hours, stirring occasionally. Salt to taste.

Mussels Marinière with Tomato and Onion | Serves four

Vigneti Zanatta, Duncan, British Columbia

THE FIRST FARM WINERY on Vancouver Island, Vigneti Zanatta has 24 acres of vineyard planted to the grape varieties Ortega, Cayuga, Auxerrois, Pinot Gris and Pinot Noir. They make a white wine called Ortega and a bubbly called Glenora Fantasia and plan to increase production by 1994 when the other vines will have reached sufficient maturity and are able to produce quality grapes.

1 cup	Vigneti Zanatta Ortega (white wine)	250 mL
2	cloves garlic, minced	2
2 lb	West Coast mussels, scrubbed and debearded	1 kg
3	fresh tomatoes, seeded and chopped	3
½	small onion, thinly sliced	½
2 tbsp	minced fresh basil	25 mL
2 tbsp	unsalted butter, cut into bits	25 mL
2 tsp	lemon juice	10 mL
4	sprigs fresh basil (for garnish)	4

1 In a large saucepan combine wine and garlic; bring to a boil and simmer 2 minutes. Add mussels; cover and steam 3 to 5 minutes or until mussels have opened. Discard unopened mussels. Transfer mussels to a warmed bowl and keep warm. **2** Strain cooking liquid into a bowl through a fine sieve lined with rinsed and squeezed cheesecloth. Return liquid to cleaned pan. **3** Add tomatoes, onions and basil; bring to a boil. Swirl in butter in two batches and add lemon juice. **4** Divide mussels among four bowls, pour sauce over them and garnish with basil sprigs.

Vigneti Zanatta Ortega

Ortega is said to have been named after the Spanish philosopher José Ortega y Gasset. Vigneti Zanatta's Ortega has a peach and apricot bouquet with fresh acidity and dryness on the palate. The wine is full and flowery, complementing the sauce surrounding the mussels. It has a crisp, dry finish that cleans the palate.

WINEMAKER'S TASTING NOTES

FRUITS DE MER ST. JACQUES | Serves six

L'Auberge de la Bastille, Windsor, Ontario

ONE OF THE CITY's best-known restaurants and one frequented by neighbouring Americans, la Bastille was opened in the early 1970s by Kurt Deeg, owner of the perennially popular Ye Olde Steak House. As its name suggests, la Bastille offers classic French dishes and a selection of good wines, many of them from Ontario. This version of Coquilles St. Jacques is one of the diners' favourites.

Pelee Island Winery Chardonnay

KINGSVILLE, ONTARIO

Fermented and aged in French oak barrels, this wine has the classic Chardonnay fruit and flavours and a hint of oak that marry well with the velvety cream sauce and the sweetness of the seafood.

WINEMAKER'S TASTING NOTES

I cup	cooked lobster meat	250 mL
8 oz	cooked peeled shrimp	250 g
I cup	cooked Alaskan crab meat	250 mL
12	sea scallops, poached and quartered	12
½ cup	sliced mushrooms, blanched	125 mL
SAUCE:		
½ cup	butter	125 mL
2 tbsp	flour	25 mL
2¼ cups	whipping cream	550 mL
I tsp	cognac	5 mL
½ tsp	Madeira	2 mL
I tsp	finely chopped fresh parsley	5 mL
I tsp	finely chopped chives	5 mL
	Salt and white pepper to taste	
3	egg yolks, beaten	3
2 tbsp	table cream	25 mL
2 tbsp	shredded Swiss cheese	25 mL

1 Stir together lobster, shrimp, crab, scallops and mushrooms; divide among six heatproof individual serving dishes. **2** To prepare sauce, melt butter in a saucepan over medium heat. Whisk in flour and cook 4 to 5 minutes, stirring frequently. Reduce heat to low; gradually whisk in 2 cups (500 mL) whipping cream and cook 5 minutes, stirring constantly. Season with cognac, Madeira, parsley, chives, salt and pepper. **3** Stir together yolks and table cream; whisk into sauce. Whisk in cheese. Reserve ¼ cup (50 mL) sauce; divide remainder among serving dishes, covering seafood. **4** Mix reserved sauce with remaining ¼ cup (50 mL) whipping cream. Pour over the six dishes. Place under a preheated broiler until golden, about 2 minutes.

CHAPTER TWELVE

POULTRY

COCONUT LEMON CHICKEN | Serves six

Miestro Restaurant, London, Ontario

ECLECTIC IS THE BEST DESCRIPTION of the cooking of chef/owner Mies Bervoets. An interest in Indonesian and Asian cooking shows up on her always innovative menus. A focus on fresh local ingredients and Ontario wines adds to the calibre of the menu in this tiny bistro.

Stoney Ridge Cellars Chardonnay

(PUDDICOMBE VINEYARD), (BARREL FERMENTED AND AGED), WINONA, ONTARIO

Soft and oaky, this Chardonnay has a coconut bouquet and sweet apple taste that picks up the coconut and sweetness of the sauce in this dish.

WINEMAKER'S TASTING NOTES

6	boneless skinless chicken breasts	6

MARINADE:

½ cup	fresh coconut milk (recipe page 49), OR canned	125 mL
1	lemon, thinly sliced	1
1	stalk lemongrass, cut into 1-inch (2.5-cm) pieces	1

SAUCE:

¼ cup	olive oil	50 mL
2 tbsp	gin	25 mL
1 tbsp	finely chopped shallots	15 mL
1 cup	whipping cream	250 mL
2 tbsp	honey	25 mL
½ cup	coconut milk	125 mL
1 tbsp	ground coriander	15 mL
	Salt and pepper to taste	
	Juice of 1 lemon	

1 In a shallow dish, combine coconut milk, lemon slices and lemongrass. Add chicken breasts and marinate, covered, in refrigerator overnight. **2** Drain chicken. In a large skillet, heat olive oil over medium-high heat. Lightly brown chicken breasts on each side, about 2 minutes. Transfer to heatproof platter and bake at 400°F (200°C) until chicken is white inside, about 15 minutes. **3** Meanwhile, deglaze skillet with gin; reduce by half. Add shallots and

cook over medium heat until glossy. Add cream, honey and
½ cup (125 mL) coconut milk; reduce until thickened.
4 Add coriander, salt, pepper and lemon juice. Reduce
until desired thickness. Serve sauce over chicken breasts.

ORANGE CHICKEN | Serves four

Michelle Ramsay / Vignoble Les Blancs Coteaux

LES BLANCS COTEAUX (the white hills) is a most suitable name for a winery in Dunham,
Quebec: every winter the surrounding hills fall asleep under a blanket of white snow, and in
spring they burst alive with white apple blossoms. Marie-Claude Lizotte and Pierre Genesse
are the proprietors of Vignoble Les Blancs Coteaux.

3 lb	chicken, cut into pieces	1.5 kg
2 to 3	cloves garlic, minced	2 to 3
½ tsp	each chopped tarragon and chopped thyme	2 mL
2 tsp	each paprika and salt	10 mL
½ tsp	pepper	2 mL
½ tsp	each grated orange peel and lemon peel	2 mL
½ cup	orange juice	125 mL
¼ cup	lemon juice	50 mL

GARNISHES:

Orange slices
Tarragon leaves and thyme sprigs

1 Rub chicken pieces with minced garlic. Season with
tarragon, thyme, paprika, salt and pepper. Place in a shallow
heatproof dish, skin side down. **2** Combine orange peel,
lemon peel, orange juice, lemon juice and ¼ cup (50 mL)
water; pour over chicken. Bake, uncovered, at 375°F
(190°C) for 10 minutes. Turn chicken and bake 30 minutes
or until chicken is cooked through, basting with pan juices
several times during cooking. Transfer chicken to serving
platter and garnish with orange slices and fresh herbs.

Vignoble Les Blancs Coteaux La Taste Seyval

DUNHAM, QUEBEC

This dry, well-balanced white
has pear and citrus aromas and
palate that match the citrus
flavours in this chicken dish.
Crisp and clean.

Suggested Varietals: Seyval
Blanc or Müller-Thurgau

WINEMAKER'S TASTING NOTES

CHICKEN STE. CLAIRE | Serves four

Château Ste. Claire Estate Winery,
Peachland, British Columbia

CHÂTEAU STE. CLAIRE ESTATE WINERY is owned by the Smitlener family. Goldie operates the winery while son Borris, a self-taught winemaker, produces the wines—Muscat, Sauvignon Blanc, Maréchal Foch and Johannisberg Riesling. Latest proof of his talent and expertise is a silver medal for his 1989 Gewürztraminer and a bronze for the 1989 Johannisberg Riesling from the 1991 Pacific National Exhibition Wine Festival.

Château Ste. Claire Estate Winery Gewürztraminer

Made in the Germanic style and aged in French Limousin oak, this Gewürztraminer has a hint of sweetness and slight oak overtones. It shows floral on the nose with spicy, varietal fruit on the palate that matches the cayenne spice in the dish.

WINEMAKER'S · TASTING NOTES

I	bottle Château Ste. Claire Gewürztraminer (white wine)	I
I lb	boneless chicken breasts, diced	500 g
½ tsp	garlic powder	2 mL
¾ tsp	garlic salt OR celery salt	4 mL
I tbsp	vinegar	I5 mL
Pinch	cayenne	Pinch
½	each large green and red bell peppers, sliced	½
I	large onion, chopped	I
¼ cup	cashews, ground	50 mL
3	large eggs, slightly beaten	3
¼ cup	honey	50 mL
	Juice and grated rind of ½ lemon	
4 cups	steamed rice	I L

1 Set aside 2 cups (500 mL) wine. Pour remainder into large skillet. Add chicken, garlic powder, garlic salt, vinegar and cayenne. Boil chicken until most of wine has evaporated. Add red and green peppers, onion and cashews. Simmer, uncovered, I0 to I5 minutes. **2** In a saucepan, combine reserved wine, eggs, honey, lemon juice and lemon rind. Stir over low heat for 5 minutes or until hot. Do not boil. **3** Arrange chicken over steamed rice. Dribble wine sauce over chicken.

POLLO PICCANTE | Serves four

Café Roma, North Vancouver, British Columbia

BROTHERS MARIO AND ANTONIO CORSI have captured the palates of Vancouverites with their exuberant interpretation of the food of Italy. Proof of that success came with Café Roma and Corsi Trattoria's 1992 induction into the Ordine Ristoratori Professionisti Italiani (ORPI). The Italian organization honours restaurants that produce a consistently high standard of authentic Italian cuisine and lists them in an annual international guide.

¼ cup	olive oil	50 mL
2	cloves garlic, peeled	2
½	onion, chopped	½
1 lb	skinless boneless chicken breasts, cut in strips	500 g
3 oz	Calona Varietal Chelois (red wine)	90 mL
¼ cup	dry porcini mushrooms, soaked in warm water for 30 minutes	50 mL
2 tbsp	sun-dried tomatoes, marinated in olive oil, garlic and basil	25 mL
1 tsp	crushed hot pepper flakes	5 mL
1 tsp	chopped fresh rosemary	5 mL
	Salt and pepper	
1 cup	tomato sauce	250 mL
12	fresh basil leaves	12

Calona Wines Varietal Chelois

KELOWNA, BRITISH COLUMBIA

A berry bouquet and raspberry and black currant flavours characterize this dry red wine. This wine has good length. Being a medium red, the Chelois marries well with the chicken's tomato-based sauce.

WINEMAKER'S TASTING NOTES

1 In a saucepan over high heat, heat olive oil. Add garlic and onion; cook for 3 minutes. Add chicken and cook for 5 minutes. **2** Add wine and cook until evaporated, about 4 minutes. **3** Add drained mushrooms, drained sun-dried tomatoes, pepper flakes, rosemary, salt and pepper; cook 5 minutes. Add tomato sauce and basil; cook for 2 minutes. Serve immediately.

*I*NVOLTINI DI POLLO AL GAMBERI | Serves six

*La Perla Dining Room,
Dartmouth, Nova Scotia*

ONE OF THE HALIFAX-DARTMOUTH area's top restaurants, La Perla specializes in northern Italian cuisine, using locally grown products. Involtini, fried rolls of meat containing various stuffings, is a favourite of La Perla patrons.

Sainte Famille Wines Chardonnay

FALMOUTH,

NOVA SCOTIA

This crisp, dry white is vinted in the nouveau California style with no oak. The slightly green apple-pear flavour and bouquet are an ideal match for this chicken and seafood combination. The crispness works well with this rich sauce.

WINEMAKER'S TASTING NOTES

6	skinless boneless chicken breasts	6
6	large shrimp, peeled and deveined	6
	Salt and pepper to taste	
	Flour for dredging	
2 to 3 tbsp	olive oil	25 to 50 mL
4 tsp	unsalted butter	20 mL
½ tsp	mashed garlic	2 mL
⅓ cup	Sainte Famille Wines Chardonnay (white wine)	75 mL
I cup	whipping cream	250 mL
	Fresh basil (for garnish)	

1 Pound chicken breasts into scallopine about ¼ inch (5 mm) thick. Roll one piece of chicken around each shrimp. Sprinkle with salt and pepper. Dredge in flour. **2** In a large skillet over medium heat, heat oil and brown chicken on all sides, 5 to 7 minutes. Remove chicken from pan. **3** Drain oil from pan. Blend butter and garlic; melt garlic butter over medium heat. Return chicken to pan and cook 5 minutes, turning frequently. Transfer chicken to warm platter. **4** Increase heat to medium-high. Add wine to pan and reduce to about 2 tbsp (25 mL). Pour in cream; reduce to half. When sauce is thick enough to coat the back of a spoon, pour over chicken. Garnish with fresh basil.

CURRIED HONEY CHICKEN | Serves four

Calona Wines,
Kelowna, British Columbia

FROM ITS HUMBLE BEGINNINGS in 1932, Calona Wines has become British Columbia's largest winery, holding 40 per cent of the province's market share in wine. Although they've made varietal wines since the 1970s, Calona is best known for their blends, Sommet Rouge and Sommet Blanc. These two wines have transformed many a beer and spirit drinker into a wine-lover. Today, Calona takes pride in making a wide spectrum of reasonably priced products, from such varietal wines as Chardonnay, Chenin Blanc and Gewürztraminer to ports, sherries and fruit wines. Winemaker Howard Soon suggests you marry this dish with the same wine used in the recipe.

1 tsp	salt	5 mL
¾ tsp	ground ginger	4 mL
½ tsp	ground pepper	2 mL
1	chicken (about 3 lb/1.5 kg), quartered	1
1	medium onion, thinly sliced	1
2 tbsp	butter OR margarine	25 mL
¾ cup	Calona Wines Pinot Blanc (white wine)	175 mL
¼ cup	honey	50 mL
1 tbsp	curry powder	15 mL

Calona Wines Pinot Blanc

Pinot Blanc is one of Alsace's most established varieties. Calona's Pinot Blanc was fermented and aged in stainless steel, making it a light-bodied white with hints of apple on the nose and palate that complement the honey glaze in this dish.

WINEMAKER'S · TASTING NOTES

1 Combine salt, ginger and pepper; rub over chicken pieces. **2** Place onion slices in a greased 13- by 9-inch (3.5-L) baking dish. Arrange chicken on onions, skin side up; dot with butter and pour wine over top. **3** Bake, uncovered, at 400°F (200°C) for 50 minutes or until chicken is white and tender. Blend honey and curry powder. During last 20 minutes of baking, baste several times with curried honey.

Breast of Chicken Chardonnay | Serves six

Lakeview Cellars Estate Winery, Vineland, Ontario

ONE OF THE NEWEST WINERIES in Niagara, Lakeview Cellars is owned by Eddy and Lorraine Gurinskas. Eddy, who can boast 30 years of amateur winemaking experience and several awards, produces such varietals as Chardonnay, Riesling, Welschriesling and Cabernet Sauvignon. The Gurinskas' newly renovated barn houses a retail store, an upstairs loft for group tastings and a barrel-ageing cellar.

Lakeview Cellars Gurinskas Vineyard Chardonnay

(AGED IN AMERICAN AND FRENCH OAK)

As a popular variety, Chardonnay is grown in most countries, including Italy, Spain, Austria, Chile and, of course, Canada. With its pale golden colour, light oak and buttery nose and ripe fruit palate, Lakeview Cellars Gurinskas Vineyard Chardonnay adds considerable flavour to this dish.

6	boneless double chicken breasts	6
3	slices cooked ham, halved	3
3	slices Gouda OR Swiss cheese, halved	3
	Chopped fresh parsley	
	Flour for dusting	
1	egg, beaten with 1 tbsp (15 mL) water	1
	Fine dry bread crumbs	
3 tbsp	butter	50 mL
2	green onions, sliced	2
1 tbsp	flour	15 mL
½ cup	Lakeview Cellars Gurinskas Vineyard Chardonnay (white wine)	125 mL
2 cups	chicken broth	500 mL
Pinch	thyme	Pinch
1 tbsp	whipping cream	15 mL
	Salt and pepper to taste	
	Sautéed sliced mushrooms and watercress (for garnish)	

1 Cut each double breast in half lengthwise. Place chicken breasts skin side down. Cover six breasts with ham slices, cheese slices and a sprinkle of parsley. Top with remaining chicken breasts. Dust both sides with flour. Dip in egg, then dredge lightly in bread crumbs. Let coating set about 30 minutes. **2** In a large skillet over medium-high heat, melt 2 tbsp (25 mL) butter. Sauté chicken 5 minutes or until golden on both sides. Transfer chicken to a shallow baking dish. **3** In same pan, stir together remaining 1 tbsp (15 mL) butter, onions and 1 tbsp (15 mL) flour until whiteness disappears. Whisk in wine and chicken broth. Stir over medium heat until smooth and thick. Boil for 3 to 4 minutes. Add thyme, cream and salt and pepper to taste. **4** Pour sauce around chicken. Bake, covered, at 350°F (180°C) for 1 hour or until chicken is white and tender. Garnish with sautéed mushrooms and watercress.

CHICKEN IN RIESLING | Serves four

*Stoney Ridge Cellars,
Winona, Ontario*

ONCE A FARM FACILITY, Stoney Ridge Cellars is now a handsome winery surrounded by dense woodlands and vineyards at the foot of the Niagara Escarpment. The barn houses a fruit market that offers local fruits, pâtés and preserves and a wine boutique selling winemaker Jim Warren's 35 varietals; 20 of these have achieved VQA excellence. Their wines are made from French hybrid and vitis vinifera grapes grown on co-owner Murray Puddicombe's vineyard or by local growers. Although modest in size, Stoney Ridge Cellars produces more than 30,000 gallons of wine each year.

Stoney Ridge Cellars Dry Riesling

Grapes from the Niagara Bench were vinified dry- and cool-fermented to produce Stoney Ridge Cellars' Dry Riesling. The wine's crisp acidity cuts through the richness of cream, while the wine's floral bouquet and fruity flavours coincide with the same Riesling flavours found in this chicken dish.

WINEMAKER'S · TASTING NOTES

½ cup	butter	125 mL
1 tbsp	vegetable oil	15 mL
1	chicken (3 lb/1.5 kg), cut into 8 pieces	1
2 tbsp	cognac	25 mL
2	shallots, chopped	2
1¼ cups	Stoney Ridge Cellars Dry Riesling (white wine)	300 mL
⅔ cup	whipping cream	150 mL
¼ lb	fresh mushrooms, sliced	125 g
	Salt and pepper to taste	

1 In a large saucepan over medium heat, heat butter and oil. Fry chicken until golden brown. **2** Warm cognac in a ladle and flame; pour flaming cognac over chicken; let flames die down. Remove chicken pieces and set aside.
3 In same pan, gently fry shallots for 1 minute. Add wine, cream, mushrooms, salt and pepper; stir until sauce is smooth. **4** Add chicken pieces to sauce. Cover and cook over low heat for 40 minutes or until chicken is tender. The sauce should be reduced. If not, cook a minute more, uncovered. Adjust seasoning to taste.

HONEY HOISIN CHICKEN | Serves six

Michelle Ramsay / Vignoble Le Royer St. Pierre, Napierville, Quebec

ONE OF THE NEWEST ADDITIONS TO Quebec's growing wine industry, Vignoble Le Royer St. Pierre, in Napierville offers three white wines called Les Trois Sols, two reds labelled Terre St-Cyprien and a Trois Sols rosé. Seyval, Maréchal Foch, Chancellor, Cayuga and Aurore are the grape varieties vinified by self-taught winemaker Robert Le Royer.

2 tbsp	hoisin sauce	25 mL
2 tsp	honey	10 mL
I tbsp	rice vinegar	15 mL
½ tsp	cinnamon	2 mL
¼ tsp	crushed hot pepper flakes	I mL
¼ tsp	vegetable oil	I mL
6	skinless chicken breasts	6
Pinch	salt	Pinch
	Freshly ground pepper to taste	

1 Stir together hoisin sauce, honey, rice vinegar, cinnamon, pepper flakes and vegetable oil. **2** Arrange chicken in lightly oiled large baking dish. Brush with some of the hoisin mixture. Sprinkle with salt and pepper. Bake at 350°F (180°C) for 20 minutes. Brush again with some of the hoisin mixture and bake 15 to 20 minutes. **3** Brush with the remaining hoisin mixture and bake just until the chicken starts to blister and brown.

Vignoble Le Royer St. Pierre Les Trois Sols Blanc

With kiwi, honeydew and lemon showing on the nose and palate of this dry white wine, it is a sound mate for this exotic, sweet chicken dish.

Suggested Varietal: Off-Dry Riesling

WINEMAKER'S TASTING NOTES

CORNISH GAME HENS WITH PISTACHIO DRESSING | Serves eight

The Oban Inn,
Niagara-on-the-Lake, Ontario

BUILT FOR CAPTAIN DUNCAN MILLROY from Oban, Scotland, in 1824, the charming little inn is set in manicured English gardens and overlooks the lush fairways of the Niagara-on-the-Lake golf course. Although damaged by fire in 1992, the owners hope to return it to its former splendour and continue the tradition of serving good unpretentious food and a selection of wines, including the area's best.

Inniskillin Wines Chardonnay

(SEEGER VINEYARD), NIAGARA-ON-THE-LAKE, ONTARIO

Aged in French oak barrels, this creamy-textured white wine has great depth and complexity with oaky aromas and apple fruit, enabling it to stand up to the zesty fruit sauce and not overpower the tender meat of the hens.

WINEMAKER'S TASTING NOTES

8	Cornish game hens, deboned	8
	Salt, pepper, sage, paprika and chopped parsley to taste	

STUFFING:

I cup	coarsely chopped pistachios	250 mL
I	medium onion, chopped	I
½ cup	chopped fresh parsley	125 mL
½ lb	butter, melted	250 g
I cup	milk	250 mL
	Salt and pepper to taste	
½	loaf bread, crusts removed, torn in bits	½

GAME PRESERVE SAUCE:

I cup	red currant jelly	250 mL
½ cup	orange juice	125 mL
	Zest of I lemon and I orange	
I tsp	arrowroot powder	5 mL

1 Season hens with salt, pepper and herbs. Combine all stuffing ingredients; stuff hens. Roast at 375°F (190°C) for 30 minutes. **2** In a small nonaluminum saucepan combine jelly, orange juice, lemon zest and orange zest. Bring to a boil; reduce heat to a simmer. **3** Whisk arrowroot powder into I tbsp (15 mL) water; stir into sauce. Cook for 5 minutes or until sauce thickens. Serve sauce over hens.

COGNAC-BRAISED OKANAGAN QUAIL | Serves six

Wild Goose Vineyards and Winery,
Okanagan Falls, British Columbia

JUST SOUTH OF Okanagan Falls, Wild Goose Vineyards and Winery grows premium vinifera grapes on their nine-acre vineyard. Here, the valley's southerly exposure to the sun and its rocky-gravel soil provide grapes with the elements they need to develop concentrated flavours. Winemaker Adolf Kruger transforms these grapes into delectable wines. From his estate vineyard and a few local vineyards he makes dry and semi-dry Johannisberg Riesling, Gewürztraminer, Pinot Blanc, Maréchal Foch and Pinot Noir.

2 tbsp	butter	25 mL
6	quails	6
3	onions, chopped	3
2	cloves garlic, chopped	2
3 tbsp	cognac	50 mL
½ cup	Wild Goose Vineyards Maréchal Foch (red wine)	125 mL
½ tsp	basil	2 mL
¼ tsp	thyme	1 mL
2	bay leaves	2
2 cups	beef gravy	500 mL

Wild Goose Vineyards Maréchal Foch

Considered one of Wild Goose Vineyards' best varietal wines, Maréchal Foch is full bodied with an intense berry nose and a hint of burnt oak on the palate—characteristics that give this recipe an exotic flavour. Being a young red with good tannin, Maréchal Foch lessens the taste of fat found in this oily bird.

1 In a 9-inch (2.5-L) square baking dish, melt butter over medium-high heat. Sear quails until brown on all sides. Add onions and garlic; cook for 5 minutes. **2** Increase heat to high. Add cognac and cook 2 to 3 minutes to evaporate alcohol. Add wine, basil, thyme and bay leaves; bring to a boil. Slowly stir in gravy; cover and cook for 30 to 40 minutes. Discard bay leaves.

ℛOAST CHICKEN | Serves four

Brad Ovenell-Carter

BRAD OVENELL-CARTER is the food editor for *Vancouver* magazine. Before turning to a career as a writer, he worked for 15 years in the food service industry as a chef and as a hotel and restaurant manager. He regularly shares his passion for food and wine with the listeners of CBC Radio's "Early Edition" in British Columbia.

Roasting a chicken is an exacting business that compels a cook to continually turn and baste until the bird is juicy, brown and crisp-skinned. Brad once worked in a kitchen with a generously proportioned grandmotherly French woman who told him the birds she roasted to perfection talked to her while they cooked. She was right—a chicken gives a sudden rain of splutters when it is almost done.

4 tbsp	butter	50 mL
I tbsp	olive oil	15 mL
I	chicken (3 lb/1.5 kg)	I
	Salt and pepper to taste	
I	clove garlic, unpeeled	I

1 In a small pan melt 2 tbsp (25 mL) butter with olive oil. Set aside. **2** Smear the inside of the chicken with I tbsp (15 mL) butter. Sprinkle inside with salt and pepper; place garlic inside. Rub the chicken with remaining butter. **3** Place chicken, breast up, on a rack in a roasting pan. Brown in the middle of a 425°F (220°C) oven for 5 minutes. Turn the bird onto one side, baste with reserved oil-butter mixture and brown for 5 minutes. Turn bird onto other side, baste again and brown for another 5 minutes. **4** Leaving chicken on its side, reduce heat to 350°F (180°C). Baste every 10 minutes. After 20 minutes, turn chicken onto its other side. Cook another 20 minutes, basting frequently. Turn the chicken breast side up and cook 15 minutes. (Total cooking time is 1 hour and 10 minutes.) **5** Let chicken cool to room temperature before serving.

NOTE: If they're available, use a free-range, organically raised chicken for its superior flavour.

Hillside Cellars Pinot Auxerrois

PENTICTON, BRITISH COLUMBIA

Brad Ovenell-Carter notes that this Pinot Auxerrois is an exciting example of the next generation of West Coast wines emerging in an industry recently deregulated under the Free Trade Agreement. It is a straightforward, well-built wine, slightly sweet and characteristically fruity. Winemaker Vera Klockocka is rightly shy of oak, so she uses steel tanks to produce very clean wine. This has a lightly framed body—it's something like a Muscadet in weight—which shoulders a fresh dose of acidity, making this a good match for foods with some fat in them—such as deliciously simple cold roast chicken.

WINEMAKER'S · TASTING NOTES ·

SMOKED BREAST OF TURKEY WITH SPINACH AND SWEET PEPPERS WRAPPED IN PANCETTA | Serves two

Cartier Wines and Beverages, Penticton, British Columbia

AS A PARENT COMPANY, Cartier Wines and Beverages has many notable wineries under its umbrella, the most recognized being that of Château-Gai in Niagara Falls, Stoneycroft in Calgary and Casabello in Penticton. Bruce Nicholson is chief winemaker in Penticton. He studied engineering and chemistry and, after many years of home winemaking, went to work for Château-Gai in 1986 under the direction of chief winemaker Mira Ananicz. One year later Nicholson transferred to Casabello in Penticton to become cellar master, eventually taking over as winemaker. He is most proud of his 1989 Gewürztraminer, which won him three awards in 1991 (People's Choice Best White at the O.S.T.A.'s Winter Wine Festival, Bronze medal at the Rossland Winter Carnival and Best White at the Vernon Winter Carnival).

	Fresh herbs of choice	
I cup	olive oil	250 mL
2 tbsp	crushed black peppercorns	25 mL
4	cloves garlic	4
I	boneless turkey breast	I
I tbsp	olive oil	15 mL
I	large onion, diced	I
I	clove garlic, chopped	I
I tbsp	chopped fresh sage	15 mL
I	bunch fresh spinach, chopped	I
I	red bell pepper, roasted, peeled and finely diced	I
I	yellow bell pepper, roasted, peeled and finely diced	I
	Salt and pepper to taste	
8	thin slices pancetta	8

1 In a shallow bowl, stir together herbs, I cup (250 mL) olive oil, peppercorns and 4 cloves garlic; marinate turkey breast for I hour in refrigerator. **2** To make stuffing, in a skillet heat I tbsp (15 mL) olive oil and sauté onion, I clove garlic and sage until onion is translucent. Add spinach and peppers. Season with salt and pepper.

3 On a barbecue, smoke the turkey over alderwood chips for about I hour. **4** Cut breast into I-inch (2.5-cm) medallions. Cut a small slit in the side of each medallion and stuff with 2 tbsp (25 mL) stuffing. Wrap each medallion with a slice of pancetta and secure with a toothpick.

5 Grill medallions over hot coals for 4 minutes. Turn and cook another 4 minutes. Remove toothpick before serving.

Cartier Wines Okanagan Reserve Gewürztraminer
(CORNISH VINEYARD)

Gewürztraminer is best served chilled to 45°F (7°C). Because of its natural spicy flavours, it marries well with Oriental and curry dishes. Made from grapes grown exclusively in Kaleden, British Columbia, Cartier's Okanagan Reserve Gewürztraminer is pale gold with aromas reminiscent of pepper, clove and grapefruit, with a hint of smokiness. These aromas, along with the wine's spicy, smoky taste, enhance the smoked-peppercorn flavours found in this meat.

WINEMAKER'S TASTING NOTES

ROAST QUAIL ON POTATO PANCAKES WITH WILD MUSHROOM FRICASSEE | Serves four

Inniskillin Wines,
Chef Izabela Kalabis

THE DISTINGUISHED REPUTATION and savoir-faire of Inniskillin Wines can be attributed in part to resident chef Izabela Kalabis. This Niagara native studied at La Varenne Cooking School in Paris, L'Académie du Vin and Ecole de Gastronomie Ritz-Escoffier, and apprenticed under such culinary artists as chef Fernand Chambrette from La Boule d'Or and chef Claude Vauguet. As her last French assignment Kalabis served as private chef to the publishers of the *International Herald Tribune*. In 1987 she joined Inniskillin and now spends her summers preparing and hosting a series of gourmet fairs in the winery's exquisite champagne loft.

Inniskillin Wines Pinot Noir

NIAGARA-ON-THE-LAKE, ONTARIO

Izabela Kalabis notes that Inniskillin's Pinot Noir has a brilliant ruby colour and is light bodied with soft texture and good fruit-oak balance. Berries show on the nose, cherries on the palate. The wine's delicate flavours complement the delicate nature of quail. The wine's complexity and spiciness also work with the light spiciness of mushrooms, while its soft texture contrasts with the crispness of the potato pancakes.

PANCAKES:

3	large potatoes, peeled and grated	3
¼ cup	finely chopped onions	50 mL
4 tsp	flour	20 mL
I	egg, beaten	I
½ tsp	salt	2 mL
¼ tsp	pepper	I mL
Pinch	nutmeg	Pinch
¼ cup	vegetable oil	50 mL

QUAIL:

4	quails	4
2 tbsp	unsalted butter	25 mL
2 tbsp	vegetable oil	25 mL
2 tbsp	sherry	25 mL
3 oz	chicken OR veal stock	90 mL
	Salt and pepper to taste	

WINEMAKER'S TASTING NOTES

MUSHROOM FRICASSEE:

2 tbsp	extra virgin olive oil	25 mL
1	clove garlic, minced	1
¼ cup	finely chopped fresh wild mushrooms	50 mL
Pinch	crushed hot pepper flakes	Pinch
	Salt and pepper to taste	
1 tbsp	sherry	15 mL
3 oz	whipping cream	90 mL
1 tbsp	chopped parsley	15 mL

1 In a bowl, combine potatoes, onions, flour and egg. Season with salt, pepper and nutmeg. **2** In a large skillet over moderate heat, heat ¼ cup (50 mL) oil. Spoon 2 tbsp (25 mL) potato batter into skillet, flatten with back of spoon and cook for 3 minutes on each side or until golden. Prepare four pancakes. Drain on paper towels and wrap in foil to keep warm.
3 Debone quails if desired. Tie each quail with string to keep shape while roasting. **4** In same skillet, heat butter and 2 tbsp (25 mL) vegetable oil over moderate heat. Sauté quails until golden on all sides. Transfer to small roasting pan and roast at 400°F (200°C) for 5 to 8 minutes or until well browned. Wrap quails in foil to keep warm. **5** Drain grease from skillet and deglaze with 2 tbsp (25 mL) sherry and stock. Reduce by half. Season with salt and pepper and remove from heat; keep warm.
6 To prepare mushroom fricassee, in a small skillet, heat 2 tbsp (25 mL) olive oil over high heat. Add garlic and mushrooms. Sauté for 1 minute, then reduce heat to medium. Stir in pepper flakes, salt and pepper. Cook until mushrooms are soft. Add 1 tbsp (15 mL) sherry; cook for 1 minute more. Add cream; reduce slightly. Stir in parsley and remove from heat. **7** Place one pancake on each plate. Spoon mushrooms over pancakes, place quail on top and spoon reduced sauce over quails.

CANARD DU LAC BROME, MÉTHODE VIGNERONNE (BROME LAKE DUCK THE WINERY'S WAY) | Serves six

Vignoble Les Arpents de Neige, Dunham, Quebec

TRANSLATING AS "Snow Acre Vineyard," Vignoble Les Arpents de Neige is located in an 1837 Loyalist home. Occupying most of the ground floor is a wine boutique, modern kitchen and dining facility that seats 60. Here, guests have enjoyed such exotic dishes as wild boar. Proprietor Jacques Breault planted his first vines in 1986 and opened the winery two years later. Production has now reached 25,000 bottles annually, mostly whites with a rosé, dessert wine and, depending on the year, a few reds.

Vignoble Les Arpents de Neige Vendange Sélectionné

A blend of Seyval and Vidal. Partial ageing in French oak has added complexity to this wine. Vendange Sélectionné (selected grapes) has a clear, slightly yellowish robe. Flowers and a hint of tropical fruit and pineapples come through on the nose, while the mouth has good sugar-acid balance and a hint of pineapple on the aftertaste. These pineapple characteristics enhance the hint of sweet maple syrup.

3	Brome Lake ducks (5 lb/2.2 kg each)	3
1	bottle Vendange Sélectionné (white wine)	1
1½ cups	maple syrup	375 mL
5	cloves garlic, minced	5
1 tsp	oregano	5 mL

1 Place ducks in a large nonaluminum container, cover with wine and weigh down with a heavy plate. Refrigerate 36 hours. 2 Remove ducks from wine; reserve wine. Wash ducks and pat dry. 3 In a saucepan combine maple syrup, garlic and oregano. Warm glaze slightly and brush over ducks.

For Water Smoker: Place reserved wine in smoker pan and fill pan with hot water. Place ducks, breast side up, on grill. Cover and smoke between 200°F and 250°F (90°C to 120°C), adding charcoal and/or vine branches and water as needed. Check the internal temperature of ducks after 3 hours; the ducks are done when the internal temperature is between 155°F and 165°F (70°C to 75°C). Let ducks rest 10 minutes before carving.

DUCK BREASTS WITH BLACK CURRANT PRESERVES | Serves six

Shari Darling / Sainte Famille Wines, Falmouth, Nova Scotia

AFTER 20 YEARS of amateur winemaking, Suzanne Corkum decided to open a winery. In 1990, Sainte Famille opened its doors to the public with a 1989 vintage of Seyval Blanc, Maréchal Foch, dry Riesling, Chardonnay and Michurinetz. In 1991 Suzanne entered her 1989 Michurinetz in the International Eastern Wine Competition and came away with a gold. With the help of winemaking consultant Allan Schmidt of Vineland Estates in Ontario, Suzanne Corkum produces a variety of red and white varietal wines, all made from grapes grown on her 17-acre estate vineyard, all treasured by her faithful clientele.

¼ cup	black currant preserves	50 mL
4 tsp	Dijon mustard	20 mL
6	duck breasts	6
	Salt and freshly ground pepper to taste	
⅓ cup	Sainte Famille Wines Michurinetz (red wine)	75 mL
	Watercress (for garnish)	

1 In a small bowl, mix together preserves and mustard. Set aside. **2** Heat a lidded nonstick skillet over moderate heat and brown duck breasts lightly on both sides. Season with salt and pepper; spoon preserve mixture evenly over breasts. **3** Reduce heat and cook, covered, 10 minutes or until breasts are pink inside. Transfer them to a heatproof platter and keep warm in oven. **4** Drain excess fat from skillet. Add wine and deglaze pan over medium heat, scraping up any meat. When sauce is reduced by one-third, pour it over the breasts. Garnish plate with watercress and serve immediately.

Sainte Famille Wines Michurinetz

Michurinetz juice was macerated on the skins for three weeks during fermentation. The wine was aged in French Limousin oak for eight months. Full-bodied with intense black currant and raisin aromas and flavours, this wine works hand-in-hand with the black currant preserves in the recipe. Because of its tannins, Michurinetz lessens the perception of oil found in this bird.

WINEMAKER'S TASTING NOTES

Suprême de Canard Façon du Chef (Breast of Duck in the Way of the Chef) | Serves two

Chef David Traquair, London Hunt Club, London, Ontario

COOKING UTENSILS HAVE ALWAYS BEEN an integral part of chef David Traquair's life. At age six he apprenticed under his grandfather, who spent most of his time in the kitchen, cooking and baking. After high school, several cooking courses and a four-year apprenticeship at the London Club, David went on to work as sous chef at Cherry Hill House. He is now executive chef at the distinguished London Hunt Club in London, Ontario.

Inniskillin Wines Proprietors Reserve Cabernet

NIAGARA-ON-THE-LAKE, ONTARIO

Made from 70 per cent Cabernet Sauvignon, 29 per cent Cabernet Franc and 1 per cent Merlot, this wine underwent only malolactic fermentation, giving it a smooth, velvety texture. Full-bodied and well-balanced, this red shows black currants on the nose with a hint of earthiness. The palate shows similar fruit with robust tannins that can cut through the oiliness of duck.

Suggested Varietal: Cabernet Sauvignon

WINEMAKER'S TASTING NOTES

I	duck (5 lb/2.2 kg)	I
2 tbsp	butter	25 mL
¼ cup	shallots, chopped	50 mL
¼ cup	pine nuts, sliced	50 mL
I tbsp	each tarragon, thyme, basil	15 mL
I tsp	minced garlic	5 mL
¾ tsp	Marsala	4 mL
I tbsp	brandy	15 mL
2	egg whites	2
	Salt and pepper to taste	

SAUCE:

	Duck carcass	
½ cup	finely chopped leeks	125 mL
½ cup	finely chopped onions	125 mL
½ cup	each finely chopped carrots and celery	125 mL
¼ cup	Inniskillin Wines Chardonnay (white wine)	50 mL
Pinch	thyme	Pinch
I	bay leaf	I
I tbsp	cornstarch	15 mL
2 tbsp	Armagnac	25 mL

1 Cut legs and breasts from duck. Skin and debone legs. **2** In a skillet over medium heat, melt butter. Sauté shallots, half the pine nuts, the tarragon, thyme, basil and garlic. **3** Deglaze pan with Marsala. Flame with brandy. Over low heat reduce liquid until pan is almost dry. Set aside to cool. **4** Cut a pocket in large end of each duck breast. Set aside. **5** In a food processor or blender, purée leg meat with contents of skillet. Add egg whites, salt and pepper; purée again until well blended. Stir remaining pine nuts into purée and place in a piping bag. Pipe purée into the cut pockets. **6** Roast stuffed breasts, skin side down, in the bottom of a 450°F (230°C) oven for 13 to 15 minutes or until skin is crispy. **7** Meanwhile, make sauce. In a large baking dish combine duck carcass, leeks, onions, carrots and celery. Bake at 450°F (230°C) for 7 to 10 minutes or until meat is brown. Remove and reserve vegetables; discard carcass. **8** Over medium heat, deglaze baking dish with white wine, scraping up brown bits. Return vegetables to baking dish; add 1¼ cups (300 mL) water, thyme and bay leaf; bring to a boil. Reduce heat and simmer until reduced to ¾ cup (175 mL). **9** In a small bowl, whisk together cornstarch and 2 tbsp (25 mL) water. Stir into sauce and simmer a few minutes longer. Stir in Armagnac. **10** Let cooked duck rest for 5 minutes. Slice breasts and fan out on plates. Spoon duck sauce over meat.

Magnet de Canard Sauce Fines de Champagne | Serves six

*Hermitage Restaurant,
Vancouver, British Columbia*

HERMITAGE IS A SPLENDID PLACE to enjoy French gastronomy in a warm, cosy setting. Medallion of lamb with papaya coulis served with a corn galette, and sautéed prawns with sweet and sour apples and pomegranate nectar are but two of the fabulous fares offered on the extensive menu.

Before establishing the restaurant, chef/owner Hervé Martin worked in some of the finest kitchens around the world, including the Palace Hotel in the south of France, the Hotel Place de la Chaudière in Hull, Quebec, and the Pan Pacific Hotel in Vancouver, British Columbia. His most prestigious position, however, was private chef for King Léopold of Belgium.

Domaine de Chaberton Madeleine Angevine

**LANGLEY,
BRITISH COLUMBIA**

Crisp and aromatic, this white shows sweet apple on the nose with apple-spice on the palate. An excellent accompaniment to duck.

WINEMAKER'S · TASTING NOTES

5 lb	duck bones	2.2 kg
8 cups	duck stock	2 L
2 tbsp	clarified butter	25 mL
½ cup	chopped carrots	125 mL
½ cup	chopped onion	125 mL
1 tbsp	chopped celery	15 mL
1	bay leaf	1
1	sprig fresh thyme	1
1 tbsp	clarified butter	15 mL
¼ cup	minced shallots	50 mL
1 cup	Domaine de Chaberton Estate Winery Madeleine Angevine (white wine)	250 mL
½ cup	whipping cream	125 mL
3 tbsp	unsalted butter, softened	50 mL
2 tbsp	all-purpose flour	25 mL
6	duck breasts (½ lb/250 g each)	6

1 To make sauce, roast duck bones at 450°F (230°C) for 30 minutes or until golden brown. Transfer bones to a large saucepan. Add stock. Bring to a simmer. **2** In a second saucepan, melt 2 tbsp (25 mL) clarified butter over medium heat. Sauté carrots, onions, celery, bay leaf and thyme until vegetables are tender, about 3 to 5 minutes. Drain excess fat from saucepan; add vegetables to stock. **3** Simmer stock for 2 hours or until reduced to 3 cups (750 mL). Strain stock. **4** In a skillet, melt 1 tbsp (15 mL) clarified butter over medium heat. Sauté shallots for 2 minutes or until translucent. **5** Deglaze pan with wine, scraping up any bits. Cook over high heat until wine is reduced by half; stir into stock. **6** Simmer stock for 5 minutes or until reduced by half. Add cream and simmer 1 minute. **7** Knead 3 tbsp (50 mL) butter and flour with fingers until combined. Whisk beurre manié a little at a time into sauce. Simmer for 2 minutes, until sauce is smooth and thickened. (If sauce is too thin, whisk in more beurre manié.) Keep warm. **8** In a hot roasting pan, place duck breasts, skin side down. Roast at 375°F (190°C) for 3 minutes; turn and cook 2 to 3 minutes or until meat is pink. **9** Remove skin from breasts. Scrape fat from skin and slice skin into strips. Discard any fat from meat. **10** Spoon a pool of sauce on each plate. Slice breasts and fan out the meat on the sauce. Spread sliced skin over meat.

ROAST PHEASANT WITH PEPPERCORN CRUST | Serves four

Shari Darling / Brights Wines, Niagara Falls, Ontario

BRIGHTS WINES IS CANADA'S OLDEST and largest winery, producing more than 8.8 million gallons of wine a year. With operations in eight provinces, they continue to hold a third of the domestic wine market. Bright's latest venture is the creation of a sister company called Sawmill Creek. This line consists of 11 wines that blend 30 per cent domestic juice with 70 per cent imported juice from Chile, Yugoslavia, Washington State, Bordeaux and Beaujolais. Brights concentrates on meeting the changing demands of North American customers, winemaking in the North American style.

Sawmill Creek Merlot/Baco

This blend combines 30 per cent Ontario Baco Noir with 70 per cent Chilean Merlot. Baco Noir gives body and grassy, almost vegetative aromas to this blend. However, predominated by Merlot, this wine has forward fruit flavours and a spicy finish that corresponds with the marinade and peppercorn crust in this entree.

Suggested Varietal: Merlot

3 tbsp	crushed white, black and green peppercorns	50 mL
1½ tsp	rosemary	7 mL
½ cup	fresh mint	125 mL
5	cloves garlic, crushed	5
½ cup	raspberry vinegar	125 mL
¼ cup	soy sauce	50 mL
½ cup	Sawmill Creek Merlot/Baco (red wine)	125 mL
2	young pheasants (4 lb/2 kg each), quartered	2
2 tbsp	Dijon mustard	25 mL

1 In a shallow bowl, combine 1 tbsp (15 mL) crushed peppercorns, rosemary, mint, garlic, vinegar, soy sauce and wine. Marinate pheasant pieces, refrigerated, for at least 8 hours, turning occasionally. **2** Drain pheasant pieces, reserving marinade. Spread mustard over pheasant pieces and pat remaining 2 tbsp (25 mL) crushed peppercorns into mustard. Set pheasant pieces in a shallow roasting pan and pour marinade carefully around, but not over, pheasant. **3** Bake pheasant at 375°F (190°C) for 18 minutes, basting occasionally. Let meat stand 20 minutes, kept warm, before serving with pan juices.

ℱILET DE PINTADE FRAMBOISE | Serves two

Michelle Ramsay / Vignoble St. Alexandre, Iberville, Quebec

AT VIGNOBLE ST. ALEXANDRE in Iberville, Quebec, Domenico Agarla, a self-taught winemaker, understands the art of focusing. Since 1980 he has concentrated his efforts on making one red table wine. Named Domar, this red is made from de Chaunac grapes. More unique than the wine is the creator himself, who speaks a mixed dialect of French and Italian.

	Flour for dredging	
	Salt and white pepper to taste	
2	guinea fowl breasts, deboned	2
1 tbsp	vegetable oil	15 mL
2 tbsp	raspberry vinegar	25 mL
⅓ cup	whipping cream	75 mL
¼ cup	fresh raspberries (for garnish)	50 mL

1 In a wide shallow bowl, combine flour, salt and pepper. Flatten guinea fowl breasts slightly with mallet. Dredge in seasoned flour. **2** In a skillet, heat oil over medium heat. Sauté breasts on both sides until golden and cooked through, about 8 to 10 minutes. Remove breasts from pan and keep warm. **3** Increase heat to medium-high. Deglaze skillet with raspberry vinegar, scraping up brown bits. Reduce liquid to 1 tbsp (15 mL). Add cream and reduce until sauce is thick enough to coat the back of a spoon. **4** To serve, spoon sauce over breasts and garnish with fresh raspberries.

Vignoble St. Alexandre Domar

Produced from de Chaunac grapes, this red table wine is light bodied with raspberry aromas and flavours that marry well with this dish. The wine's tart acidity also works with the natural acidity found in raspberries.

Suggested Varietal: de Chaunac

WINEMAKER'S · TASTING NOTES

PRESERVED GOOSE PIPERADE | Serves three

Shari Darling / Quai du Vin Estate Winery, St. Thomas, Ontario

TRANSLATING AS "the wine dock," Quai du Vin Estate Winery is just outside the century-old hamlet of Sparta, in southwestern Ontario. Roberto Quai began as a prize-winning amateur, vinifying grapes from his father's 18-acre vineyard. In 1988 he and wife, Lisa, opened the winery with 5,000 gallons of Vidal, Riesling and a blend. Word soon spread that Quai's wines were tasty and in less than a year he had doubled production. Most unique are their two blends, Chatelle and Aurore-Musce. Chatelle is a semi-dry, light-bodied white made from a blend of Seyval, Villard, Aurore and Chardonnay grapes. Aurore-Musce is a semi-sweet white made from the Aurore and New York Muscat grape.

Quai du Vin de Chaunac Blush

Made entirely from de Chaunac grape. This young rosé has sufficient acidity to cut through the fattiness in goose, while being able to stand up to the acidity in tomatoes. Being semi-dry, de Chaunac Blush brings out the slight sweetness in green peppers; being light bodied, it works with this light egg dish. The nose and palate show typical varietal fruit.

WINEMAKER'S TASTING NOTES

3	pieces preserved goose (I wing, I leg, I breast)	3
½ cup	fat from preserved goose	125 mL
2	green onions, white part only	2
I cup	green bell peppers, sliced lengthwise	250 mL
8 to 10	tomatoes, skinned, seeded and crushed	8 to 10
4	eggs, slightly beaten	4
½ cup	veal stock	125 mL

1 Place goose pieces in a roasting pan with ¼ cup (50 mL) fat from the preserved goose and heat through in a 300°F (150°C) oven. Pour off fat and keep goose pieces warm. **2** In a skillet over medium heat, melt remaining ¼ cup (50 mL) fat. Add thinly sliced onions and fry until golden. Add green peppers and tomatoes. Cook until peppers are tender. **3** Add eggs, stirring until they are cooked but soft. Stir in stock. Cook until stock is heated through. Ladle mixture into separate bowls and top each dish with one piece of preserved goose.

RACK OF LAMB WITH MINT CHILI CHUTNEY | Serves two

Lotus, Toronto, Ontario

CHAPTER THIRTEEN

MEAT

CHEF/OWNER Susur Lee combines East and West flavours in this exotic rack of lamb. The lamb must marinate three days before being cooked.

I tsp	curry powder	5 mL
2 tsp	finely chopped fresh coriander	10 mL
2 tsp	minced garlic	10 mL
½ tsp	each salt and freshly cracked pepper	2 mL
I	rack of lamb (2 lb/I kg)	I

CHUTNEY:

I cup	fresh mint leaves	250 mL
½ cup	chopped green onion	125 mL
I tbsp	sugar	15 mL
I	fresh Thai or Asian hot green chili, minced	I
4 tsp	white wine vinegar	20 mL
	Salt and pepper to taste	

Cave Spring Cellars Merlot

JORDAN, ONTARIO

Light-bodied, this Merlot has a slight spicy nose and palate with slight acidity, moderate tannin and a sweet, oaky finish. The wine is complex enough to hold its own with the curry-marinated lamb and mint flavours.

WINEMAKER'S TASTING NOTES

■ In mortar and pestle or food processor, grind together curry powder, coriander, garlic, salt and pepper. Rub on both sides of lamb; cover and refrigerate for 3 days. ■ Combine chutney ingredients in food processor and purée. ■ In a large cast-iron pan, roast lamb, fat side down, at 400°F (200°C) for 20 minutes or until medium rare. Serve with chutney.

RACK OF SALT SPRING LAMB WITH ROAST PEANUT AND CURRY SAUCE | Serves four

Hastings House, Ganges, Salt Spring Island, British Columbia

OCEANSCAPES, LUSH COUNTRY GARDENS and elegantly appointed suites housed in five lovingly restored buildings—this is Shan and Donald Cross's Hastings House. Since its opening in 1981, the House has won numerous awards and accolades for its accommodations and its special brand of West Coast cuisine. Operated by Pam and Hector De Galard, Hastings House is now a member of the prestigious Relais & Chateaux. One of the specialties of the dining room is this recipe for Salt Spring lamb, offered by Hastings House chef Jorgensen. Raised on Salt Spring Island, the lamb is a special breed of Jacob's lamb, crossed with Suffolk Hampshire, and is totally free ranging on 140 acres of pasture, forest and meadow.

Mission Hill Private Reserve Cabernet Sauvignon/Merlot

WESTBANK, BRITISH COLUMBIA

This rich, fruity wine with a long spicy-berry finish complements the spicy Asian tones of the sauce. Lively, yet elegant, this blend of Cabernet Sauvignon and Merlot is suitable for sipping, for a hearty meal or for ageing in the wine cellar. The 1989 Private Reserve won a gold medal in the 1992 International Eastern Wine Competition.

Suggested Varietal: Cabernet Sauvignon

I	rack of lamb (2 lb/I kg)	I
	Soy sauce for basting	
STOCK:		
2 tbsp	clarified butter	25 mL
2 tbsp	Madras curry powder	25 mL
4	cloves garlic, chopped	4
I	onion, diced	I
2	carrots, diced	2
I	leek, diced	I
I	stalk celery, diced	I
I	banana, chopped	I
I	apple, diced	I
I quart	chicken stock	I L
SAUCE:		
2 tbsp	clarified butter	25 mL
3	cloves garlic, finely chopped	3
8 oz	unsalted peanuts, lightly roasted and coarsely chopped	250 g

3 oz	fresh coconut milk (recipe on page 49), OR canned	90 mL
3 tbsp	soy sauce	50 mL
1	tomato, diced	1
	Salt and pepper to taste	
2 tbsp	chopped mixed fresh herbs (thyme, basil, tarragon, parsley)	25 mL
	Fresh chopped coriander (for garnish)	

1 With a little soy sauce basted over it, roast the rack of lamb at 400°F (200°C), fat side down, for 20 minutes or until medium rare. Keep warm. **2** Meanwhile, to make the stock, in a saucepan over high heat, melt butter. Add curry powder, garlic, onion, carrots, leek, celery, banana and apple; sauté until vegetables are lightly browned. Add chicken stock; simmer slowly, uncovered, for 1 hour. Strain stock over a bowl, squeezing all the juice out of the vegetables. Set aside. **3** To make the sauce, in a large saucepan over medium-high heat, melt butter. Sauté garlic and peanuts. Add reserved stock, coconut milk, soy sauce, tomato, salt and pepper. Bring to a simmer and let reduce 20 minutes or until desired consistency. Stir in fresh herbs. **4** Serve slices of Salt Spring lamb with sauce and garnish with fresh coriander.

BRAISED LAMB SHANKS, BUTTERMILK MASHED POTATOES AND TOMATO BASIL DRIZZLE | Serves six

Studio Café, Four Seasons Hotel, Toronto, Ontario

EXECUTIVE CHEF Susan Weaver combines comfort food with a modern touch in this easy-to-prepare dish.

Inniskillin Wines Cabernet Sauvignon/ Cabernet Franc

NIAGARA-ON-THE-LAKE, ONTARIO

This deeply complex wine is rich in aromatics, tannins and colour, with a decadently smooth and subtle finish, complementing the flavourful hearty lamb shanks, and with enough fruit and acidity to match the tomato basil drizzle.

Suggested Varietal: Cabernet Sauvignon

WINEMAKER'S TASTING NOTES

6	lamb shanks	6
	Salt and freshly ground pepper to taste	
¼ cup	olive oil	50 mL
2	onions, roughly chopped	2
3	carrots, roughly chopped	3
4	stalks celery, roughly chopped	4
6	cloves garlic	6
1 tsp	peppercorns	5 mL
1	bay leaf	1
1	sprig fresh thyme	1
2 cups	Inniskillin Wines Cabernet Sauvignon/ Cabernet Franc (red wine)	500 mL

1 Season lamb shanks with salt and pepper. **2** In a large sauté pan, heat olive oil over medium heat. Sauté each shank until brown all over. Transfer shanks and all cooking liquids to a large stock pot. Add onions, carrots, celery, garlic, peppercorns, bay leaf and thyme. **3** Simmer until vegetables are soft. Add wine and roll shanks in the pot so that each piece can absorb wine. **4** Cover shanks with cold water. Over medium heat, simmer for 1½ to 2 hours or until lamb is very tender and almost ready to fall from the bones. **5** Remove shanks from braising liquid and pass liquid through a strainer. **6** Season sauce to taste. Return shanks to sauce to coat all over. Transfer shanks to plates. Spoon tomato basil drizzle over shanks and accompany with buttermilk mashed potatoes.

BUTTERMILK MASHED POTATOES:

8	baking potatoes, peeled and coarsely chopped	8
1 cup	milk	250 mL
½ cup	butter	125 mL
¼ cup	buttermilk	50 mL
	Salt and freshly ground pepper to taste	

1 Cook potatoes in boiling salted water until very soft; drain. **2** In a small saucepan, warm milk. Add butter and stir until melted. **3** Combine potatoes and milk; mash. Season with salt and pepper. Stir in buttermilk just before serving.

TOMATO BASIL DRIZZLE:

½ cup	extra virgin olive oil	125 mL
2	plum tomatoes, diced	2
2 tbsp	chopped fresh basil	25 mL
6	sprigs fresh basil	6
	Salt and freshly ground pepper to taste	

1 Combine all ingredients. **2** Spoon onto each lamb shank just before serving.

NOTE: The lamb shanks may be cooked ahead and reheated before serving. The buttermilk mashed potatoes may also be prepared in advance, but use only half the milk and butter. When reheating the potatoes, add the remaining half of milk and butter. Add the buttermilk just before serving.

Susan Weaver, the first female executive chef in the Four Seasons chain of hotels, has taken Toronto by storm with her sensational cooking. One of the new breed of chef in North America, she has broken the traditional sex barrier that has kept women from the upper echelons of the professional kitchen. Under her direction, the Four Seasons Truffles and the Studio Café have flourished. Imaginative menus and extensive wine lists offer a prominent place to local ingredients and wines. Truffles recently won the Distinguished Restaurants of North America award for providing the highest level of cuisine and service.

Salt Spring Lamb Loin en Croûte | Serves four

The Tudor Room, Park Royal Hotel, West Vancouver, British Columbia

SET ON THE BANKS OF THE Capilano River in West Vancouver, this cosy country inn oozes old world charm. Owned and operated by the Corsi brothers (of Corsi Trattoria and Café Roma), the two-storey Tudor-style Park Royal combines comfort with chef Hans Schaub's updated French-inspired cuisine. Fresh herbs and vegetables are grown in the hotel's own garden, and most of the products used in the menu are produced locally.

Gray Monk Cellars Pinot Noir

OKANAGAN CENTRE, BRITISH COLUMBIA

Without the use of oak, wine-maker George Heiss, Jr., has achieved a fresh-fruit, low-alcohol, slightly tart style, emphasizing the fresh raspberry fruit of a Beaujolais. A versatile wine that matches well with fresh lamb, game birds, turkey and salmon poached in the wine.

WINEMAKER'S TASTING NOTES

I tbsp	olive oil	15 mL
2	lamb loins (1½ lb/750 g each)	2
Pinch	each salt, pepper, rosemary	Pinch
½	celery stalk, chopped	½
¼	onion, chopped	¼
½	carrot, chopped	½
I	clove garlic, crushed	I
2 tbsp	white wine	25 mL
I tbsp	Dijon mustard	15 mL
½ cup	spinach	125 g
½ lb	puff pastry	250 g
I	egg yolk, slightly beaten	I

1 In a skillet over medium heat, heat olive oil. Brown loins all over. Remove from skillet. Set aside. **2** Remove loins from bone. Trim any meat from fat cap; chop finely and set aside. Season with salt, pepper and rosemary. **3** In same skillet, sauté chopped meat from fat cap with celery, onion, carrot and garlic. Add wine and mustard; reduce to a paste. **4** Blanch spinach and refresh in cold water. Spread paste evenly on each loin and wrap spinach around it. **5** Roll out puff pastry on a floured surface to

½-inch (1-cm) thickness. Wrap around each loin. Brush pastry with egg yolk. **6** Bake at 350°F (180°C) until golden brown, about 25 minutes.

RACK OF LAMB | Serves two

Michael Roberts

AN AVID WINE-LOVER, Michael Roberts writes articles on wine for dozens of magazines. He is wine columnist for the Ottawa *Sun* and wine editor for *Ottawa* magazine. This is Michael's favourite lamb recipe.

1	rack of lamb (with six small chops), well trimmed	1
1 tbsp	unsalted butter	15 mL
1	clove garlic	1
	Salt and pepper	
1 tbsp	finely chopped parsley	15 mL

1 Rub lamb with butter and garlic. Sprinkle with salt and pepper. Place in shallow roasting pan and roast at 400°F (200°C) for 20 minutes or until meat is pink.

2 Transfer lamb to hot platter and sprinkle with chopped parsley. Let stand 5 minutes. Carve meat parallel to bones in long strips. Cut bones into separate ribs and serve with pan juices.

Inniskillin Wines Pinot Noir

NIAGARA-ON-THE-LAKE, ONTARIO

Michael Roberts notes that Pinot Noir is the grape of Burgundy, now successfully grown in the Niagara Peninsula. Inniskillin's Pinot Noir is light bodied with berry aromas and raspberry-cherry flavours that accent this simple lamb dish without overpowering it.

WINEMAKER'S · TASTING NOTES

LAMB MEDITERRA | Serves three to four

Michelle Ramsay

Château des Charmes Estate Pinot Noir

NIAGARA-ON-THE-LAKE, ONTARIO

This wine boldly displays the intense raspberry nose with sweet, red fruit on the mouth that picks up the honey and fruit in the recipe. Bold enough for the lamb but light enough in the texture and tannins that it doesn't overpower the sauce.

I	leg of lamb (1½ lb/750 g)	I
¼ cup	olive oil	50 mL
I	large red onion, chopped	I
2	medium cloves garlic, minced	2
½ cup	Château des Charmes Estate Pinot Noir (red wine)	125 mL
2 tbsp	balsamic vinegar	25 mL
I	large tomato, peeled, seeded and chopped	I
⅓ cup	currants	75 mL
I tbsp	honey	15 mL
I tsp	cinnamon	5 mL
¾ tsp	cumin	4 mL
½ tsp	cloves	2 mL
I	bay leaf	I
2	large strips orange peel	2
	Salt and pepper	
1½ cups	orzo*	375 mL
	Fresh chopped mint and thin orange slices (for garnish)	

1 Remove fat and bone from lamb leg. Cut meat into 1½-inch (4-cm) cubes. **2** In a large saucepan over medium-heat, heat oil. Sauté lamb cubes, turning until browned. Add onion and garlic; sauté about 3 minutes, stirring frequently and taking care not to burn the garlic. **3** Add wine and vinegar; bring to a boil for 1 minute. Reduce heat to medium-low. Stir in tomato, currants, honey, cinnamon, cumin, cloves, bay leaf and orange peel.

*Orzo is a pasta that looks like rice.

Season with salt and pepper to taste. Add ¾ cup (175 mL) water and simmer, covered, 45 minutes. **4** Cook orzo in boiling salted water. Serve lamb over the pasta. Garnish with mint and orange slices.

*L*AMB SAUSAGE WITH ORANGE CHILI BEURRE BLANC | Serves two to three

Michelle Ramsay

1 lb	lamb sausage	500 g
1 tbsp	white wine vinegar	15 mL
2 tbsp	Gehringer Brothers Ehrenfelser (white wine)	25 mL
3 tbsp	freshly squeezed orange juice	50 mL
2	shallots, finely chopped	2
Pinch	crushed hot pepper flakes	Pinch
1 cup	very cold butter, cubed	250 mL
	White pepper to taste	
	Orange slices and fresh coriander (for garnish)	

1 Score sausages so they won't burst, and either broil or fry for 5 to 7 minutes on each side or until golden brown. **2** To make sauce, in a small, heavy pot, boil vinegar, wine, orange juice, shallots and pepper flakes. **3** Remove from heat and gradually whisk in butter, one cube at a time, until well blended. Season with pepper. **4** Serve whole sausage on platter and nap with sauce. Decorate platter with orange slices and coriander leaves.

Gehringer Brothers Ehrenfelser (Dry)

The Orange Chili Beurre Blanc in this dish goes well with a rich white wine. Ehrenfelser, with its citrus bouquet and powerful fruit extract on the palate, works well with the orange juice and orange slices. Enough acidity to cut through the oil in the sausage. A good finish.

WINEMAKER'S · TASTING NOTES

*V*INEYARD **LAMB** | Serves four

Reif Estate Winery,
Niagara~on~the~Lake, Ontario

FOR MORE THAN 200 YEARS the Reif family has been transforming the grape into wine, first at Wein Reif in Germany and for the past 10 years at Reif Estate Winery in Niagara-on-the-Lake. The company's president and winemaker, Klaus W. Reif, is a graduate of Geisenheim University in Germany. Using traditional methods, he makes varietal wines from 100 per cent of a specified grape variety, ages all his whites in oak and sweetens his medium and late harvest wines with sweet reserves. All 27 products are made according to VQA standards. These techniques have proved successful for Klaus; every year he brings home at least one gold or silver medal from InterVin and other international wine competitions. In 1991 the winery expanded to include a barrel-ageing cellar and hospitality room where the winery hosts gourmet dinners and wine tastings.

Reif Estate Winery Cabernet Sauvignon

Made entirely from estate-grown grapes, this Cabernet Sauvignon was fermented and aged in American oak. Being full bodied and rich, it stands up to the heavier, rich meats like lamb. The wine's aromas and flavours marry well with the brandy-wine flavours in the marinade.

WINEMAKER'S · TASTING NOTES

I	Ontario lamb leg (5 lb/2.2 kg)	I
2	cloves garlic, sliced lengthwise	2
½ cup	brandy	125 mL
I tsp	oregano	5 mL
I tsp	salt	5 mL
2 tsp	black pepper	10 mL
¼ cup	sherry	50 mL
½ cup	Reif Estate Winery Cabernet Sauvignon (red wine)	125 mL

1 Using a pointed knife, make small slits in lamb and insert garlic slivers. Soak cheesecloth or tea towel in brandy and wrap around lamb. Cover with plastic wrap and marinate, refrigerated, for 4 hours. **2** Mix oregano, salt and pepper in a small bowl. In another bowl combine sherry and wine. **3** Unwrap lamb and place, fat side up, on a rack in a roasting pan. Press oregano mixture onto the lamb, covering evenly. Roast lamb at 450°F (230°C) for

30 minutes. **4** Reduce heat to 350°F (180°C). Using a basting brush, baste lamb with sherry-wine mixture. Continue to roast, basting frequently, for I hour or until desired doneness. A meat thermometer should read 135-140°F (55-60°C) for rare; 140-145°F (60-65°C) for medium rare; 150-155°F (65-70°C) for medium. Let roast stand 10 minutes before carving.

VEAL STEAK WITH PEACH AND BRANDY SAUCE | Serves four

The Tudor Room, Park Royal Hotel, West Vancouver, British Columbia

THIS IS ANOTHER of chef Hans Schaub's wonderful recipes, using local veal and Okanagan peaches.

4	veal steaks (6 oz/150 g each)	4
	Salt and pepper	
2 tsp	flour	10 mL
⅓ cup	butter	75 mL
I oz	brandy	25 mL
2	peaches	2
I cup	whipping cream	250 mL

1 Season veal with salt and pepper; dust with flour. In a large skillet over medium heat, melt the butter. Sauté veal steaks for 4 to 5 minutes each side or until pink. Flambé with the brandy. **2** In a food processor or blender, purée peaches; add to steaks. Stir in cream and simmer for 4 to 5 minutes. **3** Place steaks on plates, cover lightly with sauce and pass remaining sauce in a gravy boat.

Gray Monk Cellars Pinot Auxerrois

OKANAGAN CENTRE, BRITISH COLUMBIA

Distinctly fruity and refreshing, this wine is cousin to the Pinot Gris. It is crisp to the palate, cutting through the cream, yet complementing the peach in this recipe.

WINEMAKER'S · TASTING NOTES ·

Barbecue Roast of Ontario Beef with Cabernet Sauvignon Marinade | Serves six to eight

Stonechurch Vineyards, Niagara-on-the-Lake, Ontario

Nestled between vineyards at the junction of Lakeshore Road and Irvine Street in Niagara-on-the-Lake, Stonechurch Vineyards is Ontario's tiny cottage winery with big appeal. Just three years old, Stonechurch is quickly gaining renown for their wines from fellow winemakers, as well as critical acclaim. At the 1992 InterVin International Wine Competition, the winery was honoured with a silver medal for their 1990 Reserve Chardonnay. Their vines are reaching two decades of maturity and, since the winery's inception, owner and grower Rick Hunse and winemaker David Hulley have shared an uncompromising passion for producing the finest limited edition varietals made exclusively from Ontario grapes.

Stonechurch Vineyards Cabernet Sauvignon

Bell peppers and red currants dominate the nose of this red. Ripe raspberry and vanilla come through in the taste. Full-bodied and rich, this wine marries well with the strong smoky barbecue flavours in the roast. Using the Cabernet Sauvignon in the marinade also helts to make the union complete.

WINEMAKER'S · TASTING NOTES

I	rump roast (about 5 lb/2.2 kg)	I
MARINADE:		
1 cup	olive oil	250 mL
½ cup	Stonechurch Vineyards Cabernet Sauvignon (red wine)	125 mL
3 tbsp	soy sauce	50 mL
5	dashes Worcestershire sauce	5
	Freshly ground pepper to taste	
2	cloves garlic, minced	2
	Basil to taste	

1 In a large shallow bowl combine marinade ingredients. Marinate roast, covered and refrigerated, overnight, turning occasionally. **2** Place roast on a rotisserie and barbecue at 325°F (160°C) until meat is cooked and slightly pink inside.

NOTE: If you can find vine cuttings, chop them into 1-inch (2.5-cm) pieces and soak in water for a few days. Place some of the drained clippings in a heavy pan and place on the coals. The smoke from the clippings will flavour the roast.

TONY ASPLER'S MUSTARD LAMB | Serves six

Tony Aspler

TONY ASPLER IS PERHAPS Canada's most widely read wine writer. He is the wine columnist for the Toronto *Star* and writes for wine magazines around the world. His wine books include *Vintage Canada*, *The Wine Lover Dines*, *The International Guide to Wine*, *The Wine Lover's Companion* and *Vintage Canada II*. He has written the wine component for *Madame Benoit's Illustrated Encyclopedia of Microwave Cooking*, *Air Fare* and *How to Make Love to a Lobster*. He is currently working on *The Entertaining Guide* with food writer Rose Murray.

"This is a great recipe to make frozen leg of lamb more succulent and tasty," says Tony.

1	boneless leg of lamb (4 to 6 lb/2 to 2.5 kg)	1

MARINADE:

½ cup	Dijon mustard	125 mL
2 tbsp	soy sauce	25 mL
1	clove garlic, minced	1
1 tsp	ground rosemary	5 mL
¼ tsp	ginger	1 mL
1 tbsp	olive oil	15 mL

1 To make marinade, in a bowl blend together mustard, soy sauce, garlic, rosemary and ginger. Beat in olive oil, a few drops at a time, until creamy. With a rubber spatula spread mixture over leg of lamb and refrigerate for several hours. **2** Roast at 350°F (180°C) for 25 minutes per pound (500 g) for medium rare or until meat thermometer reaches 155°F (70°C).

Hillebrand Estates Trius Red

NIAGARA-ON-THE-LAKE, ONTARIO

Tony Aspler notes that this wine has a dark ruby robe with a black currant and raspberry bouquet and black cherry, black currant and a hint of oak on the palate. This blend works beautifully with the leg of lamb.

WINEMAKER'S TASTING NOTES

LAMB-BEEF BURGERS WITH ORANGE MINT MAYONNAISE | Makes six burgers

Michelle Ramsay

Konzelmann Estate Winery Pinot Noir

NIAGARA-ON-THE-LAKE, ONTARIO

One of the finest velvety soft, well-balanced red wines. This wine marries well with the creaminess of mayonnaise while enhancing the lamb flavour. Its fruit works with the flavours of orange as well. Slightly chilled (55°F/12°C), the wine adds contrast in temperature to barbecued food.

WINEMAKER'S · TASTING NOTES ·

1 lb	lean ground lamb	500 g
½ lb	extra-lean ground beef	250 g
1	medium sweet onion, minced	1
1	large clove garlic, minced	1
	Salt and pepper to taste	
2 tbsp	minced fresh oregano	25 mL
1	egg	1
6	onion buns, halved	6
	Leaf OR Bibb lettuce	
	Orange Mint Mayonnaise (recipe follows)	

1 Combine well all ingredients, except buns and lettuce. Form into six patties and refrigerate until firm, at least 30 minutes. **2** Grill over medium-high heat to desired doneness. Place lettuce on bun. Arrange grilled meat patty on top of lettuce and top with orange mint mayonnaise.

ORANGE MINT MAYONNAISE:
Makes 1 cup (250 mL)

½ cup	yogurt cheese	125 mL
½ cup	low-fat mayonnaise	125 mL
1 tbsp	finely minced orange zest	15 mL
2 tbsp	fresh orange juice	25 mL
1 tbsp	finely chopped fresh mint	15 mL
	Salt and white pepper to taste	

1 To make yogurt cheese, drain low-fat yogurt through cheesecloth or a paper coffee filter for several hours or overnight in fridge. The yogurt will become very thick, like a cheese. **2** Stir together yogurt cheese, low-fat mayonnaise, orange zest, juice, mint, salt and pepper.

Mustard Herb Flank Steak | Serves six

Michelle Ramsay

½ cup	grainy Dijon mustard	125 mL
½ cup	tarragon mustard	125 mL
⅓ cup	olive oil	75 mL
	Juice of ½ lemon	
¼ cup	finely chopped shallots	50 mL
3	medium cloves garlic, minced	3
I tbsp	finely chopped fresh rosemary	15 mL
I tbsp	finely chopped fresh oregano	15 mL
I tsp	finely chopped fresh sage	5 mL
2	flank steaks (I½ lb/750 g each), trimmed	2

1 In a bowl combine mustards, olive oil, lemon juice, shallots, garlic, rosemary, oregano and sage. **2** Coat steaks with mustard mixture and refrigerate, covered, several hours or overnight. Remove from fridge I hour before grilling. **3** On a preheated barbecue or under an oven grill, cook meat 5 minutes on each side or until medium rare. Cover loosely with foil and let stand 5 minutes before slicing thinly across the grain.

CedarCreek Reserve Merlot

KELOWNA, BRITISH COLUMBIA

This full-bodied red has ripe berry and clove aromas with hints of leather and cedar. The rich, full flavour, reminiscent of oak and smoke, perfectly complements this barbecued dish. Hearty enough to stand up to the sage and mustard flavourings.

WINEMAKER'S TASTING NOTES

VEAL TENDERLOIN WRAPPED IN SAGE AND PROSCIUTTO WITH SAGE ASPARAGUS SAUCE | Serves four

The Millcroft Inn, Alton, Ontario

A RESTORED HISTORIC KNITTING MILL, this Relais & Chateaux inn is set near the Credit River waterfall in the Caledon Hills. Rooms and two-storey lofts are furnished in a rustic Canadiana style. The expansive dining room has a special glass-enclosed pod offering a spectacular view of water splashing over the old mill wheel. The foods and wines of Ontario are very much in evidence at The Millcroft Inn. Chef Antonio de Luca offers sophisticated seasonal cuisine using top-quality regional ingredients. This Italian-inspired recipe is an innovative treatment of veal.

Pelee Island Winery Chardonnay

KINGSVILLE, ONTARIO

Although red wine is traditionally paired with veal, The Millcroft suggests this firm, dry Chardonnay. It is aged in French oak barrels, and its classic butter texture and fruit flavours marry well with the delicate veal. Strong enough character to handle the smokiness of the prosciutto.

1½ lb	veal tenderloin, trimmed of fat	750 g
2 tbsp	olive oil	25 mL
	Salt and pepper to taste	
16	large sage leaves	16
8	slices prosciutto	8
½ lb	pork caul fat	250 g

SAGE ASPARAGUS SAUCE:

½ cup	Pelee Island Chardonnay (white wine)	125 mL
½ cup	chicken stock	125 mL
2	shallots, thinly sliced	2
2 cups	peeled, chopped asparagus	500 mL
4	sprigs sage, shredded	4
½ cup	whipping cream	125 mL
	Lemon juice to taste	

1 Cut veal into four equal portions of 6 oz (190 g) each. Rub with olive oil and sprinkle with salt and pepper. Place two sage leaves on top and two leaves on the bottom of each portion of tenderloin. Wrap each portion with two slices of prosciutto; cover with pork caul fat (approximately 2 oz/50 g per portion). **2** In a large oven-safe skillet over high heat, sear veal for 2 to 3 minutes each side. Transfer to oven and bake at 350°F (180°C) for 15 minutes or until meat is pink. Keep warm. **3** To make sauce, in a saucepan combine wine, stock and shallots. Bring to a boil; reduce by half. Add asparagus. Cook until asparagus is soft. **4** Purée sauce in food processor; return to stove. Stir in cream and lemon juice to taste. Bring to boil; strain through a fine sieve. To serve, put sauce on plates. Slice veal. Arrange slices on top of sauce.

ROAST VEAL LOIN WITH FILET OF BEEF CENTRE ON CABERNET SAUCE | Serves six to eight

Astina's Dining Lounge, St. Catharines, Ontario

WHAT MAKES ASTINA'S particularly special is its owner/chef Walter Vaz. Humble and quiet, Walter saves his flamboyance and energy for his work, which happens to be his life-long passion. The time he has spent upgrading his skills has paid off; Walter is one of St. Catharines' most renowned chefs—not to mention a pretty good amateur beer- and winemaker. Broiled grape leaves cheese parcels with tomato concassé and cream of pheasant with black currant soup are but two of the many wonderful dishes served at Astina's.

Stonechurch Vineyards Cabernet Sauvignon

NIAGARA-ON-THE-LAKE, ONTARIO

This is an impeccable match! Full-bodied, this red has red currants, blueberries and green beans on the nose. Blackberry and vanilla come through on the palate with a light peppery finish that parallels the veal's peppercorn crust.

2 lb	veal loin (6 inches/15 cm long)	1 kg
2 lb	beef tenderloin (6 inches/15 cm long)	1 kg
1 tbsp	Dijon mustard	15 mL
1½ tsp	peppercorns	7 mL
1 tbsp	safflower oil	15 mL
1 tbsp	unsalted butter	15 mL

CABERNET SAUCE:

3 cups	beef stock	750 mL
¾ cup	Stonechurch Vineyards Cabernet Sauvignon (red wine)	175 mL
2 to 4 tbsp	cold unsalted butter	25 to 50 mL
	Salt and pepper to taste	

1 Using a slender knife, cut a slit lengthwise through the centre of the veal loin, forming a tube, being careful not to cut through the sides. **2** Cut beef tenderloin in half lengthwise (or in thirds if thick). Set aside one strip. (Reserve remaining tenderloin for another use.) **3** Tie kitchen twine around one end of tenderloin, about 1 inch (2.5 cm) from end. Using fingers, push twine through veal tube and slowly pull tenderloin through veal.

Gently press down on veal as you pull tenderloin through. If tenderloin is too large, cut larger slit in veal or trim tenderloin. **4** Cut twine from tenderloin and trim off any overhang. Tie veal ends four or five times with kitchen twine to ensure a snug round shape. **5** Generously rub mustard over veal. Set aside. Grind peppercorns in food processor or blender. Roll the mustard sides of the veal in ground peppercorns until all sides are coated. (The meat may be covered and refrigerated several hours or overnight at this point.) **6** In a large heavy skillet over high heat, heat oil and butter. Sear veal for 4 minutes, turning frequently until browned on all sides. Place veal on a rack in a roasting pan and roast at 375°F (190°C) for 20 to 25 minutes or until medium rare. Let rest a few minutes before cutting strings and slicing into medallions 1½ inches (4 cm) thick. **7** To make Cabernet sauce, in large saucepan over high heat, bring beef stock to a boil. Simmer for 20 minutes or until stock is reduced to ¾ cup (175 mL). Remove from heat and whisk in butter, 1 tbsp (15 mL) at a time. Season to taste. **8** To serve, place two medallions on each hot plate. Nap each medallion with 3 or 4 tbsp (50 mL) Cabernet sauce.

BEEF AND KIDNEY STEW | Serves six

Ye Olde Steak House,
Windsor, Ontario

ONE OF THE CITY'S MOST POPULAR restaurants with beef-lovers, Ye Old Steak House has been serving great steaks and beef dishes for close to 30 years. Local wines from Pelee Island and Lake Erie's North Shore play a prominent role on the wine list.

Colio Wines Cabernet Franc

HARROW, ONTARIO

Ruby red, full-bodied and slightly tannic, this wine has a raspberry and herbaceous aroma with vanilla and oak flavours that work well with the dark, strong meats in this simple dish. This wine has excellent ageing potential.

WINEMAKER'S TASTING NOTES

I lb	veal kidneys	500 g
6 tbsp	butter	90 mL
I	large onion, thinly sliced	I
2 lb	lean beef, cut into I-inch (2.5-cm) cubes	I kg
I tbsp	flour	15 mL
I cup	Colio Wines Cabernet Franc (red wine)	250 mL
4	sprigs parsley	4
I	sprig thyme	I
I	bay leaf	I
½ lb	mushrooms, sliced	250 g
½ cup	beef stock OR water	125 mL
	Salt and pepper to taste	

1 Bring veal kidneys to a boil in just enough water to cover. Simmer 5 minutes. Cut into I-inch (2.5-cm) cubes, removing any tendons or gristle. Set aside. **2** Melt butter in a heavy deep pan or Dutch oven and sauté onion until tender. **3** Add beef and cook, stirring frequently until browned. With a slotted spoon transfer beef to a bowl. **4** Add flour to pan and stir until brown; add wine, parsley, thyme, bay leaf and mushrooms. Stir gently for a few minutes. **5** Add stock; stir until mixture comes to a simmer. Add beef, kidneys, salt and pepper. Bring stew to a boil. **6** Cover tightly and simmer for 2½ hours, checking periodically to see if mixture becomes dry. Add stock if needed. Adjust seasoning before serving.

STEAK CREOLE | Serves four

Pelee Island Winery and Vineyards, Kingsville, Ontario

PELEE ISLAND WINERY is acclaimed for its delicious wines and its spectacular touring facility. Although the winery is in the town of Kingsville, the 200-acre estate vineyard and new Wine Pavilion are on Pelee Island. The Wine Pavilion, which can be reached via the Pelee Island Ferry, offers everything from a vineyard tour and audio-visual presentation on winemaking to a do-it-yourself barbecue lunch and a visit to the tasting bar. At this tasting bar visitors can sample topnotch varietal and blended wines, all produced by winemaker Walter Schmoranz.

CAJUN SEASONING:

1 tbsp	each cayenne, chili powder and thyme	15 mL
1	basil leaf	1
1 tsp	ground pepper	5 mL
1 tsp	commercial Cajun seasoning	5 mL
1	green bell pepper	1
1	red bell pepper	1
1	yellow bell pepper	1
1	purple onion, cut into rings	1
½ cup	sliced mushrooms	125 mL
4	beef tenderloin steaks (5 oz/125 g each)	4

1 Cut peppers into julienne strips. Place onion rings, pepper strips and mushroom slices on a baking sheet and bake at 350°F (180°C) for 15 minutes or until tender. Keep warm. **2** Meanwhile, combine Cajun seasoning ingredients. Sprinkle one side of steaks with Cajun seasoning mix. Grill steak for 5 minutes on each side or until medium rare. Serve grilled vegetables on top of steak.

Pelee Island Winery Fenian's Cuvée

KINGSVILLE, ONTARIO

Fenian's Cuvée is a half-and-half blend of Zweigelt and Gamay Noir. The Zweigelt grape brings to this wine a deep ruby robe, full-bodied flavour and heavy tannins. Gamay Noir gives the wine a berry-like bouquet and palate. Only robust reds like Fenian's Cuvée should be matched to spicy red meat dishes.

Suggested Varietal: Cabernet Sauvignon

WINEMAKER'S · TASTING NOTES

CARRÉ DE COCHONET À L'AIL DES BOIS (RACK OF PIGLET WITH GARLIC BEURRE BLANC) | Serves four

L'Eau à la Bouche, Ste.-Adèle, Quebec

PERCHED IN THE HEART OF THE Laurentians, this Relais & Chateaux inn provides a fabulous escape for those with discriminating palates and a love of the great outdoors. The kitchen is meticulously tended by co-owners and chefs Anne Desjardins and Pierre Audette. The award-winning inn and restaurant is committed to using local quality products. This recipe uses a new variety of pork raised on the south shore of the St. Lawrence River, weighing in at only 50 pounds and characterized by a white, tender meat with a delicate flavour.

Vignoble Les Arpents de Neige Vendange Sélectionné

DUNHAM, QUEBEC

Produced mainly from Seyval grapes and supplemented with Vidal, this wine is aged in oak barrels. The slight oaky flavour combines well with the garlic tones and stands up to the cream in this dish. Flowery nose with touches of tropical fruit.

WINEMAKER'S • TASTING NOTES

I	rack of pork (2 lb/I kg)	I
	Salt and pepper to taste	
4 oz	wild OR regular garlic cloves, halved	125 g
I cup	white port	250 mL
½ cup	cold unsalted butter, cubed	125 mL

1 Insert a few of the garlic halves in fleshy part of pork. Sprinkle meat with salt and pepper. **2** Blanch remaining garlic for I minute; reserve for sauce. **3** In a large, greased, oven-safe pot or roasting pan over high heat, brown pork well on all sides. Transfer to oven and cook at 350°F (180°C) for 20 minutes. **4** Remove pork from pan and keep warm. Add white port to pan juices and over high heat reduce to about 2 tbsp (25 mL). Stir in reserved garlic. Reduce heat to low. **5** Slowly whisk in butter, one cube at a time, until well blended. When sauce has thickened, adjust seasoning with salt and pepper if necessary. **6** To serve, carve pork into four portions, cutting between the ribs. Place sauce on each plate, reserving a small amount for garnish; arrange pork on top of sauce. Garnish with remaining sauce.

CONVENTIONAL BAKED HAM | Serves 20 to 25

*Shari Darling / A & H Vineyards,
Peachland, British Columbia*

A & H IS A NEW FARM WINERY located in Peachland, in the Trepanier Valley where vitis vinifera grapes thrive in the warm microclimate and stony soil. The winery's eight-acre estate vineyard is planted to Riesling and Kerner. Winemaker Henry Moeller produces 5,000 gallons of two Riesling wines, a dry and a semi-dry.

I lb	dried pineapple	500 g
I cup	sherry	250 mL
I	ham (12 lb/5.5 kg)	I
	Whole cloves to cover ham	
¼ cup	Dijon mustard	50 mL
I cup	dark brown sugar	250 mL
4 cups	apple juice	I L

1 In a small saucepan, combine pineapple and sherry. Bring to a boil, cover and remove from heat. **2** Peel skin from ham and trim fat, leaving ¼-inch (5-mm) layer all over. With a sharp knife, score fat in a diamond pattern. **3** Set ham in a shallow baking pan. Insert a whole clove in the crossed point of each diamond, and pat mustard evenly over top and sides of ham. Sprinkle with brown sugar. Pour apple juice into pan. **4** Bake ham at 350°F (180°C) for I hour, basting frequently. After I hour, add pineapples and their liquid to the roasting pan. Bake, basting, a further 30 minutes. **5** Transfer ham to a large platter. Decorate top of ham with pineapple, attaching pieces with toothpicks. Skim fat from pan juices and pour juices into sauce boat. Serve ham with a variety of mustards, chutneys and the pan juices.

A & H Vineyards Dry Riesling

A dry Riesling is the ideal partner for this dish. The wine's tart acidity reduces the perception of sweetness and cleans the palate between bites. A & H Vineyards Dry Riesling is pale straw in colour, medium bodied and has citrus on the nose and palate. These elements complement the fruit flavours in this dish.

WINEMAKER'S · TASTING NOTES

APPLE-STUFFED PORK LOIN | Serves eight to ten

CedarCreek Estate Winery, Kelowna, British Columbia

CEDARCREEK, WITH ITS 30 ACRES OF VINEYARD and spectacular view of Okanagan Lake, is situated south of Kelowna. As an estate winery, production is limited to 40,000 gallons a year, making quality the winemaker's priority. Winemaker Ann Sperling uses exclusively British Columbia-grown grapes to make classic wines such as Chardonnay, Auxerrois, Gewürztraminer, Johannisberg Riesling, Semillon and Pinot Blanc, as well as limited releases of Merlot, Pinot Noir and Icewine. Many wine-lovers insist that CedarCreek makes the best Riesling in the Okanagan Valley.

CedarCreek Estate Winery Johannisberg Riesling Dry

This great white grape of Germany has found its second home in the Okanagan Valley. CedarCreek's Johannisberg Riesling Dry is pale straw in colour, well balanced and rich with aromas resembling apple and sage and flavours showing herbal and pear. The apple-sage aromas and fruit flavours have a natural affinity with the apple flavours in the dressing.

WINEMAKER'S · TASTING NOTES

I	boneless pork loin (5 lb/2.2 kg), well trimmed	I
¼ cup	minced Spanish onion	50 mL
¼ tsp	rosemary	1 mL
¼ tsp	thyme	1 mL
4	slices white bread, cubed	4
2 cups	diced peeled apples (substitute all or part with pears, peaches, blueberries or plums)	500 mL
½ cup	crumbled strong cheese (blue, Brie or Asiago)	125 mL
¼ cup	applesauce	50 mL
½ tsp	freshly ground black pepper	2 mL
½ tsp	white pepper	2 mL
I tsp	finely chopped fresh parsley	5 mL
½ tsp	salt	2 mL
½ tsp	freshly ground pepper	2 mL
3 tbsp	applesauce (optional)	50 mL

■ Trim any excess fat from pork loin. Feel the loin for hard nuggets of cartilage; cut them off. Flatten the loin by cutting three-quarters of the way through lengthwise and opening it up. Flatten meat with mallet. Halve the loin lengthwise. **2** To prepare stuffing, in a large bowl combine onion, rosemary and thyme. Toss in bread crumbs, apples, cheese and applesauce. Season with black and white pepper and parsley. Combine mixture thoroughly.

3 Lay one half of the loin flat and mound the stuffing evenly on it. Top with second loin, making sure meat entirely encases the stuffing. Tie meat with string. Set loin on a large sheet of foil, with shiny side up. Sprinkle loin with salt and pepper. Spread with additional applesauce, if desired. **4** Wrap snugly and set in a large baking pan. Bake at 350°F (180°C) for 1 hour. Loosen foil and baste with pan juices. Continue roasting and basting for another 90 minutes. The total roasting time is 2½ to 3 hours. Cover the meat with a towel and allow to stand 10 minutes before untying and slicing.

Shin of Pork | Serves four

*Colio Wines,
Harrow, Ontario*

HARROW HAS GROWN INTO a thriving resort town, and Colio Wines is one of its major attractions. Established in 1980, this winery can boast a production of more than 416,000 gallons of wine each year. With the recent purchase of a 100-acre vineyard in Kingsville, in the Lake Erie North Shore region, Colio Wines will soon be releasing estate-bottled wines. Master winemaker Carlo Negri prefers the traditional Italian style, fermenting his juice and ageing his wines in stainless steel. He also makes an Icewine, Château D'Or Canadian Champagne and Spumante Ontario. All three products have won Negri bronze medals at the 1992 International Eastern Wine Competition.

Colio Wines Cabernet Franc

LAKE ERIE NORTH SHORE

Aged in new American oak barrels for one year, Colio's Cabernet Franc is full bodied and slightly tannic. It shows raspberry and herbaceous aromas with raspberry, vanilla and oaky flavours and a peppery finish that accentuates the potpourri of herbs and peppercorns in this dish.

4	meaty pork shins	4
	Salt and pepper to taste	
¾ cup	flour	175 mL
½ cup	olive oil	125 mL
2	large onions, sliced into rings	2
2	stalks celery, diced	2
3	carrots, sliced	3
Pinch	thyme	Pinch
Pinch	parsley	Pinch
2	bay leaves	2
I tbsp	green peppercorns	15 mL
½ cup	Colio Wines Cabernet Franc (red wine)	125 mL
I cup	veal stock	250 mL
2 tbsp	brandy	25 mL
I cup	cooked rice	250 mL

1 Season pork shins with salt and pepper. Coat with flour. In a heavy pot over medium heat, heat oil. Brown shins on all sides. Add onions, celery, carrots, thyme, parsley, bay leaves, peppercorns, wine and stock. Simmer for 90 minutes, turning frequently. Add brandy. Simmer another 90 minutes, turning frequently. **2** Discard bay leaves. Pour pan juices over rice. Top with shins.

PORK ROAST WITH BACCHUS GRAVY | Serves 8 to 10

Domaine de Chaberton, Langley, British Columbia

DOMAINE DE CHABERTON is Langley's first farm-gate winery, located in the Fraser Valley of British Columbia. With the help of consultant Dr. Elias Phiniotis, winemaker Claude Violet produces five white wines: Madeleine Angevine, Madeleine Sylvaner, Bacchus, Ortega and Chaberton Blanc. Only two years in the business, Violet has already acquired a notable reputation in British Columbia's wine industry by capturing two silver and one bronze medal for his Ortega dessert wine at the 1992 Pacific National Exhibition Wine Competition, the 23rd International Wine and Spirits Competition and the 1992 InterVin International Wine Competition.

Domaine de Chaberton Bacchus

Made with grapes grown in the Fraser Valley, Domaine de Chaberton's Bacchus is light golden in colour and full bodied, with nuts and Muscat on the nose and floral and peach on the palate and a tinge of sweetness. These elements lift the gravy and complement this sweet meat.

1	pork roast (4 lb/1.75 kg)	1
2 tbsp	vegetable oil	25 mL
	Salt and pepper to taste	
1	onion, quartered	1
4	carrots, quartered	4
2	leeks, cut in chunks	2
2 cups	chicken stock	500 mL
1 tbsp	flour	15 mL
1 cup	Domaine de Chaberton Bacchus (white wine)	250 mL

1 In a large skillet, over medium heat, brown roast on all sides in vegetable oil. Sprinkle roast with salt and pepper and place in roasting pan. Roast at 350°F (180°C) for 30 minutes, turning every 10 minutes. **2** Add onions, carrots, leeks and ¼ cup (50 mL) chicken stock to roasting pan. Roast another 30 minutes or until pork is white. **3** In a bowl combine flour with remaining stock; mix until smooth. Stir in wine. **4** Remove roast from pan; keep warm. Stir wine mixture into pan juices. Stir over medium heat until completely smooth and thickened to a creamy gravy. Return roast to the gravy, turning constantly to coat.

$\mathcal{V}$ENISON STROGANOFF | Serves six

Shari Darling / Grand Pré Estate Winery, Grand Pré, Nova Scotia

OF ALL THE WINES produced at Grand Pré Estate Winery, Michurinetz is the most celebrated. The 1983 vintage was chosen to be served at Canadian embassies around the world and later won a gold medal at the 1986 InterVin International Wine Competition. Grand Pré produces other varietal wines, such as Seyval, Vidal and Maréchal Foch.

I	saddle venison	I
2 tbsp	oil	25 mL
I	large onion, thinly sliced	I
I	clove garlic, minced	I
2 cups	sliced mushrooms	500 mL
3 tbsp	all-purpose flour	50 mL
¼ tsp	pepper	I mL
¼ cup	Grand Pré Wines Michurinetz (red wine)	50 mL
¼ cup	tomato paste	50 mL
I	bay leaf, crumbled	I
½ cup	beef broth	125 mL
½ cup	sour cream	125 mL

Grand Pré Wines Michurinetz

Aged for five years in oak, this Michurinetz has a deep burgundy robe. The nose shows pepper and oak, while the palate resembles black currant and black cherry with pepper and spice. Ideal with this game meat.

WINEMAKER'S TASTING NOTES

1 Cut small medallions from the saddle of venison. In large skillet, heat oil over medium heat. Fry venison until golden on both sides, about 4 to 5 minutes. Transfer venison to a 3-quart (3-L) baking dish. Set aside. **2** In same skillet, sauté onion, garlic and mushrooms until tender. Remove pan from heat and add flour, pepper, wine, tomato paste and bay leaf. Whisk in beef broth to prevent lumps. Stir until ingredients are well blended. **3** Pour over meat. Cover and bake at 350°F (180°C) for I hour or until meat is tender. Gently stir in sour cream and serve.

MEDALLIONS OF VENISON | Serves four

Carley House, Lambeth, Ontario

AFTER 20 YEARS OF hotel management, Noel Samuels opened Carley House. Located in the small hamlet of Lambeth on the outskirts of London, Ontario, Carley House has become a regular stop for those who enjoy upscale dining in a casual atmosphere. Continental dishes such as seafood, steak and lamb can be found on the menu, along with a few "class act" Ontario wines.

Inniskillin Wines Pinot Noir

NIAGARA-ON-THE-LAKE, ONTARIO

This red has a brilliant robe and is light bodied with soft texture and good fruity-oak balance. Berries show on the nose, cherries on the palate. Being a delicate varietal, this wine is a good partner for this tender venison dish.

WINEMAKER'S TASTING NOTES

2 lb	venison slices from the leg	1 kg

STUFFING:

1	skinless boneless chicken breast (6 oz/175 g), cubed	1
1	onion, sliced	1
6	cloves garlic	6
¼ cup	whipping cream	50 mL
½ tsp	each salt and pepper	2 mL
½ tsp	sage	2 mL
¼ tsp	basil	1 mL
½ cup	dried bread crumbs	125 mL

GRAVY:

1 cup	Inniskillin Wines Pinot Noir (red wine)	250 mL
1 cup	veal OR chicken stock	250 mL
2 tbsp	cornstarch	25 mL
1 tbsp	vegetable oil	15 mL
1	onion, thinly sliced	1
½ cup	sliced mushrooms	125 mL

1 Slice venison into 2-oz (50-g) pieces. Set aside 4 oz/(100 g) venison scraps. Flatten pieces with a mallet until thin. Wrap in plastic wrap and refrigerate. **2** To make stuffing, combine in a food processor the chicken cubes, reserved venison scraps, onion, garlic, cream, salt, pepper, sage and basil; blend at high speed. Transfer to bowl and fold in bread crumbs. **3** Place 1 tbsp (15 mL) stuffing on each slice of venison and fold over. Place in well-greased roasting pan and bake at 350°F (180°C) for 20 minutes or until pieces are brown and firm.

4 To make gravy, remove venison from roasting pan; keep warm. Deglaze pan with wine, cooking over high heat for 2 minutes. Add stock to wine mixture and bring to a boil. In a small bowl blend cornstarch with ¼ cup (50 mL) water; pour into wine mixture and cook, stirring constantly, until thickened, about 2 minutes. **5** In a skillet, heat oil over medium heat. Sauté onion and mushrooms and add to gravy. **6** Spoon sauce onto each plate and arrange medallions on top, napped with gravy.

QUADRA ISLAND VENISON | Serves six

April Point Lodge & Fishing Resort, Campbell River, Quadra Island, British Columbia

WITH ITS UNIQUELY FURNISHED ocean-view rooms, April Point Lodge is always in demand among discerning travellers who enjoy the great outdoors as much as comfort. Fireplaces, hot tubs, jacuzzi baths and co-owner Eric Peterson's wonderful barbecues are only some of the attractions of this rustic resort. Eric and brother Wayne offer an extensive seafood menu, which includes Coho and spring salmon, Dungeness crab, cod, oysters and clams. Mother Phyllis's desserts—especially her sumptuous rhubarb pie—are legendary.

Quails' Gate Estate Winery Pinot Noir Reserve

**WESTBANK,
BRITISH COLUMBIA**

This variety was grown on special root stocks in bright sunshine and well-drained soil. Aged 12 months in small French oak barrels, this dry wine has a hint of cherry on the nose and raspberry on the palate. Its vigour creates a superb balance with the venison.

WINEMAKER'S TASTING NOTES

2 tbsp	white wine	25 mL
¼ cup	extra virgin olive oil	50 mL
1 tsp	fresh thyme	5 mL
1 tsp	fresh tarragon	5 mL
1 tsp	chopped fresh parsley	5 mL
3	large cloves garlic, minced	3
2 tbsp	soy sauce	25 mL
1	boneless venison tenderloin (4 lb/2 kg) OR	1
6	venison leg steaks	6

1 In a large shallow nonmetallic container, combine wine, oil, thyme, tarragon, parsley, garlic and soy sauce. Add venison, turning to coat on all sides. Cover and refrigerate overnight. **2** On a preheated barbecue, grill venison over medium-high heat until medium rare (130-140°F/55-60°C on a meat thermometer), basting often with the marinade. (If using steaks, sear 1 minute on each side and grill 4 to 5 minutes longer.) Let stand a few minutes before serving.

ONTARIO RABBIT IN MAPLE ICEWINE GLAZE | Serves six

Metropolis Restaurant/Grill, Toronto, Ontario

CHEF TERRY KENNEDY enjoys pairing Ontario wines with local game. This simple recipe illustrates the delicious potential of pairing a sweet table wine with a delicate meat like rabbit.

12	rabbit loins	12
1 cup	maple syrup	250 mL
¼ cup	Inniskillin Wines Icewine	50 mL
¼ cup	lemon juice	50 mL
	Salt and pepper	
1½ lb	vegetables of choice, coarsely chopped	750 g
	Toasted slivered almonds (for garnish)	

Cave Spring Cellars Riesling Off-Dry

JORDAN, ONTARIO

This intensely aromatic wine, with its exotic fruit flavours of pineapple and grapefruit, complements this mild-flavoured dish without overpowering it.

WINEMAKER'S TASTING NOTES

1 Sliver rabbit loins. Set aside. **2** In a bowl, combine maple syrup, icewine and lemon juice. **3** Heat a large skillet over high heat. Lightly season rabbit with salt and pepper. Place rabbit in pan and sear until all sides are lightly browned. **4** Toss in vegetables. Add ¼ cup (50 mL) of the maple syrup mixture. Simmer for 1 minute. Transfer rabbit and vegetables to plates. Add remaining syrup mixture to pan and reduce to a glaze. Pour glaze over rabbit. Garnish with toasted slivered almonds.

PRINCE OF WALES ROAST RABBIT WITH SPICED SAUSAGE AND CAPSICUM SAUCE | Serves two

Prince of Wales Hotel, Niagara-on-the-Lake, Ontario

MARK WALPOLE, chef at the Prince of Wales Hotel, has had more requests for this updated classic recipe than he can count. It is not as difficult to recreate at home as you might think.

Stoney Ridge Cellars Chardonnay

(EASTMAN VINEYARD), WINONA, ONTARIO

Heavy with a smoky aroma from oak barrel ageing, this full-bodied wine combines a complex citrus and a buttery richness that marry well with the spiciness of the sausage and velvety sauce.

I	rabbit (3 lb/1.5 kg)	I
3 oz	lean ground pork	90 g
3 oz	pork fat, ground	90 g
2 tsp	minced garlic	10 mL
½ tsp	crushed hot pepper flakes	2 mL
	Ground fennel to taste	
	Sage to taste	
	Salt and freshly ground black pepper to taste	
2	crepenetti casings, soaked	2
SAUCE:		
I	red bell pepper, roasted until skin is black, peeled and seeded	I
¼ cup	warm chicken OR rabbit stock	50 mL
	Salt and pepper to taste	
I tbsp	butter, softened	15 mL
I tsp	flour	5 mL

1 Debone rabbit legs, leaving shin bone in. **2** Remove meat from rabbit loin and grind in food processor. Combine in a bowl with ground pork and pork fat. Add garlic, pepper flakes, fennel, sage, salt and pepper; combine well. Fry a bit of the mixture until brown, taste and correct seasonings if necessary. **3** Divide mixture and stuff into crepenetti casings. Stuff sausages into deboned legs. Roast rabbit at 350°F (180°C) for 18 to 20 minutes. **4** While rabbit is cooking, make sauce. In a food processor, combine roasted pepper with warm stock; process to a fine purée. Season with salt and pepper. Strain through a fine mesh strainer into a small saucepan. Place over low heat. **5** Blend butter and flour together with the fingers. Whisk beurre manié into purée, cooking 5 minutes or until sauce thickens. Keep warm. **6** Leaving shin bone of rabbit leg intact, slice meat crosswise, with stuffing displayed in centre. Place sauce on the plates. Stand shin bone upright in centre of plate and surround it with fanned slices of rabbit.

NOTE: Order the rabbit from a butcher and ask to have the legs boned out, leaving the shin bone in. If you're proficient at deboning, do it yourself. Reserve the rabbit loin for the sausage. Pick up crepenetti (the string-like casing for the sausage) at the butcher shop and soak in cold salt water at least one hour.

RABBIT IN DOIS AMIGOS | Serves six to eight

*Shari Darling / De Sousa Cellars,
Beamsville, Ontario*

ESTABLISHED IN 1987, De Sousa Cellars caters to the Portuguese community of Ontario. Under the direction of wine consultant Dieter Guettler, John De Sousa and son John Jr. produce 21,000 gallons a year of two blended wines, Dois Amigos white and Dois Amigos red. The grapes used to make these delicious wines are grown on the 66-acre estate vineyard. Recent renovations at the winery have added a wine store and tasting room.

De Sousa Dois Amigos Red

Similar in style to a Tawny Porto from Portugal, Dois Amigos is a blend of three grape varieties from three vintages (1989, 1990, 1991). Blending different grapes and years gives the wine the very best qualities from each of the varieties, in this case de Chaunac, Villard Noir and Maréchal Foch. Soft, delicate and dry, this wine lends itself to this delicate, flavourful dish.

2	large onions	2
2	fryer rabbits (2½ lb/1.25 kg each), livers reserved	2
1	bay leaf	1
2½ cups	De Sousa Cellars Dois Amigos (red wine)	625 mL
1 tbsp	red wine vinegar	15 mL
3 tbsp	lemon juice	50 mL
¾ tsp	whole thyme leaves	4 mL
½ tsp	salt	2 mL
½ tsp	freshly ground pepper	2 mL
5 tbsp	butter	75 mL
1	large tart apple, peeled and chopped	1
2	shallots, finely chopped	2
1 cup	beef broth	250 mL
2 tsp (25 mL) cornstarch blended with 1 tbsp (15 mL) water		
1 tsp	bottled brown gravy sauce	5 mL

1 Peel one of the onions, slice it thinly, and separate into rings. Place rabbits, onion rings and bay leaf in large shallow bowl. Combine wine, vinegar, lemon juice, thyme, salt and pepper; pour over rabbits. Cover and refrigerate 24 to 36 hours. **2** Drain rabbits, reserving marinade and onion rings. Discard bay leaf. Finely chop rabbit livers. In a skillet over medium heat, melt 2 tbsp (25 mL) butter. Sauté livers until lightly browned. Chop remaining onion, add with apple to livers. Sauté until onion is soft. Add 1 cup (250 mL) reserved marinade; simmer, covered, for 1 hour.

3 Meanwhile, melt remaining 3 tbsp (50 mL) butter in large skillet over medium heat. Brown rabbits well on all sides. Add shallots, reserved onion rings, remaining marinade and beef broth. Simmer, covered, for 1 hour or until rabbits are tender. Remove rabbits from pan.

4 Purée liver mixture in blender. Stir liver purée, cornstarch mixture and brown gravy sauce into liquid in pan. Cook, stirring constantly, until thickened. Add rabbit to sauce; simmer, covered, for 10 minutes. Spoon sauce onto each plate. Slice rabbits and arrange on top of sauce.

WILD BOAR RAGOUT | Serves six

Granny Bogner's, Penticton, British Columbia

SET ON HALF AN ACRE of park-like ground, Granny Bogner's is housed in an 80-year-old home that is a local landmark. Owned and operated by chef Hans Strobel and his wife, Angela, who manages the dining room, Granny Bogner's is named after the chef's grandmother, who was a chef in the Black Forest area of Germany. A founding member of Distinguished Restaurants of North America, Granny Bogner's is well known for its wonderful game recipes.

Hainle Vineyards Baco Noir

PEACHLAND, BRITISH COLUMBIA

This wine is deep garnet in colour with rich, fruity aromas reminiscent of blackberries, and hints of chocolate and a smokiness often found in Baco. Soft and full with a fruity and mildly peppery finish, this wine is an ideal mate to boldly flavoured dishes like this boar ragout. It also works well with game, red meat, sausages, bacon and Mediterranean cuisines.

WINEMAKER'S · TASTING NOTES

I	shoulder of wild boar (5 lb/2 kg), trimmed of fat and skin, meat cubed	I

MARINADE:

2 cups	Hainle Vineyards Baco Noir (red wine)	500 mL
I	large onion, chopped	I
I	carrot, chopped	I
I	stalk celery, chopped	I
4	bay leaves	4
5	whole cloves	5
2 tbsp	juniper berries	25 mL
I	clove garlic	I
I cup	milk	250 mL

SAUCE:

2 tbsp	vegetable oil	25 mL
2 oz	bacon ends	50 g
½ cup	mushroom stems	125 mL
¼ cup	flour	50 mL
I quart	pork stock OR water	I L
2 tsp	tomato paste	10 mL

Salt, pepper and paprika to taste
Flour for dredging meat
Sautéed chanterelle mushrooms (for garnish)

1 Place meat in a deep heavy pot. In a bowl combine all marinade ingredients; pour over meat. Cover and refrigerate 24 hours. **2** Drain meat, reserving 1 cup (250 mL) liquid and all the vegetables and spices. Refrigerate meat until needed. **3** To make sauce, in a large pot, heat oil over medium heat. Add bacon ends and sauté until the fat runs. Add reserved vegetables and spices and mushroom stems; sauté until golden brown. Add flour, cooking for 5 minutes and stirring constantly. Gradually whisk in reserved marinade and stock, whisking well to prevent lumps. Stir in tomato paste and simmer, uncovered, over very low heat for 2 to 3 hours, skimming often and stirring occasionally. **4** Season marinated meat lightly with salt, pepper and paprika. Dredge in flour. In a skillet over medium-high heat, brown meat on all sides. **5** Add meat to sauce and simmer until meat is tender. Transfer meat to plates. Strain sauce, pushing all vegetables through sieve for thickening and flavouring sauce. Adjust seasoning and pour over meat. Garnish with chanterelle mushrooms.

Sumac Ridge Estate Winery Gewürztraminer Dry

SUMMERLAND, BRITISH COLUMBIA

It has a slight dusty rose colour. Made in the Alsatian style, this dry wine has a tantalizing spicy grapefruit nose and is well balanced and full enough on the palate with spicy, smoky, lean tastes to work with this ragout.

WINEMAKER'S · TASTING NOTES

MARINATED WILD BOAR STEAKS | Serves six

Blue Mountain Vineyard and Cellars, Okanagan Falls, British Columbia

LOCATED IN THE HEART OF THE Okanagan Valley, Blue Mountain Vineyard and Cellars is one of British Columbia's newest wineries. Owners Ian and Jane Mavety make the classic varietals Pinot Blanc, Pinot Gris and Pinot Noir, and they are about to release their bubbly, done in the traditional méthode champenoise.

Blue Mountain Vineyard and Cellars Pinot Noir

The complex layering of berry flavours in the marinade and Pinot Noir sauce complement the black cherry, raspberry, spice and oaky aromas and flavours found in Blue Mountain's Pinot Noir.

WINEMAKER'S TASTING NOTES

6	wild boar steaks	6

MARINADE:

2 tbsp	olive oil	25 mL
2 cups	Blue Mountain Pinot Noir (red wine)	500 mL
3	cloves garlic, minced	3
	Salt and pepper to taste	

PINOT NOIR SAUCE:

2 tbsp	olive oil	25 mL
I	Okanagan sweet onion, chopped	I
3	cans (7½ oz/213 mL) tomato sauce	3
2 cups	Okanagan Bing cherries	500 mL
I cup	Blue Mountain Pinot Noir (red wine)	250 mL
½ cup	brown sugar	125 mL
2 tbsp	Worcestershire sauce	25 mL
I tsp	pepper	5 mL
½ tsp	ground aniseed	2 mL
I tsp	cinnamon	5 mL

1 In a bowl, mix together marinade ingredients. Place wild boar steaks in a shallow dish and cover with marinade. Cover and refrigerate, turning once or twice, at least 8 hours. **2** To make sauce, in a large saucepan heat oil over medium heat. Add onion, stirring often until soft. Stir in tomato sauce, cherries, wine, sugar, Worcestershire sauce, pepper, aniseed and cinnamon. Bring to a boil and simmer, uncovered, until thickened, about 40 minutes, stirring occasionally. **3** Prepare barbecue using Okanagan fruit wood (cherry or apple). Light fire well in advance so coals are white and produce even, medium heat. **4** Brush steaks thoroughly with marinade and barbecue slowly, about 40 minutes, basting often with marinade in the first 25 minutes. **5** During last 15 minutes baste both sides of steaks with Pinot Noir sauce. Sauce will slowly caramelize on steaks. Transfer to plates. Pour sauce over steaks. Garnish with the cherries from the sauce. Serve immediately.

CHAPTER FIFTEEN

Dessp

$\mathcal{D}$ESSERTS

$\mathcal{P}$EACHES AND CREAM TORTE

S h a r i   D a r l i n g

CRUST:

2 cups	flour, sifted	500 mL
½ cup	butter, chopped and softened	125 mL
2 tbsp	sugar	25 mL
½ tsp	salt	2 mL

FILLING:

⅓ cup	flour	75 mL
½ cup	sugar	125 mL
¼ tsp	cinnamon	1 mL
½ tsp	vanilla extract	2 mL
1	egg, slightly beaten	1
½ cup	sour cream	125 mL
6	Niagara peaches, peeled and sliced	6

1 Pour sifted flour on a work surface. Make a well in the centre and add softened butter, sugar, salt and 1 tbsp (15 mL) water. Gently knead mixture, adding a little more water if necessary, until dough is firm and forms a ball. Cover dough with plastic wrap and refrigerate at least 2 hours. **2** On a floured surface, roll out dough. Press into 12-inch (30-cm) flan pan with removable bottom. Reserve unused dough and trimmings. Refrigerate dough in flan pan for 30 minutes. **3** Combine all filling ingredients. Pour into torte shell. Roll out reserved dough and cover torte with a lattice. **4** Bake at 425°F (220°C) for 45 minutes or until pastry is golden.

OVEN-BAKED PEACHES WITH PISTACHIOS, HAZELNUTS & BASIL CARAMEL SAUCE | Serves four

The Millcroft Inn, Alton, Ontario

LOCAL PEACHES AND BASIL are teamed with two types of nuts for this Italian-inspired dessert.

¼ cup	sugar	50 mL
6 tbsp	butter	90 mL
10	large basil leaves, shredded	10
¼ cup	whipping cream	50 mL
	Juice of ½ lemon	
4	Ontario peaches, peeled	4
½ cup	sliced hazelnuts	125 mL
¼ cup	skinned pistachios	50 mL
4	basil leaves (for garnish)	4

1 To make caramel, combine sugar and butter in skillet over low heat and cook, stirring, until golden brown. Remove from heat; stir in shredded basil, cream and lemon juice. Keep warm. **2** Halve peaches and remove stones. Arrange in a roasting pan, hole side down. Spoon caramel basil sauce over, sprinkle with nuts and bake at 475°F (240°C) for 5 minutes, basting with juices. Garnish with fresh basil leaves and serve.

Cave Spring Cellars Riesling B.A.

(FRENCH OAK VINEYARD), JORDAN, ONTARIO

A medium- to full-bodied deep gold wine with apricot flavour and forward aromas of apricot, honey and citrus, which enhance the peach and caramel in this dessert. Botrytis mould affects late-harvested grapes, resulting in concentrated grape sugars and flavours.

WINEMAKER'S TASTING NOTES

GINGER PEACH CRISP | Serves six

Michelle Ramsay

8	peaches, peeled and sliced	8
I tbsp	lemon juice	15 mL
⅓ cup	brown sugar	75 mL
½ cup	pecan pieces	125 mL
2 tbsp	crystallized ginger, finely chopped	25 mL
	Cinnamon to taste	
2 tbsp	flour	25 mL

TOPPING:

I cup	flour	250 mL
½ cup	rolled oats	125 mL
⅔ cup	brown sugar	150 mL
½ tsp	baking soda	2 mL
½ tsp	salt	2 mL
¾ cup	butter pieces	175 mL

1 Combine peaches, lemon juice, brown sugar, pecans, ginger, cinnamon and flour. Pour into 11-inch (27-cm) deep-dish pie plate. **2** To make topping, combine flour, oats, brown sugar, soda and salt. Cut in butter pieces until mixture is crumbly. **3** Pour topping over peaches. Bake at 350°F (180°C) for 30 minutes or until topping is golden.

BRANDIED PEACHES | Serves four

*Brights Wines, Oliver,
British Columbia*

BRIGHTS WINES was the first to produce premium varietal wines from British Columbia-grown grapes. They now purchase more than 800 tons of Okanagan grapes annually to produce their VQA wines—Chardonnay, Pinot Blanc, Riesling and late harvest Vidal. Brights also bottles wines from Chile, France, Australia and California, which they label TGB International. Most popular of all, however, are their house blends, Entre-Lacs, Toscano Bianco and Rosso. Winemaker Lynn Bremmer chose this recipe to accompany her VQA Proprietors Reserve Johannisberg Riesling.

¼ cup	butter	50 mL
½ cup	brown sugar	125 mL
¼ cup	brandy	50 mL
¼ tsp	cinnamon	I mL
4	Okanagan peaches, peeled and halved	4

1 In a small saucepan, melt butter. Stir in brown sugar, brandy and cinnamon. **2** In a shallow baking dish, arrange peaches, cut side down, and spoon brandy mixture over them. Bake at 350°F (180°C) for 25 to 30 minutes, basting occasionally. Serve with vanilla ice cream or frozen yogurt.

Brights Wines Proprietors Reserve Johannisberg Riesling

Harvested from South Okanagan Vineyards, Brights Proprietors Reserve Johannisberg Riesling is light gold with a floral, fruity nose and hints of honey, apples and spice on the palate. Its tart acidity cleans the palate while adding a refreshing contrast to this sweet dessert.

WINEMAKER'S · TASTING NOTES

FONDUE OF PEACHES À LA BOSC | Serves four

Château des Charmes,
Niagara-on-the-Lake, Ontario

CHÂTEAU DES CHARMES' proprietor/winemaker Paul Michel Bosc, Sr., could be called a visionary. When growers were only experimenting with European vines, Bosc was planting his entire 60-acre vineyard with these varieties. He was also the first in Ontario to perfect his use of carbonic maceration, a vinification process used extensively in Burgundy. (In Ontario this technique produces a young, easy-drinking red called Gamay Beaujolais.) Bosc makes a wide range of varietal wines, some rarely found in Ontario (such as Sauvignon Blanc). Château des Charmes' gold and silver medals are proof enough that Bosc takes great pride in his work. He is especially proud of his Estate labelled wines, for they must attain and even surpass the regulations set out by the VQA.

Château des Charmes Champagne Brut

Champagne Brut is the driest of all champagnes, making it a perfect aperitif, the ideal partner for main dishes and a suitable dessert wine. Château des Charmes Champagne Brut is a blend of estate-grown Chardonnay and Pinot Noir grapes. It was made in the traditional méthode champenoise and spent three years in the bottle before being released. With a golden yellow robe, firm Chardonnay fruit overlaid with rich, creamy vanilla flavours, this delicious bubbly works with the natural sweetness found in peaches.

I cup	Château des Charmes Champagne Brut (sparkling wine)	250 mL
2 tbsp	lemon juice	25 mL
2 lb	Niagara peaches, cut in chunks	1 kg
½ lb	cream cheese, softened	250 g
6	squares Baker's White Chocolate, melted	6
¾ cup	sour cream	175 mL
I tsp	vanilla extract	5 mL
2 tsp	butter	10 mL

1 In a bowl combine Champagne Brut and lemon juice; marinate peach chunks at least 5 minutes before serving with fondue. **2** To prepare fondue, combine in fondue pot cream cheese, melted chocolate, sour cream, vanilla and butter. Heat and keep warm.

WINEMAKER'S TASTING NOTES

STRAWBERRIES IN PEPPER AND RED WINE | Serves four

Brights Wines, Longueuil, Quebec

FOR EVERY SEVEN BOTTLES OF WINE sold in Quebec, at least one comes from Brights Wines or their sister company, Les Vins La Salle. About 3 million gallons of wine are made annually by Brights wineries across the country.

2 cups	L'Entre-Côte (red wine)	500 mL
2 tbsp	freshly ground pepper	25 mL
¾ cup	sugar	175 mL
3 cups	strawberries	750 mL

1 In a saucepan, boil wine to evaporate alcohol, about 2 minutes. Lower heat; add pepper and sugar, stirring until sugar is dissolved. Let mixture cool. Filter through a paper coffee filter. **2** Wash and hull strawberries; add to filtered wine. Refrigerate at least 1 hour. Serve cold.

Brights Wines L'Entre-Côte

L'Entre-Côte is a full bodied, well balanced red. With an aroma reminiscent of fresh herbs, wood and spice, this wine is an ideal partner for this peppery dessert.

Suggested Varietal: Cabernet Sauvignon

WINEMAKER'S · TASTING NOTES

FRESH APRICOT AND HAZELNUT TART

Scaramouche, Toronto, Ontario

PASTRY CHEF EXTRAORDINAIRE Joanne Yolles developed this winning combination of fresh apricots and hazelnuts. Her wonderfully innovative desserts have gone a long way towards making Scaramouche one of Toronto's best restaurants.

TART PASTRY:

3 cups	cake-and-pastry flour	750 mL
½ cup	sugar	125 mL
1 cup	cold butter, cut into pieces	250 mL
1	egg	1

FILLING:

½ cup	butter, at room temperature	125 mL
½ cup	sugar	125 mL
2	eggs	2
½ tsp	vanilla extract	2 mL
1 cup	ground lightly toasted hazelnuts	250 mL
2 tbsp	flour	25 mL
¾ cup	apricot jam	175 mL
16 to 18	medium apricots	16 to 18
	Sugar	

1 To make pastry, fit the bowl of a food processor with the metal blade. Place the flour, sugar and butter in the bowl. Process on and off for 10 seconds, until the mixture resembles a coarse meal. Add the egg and process until the dough comes together. If the dough is not too soft, it can be rolled right away. If necessary, flatten into a disc, wrap in plastic wrap and refrigerate for about 1 hour. **2** On a floured surface, roll out the dough about ⅛ inch (3 mm) thick; line a 10-inch (25-cm) flan pan with removable bottom. Chill tart shell for about 1 hour. **3** While tart is chilling, make the filling. In the bowl of a food processor, cream butter and sugar until combined. Add eggs and vanilla. Pulse until eggs are incorporated. Add the ground hazelnuts and flour. Process until smooth. Set aside.
4 Line pastry shell with aluminum foil and pie weights. Bake at 375°F (180°C) for 15 minutes; remove the weights and foil. Prick the pastry with a fork and bake 12 to 15 minutes or until crust is light gold and resembles crispy shortbread. Cool on a rack. **5** Spread ¼ cup (50 mL) apricot jam in tart shell. Spoon filling into the shell, spreading evenly with a spatula. **6** Halve the apricots, remove stones, and cut each half into thirds. Arrange apricots in concentric circles on the hazelnut filling. Sprinkle with sugar. **7** Bake at 375°F (180°C) for 30 to 35 minutes or until filling puffs up. **8** In a small saucepan, heat remaining apricot jam with 2 tsp (10 mL) water, stirring constantly until simmering. Strain through a fine sieve; discard solids. Brush tart with strained preserves. Serve warm or at room temperature with whipped cream or ice cream.

Apple-Grape Tart with Apple Riesling Sabayon

Inniskillin Wines,
Niagara-on-the-Lake, Ontario

THE NAME INNISKILLIN HAS BECOME synonymous with quality throughout the world. Co-owners president Donald Ziraldo and Austrian-born winemaker Karl Kaiser have captured countless gold medals for their varietal wines, the most noteworthy being the Grand Prix d'Honneur for their 1989 Icewine from 1991 VinExpo, the largest international wine competition. With quality as their focus, this dynamic duo has done an exemplary job of distributing their wines to the finest restaurants and wine boutiques in the United States, five European countries and Japan.

The winery possesses a lofty charm. Fronting the meandering Niagara River, the stucco edifice and historic barn are surrounded by lush vineyards. Now under renovation, the winery will soon include a two-storey building containing an atmospherically controlled barrel-ageing centre and underground wine library.

Inniskillin Wines Late Harvest Riesling

This Late Harvest Riesling is light golden in colour and has floral aromas and honey flavours. It has enough sweetness to match the caramel flavours of apples and grapes, yet enough acidity to cut through the richness of the caramel-butter combination.

WINEMAKER'S TASTING NOTES

This recipe is one of the many wonderful entrees served at Inniskillin's gourmet fairs, which are scheduled throughout the year.

SWEET PASTRY:

2 cups	flour	500 mL
Pinch	salt	Pinch
½ cup	cold unsalted butter, cubed	125 mL
⅓ cup plus 1 tbsp	icing sugar, sifted	90 mL
2	egg yolks, lightly beaten	2

FILLING:

⅓ cup plus 1 tbsp	unsalted butter	90 mL
¼ cup	sugar	50 mL
1	vanilla bean split	1
2 cups	peeled and thinly sliced apples (Golden Delicious or Granny Smith)	500 mL
¼ cup	apple brandy	50 mL
⅓ cup plus 1 tbsp	apricot jam	90 mL
7 oz	seedless red grapes, halved	200 g

SABAYON:

5	egg yolks	5
¼ cup	sugar	50 mL
¼ cup	Inniskillin Wines Late Harvest Riesling (white wine)	50 mL

1 To make pastry, sift flour into a large bowl. Add salt and butter. Work lightly and quickly with fingers or pastry cutter until mixture resembles coarse meal. Add icing sugar and egg yolks. Knead lightly until dough just holds together. On a clean surface knead with palm of hand to blend in butter. Do not overwork. Wrap in waxed paper and chill for at least 30 minutes. **2** To make filling, in a large skillet melt butter over moderate heat. Add sugar and cook for 2 to 3 minutes, stirring constantly. Split vanilla bean lengthwise and scrape seeds into mixture. Add apples, increase heat to high, and turn apples to coat well with butter mixture. When apples begin to turn golden, add 4 tsp (20 mL) apple brandy; stir and remove from heat. Set aside to cool. **3** On a floured surface, roll out dough and line a 9-inch (23-cm) tart pan. Bake pastry at 425°F (220°C) for 10-12 minutes. Cool. **4** In a non stick skillet over low heat, melt apricot jam. Brush 2 tbsp (25 mL) melted jam over crust. Keep the rest warm. Arrange apple slices, overlapping slightly, around outside of tart. Arrange grape halves in a ring, and fill centre with apple slices. **5** Bake tart at 425°F (220°C) for 20 minutes. Brush with remaining melted jam. **6** Just before serving, make sabayon. In a medium saucepan, combine egg yolks, sugar, wine and remaining apple brandy. Whisk vigorously over low heat until thick and frothy, about 10 minutes. Serve immediately with tart.

TARTE AU VIN À LA VOUDOISE

St. Hubertus Vineyard,
Kelowna, British Columbia

FOR THE PAST SIX YEARS, Leo and Barbara Gebert have grown premium wine grapes on their 25-acre vineyard in Kelowna for such important clients as Mission Hill Vineyards. In 1992, they embarked upon the biggest venture of their lives: they opened their own winery, St. Hubertus Vineyard. With a maximum tank capacity of 10,000 gallons, this farm winery will produce many fine vintages of Maréchal Foch, Johannisberg Riesling, Verdelet and Pinot Blanc. Their 1991 Maréchal Foch won first place at the 1992 Winemasters' Selection.

St. Hubertus Vineyard Pinot Blanc

Normally, dry white wines taste too acidic when served with desserts. This dessert, however, calls for wine in the recipe, which brings to this particular marriage a common denominator of acid and fruit. St. Hubertus Vineyard Pinot Blanc has a honey nose and buttery palate that also enhances the creamy texture of this wine cake.

WINEMAKER'S TASTING NOTES

SHORTCAKE:

2 cups	flour	500 mL
½ tsp	salt	2 mL
2 tsp	sugar	10 mL
¼ cup	butter, cut in pieces	125 mL
I	egg, beaten	I

FILLING:

½ cup	sugar	125 mL
¼ tsp	cinnamon	I mL
I tbsp	flour	15 mL
1⅔ cups	St. Hubertus Vineyards Pinot Blanc (white wine)	400 mL
	A few butter flecks	

1 To make shortcake, in a bowl mix flour, salt and sugar. Add pieces of butter and work in with hands until mixture is crumbly. Add egg and mix into a paste. Refrigerate for 30 minutes. On a clean surface, roll out the cooled paste; fit it into an 11-inch (28-cm) round cake pan. **2** To make filling, combine sugar, cinnamon and flour; pour over the paste. Carefully pour wine over top. Spread butter flecks over batter. **3** Bake on the bottom rack at 425°F (220°C) for 35 minutes or until light golden. The cake will still be moist and viscous.

Mascarpone all'Arancia con Frutti di Bosco | Serves four

Café Roma, North Vancouver, British Columbia

THE CORSI BROTHERS, Mario and Antonio, have found that this Italian trifle-like recipe is a winner at their café.

2	egg yolks	2
2 tbsp	sugar	25 mL
2 tbsp	Grand Marnier	25 mL
7 oz	mascarpone cheese	200 g
½ cup	whipping cream	125 mL
8	ladyfingers	8
½ cup	orange juice	125 mL
I cup	blueberries, strawberries or raspberries	250 mL
2 tsp	shaved chocolate	10 mL

1 In a mixing bowl, whisk together egg yolks and sugar until sugar is completely dissolved and a long ribbon is formed when the whisk is lifted from the mixture.
2 Beat in Grand Marnier until the mixture is very thick and doubled in volume. Stir in mascarpone and cream.
3 Soak ladyfingers in orange juice. Place two fingers on each plate, top with berries and pour cream mixture over all. Sprinkle with shaved chocolate and serve.

Quails' Gate Estate Winery Late Harvest Optima B.A.

WESTBANK, BRITISH COLUMBIA

Inspired by the great Tokaji of Hungary and the great Sauternes of France when developing this wine, Quails' Gate has come up with an ambrosia-like wine that is ideal with coffee, dessert or for sipping. The distinct fruity flavours of peach, apricot and nectarine combine well with the fruit in this dessert. A slightly nutty taste and toasty bouquet and a good acidic balance cut through the creaminess of the mascarpone cheese.

THE STUDIO CAFÉ'S WARM MANGO RICE PUDDING WITH COCONUT ICE CREAM AND COCONUT CURLS | Serves four

Four Seasons Hotel, Toronto, Ontario

ONCE AGAIN EXECUTIVE CHEF Susan Weaver has come up with a winning combination. This East-West recipe uses tropical ingredients in a simple rice pudding recipe, creating an exciting and exotic dessert.

Vineland Estates Riesling Late Harvest

(ST. URBAN VINEYARD), VINELAND, ONTARIO

A perfect medium between Vineland's 1989 Riesling Icewine and 1989 Riesling Late Harvest, this wine has a distinct violet nose with kiwifruit aromas that bring out the exotic mango flavours of this dessert. A succulent, sweet taste is offset by a young but pointy acidity that provides a counterpoint to the coconut ice cream and enhances the mango flavours.

WINEMAKER'S · TASTING NOTES

PUDDING:

2¾ cups	milk	675 mL
½ cup	long-grain rice	125 mL
I	vanilla bean, cut in half	I
Pinch	salt	Pinch
2½ tbsp	butter	35 mL
⅓ cup	sugar	75 mL
I	mango, peeled, flesh chopped and puréed	I
¼ cup	whipping cream	50 mL

PASSION FRUIT PURÉE:

I cup	orange juice	250 mL
3	passion fruits, halved and pulp removed	3
⅓ cup	sugar	75 mL
2½ tbsp	butter	35 mL

GARNISHES:

	Fresh berries of choice	
	Mint leaves	
4	thinly sliced fresh coconut curls, toasted	4
	Coconut ice cream	

1 To make rice pudding, in a medium saucepan, combine milk, rice, vanilla bean and salt; simmer over medium-high heat until rice is tender, about 8 to 10 minutes. Stir in butter, sugar and mango purée. Simmer for 5 minutes; discard vanilla bean. Let cool. **2** In a small bowl, whip cream until soft peaks form; fold into rice mixture. Spoon pudding into serving dishes and refrigerate for 2 hours. **3** Just before serving, make the passion fruit purée. In a medium saucepan, combine orange juice, passion fruits, sugar and butter. Cook over low heat until sauce thickens, about 20 minutes. Spoon warm passion fruit sauce onto puddings. Garnish with berries, mint and coconut curl. Serve with coconut ice cream.

Green Apple Crème Brûlée | Serves six

Bishop's, Vancouver, British Columbia

Chef Adam Busby takes a twist on crème brûlée by flavouring it with tart green apples.

6	Granny Smith apples	6
	Lemon slices	
I cup	whipping cream	250 mL
4	egg yolks	4
2 tbsp	sugar	25 mL
Pinch	salt	Pinch
I	vanilla bean	I
	Zest of I orange	
	Sugar for dusting	

1 Using a sharp paring knife, slightly trim apple bottoms so apples stand upright. Slice off top one-quarter of apple. Using a sharp scoop or melon-baller, carefully scoop out each apple, leaving walls ¼ inch (5 mm) thick. Rub the inside of each apple with a slice of lemon to prevent browning; arrange apple shells in a baking pan. **2** In a large mixing bowl, whisk together cream, egg yolks, sugar and salt. Slit vanilla bean down one side and scrape seeds into custard mixture. Stir in orange zest. **3** Pour custard into the apple shells and bake, on the middle rack, at 300°F (150°C) for 20 minutes. Let apples cool to room temperature, then refrigerate. **4** Using a sieve, sprinkle a fine coating of sugar on the top of each custard. Place under a very hot grill until the sugar is evenly caramelized. Refrigerate again until the caramel is cool and set.

TIRAMISÙ | Serves eight to ten

Ristorante Giardino, The Gate House Hotel, Niagara-on-the-Lake, Ontario

CHEF TULLIO CALVELLO says the secret to this dessert is the freshest eggs and mascarpone. The biscuits are sold at Italian grocery stores and large supermarkets.

CREAM MIXTURE:

1½ cups	sugar	375 mL
13	egg yolks	13
3 cups	mascarpone cheese	750 mL
2 cups	whipping cream	500 mL
7	egg whites	7
¾ cup	espresso coffee, cooled	175 mL
¾ cup	Marsala	175 mL
2 cups	sugar	500 mL
3	pkg (500 g) Savoiardi cookies	3
Unsweetened cocoa powder for dusting		

Inniskillin Wines Icewine (Vidal)

NIAGARA-ON-THE-LAKE, ONTARIO

Richly aromatic with concentrated flavours and tropical aromas, this wine has a sturdy acidity that balances the lofty level of residual sugar. A potent enough wine for this sweet dessert.

WINEMAKER'S TASTING NOTES

1 In a bowl, beat 1½ cups (375 mL) sugar and egg yolks until fluffy. Slowly incorporate mascarpone cheese and beat for 30 seconds. Set aside. **2** Whip cream until stiff. Whip egg whites until stiff. **3** Fold whipped cream and egg whites into mascarpone mixture; refrigerate for 5 to 10 minutes. **4** In a shallow dish, combine coffee, Marsala and 2 cups (500 mL) sugar until sugar is dissolved. Soak Savoiardi cookies in coffee liquid. Drain off excess coffee. **5** Layer about half the cookies in an 11- x 7-inch (2-L) shallow dish, covering entire bottom. Cover with half the cheese mixture. Dust evenly with cocoa. Cover with remaining soaked cookies; top with remaining cheese mixture. Allow to set in refrigerator for at least 2 hours. Before serving, dust with sifted cocoa.

Housed in the elegant, refurbished Gate House Hotel, Giardino's serves superb Italian food in a setting of polished Italian marble and black leather. Operated by the Dalavalla family, the 10-room inn and restaurant places a premium on quality. Carpaccio served with colourful marinated vegetables, smoked goose breast with sautéed mushrooms, and an authentic Osso Bucco are carefully created by chef Tullio Calvello.

RAINTREE BREAD AND BUTTER PUDDING WITH DRIED FRUIT WITH PINOT NOIR | Serves six

Lang Vineyards, Naramata, British Columbia

RUNNING PARALLEL TO Okanagan Lake, Naramata Road passes vineyards, abundant orchards and some of the prettiest countryside in the south Okanagan Valley. Amongst this inherent beauty you'll find a treasure called Lang Vineyards. This farm winery concentrates on producing limited quantities of premium varietal wines, such as Maréchal Foch, Pinot Noir, Pinot Meunier, Gewürztraminer and Riesling. Winemaker Guenther Lang uses 100 per cent of a specified grape variety to make his wines, all produced according to VQA standards.

Lang Vineyards Pinot Noir

Medium in colour and body, Lang Vineyards Pinot Noir has a silky texture and exhibits intense cherry aromas and ripe cherry-spicy flavours that heighten the taste of dried fruit in this dish. It should be served slightly chilled, which adds a refreshing contrast to this warm dessert.

Developed by chef Anthony Hodda of The Raintree Restaurant in Vancouver, this recipe is a superb companion to Lang Vineyards' 1991 Pinot Noir.

3 oz	prunes, pitted and chopped	90 g
2 tbsp	red wine	25 mL
2½ cups	milk	625 mL
4	eggs	4
1 cup	confectioners' sugar	250 mL
1 tsp	cinnamon	5 mL
1 tsp	nutmeg	5 mL
10 oz	stale ladyfingers	300 g
¼ cup	unsalted butter, cut into bits	50 mL

DRIED FRUIT COMPOTE:

2 cups	Lang Vineyards Pinot Noir (red wine)	500 mL
¼ cup	brown sugar	50 mL
¼ cup	unsalted butter	50 mL
	Nutmeg to taste	
1 lb	mixed dried figs, plums, apricots, pears and raisins	500 g
	Whipped cream OR crème fraîche (for garnish)	

1 Soak prunes in 2 tbsp (25 mL) red wine overnight.
2 In a saucepan, boil milk. In a bowl, beat together eggs
and sugar; whisk into milk. Add cinnamon and nutmeg.
Set aside. **3** Layer prunes and biscuits in individual
ramekins. Dot with butter. Fill ramekins with the custard.
4 Bake at 350°F (180°C) for 30 to 40 minutes or until
top is golden. **5** In a saucepan, heat red wine; stir in
brown sugar until dissolved. Stir in butter, nutmeg and
dried fruit. Simmer for 10 minutes. **6** Unmould puddings onto serving plates and spoon dried fruit compote
around them. Garnish with dollop of whipped cream or
crème fraîche.

*I*CEWINE SUNDAE | Serves four

Vineland Estates, Vineland, Ontario

WHAT COULD BE MORE ROMANTIC than sipping a crisp, dry Riesling and nibbling a slice of smoked salmon while watching a brilliant sun sink behind rolling vineyards and disappear into the blues of Lake Ontario? This is the setting of the wine deck at Vineland Estates. There is more to this winery than its postcard beauty, however. Vineland Estates' varietal wines have been described as some of the best Ontario has to offer. Winemaker Allan Schmidt produces a wide range of whites and reds, all made from grapes grown in the St. Urban Vineyard on the bench in Niagara. The winery is best known for their Riesling, Chardonnay and Icewine.

Vineland Estates Vidal Icewine

Vineland Estates Vidal Icewine is made from frozen grapes hand-picked in winter in temperatures a little below freezing. The berries are pressed immediately, releasing a syrupy juice with concentrated flavours, sugar and acidity. Fermented for six months in stainless steel, this wine is well balanced with peachy aromas and lush, tropical fruit flavours that please the palate when consumed alone or when married with fresh fruit.

WINEMAKER'S TASTING NOTES

2	mandarins	2
2	oranges	2
2	Niagara peaches	2
2	kiwifruits	2
I	cantaloupe	I
½ lb	seedless green grapes	250 g
2 cups	strawberries	500 mL
½ cup	Vineland Estates Vidal Icewine	125 mL
	Vanilla ice cream	
	Whipped cream and mint leaves (for garnish)	

1 Peel and slice mandarins, oranges, peaches and kiwifruits. Use melon-baller to cut up cantaloupe. In a bowl, blend prepared fruits, grapes and strawberries. **2** Pour icewine over fruit and marinate overnight in refrigerator. **3** In individual sherbet dishes, place a scoop of vanilla ice cream and top with fruit. Pour I oz (25 mL) marinade over each dish of fruit. Garnish each dish with whipped cream and a mint leaf. Serve immediately.

FRESH SUMMER PLUM SOUP WITH SOUR CREAM AND LEMON ICE CREAM | Serves four

Café Bruges, London, Ontario

THIS UNUSUAL RECIPE BY chef/owner Steve James is a delicious combination of tart and sweet.

SOUR CREAM AND LEMON ICE CREAM:

2 cups	sour cream	500 mL
⅔ cup	sugar	150 mL
¼ cup	whipping cream	50 mL
	Zest and juice of 1 lemon	

1 In a large mixing bowl, whisk together sour cream, sugar, whipping cream, lemon zest and lemon juice. Chill for 30 minutes. **2** Freeze in ice-cream machine according to manufacturer's instructions.

PLUM SOUP:

2 cups	pitted sugar plums	500 mL
2 cups	Inniskillin Wines Vidal (white wine)	500 mL
⅔ cup	sugar	150 mL
1	vanilla bean	1
1 tsp	gelatin	5 mL
1½ tsp	plum liqueur	7 mL
	Fresh mint (for garnish)	

1 Place the plums, wine, sugar and vanilla bean in a saucepan. Cook until plums are soft and tender. Remove vanilla bean, split lengthwise and scrape seeds into plum mixture. In a food processor or blender, blend plum mixture and pass it through a fine sieve. Discard pulp. **2** Dissolve gelatin in ½ cup (125 mL) warm water. Stir into plum mixture. Stir in plum liqueur. **3** Ladle into chilled bowls and top with Sour Cream and Lemon Ice Cream. Garnish with fresh mint.

Château des Charmes Canadian Champagne Sec

NIAGARA-ON-THE-LAKE, ONTARIO

A blend of estate-grown Riesling, Gamay Beaujolais and Chardonnay grapes, this wine is made in the méthode champenoise. Straw-coloured with fine persistent bubbles, it has a candied floral bouquet and predominant Riesling fruit. This wine has enough acid to cut through the creaminess of the dessert, while its fruit flavours work with the plums.

WINEMAKER'S · TASTING NOTES

Despite the sophistication of a big-city restaurant, Café Bruges retains its small-city friendliness, making for a relaxed foray into exceptional cuisine.

LEMON AND BLUEBERRY MOUSSE | Serves eight

Silver Spoon Restaurant and Café, Halifax, Nova Scotia

DEANNA SILVER HAS BEEN satisfying the Halifax sweet tooth with her amazing desserts for more than a dozen years.

Jost Vineyards Blush

MALAGASH, NOVA SCOTIA

Produced from freshly pressed Nova Scotia grapes and blueberries, this wine has a fruity sweetness that offsets the lemon yet complements the blueberries in this dessert.

4	large egg yolks	4
½ cup	sugar	125 mL
Pinch	salt	Pinch
¼ cup	lemon juice	50 mL
½ tsp	grated lemon rind	2 mL
½ tsp	vanilla extract	2 mL
4	egg whites	4
½ cup	whipping cream, whipped	125 mL
2 cups	blueberries	500 mL

1 Beat egg yolks in top of double boiler. Gradually add sugar, salt, lemon juice, lemon rind and vanilla extract, beating constantly. Place over hot, not boiling, water; cook, stirring, until mixture is thick and smooth. Remove from heat and cool, stirring occasionally. **2** Beat egg whites until stiff. Fold whites and whipped cream into cooled yolk mixture. **3** Spoon some of the pudding into one large serving bowl or eight tall goblets; top with a layer of berries. Spoon on remaining pudding and top with remaining berries.

RASPBERRY HAZELNUT MERINGUE | Serves six to eight

The Angel Inn,
Niagara-on-the-Lake, Ontario

THIS LIGHT AND DELICIOUS dessert is a favourite of patrons at The Angel Inn.

6	egg whites	6
I cup	sugar	250 mL
½ tsp	vinegar	2 mL
3	drops vanilla extract	3
¾ cup	toasted ground hazelnuts	175 mL
I cup	whipping cream, whipped	250 mL
I cup	fresh raspberries	250 mL

1 Whip egg whites until soft. Add sugar I tbsp (I5 mL) at a time, beating until very stiff. **2** Blend in vinegar, vanilla and ground hazelnuts. **3** Pour into three well-greased and floured nonstick 8-inch (I.2-L) round cake pans. Bake at 350°F (I80°C) for 20 minutes. Reduce heat to 300°F (I50°C) and bake I0 minutes. Turn out onto racks and let cool. **4** To assemble the cake, cover a meringue slab with ⅓ of whipped cream and raspberries. Cover with second meringue slab and repeat. Decorate top slab with remaining cream and berries. Chill before serving.

Marynissen Estates Chardonnay

(BARREL-FERMENTED),

NIAGARA-ON-THE-LAKE,

ONTARIO

One of the least dry Niagara Chardonnays, this wine's complex taste is a piquant complement to the sweetness of the meringue. A full-bodied Chardonnay full of nuance, it has tropical banana, melon and apple flavours with a smoky, buttery character and a long finish with butterscotch overtones.

WINEMAKER'S TASTING NOTES

BLUEBERRIES AND CREAM CHEESE
CRÊPES | Serves eight

*Shari Darling / Magnotta Winery,
Vaughan, Ontario*

WINE BARONS Gabe and Rossana Magnotta have become major players in Ontario's wine industry. In 1992 they entered their 1990 Cabernet Sauvignon Limited Edition in the InterVin International Wine Competition and the International Eastern Wine Competition and prevailed with two gold medals. Some of this success can be attributed to Alejandro Di Miguel, winemaker at Magnotta. He graduated from the Faculty of Oenology, Fruit and Horticultural Industries of Don Bosco at the University Juan A. Maza Mendoza in Argentina and has more than twenty years of practical experience in winemaking. Among their many products, Magnotta produces topnotch varietal wines exclusively from Niagara Peninsula grapes. Consequently, two of these wines—the 1991 Icewine Vidal Limited Edition and 1991 Chardonnay Lenko Vineyards—were awarded VQA Gold Medallions.

Magnotta Icewine Vidal Limited Edition

Golden in colour, this dessert wine is lusciously rich. Possessing concentrated tropical fruit aromas and flavours, it is the perfect partner for this rich, fruity dessert.

WINEMAKER'S TASTING NOTES

½ lb	cream cheese, softened	250 g
1 tbsp	sugar	15 mL
¼ tsp	salt	1 mL
1 tbsp	whipping cream	15 mL
3	eggs, beaten	3
3 tbsp plus 1 tsp	flour	55 mL
1 tbsp	brandy	15 mL
¼ tsp	vanilla extract	1 mL

FILLING:

2 cups	blueberries	500 mL
½ cup	sugar	125 mL
1 tbsp	grated orange peel	15 mL
Pinch	cinnamon	Pinch
¼ cup	Magnotta Icewine	50 mL

■ To make crêpes, in a bowl beat softened cream cheese until fluffy; stir in sugar and salt. Add cream and beat mixture until soft. Stir in eggs a little at a time. Add flour, brandy and vanilla; blend until batter is smooth. Let batter rest for 30 minutes. **2** Wipe a 6-inch (15-cm) nonstick crêpe pan or skillet with 2 tsp (10 mL) butter and set pan over medium heat. Spoon in 2 tbsp (25 mL) batter and cook crêpe until surface looks dry, about 30 seconds. Make eight crêpes. Cover and keep warm in oven.

3 To make filling, in a blender or food processor purée ½ cup (125 mL) blueberries. Set aside. **4** In a saucepan over medium heat, blend sugar and 1 cup (250 mL) water; stir until sugar is dissolved. Bring to a boil. Reduce heat to low. Stir in purée, orange peel, cinnamon and icewine. Bring to a simmer. Add remaining berries and stir until they begin to burst, about 2 minutes. Set berries aside to steep in syrup for about 5 minutes. **5** Gently reheat stewed blueberries. Place finished crêpe, pale side up, on a serving plate and spoon a generous measure of berries in a thick line across centre of crêpe. Fold one edge of crêpe so that it covers some of the filling, then bring up the opposite edge. The two edges should overlap slightly in the middle.

RASPBERRY YOGURT CHEESE NAPOLEONS | Serves six

Drawbridge Inn, Sarnia, Ontario

THIS LOW-CALORIE DESSERT was developed by Doug Tarry, the creative young chef at the Drawbridge Inn. He is a proponent of the freshest local ingredients and grows his own herbs and organic vegetables.

This dessert must be started the day before. Make the yogurt cheese, raspberry purée and lemon sauce. The next day finish the filling, bake the phyllo and assemble the dish.

2 cups	plain low-fat yogurt	500 mL

RASPBERRY PURÉE:

¼ cup	sugar	50 mL
1 cup	raspberries	250 mL
	Juice of ½ lemon	

LEMON SAUCE:

	Juice and rind of 1 lemon	
3 oz	orange juice	90 mL
½ cup	sugar	125 mL
3	egg yolks	3

FILLING:

¼ cup	sugar	50 mL
1 tbsp	gelatin	15 mL
	Juice of ½ lemon	

PASTRY:

¾ cup	ground almonds	175 mL
2 tbsp	brown sugar	25 mL
4	sheets phyllo pastry	4
½ cup	unsalted butter, melted	125 mL
½ cup	sliced almonds	125 mL
2 tbsp	icing sugar	25 mL

1 To make yogurt cheese, place yogurt in strainer lined with cheesecloth or in paper coffee filter and drain overnight, refrigerated. **2** To make raspberry purée, in a small saucepan combine sugar and ¼ cup (50 mL) water; bring to a boil and reduce by one-third. Let cool. **3** Combine raspberries, lemon juice and ¼ cup (50 mL) cooled sugar syrup. Process in blender and pass purée through strainer. Refrigerate overnight. **4** To make lemon sauce, in a small saucepan bring to a boil lemon juice, rind, orange juice and 3 oz (90 mL) water. In the top of a double boiler, cream sugar and yolks well. Gradually whisk in boiled lemon mixture. Place over hot, not boiling, water, and cook 5 minutes, stirring often as sauce thickens. Let cool and refrigerate overnight. **5** The next day, make the filling. In a bowl, dissolve sugar and gelatin in I cup (250 mL) boiling water. Add lemon juice and I cup (250 mL) raspberry purée. (Reserve remaining purée for garnish.) Refrigerate, stirring occasionally; when almost set, fold in yogurt cheese completely. Spread in a 13- x 9-inch (3.5-L) baking dish and refrigerate at least 2 hours. When thoroughly chilled, carefully cut into twelve 3-inch (8-cm) squares. You will have a I-inch (2.5-cm) ridge of filling left over. **6** In a bowl, combine ground almonds and brown sugar. **7** Spread one sheet of phyllo onto a work surface; brush with melted butter. Sprinkle with one-third of almond mixture. Repeat with next two layers of phyllo. Top with last layer and brush with remaining melted butter. Carefully cut layers into 18 3-inch (8-cm) squares. Sprinkle six of the layers with the sliced almonds (these will be used for the tops of napoleons.) Bake layers on baking sheet at 350°F (180°C) until golden brown, about 3 minutes. Cool on rack. Dust the six top pieces with icing sugar. **8** To assemble, pour a pool of lemon sauce onto each plate. On sauce, place one layer of phyllo, top with square of raspberry yogurt filling, cover with another layer of phyllo and another square of filling. Top with the phyllo pieces covered in sliced almonds and icing sugar. **9** To garnish, on perimeter of lemon sauce, drop several small dollops of remaining raspberry purée. Using a butter knife, pull on drops to create teardrop effect. Serve immediately.

PULLED APPLE STRUDEL WITH
CUSTARD | Serves ten to twelve

*The Cellar Bench Restaurant Wine Bar,
St. Catharines, Ontario*

CHEF GREGORY WILLIS has had many requests for this old-fashioned strudel recipe. The abundance of cinnamon creates a spicy dessert.

Cave Spring Cellars
Indian Summer Riesling

JORDAN, ONTARIO

Estate-bottled, this wine has signature Riesling fruit character with pear and lichee predominating. This wine is acidic enough to balance the sugar and cut through the custard in this dessert. The fruitiness perfectly offsets the pastry.

WINEMAKER'S TASTING NOTES

STRUDEL PASTRY:

2 tbsp	sugar	25 mL
2 tsp	salt	10 mL
2	eggs	2
¼ cup	oil	50 mL
2¼ cups	hard flour	550 mL
¾ lb	butter, melted	375 g
1½ cups	ground hazelnuts	375 mL

FILLING:

6 cups	peeled, sliced apples (preferably Gravenstein)	1.5 L
1 cup	raisins	250 mL
⅔ cup	brown sugar	150 mL
6 tbsp	cinnamon	90 mL
	Icing sugar (for garnish)	

CUSTARD:

5	egg yolks	5
⅔ cup	sugar	150 mL
1 tsp	vanilla extract	5 mL
1 tbsp	cornstarch	25 mL
2 cups	milk	500 mL

1 To make the pastry, blend sugar, salt, eggs, oil and I cup (250 mL) water. Sift in the flour, mixing to a smooth texture. Place on an oiled baking sheet and brush with additional oil. Let rest at room temperature I hour.

2 To make the filling, in a bowl combine apples, raisins, brown sugar and cinnamon. **3** Cover a table with a cloth and work flour into it. Place dough on cloth and gently pull dough to edges of table, being careful not to tear it.

4 Brush most of melted butter over dough; sprinkle with hazelnuts. Cover one edge of the dough, in a lengthwise band, with the apple filling. Hold the cloth at the leading edge and lift so the dough and filling flip over. Tightly roll the strudel until it is straight and rolled up snugly.

5 Line a baking sheet with parchment paper. Cut strudel to fit baking sheet. Brush with remaining melted butter. Bake at 425°F (220°C) for 20 minutes or until golden.

6 To make custard, in a saucepan blend egg yolks, sugar, vanilla and cornstarch. In a second saucepan, scald milk. Gradually whisk scalded milk into egg mixture. Bring just to a boil, stirring. Remove from heat and whisk. Chill.

7 To assemble, smooth some of the chilled custard onto each plate. Slice strudel and place on custard. Sprinkle strudel with icing sugar and serve.

TWO-LAYER CHERRY TORTE

Shari Darling / Montravin Cellars, Beamsville, Ontario

MONTRAVIN CELLARS IS Ontario's leading producer of sparkling wines. Winemaker Romi Szydelko produces four bubblies, ranging from Podamer Brut (Dry) to a sweet Podamer Special Reserve. Made exclusively from Ontario grapes, mostly Pinot Noir and Chardonnay, the Podamer sparkling wines are made in the traditional méthode champenoise. Podamer sparkling wines are aged between three and five years before being released to the public. Romi Szydelko feels there's a natural affinity between the wines and fruits produced in the Niagara Peninsula. This dessert perfectly combines both.

Podamer Special Reserve

Because of its effervescence, sparkling wine has the ability to cut through rich, fatty or sweet foods. For this reason it is the perfect accompaniment to most meals, from breakfast to dessert. Montravin's Podamer Special Reserve is a full-bodied sparkling wine made from a blend of French hybrid and vinifera grapes. It has a toast-like yeasty character, a hint of sweetness and a soft finish, accompanied by a long-lasting mousseux. These elements marry well with this sweet dessert, while cleaning the palate between bites.

PASTRY SHELL:

1	moist vanilla bean	1
¼ cup	unsalted butter, softened	50 mL
½ cup	icing sugar, sifted	125 mL
2	large egg yolks, room temperature	2
1 cup	flour, sifted	250 mL
Pinch	salt	Pinch

FILLING:

1 lb	sweet cherries, pitted	500 g
1 tbsp	cherry brandy	15 mL
2 tbsp	sugar	25 mL
1 cup	toasted sliced almonds	250 mL

BATTER:

2	large eggs	2
½ cup	sugar	125 mL
⅓ cup	whipping cream	75 mL
⅓ cup	homogenized milk	75 mL
1 tbsp	cherry brandy	15 mL

¼ tsp	almond extract	I mL
	Icing sugar (for garnish)	

1 To make pastry shell, cut vanilla bean lengthwise and scrape seeds into a food processor. Add butter and mix until smooth and aerated. Add icing sugar and process until completely blended. Add egg yolks and process again. Add flour and salt; process until flour is moist. (If dough is sticky, add more flour and process again.) The dough should not form a ball. **2** Transfer dough to a sheet of waxed paper. With hands, gently form dough into a ball, then flatten into a circle. Wrap in plastic wrap and refrigerate for at least I hour. **3** Butter bottom and sides of 9-inch (23-cm) tart pan with removable bottom. On a clean piece of waxed paper, carefully roll out dough into an II-inch (28-cm) circle. Lifting it by the waxed paper, invert dough into the pan. Discard waxed paper. Without stretching the dough, pat it into the rim of the pan, allowing a I-inch (2.5-cm) overhang. Prick dough all over and refrigerate at least I hour. **4** Remove tart shell from pan and place on baking sheet. Bake at 375°F (190°C) for 5 minutes until pastry begins to firm up. Trim off the overhanging pastry; crumble pastry trimmings and set aside. Return shell to oven and bake for I5 minutes more, until pastry is brown around edges. Cool on a rack.
5 To make filling, in a heatproof baking dish, combine cherries, cherry brandy, sugar and almonds; stir to dissolve sugar. Bake at 425°F (220°C) for 5 minutes or until cherries are steaming. Drain off juice. **6** To make batter, with an electric mixer beat eggs until frothy. Add sugar, cream, milk, cherry brandy and almond extract. Blend well. **7** Pour cherry filling into pastry shell. Sprinkle with crumbled pastry trimmings. Carefully pour batter over trimmings. Bake for 35 to 40 minutes or until batter is golden and firm. Let cool on baking sheet. **8** When torte is cool, sprinkle top evenly and generously with icing sugar. Place under broiler, about I inch (2.5 cm) from heat; broil for I minute or until sugar is caramelized and golden. Cool on a rack. Serve at room temperature.

GELATO DI NOCCIOLE (HAZELNUT ICE CREAM) | Makes 1½ pints (625 mL)

Michelle Ramsay

FOR BEST RESULTS, serve gelato on the day it is made.

London Winery Cream Port

LONDON, ONTARIO

Aged in white oak casks, this sweet, tawny wine has rich, robust and mellow flavours that complement the nutty flavour of this ice cream.

1 cup	whole hazelnuts	250 mL
2 cups	homogenized milk	500 mL
¾ cup	whipping cream	175 mL
3 tbsp	corn syrup	50 mL
⅔ cup	sugar	150 mL
⅓ cup	nonfat dry milk powder	75 mL
½ tsp	granulated gelatin	2 mL
2 tsp	vanilla extract	10 mL

1 Toast hazelnuts in a 350°F (180°C) oven for 10 minutes. Wrap in a tea towel and rub to remove skins. Grind finely in a food processor. Let cool. **2** In a saucepan, combine milk, cream and corn syrup. In a bowl, mix sugar, milk powder and gelatin. Add dry ingredients to milk mixture, whisking to prevent lumps. Place saucepan over low heat and bring to a simmer. Whisk in hazelnuts. Remove from heat, cover and steep for 10 minutes. **3** Pour mixture through a fine mesh strainer; let cool. Freeze in an ice-cream maker, following manufacturer's instructions. When gelato is frozen, transfer to an airtight container, packing it down and pressing plastic wrap against the surface. Cover and store in freezer until served.

*F*ROZEN MAPLE HAZELNUT SOUR CREAM | Serves four to six

The Britton House, Gananoque, Ontario

MARK BUSSIÈRES updates the French-Canadian sugar pie with this creamy concoction. This "ice cream" has a lovely sweet/tart balance and can be used in place of vanilla ice cream.

¼ lb	hazelnuts	125 g
6	egg yolks	6
I cup	maple syrup	250 mL
2¼ cups	sour cream	550 mL
3 oz	sugar	90 mL
2 tbsp	maple liqueur	25 mL
I tbsp	lemon juice	15 mL

1 Toast hazelnuts in a 350°F (180°C) oven for 10 minutes. Wrap in a tea towel and rub to remove skins. Coarsely chop in a food processor. Let cool. **2** Using an electric mixer, beat yolks until light and fluffy. While beating, add syrup in a steady stream until fully incorporated.
3 Add sour cream, sugar, maple liqueur and lemon juice; beat until well mixed. Fold in nuts. **4** Freeze mixture in an ice-cream maker, following manufacturer's instructions.

Cave Spring Cellars Riesling B.A.

JORDAN, ONTARIO

The excellent sweet-tart balance in this dessert wine complements the "ice cream." Undertones of peach and apricot plus the acid backbone and the distinct flavour imparted by "noble rot" help cut through the richness of maple syrup and sour cream.

WINEMAKER'S TASTING NOTES

BELGIAN CHOCOLATE SIN CAKE

The Cannery,
Vancouver, British Columbia

FAMOUS FOR ITS FISH AND SEAFOOD and a breathtaking waterfront view, this member of the Bud Kanke seafood group creates some deadly decadent desserts.

Calona Wines Late Bottled Vintage Port

KELOWNA, BRITISH COLUMBIA

This vintage port has a spicy aroma that is a complex mix of vanilla and cherry with oak, providing an ideal complement to desserts rich in chocolate, fruit and nuts. This port won a bronze medal for Winemaster's Selection at the Okanagan Wine Festival in 1990.

CAKE:

I cup	flour	250 mL
½ cup	Dutch-processed cocoa	125 mL
Pinch	baking soda	Pinch
6	extra-large eggs	6
½ cup plus 2 tbsp	sugar	150 mL

ICING:

I lb	semi-sweet chocolate (preferably Callebaut)	500 g
4 cups	whipping cream	I L

I cup chocolate shavings (make with vegetable peeler)	250 mL

1 Lightly grease bottom and sides of a 9-inch (2.5-L) springform pan. **2** In a bowl, sift flour, cocoa and baking soda. **3** Beat eggs on high speed for 5 minutes. Add sugar gradually. Continue beating until a slowly dissolving ribbon of batter falls from lifted beaters. **4** Gently fold in dry ingredients, I tbsp (15 mL) at a time to prevent lumps. Pour into prepared pan. Bake at 350°F (180°C) for 50 to 60 minutes or until a toothpick inserted into the centre comes out clean. Cool on a rack. Turn out of pan and freeze for I hour before assembly. **5** To make icing, melt chocolate with cream in top of a double boiler over boiling water, stirring occasionally. Refrigerate, preferably overnight, until mixture is very cold. Whip to spreading

consistency. **6** To assemble, slice cake into six thin layers
each about ½ inch (I cm) thick. Spread each layer with
chocolate cream, building alternate layers of frosting and
cake, covering sides as well. Garnish with chocolate shavings.

$\mathcal{F}$LAMBÉ OF FIGS | Serves four

Chef Walter Vaz and
winemaker David Hulley

This delicious dessert was served at Stonechurch Vineyards' White Linen Dinner during the
1992 Grape and Wine Festival. The recipe was created by chef Walter Vaz from Astina's
Restaurant in St. Catharines and winemaker David Hulley of Stonechurch Vineyards.

¼ cup	unsalted butter	50 mL
16	Ontario figs	16
3 tbsp	brown sugar	50 mL
¼ cup	honey	50 mL
3 oz	brandy	90 mL
I cup	whipped cream	250 mL

1 In a large skillet over high heat, melt butter. Add figs
and sauté for 3 to 5 minutes, turning constantly, until nicely browned all over. **2** Sprinkle brown sugar over figs and
turn for I minute. **3** Make a well in centre of pan and
add honey; simmer honey rapidly. **4** Turn figs two or
three times to build heat again. Add brandy to pan and
flambé. (If using an electric stove you may have to ignite
the brandy in a ladle and pour over figs.) Reduce heat to
low and continue to turn figs until flames die. **5** Arrange
figs on serving plates. Pour sauce over figs and serve immediately with a dollop of whipped cream.

Stonechurch Vineyards Vidal Icewine

NIAGARA-ON-THE-LAKE, ONTARIO

This dessert and wine combination can only be described
as heavenly. The wine's honey
nose is accented by dried
apricots and raisins, complementing the fresh figs. The
wine's nectar palate marries
well with the honey
sauce.

WINEMAKER'S TASTING NOTES

APPLE CAKE WITH ONTARIO FRUIT AND MAPLE ICE CREAM | Serves twelve
Le Resto Palmerston, Toronto, Ontario

JAMIE KENNEDY, chef at Le Resto Palmerston, and one of Toronto's best-loved chefs, combines truly Canadian products in this heavenly dessert. After a two-year absence, chef Kennedy returned to Palmerston, now owned by Marcel Réthoré. As a co-founder of the Knives and Forks Club, an organization of chefs and organic food producers, Jamie Kennedy naturally uses a liberal amount of organics on his market-fresh menu. The neighbourhood bistro is at its best in the warmer months when two garden areas come to life with tables of enthusiastic patrons. Moderate prices, local ingredients transformed into Canadian masterpieces and an abundance of local wines are the hallmarks of the ever-changing menu.

Hillebrand Estates Late Harvest Vidal

NIAGARA-ON-THE-LAKE, ONTARIO

A perfect accompaniment to this fruity dessert, with its apple, quince and apricot aromas. The nutty flavours balance well with the maple ice cream and tuiles. This wine is full enough to accommodate the variety of flavours in this dessert.

APPLE PURÉE:

5	Spy or Spartan apples	5
½ cup	apple cider	125 mL
	Juice of ½ lemon	

APPLE CAKE:

8	eggs	8
1 cup	sugar	250 mL
1 cup	pastry flour	250 mL
⅔ cup	apple purée	150 mL
⅔ cup	butter, melted	150 mL

CIDER GLAZE:

4 cups	cider	1 L

RIESLING POACHED PEARS:

2	bottles Riesling (white wine)	2
½ cup	sugar	125 mL
1	vanilla bean	1
6	Bosc pears	6

PINOT NOIR GLAZE:

2	bottles Pinot Noir (red wine)	2
½ cup	sugar	125 mL
½ cup	butter, cubed	125 mL

MAPLE TUILE:

¼ cup	soft butter	50 mL
¼ cup	sugar	50 mL
I tbsp	maple syrup	15 mL
2	egg whites	2
¼ cup	pastry flour	50 mL

Maple Ice Cream (recipe follows)

1 To make apple purée, roughly chop apples without peeling or coring. Place in a saucepan with cider and lemon juice. Simmer, covered, over low heat until very tender, about 10 minutes. Purée in a food processor and pass through a fine sieve. **2** To make cake batter, in a large bowl whisk eggs and sugar for 10 minutes. Sift flour and fold into egg mixture alternately with ⅔ cup (150 mL) apple purée. (Reserve remaining purée.) Fold melted butter into batter. Pour into 8- x 4-inch (1.5 L) greased loaf pan. Bake at 350°F (180°C) for 45 minutes or until golden brown and a knife inserted in the centre comes out clean. Cool on a rack and turn out of pan. **3** To make cider glaze, in a saucepan over medium heat, simmer cider, uncovered, until reduced by two-thirds. **4** To poach pears, in a saucepan combine Riesling and sugar. Simmer, uncovered, until reduced by two-thirds. Add vanilla bean and unpeeled, uncored pears. Simmer, covered, turning periodically until pears are soft. Cool pears in cooking liquid. **5** To make Pinot Noir glaze, in a saucepan over medium

Reif Estate Winery Vidal Icewine

NIAGARA-ON-THE-LAKE, ONTARIO

Rich, with a great intensity of aromas and flavours. Concentration of tropical fruit dominates the sweet honey nose, while an abundance of apricots, peaches and honey almost overwhelm the body. Rich and big without being cloying.

WINEMAKER'S TASTING NOTES

heat, combine Pinot Noir and sugar. Simmer, uncovered, until syrupy. Whisk in butter, one cube at a time. **6** To make maple tuile, in a bowl, cream butter with sugar and maple syrup until light. Alternately beat in egg whites and sifted pastry flour. Refrigerate 2 hours. Cut a maple-leaf template out of a yogurt lid. Butter an inverted baking sheet. Spread 1 tbsp (15 mL) tuile batter over template. Lift template and repeat until baking sheet is filled with maple leaf cookies. Bake at 375°F (190°C) for 5 minutes. While still warm, remove leaves from pan and drape over shallow cups to simulate leaf shape. Let cool. Store in an airtight container until ready to serve. **7** To assemble, slice cake into 12 equal slices and place on a baking sheet. Brush cider glaze onto each slice, soaking thoroughly. Drain pears, reserving poaching liquid. Slice pears in half lengthwise; slice each half into thin slices. Place a dollop of apple purée in the centre of each of 12 dinner plates. Pour a thin bead of Pinot Noir glaze around perimeter of apple purée. Place a slice of soaked apple cake on the purée. Arrange sliced pears in fan shape on either side of apple cake. Drizzle reserved poaching liquid over pears. Place one maple tuile on each slice of apple cake and one large scoop of maple ice cream on each tuile. Serve immediately.

MAPLE ICE CREAM:

4 tsp	crème fraîche	20 mL
12	egg yolks	12
1⅓ cups	maple syrup	325 mL
2 cups	milk	500 mL
2 cups	whipping cream	500 mL
1	vanilla bean	1

1 Place crème fraîche in a 4-quart (4-L) bowl. **2** In a separate bowl, combine egg yolks and maple syrup. **3** In a stainless steel saucepan, scald milk and cream with vanilla bean. Remove from heat and remove vanilla bean. **4** Slowly pour some milk into yolk mixture, stirring well; add yolk mixture to remaining hot milk. Heat mixture slowly, stirring constantly. When thick enough to coat the back of a metal spoon, strain mixture into crème fraîche and stir to combine. Let cool. **5** Process in ice-cream maker, following manufacturer's instructions. Store in freezer until ready to use.

LOUISE BEAULNE'S LIGHT-AS-A-CLOUD CAKE

Restaurant Clementine, Oka, Quebec

LOUISE BEAULNE, award-winning pastry chef and co-owner of this critically acclaimed restaurant, has created a delicate flourless cake that really is as light as a cloud.

CAKE:

2 tsp	cornstarch	2 mL
10	egg whites	10
¼ tsp	cream of tartar	1 mL
1½ cups	sugar	375 mL
1 tsp	vinegar	5 mL
½ tsp	white OR regular vanilla extract	2 mL

SAUCE:

1	pkg (10 oz/300g) frozen raspberries	1
½ cup	sugar	125 mL
3 tbsp	lemon juice	50 mL
	Whipping cream to taste	
	Sugared whipped cream and fresh raspberries (for garnish)	

Hillebrand Estates Late Harvest Vidal

NIAGARA-ON-THE-LAKE, ONTARIO

Golden yellow with apricot, apple and quince aromas, this full wine has caramel, banana and hazelnut flavours that work with the richness of this cake.

WINEMAKER'S TASTING NOTES

1 Spray a 9-inch (2.5-L) springform pan with vegetable spray and dust with cornstarch. Preheat oven to 450°F (220°C). **2** In a large bowl, beat egg whites with cream of tartar until foamy. Beat in sugar, 2 tbsp (25 mL) at a time, until stiff and glossy. Beat in vinegar and vanilla. Spread evenly in pan. **3** Place in oven and immediately turn off heat. Leave cake in closed oven 8 hours. Refrigerate 1 hour. **4** To make sauce, in a blender, process raspberries, sugar and lemon juice. Add cream to obtain pink colour. **5** Cover cake with sauce, whipped cream and fresh raspberries.

A GLOSSARY OF WINE TERMS

Acidity – The agreeable sharp taste caused by natural fruit acids. In moderate amount it is a favourable characteristic, and is not to be confused with sourness, dryness or astringency.

Ageing – The process of allowing time to fully blend and develop the character of a wine. The span differs greatly with different wines.

Aroma – The fragrance of fresh fruit directly related to the variety of grape used to make the wine. The aroma of wine will change as the wine ages to its final bouquet.

Astringency – A normal characteristic of some young wines, usually caused by an excess of tannin, lessening with age. It has a puckering effect on the mouth. It is more noticeable with red wines.

Balance – A term of high praise denoting a wine whose sugar content, acidity and the many odour and taste elements are present in such proportions as to produce a harmonious and pleasant sensation.

Blending – The specialized craft of combining two or more wines to achieve a batch of wine of high standard and uniform quality.

Body – The taste sensation of substance in a wine, which can be related to alcoholic content. Wine may have a heavy body or a light body. This cannot be measured. It is a matter of taste.

Bouquet – The complex of odours given off by a mature wine when it is opened.

Breathing – Wines breathe when they are in contact with the air. A young red wine will benefit from being given at least half an hour to breathe.

Brut – French term designating driest (least sweet) grade of Champagne or sparkling wine.

Character – The combination of taste, bouquet and colour in a wine.

Cooperage – The general term used to designate containers in which wines are stored and aged. It includes casks and wooden or stainless steel ageing tanks. The terms derives from the occupation of cooper, one who makes or repairs wooden containers.

Corked or *Corky* – A "corked" or "corky" wine is very rare and may occur from a faulty cork. A musty, unpleasant smell and taste will be present.

Decant – To pour wine from one container to another.

Dessert Wines – Wines fortified with alcohol to give them a final high alcoholic content of 14 to 20 per cent alcohol by volume, they can be either sweet or dry, e.g., port, sherry.

Dosage – The sweetener added to bottles of sparkling wine or Champagne after degorging of sediment accumulated during secondary fermentation in the bottle.

Dry – This much-abused word means nothing more than lacking in sweetness. The degree of dryness is determined by the proportion of total grape sugar converted to alcohol.

Estate-Bottled – These words indicate that the wine was produced and bottled on a property controlled by the winery.

Extra Dry – A contradictory term used on Champagne labels meaning somewhat sweet. The degree of sweetness varies.

Fermentation – A process whereby yeasts interact with sugars to produce alcohol and carbon dioxide. It is through such a process that grape juice is transformed into wine.

Fining – A traditional process of clarification. The fining medium settles to the bottom carrying with it the fine suspended particles.

Flor – The variety of yeast giving the character peculiar to dry sherries.

Flowery – A term denoting the fragrance of blossoms in a wine's bouquet or aroma.

Fortified Wine – Wine such as sherry, port and muscatel to which alcohol has been added, usually in the form of brandy or grape spirit, to increase their alcoholic content. This is a world-wide practice.

Frappé – The notation *servir frappé* is sometimes found on white wine labelling; it means serve iced or chilled.

Fruity – Term applied to a fine young wine which has the aroma and flavour of fresh fruit.

Full – Pleasingly strong in flavour, bouquet or taste.

Green – Term applied to young wine of excessive acidity.

Hard – Winetaster's term for a wine with excessive tannin. Not necessarily a fault in a young wine, where it may indicate a long maturity.

Heavy – Excessive alcohol content without a corresponding balance of flavour.

Lees – The sediment deposited in the storage vats before bottling. The lees are left behind by racking.

Light – A complimentary term applied to pleasant refreshing wines; the opposite of full-bodied.

Maturity – A state reached by wine through ageing.

Mousseux – A French word, on a wine label, that indicates a sparkling wine.

Must – The grape juice before it is fermented.

Musty – Unpleasant "mousy" odour and flavour, similar to mouldy, usually due to unclean cellar.

Nose – Professional winetaster term describing quality of bouquet.

Oxidation – Exposure of wine to air, resulting in deterioration over a long period of time.

Pétillant – Lightly sparkling or crackling wine.

Press – A machine which, by applying direct pressure, forces the juice from the grapes. There are many types of presses, ranging from the ancient hand-operated wooden press to sophisticated hydraulic machines made of stainless steel.

Racking – The process whereby clear wine is drawn off its lees and sediment, and transformed from one storage container to another.

Riddling – In Champagne-making, the process of working the sediment into the neck of the bottle during the second fermentation. Traditionally a hand operation, it is now being done mechanically in many wineries.

Rounded – A complimentary term for a wine whose qualities, while not necessarily individually great, are in balance.

Sec – French word for dry. *Secco*, in Italian, is used similarly.

Sediment – The harmless solid matter thrown by wine during fermentation and ageing. It is more pronounced and abundant in red wines than in whites. In the ageing process it sometimes forms a crust on the wall of the bottle. Wines with heavy sedimentation must be decanted before serving.

Soft – Term describing the pleasant smoothness of wines of low astringency. Not related to sweetness.

Sour – A disagreeable taste sensation, acid and vinegary, indicating a spoiled, undrinkable wine. Not to be confused with tartness, astringency or dryness.

Spicy – A term used to describe the taste of some wines although no spices have in fact been added to them.

Still Wine – A non-effervescent wine in which the carbon dioxide gas, formed during fermentation, has all escaped. The opposite of sparkling wine.

Table Wine – A wine with a maximum of 14 per cent alcohol by volume. It may be red, white or rosé.

Tart – The sharp, astringent taste of fruit acid, like the taste of a McIntosh apple. When present in a moderate degree, tartness lends a pleasant freshness to a wine.

Tawny – The brownish-red colour acquired by some red wines in ageing. The characteristic colour of Tawny Port.

Tannin – An astringent acid found to some degree in all wine, but more in red than white. The proper degree of tannic acid is essential to aged, high-quality red wines; an excess can ruin any wine.

Varietal – The wine name taken from the grape variety used to make it. The following are some varietal names: Delaware, Chardonnay, Riesling, Maréchal Foch, de Chaunac.

Vinifera – The most important of the 32 species of vines making up the genus Vitis in the botanical classification. Vitis vinifera is the species of grape from which all the wines of Europe are made. It is being successfully introduced into British Columbia, Ontario, Quebec and Nova Scotia.

Vinifera Hybrid – A cross between the Labrusca and the vinifera families. Used in many of Canada's premium table wines.

Vinification – This broad term covers the whole process of turning grapes into wine, except for the vineyard operations. It includes fermentation, clarification and ageing.

Vintage – The harvesting, crushing and fermentation of grapes into wine. This term is also applied to the crop of grapes or the wine of one season.

Vintage Wine – A wine labelled with the year in which most of the grapes from which it was made were harvested and made into wine. When supported by other information, it usually implies a better quality than its non-vintage counterpart.

Vintner – This broad term, once applied only to wholesale wine merchants, now includes wine growers, wine makers, wine blenders, etc.

Viticulture – The cultivation of the vine, also the science of grape production.

Woody –Term describing the characteristic odour of wine aged in wooden vats and barrels for an extended period. The odour is like that of wet wood.

Yeast – A natural bloom found in grapes, whose fermentive qualities cause sugar to break down into alcohol.

INDEX OF RECIPES AND CONTRIBUTORS

Also by Rachel Hore

The Dream House
The Memory Garden

The
Glass Painter's
Daughter

RACHEL HORE

POCKET
BOOKS

LONDON • SYDNEY • NEW YORK • TORONTO

First published in Great Britain by Pocket Books UK, 2009
An imprint of Simon & Schuster UK Ltd
A CBS COMPANY

1 3 5 7 9 10 8 6 4 2

Simon & Schuster UK Ltd
1st Floor
222 Gray's Inn Road
London WC1X 8HB

www.simonandschuster.co.uk

Simon & Schuster Australia
Sydney

A CIP catalogue record for this book is available
from the British Library

ISBN: 978-1-84983-092-8

Typeset in Palatino by M Rules
Printed by CPI Cox & Wyman, Reading, Berkshire RG1 8EX

To Felix, Benjy and Leo – *non angeli sed Angli.*
(Not angels but Englishmen.)

In old days there were angels who came and took men by the hand and led them away from the city of destruction. We see no white-winged angels now. But yet men are led away from threatening destruction: a hand is put into theirs, which leads them forth gently towards a calm and bright land, so that they look no more backward; and the hand may be a little child's.

George Eliot, *Silas Marner*

Woman is like the Archangel Michael as he stands upon Saint Angelo at Rome. She has an immense provision of wings, which seem as if they would bear her over earth and heaven, but when she tries to use them, she is petrified into stone, her feet are grown into the earth, chained to the bronze pedestal.

Florence Nightingale, *Cassandra*

Acknowledgments

I wish to thank all the people who helped me during the research and writing of this novel. Susan Mathews, Curator of the Stained Glass Museum at Ely Cathedral, gave generously of her time and expertise. Ian de Arth taught a lively and interesting evening class in copper foil and lead work. Colin Dowdeswell provided useful tips about playing the tuba. The Reverend Colin Way, Victoria Hook, Juliet Bamber and Dr Hilary Johnson all read the script with an eagle eye. The Eaton Parishes Choir provided an enjoyable experience of choral singing.

Immeasurable thanks are due to my agent Sheila Crowley and her colleagues at A. P. Watt and Curtis Brown. At Simon & Schuster, I am indebted to Suzanne Baboneau and Libby Vernon's excellent editing, and to the rest of the team there, especially Sue Stephens and Jeff Jamieson.

Lastly, but by no means least, thanks to my family. My mother Phyllis is my number one fan; my children have several times saved my memory stick from the jaws of their puppy; my husband David helps in more ways than he knows.

I consulted a wide number of books and websites. The following were especially helpful: *Victorian Stained Glass* by Martin Harrison, *Stained Glass in England* by June Osborne, *Edward Burne-Jones* by Penelope Fitzgerald, *Perceptions of Angels in History* by Henry Mayr-Harting, *A Treasury of Angels* by Jacky

Newcomb, *Teen Angel* by Glennyce S. Eckersley, *Westminster and Pimlico Past* by Isobel Watson, the Canterbury Cathedral Stained Glass Studio website (www.stained-glass-studio.org.uk) and www.williamsandbyrne.co.uk.

Prologue

London, 3 September 1993

The stained-glass shop had worn its Closed *sign for nearly a week, though that hadn't stopped people from testing the door handle or staring in through the window, hoping for signs of life. Some of the lights were on, after all, and passers-by were startled from their early-morning stupor by the exquisite items on display: the angel glowing centre stage in its arched pane; delicate suncatchers – dragonflies and fairies – quivering in some draught; myriad Tiffany-style lampshades receding across the shop ceiling like lush flowers studding a tropical rainforest canopy.*

One very young woman who stopped by every day noticed that sometimes the door at the back of the shop stood open and sometimes it was closed, that sometimes there were two or three cardboard boxes stacked on the counter and sometimes none.

Someone visited the shop several times that week: a middle-aged man with a military bearing, dressed in a tweed jacket and clerical collar. The first morning, he tried the door and found it locked. He stepped back to inspect the words Minster Glass *gleaming over the shop-front, adjusted his spectacles to read the opening times listed beneath the* Closed *sign, then frowned before setting off back across the public garden of the Square. The next day he pushed a white envelope through the letterbox. On the third occasion, as he scrawled the phone number given on the sign into a small notebook, a woman in a plastic apron and with a fat purse in her hand emerged from the coffee shop next door.*

'You wanting Mr Morrison?' she asked, looking the man up and down as if to satisfy herself that he wasn't one of them down-and-outs. 'He's not at all well. The ambulance come last week.' She knew no more. He thanked her anyway as he pocketed the notebook and turned away.

Eventually, mid-afternoon on Friday, a black cab sailed out of the traffic and pulled up outside the shop. A slight, neat woman with shoulder-length dark hair and a pale complexion climbed out and started dragging an assortment of baggage onto the pavement.

Anita in the café, glancing out of the window as she waited for the coffee machine to deliver an espresso, surveyed the scuffed leather holdall and the overflowing rucksack, and wondered what could be in the hard, odd-shaped case. Must be a musical instrument of some sort, she supposed. Either that, or the shape suggested a very small elephant.

The girl dismissed the cab and stood among her belongings gazing wistfully at Minster Glass. In her short tailored coat and striped scarf, and with her brown eyes soulful below her fringe, she looked like a reluctant schoolgirl returning to her institution after a glorious summer break. Anita was new to the café, otherwise she might have guessed the younger woman's identity, and realised that, as she contemplated her father's shop, Fran Morrison's entire life was passing before her eyes.

Chapter 1

Tears, such as angels weep, burst forth.

John Milton, *Paradise Lost*

Sometimes, if I wake early on a summer's morning, I lie in a day dream whilst the rest of the household slumbers, remembering how it all started. I pinpoint that moment, ten years ago now, that precise milli-second when, staring at the closed and empty shop, I recognised that everything had changed, changed irrevocably and for ever.

We talk about going 'back home' as though it's a regression, and that's what I'd believed, but on this occasion it turned out to be a step forward into a new life. It's been on my mind a great deal, this story that is my – my 'angel reach' story. Now that I've brooded about it for so long, seen its consequences, like ripples spreading outwards on a pond after the stone is thrown, the time has come to write it all down. And so each evening, while the light is long in the sky, I climb the stairs to the attic, sit at Dad's old desk and take up my pen. How quickly I am absorbed in my task.

Home was absolutely the last place I wanted to be, that gloriously balmy autumn of 1993. Given the choice, I'd have picked an old *palazzo* apartment in Venice perhaps, or a neat townhouse *Pension* in Heidelberg, or some glittering high-rise hotel in New York or Tokyo. Somewhere different, exotic, where I could live entirely in the present and forget the past. But sometimes life doesn't give us a choice. And so I found myself in London again – a desolate homecoming, given the circumstances. Yet, knowing what I do now, I can see that the timing was exactly right.

The day before, when Zac finally tracked me down with the news, I had been in Athens, dozing away a baking afternoon in a hostel in the older part of the city. The caretaker's son, a wary, tonguetied sixteen year old, had tapped on the door then led me to the phone in a cool tiled recess of the reception lobby.

'*Fran!* Finally,' cried the voice down the line.

'Zac, what's the matter?' I'd have known that Scottish burr anywhere. Zac was Dad's assistant at *Minster Glass*.

'Why the heck don't you pick up your messages?'

No 'How are you?' or 'I haven't seen you for months.' In fact, he sounded so agitated that I didn't bother to ask where he'd left messages or how he'd found my number here.

'I didn't get any messages, that's why. Zac, what is it?' But I knew instinctively what was wrong.

The annoyance went out of Zac's voice, to be replaced by desperation. 'You've got to come home. *Now*. Your father's in hospital – and this time it's not just one of his funny turns. Fran, it's a stroke, a bad one.'

As I packed that evening, I tried to think straight. There was no one in Athens I needed to contact. The concert tour had finished a few nights ago. The orchestra had dispersed the next morning, everybody air-kissing in the hotel lobby and promising to keep in touch. Nick went too. I had decided some time before to find somewhere cheaper to stay on for a few days' holiday, and he found me out as I loitered miserably, envying other people's excitement at going home. He smiled, his expression soft, then kissed me chastely on the cheek and muttered, 'Goodbye. Watch out for yourself. It's been . . .'

'I always do. Goodbye, Nick,' I cut in, as coolly as I could, and watched him heft his luggage outside. To torture myself further I peeped between the pot plants in the window, saw him stow his cello in the boot of the taxi and drive off, out of my life.

After everyone had gone I removed myself with my bags and my tuba to the shabby Aphrodite Hostel. My original plan had been to mosey about sightseeing until my diary service told me where I might be required to play next on someone else's expenses – somewhere glamorous, I hoped, Munich, Rio or Paris – but in the event I was so downcast I couldn't summon the energy to trudge round the tourist spots. And then Zac rang and everything changed once more.

So here I was outside our old shop in Greycoat Square, my fingers remembering the trick of working the keys. *Minster Glass*, the place where I was born. I don't mean that literally, of course. That had been thirty years ago in the same hospital where my father lay now, the same hospital probably where my mother had died when I was tiny.

It is a strange secret area, this part of Westminster, bounded by the looming gothic Abbey and the ornate Italian-style Catholic Cathedral, tucked away between busy Victoria Street to the north and the River Thames to the south; an area of hidden garden squares like ours, of rows of Victorian terraces cut off from the pavement by black iron palings, the office doorways often studded with polished brass plates advertising the most unlikely sounding organisations – the London Theosophical Society, the Royal Order of Griffins, the *Bookbinders Gazette*. I suppose *Minster Glass* was itself another oddity. I loved it all.

A Victorian stained-glass shop, with bay windows and a tiled porch, though delightfully quaint, wouldn't be most people's idea of home. Dad and I had camped – I can't think of a better word for our haphazard living arrangements – in the flat above the shop. There should have been plenty of space for the two of us, given the living room, large kitchen, three bedrooms and enormous attics. But every spare nook and cranny was crammed with stuff: books, boxes, files and papers, together representing the entire history of *Minster Glass*.

The door leading up to the flat was accessed from the workshop behind the front shop. I remembered how I'd creep down the bare wooden stairs of a gloomy winter's morning and through the icy workshop, braving its dark corners and sinister acrid smells, terrified of Dad's temper should I break anything, to meet my friend Jo and walk to school. Jo's family lived in a mansion block nearby, her father being a hotshot City lawyer.

On my way out to the street I loved to linger in the front shop, for it was beautiful, a fantasy of ever-changing coloured light, especially when the sun slanted through the window, setting the suncatchers turning, pouring dusty pools of ruby, emerald and sapphire upon the wooden floor so it seemed a hallowed place.

It was this peaceful beauty that soothed my troubled feelings now, as I turned the key in the shop door, pushed down the handle and walked in, the bell jangling mournfully overhead. For a moment I stood breathing in the familiar smells, the fustiness of old wood overlaid by a hint of something chemical. And for that moment I could have been a little girl again, dancing in the dusty shafts of coloured light.

Something caught my eye – a stiff white envelope lying on the mat. I picked it up, noticing a crest embossed on the back, but it was addressed to Dad so I dropped it unopened on the counter.

Locking up – the last thing I could cope with right now was some demanding customer – I left my luggage in the shop, opened the door behind the counter and walked into the workshop.

If the front shop always felt like a welcoming church, the workshop was its chilly crypt. I flipped on the ceiling lights, temporarily dazzled by the bright whiteness. Fragments of glass crunched under my feet as I crossed the concrete floor.

Through the rectangle of window I glimpsed the same old scrubby yard and garage, accessed by a drive to the right of the shop. On a worktop next to me, pinned to a wooden board the size of a tea tray, lay a leadwork window, partly soldered. This must have been what Dad had been working on when it happened. Zac said he'd been sitting in the cubbyhole of an office when he'd heard Dad groan, had seen him crumple to the floor, the stool spinning over the concrete.

I perched on this stool now with a feeling of heaviness. With one finger I traced the Celtic knot pattern Dad had made; one of his favourite devices for borders and filling in small spaces, and which he used on occasion as his craftsman's signature. He liked it, he always said, because he could draw it in a single, continuous line. Under the bench my foot struck something, sending it rolling. I bent down to look. It was the tip of a broken soldering iron. The rest of it was there, too. Zac must have unplugged it, but in the confusion, left it where it lay. I picked up the pieces and examined them, then noticed something else glinting amongst the dustballs under the bench. I reached for it.

It was a small brooch wrought in gold, set with glittering blue stones, shaped in the figure of an angel. Pretty and perhaps valuable. Where it came from I'd no idea – I'd never seen it before. I laid it on the work surface next to the jagged bits of soldering iron and Dad's stained craft-knife.

A blob of paint on the knife bore Dad's fingerprint, and suddenly his absence shifted sharply into focus. Covering my face with my hands, I finally allowed myself to remember how I'd seen him a couple of hours before.

There'd been no one at Heathrow Airport to meet me, but then I hadn't even told Zac the time of my flight. I'd travelled straight to the hospital, where a nurse led me down a small ward to a bed at the far end.

It took me a moment to adjust to the fact that the figure in the bed was Dad, my dad, helpless as I'd never seen him before. His eyes were closed. Tubes, running from cannulas on the back of his hand, were looped above his bed, reminding me for all the world of the long strips of lead solder draped over hooks in his workshop. A monitor beside him pulsing steady red zigzags was the only clear sign of life.

I sat down on a chair beside the bed and studied the pale sleeping face. 'Dad, Daddy,' I whispered, with a flutter of unease. There was no indication that he had heard. I touched his cheek. It was cool against the back of my hand.

In some ways he was the same, I thought, trying to calm myself. His sparse greying hair was combed back in its usual neat style; the long skull with its high cheekbones and hawkish nose still conveyed an air of dignity. But his pallid skin, the thread of saliva between greyish lips, a twitching eyelid, all these made me fear that some dreadful, strange being now lurked beneath his skin. I asked myself, not for the first time in my life, what was he really like, this man, my father?

They say you can never truly know anyone, and there were great swathes of Edward Morrison's inner life that he had never allowed even me, his only child, to penetrate. He was not a cruel man, but often distant, lacking in tenderness and easily irritated. Anything could annoy him – someone ringing up while we were eating, a neighbouring shopkeeper piling rubbish on the pavement when it wasn't collection day. This worsened as he got older, and I wondered how Zac put up with it.

Dad was peaceful enough now. I sat waiting for a rush of emotion, a release of tears. Instead, there was only numbness.

'We think he will come round before long.' Mr Bashir, the consultant, who arrived a moment later, was a calm, portly, middle-aged Pakistani. 'There are signs that his coma is lightening, but the scans indicate that the stroke was a serious one. We do not know how he will be when he wakes.'

'He's only sixty-one,' I managed to blurt out. 'Isn't that still young for something like this?'

'I am afraid it is not so unusual. Especially with your father having type one diabetes. His high blood pressure was a contributory factor.' Diabetes was something Dad had suffered from since his teens. I remembered the bad spells on the rare occasions when he was late with his insulin injections. This stroke, however, was uncharted territory.

After Mr Bashir had gone I stared out of the window at the great expanse of clear sky. At least when Dad woke – and he would wake, I told myself fiercely – he would be able to see the changing light he loved, watch birds and clouds crossing the heavens, twilight fading into darkness, the lights of planes winking against the stars.

And as I whispered goodbye, stroking his hand, dry and callused, this thought comforted me.

It wasn't until late afternoon that I remembered the formal-looking letter I'd left on the shop counter. I'd inspected the flat, finding it tidy though not very clean, made up the bed in my old room, unpacked, then gone to buy some supplies from the express supermarket around the corner. It was when I returned with my carrier bags that I noticed the letter again. With that crest it might be something important. I tore open the envelope.

The single page inside was headed *The Rectory, Parish of St Martin's Westminster*, the letter obviously typed by the rector himself for it paid no heed to layout or margins.

> *Dear Ted,*
> *I called by yesterday but the shop was closed. Perhaps you're away? If so, I hope this letter will find you on your return. I wonder whether you would telephone me at an early opportunity as I've made a discovery I think will interest you and which certainly needs your expertise, given that your firm was responsible for some of our stained glass. This might also be a good time for you to inspect the windows, as I have already mentioned to you, in line with the findings in our recent quinquennial buildings report.*
> *Look forward to hearing from you. I so enjoy our conversations.*
> *Kind regards,*
> *Jeremy*
> REV. JEREMY QUENTIN

St Martin's was the sandstone Victorian-gothic church in Vincent Street, which skimmed the opposite corner of Greycoat Square, running roughly parallel to Victoria Street. I don't remember ever going inside the church – it always appeared locked up when I passed – but I'd noticed coloured glass behind several of the metal grilles that shielded the windows and had wondered vaguely what scenes they depicted. I had a faint memory, come to think of it, of Dad telling me *Minster Glass* had been responsible for their creation back in Victorian times.

I'd also been christened in the church as a baby, he told me,

yet on the odd Sunday we attended a service when I was growing up, we always went to Westminster Abbey. We both loved
the music and Dad found the sermons suitably intellectual. It
was also easy to creep out after the service without anybody
engaging him in intrusive conversation. In matters spiritual, as
in everything else in life, he liked to keep himself private. It
intrigued me how he'd become so friendly with the Reverend
Quentin.

I stuffed the letter back in its envelope and left it on the
counter, resolving to ring the vicar myself when I had a moment
and break the news about Dad's illness.

That evening, partly to take my mind off my troubles, I gave
the flat a thorough clean, throwing old food out of the larder,
mopping the faded lino, scrubbing the chipped old bath and
vacuuming the living room as best I could with Dad's whining,
worn-out machine. Afterwards, exhausted by emotion, by the
day's early start and the unaccustomed physical labour, I collapsed into the armchair by the living-room window and picked
at a pre-packed chicken salad.

The gardens turned golden in the sunset, then silver, as darkness fell. One by one, lights came on in the windows of houses
all around and the pavements glimmered in the soft yellow sul-
phur streetlamps. I'd forgotten how beautiful and peaceful the
Square could be. It was difficult to believe it was in the heart of
a huge city.

Half a dozen doors down, next to an antiquarian bookshop,
was a new wine bar, where people spilled out into the warm,
still evening. Above the murmur of voices I became aware of the
distant soaring notes of Elgar's Cello Concerto. I got up to listen,
as its heartrending phrases wafted from somewhere across the
Square. And suddenly I longed to speak to Nick again so desperately, the pain was almost physical.

I'd met him in Belgrade three weeks before, when I'd joined the Royal London Orchestra on its tour of Eastern Europe. Nick Parton was a couple of years younger than me, a liberally talented cellist and very ambitious. His energy was one of the things I found most attractive about him: that, his soft teasing voice, and – for I had the opportunity to gaze at him night after night from my place at the back of the orchestra – his smooth olive skin and perfect profile.

'I can't believe you're strong enough to play that monster,' were his first, careless words to me, eyeing the tuba cradled in my arms.

'Just watch me,' I sparked back. I pursed my lips and delivered such an ear-shattering blast on the instrument that the crusty leader of the orchestra knocked over his music stand and swore. Nick merely threw back his head and laughed.

I was aware of his eyes on me all the time after that. He sought me out with exaggerated solicitousness, teasingly offering to carry my instrument case for me because I was 'too delicate', then, when I irritably refused, holding open the door with a gallant bow to allow me through first, despite his own considerable burden. After a few days of this I allowed myself to melt slightly. We got together properly one night when, both a little the worse for wear after a late meal in a restaurant, we shared a taxi back to the hotel and a nightcap in the bar.

There was only one evening left after that in Belgrade, but then the orchestra moved on to Prague, Zagreb and Budapest – one glorious setting after another, so that our romance never had the opportunity to grow routine. There was one little problem, however, which I didn't identify until our last night in Athens, and that was the existence of a fiancée, Fiona, back home in Birmingham. It turned out that Nick saw our little duet as his final 'fling' before they married in October. And so the last night

of the tour was our finale too, ending in tears and recrimina-
tions – mine – and sulks – his.

As I lay on my rickety bed in that Greek hostel, going over
and over everything Nick had said and done during the previous few weeks, I realised that he had dropped various hints but
that I had blanked out their meaning. For though I was angry
and upset when he told me about Fiona, part of me hadn't been
surprised, and now a lot of things began to make sense. His
refusal to stay on with me in Athens, for instance, the frequent
phone messages he took, his avoidance of any discussion about
what would happen after the tour.

I tried to make myself feel better by concentrating on how
horrible it must be for poor duped Fiona, imagining how I
would feel if our positions were reversed and I found that my
fiancé had been playing away. Surely, I told myself, she must
suspect. Was it worse that she didn't, or that she did and would
marry him anyway? I couldn't decide. At least I knew the truth
and had discovered it before I was in too deep. Though it wasn't
the first time I had got myself in a mess like this. You could say
I had a gift for it.

I didn't mean to fall in love with unobtainable men, it just
happened that way. Perhaps I was hard-wired to respond to
some strange pheromone that they exuded, these men who were
married or who never intended to stay the course.

I listened to the soaring song of the cello and mulled over my
love of movies in which lovers came together on sinking ships
or as cities fell to the enemy or an asteroid was about to hit the
earth . . . situations in which love was desperate, snatched, a
long way from humdrum reality.

I was mature enough to recognise this painful cycle I put
myself through over and over again, and I knew it was about
time I broke it. Sitting alone in this scruffy old flat, which I still

called home despite everything, for I had nowhere else, I fought the urge to look up Nick's number and ring him. What finally stopped me was the thought of poor Fiona answering. I wanted Nick badly. But not a Nick who would up and leave. I knew now that I wanted someone who was wholly and eternally mine.

Chapter 2

And the angel said: 'I have learned that every man lives not through care of himself, but by love.'

Leo Tolstoy, *What Men Live By*

I slept that night as though I'd been drugged and woke up miserable and starving hungry. It was while I was still in my pyjamas, scraping half an inch of fat from Dad's grill pan, somehow missed in my whirlwind purge of yesterday evening, that the telephone rang. It was the hospital. Dad had woken briefly during the night, the nurse at the other end said. The relief was overwhelming. He would recover. Everything would be all right!

I swallowed some toast, pulled on my jeans and a jacket, and set off at a fast walk down Horseferry Road, passing early-morning joggers and a team of dustmen feeding their van. A plump Indian lady was sweeping the pavement outside a flower shop with long slow movements, and on impulse I asked her to wrap me some freesias. Maybe the fragrance would please Dad, even if he couldn't focus on the colours.

On Lambeth Bridge, a bracing wind whipped off the river, chilling all optimism and inducing a mood of anxiety.

When I walked in, I saw the curtains were closed around Dad's bed and my anxiety turned to panic that he'd had a relapse. Then a nurse emerged, carrying a bowl of soapy water, a towel over her arm. She smiled as she moved past me, and my panic ebbed, but too soon. I saw immediately that everything was not all right.

Dad seemed exactly like the day before, eyes closed, his mouth open, snoring slightly. I pulled the chair up, and sat looking for signs of change. Did he have more colour in his face? Possibly. Suddenly his eyes half-opened. He blinked, dazed by the light.

'Dad,' I whispered, leaning into his line of vision, and I was sure he looked directly at me. He seemed puzzled; a muscle twitched by his mouth as though he was trying to speak.

'Don't,' I said, forlorn. His left hand, the one nearer me, trembled slightly, and I placed mine over it. We contemplated one another, he with the guileless gaze of a very young child. I turned away first, to hide my brimming eyes.

There was one good thing, though. He recognised me, I knew he did. He was, despite all my fears, himself. Yet I had the strange feeling that he was pleading with me, like a trapped animal.

'Dad, it's all right, I'm here.' What could I tell him that was reassuring? 'I'll look after everything, don't worry. I'm sure Zac'll help, too.' Though I'd still heard no word from Zac since my return.

I stayed until Dad was asleep once more. My walk back from the hospital took twice as long because I dawdled on Lambeth Bridge watching the gunmetal-grey water swell beneath, glad of the biting wind that dulled my anguish. Some tide was rising within me, too, carrying me – where? I had no idea. My life was hopelessly adrift.

Zac was in the workshop when I walked back in, cutting shapes from a piece of glowing red glass. He looked up as I entered, his glass-cutter poised, his long lean body bent, ready to score the glass. I hovered in the safety of the dividing doorway. The old awkwardness swirled between us, as thick and mysterious as fog.

'Hello, stranger,' he muttered finally, managing a smile. 'How are things?'

'I've just been to see Dad,' I said, trying to hold my voice steady. Zac laid down his cutter and studied me, absent-mindedly rubbing at a callus on his forefinger.

'How is he?' he asked, his voice gruff as though he hadn't spoken since yesterday. That would be quite believable. I had never found out much about Dad's assistant. He'd come to work for Dad shortly after I left home twelve years ago, a thin, dark-eyed, pale-skinned man, then in his early twenties, with a Glasgow accent, a mop of thick black hair and that Celtic brooding air of mystery. He'd kept himself to himself. Now, a dozen years on, he had filled out a bit and the accent was less pronounced, but otherwise, like *Minster Glass*, he was exactly as always.

Zac had never seemed bothered by the odd hours Dad asked him to work, was apparently happy to take afternoons off when business was slow, and ready to toil a seven-day week in the event of a tight deadline. At other times he came and went as it pleased him, which seemed to suit them both, though if I'd been his boss I'd have found it disconcerting. In Dad's absence, I supposed I was his boss. The thought bothered me. What could I possibly teach Zac? Apart from a bit of charm, that is. He could at least try to look pleased to see me.

'You were right about the stroke, Zac,' I said. 'It's serious.'

I explained how Dad had come round, but that the doctor I'd spoken to today – not the nice Mr Bashir but a young woman with spiky hair – said the tests were inconclusive about how bad the stroke damage was. She refused to guess when I asked how quickly Dad might recover, though agreed that his waking was a positive sign.

Zac thrust his hands in the pockets of his shabby moleskins and stared at the floor. After a moment he said, 'That's terrible. I'm sorry, Fran.' After another moment he added anxiously, 'I did what I could, you know. Checked his breathing, called the ambulance right away. They were here in a few minutes. Perhaps if I'd done something different . . .' His face showed naked distress.

'I'm sure you did everything right,' I said. 'And you were here with him, that's the important thing. God knows what would have happened if he'd been alone.'

'Aye, you're right there,' he said gloomily. We stood for a moment, each lost in our own thoughts, then he spoke again. 'What are your plans?'

'Plans?' I echoed.

'I mean, how long are you back for? You know I'll do what I can, but . . .' He spread his hands in a helpless gesture.

'I hadn't thought about it. I suppose I'll stay here for the time being. We don't know how long Dad will take to get better.' There was another short silence during which I was aware of his eyes on me, sympathetic, but searching. I tried to consider the concept that it might be a long, long time – if ever – before Dad could work again, and pushed it away.

'There's plenty of work around to keep the business going,' said Zac softly. 'And I could do with assistance in the shop.'

Thoughts started rushing in with dizzying force. Was this what Dad's illness would mean? Being here, giving up music for the duration?

'What sort of work are we talking about?' I asked, to buy time.

'There's this.' He lifted up the sheet of red glass so I could see the template drawing underneath. 'A window for one of those penthouse flats by the river. The lady wants a sunrise. Not happy with her view of the real one, obviously. Look.' He took a smaller roll of paper from another table and showed me the design he'd made – a colour sketch of the sun rising over a country scene.

'That's lovely,' I said. 'What else?'

He described a few other similar commissions awaiting his attention. I then inspected the repair jobs lined up on the shelves. There were broken lampshades, dusty mirrors and picture frames with chipped decoration. An ugly folding screen with a caved-in middle section leaned against one wall. Despite myself, the years rolled away and I found myself assessing the work involved. All these I probably still had the skills to fix – if I wanted.

'And there's a whole list of domestic window repairs,' Zac was saying.

'What about this one?' I moved over to Dad's Celtic design, still lying beneath the window. Suddenly I wanted to do something useful. 'Shall I finish it off?'

'If you want,' said Zac, looking surprised. 'But don't rush yourself. You've only just—'

'I'd like to, when I've got a moment. It's something I can do . . . for Dad.'

'Fine.' He shrugged. 'I'll look up the paperwork now, if you like.'

'Thanks. Oh.' My eye fell on the brooch I'd left by the unfinished panel. 'By the way, do you know anything about this? Perhaps Dad dropped it.'

Zac took the brooch, studied it for a moment then returned it to me with a shake of his head. I turned the brooch over, still puzzled about its significance, then slipped it safely in my pocket.

He wandered over to the office and started flicking through Dad's big Day Book on the desk.

'Looks like that panel's the last part of an order for a new church in South London,' he said after a minute.

A church. I suddenly recalled the vicar's letter.

'That reminds me.' I went off to fetch the Reverend Quentin's missive from the shop counter. It wasn't there, nor on the floor either.

'Have you seen a white envelope?' I asked, going back into the workshop.

'This what you're looking for?' Zac fished the letter out of his overall pocket. 'You don't need to worry, I've already rung him.'

'You have?' I knew my annoyance was unreasonable, especially given my previous panic about getting involved, but Zac's dismissive tone got under my skin. 'What did he have to say?'

'He didn't mention anything about the "exciting discovery". Just asked how your father was. Anita from the café had told him he was ill. I said I'd visit the church myself and report on the state of the windows. I'm going round there Monday at five.'

'Will the light still be good enough to see properly then?' I said sharply. It might sound ridiculous – but I felt excluded. It was I, after all, who had opened the letter, my father who was a friend of the writer, and if I'd rung the vicar I'm sure I would have got out of him what the mysterious discovery was.

'I expect it'll be all right.' We were suddenly circling like a pair of prize-fighters. It was silly. I knew Zac was merely doing his job, but some small stubborn part of me wanted the upper hand.

'I'll go with you,' I said, to settle the argument, and walked away into the shop before Zac could object.

Silence followed, then after a moment came the teeth-jarring sound of tungsten scoring glass. I had been rude and I felt ashamed of myself. But, looking back now, I see that I was too unhappy and worried about Dad to act rationally.

I tried to make amends by being helpful, opening up the shop and turning on the main lights. There were several new boxes of glass left by our wholesaler, stacked on the floor. I cut open the top one. Today at least, I told myself, it would be business as usual for *Minster Glass*. I would take my father's place at the counter.

From time to time, as I slotted the coloured squares sideways into their compartments on the shelves, so they could be easily flicked through, like old vinyl records, Zac came through to fetch something he needed, and he seemed pleased to see me there.

I unwrapped a batch of small decorated mirrors and hung them on the back wall, thinking of my tuba upstairs. I had not taken it out of its case for several days now. Nor had I rung Jessica at the diary service that organised my bookings, to tell her what had happened and where I could be contacted. I thought of Dad, lying in his hospital bed, and again that dark tide rose up inside, choking me. I was terrified for Dad, but also for myself. My life was on hold – but for the moment, what could I do about it? Nothing, except wait and occupy myself unpacking glass.

Zac left at lunchtime, muttering something about calling in on Dad on the way to a business appointment. I watched him walk quickly across the Greycoat Square gardens and was glad to be alone.

It was a quiet afternoon in the shop. When I'd checked the supplies of the tools we sold, making notes for re-orders, I parked myself at a table just inside the workshop, from where I could see anyone who came in, plugged in a solder iron and tried to mend a lampshade. I hadn't soldered lead for so long that it took me several practice runs on some pieces of foiled scrap glass before I dared attempt a fine line across the joins on the shade. Contemplating my work, I decided that the result wasn't too bad. I put the shade to one side, then picked up a mirror with a broken border and started on that. It was absorbing, soothing work.

There weren't many customers. A small boy with his father bought one of the little mirrors for his mother's birthday. A middle-aged woman with faded ginger hair and hoop earrings wanted some glass for an evening-class project. She pulled out every piece in the shop before selecting a perfectly ordinary square of streaky cathedral blue. A young woman in track pants, with straggly black hair and dark eyes, hung about outside, staring at the window display and chewing her nails. When I stepped out to get a cappuccino from the café next door, she returned my smile fearfully before scurrying off. She kept to the shadows, looking behind her from time to time. Like a stray cat, I thought with a rush of pity. Used to being driven away.

That evening, visited by loneliness, I extracted my address book from my handbag and tried the number of a friend from music college I'd not spoken to for years, only to be told she had moved away, whereabouts unknown. Next I called a fellow brass player in South London, then a woman from the concert promoters I was friendly with, but it was Saturday night and no one, it seemed, was in except me.

As I leafed through the dog-eared pages, I was struck by the realisation that I had too easily let old friendships lapse. I had hardly anyone left at all.

I reached 'P' and saw my old schoolfriend Jo Pryde's name. Eleven Rochester Mansions, her parents' flat, was still the only address given. But then I hadn't seen Jo in years, so she probably wouldn't have bothered telling me if she had moved. I thought about ringing the number, but imagined a stilted conversation with one of her parents. Perhaps too much time had passed. I hadn't contacted her since I left school, dropped her along with everyone else since I began my peripatetic working life. I felt bad about it now, but it had seemed necessary to get away then, to cut my ties and launch out on my own.

I gave up trying to track down friends and instead went upstairs to pack a bag of Dad's things to take with me when I visited the hospital tomorrow.

His bedroom had a sad, abandoned air. I'd placed the gold angel brooch on his bedside table, next to the photograph of me, aged twelve, sitting on a Welsh pony, taken on a rare holiday near Aberystwyth. This photo was the only truly personal item on display. There was one picture on the wall – a framed print of an Alma Tadema painting – unnaturally pale women bathing in a Classical setting, the waters of the pool a storybook blue. Perfectly executed, but I always thought Alma Tadema's work chilly, devoid of emotion. Perhaps that was why Dad liked it, for he, too, betrayed little of his feelings. And yet I knew that he wasn't a cold man. It was rather that he had locked his feelings away.

There were no photographs of my mother, a lack I had brooded upon since I was very young. I simply didn't remember her, and Dad made sure there was nothing around the flat to remind me. He hardly ever mentioned her and would deflect any questions about her. Once, at suppertime, I mentioned a friend at primary school who had a birthday on Christmas Day. 'It's so mean,' I said. 'Some people still only give her one present.' I was horrified to see anguish cross his face.

'That's what your mother complained about,' he mumbled,

putting down his knife and fork. 'Christmas Day was her birthday, too. She was upset when I did that once. Gave her one present, I mean.' He stared at the food I'd cooked for him, lost in misery. Then, as though I wasn't there, he got up slowly, scraped the food into the bin and left the room. Sitting alone at the table I let the unseen tears drip down my face, knowing I'd said the wrong thing but not sure why I should bear the blame.

I only learned something of how she'd died by listening at doors. When I was in my first year of senior school we had a visitor at home, a rare event in itself. It was Mrs Webb, my form teacher, who came to see Dad after he refused to sign the form allowing me to go on a week's field trip in the Peak District. He seemed worried about letting me go away for so long. 'She's all I've got,' I overheard him tell Mrs Webb from my hiding-place outside the living-room door, and I glowed with pleasure at what I took to be evidence of his love. I wouldn't have minded not going on the trip if it was because he couldn't stand to be without me. But what they discussed next was unsettling.

Mrs Webb asked what had happened to my mother. 'An accident when Frances was small.' Dad's voice drifted to me, almost inaudibly. 'She died in hospital. I haven't talked about it to my daughter; it would only upset her.'

Where, how and when the accident had happened Dad didn't volunteer, but Mrs Webb persuaded him to sign the form and was sensitive enough not to ask any more questions.

My mother. I yearned to know more, but was not sure how to find out. Out of respect for Dad I hadn't liked to try.

Though I couldn't remember her, I always felt her absence keenly. 'Make a card for Mother's Day,' some teacher would say, before noticing my confused expression and stuttering with embarrassment, 'Er, how about for a g-grandmother, Frances?' while the other children stared at me curiously.

Sometimes as a child I'd lie on the borders of sleep and try to remember something – anything – about her, but I couldn't. Occasionally, I'd be caught unawares by the pattern on a dress or a whiff of a particular perfume . . . but I could never catch the coat-tails of the memory before it was gone.

Once, when I was about ten, I dredged up the courage to ask Dad what my mother had looked like and he said, 'Like you,' which pleased me. But he couldn't look at pictures of her, he added. It made him too sad. At the time I accepted this. It didn't occur to me that I had any rights in the matter. By my mid-teens, however, I became angry, mutinous, told myself I hated him – for clearly, any sadness *I* might have didn't count!

Not long afterwards I discovered a photograph album full of pictures of me, first as a baby, then as a fat laughing toddler. There were blanks in the album where, here and there, photos had been torn out. Photos of my mother, I supposed. I had to content myself with learning about her in parts – her arms cradling me, a graceful pair of legs visible where she stood behind me as I staggered my early steps, wavy dark hair, a pair of lips curving above my baby curls.

Then, one day, a few months later, I struck gold. I was becoming interested in Dad's work, was teaching myself art history out of the many books he kept in the flat. I lifted an outsize volume on Edward Burne-Jones down from a high shelf and opened it. On the title page was inscribed:

> *To my own darling Edward on his birthday.*
> *All my love, Angie, 29 March 1963.*

I turned the pages wonderingly, feeling the precious weight of this evidence of my parents' love for one another, until I reached a series of angel paintings. There, sandwiched between one named *Faith* and another called *Hope*, lay a small black and white photograph of a woman's face. I'd know those smiling lips anywhere, that cascade of hair.

I replaced the photo between the pages and slid the book under my bed, taking pleasure in the fact that I slept with it there every night. When I left on tour for the first time I had moved the book for safety to a shelf in my wardrobe. After I'd packed Dad's hospital bag I went to check. The book was still there. I sat on the bed to study the photograph.

It was a studio shot taken at a three-quarter angle, the light falling softly on her upturned face. I suspected some touching up, since her skin was so flawless, though no one could deny that she was lovely, the long dark hair cut into a heavy fringe at the front, as was the fashion in 1963. It was the style of photo you see in concert or theatre programmes, and it occurred to me that I'd never properly considered what she did before she became my mother. To me she'd always first and foremost been my mother, never a person in her own right, with her own story.

How can I describe the isolation of my childhood? My father loved me, I knew that in the way he looked after my every physical need, his protectiveness. Later he showed it in the thorough training he gave me in the workshop, gradually giving me more responsibility, letting me serve in the shop, create my own design commissions, which he would soberly carry out, giving me the credit with the customers when he might have kept it for himself.

On the one hand, I trusted him, looked up to him, but as for what was going on in his mind those days when he seemed dragged down in depression or snapped at me irritably, I could never discover. I learned not to ask questions. It might have been different if I'd had a brother or sister with whom to share this burden of loneliness, even another grown-up who might take an interest, but Dad had been an only child himself, his parents both dead before I was born, and if my mother still had any living relations, well, we had lost touch. I knew no grandmother to make a Mothering Sunday card for. I used to make one for Dad instead.

I remembered him as proud, dignified, always well turned out. Under his work overalls he'd always wear a shirt and tie, and his leather shoes were kept polished. Even at sixty, it was obvious why women might be attracted to him. His deepset eyes had a faraway, unreadable look, his low, well-spoken voice hinted at untapped passion. With his physical presence – he was over six feet tall – and his obvious standoffishness he was someone people took notice of – and treated with wariness.

I believe he never looked at another woman after my mother. He threw himself into the design and creation of beautiful stained glass with complete and utter absorption, always aiming for the highest standards. It was with his craft that he and I came to have something in common. We could talk about the whereabouts of obscure church stained-glass windows for hours; his memory was phenomenal. His other great interest was classical music, and it was he who insisted that I learn first the piano and then an orchestral instrument of my choice. He seemed faintly surprised when I decided on brass, but he paid for the lessons and came to every concert I was in at school, though he would spare me no criticism afterwards until I would almost wish he hadn't come. On any more personal or emotional aspect of my upbringing, he said little or nothing. I never remember him saying he loved me.

Dad was plainly jealous of boyfriends. I was sixteen when a fellow horn player in the local schools' orchestra plucked up courage to ask me out. I was so astonished that anyone had breached my shyness that I said yes. We went to the cinema once or twice, and to a concert, but the relationship faltered after Dad insisted on Alan picking me up from the house so he could meet him. Dad was surly and Alan meek and over-awed, so the poor boy seemed diminished in my eyes and I finished the relationship soon after. Still, wary of Dad, I declined to bring anyone home after that and so began my habit of conducting my affairs deliciously in secret.

I mustn't exaggerate the difficulties. Much of the time Dad and I got along well enough. So what was it that finally caused me to seal myself off and seek a separate life from him? The patterns laid down in childhood, the ebbs and flows of relationships, are not always easy to put into words, but I'll try.

I suppose I became more aware of the spreading pool of silence and deception between us. As I grew up and sought new experiences, I had to conceal so much from him – as he had always concealed things from me. I resented his unhappiness about me growing up, his own obstinate refusal to embrace change. So even if we hadn't quarrelled so badly when I was eighteen, I think leaving would have been inevitable. Going away was what I had to do then, just as now I'd had to come back.

Chapter 3

What angel nightly tracks that waste of frozen snow.

Emily Brontë, *The Visionary*

The next morning I woke as I had every Sunday throughout my childhood to the sound of church bells rippling from near and far across the city. During my walk to the hospital to visit Dad, the single clear bell of St Martin's tolled an insistent summons to worship.

I found my father propped up on pillows, staring out of the window with a sad unfocused gaze. It was appalling to see how one side of his face sagged. At least he was awake, and when I caught his attention, it surely wasn't my imagination that his eyes seemed to brighten.

I brought out his washing kit, clean pyjamas, a dressing-gown. I'd even put in an adventure novel by an author he loved, thinking I could read to him when he was up to it. How long might that be? I placed it on the bedside cabinet next to the jar of freesias.

At the bottom of the bag, my hand closed over a wad of tissue paper. I hesitated, then unwrapped the blue and gold brooch and held it out.

'Is this yours?' I asked him.

His eyes told me *yes* – the anxiety clear in them.

'Is it special?'

An anguished sound in his throat was his answer.

'Don't try to talk,' I said swiftly. 'I won't leave it here, it might get stolen. I'll keep it safe at home.'

I cast around for another topic of conversation. The man in the next bed cried out suddenly in his sleep, like a child having a bad dream.

'We're getting on beautifully at the shop,' I ventured, trying to moderate my false brightness. 'I'm finishing that window for you.' That was to be my task that afternoon. 'And Zac's working on a beautiful sunset. I sold some glass yesterday.' I rushed on now, telling him anything that came to mind. About the ginger-haired woman who had browsed so long, the lampshade I'd mended, that Anita who ran the café had asked after him.

His eyes eventually fluttered shut. I waited a few minutes, but he had sunk into a deep sleep. Putting the brooch safely away again in my handbag, I bent to press my lips against his cheek. How many years was it since I had last done that? He smelled strongly of hospital soap.

I wanted to ask about his progress, but there was no sign of a doctor. On my way out I consulted the staff at the nurses' station and was told to ring in the morning when Mr Bashir would be on duty.

Only as I left the hospital did I remember that I hadn't told Dad about the Reverend Quentin's mysterious discovery or our proposed visit to St Martin's.

After a snack lunch, I examined the paperwork for the Celtic window, checking the exact dimensions required. Then I measured the panel Dad had assembled and made some slight adjustments before soldering everything together and cementing it. I was quite pleased with the result. I didn't seem to have lost my touch at all. Whether this would happen with my tuba was a different matter. I went upstairs that very minute to take it out of its case, and spent a pleasant hour taking it apart, cleaning it thoroughly, oiling the valves and playing a few exercises.

Late in the afternoon, I went out for a walk, up past the Home Office and on to Parliament Square. Dad and I often used to go this way, and sometimes he'd explain what the area used to look like. 'Where we live was once orchards,' he'd say. Or, 'In Victorian times the Royal Aquarium stood on the site of that hotel.'

On the way back today I passed St Martin's Church, where evening service was clearly underway. I studied its exterior with new interest. A stone over the porch proclaimed its foundation in 1851. When exactly might *Minster Glass* have made the windows? Who was the artist, I wondered, as I made my lonely way home. I ought to find out.

Dad had always been meticulous about researching such jobs, and I knew it would be important at some point for us to find the original paperwork in order to establish the materials and processes we would need to use in any properly conducted restoration. There were strict rules in place about these matters now. Conservation – stopping further deterioration – was the watchword. Restoration processes had to be documented, non-intrusive and reversible.

Minster Glass had been in business since 1865. I had known that since my early teens, that far-off time when I'd been content, homework permitting, to help Dad in the shop, learning the techniques of glass-cutting, painting, leadwork and using copper foil, and hearing anecdotes about the shop's history. It wasn't long before I recognised with ease the different kinds of potmetal glass and could calculate the amount of lead required to complete even a complicated design. I knew my grandfather lent his services during the glazing of the new Coventry Cathedral after the war. That, going further back, his grand-mother ran *Minster Glass* after my great-great-grandfather died falling from scaffolding.

The books, papers and files that filled our flat to overflowing represented most of the paperwork documenting the firm's his-tory – though only Dad knew where everything was. Somehow it had survived damp and the Blitz, the transition from father, or mother, to son to grandson. Dad had converted the huge attic into extra office space after Grandad died, several years before I was born. There, along with much else, he kept the original car-toon drawings and handwritten Day Books that listed every job the firm had ever undertaken.

A year ago, Zac persuaded him to install a computer in the office downstairs. However, Dad still liked to keep up his Day Books, recording the nature of each job in a flourish of loopy black letters. 'Much quicker than waiting for this booting up nonsense,' he grumbled when I spoke to him a couple of months ago from Paris after one of his dizzy spells.

When I returned from my walk I climbed the wrought-iron spiral staircase and pushed open the fire door into the attic. It opened with a little sigh.

Through the skylight the setting sun bathed the boxes and filing cabinets, filling the huge room from boarded floor to sloping ceiling in an orangey glow. I switched on the single light bulb and the long black line of Day Books on their deep wall shelves loomed into focus.

Where the two earliest volumes should have been there was a gap. After a moment I spotted them on Dad's mahogany desk, amongst the books, papers and cardboard folders arranged in piles across the leather top.

One Day Book lay open. When I pulled it towards me, another cloth-covered book was revealed underneath, the pages, relieved from the weight, fanning up suddenly. They were filled with Dad's distinctive black handwriting.

I picked up this curious new find and turned to the front page. There was a title there in printed capitals, carefully under-lined. Reading it, I was amazed. Dad hadn't told me that he was engaged in writing a history of *Minster Glass*. I flipped open a page at random and a familiar name caught my eye:

During January 1870, Mr Ashe was requested by the patron, Lady Faulkham, to create three windows for the North Chancel of St Barnabas's Church in Wandsworth, the theme to be The Last Supper. *He immediately wrote to Edward Burne-Jones asking him to submit designs. The artist supplied some within two weeks but a letter from Lady Faulkham reveals that she took exception to the faces . . .*

The firm had actually tried to commission Edward Burne-Jones, my favourite artist! I hadn't known that before.

I pulled out a thin torn cardboard folder from a stack on the desk and looked inside. It contained drawings for a triptych of saints. In the file underneath I found bills and letters all fastened together in a yellowing age-curled wodge. Dad had clearly been doing his homework. I flicked through his notebook once more and scanned the opening page.

The first date mentioned was May 1865 when one Reuben Ashe set up the firm. But Dad had gone further back in time, tracking Ashe's career up to this point. It was some pages before he returned to the progress of the new business in Greycoat Square. I jumped to the place in the book where he had last laid down his pen.

Although the thick notebook was half-filled he had only

reached . . . no, it couldn't be. A moment passed before I appreciated the coincidence. I looked again. Dad had reached 1880 and the last paragraph he had written concerned the very building Zac and I were going to see, St Martin's Church. Then I remembered Jeremy Quentin's letter, the reference to discussions they'd had, and saw that it wasn't so surprising after all.

I read on.

The subscription to build St Martin's Westminster had been raised by a benefactress keen to minister to those thousands of the godless poor who huddled in their rookeries in the shadows of Westminster Abbey and the Houses of Parliament, under the disdainful noses of the rich and powerful.

Its great East Window, a powerful Crucifixion *scene, was designed for* Minster Glass *by Charles Kempe in 1870, replacing a pattern-book* Nativity *that by this date was considered workaday and old-fashioned. Then, in 1880, the rector, a Mr James Brownlow, had the opportunity to order new windows for the Lady Chapel . . .*

Frustratingly, the account ended here, though Dad had pencilled a couple of queries in one margin. *Check when Burne-Jones worked for Morris & Co.* was one. *Who was Laura Brownlow?* was another.

I pulled the Day Book over, intending to cross-reference some of the entries. The East Window, it turned out, had been commissioned by a Reverend Truelove in 1870. It took me a while longer to find the others. Here they were in April 1880: *Two leaded lights for St Martin's Westminster, ordered by Mr Jas. Brownlow, subjects to be discussed.* But that was all.

I regarded the piles on the desk thoughtfully. Somewhere in these mounds of paper would be useful information. I began to sort through the dusty files, taking care not to disturb the order they were in. Nothing of obvious relevance rose to the surface and since I wasn't sure what I was looking for anyway, I soon gave up.

Turning off the light I took Dad's notebook down to the living room, where I curled up in the chair by the window and began to read.

Reuben Ashe, I learned, had started the firm in a modest way at a time when coloured glass was all the rage again. A rash of church-building had fuelled a newfound Victorian obsession with the medieval. Dad described small restoration projects, modest commissions for public halls, then a church window or two over the river in Vauxhall, several for the chapel of a large country house in Essex, a triptych for a City guildhall.

The firm grew quickly in size and reputation until it occupied the adjoining building – where the café was now. By mid-1870, Dad wrote, Ashe employed ten men on and off, and many larger jobs were being requested – leadwork for the new suburban churches and public buildings being relentlessly rolled out across the green fields beyond London. They bought their glass from manufacturers like James Powell in the East End.

Dad described many of these commissions in meticulous detail. Too meticulous, I thought fondly as I turned the pages, remembering his favourite aphorism: the devil is in the detail. Any reader unacquainted with the trade would quickly weary of the lists of materials, the quoted letters from architects. I thought of him sitting up in his attic alone for hour upon hour, like Mr Casaubon in *Middlemarch*, filling the lonely hours with endless research into the dusty past. Perhaps I was wrong about him being lonely, but even so the thought made me feel even more guilty that I had seen so little of him over the last eleven or twelve years.

The paragraphs about the *Crucifixion* window were interesting. *Minster Glass* had been paid to use the best antique glass, no

expense spared, and the splendid result had led to many more
church commissions. I wondered what designs the Victorian
Reverend Brownlow had requested. Well, I'd find out tomorrow.
I was surprised to realise how much I was looking forward to
the visit.

Chapter 4

Angels are intelligent reflections of light, that original light which has
no beginning. They can illuminate. They do not need tongues or ears,
for they can communicate without speech, in thought.

John of Damascus, *Exact Exposition of the Orthodox Faith*

'Did you know Dad was writing a history of the firm?' I asked
Zac's back view on Monday morning, in between bursts of noise
from the electric grinder. Having cut all the pieces for his sunrise
window, Zac was filing rough edges.

'He told me, yes,' said Zac, pausing briefly in his task. He was
no more friendly this morning than he'd been on Saturday, and
it was really beginning to irritate me.

'Has he been doing it for long? He doesn't seem to have got
very far.'

'A few months maybe, I'm not sure.' The grinding started up
once more.

'Zac!' I said, raising my voice. The grinding stopped.

'Mm?' he said, without turning round.

'Zac, do stop a moment and listen. I've been thinking.' I knew
I sounded nervous. 'I will stay and help you here – at least until
Dad gets a bit better. But I can't leave my music for too long.' My
speech lacked conviction. I cursed myself, for I'd lain awake half
the night settling all this in my mind.

Zac finally turned to face me, but as he was wearing safety goggles I couldn't discern his expression. Suddenly he ripped them off, tossing his head to free the strap from his dark curls. His eyes met mine and I was shocked at the fury in them.

'Then I suppose you'll be off and we won't see you again till kingdom come.' His words were like a dash of cold water.

'Don't be silly,' I snapped back. 'Why are you so angry? You must see the sense of what I'm saying.'

'You can do what you damn well like. It's not up to me, is it?'

'What's not up to you?' How dare he be so rude?

'When you come, when you go. It's just that your dad's managed on his own for too long. He hasn't been well for years.'

'He hasn't been on his own. He's had you.'

Zac rolled his eyes and said, 'You're being obtuse, excuse my plain-speaking. I'm not talking about work. He needs family, Fran. He needs you. You should have been around more. I've tried to do my bit, keeping an eye on him, but it isn't easy. It's not my place to remind him to take his medication or to nag him to eat properly.'

So that's why he was angry. Because he thought I was an undutiful daughter. Well, he was right to some extent, but he didn't know the background. I should have explained it to him then, but I was too angry and too proud. I'd never really talked to anyone about my relationship with my father, not even my old best friend Jo. It was all too private, too complicated.

Instead I said in a low voice, 'You don't understand. What about *my* life, Zac? I've done what children do. They grow up, they leave, they make their own way in the world.'

'Yeah, but they shouldn't just abandon their parents. He had no other family.' He glowered at me, his hands planted on the worktop in front of him.

'Zac, you're overstepping the mark. Anyway, you're a long way from Glasgow. What about your parents, then?'

'I'm sorry I spoke so plainly. My ma died a long time ago now . . . twelve years. My da's married again, someone much younger. We don't get on particularly well, Sally and me. She doesn't like to think Dad's old enough to have a son in his thirties, I reckon. At any rate, he doesn't need me. It's not the same thing at all.'

So his family life was as lonely as mine. Still, I reckoned he didn't have the right to lecture me about my obligations.

I tried again to put my side. 'Zac, when you're a musician, you have to go where the work is.' He had an answer to that one, too.

'You had plenty of opportunity to come home and visit between jobs. Or, I don't know, couldn't you have played with orchestras in London? Whatever, you've rarely visited in all the years I've worked here.'

'Yes, I have.'

'You haven't been back since the Christmas before last. And before that . . . I can't remember.'

Nor for the moment, could I, but that was hardly the point. I was working. Or travelling. Doing the things you're supposed to when you're young and building a career.

At the same time, I couldn't deny that when I had spoken to Dad recently, he had seemed a little frail. I knew I should have made more effort to come home. Zac was right. I'd neglected Dad in the same way that I had neglected my old friends. With that moment of revelation, desolation swept over me.

I said wearily, 'I'm here now, aren't I? Visiting him, looking after things. And as I told you, for the moment I'll help you keep the business afloat . . .'

'And what will happen if . . . *when*,' he corrected himself, 'he comes out of hospital and needs looking after full-time? You know, nursing and stuff.'

'I . . .' The thought panicked me. 'Well, of course I'd stay and help him if I could. But I wouldn't be any good at nursing.' The thought of looking after a chronic invalid, especially in the shabby conditions upstairs, was horrifying. 'Listen, Zac, I don't know, OK? I'll have to deal with that when we come to it. But we haven't got to that point yet, have we?'

Zac sighed. 'No,' he said, 'we haven't.' And suddenly the fight went out of him. 'I'm sorry. Perhaps I shouldn't have said all that. I'm upset, that's all. I hate seeing your dad how he is. In the hospital yesterday . . . He's like a wreck of himself.'

'I know.' I could see the misery in Zac's face and forgave him.

'He's been good to me, your dad. I suppose you could say he rescued me.'

'Really?' I asked, interested. Perhaps Zac saw a different side to Dad. Just then, the tinkling shop bell put a stop to further conversation. 'Sorry, I'd better see who it is.'

'Of course,' he said, and returned to his grinding while I stepped into the shop to serve the customer.

It turned out to be a busy day, but just before five o'clock we managed to shut up shop in order to visit St Martin's Church. Zac packed his toolkit and we set off together across the public garden to the opposite corner of the Square and Vincent Street. It felt companionable. Our discussion had definitely cleared the air.

'Have you ever met this man we're going to see?' I asked him.

'Jeremy Quentin? Never set eyes on the guy. Sounded all right on the phone.'

'I don't know him either, but his letter makes him and Dad seem great friends. It's odd, isn't it? What I think is that Dad must have been to see him about that history he's working on. He stopped in the middle of writing a section about St Martin's, you see.'

'I didn't know about their friendship either,' he said. 'Your dad's never mentioned it. You know how secretive he can be.'

'Tell me about it,' I said feelingly. 'Just think, maybe the history of those windows is up in the attic somewhere, waiting to be discovered. Oh, and did you realise Burne-Jones actually drew some designs for *Minster Glass*? Burne-Jones! Isn't that brilliant?'

'Oh, I know about your obsession with Burne-Jones,' Zac said, his eyes glinting with humour. 'Your dad's mentioned that all right.'

I laughed, wondering what else my father had told this man. After all, for the last dozen years he'd been closer to Dad than I had. Zac had his secrets, too. What had he started to say this afternoon – about Dad rescuing him? I wanted to ask, but we'd already reached the church.

St Martin's Church and its hall turned out to be linked by a lobby whose double doors onto the street were the main access to both. These doors stood open, and we walked through the lobby and right through the door that led into the back of the church. A deep peace stole over us as we passed from sunlight into gloom, the sounds of the traffic suddenly muffled. We lingered in the huge space listening to the echoey stillness, breathing the faint scent of incense that hung in the air. I wished I hadn't worn high-heeled shoes for they clacked horribly on the tiles.

There was no sign of the Reverend Quentin, so we pottered about by ourselves, admiring the high, clear-glass windows of the nave, the pointed Victorian-gothic arches, the vaulted ceilings like great stone forest trees meeting overhead.

Memorials to lost soldier sons, to benefactors and previous incumbents decorated the cream-stone walls. Up ahead, the arched stained-glass window above the high altar drew us inexorably east.

'That might be one of ours,' I whispered to Zac. 'Come on.'

Zac followed me between the carved choir stalls until we stood before the altar rail, gazing up. And were transfixed.

It was Kempe's *Crucifixion* scene. Nothing unusual in the subject. But this was no bland, stylised tableau with a flaccid Christ, arms stretched as though in blessing. This communicated the full agony of the moment of death, the central figure hanging racked and exhausted. On one side, Mary His mother pleaded uselessly to a God Who didn't seem to be listening; on the other St John gazed on in horrified pity, whilst below the plinth on which the cross stood, an hysterical Mary Magdalen was being hauled back, struggling, by bemused soldiers. The pale late-afternoon light fell on the passionate white faces. Emerald, ruby, blue and gold glowed with life. In full morning light this scene must blaze with drama. We stood for a long moment without speaking, gripped by it all.

The sound of the church door opening released us from our trance.

'I'm so sorry to keep you both.' The vicar's voice, warm and vital, carried across the nave. He dumped a couple of books he'd brought onto a pile at the back of the church, flicked some light switches on and off until he was satisfied with the result and hurried down the aisle to meet us, a blue plastic folder poking out from under his arm. He laid this down on a pew.

'There's always something to upset one's best-laid plans, isn't there?' he said, shaking our hands, his hazel eyes bright in his lively, creased face. 'This time some girls from the homeless hostel, all up in arms about something. Fortunately Sarah, my wife, is dealing with them.' He kept hold of my hand in both of his and looked straight into my eyes. 'I'm most sorry to hear about your father, Miss Morrison.'

'Fran.' A whisper was all I could manage, moved as I was by the sadness of his expression.

'Fran. I so value his friendship and it's heartbreaking to think how interested he'd have been in my recent find. I particularly wanted to show him, you see.'

I wanted to ask him what it was, but he rushed on. 'I'm so pleased to meet you at last, my dear. Edward has told me so much about you.'

He patted my hand several times in a comforting way then, recovering himself, turned to Zac. 'Now, Mr McDuff, I suppose we must get down to business. The report, the report.' He picked up the folder, extracted some papers from it and looked at each of us in a fatherly fashion over his glasses, as though about to deliver a sermon.

'You perhaps know that Anglican churches are required to have a full structural inspection every five years. This is the report on the recent one. The architect has raised a question or two about the windows. I'd like you to look at the altar window first to determine its condition.'

He read out the architect's general comments concerning wear and tear on the East Window, then he and Zac moved the heavy altar table forward. Zac stood on a chair behind it, from where he could examine the lower parts of the window, but it wasn't high enough to see further up.

'I meant to fetch the ladder. You wouldn't give me a hand, would you? We'll have to interrupt the Choral Society setting up next door.' Zac followed him out into the lobby. I heard the door to the hall opposite open, a muffled echo of voices and a lot of banging and scraping before they returned bearing a long aluminium ladder.

Rachel Hore

A few minutes later, Zac called down from a rung halfway up, 'There's certainly some deterioration in the paint. See, here, by St John's head. And down there, look at this soldier. You're losing the details of one side of the face. But I've seen a lot worse than this. With luck we won't even need to remove the glass.'

'That's the sort of news I need to hear,' said the vicar.

When Zac had finished making notes in his pocket book, we pushed the altar table back into place.

'The other windows are in here.' The vicar opened the door to a small side chapel on the south side of the nave. 'This is the Lady Chapel, dedicated to the Blessed Virgin, of course,' he said, bowing his head to the small altar's simple brass cross. A wooden statue of Mary stood to one side. She had been badly damaged at some point; a crack ran across her neck.

We looked up at the two stained-glass windows here. I barely noticed the one in the south wall, beyond registering its morass of browns and yellows. But the other, over the chapel altar, was so lovely, so poignant, it took my breath away.

As I stared, the world around me seemed to vanish.

It was the most beautiful glass picture of the *Virgin and Child* that I had ever seen. The infant – and this wasn't one of those mis-shapen painted babies that made one doubt whether the artist had ever looked properly at a child – stood on His mother's lap, His chubby arms around her neck. Mary held Him gently, protec-tively. They gazed into one another's eyes, their faces rapt, serene. Almost, but not quite, touching. She was so absorbed in her child, it was as though cherishing Him was all that she was made for. I remembered the Mary of the *Crucifixion* window. Her son – a grown man, but still her child for whom she would give up every-thing – torn from her, mutilated, brutally killed before her eyes. The contrast was too much. But there was something else the image stirred in me, some sharp longing for my own mother.

'You all right, Fran?' Zac asked, his fingers lightly touching my shoulder.

I turned, saw both men were looking at me, puzzled. 'It's lovely, isn't it?' I stumbled out finally.

'Remarkable,' agreed the vicar. 'Such a shame about this . . .' he went on and I tried to drag myself back to the technical details of the window. He was pointing at Mary's robes, where something that looked like mould was growing on the other side of the glass, over the rich flowery pattern.

'I wonder if we should try to halt this.'

'Definitely,' said Zac. 'Very curious. I'll need to study it from the outside, when I've finished here.' This time he was able to survey most of the window from the lower rungs of the ladder.

As he put away his magnifying glass and took some notes, I perused the second window.

My first impressions had been correct. Artistically speaking, it was mediocre, a Second World War memorial in browns and yellows, with a matronly Britannia dangling a sombre regimental flag. *To the brave men of the parish who lost their lives fighting for their country, 1939–45* ran the gothic lettering at the base. I suppose it would have satisfied the grieving families to see it there. But possibly not moved them.

'It was about this window that I wanted to speak to your father,' the vicar said, coming to stand beside me.

'Oh.' I was disappointed. Was this what all the excitement was about? This dull old war memorial?

'Or rather,' he went on, 'the stained glass that was here before.'

'There was another window?' I asked, my spirits instantly rising.

'Your father thought so,' he said. 'And I think I've proved him right. Look.' He crouched in front of the altar, lifted the white cloth and dragged out a large, sagging cardboard box, grey with grime. I grabbed one end to help, wondering what on earth could be in it.

'Whilst he was working on the report,' Jeremy puffed, 'our surveyor asked us to take everything out from under the stage in the hall next door so he could access a damp patch he'd detected in the outer wall. It was quite a job – there was so much rubbish. But during the process, we found this.'

The cardboard flaps, limp with age, peeled back easily. The vicar lifted a sheet of old newspaper and we all stared inside the box.

'What is it?' I asked, disappointed. Surely this was just some of the rubbish he'd mentioned – a heap of twisted metal and broken glass. Then the vicar reached in with both hands and picked up a section. He held it up and suddenly I saw why he was excited. Light glinted off a line of green studded with white flowers, and what looked like sandalled toes. I was amazed. What the box contained was a shattered stained-glass window.

'I reckon it was destroyed in the Blitz,' said the vicar, lowering the glass back into the box. 'There's a date on the newspaper somewhere. Take a look.'

Zac reached for the paper, smoothed it out and read, 'Fourteenth September, 1940. Yes,' he said, frowning with concentration, 'maybe that was the date it happened and someone rescued the pieces.'

I studied the paper over Zac's shoulder. It was the front page, and I could just make out that the yellowed photograph was of firemen picking through the ruins of a bombed-out building.

'I've been looking through some files,' Jeremy rushed on, 'but I can't find anything useful except the paperwork concerning this *Britannia* that replaced it. The Mothers Union got up the subscription for it after the war.'

'Wonder if any of your parishioners remember this old one,' said Zac, crouching down and picking out odd pieces from the box, turning them this way and that.

'There might be one or two, indeed,' the vicar muttered. 'I'll have to ask around.'

'I wonder if Dad knew all about it,' I put in. 'I don't mean at the time – he'd only have been a little kid then – but since. He knew so much about the firm.'

'That's why I thought he'd be particularly interested, Fran. While researching his book he'd read that there was another stained-glass window here before this one. He said he'd try to find out what it was – but that was the last time I saw him.'

We looked at one another sadly. I remembered what I'd read amongst his papers. 'I think this *Virgin and Child* must have been one of the windows a previous Rector commissioned in the 1880s,' I told him.

'Indeed. But your father thought another might have been made at the same time.'

'And this broken one could have been it?' Zac said. He was holding up a shard of ruby glass, which flashed gorgeously in the late-afternoon light.

'Precisely.'

'You're right,' I whispered. 'Dad would have been fascinated to see this.'

'How is he, poor chap?' the vicar asked, and again I was stirred by the deep sympathy in his gaze. 'I'd like to visit. Would that be appropriate? I'm very fond of your father. He's an interesting man, very interesting, and a brave one.'

Brave? What did he mean by that? I said hesitantly, 'I confess I hadn't known you two were so friendly.'

'Oh, we got to know one another a little recently.'

'He's . . . not an easy man to know,' I said, wondering how

much my father had told him, and the vicar caught the depth of my feeling.

'Or to live with, I imagine,' he agreed. 'He's very reserved, isn't he? And I respected that, of course. Do you think he's up to a visit?'

'I'm sure he'd appreciate seeing you, but he can't hold any kind of conversation. I'm so worried about him.'

Zac tactfully moved away, saying something about looking at the windows from the outside. He took the ladder and soon we heard him banging about, unscrewing the protective metal grilles. I talked to Jeremy about Dad's condition for a while, then we both went out to help.

When Zac had finished and put the ladder away again, we all found ourselves back in the Lady Chapel.

The vicar said, 'You know, I've been pondering an idea. There's been a recent bequest we might be able to use for work on the broken window. Stained glass is important. The windows are such an aid to worship, I find. In medieval times, coloured glass was said to inspire visions of ecstasy.'

I glanced again at the *Virgin and Child*, thinking of the agony of the *Crucifixion* window, how each scene represented a different side of perfect love, and saw his point. No one, surely, could contemplate these pieces and remain unmoved.

'If you would take the box,' Jeremy asked us, 'and see what you make of its contents, that would be marvellous. Find out what it is, for a start. Of course, if you thought it possible to restore, we'd need to consult the Parochial Church Council and the diocese. The red tape's such a bother when you're dealing with church property . . .' He trailed to a halt, gazing down at the box. I guessed we were all thinking the same thing. Was this game worth the candle? Could we really transform this mess of glass and lead into something whole and beautiful?

'Well, we can at least give you an idea of what it is,' I said, 'and go from there.'

'Yes, indeed,' said the vicar feelingly.

'You don't have anything that would help us, do you? Pictures, for instance – old guidebooks to the church?'

'I'll hunt about. But I haven't ever seen anything.'

I imagined what might be lying somewhere amidst the files in Dad's paper-filled attic. The thought of tackling them didn't fill me with joy.

Zac looked at his watch and cleared his throat pointedly. 'Do you think we've seen enough for today?'

I nodded. He bent down to close up the box, then tried to lift it.

'Oh, don't do that, for goodness sake,' said the vicar. 'It took two of us to carry it in from the hall.'

'What worries me is the box collapsing,' said Zac. 'Tell you what, I'll come by with the van tomorrow.' The two men agreed a time, then they eased the box back under the altar and the vicar straightened the cloth.

'I'll say goodbye here,' Jeremy said. 'I've some things to sort out in the vestry.'

It was after six, and for a while we had become aware of activity out in the lobby. People were beginning to arrive in some number, passing into the hall opposite.

Zac and I were leaving when he said, 'You go ahead. I've left my notebook,' and returned to the chapel.

Deciding to wait, I drifted to the door of the church to see what was going on. Someone was playing flourishes of chords on a piano in the hall. The lobby was full of people. No one took any notice of me standing inside the door.

'We pay our subscription to Dominic. He's the secretary,' one florid-faced City type was instructing another. 'He lends us the music. Some people already have their own, of course. *The Dream* is such a popular piece.'

'I'll borrow it this term, since I'm new to all this,' said the second man.

It must be the Choral Society the vicar had mentioned. So they were rehearsing *The Dream of Gerontius*, one of Elgar's most famous works and, as with his Cello Concerto, a favourite of mine. I moved into the doorway in order to see better.

Somebody said, 'Franny, is that you?'

A young woman with messy fair hair, in baggy cargo pants and a smock top, had entered the lobby. I couldn't see her face clearly against the light for a moment, but I'd know that voice anywhere. And no one else had ever called me Franny.

Chapter 5

Beside each man who's born on earth, a guardian angel takes his stand, to guide him through life's mysteries.

Menander of Athens

'*Jo!* What are you doing here?' I cried.

I saw her familiar smile, the one that enlivened her whole face, and it was as though I'd last met her yesterday.

People were pushing past us, muttering about the crush, so we moved outside onto the path. For a second or two we stared at one another nervously, but then she opened her arms and I leaned forward to hug her tightly. Considering my reluctance to ring her last night, I was surprised by how good it felt to see her again.

'You haven't changed a bit,' I said, looking her up and down. People say that lightly, but this time it was almost true. The same rounded figure, the same frizzy strawberry-blonde hair, resistant to brush or conditioner, the same freckled complexion, untouched by make-up – in short, the same Jo.

'Nor have you,' she said, slightly less convincingly, and we both knew that when we had last met, a dozen years ago, I had been very different, a shy, awkward creature with bitten nails, interested only in music and art, hardly able to open my mouth to strangers. And now . . . well, let's just say that twelve years had taught me more about presenting myself than how to tie a scarf artfully. I still bit my nails though.

'What have you been doing with yourself?' she asked. 'The last I heard, you were at music college. Your dad said you were doing ever so well.'

I recalled with guilt that she had written me several letters and postcards from university and I'd not replied to any of them. Which one had she gone to? Sussex? I couldn't remember, except that she'd long hoped to become a social worker. Always wanting to bind up wounds, was our Jo, always genuine in her desire to do good.

'I called at the shop once or twice over the years, you see,' she said, her innocent blue eyes focused on my face, 'but he always said you were away.'

'I've been working freelance, playing with any orchestra that needs me,' I explained. 'I must have taken that tuba round the world several times.'

'That explains it then,' she said, shrugging. 'Well, you always wanted to travel.'

Just then, Zac shoved his way out through the crowd. He glanced at Jo and, realising we were talking, mumbled, 'See you tomorrow.' Then he strode off, toolbag slung over his shoulder, in the direction of Vauxhall Bridge Road.

'Who's that?' Jo asked, staring after him.

'Just Zac,' I said. 'Dad's assistant. The vicar asked us to look at the windows in the church. So what are you doing with yourself these days?'

'Oh, I work at St Martin's Hostel.' This was the place for young homeless women the vicar had mentioned, back down the road, past the church. 'I'm one of the wardens.'

'Do you live in?'

'Oh no,' she said. 'That would be a bit much. I'm still at Mum and Dad's flat actually. They've got a place in Kent now but wanted to keep on Rochester Mansions as Dad still comes up to London a fair bit. I feel a bit old to be living at home still but, well, it makes sense with what I'm paid.'

'I'm at home again, too,' I said to reassure her, and told her about Dad's illness.

'Gosh, that's awful,' she said. The strength of feeling in her voice caught me unawares. 'If I can help at all . . .'

'Of course,' I said hoarsely. 'Thanks.'

Someone behind us called out, 'Isn't that the new bloke coming up the road now?' We all craned our necks, but I didn't know who we were looking at, for the street was so busy.

'I'm sorry, Fran,' said Jo. 'The conductor's here. I'd better queue up, get my music.'

'What's the choir?' I asked.

'St Martin's Choral Society. It's only the second year I've been, but I love it. We have two concerts a year in the church. The next one's in December. Ben's the new conductor – the old one had to retire. Listen, why don't you join? We're doing *The Dream*, and I know we need another soprano. You're a soprano, aren't you?'

'Yes, but I'm not sure I can commit to something like that at the moment.' It was tempting though. Although I'm an instrumentalist I've always loved singing. 'Can I think about it? How long's the rehearsal, anyway?'

'Two hours. Starts at six-thirty and some of us go to the pub after. Why don't you give it a try today? Everyone's really friendly.'

'Hi, Ben,' someone called out. 'Good summer?'

A man had turned in at the gate and I looked at him with interest. He was youngish, with very fair skin, a mane of wheat-coloured hair and finely moulded features. His was a face I'd seen somewhere before – in Italian Renaissance paintings. Yes, he would be a perfect Botticelli angel. There was an air about him that drew people's attention.

'Ben, hello,' Jo called out as he went by. He stopped, turned, looked enquiringly at her. She said a little breathlessly, 'I'm Jo, you won't know me. I've got another soprano for you here. This is Fran, an old schoolfriend of mine.'

Ben studied her solemnly. 'Jo,' he said, taking her hand. 'Of course I remember you.' She reddened and I smiled to myself at his studied charm.

Close up, I saw Ben was slightly older than I'd initially thought, more my own age, thirty. His skin had lost the glow of extreme youth and there were faint shadows under his eyes. But, if anything, that gave him a down-to-earth look that made him even more attractive.

'Fran,' he said, looking deep into my eyes for a second, and now it was my turn to be disconcerted.

'I haven't quite decided . . .' I started to say, but he hurried on.

'Great to see you. *Do* sing with us tonight. Speak afterwards maybe. The audition's not at all scary, promise.' And he swept on by. As though submitting to a higher presence, the throng parted to let him through. I felt disturbed and fascinated in equal part.

'Well . . .' I said to Jo, the decision apparently made for me.

'So you'll come?' she said, her face eager. 'There'll be the audition, of course, but I can't see you having any problems there, Fran. After all, I got through and Miss Logan once told me my voice was like bricks in a mincing machine.'

I laughed, remembering the elderly aristocratic music teacher who ran our Junior Choir.

Did I want to join a choir? It was quite a commitment. I thought of the alternative. Going home, another evening on my own. OK, why not? After all, I needn't come back if I didn't like it.

I followed Jo back into the lobby.

'Dominic, hi, how are you? This is a friend of mine from school – Fran,' Jo said to a big, smiley, round-faced man with fair baby curls and a tailored suit, who was sitting behind a trestle table on which music scores were stacked. 'I've just bumped into her after twelve years. Isn't that amazing?'

'Delighted to meet you, Fran,' Dominic said, standing up politely to shake my hand, his blue-eyed gaze as direct and guileless as Jo's. He wrote down my name and phone number, and handed me a copy of *The Dream* with a little flourish. Then he said to Jo with deliberate casualness, 'Are you up for a drink afterwards?'

'Oh yes,' she said, 'of course.'

'And you as well, Fran?' he added politely. I smiled and nodded non-committally.

The small hall was three-quarters full of chairs. The rest of the space in front of the tiny curtained stage was occupied by a grand piano and a podium for the conductor. I guessed there were as many as sixty or seventy people in the room, divesting themselves of jackets and cardigans, stowing bottles of water under chairs, looking through their music or chatting to friends they hadn't seen since the previous term. Jo and I found some free seats in the back row of the second soprano section and we talked about her work and news of old schoolfriends, until a woman in front turned round and attracted her attention. After Jo introduced me, I sat quietly as they swapped news, pretending to find my way around the familiar music, but all the time keeping an eye on the fascinating Ben, who had now climbed his podium and was adjusting his music stand.

Ben seemed oblivious to the roomful of people as he flicked

the pages of his score impatiently, tapping out different time beats to himself and scribbling little pencil marks here and there. He had removed his jacket and tie and, with his shirt open to the second button and the sleeves rolled up to his elbows, he appeared boyish once more. His wavy hair curling over the turned-up collar glinted golden against the white of the shirt.

A quick exchange of words with the pianist, a slight, grey-haired man Jo referred to as Graham, then suddenly Ben was ready. He stood calmly, frowning at a couple of latecomers who were sneaking in stagily at the back. Then he began to speak, and I only half-listened to his words as the soft musical timbre of his voice, the precise rendition of consonants, charmed me. He was so poised, so elegant to watch.

'Right, *The Dream of Gerontius*,' he said, and everyone immediately quietened. 'We've only what, twelve rehearsals, and a lot of material to get through. So if you're tempted to miss a rehearsal for any reason, then the message is *don't*. It's a big concert for us and I can't afford anything less than total commitment.' He looked round the room, but instead of seeming offended at this forthright approach, many people were nodding in earnest agreement.

'How many of you have sung this before?' He surveyed the sprinkling of raised hands. 'About a quarter. OK. For those who don't know, it's Elgar's most famous choral piece. Indeed, together with the *Messiah* and *Elijah*, it's one of *the* most popular pieces for choirs. However, that only means the audience will know it and will have high expectations of our performance.

'Just to give you a bit of background, *Gerontius* was first performed in 1900. Elgar put his absolute all into the composition, and indeed famously wrote that it represented the best of him. Unfortunately, for several reasons, the first performance was a complete disaster, something I certainly don't plan to repeat.' I admired Ben's timing. He didn't wait for the laughter to die down but went on. 'The *Dream* is a musical setting of Cardinal Newman's famous poem about man's passing through the unknown that lies beyond death, the greatest of heroic journeys.

'We'll start on page eleven with the "Kyrie". Semi-chorus, put up your hands so I can see you, please. Good. Crispin here,' he indicated a tall thin tenor with a long neck, 'has kindly agreed to be Gerontius for us during rehearsals. I am delighted to say that, having severely twisted the arm of my friend Julian Wright, I have got him to agree to take the role at the concert for a fraction of his usual fee.' There was a muttering of appreciation at this, as there should have been, for landing Julian, a fine tenor voice, was a real coup.

'There are a number of *leitmotifs* Elgar introduces in the orchestral Prelude. It'll be important to be aware of them, and I'll ask Graham to play the Prelude through for you now . . .'

Judgement, Fear, Prayer, Sleep and Despair. As Graham played through the themes, I remembered all the stages Gerontius experienced on his deathbed while we, the chorus, sang out to God to grant him mercy. Crispin led in the semi-chorus, uncertainly, with his first line, but quickly gained in confidence, and the beauty and power of the music rolled over me, caught me up. The two hours passed in a flash.

During the break, Ben asked that any newcomers requiring an audition should stay afterwards. I and the other candidate, a middle-aged Jamaican woman, waited by the piano until Ben was ready to put us through our places. She sang first, with a rich contralto voice.

'That's lovely, Elizabeth,' Ben told her. 'You're a natural.'

She nodded delightedly, whispered, 'Good luck,' to me and left to catch her train.

'See you both in the Bishop?' Dominic called out as he went

out with Jo, lugging a box of music scores, and she waved at me and said, 'You will come, won't you, Fran?'

All of a sudden, Ben and I were alone. He played a fanfare of chords on the piano and I warbled my way through a series of arpeggios.

'Sorry, bit of a frog in my throat,' I mumbled. 'But I suppose everyone says that.' Ben only smiled vaguely as he flicked through the book of sight-reading exercises.

'Try this one,' he said, passing over the book, and without waiting for him to give me a note on the piano I sang the tune he indicated without a mistake.

'You're a musician?' he asked, looking intently up at me.

'Brass player. Tuba's my main instrument.'

'Mmm, that's an unusual choice.' I was grateful that he stopped short of saying *for a woman*. I was all too used to people saying that, often adding, 'Especially one as small as you,' as though five feet two was freakish.

'I started with the French horn,' I told him. Then at college someone lent me their tuba to try and I found it much easier to play. The wider mouthpiece suits me better.'

His eyes rested briefly on my mouth. I went on quickly, 'I like its role in the orchestra too.'

'The sound underpins everything, doesn't it?'

'Exactly.'

'Who d'you play for?'

I came up with a few orchestras I had performed with.

'Who will you use for the concert?' I asked, and he named a rather good orchestra that specialised in accompanying amateur choral societies.

'And you've a lovely voice. It would be great to have you here, no problem,' Ben said, stowing his books into an ancient briefcase. His eyes met mine again and I had the weird sense that he was looking deep into my soul. 'Coming for a drink? I've got to finish up here first, if you don't mind waiting.'

I hung about while he locked up.

'I'm the new organist at St Martin's,' he said, in answer to my question about what else he did, as we walked the darkening streets towards the Bishop pub in Rochester Row. 'Conducting the choir's part of the job. Otherwise, I'm a pianist and take private pupils at a local school.'

Stepping out of his conductor role he had a disarming way of speaking, quite different from the maestro act on the podium. There was still something there, an edge, a slight arrogance, and I was definitely wary of that searching way he had of looking at me, but I found myself warming to him more.

'So how come you let Jo drag you along to the choir?' he enquired, and I explained about recently coming home and that I'd only bumped into her by accident.

'Dad owns the stained-glass shop in Greycoat Square,' I concluded. 'I came to look at the windows in the church this afternoon.'

'Ah, so you'll have met Jeremy Quentin,' he said. 'What d'you make of him?'

'He seems . . . nice. Is he?'

'He's all right.'

He didn't sound enthusiastic, and I wondered if there was something else there behind his words. At that point we reached the pub.

He held the door open for me and his arm accidentally brushed mine as I went through. Then we were swallowed up in a warm and welcoming crowd of choir members.

I hardly saw Ben again that evening, though once I noticed him standing with two or three other men by the bar, a tall graceful figure deep in animated conversation.

Somebody in the group round a big table moved up to allow me to squash into a corner next to Jo. Dominic got up to fetch me a glass of white wine.

So there I was, in the middle of a throng of people again, friendly people, but all except Jo strangers who would no doubt forget my existence as soon as the evening ended. So many new people, all talking at once, asking me the same questions about how I knew Jo and what I thought of the choir. It was exhausting, bewildering. The wine tasted acidic and I felt panicky, wanting to be alone. Perhaps I'd been wrong to come in the first place. Maybe the choir wasn't for me.

I stood up to leave as soon as was polite, echoing everyone's goodbyes, kissing Jo and arranging that I would ring her during the week. When I reached the door, someone touched my arm. It was Ben. I was surprised to see him and asked him if he was leaving too, but no, he had come over specially to say goodbye.

'We'll see you next week, won't we?' Again, that soul-searching look.

'Of course,' I managed to say. All my previous doubts about the choir mysteriously vanished. 'You told us not to miss any rehearsals.'

'Wonderful,' he said warmly. 'It's lovely to have you. Take care now.'

The few minutes' walk home calmed me. Back in the safety of *Minster Glass*, I rejoiced in my own company. But the flat, as ever, was full of echoes. I lay on my bed thinking of Dad, probably asleep, an old man surrounded by other old men in the shiny white hospital sterility. I thought about the windows of St Martin's Church, about seeing Jo again, about the noisy camaraderie I had briefly been a part of this evening. I'd done nothing – yet a new life was assembling itself around me. I was being swept along by it all. I wasn't sure how I felt about it.

When I finally fell asleep I dreamed I was cradled in the arms of a great angel flying high over the city, with the flashing jewels of lights, the dark glistening snake of the river, the silver towers of churches, the glint of glass from high-rise offices, all laid out beneath me. So high were we that the only sound I could hear was the rhythmic beating of wings.

Chapter 6

Do not neglect to show hospitality to strangers, for thereby some have entertained angels unawares.

Hebrews XIII. 2.

During school holidays in my late teens, when I wasn't practising my music or helping Dad in the shop, I used to walk down to the Tate Gallery – now known as Tate Britain – only a few streets south towards the river. My favourite rooms were where the pre-Raphaelite and late-nineteenth-century paintings hung, and the painting I loved above all others was, of course, a Burne-Jones, *King Cophetua and the Beggar Maid*. In it the beggar maid sits in a wooden boudoir staring out at the observer, her bearing, despite her rags, that of a Queen. Below her on the step, the handsome King, his crown doffed in his lap, gazes up at her adoringly. But she will not even look at him. Instead she holds a bunch of anemones, telling him through the flowers that she rejects his love.

This dramatisation of unrequited passion stirred up such deep feelings in me that I read up all about the picture in the book on Burne-Jones that hid the photo of my mother.

It was based on an old legend of a King who found his love for a beautiful beggar maid was greater than all his power and wealth. Burne-Jones probably learned of the legend by reading

Tennyson's poem, 'The Beggar Maid', and he cast it in a setting inspired by fifteenth-century Italian painting. He apparently created the picture after a time of considerable strain in his marriage, and some say the artist is the King and the beggar maid Georgiana, his wife, whom he betrayed by his affair with the stormy beauty Mary Zambaco. But others hold that the maid must be Frances Graham, a girl with whom Burne-Jones went on to conduct an intense romantic friendship and who, to his distress, got married in 1883, while he was working on the picture. Did the painting become an expression of his feelings about the loss of Frances?

I bought a poster of *Cophetua* and hung it on my bedroom wall. By then my father, in respect for my womanhood, rarely entered my room, but once he did to give me a magazine that had arrived in the morning post. He stared at my poster with a stunned look on his face. When I asked him what the matter was, he snapped, 'Nothing,' and, as ever, the shutters came down.

The next day, when I came home from school, the poster had disappeared and, although this might seem strange, I didn't even question the matter. I was angry, yes, disturbed certainly, but I had just enough compassion in my selfish teenage soul to realise that my poster had touched some terrible sadness in him. So I bit my lip and let the matter go.

The day after our visit to St Martin's, Zac arrived at the shop at nine, but didn't bother to remove his jacket.

'Fitting some windows this morning,' he said. 'Give me a hand getting them in the van?'

'Oh. Yes, of course.' This meant that I'd be stuck looking after the shop, but I bit back my complaint and went out to help him polish and pack up two panels representing a pair of gorgeous peacocks, which had been drying in the garage in our yard, then to carry out the sunrise, which he'd finished the day before, and Dad's Celtic knot to take their place. He backed the van out of the drive at a lick. Locking the garage door, I went through to open the shop.

It was a glorious morning, the kind of morning when I used to shirk my music practice, but today I forced myself to sit in the shop and make suncatchers. We had sold a dragonfly and a fairy yesterday from the line-up in the window and they were easy to replace using Dad's old pattern-book for inspiration. Cutting out simple glass shapes, edging them with copperfoil and soldering them together to make fairies, birds or butterflies, adding a copper loop to hang them by, came so naturally to me it was almost a meditative task.

The bright sunshine made everything look dirty, so after I'd arranged my suncatchers in the window I found a brush and a soft cloth and set about cleaning the shop, stopping only to sweettalk an indecisive customer into buying a pair of poppy-patterned lampshades as a wedding present for her niece.

The shop obviously hadn't had a thorough clean for ages, for I was soon coughing at the dust I stirred up with my broom. I wedged the door open to clear the air, then one by one unhooked the items in the window to wipe them over carefully. It was while I was removing our lovely angel from the chains by which she hung that I looked through the window to meet a pair of dark eyes. It was the stray-cat girl I'd seen a few days ago; then she'd seemed wary, now she was agitated. Even before I'd laid the angel on the counter she had moved into the open doorway.

'Hello,' I said, trying to sound friendly. 'Can I help?'

'You're not, like, sellin' it, are you? Oh, please don't let some-one else have it.' Her voice was shaking and her black-lashed eyes great pools of pleading.

'I'm only cleaning it,' I said gently.

'Oh, I thought . . . That's OK then.' She smiled and it was impossible not to smile back, there was something so sweet and fragile about her. If I'd had to guess her age, I'd have said seventeen or eighteen, but it was hard to tell. Aware of her watching, I laid the angel on the counter and began to work away at the layer of greasy grime.

Now she was in the shop the girl seemed unsure whether to stay or go. I said, 'You like her, do you? Well, she certainly is lovely. My dad made her. Come and have a proper look.'

Shy again, she stepped inside, glancing about at the mirrors and the lampshades and the shelves of glass like Alice entering Wonderland, her mouth slightly open in amazement. Then she tiptoed, as much as one can tiptoe in trainers, over to the counter. I carefully raised the arched window, tilting it until the light brought it to life, and we studied the angel together.

Clothed in white and pink and gold, the tips of her wings pink also, she stood in a field of flowers, her caramel hair blowing around her heart-shaped face. Dad had made her shortly before I left home, from a design of his own that had a kind of 1970s style, something about the way the hair waved across the face.

'Do you know anything about how stained-glass windows are made?' I asked the girl.

She shook her head. 'No. I . . . I just like angels. And the glass – it's so pretty. I really wish I could buy her. Is she a lot of money?'

'She's not for sale, I'm afraid,' I said, and watched disappointment and relief struggle in her countenance. Eventually relief won.

'At least I can always come and look at her, then.'

'That's right. She'll be here.'

'You see, she's my angel.'

Now it was my turn to be confused.

'Everybody has a guardian angel, didn't you know? And she's mine.'

'I'm sure we could all do with a little extra help in life,' I said, wanting neither to encourage this unusual line nor to upset the girl.

'That's right.' Her smile transformed her face. All her wariness was gone now. 'Our angels watch over us wherever we go. So we're not hurt, see. Or . . .' she paused and looked away. 'They help us if we are hurt.'

She seemed so unhappy suddenly, that I knew she was talking about herself. Oh heck, now she would come out with some terrible story that I wouldn't know whether to believe and then I wouldn't know what to do about it.

'What's your name?' I asked, and told her mine.

'Amber,' she answered. 'I live at St Martin's – you know, the hostel?'

I nodded slowly. 'My friend works there. Do you know Jo Pryde?'

'Oh yes, she's nice.' This response didn't surprise me one bit. I couldn't imagine anyone not liking Jo. 'I'm just there till I get myself sorted out. Find a job and that.'

'Of course,' I said. 'Well, Amber, I ought to get on. It's lovely meeting you.'

'Thanks for showing me the angel.' And she was gone, slipping out in a little sparkling cloud of dust. A trick of the light, of course.

I considered the question of guardian angels as I finished cleaning this one, which I must now think of as Amber's. It was a sentimental idea, something out of a Victorian children's book. Yet what about all those children who fell in the fire, or under horses' hooves, or who died of scarlet fever? Were their angels looking the other way at the time? Dad used to talk about angels as a source of inspiration. Sometimes when he'd had a good idea for a design he would say, 'An angel must have passed overhead.'

Really, I told myself as I hung our angel back in the window, they were beautiful, but the world had moved on. Angels belonged to pictures and stories – and dreams – but surely that was all.

It wasn't until late afternoon that I heard Zac's van in the yard. I opened the back door to see him edging a box out of the boot, and ran out to help. I'd forgotten he had collected the bombed-out window. The box bulged dangerously and I grabbed one splitting side. Together we brought it in and rested it on a table.

We stood and looked at it for a moment, then Zac opened the flaps, pushed aside the newspaper and drew out the long twisted section from the top. A piece of glass immediately started to fall away, so he hastily laid the whole thing back into the box.

'Haven't got time to look at it now anyway,' he said, reaching for Dad's Day Book, but he couldn't stop himself glancing back at the box with a look of longing.

I shut up shop at five, intending to go straight away to see Dad. When I went to say goodbye to Zac though, I found him lifting strips of glass and lead out of the box and laying them out on a length of creamy lining paper that he'd taped onto the table.

Why couldn't he have waited? I put down my bag, deciding to see Dad later.

'Shall I help?' I asked tentatively and was pleased when Zac smiled.

'Good at puzzles, are you?' he said, moving pieces around on the paper with his long strong fingers.

In silence we contemplated the elements he'd assembled. There were a number of gold fragments clearly representing drapery. One cluster of white and red was recognisable as a hand curled round a stick. A tinted white piece painted with wavy gold lines must be hair. Zac shifted these around into likely places on the paper, then we tried to build on them using smaller pieces.

'This drapery's like doing bits of sky in a jigsaw,' I moaned. 'There's a bit with an eye here, look, and this must be the nose. Can you hunt for more face?'

Zac lifted out all the larger sections from the box and started carefully sifting through pieces at the bottom.

Eventually we assembled a large part of the face, but this area of the window had suffered the greatest damage. Although it must once have been a single piece of glass, half the features had fragmented. It was like viewing a face beneath a heavily patterned lace veil, impossible to grasp it as a whole. We stared at it glumly for a while. Then Zac unfolded the soft lead around a large section of painted gold that so obviously represented feathers that we both grinned at one another and said together, 'An angel.'

Angels, it seemed, were gathering all around me.

We worked on for another half hour, until there came a point where we ran out of pieces and the picture was only three-quarters complete. Some of the large areas of patterned background and the robes we hadn't made much sense of, and we couldn't tell exactly where hands and feet or head should be, though Zac clipped back some of the worst-twisted lead to enable us to try.

'Most of the glass is not in bad condition, really,' he noted. 'I reckon the window must have caved in from the force of a nearby explosion rather than receiving a direct hit. What do you think? There's no blackening, is there?'

'Whatever, we can only go so far without an illustration,' I said with a sigh.

Zac looked utterly fed up. 'Let's hope the vicar finds an old guidebook then or we'll have to start searching libraries. Is there anything upstairs here? Didn't you say your dad had got out all the papers?'

'The original cartoon, you mean? There might be. I'll look when I get back later. Not now though. I must go to the hospital.'

When I returned from seeing Dad, it was nearly nine and the phone was ringing in the flat. I snatched up the receiver, anxious that it might be about Dad. But it was Jo.

'It was so lovely to see you last night,' she said. 'I've got the evening off tomorrow. Would you like to meet up?'

'That would be great,' I said happily.

After I'd put the phone down, I tried some scales and arpeggios on my tuba for a while. Tonight the sound was overwhelming in this limited space. Goodness knows what anyone next door must think. I returned the instrument to its case.

Remembering the broken angel, I climbed up to the attic, sat down at Dad's desk and, with a sense of foreboding at the immensity of the task, began sorting through the stacks of ancient files there. Some were dated in a faded copperplate, others bore Dad's pencilled scribbles – *mostly bills* or *St Ethelberga's* or just a date. Some were merely fragments of paper tied together with rotting ribbon. There were scrolls of all sizes jumbled on the floor by the desk, some of which I unrolled. Designs for windows, none of which I was looking for. In a huge cupboard at the far end of the attic I knew there were hundreds of others like these. And big pattern-books. The phrase 'needle in a haystack' was certainly apt in this case.

What information did I have so far? The entry in the Day Book indicated that the Lady Chapel windows of St Martin's were made during 1880 and that there had been two of them. There were no further details given, so I picked up several files that bore 1880 dates and started to go through them methodically.

As I feared, it wasn't a straightforward job. *Minster Glass* had, it seemed, conserved every scrap of paper relating to its commissions. Much of the material was uninviting – accounts from suppliers, estimates – I had only to cast my eye over it and move on, but then came something more interesting: a letter from the then vicar of St Martin's, the Reverend Brownlow previously mentioned in Dad's history. It was dated April 1880.

> *Dear Sirs,*
> *Further to our recent discussions I am at last in a position to*
> *request that you commission Mr Philip Russell to draft*
> *drawings for two windows in the Lady Chapel of St Martin's*
> *Church, one over its altar to depict the* Virgin *and Child in*
> Glory, *the other being for the south light to represent an angel.*
> *I look forward to hearing from you soonest on this matter.*
> *Yours sincerely,*
> JAMES BROWNLOW (REVD.)

An angel. Our broken window was definitely an angel. At last I had found a thread leading into the past. A thread which, if I pulled, might begin to unravel a story.

As I laid the letter carefully in its place in the unwieldy file, the whole thing slipped from my grasp. I caught it before it fell and shuffled the contents safely back inside, but a sheet of cartridge paper escaped and sailed down onto the floorboards.

I lifted it delicately with the tips of my fingers. Turning it over, I saw at once it was probably cut from a small sketchbook. It featured a rough pencil drawing for an arched window. A speculative study, I imagined, for it was covered with scribbled notes and figures that could only have meant something to the artist.

There were other sketches on the page. A young woman's face in one corner, a sort of pattern in another. The pattern reminded me of something – Dad's Celtic knot – and then I realised that was exactly what it was, a Celtic knot. The *Minster Glass* signature. As I savoured this find, my attention drifted to the thumbnail sketch of the girl. She was deftly drawn, vitality in the tilt of her strong square face, intelligence and humour in her direct gaze. Thick hair sprang back from her forehead. She wasn't conventionally beautiful, but the bloom of youth was still upon her and there was something arresting about her expression. The artist had scrawled something underneath in his odd spindly writing. *Lana* it might have been, or *Laura*, then another word, something beginning with B. A note in Dad's handwriting teased my memory. What was it he'd written in the margins of his notebook? *Who was Laura something . . .?* Of course, the name in the letter I'd just read. Brownlow, that was it. *Who was Laura Brownlow?* Dad had written. He must have seen this sketch, too, and wondered. So who was she? James Brownlow's wife, perhaps? Or his daughter. And why had this *Minster Glass* artist drawn her?

I studied her portrait once more and her eyes seemed to stare into mine. As though she would speak, could tell me her story.

I replaced the sheet of paper in the folder and laid the folder on the heap of others. Where I should search now, I wasn't sure.

I was tired, anyway. Perhaps it would be helpful to return some of these files to their drawer?

I stood, stretching, stiff from hunching over the desk for so long, then went over to the lines of tall metal filing cabinets. The drawer labelled *1879–81* opened easily, felt light, and when I peeped over the top I saw why. Only the hanging files at the back of the drawer contained any folders.

I returned to the desk and arranged the folders there into date order, then took them over one by one to slip into their hanging files. But when I came to the one dated 1880, in which I'd found the Reverend Brownlow's letter and the sketchbook page, it wouldn't go. I laid it on the top of the cabinet and investigated the hanging file.

My fingers scraped on something hard – a book of some sort. I gripped it and pulled it out. It was the size of a slim hardback novel, and when I turned the pages I saw immediately that it was a diary or journal, completely filled with neat feminine handwriting. There was a name inside the front cover – and for a moment I couldn't take it in.

It was the name I'd read before, the name under the sketch of the young woman, the name that had excited Dad's curiosity. Laura Brownlow. *Who was Laura Brownlow?* At last it seemed I would find out.

The entries began in June 1879, but the first page had faded a bit and was hard to read. I sat down at the desk once more, and in the light of Dad's lamp, began to decipher the even, sepia italics.

Sunday, 18 May 1879
Happy Birthday, dear sister Caroline! To think that you would be eighteen! We celebrated a special service in the church for you today, Mama and Papa, Harriet and George and me. And

Tom journeyed home from Oxford. Did you see us and hear us? I believe you did. You felt so close, as though you were there, 'betwixt air and angels', just beyond our reach.

I still think about you all the time. When I rise, I have to tell myself that the bedroom next door is empty, that you will not need me to go to you today, to read or play games. I wake in the night, sure that you have called my name, and the truth weighs on me like the darkness.

So many little things remind me of you. A snatch of a song that you used to sing, the precise shade of a girl's hair. Last week Mrs Jorkins found a pair of your old boots and asked Mama if she should give them away, but I would not let her and cried over them. Three months you've been gone and now the numbness I felt after your passing has lifted. Instead there is the constant ache of missing you, the awareness that our time together is past, left far behind in life's rushing stream. When I saw those boots, for one moment I was sure I could catch hold of you once more. I was wrong.

I turned the pages slowly, moved by the rawness of the writer's grief. So Laura Brownlow must be the daughter of the Reverend James Brownlow, the man who commissioned the windows of St Martin's. But she addressed her diary entries to Caroline, the dead sister in whose memory the angel window was made. Laura was writing to Caroline as though she still lived – or as though she believed she could reach her beyond the grave. How deeply she must have mourned.

I read on. The entries were sporadic as though Laura only wrote when she felt she needed to or when there was some notable event to communicate to Caroline. In June 1879, Laura was excited about their brother Tom's academic success. In August she reported the placing of a memorial stone on the dead girl's grave. In November came the thrilling news that their married sister Harriet was to give birth the following April.

But in the New Year of 1880, Laura began to write more regularly and at greater length, and soon I became completely absorbed in her story . . .

Chapter 7

The angel in the house

Coventry Patmore

LAURA'S STORY

That chilly February morning, Laura hoped they would see the lion cub again. The walk to Westminster Hospital took them up Victoria Street towards the Abbey, and when they had passed this way yesterday, she and Mama had viewed a reedy youth with a broken nose and a mutinous expression dragging the poor beast around the perimeter of the Royal Aquarium. The cub, though only a little past babyhood, had looked confused rather than frightened. It dodged about on its rope, tripping over its too-large paws. The youth hauled it back while scowling and cursing at a handful of urchins who alternately made cajoling noises and shied pebbles at the animal from a safe distance.

'Oh, the poor thing.' Laura had made Mama stop to watch for a moment, touched to the quick to see this beast trapped in a life it wasn't made for, no doubt forced to parade with the other lions in front of a howling crowd. Not, of course, that she had experienced the crowd. She'd never set foot in the Aquarium to see the circus or the freakshows, to skate on the ice-rink or gawp at the fish. 'Third-rate entertainment for third-rate people,' was how her pompous brother-in-law George settled the matter when she'd raised the subject at dinner yesterday evening – but she could imagine it all from the lurid headlines on the posters.

Disappointingly, the cub wasn't there today. Perhaps an airing in today's freezing fog was considered a step beyond the cruelties it commonly endured. If that was the reason, Laura was glad. Or maybe the lion troupe had simply moved on, taking the cub with them. She paused to accept a flyer from a shivering young boy: tonight's entertainment seemed to be 'Two Astonishing Aerial Acts'. No mention of lions.

'Don't dawdle, Laura, dear,' Mama called, her voice dead-sounding in the icy air. 'Here, let me take the bag.' Laura gratefully passed over the heavy canvas grip and followed in her mother's neat footsteps towards the next building which, with its ramparts and flags, always looked to her more like a castle than a hospital.

Visiting the women in the Incurables Ward of Westminster Hospital turned out to take twice as long as Mama had planned today, for after the usual Bible readings and prayers, one distressed young mother poured out her heart to Mama about her anxieties for her family, and another dictated to Laura a rambling letter of farewell for a sailor son she'd not seen in years.

Mother and daughter finally emerged just as Big Ben, wreathed in mist, struck a muffled eleven. Laura asked hopefully, 'Will we still have time for shopping, Mama?' Her mother had promised her material for a new serge dress to replace one four years old and worn almost to holes, but with most of the morning gone she already guessed the answer.

'The dress will have to wait until another day now, I'm afraid, dear. We barely have time to call on the Coopers – and you must remember your father has invited Mr Bond for luncheon.'

Laura sighed, but seeing the two worry lines between her mother's brows deepen, she stifled her disappointment.

They wove their way back through the crowds on Victoria Street, where brass plaques of architects and lawyers – one of these Mr Bond's – shone at nearly every doorway, before turning left, heading south towards the river. Almost immediately they found themselves in a different world, where men loitered, as grey and grimy as the filthy street, and where a dismal cacophony arose, of wailing infants, arguing voices, and the banging of ill-fitting doors. The stink was indescribable. Laura always fancied her clothes reeked long after one of these visits to the slums of her father's parish. To her, these back streets spoke of the most desolate regions of Hades in the book of Greek myths she had read aloud to her younger sister during the days of Caroline's long illness.

As the two women picked their way through the muddy rubbish, a thickset lout lolling in a doorway called out something menacing, and Laura glanced at her mother for guidance. Mama's head was held high, like a thoroughbred on a tight rein, but two angry red spots on her cheeks betrayed her agitation.

'Come along, Laura,' she snapped, leading her on, past a building site where some of the more dilapidated housing had been pulled down to make way for new, but where whole families had broken in and erected makeshift shelters for themselves. Past the ragged school through the broken window of which birdlike Miss Pilkington could be glimpsed pointing a cane at a tattered map on the wall. Down an even narrower, darker lane, through a battered door and up some steps into a tiny hallway that smelled of damp and rotten wood on top of other, more repulsive odours. Laura remembered to breathe only through her mouth as she followed her mother up another flight of stairs.

The door to the Coopers' rooms was ajar, but Mama politely knocked and waited. A small girl peered out, fearful, before admitting them.

'Hello, Ida,' Mama said. 'This is my daughter, Miss Laura. How's your mother today, dear?'

'Not good, mam, but she ate the broth you and the other lady left,' the small girl said, peeping shyly at Laura. Mama had taken their maid, Polly, with her last time.

Her eyes getting used to the dingy light, Laura became aware that the room was full of children lying on revolting-looking straw pallets or sitting wrapped in ragged blankets on the bare wooden boards, hungry eyes staring out at the visitors. As for Ida in her filthy torn dress, Laura remembered Mama had said she was twelve. She would have looked puny for eight.

Mama handed Laura the bag and Laura brought out the parcels of bread and dripping packed by Mrs Jorkins the cook and handed them round to the children, who had hardly the energy to receive them. There was a flask of milk, too, which Laura poured into enamel mugs and administered to the smallest of the children. It was all too quickly gone. Next, she knew she was to ask Ida for help washing them, but in the meantime she couldn't resist looking where her mother had gone.

Through the doorway of the second room, a woman with a mass of untidy red hair could be seen lying under a thin blanket on a mattress on the floor, her face flushed with fever. Mama was shaking out a fresh bedsheet and Laura helped her carefully roll the sick woman over so Mama could peel away the soiled bedding. Laura felt her gorge rise when she glimpsed the pool of fresh blood.

'We must fetch the doctor to you, Molly,' Mama said gently,

then as the woman murmured something about the cost, 'Don't worry, we will take care of that. You must think of yourself. And the baby.'

Laura knelt by the littlest Cooper, a newborn boy who lay still in a wooden box next to the mattress, his skin sallow, his eyes roaming unfocused, as though searching for something he would never find in this derelict house he had been unlucky enough to get born in. She lifted out the child tenderly, remembering with a bittersweet pain how she'd once held her little brother Ned when he was a sunny, chubby baby, and her heart swelled with pity for this tiny silent scrap. The cloth that swaddled him was soiled. She called out to Ida to fetch water, searching in the bag for clean napkins.

After everybody was fed, washed and changed, they left, Mama promising again to send for the doctor.

'Out looking for work, is what she always says when I ask,' was Mama's bitter answer to Laura's enquiry about Mr Cooper's whereabouts as they hurried home to Greycoat Square. 'I've certainly never set eyes on the wretched fellow.'

Laura was shocked by the anger in her mother's usually mild voice. They were both subdued after this visit but Laura thought that although her mother must be tired, she seemed less tense now.

'Thank you for coming with me, Laura. You have a natural compassion and you see how much there is to do here in this parish.'

'Yes, Mama,' Laura sighed, immediately guilty that instead of glowing with satisfaction, she merely felt relieved to be on the way home. They passed a boy with a scruffy puppy on a string and she thought of the lion cub, confused, trapped in a world where it didn't belong. Like the newborn Cooper, his eyes shining like starlight, whose visit to this earth might only be a short one. There seemed too much unbearable pain for anyone to deal with in this world.

Laura's father was the Reverend James Brownlow and the family had lived for eight years at St Martin's Vicarage in Greycoat Square, around the corner from the church in Vincent Street. The Square itself was a quiet, genteel place with a central garden where nurses pushed perambulators and children ran about the grass in summer. Amongst their neighbours were doctors, lawyers, gentlemen in trade, the occasional Member of Parliament, but many of these attended the more fashionable St Mary's Church on the far side. St Martin's, on the other hand, had been erected by public subscription some thirty years before to minister to the poor. It had been built facing away from the well-to-do townhouses of the Square, towards the slums of Old Pye Street and Duck Lane, now at last being cleared, but slowly, too slowly for the likes of the Cooper family.

As Laura changed out of her work dress, nose wrinkling at the dirty splashes and lingering smells, real or fancied, she glanced out of her bedroom window. A little boy was tripping along the path in the garden of the Square, hand-in-hand with his nurse. A boy with a burnished bell of gold hair, who laughed and tugged at the girl's hand. For the second time that day she was reminded of Ned.

He had been about that age, only four, when he died. Now he was fixed in her memory as a bright laughing child who would never grow any older but who was as much a part of their thoughts as Tom, her elder brother, now away studying Theology at Exeter College in Oxford, preparing to follow in the steps of their father.

She watched the child until he disappeared from view then went to peer in her tiny looking glass (tiny because her mother disapproved of studying one's appearance), beholding first one side of her head then the other, to replace the loose pins in her hair.

The house was quiet; it being a Friday in Lent and hence a day of fasting, a nasty smell of boiled fish was seeping up the stairs. On the landing Laura paused outside Caroline's room, noticing that the door, normally kept shut, shivered ajar. She pushed it slightly and peered round, half-expecting to see her mother, or Polly with her duster, but there was nobody. She walked in, closing the door behind her, sniffing at the faint aroma of beeswax.

Within, all was as Caroline had left it. The bed was neatly made, the fireplace swept, the furniture dusted. Caroline's array of childish treasures – a teddy bear, her doll with the white china face, a box of pretty buttons – lay on the chest of drawers. The sampler on the wall she had painstakingly stitched when she was eight gave her name and her birth date, 18 May 1861. Books, scrapbooks, a pressed-flower collection, were lined up on the bookcase. Fanned out on the lace dressing-table mat she'd knotted were the silver-backed hairbrush, comb and mirror she'd been given for her sixteenth birthday.

All appeared as though Caroline herself might walk back through the door.

But she would never walk through that door again.

Laura lay down on the bed, gingerly so as not to disarrange the bedclothes, and folded back the counterpane just a little way to press her cheek against the pillow. Eyes closed, she breathed in hopefully, but no trace of Caroline's favourite violet toilet water remained. She let her breath go, mouthed 'Caroline,' and listened, but there was no ghost to whisper an answer.

It was a year now since Caroline's death at nearly seventeen, a long, lingering death after years of a disorder of the blood that had taken her by stealth, reducing her from a lively, round-faced child to a pale willowy girl who never quite reached woman-hood.

Little Ned, by contrast, had gone quickly. One day he had been racing around the rambling vicarage garden in Hampstead after the neighbour's dog that had slipped through the fence, the next he lay sunk in a coma, a scarlet rash spreading like fire beneath the perfect lustre of his skin. Eight years ago that had been, and then their mother couldn't stand to live in the house where he died, and their father had accepted this placement. James Brownlow had hoped that if his beloved Theodora absorbed herself in her other children and could devote herself to parishioners impoverished in body, mind and spirit, she would be healed of her sorrow.

Perhaps this might have worked, had not Caroline then fallen ill.

Laura felt a tear slip down her cheek, heard it drop onto Caroline's pillow.

Deep down in the house the front door bell clanged and Mrs Jorkins called out, 'Polly? Where is the girl? *Polly!*'

Then came the clattering of the door being unfastened and a man's booming voice, and the clump of boots. Mr Bond had arrived. Laura pushed herself to her feet, wiping her eyes with the heel of her hand. She smoothed down the bedclothes then shut the door quietly behind her and went downstairs.

Anthony Bond, Papa's solicitor and principal churchwarden, was a man of five and thirty, neither plain nor handsome, nei-ther short nor tall, neither fat nor thin. Indeed, he was average in all visible respects. His straight brown hair and beard were neatly barbered, his movements were neither graceful nor clumsy. There was nothing arresting nor objectionable about him. One would pass him in the street without a second glance – and Laura frequently did.

Papa had, most unusually, invited him to lunch because he and Bond had some business to discuss in advance of a meeting with the church's architect that afternoon. Laura felt sorry that their visitor must endure the Friday Lent menu, but as a concession to the presence of a guest Mrs Jorkins was today allowed to serve a white sauce with the obligatory fish and there would be damson jam with the semolina pudding.

When she crept downstairs, it was to find that Papa had taken the guest into his study. She stood for a moment, listening to the sound of their voices – Papa's clear tones and Bond's deep ones – rise and fall through the clatter from the kitchen.

The shut door was all too familiar. Since Caroline's death Papa retreated to his study more and more. He was writing a history of the Church of England, he told them, but once when she was sent to fetch him for supper, she'd found him deeply asleep in an armchair. She'd picked up the book that had fallen from his grasp and turned it over. It was Cardinal Newman's poem about the journey of a soul, open at the page where the dead man's guardian angel bears his soul to judgement. She read the words of the angel's song:

> 'This child of clay
> To me was given
> To rear and train
> By sorrow and pain
> In the narrow way.'

Poor Papa. She watched him sleep on, lines of his own sorrow and pain etched in his face. Beneath their brave faces to the world they seemed so . . . diminished . . . her parents, since the loss of Caroline. Of course, they had their other children, but Tom had left home, would take holy orders and tread his own 'narrow way'. Harriet was married, expecting her first child, fussed over by her voluble mother-in-law. Only she, Laura, was left – 'my unplucked rose' as her father teased her sometimes. Perhaps she was meant to stay with them, never to marry. Did she mind? She did a little. She was still only twenty-two. It would be nice to know what it felt like, to be wanted by a man.

At luncheon, she and Mama sat disengaging the flesh of their cod from its gritty black skin, as Mr Bond and Papa discussed Mr Gladstone's proposals to allow married women further rights in law and property. Mr Bond had his reservations, it seemed, but was a pragmatist. Papa was concerned that giving women greater independence would chip away further at holy matrimony, which made man and woman one flesh.

Mama picked at her food, the two lines deepening on her forehead. Was she getting one of her headaches, Laura wondered anxiously. These, when they came, usually condemned Theodora Brownlow to several days in bed, the curtains drawn. But Mama was at least eating a few mouthfuls of fish, which was a good sign. It must be just weariness.

'How then would a man guide a young and wilful wife?' Papa was enquiring of no one in particular.

'Why should not an educated woman stand mistress over her own wealth, Papa?' Laura said quietly. Her father swallowed a mouthful and frowned.

'You are still very unformed for such a suggestion, dear Laura,' he said. 'Perhaps were you to be married to a man you trust with all your heart and soul, as your Mama does me, you would recognise the good sense of the current principle.'

He exchanged glances with Mr Bond, who gave an irritating little laugh. What had she said that was funny, Laura wondered.

'An educated and dutiful woman is well able to advise her husband, Miss Brownlow,' Mr Bond said gently. 'And he may then decide for the both of them.' He took his last mouthful of fish, placed his knife and fork together on the plate and dabbed his mouth with his napkin. 'In the majority of cases,' he went on, 'marital harmony will prevail. However, the new Parliament might be swayed by the need to right wrongs that result in those few monstrous exemplars when the man neglects or, ah, abuses his responsibilities.'

Laura gave up on the mess of bones and scales on her plate and, as they waited politely for Mrs Brownlow to finish, her mind drifted to a story she might write about a woman abandoned by her husband. Perhaps she would start it tonight now that the Eastertide altar linen, the embroidery of which had occupied many long evenings, was complete.

When she tuned into the conversation again, Mr Bond was discussing a recent legacy to the church. 'Mrs Fotherington's nephew has shown me her will. Coloured glass for the Lady Chapel, his aunt specified, "to represent a suitable theme".'

Laura missed Sarah Fotherington, who had dropped down dead during a ladies' missionary meeting less than two weeks ago. Not because she had liked her particularly, but because she had shared the burden of Mama's work in the parish and helped run the Sunday school, tasks that Laura seemed now to be expected to perform instead. No one had asked her; it was just assumed that she would.

Mama finally laid down her knife and fork, most of her meal uneaten, and Polly stepped forward to clear away the plates. Mama said in a dreamy voice, 'A mother and child. That would be right for the Lady Chapel – the *Virgin and Child*.'

Laura and Papa looked at one another in alarm, both sensitive to Mrs Brownlow's lapses from strong capability into melancholy. But Mama's brown-eyed gaze was firm and serious, with no sign of tears.

'A most apposite suggestion, my dear,' Papa soothed.

Mrs Jorkins bustled in with bowls of semolina, then ceremoniously laid a large pot of her best damson jam on the table.

Mr Bond glanced anxiously between husband and wife. He said, 'I can discuss Mrs Brownlow's proposal with Mrs Fotherington's nephew, Mr Stuart Jefferies, if you so wish, Rector.'

'Yes,' said Mr Brownlow, passing the jam to Mr Bond. Laura watched him take a polite amount. He looked as though he really wanted more. 'Jefferies seems a reasonable enough fellow.'

'And, James, are there not several windows in the Lady Chapel?' Mrs Brownlow said quietly, taking the minutest spoonful of jam.

'Yes, indeed, my dear, but one is half-obscured by a cupboard. The *Virgin and Child* might fill the light above the chapel altar, do you not think?'

'Oh, yes, and the child . . . James, might we choose an artist with care, find one with facility at portraying babies?'

'There are such ugly babies,' Laura said, ladling a generous helping of the purple plum over her hated semolina. 'It's as though the great artists were more interested in their female model than in evoking the Christ Child.'

'Oh Laura,' said her father, smiling. 'But, of course, the child's appearance is important. We'll seek advice, Theodora.'

'Thank you, James. One more thing. The money my own father left: would there be enough there for a second window?'

Papa waved away the jam Laura offered him and frowned. 'We haven't discussed how we should use that money yet,' he said. 'There is the – ah – vexing question of Tom's rising expenses.'

'I know, but I'd like a window for Caroline, to remember her,' Mama went on, a slight break in her voice.

'Oh, Papa,' cried Laura, 'that's a splendid idea of Mama's! Do let's have another window.'

Mr Brownlow conferred upon his wife a look of such compassion that Mr Bond, who sat patiently waiting for the signal to start eating, stared down at his semolina, his face reddening.

'It is an excellent idea that perhaps we should discuss later in private, Dora,' Mr Brownlow said firmly, and at last picked up his spoon.

'An angel, James,' whispered Mrs Brownlow, a beatific smile transforming her tired features. 'Think about it. It will be Caroline's angel.'

'It will be to the glory of God, Dora,' James Brownlow corrected her gently, and grimaced at his first mouthful of plain, lumpy milk pudding.

*

It was after eleven o'clock when Laura's voice faded in my mind. I must have read for over an hour, but hadn't noticed the time pass, so absorbed had I been. Reading her story was like entering another world.

I wanted to know more, but I was so tired. I replaced the final folder in the filing cabinet, shut the drawer and went downstairs, leaving the journal on the desk. I'd read more tomorrow, I promised myself. I remembered the entries about the proposed church windows; they intrigued me. Perhaps I'd find something in the journal to help us with our restoration work. I must let Zac and Jeremy know about my discovery.

Chapter 8

I sit on the seventh step a long time
And I am sure the angel is there.
I can tell him all the things you can't tell your mother and father.

Frank McCourt, *Angela's Ashes*

The following morning, I rang Jeremy. I'd been going to tell him about our progress with the broken window and about Laura's journal, but he cut in first.

'I went to see your father yesterday,' he said.

'Oh, did you? Thank you, I really appreciate it. Was he awake? How . . . did you think he was?'

'He was awake, yes. I'm fairly sure he recognised me. He tried to speak, but it distressed him, so I urged him not to. I sat with him for a while, poor chap. Fran, he seemed very comfortable. They're looking after him well. And many people make good recoveries. We must have hope.'

'Yes,' I echoed dully. 'We must hope.'

'It's very hard for you – I'm sorry. If Sarah and I can do anything at all to help, you know we're here for you.'

'Thank you. That's very kind.'

We were both quiet for a moment, thinking our own thoughts, then I remembered why I'd rung him.

'Zac and I have been trying to piece the window together. There are angel wings and golden hair . . .'

'So it's definitely an angel, is it? I thought it might be, and I should imagine it's Gabriel.'

'Because it was Gabriel who visited Mary to tell her she was to give birth to Jesus?'

'Indeed. See if he carries a lily, that's Gabriel's symbol. Yes, an angel would fit well with the window of the *Virgin and Child*. I'll have a look around here for old church guides, but, failing that, I might have to ask someone at the diocesan archives to dig out what they can find. Undoubtedly that will take them time.'

'There's something else. I've found a journal. It seems to have belonged to the Reverend Brownlow's daughter, Laura.'

'Oh yes?'

'It mentions plans to commission the window. Nothing really useful yet, but I'll read on.'

'Sounds fascinating. Keep me informed.'

I sat heavy-limbed after I put the phone down, thinking about Dad hovering on the border of the Land of Shadow. The vicar was right, of course. Many people did make good recoveries from strokes, but I hadn't been given that reassurance by the hospital in Dad's case. We just had to hope. And wait.

In the end I forgot to mention the journal to Zac. I hardly saw him that day, in fact. He was off in his van on various missions again. Visiting a house in Clapham to give an estimate, he said, then collecting some special materials from his friend's stained-glass workshop in North London.

I spent the day in the shop, getting through some of the repair jobs in between customers. I opened the post and wondered what to do with the bills and the payments coming in. Zac looked through them briefly when he got back, then took the day's takings and a few cheques to post in the bank deposit box.

Later, he locked up for me while I went to the hospital to sit with Dad. He woke briefly, this time, and we contemplated one another whilst I described my day. I waited until he slept before leaving, glad that I was going to spend the evening with Jo.

At half past seven I changed out of my jeans into smarter trousers and a jacket and set off through Greycoat Square garden towards a tapas bar where Jo had suggested we meet.

Passing the black railings of St Martin's Church, I saw the church door open and a man emerge, to pull it shut behind him. I registered his mop of blond hair and called out, 'Ben?'

'Hello,' Ben said, turning and looking confused for a moment. 'It's ... Fran, isn't it? Blast it!' He was trying to pull a large bunch of keys from his pocket, and several sheets of the music he was carrying suddenly fluttered out across the ground. I hurried over to help him pick it all up.

'Is this for Sunday?' I asked, spotting the titles of anthems.

'Yes. I like to play the pieces through at home before church choir practice on Friday,' he explained. 'Where are you off to, all dressed up? I'm on my way home, round the corner here.'

'Up near Victoria Street to meet my friend Jo. I didn't know you were in Greycoat Square, too. Which side?'

'Here, let me show you.' We stopped at the corner of the Square. Ben said, 'Number sixty-one, just on the left there. It's hardly a chore to slip along and use the church organ when I need to practise, but it's even easier on my own piano.'

'Of course,' I said, wondering which of the long row of Victorian terraced houses it could be.

'Don't laugh,' he went on, 'but sometimes I can't sleep in the mornings after about five o'clock and there's something very comforting about playing church music.'

'I think I understand,' I said. I imagined the subtle chord changes slipping through his long fingers in the silvery light of dawn and felt a delicious shiver. 'But does that mean the neighbours don't sleep either?'

'Fortunately the walls on one side are thick. And the elderly lady on the other is very deaf. So which place is yours?'

'Can you see the black and silver shop right over in the opposite corner, next to the orange café sign? That's *Minster Glass*. I live in the flat above. When I'm staying with my father, that is.'

He followed the line of my finger and frowned. 'Ah yes, of course, that's you. *Minster Glass*,' he said. 'Jeremy's told me about that window he's found. What do you make of it?'

'Not a great deal yet, though we do know it's an angel. We really need a picture of some sort to guide us.'

'I can imagine the difficulty,' he said. 'It's a wild-goose chase, if you ask me.'

'Oh really?' I was puzzled by the bitterness in his voice.

'It's forty years since the organ had its last overhaul,' he said, 'but they – Jeremy and the Parish Church Council, I mean – keep putting it off. And now he's talking about repairing old windows. How do they expect me to produce wonderful music when the organ creaks and groans like a stuck pig?'

'I can understand that it must be frustrating. It's an either/or, is it? The window or the organ?'

'I wouldn't put it as starkly as that. It's certainly a nuisance that a pile of old glass that we never knew existed seems suddenly to have leaped onto the agenda. Jeremy loves music but he loves his stained glass more.'

'I'm sorry,' I said, dismayed. 'I guess I'm in the stained-glass camp, but as a fellow musician, I know how you must feel.'

He gave a broad smile, pushed his hand through his thick hair and studied me once more with that searching look of his. 'Look,' he said warmly, 'I must sound rude, as though I'm criticising your work, and I don't mean to. I appreciate pretty glass with the best of 'em. Since we're such close neighbours, you must come round to supper some time.'

'Thank you, I'd love to,' I told him, pleased.

'Good, we'll fix it then, Fran. Are you a Frances or a Francesca?'

'Frances, but no one calls me that. Not if they want to live.'

'I'm the same about my name. Benedict. God.' He made a face. 'Fran, then . . .'

At that moment he glanced down Greycoat Square, then waved energetically. 'Ah, there's Nina come for our session. Better go. See you Monday – for choir, I mean?'

'Yes, absolutely,' I said. I followed his gaze. Outside what I supposed was number 61, a demure-looking young woman was waiting. She was carrying a violin case. Just a pupil probably, I imagined. But as he drew close she put her free hand to her cheek in a self-conscious gesture and her face lit up with joy. I knew even then that Ben was special to her.

I watched him kiss her cheeks. Then he turned and waved at me. I waved back, feeling left out, then continued down Vincent Street as before and yet not as before. Where a moment ago I'd felt light-hearted, now everything seemed bleak. The shiny black railings reared up oppressively, the blank front doors frowned. What was the matter with me? I was glad to reach the road Jo had named, which led into busy Victoria Street. The tapas bar was on the corner and I went in. There was no sign of Jo.

I was shown to a table by the window and sipped Rioja Arjone while I waited, trying to collect my thoughts. I was just upset about Dad, I concluded, vulnerable and uncertain about everything. I really should get a grip on myself.

'I'm *so* sorry,' Jo sighed, flopping into the chair opposite, twenty minutes later. 'Yes, please,' she said when I offered her wine. 'Shall we order food? You must be simply starving. I am.'

'Something come up at work?' I asked, pushing the bread basket towards her.

'A meeting running on.'

She signalled to the waiter. Food came quickly and we helped ourselves hungrily to stuffed olives, mountain ham and calamares, chattering all the while, trying to make up for twelve lost years. Jo had kept in touch with a number of girls from our school and as she talked about these continuing friendships I regretted that I had cut my ties.

'You must come along when we next meet up,' she said kindly. 'They'd love to see you.' But I wondered if it would be that easy after such a long gap.

We moved on to talk about her work. 'I've been a warden at St Martin's for two years,' she told me. 'I worked with AIDS patients before, then this job came up and it seemed a marvellous opportunity.' Her eyes were shining. 'What I love most is listening to people's stories and trying to help. You won't believe what some of those girls have suffered. And they respond so well to having someone to talk to.'

'I think you're a perfect angel.'

'Oh nonsense,' she said, tossing her head, but she looked pleased all the same.

'Talking about angels, I met a girl from your hostel yesterday,' I said, remembering suddenly. 'Does the name Amber ring a bell?'

'Gosh, yes,' said Jo. 'Amber Hardwick.'

'She wandered into the shop yesterday. Seemed very fascinated by everything, especially the angel in the window display.'

'That sounds like Amber – always on about angels. She's

having a difficult time. A couple of the hard cases keep picking
on her – you know, stealing her things, calling her names.' She
sighed. 'It's really unkind. The worst you can say of Amber is
that she acts young for nineteen. Lisa – she's the ringleader –
can't resist taking advantage. We had an awful incident a few
days ago when some special piece of Amber's jewellery disappeared, a pendant. She got quite hysterical. We eventually found
it in a waste-bin. Everyone knows it was Lisa, but we can't prove
it.'

'She's an awfully sweet girl, but you're right, she's young for
her age. How on earth did she end up at the hostel?'

Jo poured us both more wine.

'I shouldn't be telling you this confidential stuff but, heck,
who are you going to pass it on to? She's one of those kids who's
fallen through every net. Her mother was disabled in some way,
in a wheelchair, anyway, and Amber kept missing school to look
after her. But instead of seeking support for them both, the
mother would lie to the truant officer, say Amber was sick. They
eventually fell below the social workers' radar. The mum died
when Amber was fourteen and the girl ended up living with her
grandmother, who went into a home last year. The council took
back the house. Amber was eighteen and wasn't eligible for such
a large place by herself. She missed so much schooling that she's
found it difficult to find a job.'

'What sort of thing has she tried doing?'

'Oh, supermarket work, catering. She should be suited to
either of those. She's very practical, but doesn't cope well under
pressure. She's artistic, too, likes making jewellery from beads
and wire. Maybe she should try something like that next. I must
suggest it to her caseworker.'

'She did seem interested in the stained glass,' I said.

'Really?'

'Yes. I was explaining a bit about leadwork and she engaged with it very well.'

'That's something to consider.' I saw a light go on in Jo's eyes and realised I'd laid myself a trap and fallen right into it.

'Oh no, sorry, I'm not in a position to train anyone to do anything.' The last thing I needed at the moment was the responsibility of an apprentice.

'She could mind the shop for you and Zac, and watch what you do. You wouldn't have to pay her much and she's very sweet and willing. She'd be great with the customers.'

'Jo, look,' I said, laughing. 'You're going too fast.' I remembered how at school she was the one who wrung your pocket money out of you for the Battersea Dogs' Home, made you sign the petition against fox-hunting, talked you into doing the charity swim.

'Think about it, Fran. Just think about it.'

'Don't, you're making me feel guilty. I've got enough on my plate at the moment.'

'Of course. I'm sorry. I was quite wrong to have mentioned it.'

Jo looked so crestfallen that I sighed. 'OK, I'll think about it. Is that enough? I'm not promising anything.'

Her face broke into a happy smile. 'It's a good idea, I know it is.'

I firmly changed the subject. 'How are the parents?'

'Oh, OK. Just the same really. They're doing up this huge place in the country now, near Tunbridge Wells. Quite mixing in society down there. I'm a bit of a disappointment to them, I sometimes think, working with the underprivileged.'

'Surely they're proud of you?'

'They're still raving Tories. Dad thinks that because he had to pull himself up by his bootstraps – you remember how he talks about his council estate origins? – why should other people be "mollycoddled" as he puts it?'

I smiled, picturing Jo's father, a charming, friendly man. He and his wife had always been very welcoming to me. But I suppose being a high-flying company lawyer doesn't bring out your caring side, and Kevin Pryde had a giant chip on his shoulder, always determined to prove he was 'as good as the other chap', as I once heard him put it.

'And Mum's worried that I'm not moving in the right circles, where I'll attract the kind of man who earns enough to "look after" me. But I love my job. I know I'm lucky – living in the flat, I mean – and that my parents will bale me out if I run into serious debt. I really wouldn't mind if I had to make my own way. I'm not bothered about money, you know.'

I sighed, refraining from answering. Jo must have seen enough desperate cases at the hostel to know what destitution really meant.

'Oh, will you listen to me rattle on,' she said now, picking up the bottle and pouring us generous glasses of wine. 'That silver spoon gets in the way all the time.'

We both laughed and she reached across to touch my arm in that natural, friendly way I had always envied. 'Oh, it's so nice to see you again.'

And suddenly it was possible to forget that I had neglected our friendship along with everything else. Twelve years had separated us but we were now our own individual selves with our own paths in life. Perhaps we were ready to start again.

'Tell me about these unsuitable men,' I teased her.

'Oh, you know,' she answered with a little laugh that didn't ring true. 'It's just that Mum's got a bit of a wait for that big white wedding.' I was surprised to see sadness in her eyes.

'Perhaps you'll meet someone at work or choir,' I said, thinking about the way Dominic had looked at her, and I must have touched some tender spot, because she blushed.

'It's all women at the hostel,' she said, 'except for Ra, and he's engaged to a nice girl his family found for him.'

'I thought Dominic at choir seemed lovely,' I said encouragingly.

'Oh, he is. Really nice.'

'But you don't go for him?'

'We're just friends. I don't think he likes me that way. Ben's rather gorgeous though, don't you reckon?'

'Gorgeous is certainly the word,' I said, wondering if she was interested in him. 'Too gorgeous really, for us mortals.'

'I know what you mean,' she said, and sighed. 'Is there anyone special for you at the moment?'

I rolled my eyes theatrically but it had become too natural for me to be secretive. 'It's been a disaster area. You don't want to know. Anyway,' I changed the subject, 'there's too much else on my mind at the moment.'

She nodded, cupped her chin in her hand and gazed at me sympathetically. 'How are things with your dad?'

I picked at some blobs of wax on the tablecloth. 'If, and if is the operative word, there is going to be improvement, it will be slow. He is conscious sometimes, but I . . . I don't really know if he understands when I talk to him.'

'Oh Fran, I'm sorry.' Her voice rose in a sympathetic squeak. 'But it can't hurt to talk to him, can it? They say it helps.'

'I know. I try. It's just it's difficult . . . well, you probably remember we haven't always been close.'

Jo nodded. Although I'd never talked much about my relationship with my father or my sadness about my mother, she had often witnessed his bearishness when she came to the flat, and had often comforted me when he had made me upset.

'I haven't seen much of him since I left home, Jo.' I picked furiously at the most stubborn piece of wax.

Jo leaned forward, fixed me with her earnest blue eyes and asked, 'Why did you go away so suddenly, Fran? Was there a particular reason? You seemed just . . . to disappear, to cut yourself off from everybody.'

'I know,' I said. 'I didn't really mean to lose touch. The music was such incredibly hard work. I had to concentrate on it, immerse myself. There wasn't much energy left for anything else.'

'Was that an excuse? Did something else happen – with your father, I mean? It's just that in my first Christmas holidays at uni, I visited the shop to see if you were home. When I asked if you'd be back he shrugged, said he didn't know, was quite offhand with me. I thought then that you must have quarrelled.'

I hadn't confided in anybody about what happened, but suddenly I wanted to very badly. I knew Jo would understand.

'Did you? Well, you were right,' I said quietly. 'I'd found out he'd lied to me, you see. About something important.'

Jo didn't say anything, but waited, her eyes large with concern. And now, after twelve years of burying the memory, it all came tumbling out.

'You might not remember,' I said, taking a large gulp of wine to sustain me, 'but in our A-level year I applied to go on a two-week music course in Paris over the summer. I was due to start at the Royal College of Music in the autumn and Paris, my horn teacher said, would be a great chance to play with other students from all over the world.'

'I think I remember,' said Jo, frowning. We had been studying such different subjects for A-level that sometimes I didn't see her that much.

As I told Jo the whole story, the pain and confusion of that time came rushing back as though it were yesterday.

It was 1981 and I had turned eighteen, was an adult, but you wouldn't think it, talking to Dad. In February he said I could go to Paris and paid the deposit, but by May he seemed to regret the whole thing. It was when I asked him about applying for a passport that it all came to a head. He said he had decided that I wasn't old enough to go abroad by myself. I said that was rubbish and he sulked for a week. Finally, he seemed to accept that I should go, so I asked him for my birth certificate in order to get the passport. I couldn't believe it when he said he'd lost it – how could he have lost something as important as that when he had safely squirrelled away all the documents about the business?

In the end I had to go to Somerset House, which was where the Registrar of Births, Deaths and Marriages was back then, and request another copy. I almost expected it to reveal some ghastly secret about my birth, but it didn't. So what was all the fuss about?

It took some time for the penny to drop – years, in fact. To put it simply, he was frightened of losing me. He didn't want me growing up and going away. I think he'd hoped that I would stay with him working in the shop, take over the business one day, that the music both of us loved would be a kind of sideline, not a career. But he didn't know how to express any of this. If he had, we might have talked it all over and cleared the air. Instead, he tried to manipulate me, which was the worst thing he could have done. I stopped trusting him and became desperate to leave home.

I finished my A-levels and went to Paris, where I had a fabulous time, and when I got home at the beginning of August was relieved that Dad seemed to have calmed down. But as September passed his anxiety mounted again. One evening I came home to find him in a semi-coma and he was rushed to hospital. It turned out he'd missed a couple of insulin injections, which was very unlike him. At the time I was merely glad that my college was in nearby Kensington and that I'd be living at home, could keep an eye on him. Later, I saw this medical emergency as a deliberate, manipulative ploy. Now, looking back, I don't know. Perhaps he was genuinely distracted and muddled. Whichever, he quickly recovered.

When we fell out again, it was about money, or rather, money was the starting point. During September I learned I'd been awarded a local authority grant towards living expenses, but I still needed extra, for music and books. It was then that Dad delivered a real bombshell. He produced a building society passbook with my name on it. There was twelve thousand pounds in the account.

Twelve thousand pounds! At first, I was overcome with gratitude, thinking he must have saved it all up for me over the years, but when I looked more closely at the book I saw that apart from the interest, just one payment had been made into the account – back in 1972. So I confronted him about it. And eventually he told me. My mother's mother had died when I was nine and left me a lump sum. And Dad hadn't told me, had just dumped it in this account until I was eighteen.

This in itself was bad enough, that I didn't ever know about an important legacy. But there was something much, much worse. He hadn't even told me that my gran had died. Or rather he did, but not until some years later in my mid-teens, when I started asking about her, and then he let me think she'd died when I was quite little. I think he was embarrassed at not having told me at the time of her death, so he lied to me. It took that building society book for me to worm the whole thing out of him.

It was difficult to convey to Jo, whose father always said everything he thought straight out, my shock and confusion about this discovery. It really did feel as though my whole world had turned upside down, that our whole relationship, Dad's and mine, was built on lies.

I should have confronted him then, demanded that he tell me everything about my mother, that he lay out the whole truth. But in too many ways I was like him. I chose what seemed the easy way. A martyred silence. We hardly spoke to one another for the remaining weeks before college. Then I took my pass-book, presented it at the building society and withdrew the deposit for a room in a rented flat.

'In giving me the money,' I told Jo, 'Dad had delivered him-self a blow. He'd given me the means and the motive to leave him.'

I drifted to a halt now, drained after telling Jo all this, nerv-ous, too, of how she'd judge me. I shouldn't have worried.

'Why didn't you tell me all this at the time? I'd have helped you,' she whispered. 'I would.'

'I'd hardly seen you over the summer, what with Paris and then you going off on holiday with your parents. And I didn't know . . . if I could make you understand. You were always so happy with your family, Jo – I envied you, really. You'd all argue, everyone would say their piece, and then it would be over.'

'Still, I would have listened and tried to understand.'

'I know that now,' I said gently. 'But back then I was unsure of everything, except about music – I was so glad I could throw myself into my studies. It was the saving of me.'

'What about your dad? Didn't you see him at all?'

'Yes, I did. I couldn't abandon him entirely. I told him we needed time apart, but I left a lot of my things at home and I vis-ited him regularly. But he changed, became more miserable and silent; made me feel I'd betrayed him. And my anger made me cold. For years, we hardly talked about anything that really mat-tered, and never referred to our quarrel. It was only recently, before this happened, his stroke, that he seemed to soften. Sometimes, when I spoke to him on the phone, he seemed . . . vulnerable . . . didn't want to end the call. Perhaps he sensed something was going to happen. Perhaps if I'd come home to visit, we could have . . .' I swallowed hard and stared down at my bitten nails.

'Don't feel it's all your fault, Fran,' Jo cried. She reached out and closed both her hands over mine. Again, her tenderness touched me deeply. 'It might not be too late. Try talking to him now. It could help both of you.'

I gave her a watery smile and nodded. Despite the sadness, a feeling of deep relief was coursing through me. Telling Jo, sharing my burden, made me feel better. I wish I had told her all those years ago.

Chapter 9

Then cherish pity, lest you drive an angel from your door.

William Blake, *Songs of Innocence*

Looking back now, I can identify that conversation with Jo as a turning point. I'd opened up to my friend, and in the warmth of her response, the shard of ice that had pierced my heart, locking me up in perpetual winter, finally began to melt.

I was thinking about her words when I visited Dad the following lunchtime, leaving a reluctant Zac to serve in the shop. I loved my father. I knew that, even as we quarrelled, even after I left home, determined to lead my own life. Despite everything he was still my dad who, when I was a child, cuddled me when I was sad, encouraged me when I was down, who would smile delightedly and growl 'That's my girl!' whenever I succeeded at something, from passing exams to getting a modest role in a school play.

Today, as I sat by his bed and watched him fight his way to consciousness, I tried hard to forget where we were, and to remember the things he and I had shared together. It was difficult.

Maybe there was something in Jo's idea, about talking to him. It didn't feel right at the moment to refer to the dark stuff, the bitterness and secrets, but perhaps I could start by reminding Dad about happy times and reassuring him of my love.

'Do you remember, Dad?' I said hesitantly. 'Do you remember when I had measles, and you played board games with me and I always had to win, and you'd tell me stories about when you were little? You had that dog, didn't you, who lived in the shop – a whippet, wasn't he, called Silky? You see, I remember.'

I waited and just then – was it a coincidence? – Dad blinked and looked straight at me. I wondered desperately what else to talk to him about. The angel window . . . now that really would interest him. So I recounted the story of Jeremy Quentin's find and how Zac and I were going to try to put the window together again.

'I wish you were able to help, Dad,' I said. 'I bet you would know right away where to look for the original drawing.'

Again I halted. It was odd speaking to someone who didn't respond. I was never someone to chatter on effortlessly.

I was also aware of the abyss between us. So much needed to be said. I so badly wanted to talk to him about my mother, but how could I? I couldn't frame words that didn't sound stilted or cheesy. And, if he could hear and understand me, I was nervous of upsetting him. I might unwittingly say something hurtful or untrue and he wouldn't be able to respond. It wouldn't be fair. In the end, I merely said, 'When you're well again, Dad, we'll talk properly. I'll be around more. Really.' His eyes were locked on mine now, such pools of anguish that I felt alarmed. Was he in pain? But then his expression grew more peaceful. I whispered, my words half-choked, 'I'm sorry, Dad. I'm truly sorry.'

When I returned to the shop, Zac was deep in conversation with a youngish, expensive-looking couple. Or rather, with the wife. The man paced the shop looking at price tags and frowning whilst the woman, a lively honey-blonde with large tortoiseshell spectacles, chattered to Zac about a series of photographs she'd laid out on the counter. Zac was studying them, nodding, interrupting her flow with dogged questions. I remembered that he didn't enjoy negotiating commissions. He preferred doing the work.

I smiled vaguely at them, attempting to slip past them into the workshop, but Zac shot me a desperate look.

'Fran, Mr and Mrs Armitage here are asking if we can do something based on these. What do you think?'

The photographs were of two glass panels, one of a young boy in an alpine hat fishing in a pool, the other of a girl in a too-short skirt reaching up to catch a butterfly in a net. The borders were decorated with teddies, dolls, flowers and fruit. Very cutesy, but then that was what some people liked.

'We saw them when we were in New Jersey, didn't we, sweetheart?' Mrs Armitage said. 'Our friends only recently moved into the house and didn't know who'd made them, so we took some pictures and thought if we could get our own designed they'd go well in the twins' bedrooms, didn't we, sweetheart?'

'Sweetheart' grunted his assent.

'We could come up with our own versions, couldn't we, Zac?' I asked him.

'I've told them we could get into trouble for producing straight copies, of course. But something similar . . .'

'That would be lovely,' said Mrs Armitage, tapping the counter with her talon-like nails. 'How much do you think they might be? We were hoping they could be ready for the twins' birthday in late October.'

Zac showed them photographs from our own portfolios and gave them ball-park prices based on panels of similar size and complexity. I watched the husband carefully but, apart from

asking a couple of perceptive questions about the cost of different kinds of glass, he seemed to accept the likely damage to his
wallet.

Eventually they left and we drifted through into the workshop. While I made tea, Zac wrote down the job in Dad's Day
Book then studied the photographs again, shaking his head.

'What?' I asked him.

'Oh, nothing. Let's say these are not my idea of high art.'

I laughed and said teasingly, 'Come on, you'll do a beautiful
job.'

'Aye,' he said, 'I always try to do that.'

'What do you like doing most, then?' I asked, realising again
how little I knew about him.

'The arty stuff, my own designs. And the church work, that
means something. It isn't only decorative, is it? It has a purpose.'

'What do you mean by your own designs?' I asked. 'Like that
sunrise?'

'I drew what the lady described. No, I've started doing other
stuff but they're experiments really. We haven't got the equipment here, so I use my mate David's studio.'

'I had no idea you did other work.'

'I don't do it on company time,' he said, misreading me. 'And
I pay for my materials. Though your father lets me have odd
pieces from time to time.'

'That's fine, Zac. Honestly I wasn't accusing you.'

'I know. I wanted to be clear, that's all.'

'I'd love to see your other work.'

'Really?' he said. 'I'm putting a portfolio together – in case it's
useful here. One day, when it's ready, I'll show you.' His eyes
brightened, bringing his whole face to life, and this made me
think just how melancholy he often seemed. I wondered if that
was his whole life – working with glass. Didn't he have family

in London, or a social life? But I didn't ask. After all, I was hardly in a position to advise other people about their lives when mine was always such a muddle.

At that moment, the bell on the shop door tinkled again.

'Oh, and I forgot,' called Zac, as I went to investigate. 'Someone rang for you. Jessica Eldridge? Said will you ring her back.'

'Oh, Jessica – I meant to ring her,' I said, feeling guilty. 'She's my diary service.' Seeing his blank expression, I explained, 'She books my work with orchestras.' I must at some time have given her the *Minster Glass* number. 'Thanks, Zac, I'll call her later.'

Whilst I helped a young art student choose some cheap off-cuts of glass for a sculpture she was creating, and carefully wrapped the pieces in newspaper, I noticed Amber hovering outside.

I held the door open for the student, who had her hands full, and when she'd gone, waved to Amber and invited her in.

'Are you busy?' she asked anxiously.

She sidled into the shop and hovered, looking at everything. After a while I showed her into the workshop and introduced her to Zac, who was engaged in cutting short strips of mirror glass.

'Amber's a friend of my friend Jo,' I said.

Surprise registered on Zac's face, then he smiled hello.

'What are you doing?' asked Amber, her shyness overcome by curiosity.

'Making a kaleidoscope,' he replied, and fetched a finished example off the shelf. 'Have a peep through here,' he said, offering her the end of the Toblerone-shaped instrument.

She held it up to the light and gasped. 'Oh!'

'Here, turn the marble.' At the far end of the kaleidoscope was a large glass marble cradled in a metal coil. I knew that when you turned the marble, the colours reflected in the mirrors inside, creating magnificent patterns.

'How do you make them?' Amber asked. Just then the shop bell jingled again.

When I returned from serving a short queue of customers, Zac and Amber were absorbed in conversation. Zac was demonstrating how to hold a glass-cutter and Amber was attempting to score a piece of greenhouse glass Zac had given her.

'Don't be frightened of it,' he was saying. 'It's not going to jump up and bite you. Just treat it with respect. There, now hold it like this between your thumbs and . . . break it. Well done!'

'The glass is like it's made of sugar.'

'That's right, it just shatters down the line you made. Not all glass is that easy. With some types it can break in the wrong place and you have to start again.'

'How do you make the coloured glass? Do you do it here?'

'Oh no,' said Zac. 'It's practically all imported from abroad now. But you can get all sorts of amazing colours, patterns and textures.'

'I love this pink and gold one.' She pointed to the glass Zac had selected for the case of his kaleidoscope.

'That's one of the expensive ones. The hot colours like red always are. You need more valuable chemicals – the red often has real gold in it – and complicated processes. The blues and greens are simpler and cheaper.'

Zac sensed me standing there and looked up. 'What's the matter?' he asked.

I was leaning in the doorway, arms folded, trying to stop a grin spreading across my face.

'Nothing,' I said. 'Carry on. It's just I've never heard you say so much before.'

That rare smile lit up his eyes. He turned back to Amber.

'Look, when I've cut this last piece here I'll show you how the grinder works. And maybe we'll see how you go using copper foil.'

I left them to it, pleased that Zac had made time in his busy schedule to help the girl.

'Zac,' I said later, when Amber had left, a suncatcher we'd given her stowed carefully in her bag, 'what would you say if I told Amber she could come and help out here occasionally?'

'Work here, you mean? What could she do?' he answered, wary.

'Look after the shop when we're out, unpack stuff, answer the telephone, that sort of thing. It would free us up to do more. And we can show her simple creative tasks. Finding patterns, making easy things.'

'Train her up a bit, you mean? Aye, it's important to train new people. Let's think about it.'

'Yes. And after all, you're right, Dad won't . . .'

'I know.' There was sympathy in his eyes, and I had to look away. It felt like a betrayal to admit that Dad was unlikely to be able to work again.

'Fran, there's something we need to talk about. Did your father ever draw up one of those Power of Attorney things? It's just . . . there are unpaid bills. And I'm not a signatory for the business.'

'I don't know, Zac,' I said. 'I'll have to speak to the bank. And Dad's lawyer.'

After I'd shut up shop I remembered the message from Jessica. She was usually still in the office at this hour, so I went to find my address book.

'Fran!' she exclaimed on hearing my voice. 'I think I've rung all the numbers you ever gave me. I was getting worried – thought you'd been kidnapped or something. How are you?'

I apologised and explained to her about Dad's illness and how I needed to be here, to keep everything going. It occurred to me, as I talked, that my previous life, touring the world with orchestras, staying in a different hotel every few days, already seemed an age away. All my energies, my priorities, were becoming focused here.

'So I don't think I'll be available for anything for a bit. Except maybe in London,' I finished lamely.

'That's a shame, because I had something exciting lined up for you in New York. The Halliwell are touring, and one of their tuba players has gone down with pleurisy. But I quite understand. If something comes up locally, I'll call, but otherwise I'll wait to hear from you.'

'Thanks, Jess.'

'Don't leave it too long, will you?' she added lightly, but I picked up the veiled warning.

'No, I'm sure I won't,' I said. It was all too easy to be forgotten in the music business.

I put the phone down with a mixture of regret and relief. Regret because I still wanted to be a part of that world. Relief because I was coming to accept that, for the moment, I was a part of this one.

That evening, I was toasting a cheese sandwich for supper, when the vicar rang.

'My wife Sarah has spent most of the last couple of days going through all the boxes and filing cabinets in the church vestry and the parish office,' he told me.

'That's very good of her,' I said. 'Any luck?'

'She's found a history of the church dated 1927, but it only describes the windows. There are no photographs, I'm afraid. So I've asked a chap I know at the diocesan archives to see if he has anything but, as I thought, he says it might take him a while.'

'What does the description say?' I asked.

'Hang on a moment. Ah. "The Lady Chapel. Fine late-nineteenth-century richly coloured glass by *Minster Glass* in the *Virgin and Child Enthroned*, E. window of chapel, donor Mrs Sarah Fotherington . . . *Angel* in S. window, also by *Minster Glass*, donor Reverend Jas. Brownlow, in memory of his daughter Caroline." That's it.'

'OK.'

I must have sighed, because he added, 'Sorry. Not very helpful, is it?'

'It doesn't matter. I'll have another look through Dad's stuff later.'

I had been searching for about an hour when I struck lucky. What I found is called in the trade a vidimus, meaning 'let us look'. It was a small colour sketch for the *Virgin and Child* window, which the artist would have showed his patron to give an early idea of how the window would look. It was beautifully executed and the colours sang.

Amazingly, there was a note clipped to it that directed me to a large cupboard at the back of the room. In this were folded and filed hundreds of much larger drawings called cartoons. Twenty minutes later, with a cry of satisfaction, I extracted one labelled '*Virgin and Child in Glory*, St Martin's Church', unfolded it and spread it onto the floor. It was a larger version of the vidimus I'd found just now, the size of the actual window, but drawn in outline, without the colour. Its purpose was to be a pattern for the window. It showed clearly the shape of each piece of glass to be cut, the details of features and drapery, and where the saddle crossbars to support the whole structure should go. Looking from the coloured vidimus to the huge cartoon, I wondered if they weren't, most unusually, drawn by the same hand. Most of the time an artist would be commissioned only to create the original colour design and this would then be handed over to craftsmen who would enlarge it and make the window. Unless the artist was sufficiently interested, he might not see what happened to his design until the window was finished.

I studied the faces on the cartoon, the carefully drawn features, the attention paid to details of light and shadow. The joyful light in the Virgin's eyes was reflected in her child's, and I marvelled at the artist's ability to recreate emotion. Carefully I folded up both drawings and replaced them in their respective files. Then I continued my search for the angel. In the foolscap file where I'd found the *Virgin and Child* vidimus there were several letters, bills and lists of materials relating to that window, but nothing for the angel. It was frustrating. Still, these would help illuminate the artist's processes with the angel, which we would need to follow.

I took Laura Brownlow's journal down to the living room. There I foraged in the bureau for Dad's magnifying glass and sat down to read once more. Laura wrote so vividly it was hard to remember that everything had happened over a hundred years before. I could almost imagine I was there . . .

Sunday, 15 February 1880
Oh, that you were here, Caroline. We would have shared such confidences, for I have received my first proposal of marriage! But, Caro, I've said him nay, for I cannot love him nor indeed feel any affection towards him at all. He is Mr Anthony Bond – Papa's lawyer, you might remember – a gentleman of distinction and property with, Mama assures me, distant con-

nections to the Dukes of Norfolk! (So distant, it seems I require opera glasses to see them!)

I shall explain exactly how it came about. Such a surprise, for Mr Bond had passed no hint of his intentions towards me. He took luncheon with us on Friday and that same evening Papa told me the man intended to take tea with us on Sunday, that he wished particularly to speak to me and I should think most seriously about his purpose.

It never crossed my mind that his frequent excuses to visit our house should have anything to do with me. His countenance rarely betrays any emotion except embarrassment. Believe me when I say I imagined he merely wished to discuss a book I'd lent him.

After he arrived, Mama excused herself and we were left alone together in the drawing room. He seemed quite agitated, spilling his tea in his saucer. I reached to take the cup from him, but instead he clasped my outstretched hand and growled, 'Oh, Miss Brownlow, Laura,' in such a strange, squeaky voice that I was frightened and snatched away my hand. We both sat staring at one another in horror. Then he cleared his throat in that nervous way he has and whispered, 'Did your father not give you any intimation of my intentions?' and I shook my head, suddenly realising what he meant.

Blood rushed to his face. 'I had hoped . . .' he said, but I read terror in his features.

'No, Mr Bond, pray say no more. It cannot be!' I cried out in my panic. I was furious with Papa and Mama for not preparing me, and so it was worse for poor Mr Bond than it might have been.

I thought I would feel elated to have had my first proposal – do you remember how we talked about how it might be? Instead I feel sad. I have caused Mr Bond misery, though the fault is not mine. I never sought his attentions.

Monday, 16 February

I have finally begun the new tale. The young woman is an orphan and marries a young man for love – he believing, it turns out falsely, that she is independently wealthy. When he learns that her estate is entailed and he may not touch the money, he abandons her and she loses her position in society. I have yet to establish how matters should proceed, but I wish her to fashion her own life in the face of public condemnation.

Wednesday, 18 February

We returned from dinner with George and Harriet last evening to discover a terrible scene. Mrs Jorkins was disputing with a drunken man who, it transpired, was the mysterious Mr Cooper. Do you recall that I told you about the Coopers? It's so sad. The baby has died and the doctor has despatched poor Molly Cooper to the hospital.

Mr Cooper cursed and shouted, like you never heard, and demanded money. Papa sensibly wouldn't give him any, determining he'd only spend it on liquor; instead, he hustled us all inside and threatened to fetch a Constable. Fortunately the man went away but we could hear him banging railings and shouting all down the street. Mama was quite shaken, but you may guess how she set her mind then. 'The children will be all on their own, James,' she cried, and she wouldn't go to bed and was all for changing her clothes and setting out to see the abandoned family at once until Papa forbade her. 'They'll come to no harm before morning,' he said. 'What can you do for them now? You'll catch your own death if that man doesn't murder us first.'

So we were up early this morning and visiting the Cooper children. Such distress. No sign of their dissolute papa and, while Ida had done her best with keeping the young ones' spirits up, they'd not eaten since the doctor came the previous day. Mama made me stay and help while she took Ida with her to the hospital, but tonight the news is as bad as it can be. Molly Cooper died of her fever this evening and, for all the use their father seems to be, the children are in effect orphans, their fate to be decided by the authorities tomorrow.

Friday, 20 February
Another dreadful day, the five youngest Coopers taken to the orphanage and Ida come to be kitchen maid until we can think where else she must go. She can only sit in the kitchen and cry, poor dear. Mrs Jorkins is kindly enough and will take her in hand.

Saturday, 21 February
That rogue Cooper's been back with his shouting, demanding to see his daughter, cursing Mama and Papa for taking away his family when all they've done is make good his negligence. He even accused Mama of killing his wife – the man's demented. Eventually two Constables came to arrest him and who knows what'll happen to him now. Ida wouldn't appear to speak to him, she was so terrified. She's told Mama he used to hit their mother when he was under the influence of drink. Mama is holding herself together magnificently, as she does in times like these, but she wears the same expression on her face as the Blessed Virgin in the *Crucifixion* window; one of anguished self-sacrifice. Am I cruel to notice this? I don't know how long it will be before her health suffers.

After this, there was a gap in the journal of a couple of months. The next entry was 15 April 1880. I read on . . .

Chapter 10

We should pray to the angels for they are given to us as guardians.

St Ambrose, *De Viduis*

LAURA'S STORY

The handle turned smoothly, the door swung open with a sigh and Laura stepped into the church. The air, pungent with lilies and incense, was cool after the spring sunshine and it took a moment for her eyes to adjust to the gloom. She stood, listening to the ringing silence – 'It's the presence of God,' her mother had once whispered to her. Sounds from the street, the rhythmic scraping of a broom, the impatient trot and rattle of a passing horse and carriage, the bark of some tethered dog, barely rippled the stillness.

Laura tiptoed down the aisle, her skirt swishing on the flags. She bowed her head to the altar, with its new gold cloth, crossed herself, then knelt down awkwardly in the front pew. Gazing up at the frozen agony of the *Crucifixion* scene she tried to still her troubled mind enough to pray.

Two months after his first proposal, Mr Bond had again asked to see her on her own, had begged her hand in marriage. This time he'd been more forthright, had declared his love for her with a passion she'd not suspected in him. How had she stirred such hot feeling in this dry, serious man, she who was always plainly, even dowdily dressed, unadorned, lacking Harriet's pretty flirtatiousness or Caroline's pale-gold fragility? 'You're beautiful,' her mother always told her beloved eldest daughter, but Laura's tiny mirror gave a more honest verdict. She had the glow of youth and good health – glossy chestnut hair, bright eyes and a mercifully clear complexion. Less happily, her mouth was too wide, her nose had a bump in it, she knew her movements were gawky, without grace.

'Think carefully, my dear,' her father had said when he warned her of Mr Bond's intention to renew his suit. 'He's a good man and well situated. Your mama and I would be happy were you to accept him. Hear him out, is all we ask, but we will not press you.'

'I do not have any feelings for him . . .'

'Love can grow, my dear. Love can grow with God's help. We judge the marriage to be advantageous. He is of sound character. I rely on him in the parish.' Still, Laura could sense her father's heavy mood. He put out a hand to pat her shoulder as though comforting her. She felt bewildered.

'We would miss you, my love,' said her mother. 'But you must consider your happiness and we must be thankful that we will have both you and Harriet living nearby.'

Laura considered the face of Mary, glowing ghostly white in the window before her. Mary, who accepted everything that happened to her. Which life should she choose? To marry a man for whom she felt no warmth, and hope love might flow, or stay with her parents, comforting them in their troubles, sharing their work.

'Is there no one you have ever liked, dear?' Harriet had asked her, exasperated, the last time Laura visited. Harriet left the house rarely now that the child had dropped in her womb.

'Not so very much,' Laura answered. But there had been Papa's young curate, Gilbert Osborn, who had left two years before. For a short while he had seemed to seek her out, but then suddenly it was announced he was to be married to his second cousin in Hampshire, and was raised to a living in the patronage of the girl's father. Wasn't it obvious, Harriet had remarked – being wise in the ways of the world – that the two events were related? Laura supposed her sister was right, but could think no ill of him. She remembered his fine dark eyes, his teasing manner, the way he could make her forget her dragging fears for Caroline. The news of his engagement caused her to weep silently into her pillow every night for a week.

From the shadows of the Lady Chapel she heard a sigh, the creak of wood on stone. Someone was there. She pushed herself to her feet and straightened her skirts, thinking it must be the verger. But the figure outlined in the doorway to the chapel was not stooping old Mr Perkins but someone taller, straighter and much younger.

'I'm sorry to disturb you. I didn't realise there was anyone here,' the man said, his voice gentle, the T-sounds slightly sibilant. He bowed slightly. In one hand he clutched his hat, in the other a large book. He made to walk past her and his hair glinted gold in a sudden shaft of light, like a revelation. She gave a sharp intake of breath and lowered her gaze. The book, she saw now, was a sketchbook.

Curiosity caused her to burst out, 'Oh no, you're not disturbing me at all. You have been drawing the church? Do let me see.'

He stopped, turned and looked at her hesitantly, then down at the book, weighing something up. Finally he said, 'A few ideas for a commission. Only early sketches.'

He stepped fully into the light and she almost gasped at the beauty of him. His skin was pale against his gold-brown hair and moustache. When their eyes met, his were hazel, flecked with green. He opened the book and she peered down at the page he showed her. A pencilled arched window containing the outline of a figure was criss-crossed with scribbled notes.

'Goodness, you must be Mr . . . Russell,' she said, remembering the name her father had mentioned. 'The artist for our windows.'

'I am indeed he,' he said. 'And you are . . .?'

'Reverend Brownlow's daughter,' she rushed on. 'Miss Laura Brownlow.'

'Well, this is a most felicitous meeting then, Miss Brownlow,' he said. His hand momentarily enveloped hers. Even through her glove she felt its warmth.

'It's my first visit to the church,' said Mr Russell. 'I like to wait, to watch and listen, immerse myself in the atmosphere of a building before I begin work.'

She thought of him sitting still as a stone saint in the semi-darkness, unseen, watching and listening.

Since she didn't speak, he went on, 'It's important to view the church at different times of day, I find. To see how the light strikes the windows.'

'I understand,' she said.

'And to gauge the particular tones of the church, to imagine what will suit it best – rich rubies maybe, or silvery whites.'

'And what do you see here?'

'The limestone requires soft colour tones. Nothing too hot, too strident.'

'You must study the other windows, too, I imagine.'

'Yes, indeed. This is a fine one, this altar light. By Mr Kempe. Do you see his sign, the wheatsheaves, almost hidden in the corner there, to the left of the Magdalen?'

He moved forward and now red light and blue and green fell across him from the window, like a blessing.

Laura too stepped into the shower of colour, followed the line of his pointing finger and nodded. 'I'd not noticed before.' The sleeve of his coat, she saw, had slid back slightly, and she was strangely touched by the fact that his shirt cuff was frayed, though the dappled light transformed the threads into something fine.

'Do you have a sign, Mr Russell?' she said, looking up at him with a steady gaze.

He smiled at her, then in a flowing movement, flipped up his coat-tails and sat down in the front pew. He was left-handed, she noticed, his fingers curved like a crab's claw as he drew. A quick flourish and he was done. 'I like to use this.' He passed her the book.

Laura studied the intricate knot pattern he'd drawn. She swivelled the drawing round. 'It's the same from all sides,' she said, marvelling.

'And I can draw it without lifting my pencil from the paper,' he said. 'You'll find them on ancient Celtic crosses, though this one's of my own invention. I like the idea of the eternal line.'

Lose not the things eternal . . . Her father's reading of the old prayer, his voice deep and pure, resounded in her mind.

'I like it too,' she told Mr Russell gravely. 'It makes me think of the important things of this life, the good things that we've lost, running on beyond this world into eternity.'

They were both silent for a moment, Laura imagining her brother Ned, a little boy running for ever, laughing, across a sward of green. She wondered of what Mr Russell was thinking. His face wore a tense expression and a fast pulse throbbed in his throat. She glanced away, afraid that he'd notice her looking.

'I have in my mind's eye a vision for the *Virgin and Child* window,' he said finally. 'But the angel design – I gather the window is in memory of your sister.'

'Caroline, yes.'

'Can you tell me a little about her? If . . . that's not too hard for you, of course.'

'I like to talk about her. It feels as though she's still with us then. Caroline was four years younger than me, nearly seventeen when she died. There was something about her, I can't explain. She had a sweetness, a goodness.'

Russell, who was drawing something swiftly on a corner of his page as he listened, nodded encouragingly.

She continued, 'We were never jealous of her. We always loved her. That's surprising, isn't it, for brothers and sisters? It was Harriet I sometimes quarrelled with – she's the sister between Caroline and me. And there's Tom, the eldest. He's at Oxford learning to be a priest like Papa. We had another brother, too. Ned was the youngest, but we lost him to a fever of the brain.'

Mr Russell's expression was full of tender sympathy. Her breath caught in her throat.

'Mama says you wouldn't know it now because he's so grey, but Papa once had hair of pale gold. Caroline's was like that, too, before it all began to fall out. Her illness left her so thin, you know, her skin was transparent. You could see the blood moving in her veins.'

'Is there a photograph, or a painting of her I might see?'

'There were photographs, but my mother has hidden them away. She cannot bear to look at them. I will ask her, if you like.'

'Do you think she would like the angel to recall the image of your sister?' He seemed anxious now. 'Or maybe . . . it would be too painful.'

Laura didn't know what her mother would want. What did

she herself think? The face of Caroline in the window would be too strange. 'I don't know,' she said. 'Perhaps you should visit and ask her yourself.'

'I will do that,' he said. He closed his sketchbook.

Laura stood up to go, drawing her shawl around her. He stood, too, and when she grasped the pew end for balance, caught her arm to steady her. For a moment he was so close she felt dizzy.

'You'll come soon?' she asked him.

'Of course. Tuesday morning, perhaps, if that's convenient.' Bowing slightly, he stepped back to let her pass.

'Oh, Baby has the hiccoughs again. Look!'

Harriet was stretched out on a sofa, where Nurse Stephens had left her to rest with pillows under her feet and head. Laura stared with fascination at the mound of her sister's great belly, clearly visible beneath her voluminous skirts. After a moment the mound twitched slightly and they both laughed.

'Oh Laura, it's so tedious lying here. I see hardly anyone. And George's mother sends advice by every post. If she writes me once more about what a marvellous baby George was because she refused rich food or took fresh air or . . . I don't know, fed him nothing but blancmange, I swear I'll scream. Oh, help me up, will you? I've pain, just here, down my back. I've had it all day. So odd. Oh, that's better, Baby's moved. Put your hand here, dear, you'll feel his little foot.'

Laura tentatively laid her fingers on Harriet's stomach. It's so hard, she thought in wonder. 'Oh!' The baby kicked under her hand. 'Harriet!'

They pressed each other's hands in excitement.

'Do you think it will hurt very much? When the baby comes, I mean?' Laura asked.

'Nurse Stephens says it will, but that it is woman's lot and I must be brave. I don't feel very brave, Laura.' Harriet's once-pretty complexion, lately as blotchy as porridge, now turned the colour of whey.

'I don't think I could ever do it,' whispered Laura, more to herself than to her sister. 'But if Mama is there, perhaps it will be all right.'

'I hope she can be, but Nurse says the doctor may not allow it. Laura, I'm so scared.'

'You must send for Mama as soon as you need her. It'll help you to know she's near, at least.'

'I think it will be soon. I feel so strange today. My nerves twitch like you wouldn't believe.'

'Poor you. I'll sit and talk then, to take your mind off the strangeness.'

'Thank you, dear, I'd like that. Laura, I've been longing to ask. Mama said Mr Bond proposed again. What did you say to him?'

'I haven't given him my answer yet. I think my head tells me yes, but my heart says no.'

'I wish you would say yes. Then I could help you with your wedding clothes and arrange your house and you would live nearby and, oh, we'd have such fun.'

'But I live nearby already, and I don't think I want to have fun, Harriet. Not the kind you mean – going to people's houses and having them come to yours. I want time to myself, to read and write and to think. Anyway, I don't love Mr Bond. I don't think I even like him much. I couldn't call him "my dear heart", like you do George, and share his bed.'

Harriet laughed. 'I didn't love George when he asked me, but I do now.' She smiled a secret smile, then winced and put her hand to her belly.

George was pompous and too sure he was right, but Laura

had seen a spark between him and Harriet from the start. Harriet managed to play him skilfully, Laura always thought, bewitching him with her teasing but never flouting him, at least, not in public. The spark between them had caught, and now the sudden fire of their love had settled to a warm steady flame.

There was no spark between her and Mr Bond, decided Laura, none at all. She was simply not interested in drawing him to her. But nobody seemed to think this mattered, except her.

'You might stay at home for ever then,' said Harriet, pouting. 'Soothing Mama's headaches and arguing with Mrs Jorkins about how best to cook veal, and visiting all the Coopers of the parish.'

'Mr Bond or the Coopers,' she said lightly now. 'Mmm, that's no choice at all.' But she felt uncomfortable as she said this. The Coopers of this world needed people like the Brownlows. Papa was right. To do God's work one must be selfless.

But she'd had enough of being selfless. She wanted to live.

And so, suddenly, did her sister's child, for Harriet let out a sharp gasp of pain.

'Is it happening? Shall I send for Mama?' asked Laura, helping her sister to sit up more comfortably as Nurse Stephens bustled in tut-tutting.

The little boy was born as first light touched the morning sky. After the doctor left, Laura and Mama were admitted to the room to find Harriet lying exhausted but demanding bread-and-milk. Portly George hovered anxiously, staring into the cradle, hands in pockets. Laura gazed at tiny Arthur (named for George's dead father), sweetly swaddled, asleep, and felt her world turn on its axis. In one stroke her sister had become a mother, her mother a grandmother, she herself an aunt. The Brownlow family had taken a step into the future.

'Five minutes, that's all,' snapped Nurse Stephens, standing sentinel by the bed. 'Mother needs to rest.'

*

I read Laura's journal until the neat italics began to swim before my eyes. It was rich material, anyway; I was glad to stop and contemplate everything I'd read. I could still hear her voice in my head, almost feel her presence in the gloomy room.

How lonely Laura must have been, shut up in a house with two grieving parents, her daily task to assist in their work. Perhaps the only activity through which she could escape was her writing.

She had a natural writer's style, Laura, an ability to make a scene come alive with emotive observations and touches of humour. All this, and yet her account was imbued with deep sadness; hers was a family in mourning, divided not only by death but by other natural processes of life – the surviving children leaving home, marrying, pursuing careers – and by silence. And Laura had been left behind, perhaps destined to look after her parents – though it seemed she had had at least one chance at marriage.

As I laid the journal on the desk, by the Day Books, I wondered again what it was doing here in *Minster Glass*. And whether Dad knew about it; that was an important question. Its position in the drawer suggested no, as did his scribbled note *Who was Laura Brownlow?* Yet all the files in the cabinet had been neatly labelled in his black script, making it difficult to believe that he hadn't come across it. Perhaps he had, but didn't realise its significance to his account.

Chapter 11

'Every time you hear a bell ring, it means that some angel's just got his wings.'

It's a Wonderful Life

On Friday morning I was exasperated to find I was to be left alone in the shop again for most of the day. At eight-thirty Zac arrived, only to go straight out again in the van to take some sketches he'd done over to a house in Clapham. Later, he said, he would head further south to install Dad's Celtic window. Jo's idea of employing Amber was beginning to seem more and more attractive.

My mind still on Laura's extraordinary journal, I found the letter Jeremy Quentin had sent Dad and rang the vicarage number. There was only an answerphone message delivered in a gentle female voice. As I left my name and number, I noticed the address at the top of the letter. It was 44 Vincent Street. How puzzling. I was sure Laura had described the Victorian rectory as being in Greycoat Square.

It was a busy morning. I longed for a moment to fetch the diary from upstairs and read some more, but evening classes must have been starting in earnest because hobbyists kept arriving in a steady trickle with printed lists, wanting tools and glass and advice. It was while I was serving that our wholesaler left a large order that, when I found a moment to check it, proved to be wrong.

I was sitting in an unflattering position, legs splayed on the shop floor, surrounded by open boxes and polystyrene packaging, and talking on the phone, when a shadow fell across the window. I looked up to see Ben. I clambered to my feet and motioned to him to come in, while still trying to explain to the idiot of a boy at the other end of the telephone line that they'd given us the wrong opalescent glass, and that a Tiffany-style wisteria lampshade was not by any stretch of the imagination the same as a poppy one.

Ben walked around the shop, looking at everything before pulling up an old wooden chair and sitting astride it, watching me with a slight smile playing on his lips. I found it hard to concentrate on what I was saying.

'So I'll see you back here first thing Tuesday without fail,' I said sternly down the receiver, and ended the call.

'Wouldn't want to get the wrong side of you on a bad day,' Ben said with a grin.

'They're usually very good.' I shrugged, starting to pack up the boxes. 'Seems there's someone new getting it all wrong. Lovely to see you. Have you come for a reason or is this a social call?'

'Half and half,' Ben said, his gaze sliding to the workshop door. 'I wondered if I could see the famous exploding window.'

'Didn't the vicar show you?' I said.

'Only the box it was in. The whole thing looked a mess, frankly.'

'It still is,' I said bleakly.

The bits of angel were carefully laid out on the lining paper where we'd left them. Ben regarded them critically, one finger hooking his cord jacket over his shoulder. He was wearing a linen shirt today of a soft pale blue. I kept glancing out of the corner of my eye to see the effect of it against his hair. Like ripe corn against a summer sky.

'Correct me if I'm wrong,' he said, bringing me back to earth, 'but it does look like a lost cause. I mean, it's not just a matter of sticking all the bits together, is it? For a start, how do you know where everything goes and what's missing?'

'I know it seems like that,' I explained, defensive. 'But if we can get hold of a photograph or find the original drawing, we could have a good try . . .'

'And there's a perfectly decent stained-glass scene already in the window. Has anyone thought of what would happen to that?'

'I don't know. That's for your council to decide, isn't it?' I imagined that he was annoyed because of wanting the organ repaired, but I wished he wouldn't take it out on me.

'The PCC? I suppose.'

I watched him wander round the workshop, pulling open the doors of the kiln to look inside, prodding little tins of paint and bags of cement, asking what things were. I held one of Zac's kaleidoscopes up to the light and he muttered his amazement as he squinted through it, turning the marble.

A man came into the shop to pick up a screen I'd mended for his wife, and when I returned to the workshop, Ben was studying a row of beautiful little lozenges of multicoloured glass Zac had left on a shelf. This fusing glass was very popular with people who made their own jewellery, and it was fun to make up pieces and to fire them in a little microwave kiln, though tricky to get the temperatures and firing times exactly right.

Ben was particularly taken with a piece that glinted blue-green, as iridescent as a butterfly's wing, and, on an impulse, I gave it to him.

'Are you sure?' he said. 'Thanks ever so much.' He tucked it safely in his jacket and turned on one of his soul-searching looks. I was getting used to these by now.

I followed him out to the door, half-expecting him to mention dinner again. Instead he merely said, 'Thank you,' adding, 'see you at choir.' And he was gone. I was puzzled as to why he'd really come.

I watched him cross the road, but when he reached the path across the garden he turned to see me still watching and gave me a little wave.

When Zac returned, mid-afternoon, I showed him Laura Brownlow's journal and told him about the artist being Philip Russell.

'I haven't heard of him,' he said, frowning. He took the book from me and tried to make sense of the handwriting, but soon gave up and passed it back.

'You must tell me anything else you discover about the windows,' he said.

'I will, and I really must let the vicar look at it.' I rang the vicarage again, but this time the line was engaged. Since someone was in, perhaps I'd call round. After all, I'd been cooped up here all day. Zac agreed to keep an eye on the shop while I walked over to the vicarage, carrying the journal in a bag. Number 44 Vincent Street turned out to be a smallish Edwardian-style terraced house in red brick. Definitely not Laura's father's rectory then.

Jeremy was out, but Sarah Quentin invited me in, assuring me she was expecting him back any moment.

'He was using the photocopier in the parish office,' she said. She was a small round woman in her fifties who had a kind of stillness about her.

The moment stretched to twenty minutes. I drank tea at the big table in her messy kitchen and when I commented on a pile of paperwork she was sorting, she told me about the parish appeal for expanding facilities for the homeless.

'We're waiting for a decision about our government grant application,' she said. 'The paperwork is endless. Jeremy's at meetings about it the whole time.'

Her eyes occasionally rested on me curiously. Suddenly she said something that almost made me choke on my tea.

'You know, you are very like your mother.'

'My mother!' I cried. 'You knew my . . .?'

'No,' she said hastily. 'I never met her. But your father showed us a photograph of her once.'

'A photograph?' I repeated. Of course, my father might have photographs somewhere that he'd never shown me. But he had shown these . . . strangers.

Mrs Quentin saw immediately that she'd upset me and said gently, 'Perhaps you didn't know that Jeremy and your father have become quite close. I've no idea what they talked about, of course, because Jeremy rarely shares anything very confidential, even with me. But one day when your father came, he brought a picture of your mother, and I saw it on the desk when I took the men tea. I noticed it immediately, because she looked so striking – dark hair and eyes like yours, very lovely and vital. You are like her, you know. The shape of your face – and there's something about your expression. Oh, I don't know. I've always admired beauty. I've never been much to look at myself. And now, well, nothing to lose, growing old.' She laughed as she touched her creased, unmade-up face. No, she wasn't beautiful in the classical sense, but she had an inner beauty, a soft humility that would draw people to her more surely than looks.

'Beauty can be a curse as well, can't it?' I murmured, still wrestling with the idea that my father had probably confided in a stranger things that I, his daughter, needed to know. Especially about my mother. It comforted me that I looked like her and I remembered that my father once said that, too. Yet, despite this, I couldn't claim to have the startling beauty Sarah talked of. My hair might be dark but it was fine and flyaway, and I hated my mouth, though full lips were great for playing the tuba.

'And some they call beautiful are hard and empty,' Sarah agreed. 'Some of those Supermodels you read about – I don't know why the men go for them when there are such lovely girls around like your friend Jo.'

She'd know Jo from the hostel, of course. I smiled to myself. Mrs Quentin obviously shared Jo's mother's anxiety to see a nice girl happily married off.

There came the sound of the front door opening, then a voice urged, 'Well, are you going in or not? I haven't got all day.' A large white cat slipped into the kitchen. It regarded me with wide green eyes full of dismay and shot off through the cat flap.

'Oh, Lucifer!' Sarah scolded. 'He's wary of strangers, I'm afraid.'

Jeremy came in with a brisk, 'Hello, hello,' dropping a large brown envelope on the table. 'Wretched animal doesn't like anybody,' he remarked.

'I thought a Lucifer would be black.'

'Not at all. "Oh, Lucifer, bright Morningstar",' he intoned, then added sadly, 'No one knows their Old Testament any more. In the Book of Isaiah, the devil is portrayed as a rebellious angel, Fran, and his name means light-bearer. Our little feline Lucifer is certainly rebellious. Comes and goes as he pleases. Any tea left in the pot, dearest? Sorry I've been so long. Mrs Taylor wanted to pass the time of day.' He sat down at the table and started sorting through his post while Sarah fetched a cup. 'Anyway, Fran, it's good to see you.'

'I won't take up much of your time,' I said. 'You're obviously busy. I came to show you the journal I told you about.' I pulled out the leather-covered book and passed it to him.

'I found it in a filing cabinet,' I went on. 'Laura must be the Reverend Brownlow's daughter, and she's written the journal to her dead sister Caroline, you see, and she's the one the angel was meant to remember. So the whole story behind the window might be here, though I haven't read all of it yet.'

Jeremy turned the pages, stopping to read bits from time to time. Finally he closed the book and handed it back. 'It looks really interesting,' he said, 'and I'd love to look at it properly when you've finished. I've read a bit about Brownlow. He was vicar here in the 1870s and 1880s.'

'Do you mean actually here?' I said doubtfully. 'This house is more recent than that, isn't it?'

'You're right, of course. The old place in Greycoat Square came to be considered too big. It's divided into maisonettes now. One's kept for the curate, but we don't have one at the moment, so our organist lives there.'

'Ben, you mean?'

'Ben's been there since he joined us in June. But yes, the Brownlow family lived there at one time. He was rather a troubled man, from what I've heard. Deeply concerned with his mission to the poor, but things went badly wrong.'

'Oh? What sort of things?'

'St Martin's has always been High Church. Emphasising the mystery of God, the importance of the Sacraments – the mystical side, really.'

I nodded. 'Yes, I see.'

'Well, Brownlow took all this very seriously, as you'd hope, but he was also attracted to the idea of church tradition and doctrine. I once found a rather dry book he'd written on church history. Although he was Anglican, there was much about the Roman Catholic Church that appealed to him and he read extensively the writings of figures from the High Church Victorian Oxford Movement, especially John Newman who, as you probably know, eventually became a Catholic Cardinal. Later in his ministry, Brownlow felt led to do things in St Martin's that some of his parishioners thought were beyond the pale, setting up statues of Mary and the saints, employing what some of them saw as excessive ritual. "Idol worship", certain less sophisticated members of the congregation called it. Brownlow saw it all as being to the glory of God.' Jeremy paused. 'There was confrontation, I believe.'

'Didn't they care about all the good things he'd done?' Having read Laura's viewpoint, I immediately took her father's side.

'I think they forgot these in the upset, unfortunately. It's always important for clergy to remember that they are serving their congregation. If a priest starts acting off his own bat and fails to take his parishioners with him, he's asking for trouble.'

Poor Mr Brownlow. I looked down at his daughter's journal, wondering how it had all turned out. Slowly I said, 'One of the puzzles is, of course, how on earth did this book end up at *Minster Glass*?'

'I simply can't guess,' said Jeremy Quentin. 'Perhaps it's something to do with the making of the window.'

'I suppose so.'

'I must tell you, while I remember. I had a little chat with one of my ladies in the almshouse,' he said. 'Mrs Muriel Trask, her name is. She's lived in the parish all her life, so I always go to her if I need any local background. She's especially useful when I'm giving funeral orations, I can tell you. Memory like the proverbial elephant. Anyway, she remembers the angel window blowing in. A bomb destroyed one of the houses behind the church in 1940 and our angel got caught in the blast.'

'That's amazing. Did you ask her what the window looked like?'

'Yes, of course, but she was a bit vague. She tends to remember details about people – you know, who quarrelled with whom, whose son stepped out with whose daughter in 1957, that sort of thing. But she did say that it was very lovely, all gold and white and glowing. Made her feel very peaceful and loved. And something about being a child and believing that it was a real angel, not just a picture. Apparently she wept when it got broken.'

I knew the vicar must be busy, so I stood up to go. But there was something I was still bursting to ask, and as I looked from Jeremy to his wife, Sarah Quentin discerned that I wished to speak to him alone.

'Will you excuse me?' she said graciously. 'It's lovely to see you, but I must bring in the washing.' She unbolted the back door and we both watched her through the window, walking across the tiny garden, calm and graceful in her movements, despite her round figure.

'It's nice for her to see you,' said the vicar. 'She misses our girls terribly.'

'How many do you have?'

'Two. Fenella's twenty-five. She works in Manchester now. Engaged to a very nice young man she met up there. And Miranda. She's at college in Bristol. Well, she should be, but she's taking a year out. Miranda's given us a lot of problems, I'm sorry to say.' He trailed off sadly. 'It's been immensely upsetting. But I mustn't run on. I think you wanted to ask me something.'

'Yes, I do, though I'm sorry about your daughter.' I paused and took a breath. 'Jeremy, how well would you say you know my father?' I wanted the truth, but at the same time was frightened of it.

He was silent for a moment, folding his glasses and pushing them into his top pocket.

'I'm glad you asked that, Fran. Before last year we'd met once or twice in a professional capacity. He was interested in the windows. But then he came to see me a year ago to ask my advice as a priest. We met several times to talk. And I feel, yes, that we became friends. We're the same age, practically, and, as I've said, he's a very interesting man. Has a detailed knowledge of the history of his craft – quite fascinating. Did you know—'

'Yes, yes,' I broke in, and he must have caught my desperation, because he suddenly gave me his full attention.

'You see,' I went on, 'my father has always been something of an enigma to me and we've grown somewhat . . . estranged. I cannot truly say I know him.'

'Which of us can ever truly say we know another?' Jeremy said quietly.

'No. But he has hidden a lot from me, especially about my mother. Things I think I have a right to know.'

'You're asking me to divulge what he told me in complete confidence,' he said heavily. 'I was afraid you might. Well I'm sorry to say that I can't. You must realise—'

'I do, I do. But you've seen how he is. He may not recover.'

'Though, God willing, he might,' said Jeremy with unmistakable feeling. 'I'm deeply sympathetic, really I am. But the guidelines of my calling are clear on this matter. I would be betraying his trust.'

'But what about me? Do I need to suffer because of this principle?'

'Fran, my dear. We are all hoping that your father will be restored to us, and it seems wrong to believe otherwise whilst medical opinion is unclear. What if he gets better, then learns that I have divulged his deepest secrets? It might change his relationship with you for ever – and he would certainly never trust me again. I know this is incredibly difficult for you . . .' He sounded genuinely upset.

I was furious when I eventually stumbled out on the street, absolutely furious. I knew Jeremy was right, he couldn't break his promise of confidentiality, but in this particular situation it all seemed unfair. And how could Dad have confided in Jeremy when he never had in me? What on earth had my father done that he couldn't tell his only child? Another thought occurred to me and I tasted bitterness. I might only know Dad better after he died. But I didn't want him to die. And what about the alternative? Maybe he'd stay alive for years and years and I'd be stuck in some limbo with him, intimate with his bodily needs but never getting any closer to him as a person, never learning about my mother. Never coming to terms with who I was.

Zac had locked the door and was totting up the day's takings when I got back. He let me into the shop, and I must have looked black as thunder, because he gave me a wide berth and went off home shortly afterwards.

I locked all the doors then mounted the stairs. I couldn't face going to see Dad tonight and felt wicked for my resentment. But a sort of weary numbness was creeping over me. In the end I opened a dusty bottle of Bordeaux I found in a cupboard and curled up in the armchair by the window to weep a little. Then I went to find Laura Brownlow's journal and began to read once more.

Chapter 12

The more materialistic science becomes, the more angels shall I paint.
Their wings are my protest in favour of the immortality of the soul.

Sir Edward Burne-Jones

LAURA'S STORY

April 1880

Mr Russell called on the Brownlows on the Tuesday morning
after he met Laura and little Arthur was born. He was told that
the Reverend Brownlow was out on urgent business but that
Mrs Brownlow and Laura would see him in the morning room.
Both ladies were weary after a late night, Mrs Brownlow
explaining that they had been with the family of a parishioner
who was killed in an accident at the tanning factory the day
before.

At Russell's tentative request, Mrs Brownlow brought out
two framed photographs of Caroline from a locked drawer in
her writing bureau. One was a portrait from before her illness,
the other, unfortunately slightly blurred, had been taken in the
garden only weeks before she died. Mr Russell studied them for
some minutes and his expression softened.

He said, very gently, 'In the first she is a child, and in the
second – nay, it's extraordinary – almost a fragile spirit.' He

shook his head as though further words failed him, then passed the photographs back to Mrs Brownlow.

'My husband asked for you specifically to design the windows, Mr Russell.' Theodora Brownlow's eyes were huge in her tired face.

Mr Russell inclined his head in grave acknowledgement. Laura had as yet said little, but glanced at him where he sat, his expressive hands resting on his thighs. He conveyed such a feeling of lightness, she thought, as though his body wasn't subject to the usual rules of gravity. His back was straight, his head dipped forward, his concentration full upon Mrs Brownlow. When he stroked his cropped beard, reddish-gold against the pale skin, the slight rasping noise caused the back of Laura's neck to prickle.

Mrs Brownlow sat back in her chair. She looked exhausted, and from the way she frequently touched her temple, Laura guessed one of her headaches was developing. She vowed to coax her mother back to bed as soon as Mr Russell departed, but for the moment, the over-bright expression in Theodora's eyes told of some deep source of energy tapped, now that she was talking about Caroline.

She went on, 'Mr Brownlow and I have seen your designs for St Aloysius.'

'Ah, the Mary windows,' he said.

'Yes. We admired them, Mr Russell. Greatly. They, too, were made by *Minster Glass*, I gather.'

'It was I who made them, in their workshop, Mrs Brownlow. If you'd allow me to explain how I like to work.'

She nodded. 'Please do.'

'You see, I believe that craft only reaches the state of true art when the whole artefact is not only designed but fashioned by the same man. I wish to avoid the frustrations of the artist whose inspired vision is thwarted by the inability of mere drudges to put that vision into practice. I often used to feel angry and frustrated when the facial detail or precise colour or the spiritual energy I tried to convey in my drawings was not apparent in the final work. So I set myself to learn the craft and create windows myself.'

'Indeed,' said Mrs Brownlow absently.

Laura could see her attention had wandered to the pictures of Caroline in her lap. 'Then you are like Mr William Morris in this matter,' she broke in, and felt the warmth of his gaze on her.

'My wife is distantly related to Mr Morris. I have enjoyed many discussions with him on just this subject,' he said. 'I take commissions from his firm from time to time.'

She heard the words 'my wife' with surprise, though why she had assumed he was a bachelor she couldn't say. Something to do with the frayed shirt-cuffs, perhaps.

'Do you seek no assistance at all in making the windows?' she asked.

'I have not the skill to make the glass, of course. But I like to consult regarding the precise colours, to draw up the cartoon myself, cut the glass, paint it and fire the result. Another craftsman will help me assemble the window and install it, but these are ordinary manual tasks, and I still supervise.'

'Do you have a studio?'

'Indeed I do, Miss Brownlow. I paint in the attic of my lodgings in Lupus Street, but my labours take me frequently to *Minster Glass*, which has the tools and materials I need.'

'Your angels,' said Mrs Brownlow, looking up from her photographs. 'They are vibrant creatures, not feeble spirits of air. I like to think of Caroline . . .' She drew to a halt, as though unable to frame the right words.

'How do you like to think of Caroline, Mama?' whispered Laura, leaning forward to touch her mother's hand.

'As being somewhere more beautiful than here. Grown into the woman she should have become. Warm and full of life . . . not as a fleshless spirit.'

There was silence for a moment, then Mr Russell inclined his head and said, 'I think I can see her in my mind's eye, ma'am. But do you and your husband wish the angel's features to be in any way, ah, reminiscent of your daughter? The face in the second photograph, you see, is indistinct, and anyway you might not feel it appropriate . . .' he broke off.

Mrs Brownlow's head was bowed. By a slight shudder of her shoulders Laura was alarmed to see that she was crying. She stood up quickly.

'My mother is tired after our disturbed night. You will understand, I'm sure . . .'

Mr Russell rose immediately and said, 'Of course. I must take my leave for another appointment anyway. Mrs Brownlow – my sympathies for you in your grief. I assure you that this memorial will represent the best of me, for your daughter's sake.'

And, with a bow and a murmured goodbye, he followed Laura out into the hall, where Polly fortunately appeared straight away with his hat and his coat. He took Laura's hands in both of his and she lowered her eyes. A button on his coat hung by a thread. Perhaps his wife hadn't noticed it.

'Thank you for understanding,' she said quietly. 'I think Mama meant also to ask you about the design for the other window. And Papa, I know, wished to meet you.'

'Please reassure your parents that I shall channel my all into these commissions. As for the *Virgin and Child*, as agreed, I am to see the nephew of the benefactress, Mr Jeffrey—'

'Jefferies.'

'Mr Jefferies, indeed – tomorrow afternoon. In the morning I intend to visit the church once more to take further measurements. I wonder, Miss Brownlow, if it would not be an imposition, whether one of your family might be on hand for advice.'

'I am sure that can be arranged. Father always says morning prayer there at eight but is finished by half-past. Why don't you come then?'

'I will perhaps come in time for morning prayer. I should pay more regular attention to matters of the soul.' His eyes twinkled with humour. 'Good day, Miss Brownlow.'

With that he was gone. Once Polly vanished downstairs, Laura hurried into the drawing room to peep through the window, but the baker's cart halting outside robbed her of a last sight of him.

Chapter 13

Behold I send an angel before you, to guard you on the way and to bring
you to the place which I have prepared.

Exodus XXIII. 20.

On Saturday I had been home a whole week, though it
seemed much longer. After some discussion, Zac and I
decided to offer Amber a part-time job. We definitely needed
help. If Zac was out on his travels, I was tied to the shop. This
was sometimes lonely, and it meant that I couldn't get on with
anything else, such as dealing with paperwork or visiting
Dad. So Jo and I talked on the phone a couple of times over
the weekend, and Amber came to see me on the Sunday – and
started work with us the very next day. She was to do eighteen hours a week on a temporary basis, with part of that being
on-the-job training.

Amber was a shy scrap of a girl, but she had a natural friendliness and sensitivity, and I knew she would charm the
customers. From the start, though, I worried about her trusting
nature.

'How do you get on with the other women in the hostel?' I
asked, expecting her to complain about the bullying.

'They're all right,' she answered, shrugging. 'They're a laugh
really.' Whether she felt some misplaced loyalty towards them

or the situation had improved, I didn't know, but as she spoke her hand flew to her collarbone where a curiously-shaped pendant rested above the dip of her T-shirt.

'I like your necklace, Amber. What's it got on it?'

She showed me. It was a tiny silver angel, its head bowed and its wings folded in a point above its head. 'Gran gave it to me. I wear it nearly all the time. It keeps me safe.'

Zac was amused and bemused by Amber in equal part. He was flattered by her interest in his work. During a quiet period I watched him teach her how to edge the glass with thin copper foil and to make a simple suncatcher by soldering the pieces together. She chattered away in her excitement. 'Have I done this right? Is this how you hold the – oh! I'm really sorry! I've messed up, haven't I?' He made her try again until she got it right, exercising the patience and gentleness that a caring father might show towards a young daughter.

'You love your job, don't you?' I heard her say to him at one point. 'Your face sort of lights up when you're doing it.'

I watched Zac carefully after that whenever I passed through the workshop. Amber was right. When he was concentrating on drawing patterns or painting glass, his habitual moroseness was gone.

Late in the morning the post brought an electricity bill with an ominous red *Final Demand* slashed across it, and this was enough to galvanise me into sorting out the finances. It seemed safe enough to leave Amber alone in the shop for a few minutes whilst I scurried upstairs.

Zac's suggestion had been that I phone Dad's solicitor, but it had occurred to me to look through Dad's personal document case first. I dragged it out from under his bed, brushed off the dust and tried the catch. It was locked, but a search in the drawer of his bedside cabinet turned up a small bent key. After jiggling this in the elderly lock for a moment I managed to wrestle the case open.

It was an odd feeling, looking down at the neat row of files inside, the dividers tagged *Building Society, Health, Wills etc, Certificates* and a tantalising *Miscellaneous* at the back. I had a strong suspicion that they might contain valuable clues about Dad, and maybe my mother, and yet Jeremy Quentin's little speech about integrity the day before must have had an effect on me. I knew it would represent a betrayal of my father to rake over his life while he lay helpless in a hospital bed. I wouldn't be able to look him in the face if I did that. Another reason for holding back was more primal: simply that I was afraid of what I would find. So I did the decent thing and flipped straight to the papers behind the plastic tag labelled *Wills etc*. And here I found what Zac and I needed.

The file contained a long thin brown envelope and a couple of big white ones. On the brown one was typed *Last Will and Testament of Edward James Morrison*. One of the white ones bore *Pwr of Attorney* scribbled on it in Biro. On the third I read with an odd, prickly feeling *Living Will*.

I put the Will back in the case unopened and read the other two documents quickly. The Power of Attorney gave me the ability to act on Dad's behalf when he was incapacitated. That was good.

Reading the Living Will left me breathless and indignant for a moment. In it, he'd ticked all the boxes about not being revived when *in extremis* – and named Jeremy Quentin as the person to decide. Jeremy, not me! My resentment ebbed when I remembered that it could be problematic to give a beneficiary of one's Will power of life and death. And presumably Dad would leave his property to me.

Retaining the two documents, I locked the case, replaced it

under the bed and went downstairs to make the necessary phone calls to set the Power of Attorney in motion. The Living Will I would take with me to the hospital that evening.

I spent the afternoon in the shop with Amber, showing her, in between serving customers, all the different types of glass and their prices, some of the tools we sold, kept in cupboards in the shop. She was fascinated by all the different colour effects that could be achieved with the glass, repeating the different makes and types like a mantra.

She was also fascinated by the broken angel window. 'It's so sad,' she whispered, when Zac showed her the pieces laid out on the table pushed out of the way in the corner. 'Can you really make it again?'

'We don't know,' he said. 'We desperately need further clues about what it looked like.'

It was nearly five o'clock and I was fetching the keys from the office in order to lock up the shop. When I returned, Amber was still studying the broken angel. I watched her pick up a piece of golden glass and try, unsuccessfully, to match it with another.

'Come on,' I told her. 'It's time you went now. You've done really well today.'

'Thanks,' she said, giving me a shy smile. 'It's been great.'

'See you tomorrow,' said Zac.

'Have a nice evening,' she said, as I showed her out of the back door.

'I hope to,' I replied, remembering that it was choir practice at six-thirty.

Just time to visit my father briefly first.

When I reached the hospital I was alarmed to find that Dad had a plastic mask over his face. The nurse, who took away the

Living Will to photocopy for Dad's file, told me his breathing had grown shallow and his oxygen levels had dropped, though now they were recovering.

He was awake though and he looked at me fiercely over the mask as I took the seat beside the bed. I told him about Amber and my visit to the vicar's house, but didn't allude to the fact that I knew of his conversations with Jeremy Quentin. This time I was reluctant to leave. The feeling stole up on me, more strongly than ever before, that each time I saw him now was precious.

I walked back home in the twilight, feeling curiously sapped of energy. My enthusiasm of earlier had quite gone. I nearly didn't go to choir after all, but forced myself. I'd only droop around the flat and get miserable and guilty. Anyway, singing always cheers me up. Our Junior Choir teacher always used to say that, and many times I have proved her right.

Once I got there, a little late, I was glad I went. This time Ben fast-forwarded to the Devils' Chorus – in which demons, assembling at the judgement court 'hungry and wild to claim their property', mock the newly dead soul. When sung properly, it is chilling, but tonight many of the basses were sight-reading and the rest of the choir subsided into helpless laughter every time the men attempted their deep jeering 'Ha-has'.

'You sound more like dismal Father Christmases than devils,' Ben exploded at one point. 'Put some welly into it, for goodness sake.'

There was a tone of genuine exasperation in his voice, and I overheard someone near me whisper, 'He's taking it a bit seriously, isn't he?'

Jo coaxed me into going to the pub later, and it turned out to be the right decision, for everyone seemed determined to enjoy themselves after such a hard rehearsal. I found myself laughing at some of Dominic's anecdotes till the tears ran down my cheeks.

He was in the Home Office and, without actually divulging anything that could get him into trouble, he had some marvellous stories of personal encounters with well-known politicians and of bureaucratic incompetence. I couldn't help noticing how often he looked at Jo. She would smile back at him, but otherwise just didn't seem to notice.

Ben lounged in his usual place at the bar, nursing a pint and talking to one of the tenors, a tall lean man in a sharply tailored dark suit. He was about Ben's age, with cropped, prematurely silvering black hair and a clever, mobile face.

'Have you met Michael?' asked Ben, after I'd bought my round of drinks at the bar and passed them to Dominic.

'No. Hello,' I said, and we shook hands.

'Michael's on the choir committee,' Ben said. 'He's yet another civil servant in real life, I'm afraid.'

'Can't get away from us here in Westminster,' added Michael. He had an urbane air, but I thought it masked a sensitive nature, for there was a tautness about his mouth.

'Foreign Office, can't you guess,' Ben drawled. 'Doesn't he look the type? Actually, Michael went to school with me. Knows all my deepest secrets. Where the bodies are buried, eh, Michael?' They were sparring with one another in a way that left me feeling uncomfortable. There was something deeper, darker, going on beneath the banter.

'I used to spend school holidays at his parents' place,' Michael explained. 'Mine were abroad, you see, and Ben's wonderful mother took pity on me. So we all got to know each other quite well. His folks had this marvellous great pile in Herefordshire. Antiques and statues everywhere. I always felt like Charles Ryder visiting Brideshead.' There was a sneer in his voice.

Ben burst out laughing. 'He makes it sound much grander than it really was,' he told me. 'And sadly, my parents had to sell it in the end. Cashflow was always the problem. My grandfather had to stump up the school fees.'

I didn't immediately warm to Michael. He was friendly enough, but he was very bitter about something and I didn't understand why he was trying to make Ben sound like a spoiled rich kid. It seemed bad manners, especially if Michael had ben-efited from Ben's family's hospitality. I wondered what the real story was behind it all.

'It's good to meet you, but I ought to get back to Jo,' I said politely, and left the men to themselves again.

By half-past ten, I was weary and said my goodbyes, promising Jo I'd meet her for a drink on Wednesday. I was faintly surprised when Ben left with me. Michael was nowhere to be seen.

'Did he join the choir because of you?' I asked, as we saun-tered back towards Greycoat Square.

'He was already a member. Actually, when the previous organist resigned, it was Michael who suggested my name for the job,' said Ben.

That seemed strange to me. If Michael was envious of Ben, why would he go out of his way to see so much of him? But I didn't know Ben well enough to ask him that. And Ben changed the subject then anyway.

'How did you think the rehearsal went?'

'Fine,' I said, not liking to offer my honest opinion. 'Early days still, isn't it?'

'I suppose so,' he growled. 'But we didn't cover everything I wanted to this evening. Second rehearsal and we're already behind schedule.'

'I expect we'll catch up,' I said soothingly.

As we parted, at the gate of Greycoat Square gardens, Ben said, 'Look, I wonder if you're free on Friday. I've been given tickets for a concert at St John's Smith Square. Do you like Berlioz? It's his Symphonie Fantastique. There's a Rossini Overture, *La gazza ladra*, I think. And some Mozart.'

'I do like Berlioz, very much. And Rossini's *Thieving Magpie*,' I said, though I'm sure I'd have said yes even if I hadn't. 'I'd love to come.'

'Great. It starts at seven-thirty. I have a church choir rehearsal first but that's usually over by seven. Why don't you come along to the church, and we'll go on together?'

As I made myself ready for bed, I reflected on the invitation. It seemed a good sign that I'd hardly thought about Nick for the past week, but a little voice warned me to be careful, not just drift into some new relationship. Still, I was looking forward to going to a concert. How quickly I was sliding into this new London life, I thought as I plumped up the pillows and picked up Laura's journal. Yet, beneath the surface, I was aware, my fear and uncertainty about the future still swirled.

Chapter 14

Angels are spirits . . . They become angels when they are sent, for the name angel refers to their office . . . which is a messenger.

St Augustine, *The City of God*

LAURA'S STORY

Customarily, the Rector did not expect his family to accompany him to morning prayer. After all, there were household prayers at home at nine. But the morning after Mr Russell's visit, Laura took breakfast with her father early and went with him to church. She left Polly with strict instructions to take Mrs Brownlow breakfast in her room only when she awoke, and to persuade her to stay in bed and rest. Her mother's headache had been so bad last evening that Laura didn't think she'd need much persuasion.

They were met at the church door by Mr Perkins, the verger, his thin, stooping body trembling with distress.

'It's thieves and robbers, Reverend, robbers and thieves,' he quavered. 'No one has respect for God's House any more.'

'What's happened, man?' asked Mr Brownlow. 'Take your time now.'

Perkins finally calmed down sufficiently to explain that he'd arrived a moment ago to discover that several small clear-glass panes of the square-hatched windows in the north wall had been smashed during the night.

With considerable alarm, Laura and her father followed him inside, picking their way across the spray of broken glass to view the damage.

'They did not gain entry, did they? Has anything actually been stolen, Mr Perkins?' the Rector asked with anxiety, but the verger shook his head.

'The door was locked as usual, Rector, and they couldn't have got in through holes that small, could they?'

'I suppose not.' James Brownlow sighed and thought a moment. 'We'll send for a Constable after the service,' he said finally. 'I will not allow base vandals to interfere with daily worship. Light the candles in the Lady Chapel, will you, Mr Perkins. We'll be well away from any broken glass in there.' And he disappeared into the vestry.

Laura waited alone in the chapel, trying to calm her thoughts. Flickering candlelight reflected off the shiny new-painted figure of the Virgin on the altar. Outside, Mr Perkins clattered about, sweeping up glass and complaining loudly about 'robbers and thieves' to someone who had entered the church.

A moment later Mr Bond walked into the chapel. Seeing Laura, he immediately stiffened with embarrassment and made to retreat with a muttered apology. She summoned him back, her face burning despite the coolness of the air. They sat together self-consciously, not speaking, his marriage proposal still lying unanswered between them.

A party could be heard approaching and shortly there entered Mrs Fotherington's cousin Miss Badcoe, as severe as her angular, black-clad appearance suggested, Miss Pilkington the schoolteacher, Mr Perkins, and finally Mr Russell, somewhat out of breath. Laura's father, now wearing his robes, shepherded them in and closed the door.

'Rend thy heart and not thy garments . . .' he began to read, in a voice too loud for the small chapel.

Laura, constantly aware of Mr Bond shuffling in his chair to her right and Mr Russell thumbing the pages of his prayerbook to her left, hardly pondered a word of the service.

Afterwards, the older women ambled off chattering. Mr Bond stood up, nodded to Laura, and glanced hesitantly at Mr Russell, who acknowledged him politely. Laura introduced the two men and explained the purpose of Mr Russell's visit.

'You'll have need of a ladder,' said Mr Bond. 'I'll ask Mr Perkins to bring one.' Then, with a meaningful glance at Laura, he excused himself. She listened to the echo of his retreating footsteps.

Her father called out from somewhere, 'Did you read those letters I gave you, Mr Bond?'

Bond's deep tones came in reply. 'I did. It's a serious matter, Rector, very serious indeed. And now all this broken glass . . .' The voices drifted off into the distance and the church door clicked shut.

She was alone with Mr Russell.

He put down his hat, picked up his sketchbook and began to pace around the chapel, staring up at the windows. The sunlight bleached the colour from his skin, glinted off his hair, making an ethereal creature of him.

'See how the light shines through the south side?' he said. 'It's a bright glow rather than direct sunlight. The really strong light, you see, will come through the *Virgin and Child* pane here, from the east. But the angel will be softer. I see the light of his face radiating white and gold, don't you think? Down here will be richer, darker, more mysterious – jewel colours, ruby and deep emerald.'

Laura nodded, seeing the picture vividly in her mind's eye.

Presently Mr Perkins arrived with the ladder, then her father reappeared, looking distracted. He said, 'Mr Bond has gone to fetch a Constable about the glass and it seems I have, ah, another urgent matter to attend to. Mr Russell, my apologies, but I'm unable to speak with you now after all. Would you call on me at the vicarage later this morning if you have questions?'

'Father,' Laura broke in, 'if it helps, I am happy to stay while Mr Russell takes his measurements.'

'As you will, my dear. I am sure Mr Russell and I are most grateful. Now I must go.'

Laura held one end of the tape measure and wrote down figures while Mr Perkins steadied the ladder. When they'd finished, the verger staggered off with his burden.

Russell sat executing a series of quick sketches with that curious cramped hand movement he had.

'Do you come from a family of artists, Mr Russell?'

'Mmm? No, far from it. My father was a travelling minister for the Baptists, but recently retired from his mission because of ill-health.'

'You're a Baptist, then?' Laura wondered what her father would think if he knew that his church's windows were to be designed by a dissenter.

'Shortly before I married I was received into the Church of England,' he said – then, as though anticipating her thoughts, 'No, not merely because of Marie. I was seduced by the beauty of traditional Anglican worship, you see. I felt humbled to be able to contribute to that beauty through my work. Do you know, the Early Christian mystics believed God's light cascades through all the ranks of angels into the minds of all creatures, and as optical light into gemstones and other translucent objects. Think what this means – that the light passing through coloured glass comes directly from His angels and ultimately from God.'

'Don't the Baptists believe in angels, too?' she asked abruptly.
The sun had gone behind a cloud and she pulled her shawl
around her against the sudden chilliness.

'Well, yes, of course. They are the messengers of God. The
Bible is full of . . . Miss Brownlow, you mock me.'

'No, no, I am completely serious. It's the idea of your religion
being decided by the beauty of its trappings that I find mocking.
Is that what your belief is to you, a matter of seduction?'

'Not at all. I am stung. My soul responds to beauty, yes, how
can anyone help that? The plainness of the religion of my birth
might emanate from a sincere wish to concentrate on matters
spiritual, but it has starved me of so much. One can worship
God through beauty, I find.'

'And what if there *is* no beauty? Where is God then?' An
image of the Cooper family in their slum flashed into Laura's
mind, another of her mother sitting with bowed head, tears
falling into her lap. 'Where is God when there is only poverty
and pain and death?'

They stood together without speaking, he studying her, his
eyes full of concern. 'I know something about suffering, Miss
Brownlow,' he said in a low voice. 'Come.' Taking her arm he led
her out of the chapel and over to the *Crucifixion* window.

He said, 'You must ask the man who created this. *There*, he is
telling us – there, in the midst of pain and death – that is where
God is.'

'I . . . I know. That is what Papa says. But I . . . I don't always
see Him,' whispered Laura. 'And it makes me afraid.'

Behind them, the vestry door opened and closed again as Mr
Perkins came and went.

The church seemed to settle with a sigh. Outside, a cart clattered, metal on stone, and a woman began to laugh, a harsh
maniacal laugh that went on and on, fading into the distance.

'My parents give their lives to God's work, Mr Russell. They pour out their lifeblood to the destitute, to those with no hope. Yet they have received little thanks, little reward. Instead God takes their children from them. My mother . . . my mother, Mr Russell . . . is sick with grief. She finds no healing in her work.'

'But think of the people they help. Only one of the ten lepers came back to thank Our Lord for healing him, but that didn't mean His deed was worthless.'

'I sometimes think the poor and godless like being poor and godless,' Laura said quietly. She knew that was uncharitable. Yet some showed no gratitude; indeed, they plainly resented what they saw as interference and moralising. She thought bitterly of Mr Cooper, recently sprung, unrepentant, from his cell, at her father's pleading.

Her attention was caught by something on a pew below the broken window. It was a pebble. She picked it up and showed him. 'Some have hearts of stone.'

'Even stone wears away over time.'

'Do you know, Mr Russell, my father receives letters complaining about his ministry. Rude, hateful letters, decrying incense and statuary and decoration in the church, all of them unsigned. Whoever this ignorant person is, he does not see that these things are symbols of my father's piety. My father does not worship the statues. He does not spend money on himself, but to glorify God.'

'I am sorry to hear this. Anyone who knows your father can see that he is a man of God.'

'He is the last man in the world to deserve the blows that life has dealt him. My mother, too. They have always done their duty. I cannot bear to see their sorrow. Do you and your wife have children, Mr Russell?'

'Yes, indeed. We have a son, five years old, named John. He lives with his mother.'

'With his mother?'

'My wife and I live apart. It is a great sadness.'

'I am sorry, I intrude.'

'You don't, Miss Brownlow. I wanted you to know about this. The decision was not mine. I would have it otherwise.'

'And do you see your son?'

'I try to see him, but do not find it easy. He is too young to understand. If his mother is not near, or his nursemaid, he cries for them. I am practically a stranger to him, it seems.'

'Perhaps it will be easier when he is older.'

'I have to hope so.'

'Or maybe you will become reconciled with your wife.'

'Miss Brownlow, I have loved unwisely and too well. I adored Marie with every fibre of my being. I still adore her. If I weren't standing here in a house of prayer and if it weren't a blasphemy, I would say I worship her. Yet she is possessed of a wild beauty and a passionate temperament. Other, baser men have not been able to resist what is mine. And so I have lost her.'

'You mean . . .'

'That she left me for a lover, yes. Though she presently lodges with her parents for the fellow is penniless. He too left a wife, so there are two families brought to ruin. If I had not my work I do not know what I would do with myself. Go mad, I suppose. I have been driven to hell, Miss Brownlow. Perhaps I shock you. If so, I am sorry. But we talk of suffering.' He spoke gently and his face was expressionless.

'No, I am not shocked. Just sorry, very sorry for all your pain.' Laura could only whisper for fear her voice would break. She felt such a sudden tenderness for him.

'Thank you. Your sympathy means something to me. There

are some too ready to cast blame. My parents are ashamed. They objected to my marriage in the first place, blamed me for aspiring to a life beyond their narrow horizons. The fault is therefore all mine, they say. Their friends will not receive me, not that this is of great moment. I grieve more for John, passing beyond my reach.'

'Is there nothing more to be done?'

'Nothing that will not hurt him more. I will not try to wrest him from his mother, though the law might take my side on this, seeing as I am the wronged party.'

There were footsteps in the porch and the door opened. They turned to see Mr Bond enter, followed by a policeman.

'You are still here then,' said Mr Bond, a little abruptly, glaring at Mr Russell, who merely inclined his head.

'See, I have found one of the missiles,' Laura said quickly. Mr Bond held out his hand and Laura tipped the pebble into his palm. Their eyes met but their fingers did not touch.

A line from the story she was writing ran through her mind. *I asked for your heart and you gave me a stone.* It was as though she had spoken the words aloud, for sudden despair flared in his face.

She would have to tell him her decision, soon.

Chapter 15

Every visible thing in this world is put in the charge of an angel.

St Augustine, *The City of God*

On Tuesday Jeremy rang.

'I'm putting together an agenda for next Sunday's PCC meeting,' he said, 'and I want to raise the matter of our angel window. Have you made any progress?'

'I had another quick look at Dad's papers on Sunday, Jeremy,' I said. 'I need more time – I'm sorry. I'll let you know the minute I find anything new.'

'Thank you, Fran.' He cleared his throat and went on hesitantly, 'I could see that you were upset on Friday, and I feel bad about it. It must be hard for you at the moment. I wanted you to know that you are in my thoughts.'

'Thank you,' I said, slightly stiffly. I was still very upset that Dad had confided in him and not me, though I kept telling myself it was wrong to blame Jeremy.

'Sarah and I are here for you, you know,' he went on. 'If you need us in any way.'

'Thank you,' I said again, but this time more warmly. They were doing their best to help.

Later that morning, the redelivery from the wholesaler

arrived. Amber and I spent a couple of hours checking the order was correct, unpacking the boxes, stacking new glass and hanging the lampshades, whilst Zac settled down in the workshop, surrounded by books and papers, to draw a church window design he'd been invited to submit.

'That's beautiful,' I remarked, as I studied his drawing, the rainbow halo-ing Noah's Ark from which animals were streaming.

'They want something fairly simple in antique glass,' he told me. 'It's to complement a medieval *Adam and Eve* in the same wall. I'll have to use David's studio to do the finer cutting and sandblasting, if my design's chosen.' He gazed around the workshop as he said this and I suddenly saw what he meant. We couldn't offer any of the technical sophistication many modern pieces demanded. I realised then how loyal Zac had been to my father, staying here, using the old methods. I wondered if David had ever offered him a job. I felt a surge of gratitude.

'I'm so glad you're here, Zac,' I said.

He must have felt my sincerity for he replied, 'He's been so good to me, your dad.'

'Yes, you said.' I waited for him to go on.

After a moment, he told me, 'There was a time I was rock bottom – no money, no place to go – and he took me on, gave me a chance. I wouldn't ever want to let him down.'

'What happened?' I asked him, puzzled. Zac had never made reference to this period before, but then the phone rang and we listened to Amber answer it in the shop. After a moment she came in and said, 'It's a Mrs Armitage, wants to know how long her designs will be.'

'Mrs Armitage.' Zac and I looked at one another. I got there first.

'Oh goodness – the children's panels. We haven't done anything about them. OK, I'll speak to her, Amber.'

Mrs Armitage was naturally anxious that she hadn't heard from us, the children's birthday being only weeks away. Could they see the designs as soon as possible? I made the right soothing noises, assuring her there was plenty of time.

'I'll do them when I've finished this,' promised Zac, but he was still working up his Ark and there wasn't much enthusiasm in his voice.

'What do the people want?' Amber asked tentatively. I showed her the Armitages' photographs of the boy with the fishing rod and the girl with the butterfly.

'They're lovely,' she breathed. 'Could I try and draw a design?'

I was so surprised that I said, 'OK. They understand they can't have exactly the same thing – I've explained to them about copyright. Fortunately, they say they want to be different from their American friends.' I showed her a pile of pattern books where she might look for further ideas and she laid them out on the counter and worked on them for most of the afternoon.

I was pleased that she did a very creditable job. The little girl she drew was feeding a bird and surrounded by greenery. The boy was wearing Chelsea strip and dribbling a ball.

'I'm not sure they'll go for that one,' I said. 'I got the impression they wanted something a little more . . .' the word 'twee' came into my mind but I chose 'unworldly'.

Amber didn't seem to mind me rejecting her design. She immediately started thumbing through some of the books again and, after a while, she showed me a drawing of a boy sailing a boat on a pond.

'That's great!' I cried. 'Look, Zac, they'll go for this, won't they?'

Zac studied the drawings and nodded. 'They're very good, Amber. After I've finished this I'll teach you to work up your designs into a proper pattern. Then we can look at some glass samples and try to cost the project.'

Amber looked so happy I thought she'd burst with pride.

After she'd gone, Zac called through from the workshop, 'Fran, have you touched the angel?'

'No.'

'I expect Amber's been messing with it then.'

'Why, what's the matter?'

'Come and look.'

Zac was straightening the lining paper on the table, and I saw with a little shock that the carefully arranged pieces of glass and lead were skewed.

'I expect someone's knocked it,' I said, wondering if I could have done it while moving that screen the other day. I didn't think so. I'd tried to be so careful.

Zac grunted and started rearranging all the bits with quick fingers.

'OK,' he said, stopping suddenly. 'Where's the rest of the face?'

'What do you mean?'

'There are some bits missing. The eyes. The eyes have gone.'

'Are you sure? Are they on the floor?'

We looked. Nothing.

'In the box then.'

Zac took the box down from the shelf. Together we picked out the remaining glass fragments. No luck.

'That's weird. I might have jogged the paper by accident, Zac, but I haven't done anything else, I promise.'

'Well someone has, that's for certain.'

'Does it matter very much? The face was so battered anyway, it would have been difficult to reconstruct it.'

'We would have tried. Damn it, Fran, we should have taken more care.'

'Amber swept the workshop yesterday,' I remembered suddenly. 'Oh, don't say we've got to go through the dustbin! That's horrible.'

Zac gave me his dourest look of grim determination.

'Zac, no!'

'Aye, it's got to be done.'

There were three black bin bags to go through. One by one, Zac shook their contents onto newspaper in the back yard. There were dozens of glass chippings to go through. We turned them all over, every one. Zac made sure of that. But none of them were the missing pieces. Eventually even Zac gave up.

'We'll just have to manage, Zac. I'm sorry. I'm sure we can't use those pieces properly again anyway. Who'd want an angel with a bashed-up face?'

'That's not the point, Fran. We'd be expected to try. Fill in the gaps with resin.'

'Well, it's not as though we're getting anywhere with the thing anyway,' I said. We were both despondent now.

Apart from a couple of hours on Sunday I'd had no opportunity to go through more files upstairs. I wouldn't say I'd given up, just that I'd had other things to distract me. Zac had done his bit, visiting one or two libraries in the hope of finding a picture. But he, too, had drawn a blank.

'The mysterious disappearing angel,' I said, with a sigh.

'Aye, and now even the bits are disappearing,' he grunted, hunched up, hands in his pockets.

He mooned about all the next day. Occasionally I caught him breaking off from some other task to stand staring down at the angel, a preoccupied look on his face. When we asked her,

Amber swore blind that she hadn't been near it, and there was no reason not to believe her.

Wednesday slipped by. At six o'clock I remembered that I'd agreed to meet Jo but I hadn't heard any more from her about it. I dialled her number.

'Oh Fran, I'm sorry. I've just heard I've got to work this evening, after all.'

'What a shame.' I was disappointed.

'Are you free on Friday?' she asked.

'No, as Ben's asked me to go to a concert with him.'

'Ben?' Jo squealed. 'That's wonderful!'

'Don't get excited,' I said. 'It's only because he had a spare ticket. What about the weekend. Saturday?'

'I think I'm likely to be busy,' she said hesitantly, but she didn't say doing what. 'Sunday's no good either. Look, can we talk next week? I'm really sorry. Oh, I forgot to ask,' she rushed on. 'How do you think Amber's doing? She really loves the work, you know.'

'We're very happy with her,' I said. 'She's a fast learner.'

I came off the phone feeling disturbed and not a little hurt. Jo had been so evasive about meeting up – or was this my imagination? She had at least offered Friday, I remembered, and her excited reaction heightened the pleasurable feeling running through me at the thought of seeing Ben.

Chapter 16

Music is well said to be the speech of angels.

Thomas Carlyle

On Friday evening I left at seven-fifteen to meet Ben in the church just as heavy drops of rain started to dash onto the dusty pavements. I wished now I hadn't chosen open-toed sandals, but they were the only shoes that went with my favourite red skirt and denim jacket, and it was too late to change now.

I could hear the distant notes of the organ grow louder as I turned the corner into Vincent Street, and when I opened the door of the church, they rolled over me in a swell of sound that vibrated through my whole body. It was a Bach Fugue – in F, I worked out after a moment. The soaring scales expressed ecstatic worship in a way words never could.

From where I stood in the doorway, the organ loft rose above my head. I tiptoed down the aisle and slid into a choir stall to watch and listen, the grey evening light coming through the windows and the heavy scent of incense and lilies adding to the mystical atmosphere. Had it been just like this when Laura sat here, more than a hundred years ago?

All I could see of Ben was his bright hair as he played so I sat back and closed my eyes, letting the music course through me. When he paused at the end of a movement, I clapped.

'Hello,' he called down, his voice echoey. 'Sorry, got carried away. Didn't realise you were here. Just a moment.'

He vanished and I heard papers scuffling and footsteps on wood before he reappeared through the wooden gate below, straightening the collar of his silvery-grey sports jacket.

'That was magnificent,' I said. 'I'm no good on the subject of church organs, but it really doesn't sound too bad.'

'It's awful. Couldn't you hear the wheezing? The stops badly need renewing. It's the original Willis. Not going to be cheap to restore.' But he was smiling, exhilarated, as I was, by the music and the atmosphere. A man in his element.

His fingers brushed my arm lightly. 'Come on, we ought to go.'

We shared a red tartan umbrella, which he liberated from the vestry, and forged our way out through the lashing rain.

'You women are so daft,' he cried, as he held my arm, guiding me between puddles. 'Why do you never dress properly?'

'What – in sensible shoes? Be elegant or die has always been my motto,' I retorted and he laughed. He was close; the heady scent of lilies and incense from the church still clung about him.

We ran through the thickening downpour, madly dodging puddles and shrieking with laughter. When we reached Smith Square, our red tartan joined the sober-looking queue of black umbrellas edging its way inside St John's Church. Several people shot us looks of alarm, probably fearing we were drunk, so we did our best to calm down.

'Do you know anyone who's playing?' I asked him as we took our seats – good seats near the front – and we watched as the small orchestra assembled.

'Actually, Nina's given me the tickets. You've met her, haven't you? Well, seen her. Here she comes now.'

We clapped the leader of the orchestra as she entered and

with a small stab of unease I recognised the slim brown-haired girl I'd seen gazing up at Ben in Greycoat Square. She bowed, sat down, checked the tuning of her violin, then waited serenely for the conductor to come on, her instrument held resting on her lap. Her eyes searched out Ben and she nodded at him, her expression gravely joyful. She didn't notice me.

It was a wonderful concert, or at least I think it was. I missed a lot of it because my mind kept drifting to Ben, sitting beside me. I was trying to observe out of the corner of my eye whether he was watching Nina or looking at me, but he always seemed to be absorbed in the music, sometimes with eyes closed and a frown of concentration, sometimes staring unseeing into the dark recesses of the church roof.

During the interval we queued for refreshments and several people came up to talk to Ben. As he introduced them to me, one by one, I gradually realised that he was at the heart of a musical community. I myself only recognised a fellow soprano from the choir, here with her husband, but Ben knew them better than I did, too – apparently taught their son at school – and this heightened my feelings of isolation. It was a relief to be able to wave hello to someone Ben didn't know – another brassist I'd played with in London once or twice. But before I could go across and speak to him, a voice behind me said, 'Well, this is a surprise. Twice in one week. How delightful.' I turned to see Ben's sardonic schoolfriend Michael, his tight lips curved into a smile that didn't quite reach his eyes. He gave me a little mock bow.

'Hello, Michael!' cried Ben. 'Where are you sitting? I couldn't see you.'

'Same row as you but on the other side,' Michael replied. 'I tried to catch your eye. They're rather good, aren't they? Nina's going great guns. If I had one criticism I'd say that the last movement of the Mozart was played at a gallop.'

I hadn't noticed this myself, and thought Michael pernickety. But I didn't have time to respond as Ben took my empty glass. It was time we returned to our seats.

After an enjoyable second half in which I was finally swept up in Berlioz's wonderful Symphonie Fantastique, I hoped Ben would suggest we went off by ourselves for a cosy drink. Instead he said, 'You'll come and say hello to Nina?'

'Of course,' I replied, whilst heartily wishing I could do the opposite. For some reason, I didn't want to meet her. But it was only polite, since she had given him the tickets, so I followed him over to the green room door. Michael got there first, and it wasn't long before my hopes of a quiet drink were dashed and it had somehow been arranged that we should all go back to Ben's.

'Nina, darling, that was simply wonderful.'

Ben embraced her warmly, while Michael planted a rather formal kiss on her cheek. Finally, she gave me a limp handshake.

'Oh, you're in Ben's choir,' she said. 'I love *The Dream* but I'm so busy already this term with the violin, I simply haven't got time to sing.'

She still held herself very upright and I noticed now that it was her natural posture, for she had a long, graceful back and a slim waist that would have made her perfect to wear one of those low-waisted fifteenth-century dresses. This elegance, her long fine hair and pale ethereal prettiness gave her a languid, feminine charm.

We all walked back in the direction of Greycoat Square. The rain had stopped now, though the streets shone wet. As often happens in mixed company, the men walked in front, Michael carrying Nina's violin, leaving the women to hurry along behind.

'Did I seem at all nervous?' Nina said anxiously when I

congratulated her on her performance. I was surprised that she revealed her vulnerability to a stranger.

'Not at all,' I said. 'You seemed very confident.' Which was true. She had seemed completely involved in the music.

'It was my first time as leader of the orchestra. A bit nerve-racking with Ben and Michael sitting there. They know so much about music, you see.'

'You didn't have any family you could invite?' I was interested to know if her situation was similar to mine.

'I'm from Jersey,' she said. 'It's a long journey for my mother now. My dad died a few years ago.' She sounded a little choked and despite everything I warmed to her. She seemed a gentle person, one of deep feeling.

'When did you leave Jersey?' I asked her, and she told me about her studies in Paris and London.

'I go back to the island as often as I can,' she said. 'They're very supportive. I try to speak to my mum and my sister every night. Lily's just had her second baby, a little boy, and I've hardly seen him.' This family portrait touched a tender place in me.

'How did you come to meet Ben and Michael?' I asked. We were in Page Street now, where the black-and-white checked apartment blocks gleamed wet through the darkness, like nightmare chessboards, a threatening world through which the men marched confidently half a block ahead.

'Michael's a friend of someone in my quartet,' she said, 'and when I mentioned that I was looking for a piano accompanist, he suggested Ben. So that's how it all happened really.'

It seemed that Michael was always helping Ben. It had been Michael who'd recommended Ben as organist and choirmaster, too. They were much closer friends than one might think. I wondered what Nina meant by 'that's how it all happened'. What happened? Everything about these three was so confusing.

Perhaps it was this sense of exclusion or the mocking chess-boards, or watching Ben and Michael stride further and further away, but for a moment I felt an awful howling loneliness. 'Come on,' I said to Nina, fighting the mood, 'let's catch them up.'

By the time we reached Ben's flat, my shoes and the hem of my skirt were wet through. He ushered us up the steps and in through the front door of the large Victorian house that had once been Laura Brownlow's. Now it was divided in two, vertically, so that it was difficult to imagine how it had been originally. Through one doorway I glimpsed a shiny black grand piano, but Ben led us into the living room behind, where a pair of big padded striped armchairs and a matching sofa were arranged round a small fireplace. Books lined the walls and the room still had its original decorated ceiling. By now I couldn't disguise the fact that I was freezing.

'Fran,' said Ben sternly, 'for heaven's sake, you're shivering. Look, the bathroom's at the top of the stairs. Go and dry your-self – there'll be a clean towel in the cupboard – and I'll light the fire.'

I found the bathroom and peeled off my shoes, then opened the cupboard to search for a towel to dry my feet and the bottom of my skirt. After rejecting a couple of large bath-towels, I pulled at what I thought was a smaller pink one. When it unfurled onto the floor I saw it wasn't a towel at all, but a woman's bathrobe. Whose was it, I wondered. Nina's? Or something he kept in case of an unexpected overnight guest? I stuffed it back in the cup-board and located an innocuous beige hand-towel.

When I padded barefoot back into the living room, Ben laid my shoes by the fire then pointed me to one of the armchairs, opposite Nina. Perching on the edge of the sofa he uncorked a bottle of red wine, while Michael, who seemed to be thoroughly at home, set out glasses on the coffee-table.

'Thanks,' I said, when Ben passed me my drink. 'It's a lovely place. The ceiling is Victorian, isn't it?' I wondered if he knew the building's history.

'I think so, yes. The flat comes with the job. I've lived here since June, when I became church organist. It belongs to St Martin's, you see. Here you go, Michael.'

'Thanks. Falls on his feet, does Ben,' said Michael, with his twisted smile. 'A grace and favour home, while the rest of us have stonking great mortgages.'

'Or rents,' sighed Nina, sipping her wine and screwing up her face, whether at the wine or the idea of rent, I couldn't tell.

Ben frowned at Michael's sneering. 'Makes up for the very modest pay and the unsociable hours,' was all he said.

'Do you know,' I asked them, 'that this used to be the rectory? The vicar was telling me.'

'Yes, I did know. Back in Victorian times, wasn't it?' said Ben. He addressed the others. 'Then after the last war the diocese bought a smaller Edwardian place, where the Quentins live now, and turned this one into maisonettes. The other was sold but the vicar said they kept this on for the curate. Except the bishop can't afford to give us a curate at the moment. Long may we be without one, I say, or I'll be have to come and live with you in your bedsit, Nina.' His eyes twinkled.

Nina giggled, her hand over her mouth. 'Oh, you'd hate it,' she said. 'I do.'

I stared up at the cornices on the ceiling, trying to imagine the room as it must have been 120 years ago, but it was difficult. Possibly, facing east as it did, this had been the morning room. In which case, perhaps it was where poor Mr Bond had proposed and been rejected – or had that been in the drawing room? That would have been the room where I'd glimpsed the piano.

I decided to explain to them about Laura. 'During my research into the window . . .' I stopped and glanced at Ben, slouching languorously on the sofa. 'Has he told you about the angel window?' I asked the others.

'The one that means the organ won't get repaired? Oh, golly yes,' said Michael. 'He's moaned about it endlessly, hasn't he, Nina?' Michael had been prowling the bookcases, occasionally selecting a volume and flipping through it. Now he came to lean against the back of Nina's chair, looking down on her in a faintly proprietorial fashion. Nina hardly seemed to notice him.

'It sounds simply fascinating,' she gushed to me. 'Putting together a shattered window. Like recovering a piece of history.'

'It's going to remain a piece of history unless we can find out more about what it looked like,' I said. 'But what I have found is the journal of a woman who must have lived here. It was her family who commissioned the window.'

'Really? Who was she?' asked Nina, and soon I was telling them all about Laura and the unfortunate dead Caroline.

'It's rather spooky, if you think about it,' Nina said, looking round the room with a shiver, as though Laura might appear in a shimmer of ectoplasm.

'Ever see ghosts here, Ben?' Michael asked.

Ben shook his head. He was the only one who didn't seem to be interested in Laura's journal. After a moment he got up and fiddled about with a stereo system. Soon we were silenced by the passionate swell of Gershwin's 'Rhapsody in Blue' filling the room.

'That's chased the spooks away,' he said as he turned it down again. 'Michael, can you pour more wine? I'll get some snacks. I'm famished.'

The conversation moved on. Michael told a complicated story about one of his and Ben's schoolfriends, nicknamed Boko, who had got himself caught up in some financial fraud and looked set to go to prison. Nina listened wide-eyed, as though this tale was way beyond her cosy cottonwool-wrapped world.

I was just happy to sit in a warm room, drinking wine, eating cheese and biscuits and watching Ben, who listened gravely to Michael's sorry narrative, occasionally putting in the odd comment. They shared a kind of shorthand, these two, bound by their common background. I felt envious. I didn't have that with anyone, except possibly Jo.

At the end of the story, silence fell. Nina yawned and asked, 'So how's the *Gerontius* going?'

'All right,' said Ben, offering everyone more wine. 'But I'm appalled at how little preparation anyone does. So many people seemed to be sight-reading on Monday. It's not good enough, really.'

Michael waved away the wine bottle and said, 'It's not that sort of choir, Ben. Most people belong for the pleasure of singing, not for polished performance.'

'But we need to bring in bigger audiences to cover costs, Michael. And you can't ask an audience to pay to hear something less than polished these days. There's so much else for them to go to in London. Anyway, think of the pleasure to be had from making something the best it can be.'

'True enough,' answered Michael, taking a well-bred bite from a cheese cracker. 'But go carefully, is my advice. You don't want to alienate people.' The clock on the mantelpiece gave out a soft 'chng' as the hands moved to eleven. 'Christ!' he said, checking his watch. 'I'm catching an early train to Gloucestershire tomorrow. Haven't even packed. Nina, shall we share a cab?'

'Oh, yes,' she said, glancing from Ben to Michael to me and looking slightly helpless. 'I suppose I'd better go home now. There aren't many Wimbledon trains at this hour.'

'And you mustn't travel alone, anyway,' said Ben, standing up, yawning. 'I'll ring for a cab.'

She was going, and something relaxed inside me. But when the taxi arrived the uncertainty was back, for Ben took Nina's hands, pulled her lightly to her feet and kissed her soundly on both cheeks.

'Goodbye, darling,' he said.

'I suppose I'd better go myself,' I said, after Michael gave me a stiff little bow.

Nina hugged me in a brief, distracted fashion. 'Simply lovely to have met you,' she murmured. 'Are you sure I wasn't nervous?' She smelled of something light and flowery.

'You were wonderful,' I said gravely, and she looked pleased.

When Ben came back from waving them off, I was examining my shoes. They were still damp, but I had no choice but to put them back on.

'You're not going yet?' he said.

We stood looking at one another, his obvious tiredness lending him a soft, vulnerable look. At some point during the evening he'd pulled off his tie. His shirt was coming untucked. He looked tousled and scruffy, yet somehow inviting. I hesitated, then decided he was merely being polite.

'Saturday's a working day for me. I really ought to get to bed,' I said.

He gave a charming disappointed pout, then shrugged and opened the front door.

'Thanks very much for the concert,' I said. 'I so enjoyed it.'

'We must do it again. Sure you don't need me to see you home?'

'You can stand just where you are and watch me get there safely if you like,' I said, laughing.

'I will then.'

When I reached *Minster Glass* I turned to see him slouched in his arched doorway on the other side of the Square, haloed by the hall light, like some dissolute stone angel come to life in his niche. I waved, and the angel gave me a thumbs-up sign.

Chapter 17

See that you do not despise one of these little ones; for I tell you that in heaven their angels always behold the face of my Father, who is in heaven.

Matthew XVIII. 10.

On Saturday afternoon, I caught Zac rearranging the pieces of our broken angel once more. He had been unusually silent all day, even for him, but now he looked downright miserable. I wondered if it was merely because of the missing eyes.

'No one else knows exactly which pieces were in the box,' I said hopefully. 'They won't be missed.'

'It's enough that we know, Fran. It'll be on our conscience.'

'I suppose you're right. Zac, cheer up. Is there anything else the matter?'

'There's nothing wrong, Fran.' He shot me his most glowering of looks and tramped off to start some new task. Cutting my losses, I retreated into the shop.

Apart from Zac's stormy mood it was proving a quiet Saturday. Eventually, at about three, I said, 'Why don't we close early? We could both do with some time off.'

Zac seemed unable to forget about the angel. Earlier I caught him searching the box again, though we'd already done so twice in the last few days and shaken it out in case we'd missed something. For a while this afternoon he'd tried to sketch how he thought the angel should look. Finally he'd given up and gone back to making candle-holders. These always sold well in the run up to Christmas. He'd made a dozen by early afternoon and, when I found him once more, he was back looking at the angel, hands in his pockets.

'I'd like to visit your dad,' he said, looking up. 'Or were you going?'

'We could go together if you like,' I said, and he looked pleased.

'Let's do that.'

The leaves on the trees in the Square were tinged with red and gold now. Whenever a cloud masked the sun, the air was chilly. Down Horseferry Road, the front of the flower shop was a glorious array of dahlias and chrysanthemums, which always made me think of autumn and decay. Actually chrysanthemums are symbols of life and happiness, and Dad had always admired their complex structure, so I asked Zac to wait while I bought a bunch.

When we arrived at the ward it was to find Dad still wearing his oxygen mask. Zac sat down by the bed while I went off to find a vase. When I asked at the nurses' station what they knew about Dad's condition, they shook their heads and told me to ring tomorrow, explaining that the doctor was unavailable. I turned away, frustrated. Why was everyone so reluctant to comment?

I returned with the jug to find Zac leaning forward, talking to Dad in a low voice, apparently explaining something quite involved and complicated. It seemed that Dad, not a man who had sought out anyone's confidences when well, had become the perfect repository for their secrets, though with what anguish he might receive them in his semi-conscious state, who could say. I crept away again, to find somewhere nearby to arrange my flowers.

'Why don't you come and sit here for a bit,' Zac said when I returned a few minutes later. 'I'll wait for you in the café downstairs.'

Today all I could do was sit and be with Dad as he slept. I thought of Gerontius, the old man pleading, terrified, as death drew near. Did Dad, with what was left of his damaged mind, have any concept of his condition or was he merely drifting? I felt helpless. Yet he seemed peaceful.

Twenty minutes passed before I remembered poor Zac waiting downstairs. 'Goodbye, Dad. I'll come tomorrow.' When I kissed him, his forehead felt cool and dry against my lips.

Zac was deep in a fat paperback book when I spotted him across the crowded café, oblivious to the admiring glances of two young nurses at the next table.

'Like another coffee, Zac?'

He stuffed the book into a sagging pocket of his jacket. 'I'll fetch them,' he said, getting up.

I watched him weave his way between the tables to the counter, a graceful lean figure with his own private brooding air. His hair needs cutting, I thought maternally, and a new jacket wouldn't be out of place.

'What were you reading?' I asked when he returned with coffee and a couple of Danish pastries.

'Trollope,' he said.

'Anthony or Joanna?'

He smiled, eased the book out of his jacket and passed it to me. It was a volume of *The Pallisers*. I opened it and an envelope he was using as a bookmark slid out and would have fallen to the floor. His hand collided with mine to catch it and our heads bumped together.

'Sorry,' he said, picking up the envelope. 'Are you all right?' But it was he who looked wounded.

'I'm fine. What's the matter?' I whispered. 'Tell me.'

After a moment he sighed and passed me the envelope. I turned it over. It was inscribed to a Miss Olivia Donaldson in Melbourne, Australia, but the address was struck through, with *not known, return to sender* scribbled above.

'Olivia's my daughter,' Zac said, his voice dull.

'Your daughter? Zac, I had no idea . . .'

'That's surprised you then.' He caught my eye and tried to smile, but his eyes were sad.

I sighed. 'You are a dark horse. For goodness sake, Zac, why haven't you told me anything about it before?'

'Subject's never come up.'

'No, I suppose not.' It showed how little we communicated. 'How old is she?'

'She'll be twelve. This was a card for her birthday.'

Zac had a girl of twelve called Olivia. A pretty name, a name I'd have chosen for a daughter. Now I remembered his gentleness with Amber. He'd be a good, caring father.

'I haven't seen her since she was three months old.'

'Oh, Zac . . .'

'I've sent her a card every year but I've never heard back till now. And then this.'

We both stared at the envelope.

'I don't even know how long ago they moved.' He looked miserable.

I passed him back the card. 'How can you bear it, not seeing her?'

'Most of the time, to be honest, I try not to think about it.

But I like to acknowledge her birthday. No idea if her mother ever shows her the cards. I've never had any response. That's the worst thing – not knowing if Olivia even knows about me.'

'Wouldn't her mother have told her?' It was hard finding the right questions to ask. We were too used to keeping our private lives at a respectful distance.

He shrugged. 'I don't know. We were once so close, Shona and me, but by the end she cut herself off. I couldn't say any more what she would or wouldn't do. She'd changed, Fran.' He sat, locked in his own thoughts, a faraway expression on his face. I picked at my pastry. Zac hadn't touched his. Finally he said, hesitantly, 'I was telling your dad upstairs, you know. About the card. I expect that sounds stupid.'

'No. No, it doesn't.' I was rather moved by this. A thought came to me. 'Did he know all about Olivia?'

'Yes. It was he who helped after I lost her.'

'Is this when you were rock bottom?'

'Yes. He gave me the job. After Shona took Olivia and went back to Australia I got a bit desperate. Had nowhere to live and no proper work. Your dad rescued me, Fran.'

Twelve years ago. I'd started college. I remember coming back to visit Dad one day and seeing with a shock the notice he'd put in the window advertising for an assistant. Not long afterwards I'd called in to find Dad was out. There was only this quiet, sad-looking young man working in the shop.

'I remember meeting you for the first time,' I told him. 'You hardly said a word to me.'

'No.' He smiled. 'You looked like a scared rabbit yourself.'

'I didn't.'

'Did.'

In truth I probably had seemed nervous. I'd found Zac surly –

rude, even. And I was appalled when Dad told me Zac was sleeping in the spare room.

'It was the surprise, that's all. And Dad had given you a room in the flat. It was odd after there being the two of us for so long. I know I'd moved out. It took some getting used to, that's all.'

'I wasn't there long. It's funny, I've been thinking, I was like Amber at the time. Had nowhere to go. When I told your dad everything that had happened he said I could stay with him until I got myself sorted out. So I did.'

'Where had you been living before?'

'It's a long story, as they say. And this isn't the place.'

I looked around. The café was getting crowded. The young nurses had gone but a middle-aged couple had taken their seats. Other people with trays were roaming around looking for free tables. A vast, weary-looking woman with a clutch of dark-eyed children indicated one of the spare chairs at our table and asked in broken English, 'OK to sit here?'

'Sure,' Zac said. We piled up our crockery to make room for them. Then he picked up his book and whispered, 'Shall we go?'

When we got outside he asked, 'Are you busy now? We could walk along to the South Bank, get a proper drink.'

'Good idea.' I hadn't anything planned that evening and was curious to learn more about Zac's story.

It was early evening and still surprisingly sunny, though a cold breeze blew up from the river. We bought a couple of beers at the National Film Theatre bar and found stools by the window, where we could see the cruisers on the river. On the esplanade, a young juggler performed some pathetic antics.

'Even I could do better than that,' said Zac, sipping his beer, and I smiled. He brought out his wallet and extracted a piece of card which he passed to me. It was a colour photograph, some-what faded, of a fair-haired baby in a sunhat.

'Olivia?' I asked. He nodded and I saw the flash of pride in his eyes. She was pretty, this baby, a smile lighting up her face.

'She's gorgeous, Zac,' I said, and I meant it.

'It was her first birthday. Shona sent me it from Australia. That was the last time I heard from her.'

I passed the photograph back to him and watched as he returned it to the wallet.

'You and Shona,' I probed carefully, hoping I wasn't intruding, 'were you . . . married or anything?'

He shook his head. 'No. Though I asked her once.'

'Is she Australian by birth? Is that where you met?'

He laughed. 'I've never been further than France. She's from Melbourne and we met in Glasgow when we were both twenty. I'd been in work a couple of years then, got an apprenticeship at a stained-glass workshop up there. Shona was a barmaid in a pub I used to go to. Supporting herself through university. She was so pretty and bubbly, easy to talk to.' I imagined her drawing Zac out of himself. He must have been even shyer in those days.

'Don't know what she saw in me.' His face was suddenly alive with the memory of her. I remembered the two nurses trying to catch his attention in the hospital café and I could see. With his dark eyes, that white skin, shadowy beard and his brooding presence, many women would find Zac attractive. I suppose I hadn't noticed before, but then Zac had never made any effort to make me notice. He became aware of me staring and I said hastily, 'So you got together?'

'Yes. I told you about my mam having passed away? She had started to get sick then, was having lots of hospital tests, and it turned out Shona's dad was ill, too, so we sort of helped each other, her and me. Our worries were a bond between us. We understood what the other was going through, you see. I didn't get on too well with my dad and I had no brothers or sisters. It was great having someone to talk to.'

I thought about my own father. How difficult it could be, coming to terms with a parent's illness. Zac took a long draught of his beer. Outside, the juggler had given up and was packing to go home.

'We were together most of her last year at uni,' he went on. 'She was the first really serious girlfriend I'd had and I fell for her completely. When she talked about moving to London I couldn't accept it. Mam's motor neurone disease had been diagnosed by then and I needed Shona so much. Looking back, I should have recognised the signs, let her go. She was restless, wanted to move on. But I thought there was a future for us.'

'What about her father?'

'He had heart problems, poor guy, but he'd just had an operation, seemed better, so she didn't feel she had to rush off home. She badly wanted to live in London for a bit, for the experience of it. In the end I jacked in my job and went with her. Felt bad about leaving my mam, but I told myself I'd go back and see her often. I didn't think about what might happen long-term – whether Shona would go back to Australia and what I'd do then. You just live for the moment when you're young, don't you?'

I nodded. I'd been doing precisely that for years. Living for the moment, not knowing what else to hope for. And now time seemed precious. Time with Dad, time to think about my own future. I mused about this as Zac went up to the bar for more drinks.

When he came back I prompted, 'You were saying you moved to London.'

'Yes. We found a small flat in Cricklewood. Shona got a job in a travel agency somewhere off Oxford Street, but I didn't have any luck. I hadn't finished my apprenticeship, you see, and it was the early 1980s. There was a recession, so people were being laid off rather than taken on. It was difficult. And Shona and me, it started to fall apart. I was still crazy about her, but I could tell she wasn't so keen. She hated me hanging round the house all day. Didn't think I did enough to help. I probably didn't, but my mam had done everything at home. I didn't notice whether the bin was full or whether the washing-up was done. I thought she was fussing.'

I laughed. 'Remind me not to come and live with you then.'

'Don't worry, I'm fully housetrained now. Anyway, what happened next was, Shona announced she was pregnant. I was stunned. We hadn't planned it, you see. Once I'd picked myself up off the floor I was quite pleased. I thought it meant Shona and I would stay together. But it didn't turn out like that.'

'Did she want the baby?'

'Yes. Her dad had had another heart-attack and she was worrying about whether she would go home. The baby decided her. So in the end you could say that Olivia didn't keep us together – she pulled us apart. Shona left when Olivia was three months old. I'd got a job in a local supermarket, and one day when I came in from work, it was to find they'd gone.'

'Without telling you?' I was appalled.

'She'd left a note with her address in Melbourne but asked me not to follow her. She couldn't face telling me what she was doing, she said, because she'd be too upset. *She'd* be too upset.' His fist was clenched and I saw in his face that even now, twelve years later, the pain of that day had never left him.

'What on earth did you do?' I whispered. 'I'd have gone crazy.'

' I think I must have done. The next few months are a blur. I missed them so much, Fran – Shona and Olivia. And then I wasn't earning enough to pay the rent and had trouble with my benefits, and the landlord's patience ran out.'

'Why didn't you go back to Glasgow?'

'I nearly did, but by now Mam was dead – she died a few weeks before Olivia was born. I knew Dad wouldn't want me living at home, and anyway, I hadn't seen him since the funeral. My job in Glasgow would have been filled and it would have been like admitting failure to go back to do nothing.

'Looking back now, I can see I was grieving – for Mam and for Shona and Olivia, and I couldn't cope with it all, couldn't concentrate on anything. I made mistakes on the till in the supermarket, then couldn't be bothered to turn up at all. Finally, the landlord locked me out of the flat with virtually nothing. That night, I went to the Sally Army hostel in Westminster. The next morning, I decided I'd give London one more week, then I'd ring Dad and ask him to send me the train fare home. It was the day after that when I saw the ad on the door of *Minster Glass*. Your father offered me the job on the spot.'

'That's amazing,' I said quietly. No wonder he was so loyal to Dad.

'For a while he let me kip in the flat, but I could see he didn't take to having a lodger. A customer heard I was looking for somewhere. She had a friend in Lambeth who wanted to sublet her flat while she went to live in Spain. I grabbed at it. The area's a bit rundown but the flat's been perfect for me.'

'And you haven't seen Olivia or Shona since?'

'No,' he said quietly. 'I wrote to tell Shona my new address and after a couple of weeks I had a long letter back saying all the things she should have said to my face. That she was sorry but she knew it wasn't going to work out and there was no point in us seeing each other any more. Her dad's latest operation had been successful, but he was still very unwell. They were going to stay in Melbourne and she said again, I shouldn't come to find her. The only other time I've heard from her was when Olivia was one. That's when Shona sent me the photograph.'

He eased it out of his wallet again and we looked at it together. 'Shona wrote that Olivia looked like she did at that age. No trace of me, then.' He sounded bitter.

I stared down at this little lost angel. Of course, Olivia wouldn't look like this any more – eleven years had passed – and yet the photo of this gorgeous little girl represented something eternal. Loss. The faded nature of the print distanced her further in place and time, like one of those children lost to us on earth who never grow up, but exist in some happy limbo of our imaginations, out of our reach.

As I passed the photo back to Zac his expression was lifeless.

'Have you never tried to see her?'

'No. I was broke, though if Shona hadn't been so definite that I shouldn't go, I'd have got the money from somewhere. But she didn't want me to come. I kept having bad dreams about turning up on her doorstep like a mad person and Shona's family chasing me away. I have my pride.'

'You shouldn't allow pride to get in the way of you seeing your daughter, Zac,' I said stoutly.

He thought for a moment. 'Maybe not, but it's hard to go where I'm not wanted. And Shona may be married now. That could be awkward, me turning up and eyeballing another bloke.'

'Do you still . . . love her, Zac?'

He shook his head. 'I don't know how I'd feel though, if I saw her again. Not that there's much question of that. I don't know where they are.'

'It should be possible to track them down.' I felt angry on his behalf. I didn't see why Zac shouldn't be allowed to see his daughter. 'Did you never write to Shona and actually demand to see Olivia? Surely you have legal rights.'

'I don't think I do. It's probably easier for everybody, this way.' He sounded defeated and that made me sad. As he drank the last of his beer, I noted his strong fingers around the bottle were scarred, the nails cut short. And yet I'd seen them handle fragile shards of sparkling glass, paint delicate details of lips and eyes and flower petals, could imagine him holding the hand of a small child.

Chapter 18

And he dreamed that there was a ladder set up on the earth and the top of it reached to heaven; and behold, the angels of God were ascending and descending on it!

Genesis XXVIII. 12.

I slept fitfully that night, haunted by dreams of a lost child. I remember the first drear lightening of the sky and, next, the ringing phone dragging me out of a deep sleep to bright sunlight. I saw with horror that it was ten o'clock.

'I'm *so* sorry about cancelling Wednesday,' Jo's voice said, when I picked up the phone. 'I wondered if you were free today? I thought I'd be busy this weekend, but my arrangements fell through. Then when I rang Mum this morning, thinking I'd go down there for lunch, she said I couldn't, that they were going out!'

I had to laugh at Jo's indignant tone. I had vaguely thought of spending my Sunday sorting through more *Minster Glass* papers until it was time to go to the hospital, but now I heard myself say, 'I haven't been to the Tate for years. Would you like to do that?' I had a hankering to see my beloved *King Cophetua* painting once more.

'That's a great idea,' she said. 'How was Friday, by the way, with Ben?'

'Interesting,' I replied, explaining about going back to his flat. There was another couple there. Michael, from the choir, and a violinist called Nina.'

'But you liked him?' she pursued.

'Yes,' I told her, adding firmly, 'but he's just a friend.'

I felt such relief to see that *King Cophetua* was hanging in its usual place. I'd have felt indignant if they'd lent it out to some exhibition. We gazed at Burne-Jones's lovely beggar maid, regal, untouchable, the King worshipping unheeded at her feet, and I puzzled again why my father hadn't been able to bear the poster hanging in my room.

Jo was more attracted to *The Golden Stairs*, an enigmatic painting of eighteen lovely women descending a gold staircase. 'They're like enchanted spirits in a dream,' she said with a sigh.

'Burne-Jones only used one model for the bodies,' I said. 'Isn't that funny? She was an Italian named Antonia Caiva.' Many of the faces though were of different women Burne-Jones knew. 'It's as though he's raising them to the status of angels, isn't it? Look, this one at the top is Burne-Jones's daughter Margaret, whom he adored. Here is Frances Graham, whom he was devoted to at the time, and this is May Morris, William Morris's daughter, with whom Ruskin and George Bernard Shaw and Stanley Baldwin all fell in love.'

'How wonderful to be beautiful and to inspire that kind of love,' Jo sighed as we left. I was about to make some light reply when I saw that she meant it.

'Jo, you must know that's nonsense. You'd be in danger of becoming a "thing", an object of desire instead of a person. I should think May Morris came to find all the worship very irritating. She was said to be a discontented person.'

'Still, being worshipped sounds all right to me.'

Rachel Hore

Jo seemed so miserable that I asked her, 'Is something wrong?'

'Oh, nothing,' she said, shrugging. 'Don't listen to me. I'm just having an off-day. I don't even matter to my parents today.' We both laughed.

I squeezed her arm. 'You're nice exactly the way you are,' I said.

'Thanks,' she said, 'and I suppose I'm . . . I don't know, a useful person. But I'd rather be pretty. Like you.' Her smile was sad.

'Now you're making me cross,' I said. 'You're lovely. And I don't think I'm pretty as you call it, at all.'

She laughed. 'Will you come and have some lunch?' she asked me. 'Effie rang from work after I got off the phone to you. She hasn't got anyone to help this afternoon so I said I'd go in at three, but . . .'

'I ought to see Dad then, anyway,' I said quickly, 'but lunch would be great.' We stopped at a little supermarket to buy a few things.

Jo's parents' flat was on the first floor of an immensely solid Edwardian mansion block with a wide, carpeted communal staircase. The flat itself was much the same as I remembered it, opulently decorated with Sanderson-print wallpaper and formal brocade curtains tied back to let in what light could be gleaned from the gloomy street.

We ate in the kitchen, overlooking a communal garden where two women in full Islamic dress sat on a bench, talking animatedly. Three tiny dark-eyed children, the girls in white dresses, played on the grass nearby.

'It's funny,' said Jo, passing me the bowl of green salad, 'I always planned that by the time I was thirty I'd have children of my own. And there's not even the remotest possibility on the horizon. Do you ever want kids, Fran?'

I grimaced. 'The idea terrifies me. Think of my weird upbringing. Suppose I messed up too?'

Jo put down her fork and knotted her fingers together, frowning. 'Your dad did his best though, Fran. It's not his fault that your mum died.'

'I suppose not. But it was his fault that he erased all memory of her, leaving me with . . . a void.' I remembered my conversation with Zac yesterday. His girlfriend Shona had done the same thing with their daughter. Deprived her of a father.

'Did your parents ever say anything about my mother?' I wondered suddenly. 'I mean, Dad must have spoken to other grown-ups about her sometimes. I once heard one of the teachers ask about her.'

Jo, mouth full, shook her head slowly. It had always amazed me as a child how much power grown-ups had in situations where I felt quite helpless. I remembered how swiftly Dad dismissed my first piano teacher when I told him how the wretched woman struck my hand with a ruler if I played a wrong note. I had worried about the matter for weeks, frightened that he would belittle my suffering if I told him. But parents would keep things from you too, as I well knew, and secrets they thought small came to assume giant proportions. Mrs Pryde had intimated she knew exactly why a quiet, studious girl called Kathy hadn't returned to school after half-term one hot summer – but 'it wouldn't be fair to her mother to spread it about, darlings,' was all she'd say when Jo begged to be told.

'What about the Kathy Maybury thing?' I asked Jo, who looked understandably puzzled at the sudden change of subject. 'Do you remember, we imagined she must be pregnant, or messed up on drugs, or that she had murdered somebody?'

'Oh, Kathy. It was ridiculous how secretive everyone was. It sounds so normal now. The poor girl had just been working too hard, made herself ill. But everybody thought it was terrible back then, a nervous breakdown. It marked you as a failure. In fact, she just switched schools after the summer holidays. Mum heard she did really well in the end.'

The phrase 'ill with grief' floated through my mind. It was from Laura Brownlow's journal and Laura had been speaking about her mother. 'Have I told you about this diary I found?' I asked Jo now. She shook her head, pushing her plate away with half her food uneaten. I explained.

'Laura's mother, Theodora, lost two children to disease. Clearly something broke inside her, but no one knew how to deal with that then.'

'It must have been unimaginably awful,' said Jo, her eyes huge with concern. 'Yet people in those days said losing their children must be the will of God.'

'It does sound callous to us today, doesn't it? But how else could they deal with it when there was no cure for common childhood diseases? Laura's parents' faith was what kept them going. Think of those gravestones referring to children "fallen asleep" or graves with statues of children resting in the arms of angels. It seems sentimental to us now, but it must have helped parents express their grief.'

A cry came up from the little party in the garden below. The tiny boy had fallen and lay weeping. One of the women scooped him up and stood rocking him in her arms as though he were the most precious thing in the world. I glanced at Jo. Her expression was troubled. She looked down at her watch, said, 'We've got another hour,' then stood up and started clearing away plates with what seemed unnecessary haste.

At her request I made us a pot of tea. 'Have you practised for choir tomorrow at all?' I asked. 'Ben's sure to notice. He's grumbling about people sight-reading at rehearsals.'

'Haven't had time,' she said crossly. 'Anyway, we don't have a piano like you. I should have ordered one of those tapes Val was offering, but I didn't realise it was all going to be so serious.'

'Was the last conductor like this?' I said.

'No, much more easygoing. We thought Ben would be, too. He took us for a trial rehearsal back in June and he seemed very relaxed.'

'But now he seems more serious about it?'

'Yes, he's definitely more ambitious than we imagined. The thing is, a lot of people only come because they enjoy singing. Most of us aren't musicians or anything. We don't want to spend all our spare time practising. People won't like the conductor pushing them too hard.'

'And you think Ben's doing that?'

'Possibly. We'll see how he is tomorrow. But if he carries on like this, I don't think I'll enjoy going.'

'That's a shame,' I said. On a wicked impulse I added, 'Dominic will miss you.'

'Don't be silly.'

'He will. He can't take his eyes off you.'

'Rubbish. He's just friendly. He's never given the slightest—'

'Trust me, I notice these things. Not with regard to myself, unfortunately, but with other people.'

She smiled sadly and started to pull at a hang-nail on her thumb. 'He's a very nice man. But I think you're wrong and, anyway, I'm not interested.'

I thought of Dominic, one of those instantly likeable men, who shone with goodness and honesty. He was nice-looking, too. Not classically handsome or, it struck me now, sexy, like Ben. He wasn't aware of his attractiveness in the way Ben was.

He was just someone you warmed to instantly. A lovely person, who'd suit Jo down to the ground.

'Why aren't you interested?' I insisted, but found I'd gone too far.

She ripped at the hang-nail and it tore off. Blood welled up. 'Oh, whoever knows why someone is or isn't attracted to someone! I can't explain it.'

'Sorry,' I said, but instead of apologising profusely as she usually did if she feared she had caused offence, she merely sucked at her thumb while pouring the tea, a self-absorbed expression on her face.

She plonked a mug in front of me.

'So how's Amber getting on?' she asked, sitting down.

'Oh, she's going great guns,' I replied. 'Got Zac twisted around her little finger. He's really impressed with her progress. Do you know, she created designs for two children's nursery windows, and they're beautiful.'

'I'm so glad,' Jo said, and it was the old, upbeat Jo again, eyes shining. 'I can see it's made a real difference to her. I don't think life at the hostel is much easier for her, but she seems to be taking it better. She was going shopping for some clothes yesterday. I wonder what she's got for herself.'

'Not a great deal, on what I can pay her,' I said. 'Doesn't she have to pay the hostel rent if she's earning?'

'Only something small,' Jo said. 'Tell you what, have you seen the hostel? If you've got time now, you could come in with me, before you go to see your dad.'

'I'd like that,' I said.

Just as we were leaving the flat the telephone rang. Jo snatched it up, but when she said, 'Mum,' a look of exasperation crossed her face. 'I'm fine, really. Fran's here but we're going out now. I've got to work.'

She put the phone down. 'She was ringing from the party they've gone to, worried at the idea of me being here on my own. Honestly.'

I remembered Jo's tone of indignation, that her parents should have their own lives, and forbore to comment.

The modern brick building that was St Martin's women's hostel must have replaced the rather grim 1930s offices I remembered, sometime since I left home. For some reason I had a preconception of bare school-like dormitories or an old-fashioned youth hostel with sets of bunks. It was a pleasant surprise to be shown single rooms that were cheerfully decorated and strewn with female possessions, often with en-suite bathrooms. On the ground floor there was a kitchen and a café which was open for snacks at certain hours, and a big living room with the inevitable TV blaring away in one corner.

'It's really lovely,' I told Jo.

'It is a temporary home,' she said. 'Somewhere the girls can live until they're set up and ready to move on. We can take about thirty at a time, and, as you might imagine, there's a waiting list. If they break the rules, they're out though. We can't put up with illegal drug use or drunkenness or violence, anything like that.'

Being a Sunday afternoon, there were not many people around. Just a small huddle of girls in a corner of the café drinking fizzy drinks from out of the machine. One of them, dressed in a T-shirt and what looked like pyjama bottoms, leaned against the whitewashed wall smoking a cigarette, her black bobbed hair framing a face the colour of whey but for a slash of scarlet lipstick. She had small pretty features, but a hard twist to her mouth and cavernous dark shadows under her eyes. The look she fastened upon Jo and me showed such disdain that it hurt.

The other girls lounging, feet up on the chairs around us, glanced up briefly as Jo said hello.

'This is my friend Fran. I'm showing her round. Lisa, you know you can't smoke in here. Take it outside, please.'

There was a tense silence that seemed to go on and on. Then, slowly, Lisa took a last long drag on her cigarette and dropped the butt into a Coke can. She walked off in the direction of the stairs, all eyes on her. Nobody spoke.

'Well,' said Jo, to no one in particular, and the tension relaxed.

'You on tonight, Jo?' asked one of the other girls, a plump, unhappy-looking blonde with a little girl's voice, wearing caked make-up that failed to disguise bad acne.

'That's right, Cassie,' replied Jo. 'Anyone know if Amber's about? Fran here, her dad owns the shop Amber's working at.'

The girls glanced at me with more interest. After a moment Cassie said, 'She and Lisa had a row. Amber went out in a strop. Dunno where.'

'Ah,' said Jo. 'What were they fighting about now?'

'Oh, same as ever. Lisa calls Amber a runt or something and Amber starts whingeing. She's such a baby.'

'Oh, Cassie . . .' Jo started to say.

'She'd be OK if she stood up for herself,' said a skinny girl who was searching her hair for split ends. 'That's what Lisa hates – that Amber doesn't fight back.'

Jo and I moved on through to the entrance hall. 'It doesn't stop at name-calling, that's what worries me,' Jo said in a low voice. 'Lisa can be vicious and the others are scared of her. They're not bad girls but they're cowed by her and will do what she says. Still, we get by.'

I hugged Jo goodbye, and thanked her, then set off to see my father.

*

Dad wasn't wearing the oxygen mask today and a nurse explained that his breathing was much better. He lay against a pile of pillows, watching me with anxious eyes. Once he opened his mouth and I thought he was trying to speak, but it turned into a yawn.

'I've told you about Amber, haven't I?' I asked him. 'She's the girl who's come to help in the shop. She lives in the church hostel. I went to see it this afternoon. It's nothing like you'd expect, you know.' I sat down. 'Jo was right about employing Amber,' I went on. 'She's got something of a flair for the glass-work. She's even working on some designs with Zac. He'll do all the difficult stuff, but she's helping choose the glass.'

Dad's eyes gleamed with interest, or was I imagining it? Anyway, it motivated me to go on. 'It's making life easier, having Amber. Gives us a bit more flexibility. And the customers like her.' She was good at small talk about people's health and the weather, at which neither Dad nor Zac excelled.

I remembered Zac confiding about Olivia. 'Zac told me how you originally came to employ him,' I said to Dad. 'You never said at the time. I think it's wonderful, the way you helped him.'

I waited, as though I expected him to respond. What would he have said? 'He was obviously the man for the job.' Or, 'It seemed the sensible thing to do.' Something matter-of-fact, anyway, that allowed no room for emotion.

Ben rang early that evening.

When I picked up the phone I wandered over to the living-room window and peered across the Square, wondering if I would be able to see him. But the evening light dazzled off his windows.

'Coming to choir tomorrow?' he asked.

'The wildest of horses wouldn't keep me away,' I quipped.

'Good. I was ringing to ask your advice as a fellow musician. What do you think about singing exercises?'

'Singing exercises?'

'Yes, for the choir. If we spent, say, the first half-hour practising breathing, relaxation, scales, that sort of thing.'

'Mmm.' I tried to envisage Jo enjoying this.

'It could make all the difference to their performance.'

'Why are you asking me? I'm new. I hardly know anyone.'

'That's exactly why – you've still got some sort of objectivity about the whole thing. And, as I said, you're a musician.'

'Oh, OK. Since you ask, I suppose they wouldn't mind a few minutes, but any more than that, they might see as hard work and a bit boring. Half an hour would be too much.'

Ben gave a sharp intake of breath and said, 'That's what Michael thinks. I suppose you're both right. OK, I'll try ten minutes.' Then he said softly, 'I'm so sorry about Friday night, by the way.'

'How do you mean?'

'It must have been tiresome, listening to stories about people you don't know. Nina's used to us now, of course . . .'

'No, it was fine, honestly. Though it's nice of you to say.' I was touched by his concern.

'Good,' he said. There was a brief silence, and I wondered if he had some other motive in ringing, but then he said, 'Ought to go. PCC meeting in twenty minutes. See you tomorrow. Maybe we can fix up something.'

'Yes, let's,' I said, hoping he'd do so right away. But he'd rung off.

I put the phone down, unsure whether to feel happy or exasperated; whether to believe there was something between us or not. He was attractive, I couldn't deny that. We had a shared interest in music and, I could be wrong, but I thought there was some spark between us.

Looking back now, I realise that I'd got over Nick very quickly. It hadn't been a deep thing at all. But it had left me tender. What with that and my anguish about Dad, my guard was down.

I couldn't settle to anything that evening. I tried playing through some *Gerontius* on the old piano, but it was horribly out of tune. I contemplated my tuba case, squatting in a corner, but didn't have the will to take the instrument out. The flat looked wretched with its faded furnishings, its sense of absence. Shreds of memories from my childhood rushed in. In the end I trudged gloomily up to the attic. It turned out to be the best possible thing, for I quickly got absorbed in searching the remaining files in the cabinet where I'd found Laura's journal.

By the time I surfaced my watch said eleven o'clock, but I'd found nothing. I'd hauled files dated 1880, 1881 and even 1882 out of the drawers, trawling through them not once but several times, turning over every letter and receipt, unfurling endless drawings in my search for a cartoon for the angel window.

I'd found sketches for saints and disciples, crucifixions, Holy Families; for creations and apocalypses; and for angels, yes, dozens of angels. The Angel of the Lord – believed to be the personification of God Himself – saving Shadrach, Meshach and Abed-nego from their Babylonian furnace, messenger angels visiting Virgins and shepherds; whole choirs of angels praising God in Heaven – but not my angel.

I carefully refolded a torn sketch for a roundel of cherubs and returned it to its place, filed under *June 1882*. Apart from that letter from the Reverend Brownlow, Laura's angel seemed to have vanished from official record. Every reference to its construction had disappeared. *Why?*

Where else could I look? There must be a picture in an old book somewhere. Or maybe . . . I suddenly remembered the

Museum of Stained Glass at Ely in Cambridgeshire. Perhaps they could help me.

Telling myself that I'd ring them the next day, I went downstairs to read a page or two of Laura's journal.

Chapter 19

Four angels to my bed,
Four angels round my head,
One to watch and one to pray,
And two to bear my soul away.

Thomas Ady, *Candle in the Dark*

LAURA'S STORY

The first letter from Mr Russell arrived at the end of April and was brought by Polly to the breakfast-table. Laura recognised the curious spindly handwriting on the envelope instantly and some tension eased inside her. It was as though some deep part of her mind had been waiting. Murmuring some excuse to her mother, she took the missive up to her room, where she opened it carefully and gasped with pleasure. The margins of the thick cream paper were dotted with humorous little sketches of angels and animals.

I pray you will forgive my corresponding with you, Miss Brownlow, Mr Russell had written, *but I badly need your advice. It is the age-old problem of trying to please two masters, and since you know both parties in the case, perhaps you might graciously agree to be Solomon.*

It regards my design for the Mother and Child *window. I sent it to the benefactress's nephew, Mr Jefferies, and am pained to learn today that it does not find favour. If it is to be the* Virgin and Child in Glory, *his letter informs me, he wishes to see more of the* Glory. *Harps, cherubs and pink clouds, and all manner of sentimental pish were his late aunt's taste, it seems, but this I will not do. Your father saw my design last week and approved it, so now I am caught on the horns of a dilemma. How should I proceed?*

Laura reread the letter with surprise. Mr Russell valued her advice! She'd seen the design in question, an early colour sketch which the Rector passed to Laura and her mother. They'd admired its simplicity, its naturalness. She felt confident of her answer. Sitting at her escritoire, she took up her pen.

Sir, she wrote, *your Mary is already bedecked in rich blue and gold as befits her royal status. Perhaps a simple crown to indicate her position as Queen of Heaven would satisfy Mr Jefferies without compromising your artistic sensibilities? Two cherubs, such as the pretty ones you drew at the bottom of your letter, might hold the crown above her head. Nothing else need alter a jot.*

But Russell wasn't so easily soothed. *On my life, cherubs and crowns speak of the worst excesses of the Baroque,* came his reply that afternoon. *Perhaps we should meet to see how the matter might be settled. If the weather is clement, we might walk in the park. Will tomorrow at two o'clock suit?*

With the faintest feeling that she was being underhand, she wrote back naming a time the next day when she knew her father would be out and her mother at some meeting. Laura couldn't say why, but she wanted to see Philip Russell by himself.

The next day he arrived promptly at two and she took him into her father's study. Remarkably, his irritation about the window had vanished like the morning's last puffs of grey cloud. He'd even brought a new sketch that incorporated Laura's suggestions, though in a different way to how she'd imagined, the angels like androgynous youths rather than small children. 'Leave it for my father to see,' she suggested, and Russell readily agreed.

'Now, shall we walk?' he said. 'It's breezy, but quite pleasant out.' She fetched her bonnet and a Paisley shawl and they set off.

As they wandered through St James's Park, watching children playing tag on the grass and a giggling group of young women throwing a ball, Laura thought she'd never felt so happy.

They talked easily, she and Russell, of pictures and books they loved. Tentatively, she told him about her own endeavours. 'I don't know if what I write has any merit,' she confessed. 'I sent one of my tales to a magazine once, but it came back with a letter to say that they had no room for it.'

'I'll read your stories, if you'd permit me,' he said. 'I read occasionally for a publisher friend of mine so I know the form.'

'That's very kind of you,' she said, 'if you're sure it's no trouble.' She felt such a sympathy with him and instinctively trusted that he'd treat her writing seriously. Their milieux were so different, he moving amongst artists and writers, encountering wealthy patrons like his wife Marie's family, and yet there was much they had in common. They shared their experiences of being the children of church ministers.

'We moved around more frequently than you,' he said. 'My father was a travelling minister and rarely at home. Every two or three years he'd be directed to a different region and my poor mother would be beside herself with worry, altering curtains and measuring up the furniture for the next house, complaining about the aspect of the rooms or the run-down nature of the neighbourhood and the difficulty of finding a new cook. When I turned eight, I was sent away to school and so avoided the turbulence of these moves, but ever after it seemed that nowhere was home.' He, too, was from a family of five children, but the only son. 'My parents are most dismayed at my choice of profession, never mind my choice of wife.'

'What is the nature of their objection to her?'

'To them she seems strange, exotic, beyond their narrow experience. Her mother is Italian and although Marie was brought up in the Church of England, you'd have thought she was the Pope himself for the way my father speaks of her.'

Laura felt his anger then, his bitterness. He still spoke of his wife with deep loyalty, despite the wound she had inflicted on him. Marie's father was a wealthy shipping magnate, he told Laura, and she'd inherited her mother's passionate, unstable nature.

'Sometimes I think she can't help herself,' he said sadly. 'There's something about her that draws men to her.'

After their meeting Laura looked for another letter from him. It came the next day, once again inviting her to show him her stories. She parcelled up her notebook and dispatched it to him with a little whispered prayer that he'd like them. He did, and several days later, wrote back, asking if he could show them to his friend the publisher. 'It might take some time,' he warned. 'My friend is often inundated with work.' She was satisfied to wait and even more satisfied with his postscript suggestion to meet for another walk in two days' time.

On this next occasion, they encountered in the street two women from the church, who greeted Laura and looked at Mr Russell most curiously, so that for the entire outing Laura was anxious that they were being watched. In Greycoat Square, as they said goodbye, she was sure she glimpsed Mr Bond cross the road behind them and she hurried indoors to avoid meeting him.

Not that she was doing anything wrong in walking with Mr Russell, she assured herself, as she slipped upstairs to change her dress, which was splashed with mud. Discoursing in a public place with a married man of forty, who was a friend known to the family, hardly constituted a scandal. But something made her unsure that her parents would regard the matter in the same way. Yes, he was a friend and only a friend. She accepted that, but she was aware of a growing warmth between them, a closeness that both comforted and disturbed her.

As she tidied her hair, she told herself that by listening to his outpourings of grief about Marie, offering words of consolation, she was helping him. In return she found herself opening up to him, confiding her own grief about the loss of Caroline, something her parents rarely discussed. Mr Russell listened tenderly, and this made her realise how much she missed good friends, especially now that Harriet was absorbed in motherhood. As she stared at her flushed face in the mirror she had to acknowledge that she already longed to see him again.

After Mr Russell redrew the *Mother and Child* sketch, the work on the windows stalled. Mr Brownlow approved the changes, but Mr Jefferies disappeared abroad on business before seeing them. By the time he returned, it was Mr Russell's turn to go away. He and Laura had arranged to meet again one afternoon, but during the morning before she received a hastily written note from him.

I have bad news from home, it ran, *and I'm afraid I must break our appointment. My father is dangerously ill and I'm leaving for Manchester at once.*

Laura felt disappointed and had to remind herself to pray for Russell Senior.

The tone of his next missive, five days later, was irate. *My journey was to little purpose. My father, thank God, has fashioned a remarkable recovery from his seizure. That his strength returns is evident in his constant tirades against me. He blames me*, me, *for Marie's desertion, saying I should never have made the marriage. I can take no more of this and shall be returning to London as soon as filial duty permits.*

Please tell your father, he finished, *that I'm determined to resume work on the windows immediately.*

Chapter 20

Holy, holy, holy
Lord God of Hosts
Heaven and earth are full of Your glory.

The Angel Prayer from the Communion Service

'Are angels girls or boys?' I asked the vicar when he came into the shop early Monday morning. 'It's been plaguing me.'

'Ah,' he said, frowning. 'Religious texts usually say "he" but it's traditionally supposed that they're without gender. It is further confused by the fact that many artistic representations look feminine. I fear I'm not being very helpful. It's our angel, in fact, that I've come to see you about. Bad news, I'm afraid. We had our PCC meeting last night, as you know, and . . . well, I've been outvoted.'

'Meaning?'

'They don't see the point of restoring the window.'

'Oh no!'

'Quite. I suppose they have a case. There is the War Memorial window in its place now. The Mothers Union ladies would be most offended if that was taken out. But the main thing is money. We've got an ongoing appeal to expand our homeless projects, and in addition it's been brought to my attention that the organ needs restoring. It's difficult under these circumstances to argue that mending the angel window is really a necessity. Though we have to honour our maintenance obligations, beautifying the church building at the expense of helping people in need is not a popular option these days. There was a clear majority against it, I regret to say.'

He stared at the floor, glum.

'So I suppose I must ask for him – or her or it . . .' he laughed suddenly '. . . back from you. We're unable to pay you for the work, you see, except for what you've done so far, and for the repair work on the other windows.'

'That's a shame,' I said. As this news sank in I was dismayed to find how downcast I felt about giving up the quest. 'An awful shame. I don't know what to say.'

'So I'll bring the car over to fetch the box sometime, unless Zac is likely to be passing in his van?'

'Right,' I said vaguely. I was thinking furiously, trying to find some solution.

The vicar was staring unhappily at Dad's angel hanging in the window. I thought about Laura's journal. I felt I was on a sort of journey myself, finding out the history of the angel, becoming caught up in the search for what it looked like, learning about *Minster Glass*. I'd an idea of continuing Dad's book for him.

And I would have enjoyed reassembling the window. Zac would, too. The money would have been useful, but since I'd discovered that Dad's bank balance was healthy, that didn't really matter.

'Jeremy?'

'Hmm?'

'We can still do something, you know. I'd like to. Restore the window, I mean. We wouldn't need payment. It's just the whole thing intrigues me. I feel involved in its story somehow, especially reading Laura's journal.'

'I understand, but I couldn't ask you to do it,' he said. 'It would be such a lot of work, and there's the cost of materials.'

It would take up time, I couldn't disagree with that. There would be the research into the design of the window, never mind into the methods we would need to use, the sourcing of the right glass and lead. And that's before we actually assembled it. But suppose we achieved all that?

'It would be a labour of love,' I said. 'The sort of thing Dad would have done gladly, the sort of job he'd have enjoyed, if he were well. He'd be pleased if we did it, I know he would.'

'I think he would. Fran, it's a lovely suggestion. I'm rather overwhelmed. As you know, it's become rather a pet project of mine, too. If I can't persuade the PCC to spend parish money on it, well, maybe Sarah and I could contribute something privately.'

'That's something we can talk about, but I'd just be glad if you would agree to us doing it. I'd need to ask Zac, of course.' I laughed. 'After all, he'd be doing most of the work.'

'And I'd need to ask the churchwardens, the window being church property. But I can't see that anyone would disagree, really, can you?'

'There is one thing,' I said. 'If we do this, I'd like to think that there would be somewhere for the angel to go. I can understand if you don't want to dismantle the War Memorial window, but I would feel immensely disappointed if the angel had no home at all, just lay unseen in some museum basement somewhere.'

'I see your point. Mmm. I can immediately think of one or two possibilities, but I'd need to study them to see if they'd work. There's actually another window next to the Mothers' Union one that's currently hidden by a cupboard. It might be the right size, I'd have to check – and think about where we could put the cupboard instead. Then we'd have to ask permission, of course. But, well, my dear, I'm very pleased at your reaction. A generous offer. I feel very cheered.'

When he'd gone, setting off across the garden at a brisk pace, I smiled to see him suddenly skip to one side with the vigour of a man thirty years younger, to kick a stray ball back to a toddler.

I switched on the lights in the workshop and, energised by my offer to Jeremy, resolved to carry out straight away my promise of last night. I went into the office to find the phone number of the Museum of Stained Glass. When the phone was answered, I asked to speak to a member of staff. I told her the whole story and she asked me to spell various names and clarify dates. 'I'll call you back as soon as I can,' she said, and I put the phone down thinking that perhaps, now, I would make some progress.

'Of course we must do it,' was Zac's immediate response to the news that we wouldn't get paid for reconstructing the angel.

'We'd have to do it on top of all the regular commissions,' I said. 'You're already fairly overloaded.'

'There are some jobs that are worth doing,' he said with finality. 'I'll enjoy it.'

Good old Zac. Not that I'd really expected him to say anything else.

It was choir that night, and Ben was in full fighting mode.

'Can we take it from the *tutti* on page forty-one. "Go, In the name of Angels and Archangels".' And it's *fortissimo*. We're sending this soul from the world with a great fanfare of sound. I want to be blown away. Ready . . . three, four.'

'Go . . .' we all wobbled, having trouble pitching the note.

'No, no, no. I said blown away. You need to sound as though you mean it. Graham, play that A, please. Once again now – three, four.'

'GO!' we all shrieked. Ben rolled his eyes but let us stagger on.

'Watch your timing, tenors!'

The rehearsal had been going reasonably well. Many people looked surprised at the idea of singing exercises, but had valiantly joined in. But after ten minutes a group of altos I'd once heard Michael refer to unkindly as the 'knitting circle' started talking at the back and I noticed one of the basses looking pointedly at his watch. Sensing unrest, Ben turned swiftly to the *Gerontius* score.

'That's really not too bad,' he said, once we'd despatched old Gerontius to his death. 'Some of you have more obviously prepared than others, however.' I saw the front line of first sopranos sit up straighter. They were the keen ones, their ringleader being Val, who organised the orchestra. Jo and I felt more comfortable at the back, out of the firing line.

I was faintly surprised that Jo wasn't here, given that she hadn't rung to tell me. Perhaps I was unreasonable to have expected her to, it's only that it was the sort of thing she did. You always knew where you were with Jo.

Later, I walked to the pub with Dominic.

'A shame Jo couldn't make it,' he said, so sadly that I wondered once again whether she was special to him.

'Perhaps something came up at work,' I hazarded.

'Unusual for her to miss a rehearsal though,' he said. Then, 'I can't stay long tonight myself. I promised my sister I'd take over before eleven.'

'Oh,' I said. 'Take over what?'

'Babysitting my mother,' he said, making a rueful face. 'She's very disabled now, I'm afraid. It's a real worry. After the carer goes home my sister and I share responsibility. Monday night's usually my night off, but tonight my sister can't stay as they're going on holiday tomorrow so I must get back at a reasonable hour.'

'I'm sorry to hear about all that,' I said gently, rather moved by his story. 'I had no idea.'

'Quite honestly, Fran, I don't like to complain, but we're getting to breaking point. My sister and her husband are expecting their first, so what we're going to do when the baby's born I don't know. We've got to start thinking of a home for Mum, though it'll be distressing for all of us. I've applied for some time off work to try to sort everything out. The trouble is, the timing is really not great. I'd been hoping for a promotion to come through. But what can you do? You have to take what life deals you. She's been a wonderful mother to us, and we won't abandon her in her hour of need.'

I glanced up at him, walking beside me, expecting him to be cast in gloom, but instead he smiled at me wickedly.

'Perhaps I should bring her to work in a wheelchair. That would be fun on the Tube,' he said. 'And she'd probably sort them all out at work, too. Never stood much nonsense, did Mum! She's still got a lot of spirit.'

She'd clearly brought her children up with a strong sense of duty, too. I couldn't think of many men who would give up a chance of promotion to look after an ailing parent.

'I don't have much time for anything else though.' And so he sighed. 'Monday is my one night out. It is a shame not to see Jo.'

At that point we reached the pub. Since Ben hadn't yet arrived, we were immediately drawn into a conversation about the rehearsal. Of the dozen or so choir members thronged around the table, about half thought the singing exercises a great idea. 'Ben's right, we need to be more professional,' said Crispin, our earnest Gerontius, who was so grateful to have been given the solo part in rehearsals that he would never hear a word against Ben. But some of the 'knitting circle' thought it was a shame. 'It's too much like hard work, the whole thing.' Dominic, a tactful man, didn't say much, merely listened to the others.

When Ben hurried in shortly afterwards, agitated and short of breath, I saw two or three of the complainers go up and engage him in animated conversation. At one point he raised both hands in a calming gesture.

While this was going on, I noticed Michael was standing on his own, so I went over to say hello.

'I wouldn't say the choir are completely happy,' he said, nodding towards the group gathered around Ben. 'Well, I did warn him.'

'I expect it's a storm in a teacup,' I said, feeling defensive of Ben. I still couldn't understand the relationship between these two. On one level they seemed as inextricably linked as brothers, yet here was Michael almost taking pleasure in Ben's difficulties. It made me wary.

'I enjoyed the other evening,' I said, to change the subject. 'I hope you got your train home in the morning all right.'

'I didn't go in the end,' he said, offhand.

'Oh.'

'Nina asked me to spend the day with her.'

'I see,' I said, not understanding at all.

'It must seem confusing to you,' he went on, finally looking at me, unhappiness in his eyes. 'It is to me, too.'

'Are you a couple, you and Nina?'

He shrugged. 'Yes. Or rather, we were,' he said. 'Until she met Ben. It was silly of me introducing her to him.'

'She's . . . going out with Ben, then?' I was alarmed to feel a flood of dismay.

'I don't think Ben thinks of her that way,' said Michael. 'She's besotted, I can tell, but she won't admit it. I suppose I shouldn't hang around, but I . . . care for her, you see.' Michael's expression was suddenly so hurt, so vulnerable, that for the first time I warmed to him.

We stood in silence, a stew of emotions simmering inside me. Ben wasn't with Nina. But Nina wanted him to be. And poor old Michael was miserable. It was like a Shakespearian comedy and not at all funny. And here was I, for the moment on the outside looking in. For how long? I could feel myself being sucked in.

I went and talked to Dominic until he had to go, and then I myself left soon after. When I called, 'Goodbye,' to Ben and Michael, now in deep conversation together, Ben followed me to the door.

'Sorry I haven't had a chance to talk to you this evening,' he said. 'Are you free to come round for supper later in the week – Thursday, or Friday after church choir practice, perhaps? It would be fantastic to see you.'

'Thursday would be less rushed for you, wouldn't it?' I said, so we agreed to Thursday.

I was already looking forward to it. In my good mood I even managed to smile at the catcalls from a group of workmen who were gathered round a throbbing generator at the edge of the Square.

I let myself in through the shop door, then turned on the lights and went over to look at our angel. Zac had moved her table to a corner of the studio out of the way, and I could see he'd polished some of the larger pieces. Golds and greens glowed in the overhead light. From the box nearby, the piece of old newspaper peeped up. I pulled it out to study the faded picture of the bombsite.

I wondered who might have lived at *Minster Glass* in September 1940. My father would have been a boy of around ten. My grandfather would be the one the church contacted, though I knew nothing much about him. Where would the family have been on the night of the raid? We had no garden for an Anderson shelter and were some way from a Tube station. Perhaps the family had gone to one of the trench shelters or merely huddled under a table in the workshop until the all-clear sounded.

That night, I fell asleep and the distant hum of the workmen's generator must have got into my head because my dreams were filled with the whir of plane engines, but then there were wailing sirens, explosions and smashing glass and then a woman screaming. I woke in darkness, bathed in sweat and shouting for my mother, sure I'd dreamed of some dreadful calamity.

Outside, even the generator had stopped and there was only the distant growl of night traffic.

I lay in the darkness, which in a city is never proper darkness, listening to the quiet that is never complete silence, trying to remember my dream. Shreds came back. Something to do with bombs and the angel window breaking.

I imagined someone, maybe the vicar, picking their way through the damage next day, tenderly gathering up the clumps of glass and twisted lead. Had the window got boarded up as it was or had the remaining glass been knocked out first? Would they even have bothered to seek professional advice?

Let's suppose they did. Suddenly I had a strong sense of where to search next.

I was haunted by my strange dream all the following day, but I was so busy at work that there was no opportunity to follow up my revelation about the window.

Part of the explanation for my troubled night presented itself when I went next door to the café. Anita repeated to me something her tenant upstairs had told her.

'He saw a fight last night in the Square. Police cars an' all. Mr What's-his-name from the bookshop come in earlier an' said there was blood on the pavement. Probably something to do with that homeless place.'

'But that's for women! Surely that's not likely?'

'There's another place for blokes round the corner, isn't there?'

'Could as easily have been drunken City types, Anita. Though, granted, a Monday night would be unusual.'

'All I know is that decent folks are not safe in their beds. Now tell me how your dad is, the poor man.'

I always liked chatting to the gossipy Anita, but felt uncomfortable about these cut and dried remarks. It was too easy to blame Jo's flock for any problems, especially given that Anita knew nothing about the incident. I, it seemed, had slept through it, though perhaps the commotion, like the workmen's generator, had contributed to my dreams.

Later, as I watched a large lorry pull up outside *Minster Glass*, the shop phone rang. It was Jo.

'Jo! I can't talk for long. Our wholesale order's just arriving. Missed you last night at choir.'

'That's what I rang about. Something came up,' she said mysteriously. 'How did it go?'

'It was a tough rehearsal, but we got through,' I said.

' Shall we meet later in the week? Have you an evening free?'

'Where are we – Tuesday. How about tomorrow?'

'Possibly. I'm not sure. Shall I ring you?'

'Of course,' I replied, feeling a bit puzzled and hurt by her uncertainty. ' Oh, Jo . . .?' I'd suddenly thought to ask her if the disturbance in the Square had been anything to do with the hostel. But she'd already hung up.

It wasn't until the evening, after I'd visited Dad, that I got the chance to do what I'd been wanting to all day. I climbed up to the attic and carefully packed away most of the Victorian documents in their cabinets, to make room for what I had to do next.

Dad had been awake when I'd seen him earlier, and I'd told him all about my dream. I was certain that he understood. His mouth opened slightly and he made a sound, a sort of 'Ah.' Had he been trying to tell me something he knew? We stared at each other and I had whispered, 'Do you think I'm on the right track, Dad?' But he didn't try to say anything more.

I opened a drawer labelled 1940, flipped through the files until I came to *September*, and laid the folder open on the desk. My idea was simple: if *Minster Glass* had been contacted by St Martin's after the bombing, they might have found the paperwork and refiled it as a new commission.

Near the front of the folder was a thick manila envelope with *Re. broken light at St Martin's* scribbled on it. I pulled out the wadge of paper inside and flicked through the pile with increasing excitement. The yellowed letter on the top bore the date June 1880. I took in lists of figures relating to materials. Finally, when I unfolded a large, thick piece of cartridge paper and saw the illustration inside, I knew I'd found exactly what I'd been searching for.

Laura's angel.

Later, I sat by the living-room window. It had been raining and the Square sparkled wet in the darkness. Somewhere along the row of lights on the far side was Laura's old home. The past seemed all about me as I picked up her journal and began to read once more.

Chapter 21

Unless you can love, as the angels may, With the breath of heavens
betwixt you . . .
Oh, never call it loving!

Elizabeth Barrett Browning, *A Woman's Shortcomings*

LAURA'S STORY

June, 1880

'Oh, the darling!' Baby Arthur was definitely smiling at his Aunt
Laura from his nest of white lace in her arms, first uncertainly,
then wider and wider.

'He knows me, I'm sure he does.'

'Of course he does, silly, he's seen you ever so many times
now. Say Happy Birthday to your aunt, Arthur.' Harriet, having
installed herself in the largest armchair, signalled imperiously to
Arthur's new nursemaid, little Ida Cooper, to sit out of the way
on the footstool beneath the window.

Laura gazed down in wonder at her six-week-old nephew.
His eyes, navy at birth, were changing to a translucent sea-blue.
When she stroked his flawless skin – well, flawless if you dis-
counted the tiny milk spots across his nose – it felt even
smoother than Mr Russell's gift for her twenty-third birthday, a
silk-covered writing case, which he had sent round earlier. He

had decorated the accompanying note with an ink-drawn border of birds and plants.

I trust this will encourage you to write to me often, dear Laura. Your friendship is precious to me, the letter said. In the privacy of her room she had penned a few careful words to thank him, then hidden the gift in a drawer and taken the note down to the post herself.

'Let his grandmother have a turn with him now, Laura,' said Harriet, and Ida hurried over to transfer Arthur in his bundle of white lace to Theodora's outstretched arms.

Laura felt her throat contract with emotion as she watched her mother's expression of naked adoration for the baby. Theodora's tired face glowed with pleasure as she returned his smiles and chuckled back. Perhaps with regular doses of Arthur, Mama's spirits would improve.

'Open your present, Laura, do,' commanded Harriet. How was it that Harriet suddenly seemed older than Laura? Marriage and motherhood gave her new status. Next to her, Laura felt faded, diminished.

Even her gifts were now extravagant, compared with the modest penwipes and needlecases the maiden Harriet used to sew. Laura picked up the huge box Harriet had placed near her, unknotted the ribbon and opened the lid. She peeled back the tissue paper and shook out a beautiful golden tea dress.

'Oh, Harriet!' Laura cried. 'How wonderful!'

'Go and put it on, Laura,' ordered her sister. 'We must see how it looks. Mama gave me your old work dress so I would know the fit.'

The dress was perfect. Laura stood before the long cheval mirror in her father's dressing room, fastening the front buttons, admiring the ruched sides and the pleated layers that fell flatteringly from the hips to finish, daringly, a few inches off the ground. The gold colour exactly complemented her complexion, she was pleased to notice, and reflected the chestnut lights in her hair. She'd never had such a costume.

'Well, I never,' said her mother, frowning with amazement as Laura slipped shyly back into the room several minutes later.

Her father said, 'Laura, my goodness, child.'

Two gentlemen had entered the room. One knelt to admire Arthur, the other sat stiffly with his back to her. Both turned to look at her. She gazed in horror from Mr Russell, now rising from the floor, to Mr Bond, and almost fled. Mr Bond's eyes swept over her, his mouth a round O of surprise; Mr Russell studied her, smiling slightly. Her face flamed and for a moment she couldn't move her limbs. No one had ever made her the centre of attention before.

'Darling, you look simply beautiful.' Harriet rose and came to take her hand. 'Come and sit here, near Mama. Ida, take Arthur now. Mr Russell is going to show us his drawings, Laura.'

Mr Russell cleared his throat and foraged in a leather portfolio. Laura perched upright on the sofa, her mind working furiously. Why was that man Bond here? On her birthday, too. How could her father be so insensitive?

'This is so fine. Harriet, look.' Theodora held out the drawing for her younger daughter to see.

'Oh!' cried Harriet.

Forgetting her embarrassment, Laura leaned forwards to see over Mama's shoulder.

It was the design for the light over the altar; a more detailed draft executed in ink and a colour wash. Mary sat gently cradling the infant standing in her lap. The two gazed into one another's eyes in mutual adoration. Hovering above Mary's head, two sublime-looking angels held her crown.

'The morning light will strike the window thus,' Mr Russell

explained. 'Her cope will be pale gold – less yellow than this; the tracery antique gold and white; her gown the richest of blues. The lead will outline the Christ Child here and Mary's halo here, framing the faces thus.'

There were murmurs of appreciation.

'And Jefferies has seen this version?' asked Bond.

'Yes,' Russell replied shortly.

'He wrote to me yesterday giving his approval,' the Rector told Bond. 'Now, may we see the angel?'

Russell unrolled the second sketch and held it up. There was a little silence. Laura stared. It was different to how she had expected it, but she couldn't say why. The figure was lovely. With its wings folded above its head it filled the tall thin shape of the window perfectly. The face did not look particularly like Caroline's and she was surprised to feel a quiet relief at this. She would not, after all, have to see her dead sister's face in church every week. This angel was a solid, powerful-looking, reassuring figure, with one hand raised as though in blessing. She liked it, it made her feel calm and safe; as though she were filled with light, but it was unexpected and she didn't know how she was supposed to react.

It was her father who broke the silence, and as he spoke she understood that his expectations had been different from hers again. 'But this is not Gabriel the messenger to Mary, is it? This angel is dressed like a traveller, bears not a lily but a pilgrim's staff.'

Russell inclined his head. 'I remember no specific request for Gabriel, sir.'

'No, I suppose I made none. But in my mind's eye, it being the Lady Chapel, it was natural to imagine Gabriel, the angel who came to Mary to tell her she was to give birth to the Emmanuel.'

'Sir, I briefly wrestled with the idea of Gabriel. It was especially difficult, since there is no room for Mary in the window. I discarded several early versions before inspiration came. If I might be so bold with my opinion, I believe that Raphael is appropriate for the Lady Chapel. Raphael is the guardian angel, the special protector of the young, of travellers. It was Raphael in the Old Testament who was the companion of the young Tobias. And, sir, see this banner at the angel's feet. It's not easy to read in this sketch but the meaning of Raphael's name seems so suitable in a memorial to a beloved daughter.'

Laura's father took the paper and squinted at the scroll by the angel's feet.

'Raphael's name means "God heals",' he told the assembled family, his voice unusually reedy. He cleared his throat, passed a hand through his thinning hair. 'What do you think, my dear?' He handed the sketch to his wife.

A long minute passed as she studied the sketch, her face a blank mask as though her mind were a long distance away. Then suddenly she smiled and looked up at her husband. Laura was struck to see that her eyes sparkled with happiness.

'Raphael the guardian angel. I like it, James,' her mother said. 'It is right. We are all pilgrims and our angels watch over us. I especially approve of the patterning on the wings, Mr Russell. You have taken such trouble with the detail and I thank you.'

'It has been no trouble, madam.' His voice was soft.

Laura glanced at Mr Russell to see his golden eyes upon her. He was waiting. 'And you, Miss Brownlow? Your good opinion is important to me.'

'I like your Raphael,' she said after a moment. 'Very much.'

Everyone seemed to have forgotten that the angel had been supposed to look like Caroline. Or perhaps they, like Laura, had been relieved that it didn't.

*

'Why did you do it, Papa? Why did you invite him?' Laura cried, following her father into the study after everybody had gone.

She looked down at the brown paper package she held. As their visitors left the house, Mr Bond had pushed it into her hand '. . . a small token for your anniversary,' he had said gruffly.

'You know how uncomfortable he makes me feel. And it must be a torment for him.'

'Laura, whilst I am sorry, you must see the difficulty for me. He is my churchwarden, after all, my mainstay in these difficult times. He must share in decisions about the fabric of St Martin's. It is his right to see those drawings. And as for personal torment, he could have offered some excuse not to come.'

'But to invite him on my birthday? To a family gathering?'

Her father sat down heavily in his chair. 'Perhaps it was insensitive of me,' he said. 'I'm sorry, there is too much on my mind. However, whilst we are touching upon one delicate subject, I must raise another. Mr Bond came to me recently with a concern.'

'A concern?'

'About you, my dear.'

'Me? What right has that man to express concerns about me?'

'He has our family's best interests at heart. And he still cares for you, Laura. What he had to say alarmed your mother and me.'

'What he . . .? What do you mean?'

'That you keep such open company with Mr Russell. No,' he raised his hand to stop further interruption, 'I know you are an innocent in this matter, my dear. However, you must consider your position as a young lady with, ah, hopes and expectations.'

'Mr Russell is a married man, Papa. There is no possibility of anything else. We are friends only.'

'Yes, indeed. I know this. But worldly opinion twists that which is pure, preferring to believe the worst. And being a daughter of a Church of England clergyman you must be, like Caesar's wife, above suspicion. Bond tells me what I did not know previously. The man is the subject of a public scandal. His wife has left him, though I gather he is the wronged party. I feel it my Christian duty to receive him in the house, but it still does not do for you to be seen with him. Laura, I've never been able to forbid you to do anything, you know that. And though you are a young woman of forceful opinions, you have never before given us cause for concern.'

'Papa, I do not now.'

'Perhaps not. But I counsel you to be careful. He will make our windows and be gone from our lives. And, Laura, I accept your feelings with regard to Mr Bond's suit, but I must ask you to respect my position. He is a stalwart supporter in the parish and I can't prevent the two of you meeting from time to time.'

'I didn't mean that he should be banished from the church, Papa. Merely that I should not have to simper sweetly at him across our drawing room on my birthday.'

At this her father laughed and squeezed her hand. 'Ah, my dear, again I'm sorry. And a secret part of me is pleased that you will be with us for a while yet – despite Mr Bond being a most excellent man. Now I must wrestle with Sunday morning's sermon. A particularly difficult exposition on The Four Last Things.' And patting her shoulder, he guided her out of the room.

Laura stood in the hall, trying to collect her feelings. From the drawing room came the plaintive tones of Chopin's Raindrop Prelude played with all the passion her mother could muster.

Why did that man Bond have to interfere, to tarnish something good? She was still holding the package he'd given her. Tearing off the paper, she saw it was a copy of *Sesame and Lilies* by John Ruskin, a present she'd have welcomed if it had come from anyone else.

'Oh, confound the man!' she cried, and slapped the book down on a console table where it caught a metal statue of *St Christopher Carrying the Christ Child*. The ornament slid to the floor with a crash.

The Chopin foundered. There came a long silence, then the crashing opening chords of Beethoven's Sonata Pathétique.

Laura listened for a while, allowing the music to fill her. Then she rescued the statue, relieved to see it was not damaged, and climbed the stairs.

As she gazed once more at her reflection in her father's mirror, her thoughts swirled. The girl who looked back at her could not be called beautiful, but she had strength and spirit. The set of her chin might, however, label her stubborn. Now Laura knew what to do.

As twilight fell, she sat at the table in her room writing a letter to Mr Russell, assuring him of the family's delight in his drawings. She hesitated for a moment then wrote, *It would interest me greatly to view the construction of the window, if you would permit it.*

Chapter 22

For He will give His angels charge of you, to guard you in all your
ways.

Psalm XCI. 11.

'Zac! I've found it. Look!' I wouldn't even let him take his jacket
off the following morning. But he was as excited as I was to see
the drawings.

'Fran, it's exactly what we needed. Isn't he magnificent?'

'You think it's a he?'

Zac considered the matter and shrugged. 'Could be either.
The shape of the face is masculine, isn't it? Square-jawed, like
one of those Renaissance angels. And the hands are too broad
for a woman's.'

'But the features themselves . . .'

'Are delicate, I agree. No, it could be either.'

'It's Raphael, Zac. There's a passage in Laura's journal about
it, too. Look, here is the pilgrim's staff and the hand raised in
blessing. And the motto "God heals". Gabriel would hold a lily.'
I waved the drawing and did a little dance that made him laugh.
'Isn't it fantastic, Zac? Come on now, we must ring Jeremy.'

The vicar promised to come round as soon as he could disen-
tangle himself from a parish finance meeting.

Amber arrived late.

'Sorry, the police came this morning. Something about a fight last night. Some blokes Lisa knows, but no one's saying anything.'

'Was anyone badly hurt?' I asked and she shrugged.

'Don't think so. Ooh, what's that?' She admired the picture of Raphael and pronounced the angel a 'he'.

Jeremy, when he appeared, stuck to his line that angels were androgynous.

'Well, we can't call the angel "it". That doesn't sound right at all,' said Amber. In the end we settled for 'he' and 'he' Raphael remained.

The vicar was on his way somewhere and could only stay a minute, so we agreed to reconvene on Thursday morning to discuss how to proceed.

After he left I remembered that Jo and I had agreed to meet that evening. I hadn't heard from her, so I dialled her number, thinking I'd leave a message, but she was in. 'Oh no, that's awful. I'm really sorry,' she said, 'I'd completely forgotten and I've double-booked. I'm just getting ready to go out, Fran. Something I can't cancel.'

'Oh Jo, that's a shame.' I felt crestfallen. There was once a time when I had taken Jo for granted. Now, it seemed, the tables were turning. But as I finished the call I remembered I'd be seeing Ben the following night and that cheered me up.

At five o'clock, when I'd finally finished unpacking the morning's order and was switching the sign on the door to Closed, the woman from the Museum rang to tell me what she'd discovered about Philip Russell.

'The main thing that'll interest you,' she said, 'is the link with *Minster Glass*. Did you know that Philip Russell eventually took over the business?'

I almost dropped the phone in astonishment.

'I read it in a footnote somewhere. Reuben Ashe, who owned the firm, invited him to become a partner in 1885.'

'But that means,' I cried, trying to take this in, 'that he might be part of my family.' I explained how *Minster Glass* had been handed down through the generations, realising as I did so that I didn't know whether my predecessors had been called Ashe or Russell.

'That continuity is unusual these days,' she agreed, 'but, yes, it certainly sounds like it.'

'Since we're rebuilding practically from scratch, it's going to be challenging to treat this as a strict conservation exercise,' Zac told the vicar on Thursday. 'We will use as much of the original glass as possible, of course, and follow ethical guidelines for conservation as often as we can.'

Standing in the workshop of *Minster Glass*, with the angel on the table before us, we might have been surgeons discussing where to make the first cut on an anaesthetised patient.

'However, unless what you're wanting is a pure-Victorian half-made window to lie in some museum vault, I'm going to have to fill in the gaps using new glass. And then we will fit it into a bronze frame which can be installed in front of the present clear-glass window.'

'Will that matter?' I asked.

'Not really. We can record which bits of glass are new, you see. And mark them.'

'What do we know about the artist?' asked the vicar, awkwardly hitching his bulk onto a stool.

'I take it you're asking whether the window has any historical merit?'

'Yes. If he was an important figure – I'm not saying of Burne-

Jones's stature, but even someone well known amongst stained-glass experts – would we get ourselves in the soup if we filled in the gaps, so to speak? Have you managed to find anything out about Philip Russell, Fran?'

I'd already explained to Jeremy how Laura Brownlow's journal might help document the creation of the window, but my contact from the Museum of Stained Glass had been able to tell me very little otherwise about Russell except for the connection to *Minster Glass*.

'As well as the *Virgin and Child* window in St Martin's, she could tell me about only two or three other surviving windows directly attributable to him.' A *Nativity* window at St Helen's in Brighton was one that she'd mentioned, an *Annunciation* at St Aloysius in Islington another. 'But what is more important from our point of view is his connections to the business. He went into partnership with Reuben Ashe, the then owner, and eventually took over the firm, so he was undoubtedly responsible in some way for many more windows.'

'That's something your father might have known about . . . know about, I mean,' said Zac, blushing at his error.

'Yes,' I said softly, smiling at him, 'though I haven't found any mention of it amongst his papers upstairs.'

'What was his reputation as an artist?' Jeremy asked me.

'The woman at the Museum says he's a little-known figure. But given how wonderful the *Mary* window is, surely he deserves better?'

'So, would we all agree that his work is worth preserving?'

'Definitely,' said Zac and, 'Oh yes,' I replied, both at the same moment.

'Mmm.' We waited. Jeremy drummed his fingers on the table. Eventually he said, 'I think we should do what Zac suggests. Restore it using new glass. I want to see that window back in the church. I'm sure we can move that cupboard to free up the other light. It'll take time to talk everyone round, but we'll get there.' His eyes were bright with enthusiasm.

'Good,' said Zac. 'Do you imagine that the light you speak of is the same size as its neighbour?'

'I think so, but I'll help you measure it if you come and find me tomorrow. I'll be in the parish office, round the side of the hall, most of the morning.'

'Is that OK, Zac?' I asked anxiously. 'Of course, if Amber were in, I'd come with you. But we haven't asked her to come again until Monday.'

'I'll be fine,' he said. 'Do you think I can't manage?' He wasn't smiling.

'Of course not,' I started to say. 'I just . . .' He laughed and I frowned at his teasing.

Zac seemed happier that week. I'm sure the progress with our angel was partly responsible, but perhaps sharing his anxieties about his daughter had helped, too. I hoped so.

When Ben opened the door to me that evening, he was wearing an apron covered in little Hoffnung orchestral cartoons and an air of distraction. His hair was unusually ruffled and his face flushed.

'You'd better come down to the kitchen, Fran,' he said, after quickly kissing my cheek. 'I'm at a crucial stage with supper. Are you any good with béchamel sauce? I can never quite get the hang of it.'

I followed him down to the basement where the kitchen was a scene of havoc. A celebrity cook book spattered with flour and grated parmesan was weighted down with a pepper mill at a recipe for *Uncle Pepe's Famous Vegetable Lasagne*. A trail of ratatouille led across the floor from the table to the sink, where vegetable peelings floated amongst the dirty crockery. I stepped over a broken egg lying on the floor and inspected a saucepan of lumpy white goo on the stove.

'Where do you keep the sieve?' I asked, prodding at the sauce with a spoon.

Ben scooped up the egg in a tea towel and I watched with horror as he threw it, shell and all, into the washing machine. His only subsequent contribution to proceedings was to splash red wine into two huge glasses and amuse me with stories about his hectic day, while I strained the sauce of lumps and poured layers of vegetable, béchamel, pasta and, finally, parmesan into a waiting dish.

'Do you always expect your guests to cook their own dinner?' I asked, closing the oven door.

He laughed. 'I'm sorry. I am hopeless, aren't I? You don't know how grateful I am.' His repentant small-boy expression was so endearing that it was impossible to mind.

'Where are we eating? I mean, should we set the table? Is there any salad or anything?' Ben leaped up and delved in the cutlery drawer. Green salad and bread followed forks and spoons onto the kitchen table.

'*Et, voilà!* Now, Fran, why don't you take your wine upstairs and make yourself comfortable in the sitting room while I clear up a bit. Or have a tinkle on the piano, if you want.'

I protested but he waved me away. 'No, I insist. You've done enough.'

Today, as I wandered up the stairs and down the long thin hall, I found myself assessing the layout of the place, which I'd been too distracted to do on my last visit. I tried to imagine how Laura's home had originally been.

In converting the old rectory to maisonettes, I guessed that the developers had merely removed the old staircase and built a wall that split the property in half from front to back. Hence Ben had half the old hallway, half the rooms of the original house – all, of course, off one side of the hall, and his own street door. Presumably the other half, next door, was a mirror image. If there were any Victorian ghosts, I mused, they'd likely be seen walking back and forth through the dividing wall, wondering what idiot had put it there.

I peeped round the door of the front room to where the grand piano glinted ebony in the evening light. It was a cheerfully messy room with bare floorboards, the surfaces bestrewn with sheet music. An arrangement of wooden chairs and music stands suggested a recent chamber group rehearsal. On one wall Ben had hung an impressive array of framed degree and masters certificates. There were concert flyers and a couple of posters, too, advertising piano performances at well-known music festivals; the most recent, as far as I could see, from two or three years back.

I walked over to the piano to where a diary lay open on the top, and couldn't stop myself peeking at it. Nina's name appeared several times among the scrawled entries and I flipped the book shut, disconsolate.

I put my wine glass on a table and sat down on the long stool. The piano was beautiful, a Bechstein, kept in immaculate condition. I tried a few chords, then sight-read a hymn from the book propped up on the music rest. The descant was fiddly in the final verse – *Angels help us to adore Him* – but I staggered on until I became aware of Ben standing in the doorway, arms folded, listening.

'Come on, you play something,' I said, getting up and pulling some music at random from a huge pile on a little table. 'Piano's not really my thing. Look, here's some Ravel. Do you know this one?'

It was *Jeux d'Eau*, a sparkling, impossibly difficult piece that's meant to sound like running water. As I opened it and swapped it for the hymn book, I noticed a name pencilled on the cover. *Beatrix Claybourne*. It lingered in my mind because of its old-fashioned elegance.

'Haven't tried this piece for years,' said Ben. But he launched himself into it confidently and ignored the occasional wrong note as he plotted his way at speed through the hemi-demi-semi-quavers. By the time he'd finished we were both laughing.

'OK, so that one needs a little practice. Can I play you something else?'

'Is there anything you're rehearsing at the moment?' I asked him. 'For performance, maybe.'

'I'm accompanying Nina,' he said. 'It's an important solo outing. Only a small music festival in Sussex, but it's well regarded. Schubert and Brahms.' He started to play from memory a lovely flowing sonata of Schubert's, the plaintive melody tapping deep emotion. When he came to the end we sat quietly for a moment.

A delicious herby smell was creeping into the room. Shortly afterwards, the oven-timer began to beep rudely.

'How is your dad?' Ben asked me as we were eating, and his face showed concern as I told him about my visit that afternoon – that there had been no change. I felt I could confide in Ben.

'It sounds odd, Ben, but I feel closer to him than I have for years. We've not always had an easy relationship, but now I can sit and tell him what I've been doing and how I feel about things – and, this time, he can't change the subject or leave the room. That's what he used to do, if I said something that made him feel uncomfortable. He *has* to listen. If that's what he's doing – listening. I can't always be sure. Perhaps he is far away in some other place.'

'They say it helps the patient though, don't they? To talk, stimulate them. You don't mention your mother. Is she . . .?'

'She died when I was tiny,' I told him.

'Oh, I'm sorry,' he said, looking dismayed.

I was used to people's reactions. Sometimes they were embarrassed, didn't know what to say, and I found myself reassuring them. 'Don't worry,' I said. 'It was nearly thirty years ago. I can't remember her at all.'

'Still, growing up without a mother . . . that's a tough call,' he said.

'What about your parents?' I asked.

'Oh, I don't get up to Herefordshire to see them very often,' Ben replied, offering me more salad. 'My sister Sally lives locally so she keeps an eye. I go a few times a year, for Christmas usually, but I suppose that'll be more difficult with my organist duties. Sally looks out for them. I'm lucky really.'

'It's a shame though, if the job stops you from visiting them.'

'To be honest, we're not that close. I was packed off to boarding school at seven and got used to looking out for myself.' He pushed his plate away, his expression stony-faced.

'Seven seems awfully young,' I prompted. A picture arose in my mind of a small cherubic Ben in shorts and blazer, sitting on his suitcase at a railway station, alone, abandoned and I felt a rush of maternal feeling.

'Was that the school where you met Michael?' I asked.

'No, that was later, when we were thirteen. He had it worse. His parents were diplomats – I think he told you. In the summer he'd fly out to wherever they were, but the rest of the time he was bundled between relatives. My mother took to him, so he often stayed at my parents' place. He still goes to visit them, you know. He's a better son to them than I am.'

Ben looked so glum that I said quickly, 'I'm sure that's not true.

He works more regular hours than you, doesn't he? Don't forget, I know about being a musician – how it takes over your life.'

'You're telling me,' he agreed. 'I don't feel I have any leisure time at all. Mind you, I'm doing what I love and I don't know that Michael can say that.'

'Doesn't he like his job?'

'Oh, don't get me wrong, he finds it interesting. But you can hardly say he lives and breathes it in the way I can with music. Music is my entire life, Fran.' There was a passionate light in his eyes as he said this and even then I could see that, for Ben, music came first, above everything else. But at that moment, the passion, the intensity, made him all the more interesting.

'I've never felt that about my music,' I told him soberly. 'I love it, yes, but I could live without it.'

He shook his head. 'That's not me at all.'

'I'm pleased how much I'm enjoying the stained glass again.'

'That's two things you're good at,' he said, getting up. 'Don't they say that the happiest people have two things they can do? Now, how does zabaglione sound to you?'

'Do I have to make it?' I asked warily.

'No, no, only to eat it.' He opened the fridge door and inspected the contents of a glass bowl. 'Hope it's set all right though,' he said, looking doubtful.

Later, I slipped upstairs to the bathroom, and when I came out I noticed some pictures on the landing floor, propped against the wall, as though waiting to be hung. Aware that I was snooping again, I picked up the one in front. It was a long school photograph labelled *Wellingsbury, 1978*, and Ben was easy to spot on the back row scowling through a cloud of fair hair. Behind this picture was one I stared at for some moments, a graduation photograph of a breathtakingly beautiful Ben with shorter, spikier hair, perfectly moulded features and dewy skin, and then several more framed concert flyers. The last one was for a programme of Ravel and Debussy at a Northern music festival four years ago. Ben's name featured, but it was beneath the name of another pianist, Beatrix Claybourne. Here was a dramatically lit photograph of a serious young woman with tied-back dark hair. I studied her intense expression for a moment or two, feeling faintly troubled by it, then replaced the pictures and went downstairs.

Ben had drawn the curtains in the living room, where we sat in chairs either side of the fire like a comfortable old couple, drinking our coffee.

'So what happened in the pub after the rehearsal on Monday night?' I said, sliding off my shoes and drawing my legs up under me. 'You seemed to be under siege.'

'Ah, the knitting circle,' he said, draining the rest of his cup in a sudden gulp. 'The dear ladies who bring cushions to practices and save places for each other.'

I laughed, but remembered something Dominic had told me. 'Oh Ben, don't mock, the choir is probably the highlight of their lives.'

'Maybe, but they're the kind who like things to stay exactly the same, even if a change would be for the better. They don't see what's going on around them – realise that you have to adapt to new circumstances. It's a dog-eat-dog world out there, Fran. Especially when you're chasing Lottery grants and booking bigger venues.'

'But we're not,' I said, bewildered. 'Are we?'

'We could be. There's a lot of potential in the choir if you think about it. We've a few really good singers and musicians like yourself and Val and Crispin. And plenty of contacts and commitment. I think we should be more ambitious.'

'What does the choir committee think?' I wanted to know.

An administrative committee met regularly, I'd discovered. Michael was on it and Dominic and a few others. They organised things like the concerts and the sheet music, and assisted Val's recruitment of the orchestra.

'The first meeting of term is tomorrow, in fact, before church choir practice. I'm going to introduce a few ideas then.'

'Well, the best of luck,' I said. I stifled a yawn and glanced at the clock. 'Goodness, I ought to go. It's a whole new routine running a shop. I have to be up early.'

He laughed. 'I have to get up for school three days a week. Come on, I'll get your coat.'

At the door, when I left, he kissed me on both cheeks, for a moment holding me close. 'It's been a wonderful evening,' he said in a gorgeously husky voice. 'We must do this again.'

Halfway across the Square I turned to look back at the house and there he was in his doorway again like a charming angel. I waved and he waved back. But when I looked back again, the door was closed.

I walked home, thoughts whirling. It had been a lovely evening, but I couldn't work Ben out. Did he like me only as a friend, or was there the promise of something else? Whichever, I felt closer to him after that evening. The image of that seven-year-old Ben going off to boarding school still tugged at my heartstrings. Despite his confidence and his devastating beauty, somewhere inside, Ben was still that lost little boy, who made me want to look after him.

Chapter 23

Let triumph . . . the better angels of our nature.

Abraham Lincoln, First Inaugural Address

Zac and I had set aside Friday afternoon to start work on
Raphael. We closed the shop at three, and I helped Zac unroll a
huge sheet of white paper. On this he began to draw the outline
of the window in which our angel had to fit, using the measurements that he'd taken at the church that morning. Later, I
watched him draw a grid of squares over a photocopy of
Russell's original sketch and a similar grid over the fullsize outline. This would enable him to copy out the sketch square by
square, in the process enlarging it to a fullsize cartoon. After further searching upstairs, I'd discovered the original Victorian
cartoon, but it had been folded and refolded so many times it
was in pieces.

'Perhaps it was used as a template for other angel windows,'
I told Zac, but he wasn't sure.

'The original design might have been, but the grid would
only work on a window of exactly the same size. Thank the Lord
we have it though, as a guide,' and I had to agree with him, for
it also showed us the shapes of all the pieces of glass.

Drawing the new cartoon of Raphael took Zac most of the

afternoon, for he was always having to calculate and recalculate measurements and refer back to the Victorian cartoon to see if what he'd done looked right. Every now and then he wrote something in a hardback notebook he'd bought. He also took photographs.

'You're supposed to document everything you do when you restore a window,' he explained, when I asked him about it. 'In case future generations want to study it or further work is required.'

Between us it became known as *The Angel Book*. Over the next few weeks its pages were to be filled with Zac's neat handwriting and illustrations and photographs.

'The woman at the Museum was fascinated to hear about our archives,' I told Zac. 'Apparently very little about Victorian stained-glass businesses survives. She's offered to come and look at all the papers sometime.'

'Have you thought about donating everything to them?' Zac asked, as he copied a border pattern of fleur-de-lys. 'It's not much use to us. We know how hard it is to find anything when we want it. At least they would catalogue it, make it more accessible.'

'Zac!' I told him, hurt. 'It belongs to Dad and he's writing his history. I can't give it all away. When Dad . . .'

He said softly, 'You're right, Fran. I'm sorry.'

We continued work in companionable silence.

At the end of the afternoon, he asked, 'Will it bother you if I come in tomorrow, it being Sunday?'

'You don't want to do that, do you?'

'Why not? I'm not doing anything else particularly, and it would be good to get on with the job.'

'Tell you what,' I offered. 'I'm not doing much either, so I'll help you, if you like.'

'That would be great,' said Zac.

*

The next day, Zac transferred the fullsize drawing to a large piece of tracing paper, and by a process of half-tracing, half-copying, drew the lines showing where the lead would go and the position of the ironwork that would be required to support the finished window.

As humble assistant, my job was more mundane: to continue Zac's work preparing the old glass – a fiddly and grubby business that involved melting off old solder, detaching glass from the battered strips of lead and cleaning off cement from both lead and glass. As I finished each piece I returned it to its place on the lining paper, under Zac's critical eye.

From time to time, when concentration allowed, Zac dropped fascinating snippets of information about Victorian stained-glass methods.

'It's interesting that Victorian techniques and materials were virtually the same as in medieval times.'

'Really? You'd have thought something would have changed over the centuries,' I replied.

'Occasionally they tried to take short cuts. These would often fail. Have you heard about the great borax disaster of the 1870s? Some craftsmen mixed paint with borax, which fires at a lower temperature, so they thought they were on to something useful. Unfortunately borax is also soluble in water, which meant that when condensation ran down the inside of the windows, the figures literally wept!'

'That's awful. How do you know all this, Zac?' I'd spent hours as a teenager reading all about the period in terms of art history. I was fascinated by the gothic revival that celebrated all things medieval and which led to a renaissance in stained-glass making. I read how Burne-Jones, William Morris and their circle transformed the decorative craft into a high art form that celebrated the integrity of the materials and the romantic values of the age. But I didn't know the detailed chemical techniques as Zac did.

'I've made it my business, haven't I?' he answered. 'I've read stuff, been on courses.'

I asked Zac how he usually spent his Sundays, half-expecting him to say on his own work. But instead he said, 'It varies. I visit friends, or go to the movies. I love walking. Sometimes I take a Tube or a bus somewhere in London and get out and walk. Richmond or Hampstead, Docklands, anywhere. I like visiting all those Hawksmoor churches in the East End. The ones that are open, anyway.'

'Shame you didn't go somewhere today, given the weather,' I said. It had been sunny earlier when I ventured out to attend the eight o'clock service at St Martin's. It was a simple spoken liturgy, without organ or hymns, so there was no sign of Ben, though I told myself he hadn't been my reason for going.

We were tidying up at about four o'clock when the shop doorbell rang loudly three times. I had both my hands in the sink so Zac went to answer it. There was the sound of the door unlocking, then male voices, and he returned, followed by Ben.

'Thought I'd see if you were in,' Ben said to me. 'You left this behind on Thursday night.' He held up my striped scarf, which I hadn't even realised I'd lost.

'Oh, how stupid of me,' I said, drying my hands and taking it from him. 'Thank you. And thanks again for dinner.' I felt awkward, knowing that Zac was listening.

Ben was walking around the workshop, looking at everything. Zac watched him warily. Ben stopped to study the pieces of angel, frowning, but when he reached out to touch one, Zac called out, 'Don't . . .'

Ben contemplated Zac with a steady eye. 'Sorry, mate,' he said. He turned to me and smiled. 'So, you're both working on the Sabbath, are you?'

'*You* do,' I came back at him, and pretended to play an invisible organ.

'*Touché.*' Ben laughed. He glanced again at the pieces of glass. I was sure he was about to say something else, but then he changed his mind. I wondered if he had some reason for coming that wasn't to do with the scarf.

Zac refused to melt. He took a step nearer the worktop as though he might need to shield the angel from Ben.

Trying to lighten the atmosphere, I said quickly, 'We've practically finished for the day. Perhaps you'd both like to come up for some tea. Or is it too early for a glass of wine?'

'Thanks,' said Ben, relieved. 'Good idea. Actually,' he went on, 'I've something to ask you, Fran.'

'Oh?' I said. Ben glanced at Zac, who took the hint.

'I'll come up in a moment when I've cleared away,' he said tiredly. I felt sorry for Zac, but annoyed too. He simply made no effort to be friendly to Ben and I found that rude.

'You're not to just disappear,' I hissed at Zac over my shoulder as I followed Ben up to the flat, and he gave me one of his Celtic thundercloud looks.

Ben and I both decided on tea. 'I had a boozy lunch with some old schoolfriends,' he explained.

We were standing in the kitchen, waiting for the kettle to boil. Ben glanced at his surroundings and I felt both embarrassed and defensive about my scruffy childhood home.

'I hadn't realised you could see my place so well from here,' he said, peering out of the window.

'We could flash signals to one another at night,' I joked. But Ben seemed to consider the idea seriously.

'The light in the window signalling to a lover. Which opera's that?'

'I don't know. Is there one?' I said, trying to keep my voice steady.

I waited as he came closer. He said softly, 'And what would we signal to one another, eh?' and his finger brushed my cheek.

I looked away, suddenly dizzy, as though I'd lost control of my limbs – exactly as I remembered feeling with Nick. And suddenly I knew I wasn't ready for this. I was scared.

'Better get the kettle,' I muttered, for it had started to whistle, and Ben stepped back.

'What was it you wanted to ask?' I reminded him, trying to make things normal again as I poured water on the tea bags.

'Oh yes,' he said, not looking at all put out by my rejection. 'It's since the choir committee meeting yesterday. It has been suggested that I call together a wider group to discuss the choir's future direction.' All this sounded a bit formal. What was wrong with a chat in the pub?

'I'd like you to be involved,' he went on. 'With your musical experience and your objective viewpoint.'

'Oh,' I said, surprised, and thinking I was moving beyond being able to be objective with Ben. 'And there was me thinking this was a social visit.' I passed him his tea and we sat opposite one another at the table by the window.

He laughed. 'It is, of course,' he said, narrowing his eyes in a very attractive manner, 'but it seemed a good moment to mention it.'

'Did they like your ideas at yesterday's meeting, then?'

'They thought it sensible to take soundings,' he replied rather cagily. 'So will you do it?' He leaned forward, giving me one of his soul-searching looks.

I grinned.

'What?' he asked, smiling. '*What?*' He put out his hand and lightly brushed mine.

'Oh, I don't know. You're clever at getting round people,' I told him.

'So you will?'

'I'll think about it. I'm not very good at committees. And anyway, I might not agree with you over everything. Who else are you asking?'

'Val, Dominic – he's sensible.' He tapped the table as he thought. 'One more, maybe. Crispin, our soloist, would be best.'

'Michael?'

'I suppose so.'

'Why the reluctance?'

'I already know his opinions. He doesn't think anything should change.'

'Oh,' I said, privately thinking that Michael's views should be represented. 'What would this group do?'

'Brainstorm ideas,' he said. 'Naturally, the vicar must be on side. I'd need to invite him. But surely as long as we didn't ask the church to subsidise the whole thing he wouldn't object to us spreading our wings a bit.'

'Ben, I don't mind offering advice, but if you did make big changes you'd need to have the whole choir behind you, wouldn't you?'

'That,' he said, 'will be part of the challenge.' And this time when he smiled at me there was a glitter of resolution in his eyes. It made me uneasy.

Just then we heard slow footsteps on the stairs, followed by a gentle knock. I got up and let Zac in.

He smiled unhappily at me and nodded at Ben sitting at the table. His mood hadn't improved and this annoyed me in turn.

There were only two chairs in the kitchen so I suggested we

all move into the living room. Back in the kitchen I was glad to be alone, making a third cup of tea. I strained my ears to hear whether they were talking – they weren't. When I took the milk out of the fridge I held the carton briefly against my hot face.

Ben and Zac, Zac and Ben. They represented the two different sides of my life. Music and art, and I couldn't manage either of them. Especially when they came together. I took in the tea, to find them standing in uncomfortable silence, their bulk seeming to fill the whole room.

'Here we are,' I sang brightly. 'The drink that cheers but does not inebriate.'

They both looked at me rather oddly. We drank in awkward silence then Zac put down his mug half-finished and said he had to go. I was almost relieved when Ben followed him out a moment or two later.

'All right,' I told him, 'I'll come to your discussion group.'

'Great!' He kissed my cheek quickly and was gone.

Chapter 24

Hark to those sounds!
They come of tender beings angelical

Cardinal Newman, *The Dream of Gerontius*

'I've seen a real angel, you know.'

When she arrived at work on Monday, Amber was entranced by the reconstruction of Raphael and took every opportunity to escape from her designated post in the shop to come and watch Zac and me working. While I continued to clean glass and untwist lead, he collected up the clusters I had finished and moved them onto the tracing paper pattern, which he'd laid over the big light-box; when switched on, this provided a useful light source from below. After this stage he'd decide which pieces of new glass we'd need to find.

'Tell us about seeing an angel, Amber,' Zac said gravely, as he shuffled the glass jigsaw around. But his eyes were merry.

'I know you think it's funny, but I really have seen one. He saved my life.'

We were used to Amber's zany ideas by now. Her personal guardian angel was somebody-or-other, whose colour was red, and his special area of authority was, I'm sure she said, watching over orphans. But she hadn't shared this particular story with us before.

'It was after my mum died.' We both stopped to listen. 'I was, like, all over the place, kept forgetting things, going round in a daze. Well, once I walked into the road without looking and the next thing, it was like someone gave me a hard push, and I was back sitting on the pavement. Then this car whizzed past. It just missed me. I couldn't believe it.'

'How terrifying,' I said, wondering what she was getting at. Had the car clipped her and forced her back? Or had she seen the danger at the last minute and jumped automatically?

She saw our bemused expressions.

'When I say someone gave me a push, that's what it felt like. But there didn't seem to be anyone there. Except I know there was. It was an angel.'

'Why do you think that?'

'I was so surprised, I sat there on the pavement for a bit. I was sure I could hear music – in the distance, like. I looked up and there was this guy standing in the middle of the road holding a guitar case. And there were white feathers floating through the air around me, lots of them. And that's a sign of an angel. When I looked again, the bloke had vanished – into thin air, like. I would have seen him walking away if he'd been ... well, human, wouldn't I?'

Zac and I caught one another's eye and he raised an eyebrow very slightly at me.

Not wanting to upset her, I said, 'Well, whatever he was, I'm very glad someone or something was there and looking after you, Amber.' I wondered idly what the vicar would make of this story. I'd have to ask him. Vicars should be experts on angels – there were so many in the Bible.

'This is as far as we can get with the pieces we have,' said Zac, thankfully changing the subject, and we all three studied the mosaic of glass in front of us. Zac had made remarkable progress.

Somehow he had managed to cover most of the pattern with the original pieces of glass. Whoever had cleared up after the bombing had helped us by doing a thorough job, although some pieces were admittedly too fragmented or damaged to be able to use. The bare patches of paper for which no glass at all could be found were centred around the top half of the face, some of the grass, some red border and part of a wing. It was a pity that we never did find the broken pieces with the eyes.

'The colour's right for Raphael,' Amber volunteered.

'Angels are often dressed in gold,' I murmured.

'Yes, but Raphael's special colour is gold,' Amber insisted. 'Or sometimes emerald green. His crystal's the emerald and his element is air. That's all I can remember, except that he's an archangel. But the words are right.'

The banner was cracked, but it was just possible to make out the motto *God heals*. Amber sighed contentedly. 'I love the pretty angel in your window best – the one your dad made, Fran. But I like this one, too.'

'Thank heavens for that,' said Zac, smiling at her. 'Now could that be a customer coming in?'

'She's so sweet, isn't she?' I mouthed, when Amber had gone back into the shop.

'But such an innocent.'

'Only in some ways. Think of all she's been through.'

Later, after Amber had gone home, Zac started searching in the shop for glass that would be suitable for the bare patches on our angel. The green for the grass beneath the sandalled feet was fairly easy to match. He held to the light a piece that looked similar to the old glass, even down to the bubbles and impurities that gave it beauty and character. Trying the old next to the new on the light box confirmed the similarities.

The ruby glass gave him more difficulty. 'Colour's not quite right,' he grumbled at the pieces I passed him, or, 'This one's too transparent,' or, 'It's thinner, don't you see?' After going through all our stock without satisfaction, he carefully wrapped up several pieces of angel to take over to the other studio, where he thought his friend David would be able to advise him.

'That's where I'll be tomorrow morning, if that's all right with you,' he said, taking off his overall and pulling on his jacket. 'I might end up having to get some glass specially made.'

'I'll see you after lunch then.' I was aware of his eyes on me, and was struck by how our relationship was changing. We were more relaxed with one another now – though I was still annoyed with him for being rude to Ben.

'Busy this evening?' he asked, but his enquiry sounded too casual.

'Choir,' I told him.

'Ah.' I suppose he was thinking of Ben, but all he said was, 'Have a good sing. See you tomorrow.'

I watched him walk across the Square; a solitary figure, his jacket worn at the elbows. I felt a tug of sadness, as though I'd lost something I hadn't known I valued.

The melancholy remained, like a lump in my throat, all the evening. I hadn't visited my father for two days; this was a part of it. But everything felt as though it was shifting beneath my feet – as though my world had been hit by some great meteor and was turning differently. Some of this must be my unsettled feelings for Ben.

How can I describe my growing fascination with him? I was falling under a kind of enchantment, like one of Burne-Jones's languorous women. Perhaps it started that time in the church, with the incense and the scent of lilies and the thrilling music of the organ that caught me up in his aura. I certainly loved his intensity, his complete absorption in music, his charisma as a conductor, the way he bound our choir together, bowed us to his will. And he was so beautiful. How was it possible not to be drawn to a man who looked like an earthly version of a Florentine angel, a deliciously tainted one, one splendid in the passion of his art, yet tender and vulnerable underneath? Yet I'd little idea how he felt about me or whether there was someone else in his life.

Jo was at choir tonight, I was pleased to see, but she was late and we had to sit in different places. Once or twice I got a sideways glimpse of her. When she wasn't staring distractedly into the distance she was anxiously scrabbling through the score to find her place.

Ben took us through ten minutes of singing exercises, which everybody did without argument this time, then embarked on 'The Chorus of the Angelicals'. He seemed in a good mood this evening, but it wasn't going to last.

'Now, I know it's complicated with so many parts singing at once, but this must be absolutely sublime,' he told us. 'You must transport the audience to the heavens. Elgar was himself in a state bordering on ecstasy when he wrote *Gerontius* and virtually felt himself to be in heaven with the angels. You all have to *be* angels.'

There was much giggling at this, and a pair of the younger men made silly faces, but the laughter soon died away as we began to wade through the section in chunks, Ben frequently having to stop us as one voice-part or another lost its way. Eventually we meandered through the broad fugue of 'Praise to the Holiest in the Height' at the movement's end, and flopped down gratefully in our seats.

'That,' said Ben, looking seriously pained, 'was execrable. Simply execrable. Quite how we're going to turn this tosh into something presentable in the short time left to us, I have simply no idea. Tenors and basses, you were all over the place. Second altos, at one point you sounded as though you were moo-ing – yes, moo-ing. You're not cows, for goodness sake, you're angels! And, you, sopranos. Well, the firsts weren't too bad . . .' (here the front row smiled smugly) '. . . but watch me, seconds, can't you? What's the point of me standing here like a lemon when you take no notice of me. Now, everyone back to page ninety-five. Graham, play from bar sixty-five, please . . . and watch, all of you.'

I glanced quickly round the room to see the general reaction to this verbal battery. For a second, the only sound was the whisper of pages turning. A cloud of gloom had settled over the room. One or two people looked really upset.

That evening, Ben made us work very hard. We went over and over that wretched chorus until we couldn't bear to hear it ever again. But, watching him, pushing his hand through his hair, counting bars to himself, lost in the music, I suddenly appreciated what a good conductor he was. He had the will and the vision to get the absolute best out of us. And, what is more, he didn't care if we hated him for doing it.

'That,' he finished up, ten minutes over time, 'was almost passable. And that's the best compliment you're likely to get out of me today, if not this term. Graham, thank you, you've been amazing.' And he turned his back on the lot of us.

Collecting up my things, I expected to hear grumbling around me, but instead the choir seemed beaten into remorseful submission.

'We're rubbish, aren't we?' moaned the woman next to me, to her older neighbour. 'I'm really going to practise before the next rehearsal.'

'I thought I had practised,' said the older lady, shutting her spectacles away in a knitted case. 'But I completely lost my way at one point. I'll borrow that cassette tape off Deirdre if she'll let me.'

'What did you think, Jo?' I asked, walking over to her. She was still slumped in her chair, dazed and tired.

'Exhausted. I've got a bit of a headache, to be honest.' She smiled weakly. 'Going to give the pub a miss this evening. I'd better confess to Dominic.'

As I pulled on my jacket I watched the two of them talking. Dominic put a protective arm around her and Jo told me, 'Dom said he'd walk me home as he's got to get back early himself. I'll give you a ring, shall I?'

'Please do. Hope a good night's sleep works on the headache,' I said.

'Fran?' Ben called, and wove his way towards me between a couple of beefy baritones stacking chairs. He looked agitated and his hair reared up at the front like a breaking wave. 'Are you busy now?'

Before I could speak, Michael walked up to us and said, 'You two aren't heading for the Bishop, perchance?' I looked at him with curiosity. It didn't appear possible to me that Michael could ever lose his urbane composure, but this evening he appeared rattled. And when Ben replied curtly, 'No, I don't think so,' and the hurt leaped into Michael's eyes, I realised they must have had a bust-up.

'What about you, Fran?' Michael asked, still looking at Ben. Ben gripped my wrist as if to stop me dashing off out of the door with Michael.

'We're giving the pub a miss tonight. I'm seeing Fran home, aren't I, Fran?' he said. I didn't know what I should do. He glared at Michael. Michael stared back, his face a blank mask. Then he shrugged and left.

'What was all that about?' I asked Ben, upset that he was behaving like this.

'I couldn't stand to go to the Bishop tonight,' he said, as though he hadn't heard me. He snatched up his music and looked around. The chairs were arrayed in neat stacks now; the piano pushed back into its corner. 'Can you imagine what a hard time I'd get? Some of those altos have pretty sharp-edged handbags.' We walked out into the lobby.

'Don't be silly. They love you.'

'They hate me. Not that I give a damn.' He held open the outer door for me with a graceful flourish.

'But they respond to your leadership,' I told him. 'Some of them are finally seeing the point.'

'Do you really think that?' he asked, stopping mid-lock-up to look at me. There was a slight mist coiling in the air tonight, lending proceedings an atmosphere of unreality.

I sensed that he needed reassurance. 'Yes,' I said, 'I do.'

'Whatever,' he growled, thrusting the keys into his pocket. 'I need a drink badly. Let's crack open a bottle at mine.' He was angry, imperious, and it made me nervous and enthralled at the same time.

'I think I ought to get home.'

'No. Please?' Now he sounded petulant.

'Perhaps you need to be by yourself, Ben,' I said gently. But despite myself I couldn't walk away.

'That's the last thing I want. I'm sorry I grabbed you like that just now. Here, let me have a look – have I hurt you?' Of course he hadn't, but I let him push up my jacket sleeve and stroke my wrist, so that my skin prickled deliciously. 'Oh, come and have a drink, do,' he pleaded, this time more tenderly. 'Pretty please.' With his finger, he tipped my chin so I was forced to look at him. He was smiling wickedly and I couldn't help but smile back.

'Oh, all right,' I said, giving in, as I wanted to all along. 'A quick one.' He tucked my arm through his companionably and we set off together through the mist.

Once we were ensconced in front of the fire with a bottle of wine, I asked, 'What was your quarrel with Michael about?'

'Was it that obvious?' he said flatly.

'Yes.'

'Michael can be particularly tiresome sometimes,' he said.

I laughed. 'If it comes to that, you've been quite tiresome yourself.'

'Thanks. The word I'm looking for with regard to Michael's attitude to me is "proprietorial". I told you, he thinks he has some God-given right to interfere in my life. I think it has something to do with my parents semi-adopting him, and him spending so much time at home with us when we were teenagers. He feels he has to keep an eye on me, set me on the straight and narrow.'

'Like an elder brother, you mean.'

'Yes. Though he's not older than me and he's certainly not my brother.'

'But he feels tied to you in some way. He didn't save you from drowning or something, did he?'

'No, but he thinks he saved me from other things. The problem is that I certainly don't feel tied to him.'

'But you're supposed to be friends?'

'We are. He's the person who knows me the best in the world. Even more than my parents and sister.'

'You're lucky,' I said wistfully, thinking of my own lack of relations. 'Not something to treat lightly.'

'Lightness is not possible with Michael, I assure you.'

The alcohol and the slightly surreal tone of the evening made me bold. 'And what have you done this time to make him interfere?'

I half-hoped he'd say it was something to do with me. Some perverse part of me rather liked the idea of Ben caring enough to quarrel over me. But after a moment he disappointed me by saying carefully, 'It's something to do with Nina. He thinks I have too much influence over her, that I'm letting her get too dependent on me. He means musically, career-wise, though he's also accused me of all sorts of dreadful things that I'm not remotely guilty of.'

'How complicated!' I said. And suddenly I didn't want to know any more. I was only making a fool of myself. I finished my drink and stood up. 'I really must get back now.'

When we reached the front door, we seemed suddenly awkward with one another.

'Making sure I've got my scarf this time,' I said, wrapping it round my neck and standing tense, hands in pockets.

Ben hesitated, then pulled me to him and kissed me quickly on the cheek.

'Thank you for putting up with me tonight,' he said softly.

'That's all right,' I said gravely. 'I understand.' He opened the door and stood back to let me go.

That's it, I thought wildly as I crossed the road. I probably won't see him alone again.

I was vaguely aware of a security alarm squealing across the Square. I turned and waved to Ben, I thought for the last time. Halfway across the garden, I looked back once more, but the door had closed. I felt empty.

The security alarm whooped on and on. Why doesn't someone blooming well get out of bed and turn it off, I thought irritably, as I continued my walk.

It gradually dawned on me that the alarm was coming from my side of the Square, and when I reached the street I stopped dead. In the window of *Minster Glass*, above Dad's angel, there was a hole the size of a tea-plate. Shards of glass glittered on the pavement.

A long wail of anguish soared above the sound of the alarm. It took me a moment to realise the cry was mine. As I dashed back across the garden to Ben's flat, the alarm wailed mockingly on and on.

By the time I returned, with Ben in tow, there were half a dozen people milling around outside *Minster Glass*, all talking at once.

'I telephoned the police, of course,' said an elderly man wearing a Paisley dressing-gown and slippers whom I recognised as Mr Broadbent, the antiquarian bookseller. He had called into the shop once to ask about Dad. 'It seemed the thing to do. Or none of us will get any sleep.'

'I'm ever so sorry,' I said faintly, but a woman shivering in a short-sleeved sparkly top immediately admonished him.

'It's not *her* fault someone's tossed a blimming rock through the window.'

Ben took charge, stopping anyone from touching anything, checking round the back for signs of intruders and reporting that there were none. He wrapped a throw round my shoulders, which the woman brought out, for I was shivering from shock as much as cold.

The police arrived a few minutes later – a man and a bored-looking woman in a tiny patrol car. Under their instruction, I was allowed to unlock the shop and turn off the alarm. Then Ben and I waited whilst the policeman assessed the damage and the policewoman interviewed the neighbours. No one had seen anything suspicious. From within the shop the policeman called, 'Come and look at this.'

Inside, glass crunched under our feet.

'This is the culprit,' said the Constable, bending and picking up what looked like a glass ball with a cloth. 'Hurled with some force, I'd say.' He placed it in a polythene bag, which he held up for our inspection. The ball was about the size of a grapefruit and looked as though it was filled with a pink and purple mist.

'A paperweight, isn't it?' said Ben.

'Where did it come from?' I wondered. 'And why didn't it smash when it fell?' The answer to the second question was easy to spot – it had met a soft landing in the form of the chair that now lay on its side by the counter, a large dent in its seat.

'Here's what you need for your insurer – you are insured, I take it?' The Constable scrawled his initials on the form and ripped off the top copy for me.

'I think so,' I answered.

'And you'd better be getting a grille for your window for the future. We'll be in touch if we hear anything.'

'But . . . aren't you going to try and find out who did it?' I asked, confused.

'Of course,' answered the policeman, but he was watching his colleague, who was talking urgently into her radio.

'We're off,' she said, nodding at him. They climbed into the car and were away, siren wailing, before he'd properly closed the door.

The bookseller went off to fetch some cardboard to tape over the hole whilst I found a dustpan and broom. Everybody helped. It wasn't long before the mess was cleared up and everyone had gone home. Except Ben.

'Would you come and stay at mine tonight?' he asked.

'Oh Ben. I can't leave the shop like this.'

'Well, why don't I come and kip here, then?' he asked. 'I'll sleep on the sofa, promise.'

'You'd have to fold yourself in half. You've seen how tiny it is. Better have the spare bed.'

In the end he fetched a sleeping bag and a few things in a bag and dumped them on the spare-room bed. We huddled together on the too-small sofa and drank tea with no milk, because I'd run out. Ben had to make it, because I was still trembling.

'It feels like the last straw, after Dad and everything,' I said shakily. 'Who would do that?'

'Some loser. Happens all the time,' Ben said, putting his arm round me. I snuggled up close to him, to keep warm as much as anything. We were sitting in the dark, though every now and then some car's headlights would sweep the room.

'Thank heavens you were nearby. I'd have been terrified otherwise.'

'That's curious. You always strike me as being strong and independent. After all, you travel all over the place.'

'I am fine about most things. Then something like this happens, and it feels as if the floor's disappeared from under my feet. I'm falling and there's no one to catch me.'

'It's been my absolute pleasure to catch you tonight.'

And after that it was only natural to lean in and kiss him quickly on the cheek. 'Ben, thank you,' and I gave a great yawn. 'Oh, sorry.'

He kissed me back and squeezed my shoulders in a comforting manner. I drifted in and out of sleep, trying to sort out my confused thoughts. Ben had seemed to be so many different people that evening – the molten god standing on his platform, a domineering quarreller, a seducer. Then he'd turned into this lovely, helpful man who had taken charge and looked after me in my hour of need. Which person was he?

All these rolled into one, probably – and anyway, I didn't care. What happened then, as I lay sleepily in his arms, was that I fell in love. It's as simple and as complicated as that.

In the end I must have fallen into a deep sleep. I had a vague memory of Ben half-carrying me, and his lips brushing my fore-head, and the next moment it was eight o'clock and daylight and I was in my own bed, still fully dressed. No sign of Ben, but when I peeped round the spare-room door I could see his golden curls, just visible under the sleeping bag. I resisted the considerable temptation to put out a hand and run my fingers through them.

My next thought, oddly, was relief that Zac wasn't due in this morning and therefore wouldn't know Ben was there.

The thought after that was to go and buy something for breakfast.

Chapter 25

Just such disparity
As is 'twixt air's and angels' purity,
'Twixt women's love and men's will ever be.

John Donne, *Songs and Sonnets*

LAURA'S STORY

At breakfast one morning near the end of June, Mr Brownlow,
flicking through the post, a weary look on his face, let out an animated 'Aha! It's a letter from Tom,' he explained cheerfully. He
slit open the envelope and began to read.

Then: 'Dora!' he whispered, and the light faded from his eyes.
Laura and her mother turned rigid, a cup halfway to Laura's
lips.

'What is it?' Theodora said in a faint voice. *'James?'*

He finished the letter and passed it across to her, his face that
of a man struck down.

'What's the matter, Papa? Tell us,' Laura begged.

'What has the boy done?' he cried, and pressed his hands to
his face.

'Papa!' Laura pushed back her chair and rushed to help him.

Across the table, Mrs Brownlow read the letter and gasped
out, 'Oh, Tommy!'

It was Laura's turn to take the sheet of cheap white paper. She read it with growing horror. Her brother had given up all plans for the priesthood. Not only that, he had left Oxford. *By the time you read this, I will be in Liverpool, my plan to take ship for New York. Please don't come after me. I need to plot a different course in the world. In Oxford I could hardly breathe, was forcing myself along a path I could not, nay, must not go. I know for sure that the Church is not my calling. Better to change now before all is too late. I know this will cause you great pain, after all you've done and hoped for me. Oh, the guilt tears me apart, but the alternative, I assure you, would in the end have been much worse for everyone. A priest without faith can only damage his flock.*

The Rector left for the station without finishing his breakfast and caught a train to Liverpool, hoping, God willing, that he would reach the docks in time to prevent Tom's folly.

He hoped in vain. A salty old mariner from the shipping office pointed out the smokestacks of the SS *Alexandria* on the distant horizon. James Brownlow watched until the ship disappeared over the edge of the world.

For a long while he was unable to move or speak. Finally the mariner came and tapped him on the shoulder and took him to sit in the office, practically forcing brandy down the Rector's throat.

On the way home, exhausted and despairing, Brownlow stopped to lodge at Oxford and met with his son's tutor, hoping for some explanation of the calamity. The man, however, though highly embarrassed at his own failure, was at a loss to understand the sudden defection of his bright and previously dutiful pupil.

As Mr Brownlow left the fellow's rooms he almost collided with a young man he recognised at once as one of Tom's friends. He spoke pleadingly to him of his trouble. The boy took pity and led Mr Brownlow to a shabby sitting room, plied him with tea and stale cake and explained in the most tactful terms what he thought had been going through his friend's mind to make him take this dreadful step.

Tom had fallen in with a sophisticated crowd: a band of rationalists who admired the work of Charles Darwin and who brought Tom to question everything the young man believed in.

'He came to doubt not only his calling, but the very bedrock of his faith in God,' the spotty young man said miserably, knowing that each word was like a physical blow to Tom's father.

After that there was nothing to do but return home in the morning and wait for another letter from Tom. The weeks passed and there was nothing.

If Mr Brownlow had seemed vague and oppressed before, this latest news crushed him. The family's investment in Tom – not just a financial one, though it was undeniable that much scrimping had been necessary to see him through college, but all their hopes for the future, too – had been flung back in their faces.

Tossing and turning in her bed, Laura asked herself why he couldn't have stayed and explained everything to his parents? Was he, too, afflicted by the darkness that seemed to weigh down on their family?

Mr Brownlow now seemed unwilling even to hear Tom's name, for reasons of grief rather than anger. More and more he wrapped himself up in his *History of the Church* and in his God.

He hardly had the strength to deal with the continuing rumblings of discontent in his parish.

More anonymous letters had been arriving, complaining about matters such as incense and statues of the Virgin, which the writer, who had an educated hand, condemned as *the scarlet rags of Papists; sacrilegious, unEnglish.*

Then one evening Mr Perkins, the verger, fetched up on the Brownlows' doorstep in a terrible dither. 'They've thrown earth at un, they've thrown earth!' was all the Brownlows could get out of him. They sat him in the kitchen with a glass of Mrs Jorkins's Best Medicinal until he calmed down, then Mr Brownlow accompanied him to the church where he was shocked to find that someone had indeed scattered dirt from the street all over the high altar. Worse was to come. When they visited the Lady Chapel, they found the statue of the Blessed Virgin knocked to the floor, her head rolled into a corner amidst the mouse droppings.

Enquiries were made. The old flowerseller who sat in the street outside most days, but swore as though it were a virtue that she had never crossed the threshold of a church in her life, told a Constable she'd seen three drunks lolling in the porch the day before, but even she couldn't actually confirm that they'd entered the church.

'Could one be that rogue Cooper?' Mr Bond asked the officer, but investigations revealed Ida the nursemaid's father to be in the penitentiary, sent down for breaching the peace.

On Mr Bond's orders, Mr Perkins hammered a notice to the door: *This church will be locked when unattended due to vandalism.* Overnight the notice was defaced.

The following Sunday Laura's father delivered a fiery sermon denouncing iconoclasm as 'blasphemous and anarchic'. He instructed any in the congregation who knew the identity of those involved to give him or Mr Bond the names. The sermon proved a mistake. Some of the rougher elements of the congregation took umbrage, believing they were under suspicion. The wealthier members, who had heard about the anonymous letters, were upset that one of their number might be responsible. Everyone began to suspect everyone else, despite the Rector insisting that the vandalism was very likely the work of out-siders.

Everyone was briefly united again the following Sunday, when morning worship was interrupted by a cacophony of clanging and shouting outside.

Mr Bond and Mr Perkins hurried out to find a gaggle of small boys banging saucepans and cans by the gate. 'Run, ye beggars,' shouted the ringleader, and they scarpered, all except one, whom Mr Bond collared.

'They paid us sixpence,' squeaked the miscreant, but as to who had ordered the children to make a noise, he couldn't or wouldn't say. In the end Mr Bond took pity on the half-starved urchin and let him go.

'Some of the poor resent us,' a gloomy Brownlow said at luncheon that day, 'when they should be grateful. Now they mock the glory of God. Instead of joining our worship they drag everything down to their own godless level and destroy.'

'We have to remember it's only a few people who are respon-sible, James,' his wife replied. 'Most are appreciative of our efforts.'

'Then we must defend ourselves against the troublemakers,' said James, sighing. 'We must stand firm.'

Another anonymous letter arrived. The vicar left it open on his desk and Laura couldn't help reading it.

Disciples of the Scarlet Whore will burn in hell. The capital S of Scarlet was shaped like a small, ornate harp. *Thou shalt not make unto thee any graven image.* Had it been written by the same hand that threw earth and broke glass? Laura agreed with her father that it seemed unlikely. The writer betrayed at least some rev-erence for plain worship. The vandals didn't value anything.

'Papa has been summoned to see the Bishop,' Laura remarked

breathlessly to Mr Russell one day, when she visited him in one of the workshops at *Minster Glass*.

She had been to the shop once or twice before, and was introduced to Mr Reuben Ashe, the thin-faced, bespectacled owner of the firm, himself a skilled glass-painter. On their second visit, Polly the maid so clearly expressed her dislike of the dirt and the chemical smells that this time Laura came alone.

Today, black curtains were drawn across the windows; daylight was only permitted to shine through the middle, where Russell had propped up a large sheet of clear glass on an easel. Stuck to this with beeswax were the pieces of coloured glass that were to make up the *Virgin and Child* window. Last week Laura had watched him cut out the shapes and neaten the edges with pliers. Today he showed her how he had painted the reverse of the clear sheet with lamp black to mark the lines where the lead would come. Now, with the light shining through the sheet from behind, he stood painting detail on the coloured shapes, the original drawing by his side as guide.

Laura sat in the half-darkness and watched him, talking about anything that came into her head. Sometimes her father heard confessions from behind a screen at the back of his church; another Papist fashion that scandalised the letter-writer. Laura had never taken advantage of this herself. There were things now that she wouldn't want to tell her father; but here, sitting in the half-darkness with Philip, concentrating on his work, no more than a silhouette against the light, she could imagine what it might be like. It was easy to say too much. Words, once said, could not be taken back.

'The Bishop might blame Papa; might order him to make changes,' she confided. 'Papa fears the shame of it.'

Mr Russell didn't answer so she rose from the uncomfortable wooden chair and moved over to look more closely at what he

was doing. He was working on the faces, which until now had
been only rough circles of white-tinted glass. With the thinnest
of brushes he outlined the iris of the Madonna's eye, then, picking a fatter brush from the jar, he dipped it into the paintpot
and sketched an eyebrow like a bird's wing. As Laura watched,
the whole face came into being under his hand. But it was
unfinished, without depth or texture; just features floating.

'This brown paint has to dry first,' he explained, wiping his
brush on a cloth hanging out of his overall pocket. He selected
the fine one once more, with a quick movement of his long fingers, like a heron they'd once seen dipping for fish in the park,
Laura thought. 'When I've finished the faces I'll start work on
the lines of drapery. The borders will be done after that.
Tomorrow, I can mat the lightest of washes on the skin. When
that's dry I'll stipple it with a brush to bring out the moulding
of the flesh.'

'And the hair?'

'Silver nitrate. It turns gold when fired. That stage is last of all.'

'All that will take days. Can't you ask someone else to help –
I don't know, paint the borders for you?'

'I could,' he said calmly, as he outlined the infant's rosebud
mouth with the fine brush. 'But that's not how I like to work.'

She sighed impatiently. He was so absorbed in his work now
that he hardly looked at her. She wandered back to her chair,
careful to lift her skirts clear of the paint-splashed tins and dusty
bags lining the skirting boards and worktops.

'This must bore you,' he said after a while.

'Not at all,' she said sharply. 'But I must leave. I promised
Mama I'd accompany her to the orphanage.' They were taking
Ida Cooper to visit her brothers and sisters.

'Mmm,' was all he replied. He was contemplating the baby's
face, looking from the drawing to the glass, frowning.

She stood up, shook out her shawl and pulled it round her. When she said goodbye, he finally put down his brush and turned to face her, smiling, wiping his fingers on the dirty cloth. He looked like a common workman today, she thought, and was irritated that he didn't notice her mood.

Walking briskly across the Square she regretted her scorn, berated herself for viewing him as through her parents' eyes; in dirty overalls, at home in an industrial workshop. She had only thought like this because she was annoyed, that's all. And yet she couldn't explain her annoyance.

She still enjoyed their meetings, but she was aware that, all the while they talked, his thoughts were not really on her.

What was wrong with that? He was married. She had no claim on him. Anything more than friendship was simply not possible. She was tired of hearing about his wife, Marie, that was all. She didn't want to be reminded of how Marie still filled his dreams, even though she'd betrayed him. One day, maybe, Marie would return to him. Laura knew it to be her noble duty to pray for such a day, without any consideration for how it might affect her friendship with him. If only – if only the light glinting on his red-gold hair didn't make her heart beat so fast she would have been able to bear it all.

One balmy July afternoon, they took a walk up past the Royal Aquarium to Westminster Abbey. She was wearing her gold dress, which always made her feel more attractive.

'I came to a wedding here once with Marie,' he told her, as they stood looking up at the dizzying heights of the west front. 'It was the first time I realised what a lovely singing voice she had. Yet she rarely sang, you know, except lullabies. It was a shame.' His eyes were sad.

Laura felt a bolt of anger shoot through her; she picked up

her skirts and ran for the steps. This so startled a great flock of
pigeons that they wheeled up suddenly, and she had to put up
her arms to shield her face.

I don't want to hear about Marie any more, was what she was
telling him. He merely grabbed her, pulled her back.

'What did you do that for?' he asked angrily.

'Oh, I felt like it,' she replied, as gaily as she could, but she
meekly allowed him to take her arm once more.

'You might have been hurt,' he said, gently now, as though he
were correcting a child. 'And now I must tell you some news.'
His eyes were sparkling. Not more Marie, she briefly prayed,
but it was something else entirely. 'I showed those stories of
yours to my friend at Millner's. And he rates them, my dear.
Can't publish them himself, he says; not his sort of thing. But he
advises you to send one or two to Alfred Loseley at *Ladies' World*.
Thinks they're right up his street, especially the one with the
dead flowers and the destitute wife.'

Laura looked at him, speechless, joy and fear taking turns in
her mind. A real publisher liked her stories. But suppose the
magazine editor did not? Or suppose he did, and they were
published? How would her parents respond? Not that they
seemed to have spare energy to think about anything but their
own troubles at the moment.

'Do you think I ought to send them to Mr Loseley?'

'Of course.'

'I'll consider the matter,' she said haughtily. Then she smiled
at him. 'Thank you.'

Laura's parents might be too wrapped up in themselves to
notice their daughter's doings, but her sister was another
matter.

When Laura arrived home that afternoon it was to find

Harriet there on an impromptu visit. As Laura handed Polly her coat and gloves she could hear laughter from the drawing room, and was amazed to realise it was her mother. She peeped round the door to see Mrs Brownlow on the sofa, holding baby Arthur who, now a lusty four months of age, stood bucking, testing his strong legs on her lap, crowing with joy. He turned his head to stare round-eyed at Laura when she entered the room, then stretched his mouth in a gummy grin.

'Laura, where have you been?' Harriet asked, jumping up from her seat to hug her.

'Just out for a walk,' Laura said. 'No Ida today?'

'She's out of sorts. I sent her down to the kitchen to sit with Polly.'

'I hope she's not unwell.' They all looked anxiously at Arthur, who was now sitting on Theodora's lap.

'Best keep her away from him in case, Harriet,' said Theodora, trying to keep her voice even. 'Who's my precious one?' she whispered into Arthur's neck and laughed delightedly when he gave a sudden loud crow, which turned to a wail and soon it became apparent he was hungry. Theodora went down to speak to Mrs Jorkins about warming a bottle of milk.

Harriet walked round the room, gently jiggling her baby son to soothe him. 'Where did you go, Laura?' Her voice was stern.

'When?'

'Just now. I saw *him* out of the window. The glass man.'

'Oh, Mr Russell. We walked up to the Abbey, that's all.'

'Why didn't you take Polly?'

'She was too busy here. Harriet, don't lecture me. I haven't done anything wrong.'

'But you know what Father said. You should be careful.'

'Not you, too. Harriet, I'm acting perfectly properly.'

'Mother says you've been to the workshop. Alone.'

'There are other people around. Don't fret so.'

'Rough working men, no doubt. Laura, there's trouble enough here without you dragging the family down further . . .'

'I know. I tell you, I'm doing nothing wrong. He's a friend, that's all.'

At that moment, they were interrupted by their mother's return with a bottle of milk and soon the only sounds were Arthur's contented gulps.

A day passed after that and then another day with no word from him. Laura was miserable. By the third day, when her mother asked for her company visiting the hospital, she snapped, 'Can't one of your ladies take a turn?' then immediately felt guilty and apologised.

'I'm going mad,' she told herself. Russell irritated her with his presence and diminished her by his absence. What was she to do?

Then, finally, came a letter. She took it from the tray in the hall before her parents saw it, went straight upstairs to read.

My dearest Laura,

Mary is painted, her infant and the cherubs almost done. I have only the surrounding details and borders to complete now. I find it healing, painting a mother and child, nay, not any mother and child, not even Marie and our son, but the mother of the world with Our Saviour. It is an honour and I feel very humble.

He hadn't forgotten her. But once again his thoughts returned to Marie.

Chapter 26

In heaven an angel is nobody in particular.

George Bernard Shaw, *Maxims for Revolutionists*

'It's Lisa. It must be Lisa. She wants to get at me.'

Amber arrived just after Ben had gone and was deeply distressed to see the broken window.

'You can't go around randomly accusing people,' I said rather wearily. 'It happens to shops all the time.'

'I know it's her. She hates me.'

'Why?'

'I don't know why. I've never done nothing to her. I . . . I get up her nose without even trying. It isn't fair.'

'Life rarely is,' I said automatically. Certainly Amber hadn't had a good deal so far. This job was probably the first real opportunity anyone had given her, and so far, fingers crossed, it seemed to be going well. She had a natural facility for working with glass and plenty of artistic flair. It was indeed a shame if someone spiteful was trying to ruin it all.

'Amber, is there really any evidence to suggest that Lisa would have left the hostel late last night and come and thrown a paperweight at our window? If there is, of course, I'll pass the information on to the police, especially as they might have got fingerprints . . .' Though I somehow doubted that whoever had committed the crime had been daft enough to have left any prints on their missile. 'But otherwise . . . well, it could make life much worse for you if you accuse her of something she didn't do.'

'I suppose you're right,' said Amber, looking miserable. In addition to being shocked by the window, she felt responsible. I knew it was the way of the very young to relate everything to themselves, but even if, as I thought unlikely, Lisa had done it, that could hardly be construed as Amber's fault.

'Can you discreetly ask around? Find out where she was last night?'

'I can't ask her mates, can I? They'd want to know why I'm interested.'

'Just ask whoever was on duty then. It's a pity it wasn't Jo. She'd know right away.' Jo had been at choir last night, of course, and went straight home afterwards.

'Effie and Ra, they were on. I can ask Ra. He was on reception so he saw everyone go in and out.'

'You'll have to ask him in a clever way then, so he doesn't get suspicious about why you're asking.'

'OK, I'll think of something.'

'Remember that even if Lisa was out late it doesn't prove anything, Amber. She's free to come and go.'

'No, but it would look strange if she went out at eleven o'clock on a Monday evening.'

'Clubbing? A late-night job?'

'Yeah, I suppose so.'

We broke off to serve a customer, and then the glaziers arrived, so we had to hastily dismantle the window display – miraculously undamaged – then move into the workshop, out of their way. I helped Amber with the next stage of the windows she had designed for the Armitage children. They were coming along beautifully. With Zac's help she had cut out the pieces of glass. Now, as we tried to ignore the terrifying hammering and crashing that came from the front shop, I showed her how to stretch long floppy strips of soft lead, by securing one end in a vice and pulling on the other. The stretching made them more straight and rigid – easier to cut up and use. Zac or I would have to solder everything together for her, because it was important to do it neatly and, like any beginner, she was still splodging about with the melted metal. However, she was excited to be involved in the project as much as we could allow her.

'I used to help my mum make Christmas decorations,' she volunteered, as we started to fit the glass into the strips of lead. 'She couldn't leave the flat to work, you see. So that was her job, all year round, even when it was Easter. Every week this bloke came with boxes of stuff – you know, glass beads and gold thread and tinsel – and she'd have to thread it all together. He took away what she'd made the week before. Sometimes, if she wasn't well or her fingers were very stiff, I stayed home from school and helped her, because she was worried about losing the money.'

This wasn't the first time Amber had alluded to her childhood. I thought it sounded a lonely one – just her and her mother in a dreary high-rise flat on Commercial Road, surrounded by out-of-date Christmas decorations. But she spoke of it wistfully, as though it were a lost time of happiness.

'What about your dad?' I asked.

'I never knew him,' she said. 'They met in the doctor's surgery. It was before she got the multiple sclerosis. Mum says meeting him was the most romantic thing ever to happen to her. He held the surgery door open for her and she ended up being given a lift home in his boss's limousine. He was a chauffeur, you see. He was Egyptian.'

'Ah,' I said, 'that explains your lovely black hair.'

'Yes. Amber was *his* mum's name. Things didn't work out though, because he missed Egypt, and when he went back Mum wouldn't go with him. She found out he already had a wife. It wouldn't have been a problem there because you're allowed to have more than one wife, but Mum wouldn't stand for it. So she had me all by herself.'

My head was beginning to spin at all of this. I asked her if she had ever heard from him. 'Never,' she replied.

'Do you mind?' I enquired, thinking of Zac and his Olivia, but she insisted she had no curiosity about him.

'He can't have been very interested in me; never sent us any money or anything. He was just some bloke . . .'

'Who happened to be your father.' Maybe there'd come a time when she was older, had a child of her own, when she would want to know more about him; about the half of her that was Egyptian. I studied her sweet heartshaped face, those thick-lashed brown eyes shining softly in the glow from the light-box, and almost envied her lack of concern. In contrast, my family secrets swirled in my mind like a great malevolent maelstrom.

'How is your dad now?' asked Amber, and I could sense those eyes steady upon me as I soldered together the delicate pale circles that represented the boy's toes.

'He's holding his own. The doctors won't really say how much better he's likely to get. Damn.' A blob of solder splashed like a tear on the glass.

'It must be so hard for you,' she whispered. 'Specially not having your mum and that.' She reached out and touched my arm. And with that little gesture she told me that she really understood about Dad. She'd been through it herself with her mother. She couldn't know precisely how I felt, but she could guess, and that was comforting.

For a while we concentrated on the job at hand. I allowed Amber to fit some of the glass into the grooves in the lead strips, while I continued with soldering and daydreamed about Ben, going over everything he'd said and done the previous evening and wondering if he cared. He had had to hurry off that morning, still muzzy after the late night, but had promised to ring.

'Do you enjoy this, Amber?' I asked after a while.

'Oh *yes*,' she said. 'This is what I've always wanted to do – make beautiful things, ever since I was small. Mum always said the decorations I made were the best, the neatest, so I knew I'd be good. But then she passed away and I had to go and live with Gran and look after her, and then I messed up my exams.'

'You might be able to get on a course to supplement the training here,' I said vaguely. 'Evening classes or something.' Perhaps Zac would know.

'I'm not good at writing stuff,' she said, her eyes clouding with anxiety. 'Do you think that would matter?'

'Probably not,' I said. 'But you can get help for that, can't you? You'll be all right.'

By the time Zac returned at lunchtime, carrying a square package wrapped in newspaper, we had a lovely new shop window and the glaziers were gone. Amber and I had finished about half the panel and were happily chatting about angels again. Apparently it was Amber's gran who had got her into the idea of angels, and we were having fun trying to diagnose who my Zodiac angels might be, though I had to admit that I didn't take any of it seriously.

'It's not that I don't believe you, Amber, about you seeing an angel. It's just that . . .'

'. . . you don't believe me.' She smiled and I was forgiven.

'There might be some other explanation, that's all. How did

you get on?' I asked Zac, who looked tired and fed up as he put on his overall.

'Oh, a bit frustrating. David found me some glass for the border, but the gold stuff's more difficult. He's sending some off to a glassmaker in Hungary he thinks might give him the right match. I hope it's not pricey, but we'll have to wait and see.'

'Are there other bits of Raphael you can do in the meantime?'

'Yes, I'll get on with some of the painting and firing. But it would be best to have all the pieces in one place first.' He caught sight of our work on the Armitages' little boy. 'You've both done well this morning.'

'Haven't we? And what's more, Amber's worked out that Ambriel and the archangel Uriel are my birthsign angels. And Uriel's also the angel responsible for stained glass. Isn't that amazing?'

'We can work out yours if you like, Zac. When's your birthday?' said Amber.

'August the third, but I shouldn't go to the bother.' Zac must have realised he sounded unkind because he added gently, 'I'm really not into any of that. I was brought up to rely on myself.'

I wasn't 'into it' either, but on the other hand I couldn't agree with Zac. With Dad ill, waiting to find out which way the tide would turn, I was learning that I couldn't rely on myself as I used to. There were all these new people around me – Zac and Jo and Amber and now Ben, even the vicar and his wife – all becoming a part of my life whether I wanted them to or not. How quickly I was putting down roots.

I went to clean up the rest of the mess and to rebuild the window display. Last of all I hung Dad's angel carefully back on her hook and, stepping outside, checked the result. She wasn't quite straight. Inside again, I knelt down to adjust her slightly, and saw something I'd not noticed before. Woven into the carpet of flowers at her feet, so cunningly that it looked like foliage, was a little swirly symbol. It was a Celtic knot. The same knot that, according to Laura's journal, Philip Russell had used. How strange. I remembered the panel that Dad had been working on when he collapsed and the penny dropped. Dad must have always known about that knot. It was in the family, after all.

Much later, when I'd almost given up hope of hearing from Ben, I picked up the ringing phone.

'Fran.'

He had only to say my name in that teasing tone.

'Ben,' I replied, in that same tone, and we both laughed.

'How are you today?' he asked.

'A little weary,' I said, 'but much better for hearing from you.'

'Good. I wondered if you'd like to come over this evening?'

'There isn't much of it left.' It was already nine-thirty.

'I've only just got in from work. A little soirée at the school tonight. Pupils' concert, you know.'

'Oh? How did it go?'

'Very well. The parents seemed pleased and, let's face it, that's the main thing.'

'That's certainly one way of looking at it.'

'So you'll come?'

'Yes,' I said softly, and it was what I'd wanted to say all along.

'Thanks again for rescuing me last night.'

'Damsels in distress are my speciality.'

'You were very gallant and masterful.'

'Thank you. Window's all fixed then?'

'Mmm.' We stood in his kitchen and I took a large gulp of the rosé he poured me, which was so strong and sweet I was downing it like fruit juice.

'Heard anything from the police?' Ben was running his finger around the rim of his glass.

'Not a dicky bird.'

'Well, since whoever it was didn't steal anything, I'd forget about it. Kids, probably.'

'I don't like it though, Ben. It's not just a shop, it's my home, and I feel under attack. Amber thinks it's a girl from the hostel, but I don't know. It could be anyone.'

'You poor thing.' He hugged me quickly with his free arm.

We were heading upstairs into the sitting room when Ben said, 'Oh, I forgot. A date for our choir meeting. Let's go and find the book.' I'd half-hoped he'd dropped the matter, but I couldn't back out now.

In the music room I sat at the piano whilst he perused his black diary. There was a book of duets on the stand and I tried muddling my way through the lower part, whilst he muttered to himself. 'Tomorrow – no. Friday's church choir practice, then I'm away for the weekend . . . damn, there's a colleague's soirée after choir, that's no good. It'll have to be Tuesday.' He turned to me and said, 'I'll get back to you when I've asked the others, but why not pencil in early evening Tuesday.'

'Fine,' I said.

Tutting at my carelessness, he removed my glass from where I'd balanced it beside the keyboard and sat down next to me.

'After four,' he commanded and we started to play – he, of course, perfectly; I just managing to stagger on.

'It's the wine!' I said, when my timing collapsed completely halfway down the page.

'Nah, keep going, the wine should loosen you up,' he said, still playing. I shook my head, got up to give him more room.

He launched into something that, after a moment or two, I recognised as a Chopin Prelude – the one called the Raindrop. And then something crazy seemed to be happening to the air in the room, as though the piece was playing in stereo. Something was prodding at the edge of my mind, some resonance of long ago, something to do with Laura and the passionate music her mother had been playing. That had been the Raindrop, too.

I stood in the middle of the room with my eyes closed, just listening to the notes rolling over each other and through me until I felt I was actually vibrating. Then finally the last chords faded away and I opened my eyes to find myself looking at a pair of shoes, tucked in a corner. Women's shoes, black, with high heels and pointed toes. Not new – in fact, quite worn.

Ben watched me watching the shoes, then got up and came over to where I stood. I felt his touch on my arm, his breath on my cheek. 'Fran?' He tried to swing me round to face him, but I resisted. All I could see were those damned shoes.

'Whose are they?' I asked.

'Only Nina's,' he answered lightly.

'Why does Nina leave her shoes here?'

'She often brings a spare pair to change into if she's performing. She must have forgotten them last time.'

'Oh, I see,' I said. I wanted to believe him, but I didn't quite. I suppose it was because of what Michael had said. About Nina's crush on Ben.

'Ben, do you mind me asking, are you and Nina . . .?' I started. My mouth was dry. 'I mean . . .'

'I am Nina's accompanist and, I hope, her friend,' said Ben stiffly. 'As I've explained to Michael.'

'You've made up with him, then?' He nodded. 'Oh, good.'

He moved closer to me.

Another question popped into my mind. 'Whose is the pink

dressing-gown upstairs?' The words were out of my mouth before I could stop them, but I needed to be sure. Ben studied me in silence, a frown on his face. Then he laughed.

'My, you have been observant. It's my sister Sally's, actually. She left it last time she came to stay.'

Such an obvious explanation, so why did I still feel so tense? I suppose, looking back, that it was because of my strange experience while hearing the music, and being troubled about the shoes. And then there was Ben's charming smile, his glossy allure that said 'come here' and 'go away' at the same time. It bemused me.

'Fran. Please look at me.' It was a command.

I did so, and he was mesmerising, gazing at me through narrowed eyes, smiling slightly with that moulded, sensuous mouth; just a little bead of wine like a beauty spot on the curled upper lip. I reached up almost without thinking to brush it away with my fingertip and his hand closed around mine, warm and hard.

'Don't worry,' he whispered, imprisoning my other hand. 'There's really nothing to worry about.'

'No,' I whispered. 'Of course there isn't.' We were leaning towards one another, and then suddenly he pulled me into a long, practised and very thorough kiss. I kissed him back and he held me tighter. 'You are gorgeous,' he whispered when we came up for air.

'Mmm, so are you,' I murmured, our mouths meeting once more. At last I drew my fingers through the glorious tangle of his golden hair.

When I finally pulled away and said, 'I must go,' he gave me a pleading look and said, 'Stay longer.'

I smiled lazily and kissed him again, then shook my head. I hardly knew him yet.

'Do you know,' I confessed, as we said goodbye in the doorway, 'when you stand here like you do, watching me walk across the garden, it feels as if you're an angel keeping guard over me.'

'Angelic – that's me absolutely,' he breathed into my ear. 'Especially tonight, letting you go at all.'

Chapter 27

Saint Michael the Archangel, Defend us in battle. Be our protection against the wickedness and snares of the devil.

Catholic Prayer

I could hardly sleep for happiness that night. If I drifted into unconsciousness it was to dream of Ben, my very own earthbound angel.

'What do you make of angels?' I asked Jeremy, when he came to see Raphael the following day.

'You mean, do they really exist?'

'Yes.'

'A pertinent question this week. Tomorrow is September the twenty-ninth, the Feast of St Michael and All Angels.'

'St Michael being . . .?'

'One of the archangels. Often pictured with a sword, slaying Satan in the Last Days. Raphael's another. Then there's Gabriel. They're the angels we hear most about in the Bible. The archangels were God's messengers, you see. They had the most contact with ordinary men and women, like Tobias and Mary – which might be the reason they're portrayed in human shape, like Raphael here. But they still inspired awe and terror in those who saw them.'

'Do you mean angels might not really have looked like people?' I'd not considered the idea before.

'Who knows. Maybe they're spirits of air, usually without visible form. If you read about the visions of some of the Old Testament prophets, Ezekiel and Isaiah, for instance, angels are described as beasts, flying serpents in flames carrying God's chariot, or great living creatures bellowing out to one another in a universal shout of praise to God. Very different to how they're portrayed today.'

'Like Christmas-tree dolls,' I said, thinking of Amber's mother's work.

'Or fairy godmothers.'

'Or godfathers.' I remembered Amber's story of the young man who saved her from the speeding car.

'Yes. We've certainly dumbed-down angels; made them fit into our own manageable little boxes. My favourite story, which I heard on the radio, is about the parking space angel. There's a lady who lives in Bristol who prays to her angel every day that she'll find somewhere to park in order to get to work on time. And a space always magically appears. Marvellous!' He laughed and shook his head, then was serious again. 'I'm not saying angels don't exist. I've had no experience to speak of myself, but I do know people who have. Quite trustworthy people, sceptical people, who have subjected their experiences to the most rigorous questioning but still conclude that there's no other explanation than something . . . otherworldly. There is, to me, a further test which should be applied, that angels do not glorify themselves, only God; their actions will therefore be consistent with the character of Christ.'

'But it sounds so ridiculous in our day and age.'

'When we rationalise everything away? We're in danger of defining absolutely everything in material terms. And yet there are other ways of knowing. Go about in the world, talk to people of all backgrounds – of all religions and none – about their experiences, and you'll find that the universe is a much greater and stranger place than our minds will ever be able to fathom. I like to think of angels as a symbol of everything that is beyond our ordinary perception and understanding of the world; part of the universal song of praise that surrounds us always.'

I thought about this. In some ways Jeremy hadn't answered my question at all, but he'd made me look at it differently.

'What am I to think about Amber's stories?' I asked.

'I don't know. Clearly something happened to help her in a situation of extreme danger. Whether the feathers and the music and the appearance of a charming young man all happened and can definitely be linked with one another, who knows. Amber believes that. I don't want to fall into the trap of accepting everybody's beliefs because they happen to believe them.'

'Do you think we're all drawn towards the same thing in different ways?'

'Up to a point, yes. At the same time, we have been given the power to reason, to test our experiences, and I don't think one should explain everything unusual that happens to us in terms of magic or miracles. It's very egocentric for a start. Can the activities of the universe really be geared around a working mother's need for a parking space? I'm not sure about that.'

'But do you think we have guardian angels? Like Gerontius did – watching over us and guiding our every step?'

'It's a nice idea, isn't it? And it has some Biblical support. Although to our short-sighted selves, it sometimes seems that the angels are looking the wrong way. It's probably safest to see our lives as being important to God, but believing that we're also part of some greater plan that's ultimately good for all of us.'

'Now that sounds really patronising. As though our responsibility for ourselves is taken away and we're controlled by a Big Brother.'

'God does encourage us to grow up, but also to acknowledge our limitations and be guided by Him. How about considering Him as a Big Father?'

I thought of my own father, unable to engage with me, a distant if loving figure, and sighed.

Jeremy must have understood for he patted my shoulder and said, 'Think about it in terms of ideal fatherhood rather than one's earthly, fallible father. The best fathers help their children to grow up and live free but responsible lives.'

'I sometimes think I've a way to go there,' I said, and we both laughed.

Ben rang me late on Wednesday evening to apologise for not being able to see me for several days, then again on Sunday evening to tell me he'd definitely set the meeting for Tuesday.

'Perhaps you'd like to stay on after that for a bit,' he suggested. 'We could have snacks at the meeting as some people will have come straight from work.'

I found myself offering to come early and help him prepare them.

'And of course, I'll see you at choir practice – though I've got some tiresome work thing afterwards. I'm sorry not to be seeing you for so long, Fran.'

'Me, too,' I said wanly.

I remembered my conversation with Jeremy on Monday, when we sang of Gerontius' guardian angel bearing his soul to judgement. The angel's task, I saw clearly now, was not to whisk the old man's soul from the path of danger but to help Gerontius *through* the danger. Perhaps that was really what guardian angels did. Support their human charges through life's difficulties, through the Valley of the Shadow of Death and beyond.

Ben was much more supportive of us that evening. 'More carrot than stick,' was Dominic's comment during the halfway break. But the reason for this became clear during the notices at the end. He'd obviously felt the need to butter us up a bit.

'Some of us are having a meeting tomorrow evening about the future of the St Martin's Choral Society, and next week I will be circulating a questionnaire for you all to complete. One thing we'll be looking at is a name for the choir. Perhaps you'd all like to be thinking of a name that will give us a higher profile in the musical world here. Something like the "St Martin's Singers"?'

I was surprised that Ben seemed to be moving things forward before we'd even had our meeting.

He left us to deal with people's puzzlement. 'See you tomorrow,' he told me as he rushed away.

Dominic and I did our best in the pub to answer questions. He seemed different tonight. Jo and I kept looking at him. He'd been granted his sabbatical from work and instead of the usual dark suit wore jeans and a pale blue cashmere sweater under a corduroy jacket; his thinning blond hair curling in unruly little puffs around his face.

'I think he looks charming,' I whispered to Jo, teasing.

'Oh, shut up about Dominic,' was all she said, rather tiredly, I thought.

On Tuesday evening Crispin, our Gerontius, arrived at Ben's early and began to make his way through the Devils on Horseback I'd prepared, his prominent Adam's apple bobbing in his long neck at every swallow. At six-thirty, Val and the vicar appeared, then Michael, and finally, slightly late, Dominic. He was out of breath from running – he muttered something about cancelled trains – but he was such a pillar of normality that I almost hugged him.

It was a squash in Ben's drawing room, with everyone eating and drinking and talking at once. But eventually he shuffled us into some sort of order, onto available chairs, pouffes and sofas, and began.

He had, of course, talked to me a little about his plans, but listening to the full extent of them now, I realised how alarmingly ambitious they were.

'I would like to see us develop until we stand in terms of reputation beside, say . . .' here he named one or two of the best-known amateur choral societies. 'This means growing numbers by a third, which would involve a recruitment campaign, and we'd also need to look at our financial resources.'

Here the vicar cleared his throat and said in a mild voice, 'Of course, the choir is currently self-financing. Where do you imagine the extra money is to come from?'

'There will be the subscriptions of new members,' Ben said, 'but then, if we're to pay for bigger venues – the Queen Elizabeth Hall, for instance – we'll need fund-raising on a more significant scale. Raising the level of subscriptions would only be a start.'

Dominic, who had been slowly stroking his chin, now moved restlessly in his too-small space on the sofa. 'Raising subs would be a shame, Ben. We're already near some members' limits. I discovered that when we had a five per cent rise last year. There are a few pensioners and one or two unemployed members. Half a dozen people even pay in monthly instalments.'

'We'll need to discuss other ways, then. There might be, for instance, Lottery money available. I'm not an expert in these matters. Michael, perhaps that's something you could look into?'

Michael frowned. 'It's not my area,' he said, 'but I could find out what the procedures are.'

'What is the possibility of other sources of funding through the church, Jeremy? I know the PCC have voted to restore the organ . . .'

'Have they? I didn't know that, Ben,' I said, surprised.

'I'm sure I told you.'

'You didn't.'

Jeremy glanced from me to Ben and said heavily, 'It was last week's parish finance meeting about that legacy I told you about. I wasn't able to be there but Ben was, and I gather he argued most persuasively for the church to use the money to restore the organ. The PCC will need to ratify the decision, but I have reason to think that they'll do that. Here is not the time and place, but I need to talk to you about the embarrassing situation that puts me in with regard to the angel.'

'Oh,' I said confused, 'but I thought you'd all decided to give the legacy to the hostel appeal.'

'We had. But when the churchwarden spoke to our solicitor last week about it, she was told that the terms of the Will are that the money has to be spent specifically on the church. I'm sorry I've been hazy about that one, but I've only just heard myself.'

I thought about the time and money we'd already given towards the window and felt hurt. So there might have been money for the angel window after all, but Ben had won it for the organ. No one at *Minster Glass* had been included in discussions. Why had nothing been said?

With Jeremy it must be vagueness, but Ben? Perhaps he'd felt embarrassed that his project had won over mine. Even so, he ought to have plucked up the courage to tell me, especially since my time and money were involved. The more I thought about it, the more upset I felt. I was so absorbed that I missed some of what Val was saying about the orchestra she always booked for the concerts.

I tuned back in. 'We'll need good instrumentalists who might ask for higher fees.' Val couldn't help an exasperated whine creeping into her voice and I sympathised. I knew how much work went into organising an orchestra, and how easily egos could be upset.

Crispin, still making his way through a plate of sausage rolls, gave a sudden cough and we all looked at him, expecting him to speak, but he merely smiled encouragingly at Ben and carried on eating. I thought him rather a waste of space. I suspected Ben of inviting him because the man so clearly idolised him.

There was a short silence, then Dominic shifted forward in his chair and spoke. 'There are some good ideas here, Ben, and you're getting great things out of the choir.' He smiled. 'We certainly haven't been worked so hard before. But we need to ask ourselves, what is the purpose of St Martin's Choral Society?'

Here, the vicar weighed in. 'Perhaps I can help on that point. As some of you know, it was set up five years ago as an extra social activity. Conducting it is part of Ben's duties as organist, and we wanted it to attract people living or working locally into our church. And although we don't expect many to attend Sunday services, it does bring them into the church itself at least three times a year to perform, and I do occasionally see choir members at our lunchtime "pop-in" services. I'm rather worried, Ben, that the expansion you are suggesting, whilst admirable in its scope and imagination, is way beyond our original vision. The choir would inevitably become detached from the church, and current members who can't take the pace or afford higher subscriptions, might end up being excluded. That would be an awful shame. However, I recognise that these things should be democratic and if the choir members themselves wished to go forward in this way, well, it would be churlish to stifle the initiative.'

Michael chipped in. 'Perhaps we should wait until we've asked the members,' he said. 'Ben's drafted a questionnaire.'

'I should say,' added the vicar, in a steely voice, 'it's extremely unlikely that extra funds would be forthcoming from the church. We currently offer the use of the church buildings and our organist as conductor, charging the choir a modest part of its subscriptions to cover costs, but we have a small congregation and many big commitments, particularly with our social work in the area. It's not reasonable to expect us to supplement choir funds.' He sat back in his chair and took a large draught of wine.

Ben's face was stormy. 'There's no doubt,' he said, 'that life would get more expensive for us. We'd need to pay for better soloists – I can't keep calling in favours as we're doing with Julian for this concert – a bigger orchestra and bigger venues. There'll be publicity costs, too.'

'I'm not sure where you'd rehearse a bigger choir,' said Val mildly. 'The hall is reaching its maximum capacity as it is.'

'It must be possible to squeeze in a few more,' Ben insisted.

'I'd better check the insurance situation on that,' muttered Jeremy, scribbling a note.

Ben stood up, barely managing to control his frustration. 'So is there anybody who shares my vision?' he asked, looking round the room, meeting every eye.

Crispin was nodding enthusiastically through his umpteenth sausage roll and I said quickly, 'Ben, there definitely are ways in which you can make a difference. Don't forget, you've shown the choir that they can do better. They can improve. They don't just come along and have a jolly time any more; now they are learning something. The audience will notice this and you'll get more interest all round. Isn't this a great enough achievement?'

'Absolutely,' said Dominic. 'Fran's hit the nail on the head. We're very lucky to have you, Ben, and your ideas are fantastic. We must obviously circulate the questionnaire and gauge what the members want, but personally I don't believe expansion is right for us at the moment. As Jeremy says, it's moving away from the reason the choir was set up. OK, I know things change and we mustn't be rigid about it, but there is something about our current set-up that's valuable to the members, and it would be a shame to throw that away.'

'I'm sure I speak for everybody, Ben, when I say you're giving many people a great deal of pleasure with your leadership,' Michael said quietly, and people murmured their agreement. 'Don't underestimate the importance of that. Just go carefully.'

Ben raised both hands, then brought them down on his knees and sank back in his chair. 'OK,' he said. 'I get the drift.'

'We do value you,' Val insisted. 'And the questionnaire will be incredibly useful.'

'Amen to all that,' said Jeremy, glancing at his watch. He stood, shrugging on his jacket. 'I have to go, I'm afraid. Marriage Guidance course at eight.'

After that, no one stayed for long. Crispin helped himself to a pocketful of petits fours and nodded his thanks. Even Michael seemed to realise it was tactful to go. Ben and I were left, staring at the debris. I wondered if I ought to leave too, but thought he might need me.

'Ben,' I said, moving towards him, but he turned away, arms folded, rigid with misery. 'I'm sorry. I know how much this means to you.'

'Do you?' he said dully. 'Then why didn't you support me

more? It was the least you could have done, stood by me. I thought you were on my side, but you were just like the others.'

'That's not fair. I tried to be positive, but I can't ignore the difficulties. I couldn't lie.'

'I expected greater support from you. People are either for me or against me, I find. You were against me, this evening.' His lips formed a petulant twist. Part of me was shocked and the other part badly wanted to comfort him.

'Don't be daft. It's not personal. We were trying to discuss something objectively. And everyone was so nice about you and everything you do.'

Ben's eyes glinted like blue ice. 'You were against me, Fran, and I'm deeply hurt. I thought you were my friend.'

Now I was angry. 'That's rubbish. You're being unkind.' I was bewildered as well as angry. He was so different from the other night, acting like a toddler with a tantrum. 'If it comes to that, I could feel let down about you, arranging that the organ should be restored instead of our angel, and then not telling me.'

'But the organ's much more important than your angel. You must see that.'

'That's not the point. It feels so – underhand, that's all.'

He didn't answer that.

'Ben,' I said, recovering myself. 'Don't let's quarrel, please.'

'Who's quarrelling?' Suddenly his mood changed. 'It's always the same.'

'What is?'

'I get so far with things and then there's a brick wall. As though someone's trying to stop me.'

I wondered what things he meant – music, perhaps. I remembered all those posters and flyers in the other room advertising his solo performances. All were dated a couple of years or more ago.

'How do you mean?'

'I don't seem to get anywhere with what I do.'

'That's just not true. You've got a career many people would envy. You're involved in so much.'

'That's not what I'm getting at.' He picked up a cassette from the top of a pile and placed it in the machine with a theatrical gesture. The sounds of a concert hall suddenly filled the room, people coughing, rustling programmes, settling down. Then wild clapping as the performer arrived on stage, dying away to complete silence before the rush of liquid piano notes began, passionate, sparkling, brilliant.

I glanced at the cassette box he held in his hand – Ashkenazy, one of the world's most gifted pianists. And Ben had never made it even to the lesser ranks. Was this what he was saying?

A stab of his finger and the music was cut off. He turned and walked out. The door of the next room slammed shut. A moment later he began to play Beethoven *fortissimo*.

'Oh!' I wanted to hit something or run away, but made do with counting to ten. I'd be as childish as he was otherwise. Then, martyr-like, I started piling up plates and glasses onto a tray, resentful that he'd left me to clear up.

Loading plates into the dishwasher and hand-washing wine-glasses was soothing. There were no blinds on Ben's kitchen window and it was dark outside. Dotted around, I could see squares and rectangles of light as Londoners cooked, folded linen, put kids to bed or merely stared out at the sky, drink in hand. The tail-lights of planes winked overhead. Life went on.

When I was polishing the last glass, Ben appeared through the kitchen doorway. I watched him in the reflection of the window.

Finally he mumbled, 'Fran, I'm sorry.' I turned, the last trace of my anger vanishing when I saw his little-boy smile. He raised his hands in a sheepish gesture.

'You really hurt my feelings then,' I said softly.

'I know, I know, I am really sorry.'

'I was trying to be helpful at the meeting and you threw it back in my face.'

'Yes. I'm sorry. I don't know what came over me.'

He ambled across the kitchen and gently took the glass from me, then reached for another from the worktop. I watched him uncork a half-drunk bottle of red wine and slop some into the glasses, pushing one towards me. He took a great gulp of the other, then wiped his mouth with the back of his hand in a manner that managed to be sexy rather than sloppy. He stood grinning at me.

I folded my arms. 'Don't think you can just make it up by smiling charmingly.'

'You're smiling too.'

'No, I'm not.'

I was. He put his wine down and came over and, at last, took me in his arms. As he kissed me, I felt as though I was unfolding like a flower. A moment or two later, his hand snaked inside my top and his lips were moving down my neck, giving me the most amazing tingling feeling.

'Ben!' I remembered where we were. 'All the neighbours will see!'

'Let them,' he growled, and kissed me again. After a moment he half-carried, half-led me up to the sitting-room sofa where he kissed me very satisfyingly again. We nestled together in the gathering darkness.

'What did you mean earlier, about people stopping you doing things?' I asked him sleepily.

He pulled his arm away and sat up, was silent for a moment. Just as I began to feel panicky, thinking I'd offended him again, he kissed me quickly.

'It sounds funny, but I believe I'm jinxed,' he said. 'It's like tonight. I know I've got the talent and the ideas – I put in the hard work, but it doesn't seem to happen. There's some invisible force that says "don't let Ben succeed".'

'But surely you've succeeded at so many things,' I argued. 'The conducting, being organist, the piano, all your teaching. People think you're marvellous.'

'Yes, but it isn't what I want. I was a soloist. That's what I wanted to do most, but I never quite got there. A competition judge would take against me, or the recording never quite materialised, or there'd be some sort of favouritism involved and someone else would get the break. It's not fair. I needed that bit of luck and it never came. I love playing with Nina. That girl's got so much talent, if only people will take notice. She's brilliant, Fran, and has had some great teachers.'

'I hope it works out then – for you both,' I said softly. For although he spoke about Nina's career, I discerned that he was speaking of his, too, as her accompanist.

That evening, I felt as close to Ben as I'd been to anyone. He'd opened up to me and sought comfort, and this touched me deeply. So what if he was moody? I was used to that with my father. But where my father kept me at arm's length, tonight at least, Ben let me in.

We saw each other frequently after that evening, but I was occupied in the shop and visiting Dad, and Ben was always busy, at the school or teaching pupils at home, taking choir practice, rehearsing, sometimes with Nina. It was frustrating. Once or twice, when I rang his doorbell, he didn't hear, was caught up in some piece of music, so I leaned over the railing and knocked on the window to attract his attention. I never knew how he'd be. Sometimes, when he opened the door he'd pull me into a passionate kiss that left me breathless and laughing. At other times, he'd still be away somewhere with the music and would give me that faraway smile of his, showing me rather formally into the drawing room while he finished whatever he had been doing. Then I'd feel on a knife-edge, so I'd play the game too and be cool towards him. Not that he ever noticed.

Sometimes we quarrelled – oh, about silly things – and then, when we made up, he would hug me as though it was the end of the world. Once, at home in the bath, after such a quarrel I noticed bruises on my upper arms. But still I couldn't stay away. At other times I felt more like his mother than his lover, tidying up after him and soothing his ruffled feelings, though sometimes it was me who was badly in need of comfort because of Dad.

Looking back much later, I wondered what made me stay around. It was partly passion, pure physical passion. I longed for him, and the fact that he played with my feelings made me want him more. But I think I was crying for help, too, throwing myself into an intense relationship to forget my deep sadness and loneliness.

There was something in each of us that was alike, cried out to each other, some wound in each of us, some destructive darkness. He was a dark angel. And who were we hurting but each other?

One afternoon at the beginning of October, I sat at Dad's bedside, holding his hand. He was asleep, but his breath came in quick, shallow snores.

A shadow fell across the bed, there came a polite cough, and I looked up to see Dr Bashir reading through the papers at the end of the bed and scrawling his initials on them. 'Come,' he said, and ushered me into a small consulting room near the ward.

'Miss Morrison,' he said, 'we ran some more tests on your

father this morning and the news is not encouraging. He appears to have suffered another small stroke, and he is slipping into an unconscious state.'

I couldn't say anything. I just blinked at him.

'I am sorry to say that the prognosis is poor. I cannot tell how long it will be, days or weeks or months. We can continue the medication he is on, but I fear it will merely delay the inevitable. He will travel deeper into a state of unconsciousness and, sooner or later, there will be irreparable damage. He will not, I'm afraid, return to us.'

He passed me a wadge of tissues, for by now I was crying. 'Is there anyone you can call?' he asked, and I shook my head.

'There isn't anyone,' I said automatically, but immediately realised that this wasn't true. I knew instantly who I wanted. Not Ben, who had never met Dad, not Jo or Jeremy, but Zac. I'd ring Zac.

Dr Bashir was still speaking. 'And now I must ask you, Miss Morrison, if you would consent to your father being discharged from here.'

He paused, and a wave of panic overwhelmed me. How could I look after Dad properly in the flat, with those stairs and the seedy old bathroom and no help? I couldn't do it. But Bashir was continuing, and as he spoke I breathed again.

'He needs the level of care now that is best found in a hospice, and we can recommend one or two, if you would like us to. The beds here, you see – it's a certain kind of ward. There is great need . . .'

'Yes, yes,' I said, feeling guilty for thinking about myself, determined now to engage with Dad's needs.

'These places are very good,' the doctor continued. 'They will make your father comfortable, attend to his every need. You will see.'

We talked about Dad's Living Will, how he had stated that he didn't want to be revived if it would be to live what was in effect no life at all. We must let time and nature take their course.

And so I agreed to let them make the necessary arrangements.

I found a payphone out in the foyer and managed to punch out the number of the shop. Zac picked up on the second ring.

'Zac?' I whispered. 'Thank God. I'm at the hospital. I really need to see you. It's Dad. Things are worse.'

'Wait there,' he said instantly. 'I'll get a cab.'

I hung about inside the main doors, watching the taxis come and go. Finally Zac stepped out of one and the force of my relief at seeing his familiar lean figure took me by surprise. He hurried towards me and we hugged. Now I no longer felt alone. In the four or five short weeks that I'd been home, I'd learned to appreciate Zac as the closest thing to family I had. He and Dad had come to know each other well in their own shy ways and he cared for Dad as much as I did. More so, I sometimes thought, for he didn't carry all the baggage I did.

The hospice we found for Dad, and which could admit him straight away, was in Dulwich. It meant a train ride, but I liked the leafy suburb and the building – a gracious Edwardian mansion standing in its own grounds, the light streaming in through the windows filtered by the branches of autumn trees. Dr Bashir had spoken the truth when he said my father would be well looked after. The nurses, some of whom were nuns, went about their business with gentleness and efficiency, anticipating Dad's needs and respecting ours, too. It was a pleasant place for Zac and me just to sit and be with Dad as he slept.

The first two weeks of October passed in a sort of limbo. The leaves on the trees in the Square fell, spinning, to lie like a gentle shroud, as I watched my father slip into a deep coma. I would sometimes trudge through them in the morning on my way to get milk or a paper. Later in the day, wind and rain and people's feet would have reduced their delicate beauty to a slimy mush, to be scraped up by some passing street-sweeper.

In the first days after his arrival at the hospice Dad would sometimes seem to stir, though never to full consciousness, and when I recounted all the little things I'd been doing – how the angel was progressing, that Amber had been looking into part-time college courses for next term, that Anita next-door had become a grandmother – I could almost believe that he heard me. But as the days lengthened into weeks, he sank deeper into unconsciousness and I knew in my heart that he was beyond hearing.

Zac was the friend and colleague with whom I spent my days, but I was completely wrapped up in Ben. If Zac knew about Ben, which he must have done, he didn't mention it. Instead he absorbed himself in our angel, and during that time, inch by inch, piece by piece, we continued to recreate Raphael.

Zac was lucky finding replica glass – the glassmaker in Hungary managed to match all the specifications, and while the gorgeous colours of autumn faded outside, inside our workshop they came to life.

'There's light trapped inside,' breathed Amber, enraptured, as Zac held up the dazzling pieces one by one.

Yes, there was a kind of exhilaration about this task. We were piecing together a broken angel, but what we were creating wasn't just a beautiful picture of glass and light. It was trans-forming, as if by a miracle, into something marvellous and life-affirming.

Chapter 28

'Tis strange what a man may do, and a woman yet think him an angel.

William Thackeray, *The History of Henry Esmond*

The second Monday of October, Jo missed choir again. I rang her the next evening, but she wasn't home, and although I left a message, she didn't return my call. Somehow I got too caught up in other things to try again and, since Dominic had undertaken to drop in on her with her copy of the choir survey, there wasn't even that excuse to remind me. So when I picked up the ringing phone the following Sunday morning, my first reaction on hearing her croaky 'Fran?' was one of guilt.

'Jo? Jo, is that you? Are you all right?'

'Oh no, Fran, I'm not. I don't know what to do.'

'What's the matter?' I asked her. But instead of answering me she started crying, and I said, 'I'm coming over to see you. Stay right there.'

She buzzed me into the apartment block and waited for me at the top of the stairs, a miserable heap. Had someone died, I wondered. I believed her when she told me she'd been awake crying all night, for her face was blotchy and swollen, her eyes, without her contact lenses, large and red-rimmed behind her glasses.

'You're going to think I'm awful,' she said, throwing herself onto one of her parents' sofas. 'You're going to hate me. I hate myself. I don't know how I got into it. I'd never have thought I ever would, not me.'

I sat down beside her. 'What on earth have you done?' I asked, appalled at her distress.

'It's so awful, and there's going to be such trouble. Oh, why did I ever let it happen?'

What could she possibly have done? Jo, out of whom goodness and innocence always shone.

'Why don't you start at the beginning,' I suggested gently, passing her some tissues.

She gave a great shuddering sigh, then nodded and wiped her eyes.

'It was back in June,' she said, twisting the tissue into pieces on her lap. 'The twenty-fourth. I'll never forget the day. He came to look at the hostel.'

'Who did?'

'He's an MP who champions the needs of the homeless. I don't know if you'll have heard of him – Johnny Sutherland?' I hadn't. 'Earlier in the year, the church applied for some government grants to extend the hostel. Johnny was on the committee awarding them so he came to inspect us. I was on the team who showed him round and he was awfully nice and interested in it all. Asked some good questions, too, as though he really understood the problems we were dealing with. That was all I thought about him at the time.

'Anyway, a couple of days later I passed him in Rochester Row. He was trying to hail a taxi, except there weren't any free, and when I said hello, I was pleased that he remembered me. I suggested he try Victoria Station and since we were going in the same direction we walked together. When I got here though, we were still talking, so I invited him in. We only had coffee, but we got on so well, and he was awfully nice.

'A week later, at the beginning of July, he rang to ask if we could go for a drink. He wanted some more details from me – you know, life behind the figures on the grant submission form, that sort of thing. And that's how it started. During the evening he hinted that he wasn't getting on well with his wife, and I encouraged him to talk about it, thinking I could be helpful just by listening. I felt sorry for him, especially because he has three children. It would have been a shame for the marriage to fall apart just because he didn't have anyone to talk to.'

'Oh Jo.' How exactly like her to want to help. This time though, she'd fallen into a honey trap; the man in trouble, who apparently only needed the touch of a ministering angel to set him back on the straight and narrow.

'We met several more times, and then . . . it was the most terrible shock. He said he wanted to leave his wife. Out of the blue, he said it, just like that. He told me that he'd fallen in love with me.'

'What on earth did you say?'

'What could I say? That I was very flattered and, of course, I liked him very much, but I couldn't be responsible for the breakup of his marriage. I told him I couldn't see him any more.'

'I take it that you did though.'

'Yes. He kept ringing and sending me flowers at the hostel – it was incredibly embarrassing. I don't know what people there thought.' But Jo had this stupid smile on her face as we talked and I guessed that she'd loved being, for once in her life, the subject of all this attention.

'I only agreed to see him again in order to tell him to stop. But, of course, you can guess what happened.'

'He didn't stop.'

'I believed him, Fran. I thought he was telling the truth. I know he was. He was genuinely unhappy with his wife, he was definitely going to leave her. Suddenly we were in love and it was wonderful. I've never felt that way before. And now I probably won't ever again.' She looked desolate.

'Anyway, all the next month he kept telling me that once their family holiday in Tuscany was over, he'd sort it out with his wife. But he came back at the end of August and then the excuse was his daughter's thirteenth birthday party; she'd be traumatised if he ruined that for her with his news. And so it went on. I love him so much and I thought that's how he felt about me, too. I really, really thought it would all work out.' And Jo started to cry again.

One of the world's oldest stories, then. Despite all her high principles, poor old Jo had fallen for it.

'But it hasn't?' I asked tentatively.

'I can't believe I've put myself through all this. Fran, it was so stressful. He could only see me sometimes. It was work this or the children that, and we'd make an arrangement and then he'd cancel. Or he'd give me five minutes' warning and I'd end up changing my arrangements. I know, I'm a mug. I was like a cat on hot bricks. Every time the phone rang my heart would start pounding. I'd have gone mad if I hadn't got my work, and I made myself go to choir this term most of the time. But perhaps it's too late, I'm mad already.' Her voice rose to a sobbing squeak.

'You're upset, and not yourself, but you're not mad,' I told her soothingly.

'But you haven't heard the worst yet, Fran. I was never allowed to ring him, but last week I hadn't heard anything for days and I was worried. So on Monday I rang him at work. As soon as I said "It's me," and he hesitated, I knew that something was badly wrong. He came round here after work, and was acting strangely. He seemed in a great hurry and I could tell he didn't want me to touch him. "Yvonne knows about us," he said. "She confronted me and I had to tell her." She's threatened to leave him and suddenly he can't cope with the idea. After everything he said to me, he doesn't want her to go. He's just . . . dropped me. He puts the phone down on me if I ring. He's blanking me out. I really am going mad. I don't know what to do. You're the first person I've told.'

'I wish you'd said something before.' I was thinking about the past six weeks. Her vagueness, her unpredictability, suddenly made sense. All this because Johnny was treating her like a puppet on a string. Poor Jo.

'I wish I had, but Johnny made me promise to keep things secret.' I wondered if she'd enjoyed that aspect – the secrecy, the intrigue. Perhaps it was part of the excitement.

'Why don't you ask your parents for help?' They'd give her a hard time, I thought – but surely they'd be supportive?

'I can't. Dad would probably go and horsewhip Johnny on the steps of the Commons! I nearly told Dominic the other night when he brought the questionnaire round – he could see I was upset and he was so sweet. I just said that a relationship had gone badly wrong. He made me some tea and talked to me until I cheered up a bit. He's so nice, isn't he?'

'Yes,' I said, with a sigh. Poor Dominic. He was clearly in love with her. But I was more worried about Jo.

'I just wish Johnny would explain things properly. Why won't he talk to me? I feel so powerless.'

Whatever the rights and wrongs of their affair, he was behaving very cruelly to her. 'Do you think wanting to keep his family is the most likely reason?' I asked.

'I don't know. Probably. But he loved me, Fran. I know he

really loved me. How can I get him back? What can I do?' She looked so wan that I reached out and hugged her. She clung to me, starting to cry once more.

When she was quieter, I said, 'Jo, I can't advise you what to do, but it sounds as though he's not going to leave his home. It's going to be tough, but you might save yourself a lot of unhappiness if you accept that and let it finish now.'

It was as though I hadn't spoken. 'If only I could see him again and try to understand,' she repeated.

'Perhaps he can't see you,' I suggested. 'Do you think his wife has forbidden him?'

'I don't know. Or it could be because of his job.'

'Being an MP? Do you think he's frightened your affair would affect his career?'

'Maybe.' She was round-eyed and earnest now. 'Perhaps his wife has threatened to tell his Party, or to go to the papers about it.'

'Or maybe he's worried that you'll go to the papers,' I said, thinking this explanation more likely. Surely his wife wouldn't want the affair made public. She'd instinctively protect herself and the children.

'Oh no,' Jo said, indignant at the idea. 'Johnny knows it would be against all my principles doing something like that!'

Lucky Johnny, I thought bitterly. He'd get off scot free. Jo would never exact revenge. She was too good for someone like him.

Jo looked down at the bits of tissue in her lap and sniffed wanly. I gave her another hug and said, 'We can't sit around brooding. Let's do something fun. Have a lovely lunch somewhere and lots to drink.'

'You sound as if you've had practice,' she said, blowing her nose.

'Believe me, Jo, I have.' If only she knew how often.

So Jo tidied herself up and we took a bus up to Trafalgar Square then walked to a restaurant near Covent Garden. After fancy cocktails and her favourite comfort food of pepperoni pizza, Jo started to cheer up.

'I was out of my depth,' she explained. 'The uncertainty was awful. It'll be a relief to get back to normal.' Then she added, 'But he was so lovely,' and started sniffling again.

'He can't be that lovely if he's made life so dreadful for you,' I said, though with a sudden guilty thought of what I put up with from Ben. 'Do they know at the hostel?'

'They guess something's up, but I've not explained,' Jo said. 'Do you know something? Amber's been so sweet. I didn't tell her what was wrong, just that it was a man, but she's so . . . intuitive and kind, isn't she?'

'She is a very special person,' I agreed, and I finally plucked up the courage to tell her about Ben. 'I feel wretched burdening you with this now, but if I don't you'll think I've been hiding it from you. I'm going out with Ben.'

I needn't have worried about upsetting her. 'Really?' she said, all round-eyed. 'I thought that might happen. That's lovely. I'm so happy for you.'

'Thank you. I suppose I'm happy, too.'

She licked her pudding spoon and said, 'I'm surprised you haven't joined the adoring front row of sopranos though! You needn't slouch at the back with me any more, hoping he won't notice us.'

'I can assure you I'll be slouching at the back as usual,' I said, laughing.

It was good to hear her joke, to see her eyes sparkle. Perhaps she hadn't got in so deep after all and would recover quickly.

But I was wrong to think that the matter of Johnny was all

over. It merely waited, underground, growing canker-like in the dark.

And it wasn't long before *I* had to face the truth as well. That things were far from right between me and Ben.

Chapter 29

Beautiful and ineffectual angel, beating in the void his luminous wings in vain.

Matthew Arnold on Shelley, preface to *Byron's Poems*

One Monday, in the middle of October, Ben phoned before choir and said that he'd invited Michael and Nina over for supper the following evening. Would I like to come?

'Are you asking me to cook?' I said lightly.

'Of course not! How could you think such a thing!' He sounded genuinely indignant. But I turned up early and, sure enough, the kitchen looked like a bombsite. What's more, Ben had just cut his thumb with a vegetable knife.

I calmed him down and sent him upstairs for a plaster, then sorted out our meal, deciding to fry the chicken before casseroling everything, or we'd be waiting for ever.

This was only the bad start to an increasingly difficult evening.

Nina and Michael arrived together, but it was clear that there was some tension between them. Nina, exuding fifties' elegance in a wasp-waisted dress, sat stiffly in her seat, the nubs of her vertebrae visible through the cloth down her long back, and hardly looked at Michael or me, but shot little glances at Ben all the time. Michael couldn't take his eyes off her, the misery plain on his face. Ben didn't seem to notice that anything was amiss, while my role seemed simply to be the audience, watching the farce, whose plot I could never follow, as I moved to and from the table, serving the food, and feeling more and more uncomfortable as the evening progressed. From the conversation I deduced that something had happened, something I could guess at but didn't like to admit.

'Do you know who I saw at the Barbican last night?' said Michael. 'Bea.'

'Really?' Ben hesitated for the smallest moment as he brought his fork to his mouth. 'How the devil was she?'

'She looked very well. Her husband was with her – Ivan or Ian or something. Very charming chap. They've got a little boy.'

'Mmm,' Ben said. 'Hardly ever see her name these days.'

'Oh, she plays abroad a lot, she said. Gave every appearance of doing very well.'

'And who is Bea?' Nina asked brightly.

'Old friend of Ben's from music college,' Michael said quickly.

'Anyone for more Beaujolais?' Ben asked. 'Nina, you look as if you could do with some. Come on, don't be coy.'

'I'm fine, Ben, honestly,' said Nina, putting her hand over her glass. 'You know the effect that stuff has on me.' She stifled a little giggle.

Michael looked at her sharply. 'Perhaps she shouldn't,' he told Ben.

'I will if I want,' Nina said, and held out her glass. Michael frowned.

'I'll have some as well, Ben,' I said. Perhaps getting tipsy was the best way to get through this evening.

They left early, Nina slumped at one end of the taxi seat, Michael at the other.

'Looks like Michael's pursuing a hopeless cause there,' I remarked as Ben closed the door.

He merely shrugged. I knew it would annoy him, but the wine loosened my tongue. 'I'm not sure that I'm her favourite person.'

'Oh, why's that?' he said, throwing himself down in an armchair and yawning.

'Oh Ben, you must see it.'

'What?' he said.

'She's mad about you.'

This time, instead of laughing and denying it, he merely said, 'Oh that,' in a rather dull voice.

I sat down in the chair opposite. Why did I feel cold, even by the fire? He started drumming his fingers on the arm of the chair as though conducting music I couldn't hear. 1-2-3-4, 1-2-3-4. The clock ticked out of time so it sounded like 1-tick, 2, 3 tick, 4, 1-tick, 2, 3 tick, 4 . . . until it started to drive me mad. I stood up.

'I'll clear up,' I said.

'Oh, leave it,' Ben protested, but I started anyway, loading cutlery into the machine. After a moment, he came into the kitchen and helped by putting the odd thing away. He was whistling gently to himself. There was something faraway, unknowable about him that evening, and I couldn't think of anything to say that wouldn't seem unnatural.

Suddenly, he surprised me by putting his arm around me. 'Stay tonight?'

But I was annoyed with him. 'I shouldn't. It's a working day tomorrow.'

'One of us always has an early start whatever day it is,' he said carelessly. But he took his arm away and put his hands in his pockets. He looked sad, out of sorts.

It felt as though something was broken between us. I turned away, unable to face the thought. Ben wandered off and soon I heard the sound of the piano, played very softly. It must be one

of the hymns for Sunday – his early-morning habit – but then a
Chopin Nocturne started up, the dynamics of 'quiet and forceful' preposterously exaggerated.

I slipped upstairs to the loo.

He'd left the light on in the bathroom. There was a fresh
smear of blood on the washbasin, and a box of plasters had
spilled off the narrow wooden ledge above from when he'd cut
himself earlier. I returned the little white packets to their container and, seeing the door of the bathroom cabinet half-open,
reached up and placed it on the top shelf. As I did so, I knocked
something: a small wooden bowl. I grabbed at it too late. It fell,
its contents scattering across the floor.

'Damn.' I crouched down. Something glinted up at me in the
weak electric light. I knew it right away. The fused glass I'd
given Ben once when he visited the workshop. I held it up,
admiring its beautiful peacock blue.

Downstairs, the Nocturne crashed to its end. There came a
silence. I dropped the blue glass back in the bowl and picked up
the other bits – some safety pins, a toothpaste tube lid, a pair of
nail clippers, a buckle from a watchstrap. Gingerly I returned the
little bowl to the shelf. It wouldn't sit straight at first and I saw
it was half-resting on something. I felt around and picked up
two quadrilaterals of white-painted glass, each the size of a large
biscuit. I examined their ragged shapes with dawning recognition. One had a pattern on it. I turned over the other and was
shocked to see a pair of eyes staring at me. They were Raphael's.

Downstairs, under Ben's long fingers, a Chopin Ballade
began to leap and sob.

I stood in the bathroom for what felt like ages, looking down
at those two eyes that calmly stared back at me. My thoughts
churned. Then I carefully closed my fingers over them, picked up
the piece of peacock-blue glass, and walked slowly downstairs.

Ben was bathed in the glow of a single table lamp, his eyes closed as he played, completely caught up in the music. I watched the plaster on his thumb flash up and down as his fingers moved, felt the harmonies rampage through me. The lamplight softened the sharp angles of the music stands and glinted off the framed certificates on the walls. I leaned against the piano. Sensing my presence, Ben's eyes opened, surprised, though he kept on playing. Finally he reached an exhausting but triumphant end and we listened to the chords die away.

I showed him what I held in my hand. 'I found these,' I said. 'You took them, didn't you?'

'Oh God,' he said, his face a picture of horror. 'I completely forgot. Fran, that's awful, I'm sorry.'

'I don't understand.'

'It was that time I came into the shop and you gave me that lovely . . .' I produced the piece of blue glass. 'Yes, that,' he said. 'I took it as a sort of sign, you know. That you . . . liked me.'

'I did,' I said softly. 'But the eyes – why? We thought we'd accidentally thrown them away or something. Zac spent days looking. Why on earth did you take them? I don't get it. You must have known they're important.'

He bowed his head and shuffled his feet on the piano pedals, his arms folded. To give him credit, he looked chastened. 'I don't know. It was a sort of joke, I suppose.' He glanced up, met my eyes. 'I was furious about the wretched window at the time, and they looked so silly, mocking, those painted eyes, in the pile of broken glass. I just picked them up and . . . took them. Fran, I'm so, so sorry.'

'Ben,' I said, trying to find the right words, 'you shouldn't have taken them, not even as a joke.'

'I know, I know. I didn't mean to keep them, but then . . . well,

I forgot where I had put the wretched things. I searched everywhere. Where did you find them?'

'In the bathroom cabinet.'

'I can't think why I put them there,' he said briskly. 'Stupid, really.'

'You should have told me you'd got them,' I said, and I could hear the whine in my voice. 'Oh, never mind.' I tried to be relieved that it was a joke, rather than a deliberate felonious act. But I couldn't be. It was so casual of him.

He got up, gently lowered the lid of the piano and came around behind me, massaging my shoulders, burying his face in my hair, whispering that he was sorry. Despite still being upset I couldn't stop myself tilting into him.

'It was just a silly prank, darling, really,' he said.

It was the first time he'd ever called me darling. Come to think of it, there had been no word of endearment between the two of us before. And now 'darling'. But perhaps it was too late.

I couldn't stay with Ben that night; pretend that everything was normal. Walking back across the Square, I tried to work out what I'd tell Zac about the theft.

In the end I told him the truth. 'I think it was just a silly joke,' I said, still wanting to defend Ben.

'Very funny,' said Zac gravely, turning the battered fragments in his palm. He wouldn't look at me, but moved away to lay the pieces in their rightful place. I understood that in some way he blamed me. And I accepted that blame.

It took a chance meeting with Michael two days after the dinner-party to make me finally see sense.

I had left Amber in charge of the shop and walked up to St James's Park for a change of scene. It was one of those cold clear days when you sense autumn segueing into winter, and I pulled my coat tightly around me as I loitered watching Japanese tourists photograph ducks skid-landing on the lake.

A man was sitting on a bench nearby. Leaning forward, bent over his paper as he ate a sandwich, I didn't recognise him immediately. As he turned a page he looked up.

'Fran.' He folded his paper and rose politely, brushing the crumbs from his coat.

'Hello, Michael. No power lunch with some Ambassador today?'

He laughed. 'You've a somewhat over-glamorised view of what I do all day. I assure you, I'm just a paper-pusher.'

Despite the bright sunlight, the sadness of the other night still hung about him. He looked tired and ashen-faced, and I felt sorry for him.

'Do you have time for a coffee?' I asked.

'That would be nice.' We made our way over to the park café and sat at a table by the lake, warming our hands on our mugs. I asked him about his work and he talked for a while about government briefs and possible trips abroad, but then, inevitably, we moved on to Ben.

'I'm sorry about the other night,' he said, dabbing his upper lip with a handkerchief as white and crisp as his shirt. 'You might have gathered that Nina and I were having a misunderstanding.'

'Oh?' I said. There was something about Michael, the way he pussyfooted around emotional issues, that reminded me of Dad.

'Yes,' he said, looking down at his handkerchief with an expression of bemusement. Then slowly he put it in his pocket. 'I'm very fond of Nina. I told you, I think.'

'I can see it,' I said softly.

'Oh.' He smiled sheepishly. 'Is it that obvious?'

'It is.'

'I thought . . . that she liked me, too.'

'But she still prefers Ben.'

'Yes,' he said, his face almost crumpling.

'And he . . . likes me.'

'Quite. You know, perhaps I shouldn't be saying this to you, but he's always had this thing with women. This knack.' He gave a dry little laugh.

'I think I know what you mean.' And now I felt so cold, I couldn't sit there any longer. 'Shall we walk?'

'I'm sorry, I've offended you,' Michael said, getting up too.

'No, no, really, you haven't.' Part of me knew I shouldn't listen to what he was going to say, that at some level I was betraying Ben. I should let him tell me about himself, not hear it from Michael. But I couldn't stop myself.

'He's a golden boy, Ben is. Always has been. But you need to see, Fran, that he uses people.'

I was shocked to hear him say this. 'I thought you were his friend,' I said angrily.

'I am. I've always been there for him, and I always will be. I've helped him out many times. You know, I used to lie for him at school, when he wanted to get out of Games or needed an alibi. Once, in the Sixth Form, he went to an Oxford college ball with a girl he'd met. Sneaked out of school overnight without permission. He made me cover for him. That sort of thing.'

'Why did you do it?'

'I was fond of him. He was a kind of wayward little brother – he's always seemed younger than me, though actually, he's three months older. And I was very fond of his parents and sister; they made me feel so welcome when I missed my own family so much.'

'But surely if you felt you were an older brother you'd have

acted more responsibly. Stopped him from doing these things.'
It sounded to me as if Michael, by allowing Ben to behave badly,
had contributed to the problem.

Michael sighed. 'Maybe I should. But part of me felt sorry for
him. Ben was always outstanding at music, and never very
interested in other subjects, especially sport. And it being a
school obsessed with rugby and cricket he had a hard time of it
from some of the boys. Sometimes there was violence. That's
why we became friends in the first place.'

'You were bullied, too?'

'Not for long – I learned how to deal with it. I was good aca-
demically, so I adopted the role of class nerd and helped other
boys with their prep. We were unusually sensitive teenagers,
Ben and I. But when he was upset, he came across as arrogant,
which put people's backs up.'

It still sounded such an unlikely friendship, but then Michael
explained. 'We kept getting thrown together. We were both in
Magdalen House and shared a room in the Lower Fifth. Our
parents met on Sports Day that year – mine were in England
that summer – and I was invited over to Ben's for the first time.
It was the start of it all.'

At last I was beginning to understand this friendship. Ben
hadn't chosen it. It had happened to him. And yet they did seem
close – like brothers who irritate one another but have stuck
together anyway, though it was old experiences in this case,
rather than shared blood, that bound them.

Then Michael said something that shook me. 'I'm not sure
he'd be happy that I told you, but sometimes I didn't believe his
stories that other boys had hurt him.'

'What do you mean?' I asked, shocked.

'There were cuts on his thighs, Fran. You're not telling me
someone else did that?'

'Oh,' I said, trying to assimilate this. 'How dreadful. Poor Ben.' We were silent for a while.

'What happened after you left school?' I asked, imagining them drifting apart at university.

'We both came to London, so we saw each other often. I went to University College to read English, and Ben won a scholarship to the Royal College of Music.'

'Where I went,' I told him. 'Though I never knew him there.' He'd have been a couple of years ahead.

'Ben always worked damned hard at his music, but he also got discouraged easily and then we – his family and I – had to try to buck him up.' I nodded in recognition.

'Ben has this fear of failure, that people will laugh at him or pity him, you see, so sometimes he gives up and finds someone else to blame,' Michael told me. 'It's as though he's protecting some unhealed wound deep inside. When things get bad he doesn't see them through. Yet when things are going well, he's ecstatic; it brings out the best in him.'

I thought of him conducting, his obvious drive and talent, then of the way he had spiralled down into misery after the committee meeting about the future of the choir. 'I think I understand what you mean,' I told Michael.

'I suppose that's it in a nutshell,' he said, considering. 'He yearns for the fruits of success, for adulation, but there's some faltering in self-confidence that stops him going for it. And, well, he manipulates other people to get what he wants. I don't think he means to, but he does. Then, of course, it all goes wrong. It was like that with Bea.'

'Bea. You mentioned her the other night. Who is she?'

'Beatrix Claybourne.'

I remembered the elegant handwritten name on Ben's sheet music, the framed poster on the landing upstairs.

'Has he told you about her?' Michael went on. 'She's a pianist too, a brilliant one. He went out with her at college; there was talk of them getting engaged. But it soon became apparent that she was outshining him. Everything went right for her – she won the awards, was sought by the best teachers. And in the end she couldn't stand his jealous rages. They broke up.'

I stared at him, not wanting to believe him, but remembering something Ben had said about Nina's brilliance. His eyes had shone with ambition.

'You said he used people,' I whispered. Ben might not admit this to himself, but it was obvious he hoped to win personal success as Nina's musical partner.

'Yes,' Michael said softly.

'You introduced Nina to him, didn't you?'

He nodded miserably.

'I met her at a concert a year ago and we started seeing each another. I was so happy – but then she met Ben. Her teacher's an acquaintance of Ben's, agreed with me that they'd be good together. Of course, professionally they are. But I should have considered the possibility of her falling in love with him. There's something fatally attractive about him. You know that, Fran.'

We had stopped now, sat on a bench to watch a boy throw a stick for his dog.

'But Michael,' I said, 'if Ben's not interested in her that way, maybe she'll come to accept it. Things can't go on like this for ever. Maybe she'll come back to you.'

The boy had thrown himself on the grass, fed up with the stick game. The dog barked for more, but he took no notice.

When he looked at me this time, Michael's expression was bitter. 'What is it?' I asked, uneasily, but I read it in his face. He opened his mouth, but could say nothing.

'Michael.'

'I have to get back now, Fran. I have a meeting.' He stood up, said goodbye, and started to stride off across the grass towards St James's Palace.

I watched him go. There was no point chasing him, or begging him to tell me. I had discerned what it was he needed me to know.

'It was sometime last week. I've forgotten when. I only kissed her,' Ben said, staring at the floor. 'Nothing more. We didn't . . . go to bed or anything. I wouldn't do that to you, Fran.'

But he'd treated Nina carelessly. He'd led her on when she was besotted with him; working with him so intimately, her desire was at fever pitch. It was wrong of him. How could he be so casual to anyone? And why had it taken me so long to realise?

I squeezed my eyes closed in an effort to clear my mind. When I opened them again, there he was, lounging sulkily, mutinous. And suddenly I couldn't be bothered with him any more. I was free.

'Ben,' I said heavily. 'You've simply no idea, have you?'

I opened the front door and walked out, pulling it shut behind me with what I hope sounded like a final bang.

I was miserable for days, half-hoping Ben would ring and beg me to come back, determined that I wouldn't if he did. He didn't ring, which cast me into deeper gloom. Working in the shop I'd find tears welling, and if I were alone I'd let them run down my cheeks unchecked. I was still angry with Ben and furious with myself for having got mixed up with someone like him again, after all my promises to myself. Yet all the time, the memories would catch me unawares. Ben conducting, jacket off, sleeves rolled up, beautiful, intense, determined. Or playing the piano, eyes closed, lost in the world of the music. I dreamed of his long, slow kisses and my body cried out for his. Although I'd known him for such a short time, I'd allowed myself to get in too deep, too quickly.

It was hard living so close. Several times I caught myself staring across the Square, searching for a glimpse of him. Once, a week after our quarrel, I saw him let himself out of his flat, the long golden scarf round his neck flapping in the wind. He glanced over in my direction, but didn't notice me watching from behind the curtain in the living room. He walked off quickly in the direction of the church. I hadn't been able to face going to choir. Did he miss me? Indeed, did he give me any thought at all? I dropped the curtain and turned away.

I had better things to worry about, I told Jo, when I went round to confide in her. She, nursing her own broken heart, understood more than anyone how I felt. The most important of my worries was my father.

I visited Dad several times a week now. Zac often came with me and we'd sit at either side of the bed and converse, addressing comments to Dad as though he were listening, but of this we couldn't be at all sure.

Zac never said a word to me about Ben, but it must have been obvious I was no longer seeing him. He was particularly gentle, and sometimes in the shop I would glance up from whatever work I was doing to find him looking at me, a thoughtful expression on his face.

He'd been working on Raphael for weeks now, giving the window every spare moment. Amber and I helped where we could, but we didn't have Zac's expertise. He was at the painting stage now, which involved great delicacy, tracing the main drawing lines on the new pieces of glass and retouching some of the old in paint made with iron oxide and powdered glass.

'The gold colour of the hair was made by painting the glass with silver nitrate and firing it,' he told Amber one morning, making a note in *The Angel Book*. 'But first you had to paint the lines of hair and feathers straight onto the glass and fire that.' He wouldn't be able to refire the original glass, he added, in case future generations needed to alter what he had painted.

Because the eyes were missing he had been unwilling to do much work to the face, but now he was able to work on its reconstruction, filling in the gaps with a tinted resin. On Russell's vidimus and cartoon the features had seemed regular, but bland. There had been no life in the face. Finally Zac had the chance to make his mark.

One day near the end of October, the two of us found ourselves alone in the workshop. Zac was telling me about a customer who'd come in that morning when I was out, wanting a crystal wand. 'You wouldn't believe it,' he said. 'It was for some weird magical ritual and I didn't feel comfortable about it, so I quoted him five thousand pounds and luckily he went away.'

I laughed at Zac's ruse and it seemed it was the first time I'd laughed easily for ages. Perhaps at last I was starting to forget Ben. I smiled in relief at the thought and Zac looked at me intently.

'Stay exactly as you are,' he said. With a few quick lines he drew something on a piece of paper.

He showed me what he'd sketched. 'That's how you think I look?' I asked. I wasn't displeased, as he'd made me far prettier than the mirror ever told me, but still, I didn't think it was me.

The next day, when Amber studied the sketch, she cried, 'The angel looks a bit like you, Fran.'

'No, it doesn't. It could be anyone,' I said, somewhat grumpily. 'Anyway, you're not supposed to change Philip

Russell's version, Zac.' I wasn't sure that I wanted to be immortalised as an angel. It was too much to live up to.

'The original sketch definitely has a look of you,' said Zac, quite seriously. 'It's the fullness of the mouth Russell painted. And there's something about the eyes, too. You to a T.'

'Whoever heard of an angel called Fran?' I said.

'I read about one called Eric,' said Amber solemnly. 'A girl kept reading the name Eric around the place and her spiritual guide told her that must be what her angel was called.'

Even Amber joined in our laughter.

'It's finished,' Zac said quietly a few days later. Amber and I rushed over to look. I couldn't believe how beautifully he'd reconstructed the face. It had been a complicated process that involved creating a moulded clear glass backing plate to hold it, the original pieces painted and seamlessly stuck together with special glue. Then he had slotted the whole window into a bronze frame.

Now, using a board, we helped him transfer the heavy window onto the light table. Zac flicked on the switch and Raphael shone in all his golden glory.

Amber yelped with delight.

From the tips of his gold wings, folded to a point above his head, to his sandalled feet amidst grass and flowers, he was perfect; a tall, long-limbed figure clad in gold and white, flowing blond locks framing his calm, slightly smiling face. One hand was raised in blessing and, right at the bottom, the inscription *God heals* stood out as clearly from the window's ruby border as it must first have done a hundred years ago. The crack was hardly noticeable.

'Well?'

I broke from my reverie. Zac smiled at me, waiting.

'He's amazing. I can't believe it's not the original.'

'It is, mostly. And anyone who needs to strip it down again in the future for any reason can.'

I picked up *The Angel Book* from a nearby worktop and flicked through the pages. Zac had meticulously noted every detail of every step of his reconstruction, including drawings and photographs, descriptions of new glass and lead, of the composition of paints and resins he'd used. The whole thing had taken him five weeks.

'And under the lead here,' he bent to indicate the bottom left-hand corner of the window, 'I've painted *Minster Glass*. And there's the piece with Philip Russell's Celtic knot, so future generations can blame us if needs be.'

'There's nothing to blame us for,' I said, shaking my head in wonder. 'Zac, it's beautiful, superb. Jeremy's going to love it.'

He was fiddling with the camera again now, so my attempt to hug him got a bit confused. For a brief moment though, he hugged me back and I felt his breath in my hair, smelled the saltiness of his skin. I stepped back, both of us a little startled.

'Thank you,' he said, smiling. 'I hope Jeremy doesn't have the same reaction.'

Jeremy came that afternoon, walked around the angel several times and then finally said, 'It's magnificent. Thank you.'

During the following days, we had a steady stream of parishioners making a pilgrimage to the shop to see the window. They all agreed that it must be installed in the church. Now we had to wait for official permission.

I often found myself going over to study the angel, feeling the force of that calm, strong gaze. How close, I wondered, had Zac managed to get it to the original? Perhaps we'd never know.

Chapter 30

Somehow life is bigger after all
Than any painted angel.

Oscar Wilde, *Humanitad*

LAURA'S STORY

It was nearly the end of July when Philip Russell asked Laura to accompany him to the Grosvenor Gallery in New Bond Street, to see Burne-Jones's sensational new painting: *The Golden Stairs*. She'd never been there before. At first, her attention was caught by the Sunday crowds and the olive-green rooms cluttered with furniture and ornaments, even before she contemplated the paintings.

As they stared up at the huge, glowing picture, Laura wondered at how ethereal, how spellbinding these barefoot women were, endlessly descending their mysteriously suspended staircase. Here was mysticism of a different kind from the awe she felt in her father's church. What would James Brownlow think of it? She couldn't imagine that her father would like or even try to understand this faintly pagan scene. But nor could she name the deliciously disturbing feelings the painting inspired.

Philip explained in a whisper about the faces – that one was Mr Morris's daughter May, the girl in profile at the top Mr

Burne-Jones's own child, Margaret. Laura imagined what it must be like to be made famous in a painting. It was a form of immortality her father would definitely disapprove of, she decided.

From further down the room there came a ripple of female laughter. A tall woman in a flowing sage-green robe, all embroidered with birds and flowers, peeled away from a cluster of ladies around an Alma-Tadema painting, and Philip gave a little gasp. She was a real beauty this one, Laura thought, with that head of glossy dark curls tamed into a knot at the nape, fine sloe-black eyes, a long straight nose, perfectly moulded lips, and a lively expression. The woman's gaze darted around the room and came to rest on Philip. For a moment she grew perfectly still, then she moved towards them. To him she said gently, 'Philip, are you well?' and placed a graceful hand on his arm. He seemed agitated.

'Marie. Yes, I am quite well, thank you. This is Miss Brownlow.' The woman's eyes passed over Laura's face and figure briefly, without interest. Laura's cheeks burned.

One of Marie's companions called out, 'Mair, have you seen the King Arthur?' and she murmured, 'Goodbye, so nice to see you . . .' As she moved away Laura noticed the row of iridescent buttons marking the languorous movements of her spine.

'Was that . . .?' she muttered, turning to Philip, already knowing the answer.

Russell nodded, tearing his eyes from Marie and blinking furiously as though waking from an enchantment. 'My wife.' He looked around wildly. 'Now, there's another work will interest you,' he said, pulling her roughly into an adjacent room.

'Don't.' She felt like a pet on a leash.

Everything was ruined. *I want to go, I want to go,* thrummed

through her mind as she drifted past painted faces and land-
scapes, hardly registering artist or subject. She remembered the
way Marie had dismissed her, a dowdy brown-feathered bird
next to her own exotic plumage. When Philip suggested they
leave, she dumbly assented.

They walked across Green Park, where mist was rising from
the grass. Russell was plunged so deeply in thought that he
answered Laura's lame attempts at conversation with mono-
syllables.

On reaching Victoria Street he seemed to stir from his melancholy. 'You haven't seen my studio, have you?' he said. 'Some
artists open theirs to the public and I'm wondering whether I
should. Come and tell me what you think.'

'I should go home. My father . . .'

'Please, come with me. I don't want to be alone.' He patted
her arm in a clumsy affectionate way that brought with it a
heartbreaking sense of her brother Tom, and she relented.

'Only for a minute then.'

'It's not far. Down Wilton Street, here, towards the river.'

He drew her past the railway station down into a maze of
whitewashed terraces bathing in hazy late-afternoon sunlight.
Caged birds sang by open windows. A little girl leaning on an
upstairs sill waved to them. Laura waved back. Further on, from
the depths of a drawing room, could be heard the opening bars
of a Bach Prelude being played over and over again, the unseen
pianist tripping up at exactly the same place each time.

In Lupus Street the houses were gay with flower boxes. Philip
led her to the steps of number 13, then up a staircase to the top
of the building where a huge attic with a north-facing skylight
served as his studio.

Canvases of all shapes and sizes lined the walls. On a table a
sketchbook lay carelessly open. She glanced at this, then at the

small canvas on an easel under the skylight. Her dismay deep-
ened. Everywhere she looked was Marie's face. He could not
possess his wife in person; instead he'd trapped her image, over
and over again.

She backed away towards the door, reaching for the handle.
'I shouldn't have come.' Her voice sounded too loud in the
echoey room.

'Why not?' he said. 'What's the matter?'

'I cannot advise you about opening your studio. Or . . .
compete with your wife.'

'My wife? What is Marie to do with you?'

'Philip, she is everywhere. Look.'

He stared around the room like one enchanted, then stepped
over to the easel and gently touched Marie's painted cheek.
He'd evoked her as some wild spirit, Laura thought – a river
nymph, perhaps. His hand dropped to his side.

'All this . . .' she gestured to the portraits '. . . makes our
friendship intensely painful to me. There is no room for anyone
else in your life.'

'I need you,' he said, his voice harsh with emotion. 'Even my
old friends neglect me now. Don't you, also.'

'But you must see. You don't really care for me, you care for
her. I'm . . . someone you talk to about Marie.'

'We talk about all manner of things. Laura, I'm dismayed that
you find our friendship painful.' He came to face her now, took
her hand. 'How cold you feel,' he said, warming it in his. 'I find
I can talk to you without needing to think.'

She made a sound that might have been a laugh or a sob.
'That does not flatter me, Philip.' She pulled her hand away.

'Oh, I didn't mean . . . I just meant that I feel at ease with you.
Not constantly guarding my tongue as I am with . . . Marie.'

And yet you don't notice me, not really. You don't see me as you see

her. You don't draw me constantly, as you do her. These thoughts
shouted in her head but she didn't dare give them voice. To hide
her distress, she picked up a little wooden bird from a shelf by
the door, cradled it warm and round and safe in her cupped
hands. This was what she was meant for: to comfort; not to disturb or excite.

When she was calmer she said, 'Philip, you must learn to
forget Marie. Not forget her altogether – I don't mean that. She's
your wife and the mother of your child. But you must learn to
distance yourself from your loss. It's been over a year. She won't
come back. You will drive yourself mad if you cannot accept
this. Think of the damage you do to your son.'

His face turned to stone. For a moment she feared she had
said too much.

'I cannot forget her, as you ask. Any more than your family
can forget Caroline.'

'That's different,' Laura sighed. 'Caroline is dead. We'll never
see her again in this life.'

'At least she died in the full knowledge of your love for one
another!' he cried out. 'You have that satisfaction.'

''Which makes us miss her all the more!' Her own voice was
raised now. 'No, I don't mean that,' she added quickly, seeing
his distress. 'Only that you can't compare the two losses. But I
do know that our duty is to be thankful for what we have and
to make the best of what we are given. And I think our angel
will help us do that. When he is finished.'

'He *is* finished,' Philip said. He wandered back to the easel
where Marie's face looked out.

'What did you say?'

'I meant to tell you earlier. Your window is ready. You may
come and see it when you like.'

'Philip, that's wonderful!'

'I thought you would be pleased.' He took the painting from the easel and placed it in a drawer. Then, with slow, deliberate movements he gathered up all the other portraits of his wife and piled them in a cupboard. Laura watched, amazed.

Closing the cupboard, he turned to her and smiled. It was a dazed, unhappy smile, as though at last he was struggling to wake from the spell Marie had cast.

Chapter 31

And the great dragon was thrown down, that ancient serpent, who is
called the Devil . . . and his angels were thrown down with him.

Revelation xii. 9.

I'd have missed the story altogether if Jo hadn't rung on 28
October, gabbling hysterically about a newspaper article. After
I'd put down the phone, promising to ring back, I dashed out to
buy a copy. The piece appeared on page 8 – I spread the paper
out on the counter to read it. There was an unflattering picture
of Jo, emerging from the hostel, and a posed photograph of a
stylish couple wearing huge rosettes and waving amidst a
shower of ticker tape. *Homelessness MP finds naughty love nest* ran
the headline.

'Oh hell,' I whispered. It got worse. 'Why would he risk
everything for such a Plain Jane?' a friend of Mrs Sutherland
was reported as saying. 'A colleague describes Miss Pryde as
"earnest and wholesome. A real do-gooder. The last person
you'd expect . . ."'

When, heavy-hearted, I rang Jo back, her answermachine
clicked on with its usual friendly message, so I started to say, 'Jo,
it's me, Fran,' and a man's voice interrupted, a voice I recognised. 'Fran. Kevin Pryde here. Good to speak to you. How are

you? I take it you've seen the papers. We're under siege here. Journalists, photographers, the whole bloody crew, if you'll excuse my French. I'm trying to get rid of the bastards. Jo's with Claire. Want a word?'

It was a relief that Jo's parents were with her. Kevin Pryde, in his lawyer's hat, had long experience of dealing with the media. Jo was too upset to come to the phone again, but I agreed with Kevin to visit later in the day. By then the feeding frenzy had abated somewhat, though I had to dodge a haggard-looking man outside who was speaking quickly into a microphone.

I sat on the sofa holding Jo's limp hand. She wore a fixed look of horror, as though the sight of a ghost had sent her into a trance.

'I've seen what they've written about me,' she whispered. 'Plain and worthless. A marriage-wrecker.'

'They're not interested in portraying you as you really are,' I said fiercely. 'They just want to sell papers.'

'Hear hear,' said Kevin, absently, from his watch at the window. 'Sharks and vermin, the lot of 'em.'

'I still think if we talk to that *Mail* journalist, Kevin, then at least she'll present Jo's version of events.' Jo's mother, who sat on the sofa close to Jo, was exactly as I remembered her, expecting everyone to be as civilised as herself.

'Claire, don't be naïve. They'll mangle anything we say.'

Poor Jo. I remembered our conversation several Sundays ago, walking back from the Tate, when she had wished so fervently that she was beautiful. That must have been about the time when things started to go wrong with Johnny. Always so cheerful and positive, it turned out that Jo had a faultline running through her like the rest of us. She'd believed she would be happier if she was someone different.

'I was happy before I met Johnny,' she said brokenly now. 'I wish none of it had happened.'

Jo went down to her parents' house in Kent, and I started to think the whole thing was blowing over. But then, four days later, at Hallowe'en, the vicar called at the shop. He was carrying a copy of the *Guardian* and wore a sober expression.

'Do you know how to contact Jo?' he asked. 'We can't track her down. It's rather important.'

'Didn't she tell the hostel? She's at her parents' house,' I said. 'I'll find the number for you. Come through.'

I went to get my handbag from the office and he followed me into the workshop. As I riffled for my address book he stood looking at the angel. He touched the glass gently and rubbed his fingers, an absorbed expression on his face.

'I hope he won't be taking up valuable space here for much longer. I rang the Archdeacon yesterday to ask how the permissions procedure is going . . . ah, thank you.' Jeremy took the scrap of paper I passed him with the Kent number on it. 'I suppose you've seen this, have you?' He laid his newspaper in the only clear space on the worktop and pointed to an article headed *Homeless hostel. Allegations of MP's corruption.*

I scanned it quickly.

Following the disclosure of backbencher MP Johnny Sutherland's affair with a hostel worker, a grants committee was yesterday trying to answer accusations that Sutherland had given preference to a quarter-million-pound grant to St Martin's Hostel in Westminster, where his lover, Jo Pryde, is a careworker. 'We're not saying that St Martin's doesn't merit the grant,' said Mary Coltrane, a spokesperson from the Home Office, 'merely that the circumstances in which it is being awarded must be called into question. Any grants to St Martin's are, for the time being, suspended pending further investigation.'

'It is a bit grim, isn't it?' Jeremy said. I'd never seen him so low, not even when he delivered the news that the church wouldn't pay to restore the angel. 'There was a lot hanging on this grant. You can see why we've got to find Jo.'

'They'll need to question her.'

'Exactly.'

Shortly afterwards, he thanked me and left. There was something dejected about the set of his shoulders as he walked back across the Square.

It was an odd day. Zac didn't come in at all – his Noah's Ark design had been chosen and he was meeting people from the church who were commissioning it. And Amber didn't turn up as expected, which troubled me, as she'd always proved reliable.

At one point a skinny woman with a camera snapped a picture of the shop, but when I went out to challenge her, she merely smiled nonchalantly and marched away. A young Asian man in an overcoat climbed out of a taxi and poked his head round the door, saying that he wished to ask me a few questions about Jo, but I packed him off without even bothering to find out who he worked for or how he'd tracked me down.

In the late morning, I tried ringing Jo's parents but their phone was constantly engaged. Then Dominic rang.

'I hope you don't mind,' he said. 'I got your number from the choir register. I saw the paper today, and I'm extremely worried about Jo. Do you know how she is? I don't like to ring her myself in case I'd be intruding.'

'I haven't heard from her, but I'm sure she'd love it if you rang.' I gave him the Kent number. 'I don't suppose there's anything you can do, Dominic, being at the Home Office yourself?'

'Nothing,' he said shortly. 'It would only make things worse if I started making enquiries.'

Imaginary tabloid headlines about corruption in the Home Office danced before my eyes. 'Sorry,' I said. 'You're absolutely right.'

'I expect it will all come out in the wash,' he said, sighing. 'I only want to send Jo my warmest wishes. I'll be in touch.'

'How are things going with you, by the way?' I asked before he could hang up.

'We're making progress, thanks for asking. We've found a residential home for Mum quite near my sister's and a bed is likely to come up in the next week. So we're deep in the awful business of getting ready. Then, when she moves we'll have to clear out the house. No hurry there though.'

'It must be a weight off your minds.'

'Yes, and I think Mum is reconciled to going. The waiting's awful though. She's very unsettled.'

Unsettled, I thought, as I put down the phone. That's exactly how I felt too.

Amber appeared in the early afternoon, agitated and out of breath. As she came into the shop, she looked behind her in a furtive fashion.

'It's Lisa's mates,' she said, closing the door. 'I thought they were after me, but they've gone. There's all these people outside the hostel. Blokes with cameras, and that snotty woman from the TV news. Effie went out and shouted at them, which didn't help. Lisa's so stupid. She's, like, since I'm friendly with Jo, the whole thing's my fault. That hasn't stopped her tarting herself up and trying to get on telly though.' Here she did a not very convincing impression of Lisa, thrusting out her chest and preening her hair.

I laughed, then said gently, 'I'm glad you've made it finally.'

Amber looked instantly crestfallen. 'Yeah, I'm sorry I couldn't get here earlier. It was really difficult.'

'Don't worry,' I said. 'I thought as much. Can you give me a hand with stocktaking?'

In this troubling atmosphere it was good to have something routine to do. As the light began to fade it felt less settled still, as scattered groups of children dressed as witches and ghosts and vampires began to appear, hurrying from door to door, collecting treats, their laughter ringing out across the Square.

At a quarter to six there was a cracking noise, then an angry shout, and two young lads in flapping black robes skittered past our window. Mr Broadbent from the bookshop stumbled onto the street shaking his fist, a mess of flour and egg sliding down the front of his shop window. I went out to help him clear up.

'It gets worse every year,' he complained. 'And I'm damned if I'll give them a thing. We never had this trick or treat nonsense when I was a boy. Nasty American habit.'

Tonight, just to prove I was over Ben, I'd steeled myself to go to choir practice. Afterwards, I came straight back home. It was unbearable now to go to the pub with the others and endlessly discuss the wretched questionnaire, to see Ben and pretend that nothing had happened between us. It was bad enough watching him conduct.

It was half-past eight, a night with no moon. Now the robed figures I passed in the Square on their way to Hallowe'en parties were older, more sinister-looking.

'Want some, love?' called out one of a trio of men who were sharing a bottle of whisky, and the others cackled suggestively.

I shook my head, never so glad to reach the sanctuary of the shop.

As I drew the curtains for bed, fireworks started exploding

somewhere a couple of streets away. I watched the showers of sparks splatter the sky for some minutes before shutting them out. I could still hear distant pops and bangs as I drifted off to sleep.

I dreamed that I was walking down a tunnel of swirling psychedelic coloured light. It was warm and there was a lovely fragrance, something tantalisingly familiar, hovering just beyond recognition. A woman was singing in a rich strong voice, far away. As I walked through that swirling tunnel, the singing faded. Instead, someone gently called my name: 'Frances, Frances.' The tunnel widened into a great valley, aflame with sunset, but all I could hear was that voice, 'Frances, Frances, wake up now,' and I was swimming upwards through the sky, breaking into consciousness. '*Frances*.' I was awake. But there was no one there.

I sat bolt upright, sensing straight away that something was wrong. The air smelled acrid and felt too warm. There was a distant rushing noise, then crackling and a sudden crash. I knew what it was even before I placed my feet on the floor. Quickly, I pulled them up again. The floorboards were hot. Fire. The shop was on fire. Then came a terrible sound of shattering glass below.

It was too dark to see much. I felt around for shoes, finding some trainers under the bed. I briefly considered pulling on clothes, but immediately rejected the idea. Some mad part of my brain started listing things I ought to save; I mollified it by catching up my bag from a chair. I touched the closed door cautiously. It was cool, so I opened it. The rushing noise intensified. Moonlight shone through Dad's bedroom to the landing, silhouetting smoke coiling up from under the flat door. I rushed into the living room, threw up the sash window. A brief glance down and I recoiled from the heat, but not before I glimpsed the flames feathering the wall below, saw chunks of glass from the new window scattered on the pavement. I considered my options. There was only one and I hadn't much time. I grabbed first one sofa cushion and shoved it out of the window, then the other. Scatter cushions followed.

Thankful to be wearing pyjamas rather than a nightdress, I squeezed onto the window ledge, peered out briefly to get my bearings, then closed my eyes and jumped.

I missed the cushions altogether. The pain was awful. Everything went dark. I lay there, unable to breathe. My feet hurt, my legs hurt, my lungs were sore and my eyes burned. At last I gulped air, hot, smoky air, and sat up coughing to see the shop a wall of smoke and fire. Close by me a cushion burst into flames. I gasped and wriggled away. Amazingly, though one shoe had gone, I was still clutching my bag. Something lay on the pavement amidst the smashed glass. With a sharp little pain I realised it was Dad's lovely angel, melted into great tears of glass and lead.

Angels. Raphael. Fire brigade. There was a phone box round the corner. My brain lurched suddenly into motion. Then someone behind me said, 'Are you all right, miss?' It was a soft male voice with an Irish accent. 'Don't worry, a fire engine's already on its way.'

I shuffled round and looked up. He was a pale young man with short hair that glinted gold in the firelight. He crouched beside me and grasped my hand. 'Did you jump? You'll have had a lucky escape there. Any broken bones, do you think?'

'No, I don't think so.' I studied my hands, which hurt, and realised I was shaking, not with the cold but with shock. The man took off his coat and fitted it around my shoulders.

'Thank you. But I've got to . . .' I said. I couldn't get the words out. I struggled up, waving him away, and shuffled my shoe back on. My legs ached, they had no strength, but nothing seemed broken. 'Look,' I told him, 'I'll be back in a minute.'

'Don't – it's dangerous!' he called, as I half-ran, half-hopped around to the back of the shop. Thank goodness I had the keys in my bag. Scrabbling with the locks took a moment, but I got the workshop door open. Thick black smoke poured out and I reeled back, choking, my eyes streaming.

The man appeared at my side as if from nowhere and slammed the door shut. 'You mustn't go in there,' he said, with quiet authority. 'Breathe now. That's right.' Coughing and crying, I fell against the wall. He waited until I recovered.

'You can't be going in there. But it's all right. See? There are no flames. Only the smoke.' Together we peered through the window into the pitch blackness. He was right. The fire hadn't yet reached the workshop through the thick Victorian dividing wall and the modern fire door. We both heard the distant wail of a siren. I felt his hand on my arm. 'Come on, it'll be all right.' And, with me half-leaning on him, we made our way back to the street where a fire engine with softly flashing lights was negotiating its way past the parked cars.

'Thank you,' I gasped to the young man. He smiled and let me go. I turned back to the fire engine and completely forgot about him.

'Anyone in there, d'you know, love?' shouted the stocky fireman who jumped down first from the truck. Others, pouring out of the cab with comic swiftness, started scaling the machine, loosening catches, pulling out hoses.

'No. There was only me.' I started to shake again and pulled the coat more tightly around me.

' 'Ere, miss,' said another fireman, and he draped a blanket round me. Hoses began to jet water on the flames.

A police car arrived. All around the Square lights had come

on and people were emerging from their houses or leaning out of windows. Mr Broadbent from the bookshop tapped me on the shoulder and invited me up, somewhat bizarrely, to drink cocoa at his flat. I shook my head.

'Fran,' said a voice I knew. I whipped round. 'Ben.' I'd never felt so glad to see him. He'd pulled on jeans and a sweater over his pyjama top. I hugged him and his unshaven chin grazed my cheek. We stood, arms round each other and there was no time to think about anything but the present. I was grateful for that.

The vicar and his wife joined the throng, dressed but unkempt, and then the wine-bar owner, who looked as if he hadn't been to bed yet. A police officer made us all move further back, out of the way of the firefighters, but the fire was quickly losing the battle against the hoses and it was over in no time at all.

Two firemen sloshed through the shop to check that the flames were completely out whilst several others busied themselves with plastic tape to fence off the building. A young policeman asked me a host of questions and filled in a form with slow, careful writing while a paramedic checked me over.

'Please, can I go in? I need to see . . .' I started, still worried about Raphael, but a fireman said, 'Sorry, love, it's too hot in there. And you never know, the whole place might come crashing down.'

We watched one of the men bend down to pick up some pieces of something in the doorway. He beckoned to another officer, who walked over to look at it with him, and they both started hunting around. After a while they came over and showed us what they'd found.

'It's a firework, miss. Jammed through your letterbox. A nasty Hallowe'en trick. We've had one or two like this tonight. Fireworks start earlier every year.'

'Oh,' was all I could say, remembering the assault on Mr Broadbent's shop and all the sinister revellers passing through the Square. It seemed senseless, but I was exhausted now and I couldn't work it out.

One by one the spectators were moving away. Some, like Mr Broadbent, came up to me, saying how sad they were and offering help. I thanked them all, grateful for the second time in a month, that I had so many good neighbours.

It was only when Sarah Quentin came and put her arm around me that I finally cracked. I cried on her shoulder like a hurt child and she soothed me as she might have done her daughters when they were small.

Ben started to offer me a bed for the night but she interrupted, firmly insisting that I must go to them and stay in their elder daughter's bedroom. She'd find me some clothes, she said. Mothering was what I needed, so I told the police where I'd be and gave a fireman back their blanket. It was then I realised I was still wearing the stranger's coat. I looked round for the young man with the gold hair, but he wasn't there.

'Come on now,' said Sarah firmly, so I meekly obeyed, allowing myself to be led away across the garden, with Ben and the vicar several steps behind.

When we reached Ben's house he said, in a woeful voice, 'Well, goodbye, then. I'm so sorry, Fran. About your shop – and, well . . . everything. I mean, I know I haven't . . .' but I cut him off by hugging him again quickly. I couldn't cope with some eloquent apology right now.

It was three in the morning and I felt wide awake; my nerves were jangling. As I sat in the Quentins' kitchen nursing a cup of tea, Lucifer crouched on the table, staring at me resentfully. There was no point in going to bed, I thought, but Sarah Quentin must have put something in my tea, because when she ushered me upstairs into a pretty pink and white bedroom where she helped me into a bed warmed by a hot-water bottle, I fell immediately into a deep sleep.

Chapter 32

And there appeared an angel unto him from heaven, strengthening him.

Luke XXII. 43

My dreams were awful, full of shouting and smoke and demonic laughter. When I awoke it was light, and my hands and face were red and burning. As I held them under the cold tap in the bathroom, I thought of Zac. Somehow I had to phone him, tell him what had happened. My next thought was of Raphael. We couldn't leave him in the workshop. It probably wasn't secure.

Sarah was up and making breakfast when I came downstairs in a dressing-gown I found on the back of the bedroom door. I saw from the clock that it was nearly eight.

'We had a call from Amber,' she explained. 'We didn't want to wake you. Jeremy's gone to the hostel.'

'Why the hostel?' I repeated, more than a little dazed.

'She was hysterical,' she said. 'Someone at the hostel told her about the fire . . . she thinks it's something to do with that girl Lisa. Jeremy's gone to pour oil on troubled waters.'

'Oh,' I said. Surely oil was the last thing we needed where fire was concerned, I thought vaguely. 'He thinks Lisa might have started the fire?'

'I'm sure Amber's jumping to conclusions. The police seemed to think it a nasty prank, didn't they? Now, Fran, let's go and investigate Fenella's wardrobe. There should be something in there that'll fit you.'

The Quentins' elder daughter was a couple of sizes bigger than me, so I felt slightly ridiculous in her baggy trousers, T-shirt and sweater, but they would have to do for now. It was nine o'clock and I told Sarah I had to go over to the shop to find Zac.

It must have been one of the biggest shocks of his life. His van skewed to a halt outside and I rushed over at once as he jumped out. 'How the hell did this happen?' he demanded.

'Oh Zac,' was all I could muster, for I was crying again.

He drew me close. 'I can't believe it,' he whispered.

I stumbled out the story, and together we went to look at the ruins of *Minster Glass*.

Other people were stopping to gawp at the burned-out shop. At first sight it was awful, truly awful; a blackened morass of charred wood, broken glass and twisted metal, still smoking slightly in the cool morning air. Someone had taken a brush to the glass on the pavement, piling it all up in the doorway. Zac squatted to pull out bits of Dad's angel that were sticking up out of the heap, but shoved them back. They were clearly beyond repair. Amber would be devastated.

'Zac,' I said in a low voice, 'can we go round the back? I want to see what the workshop's like.'

He raised his eyebrows. 'You're thinking the same thing I am, aren't you?' he said. I nodded.

I slotted a key into the back door of the workshop, then discovered I'd left it unlocked after that man had helped me the night before. I wondered again who he was. His coat must be in the rectory somewhere. I should give it back.

We walked into the workshop, where wisps of smoke still hung in the air, and saw that all the surfaces were coated in a fine black dust – but nothing had actually burned. I hardly dared approach Raphael but watched Zac walk over and trace a finger lightly over the glass. He smiled and looked up. 'He's fine! He's really fine. Come and see.'

Like everything else, Raphael lay under a sooty shroud. All it would take to restore him was a soft brush and a good polish; I could see that right away. The relief was overwhelming. Once more, in his turbulent history, the angel had survived.

'Thank goodness I put this away.' Zac opened a cupboard and drew out *The Angel Book*.

'Let's take a look upstairs.' I was feeling reckless now. 'I don't think the flames got there.'

I started towards the stairs, but he shouted, 'No! Don't be a fool. We've taken enough of a risk coming in here.'

'Oh, come on,' I said, anxious now. 'I'm sure the fire hasn't destroyed the main structure.' Was my tuba OK? And I needed my clothes. The thoughts were tumbling in. What about all the books and papers and Laura's diary? And the photo of my mother?

Zac marched over and grabbed my arm. 'Fran, I know you're my boss but I'm ordering you. You're *not* to go up there.'

'All right,' I said fiercely, shaking off his arm. He looked a little hurt and I felt guilty. 'Sorry,' I said, looking around the workshop. 'It's just so awful, isn't it? To think the shop's lasted a century and a half and then this happens.' And suddenly I couldn't be brave any more. Just when I'd thought things couldn't get any worse – first with Dad, and then Ben – I'd been dealt this blow. It was a mistake to cry. My eyes, already smarting from the smoke, were now streaming and painful.

'Come on,' Zac said. We were both coughing by now. 'Let's get out of here. We can move Raphael to the garage later.'

We went next door to the café. When she brought our cappuccinos over, Anita sat down with us. 'On the house today, my loves,' she said. 'It's the least I can do. So tell me how it happened.'

'I was having some weird dream,' I said, and stopped. The dream flickered bright in my memory, then died again. 'I woke up – it must have been the smell of smoke or something. Or if it was a firework – that's what the police think – perhaps I heard it go off?'

'Did you realise it was a fire straight away?'

'Oh yes. The air smelled hot, smoky, and there were strange crackling and roaring noises.'

'I bet you were terrified,' Anita said, shuddering. 'I'd have shrieked the place down if it had been me. Here, I'll get us some more coffee.'

I told Zac about the golden-haired stranger giving me his coat and preventing my crazy plan to go into the workshop. I'd been too much in shock to think, but I might have died of smoke inhalation. 'I think my brain had really gone,' I said ruefully.

'I'm not sure it's come back, judging from just now in the shop,' said Zac.

'Charming,' I said, kicking him lightly under the table. He kicked me back and our legs locked for a moment. I felt my scorched cheeks grow hotter still.

'I could hardly believe it when I got in this morning,' Anita remarked, bringing more cappuccinos and a couple of pastries, and sliding back into her seat. 'It shocked the life out of me. You've really had it rough lately, what with your dad and everything.'

My dad. It was as though a blade had cut through me.

'We can't tell him, Zac,' I whispered.

'I know,' he replied.

By one o'clock we were all back at the vicarage eating Sarah's home-made leek and potato soup when Jeremy returned. He looked strained and exhausted.

'The police have only just gone,' he said. 'They've taken two of the girls.'

'Lisa?' I asked.

'And one called Cassie.'

'I remember her.' The pudgy girl with the miserable face and the voice of a child.

'She's a friend of Lisa's. Cassie says she and Lisa were out with a couple of young men last night. One of the boys had some fireworks. They dared Cassie to do it and she did.'

'But why our shop?'

'I think Amber's had it right all along, but not exactly right. Lisa's been very clear about her dislike for Amber and outspoken about Jo's little crisis. You're a friend of Jo's and Amber's employer. Perfect motive. The thing is, put Lisa under questioning and she gives up Cassie without a thought. She's a nasty piece of work. And now Cassie could end up in jail.'

'That's terrible.' I meant it, but my pity for Cassie was limited. I'd almost lost Dad's shop – *my* shop – and I could have been killed. I was furious. And not a little relieved that someone had been caught. 'Why've they taken Lisa?'

'They may charge her with being an accomplice. But there's something else. Another girl at the hostel was so incensed by Lisa's casual betrayal of Cassie that she revealed that Amber was right about the broken window.'

'You mean it *was* Lisa who put the paperweight through it?'

'Except it wasn't a paperweight. It was a crystal ball that

Amber's mother once gave her, and which vanished soon after Amber moved into the hostel. When you called it a paper-weight, she didn't twig what it really was. She'd given up looking for it. So Lisa is also being questioned for criminal damage. It's sad. More damaged lives and more bad publicity for St Martin's.'

'I'm sorry,' I said rather weakly. 'I seem to have caused an awful lot of trouble to you.'

'It can hardly be considered your fault,' Sarah said kindly.

'Amber must be very cut up,' I said. 'Have the police finished with her?'

'I think so, yes. They only took Cassie and Lisa down to the station. Effie, the hostel manager, has gone with them. They're meeting legal representation there.'

'Shall we go and find her, Zac?' I said. He nodded, quickly finishing his soup.

When we arrived, Amber was sitting with a member of staff in the living area. She seemed calm enough, but when we took her to see the shop she broke into racking sobs, picking up the bits of Dad's angel and trying hopelessly to fit them together.

'Amber, it's all right, really,' I said, feeling stronger as I comforted her. 'Nobody was hurt and the damage could be a great deal worse.' I hoped, as I said it, that this was indeed the case. To my untrained eye the fire had scorched the inside of the shop but hadn't burned through the beams. Everything was a disgusting mess, that was all.

We returned to the vicarage. This time, I noticed the coat I'd been lent last night, hanging on the rack in the hall, stinking of smoke. I'd need to get it cleaned before giving it back to my rescuer, whoever he was.

'I saw an angel last night,' I said to Amber, thinking it would cheer her up, but she immediately looked so enthralled that I regretted making a thing of it. I explained about the young man who had helped me but then vanished.

'Do you know anyone round here of that description?' I asked Zac, but he shook his head. 'He had an accent,' I added. 'Southern Irish, I think.'

'He could still have been an angel,' Amber said seriously.

'He didn't look angelic. Just . . . normal, really.'

'You said his hair was gold. Did you hear any music or anything?'

'Well, no, I don't think so, Amber,' I said, but something was teasing the edge of memory.

'There *was* something, wasn't there?'

'Possibly.'

'What then? A feather? Or bells? Bells is another thing people hear if they've had a visitation.'

'Definitely no bells.' But there had been singing. When was that?

'You must keep an open mind, Fran,' Amber said earnestly. 'He helped you when you were in trouble, after all.'

'If I hadn't woken up,' I said thoughtfully, 'the whole thing might have ended differently.' And now I remembered my dream – the woman singing and someone calling my name. Had it been him, the golden-haired man? No, I couldn't make it out. He wasn't the only untied end.

That evening, Jo came round to the vicarage. The Quentins tactfully left us alone together.

'I met Jeremy this afternoon,' she explained, 'and he told me what had happened. Oh Fran, I'm so glad you're all right.' She hugged me, then added, 'But I'm so sorry about the shop. Jeremy explained about Lisa and Cassie. I haven't been to work since – you know – so I'd simply no idea that all that had been brewing.'

'It's awful, isn't it?' I said. 'Of course, I don't know how extensive the damage is yet. A structural engineer is going to look tomorrow.'

'Are you all right here?' she asked, looking round the Quentins' kitchen. 'It's nice of Jeremy and Sarah to take you in, but why don't you come and stay with me for a bit?'

'Thanks,' I said, 'but I'm fine here for the moment. Can I think about it?'

'Of course.'

'How are you though?' I'd hardly seen her since the scandal broke; she'd stayed at her parents' house most of the time.

'I'm recovering,' she said. I thought she looked weary and a bit sad. 'But I've told Jeremy I want to resign.'

'Oh Jo, that's a shame. You love your job.'

'I just don't see how I can go back there. And your fire only makes it worse.'

'How do you mean?'

'Well, I suspect your shop was targeted because you were a friend of mine, and Jeremy agrees. I made him tell me.'

'*And* because I employ Amber,' I said. 'Though I suppose you'll take the blame for making me do that, too. But you'd be wrong. Lisa and Cassie are the culprits.'

'Yes, but my affair with Johnny has had its effects, hasn't it? It's made lots of other people unhappy or unsettled – his wife and family, his Party, everyone at the hostel.'

'Even so, it wasn't you who put the firework through my door.'

'No.'

'Why are you going to resign?'

'Because, intentionally or not, I've damaged the hostel and its reputation. It wouldn't feel the same working there, knowing I'd done that.'

I sighed. Put like that, I could see her point.

'Dominic's been really sweet,' Jo added. 'You know, he came down to Kent a couple of times to see me.'

'That's good of him,' I said. 'I'm sorry that I didn't. It's just been crazy here.'

'We talked on the phone though, didn't we? I didn't feel abandoned, honestly.'

'Good,' I said. 'So what are your plans now?'

'To find another job. Oh, and to catch up with what I've missed at choir. Dominic's going to help me.'

Chapter 33

What know we of the blest above but that they sing and that they love?

William Wordsworth

On Wednesday morning, the structural engineer visited and declared the building safe. I opened the door of my flat fearfully. The place stank, like the rest of the building, of smoke and damp. The carpet squelched in places as I walked through the first-floor rooms, but otherwise, amazingly, it was untouched by the fire.

The living room – the window of which I'd opened to effect my escape – had borne the worst of the water damage. Wallpaper sagged, the sofa was sodden and the carpet pooled water where I trod.

Upstairs in the attic, everything was as usual, though the appalling charred smell seemed to permeate everywhere. It seemed possible I'd never be rid of it.

I saw straight away that there wasn't much point in me trying to clear up. My business today was a rescue operation.

The night before, as we washed up after supper, Jeremy and his wife had talked seriously to me. 'We'd like you to stay with us,' Jeremy said. 'As long as you need to. I can't imagine that your flat will be liveable in now.' On that point he was certainly correct. It would feel like a derelict's squat, I thought, looking round the kitchen. I'd probably catch some horrible ague from the damp.

'Just until I can find somewhere of my own,' I said, thanking them, 'that would be lovely.'

'Now both the girls have moved out, the house feels rather empty, doesn't it, Jeremy? It would be nice to have another daughter. You can stay as long as you like.'

'That's so kind. Of course I'll give you something for my keep.' I hastily did some mental sums, wondering where the money was to come from. Nothing had really changed. All the time I'd been working at *Minster Glass* I'd not taken any wages; I'd been living off savings. Those couldn't last for ever. I'd have to find work sometime. I hoped that Jessica at the diary service hadn't forgotten my existence.

I looked round the flat now, wondering what to take with me to the vicarage. All sorts of things seemed essential – clothes, washing kit, my tuba, Laura's journal, anything really valuable. I'd have to think of Dad, too, what he might need.

I started pulling clothes out and laying them on the bed, my nose wrinkling at the smoky smell of them. My small suitcase I'd lodged on top of the wardrobe. I lifted it down and stowed the more crushable items in it. When I picked up my rucksack from the floor I found it was wet. The small bag I used to take to the hospital wasn't large enough. Did Dad keep any suit-cases? I didn't remember him using one, for he had hardly ever gone anywhere.

I went to his room. Being out of the way at the back of the flat, the carpet there was completely dry. Everything seemed undis-turbed. A brief search of his wardrobe and cupboards revealed nothing useful. I knelt down and hunted under the bed. There was his document case. I'd better take that. Behind it glinted the metal locks of a suitcase. I reached under, fumbled for the handle and pulled. The case came out easily. A good size and – I brushed off the dust and opened it – empty. Just what I needed.

I bent to take another look under the bed. There was another, smaller case, tucked right in the corner so that I had to wriggle right under the bed to reach it. The edge of the metal bedframe scraped my back painfully. This other case snagged on the springs, moved reluctantly, but then I had it. It was actually an old-fashioned vanity case of French-blue leather. At first I thought it was locked, but the catch was merely stiff; it sprang open suddenly. I lifted the lid.

Immediately I caught a faint scent of that same perfume that haunted my deepest untapped memories. It rose as though by opening her case I'd conjured the spirit of my mother. In it I saw she had kept all her make-up, glass bottles of nail varnish remover and moisturiser tethered to the side, pots of eyeshadow and lipstick and ancient crusted foundation all wiped clean, snug in tidy compartments. I lifted them out, one by one, opening some, recognising familiar names, Revlon, Max Factor, though the colours, textures and smells belonged to another age. And here was her perfume: *Arpège* by Lanvin. I eased out the stopper and sniffed. It was still strong after all these years, but not quite the same as I remembered. Not quite as it must have been on the glowing, living warmth of her skin.

But for a moment I had something: the sensation of being held close, warm and safe. A woman's laughter. A catch of husky lullaby, before the memory died.

My skin prickled. It was odd, looking round this room, to think that she had lived here, my mother. Had this been their bedroom? There was only the single bed now, though this was the biggest of the three bedrooms, so presumably it had been theirs. Not exactly glamorous. Had she minded?

As I lifted the lid to close the case, I saw a long slit in the ruffled blue lining. A pocket. My fingers slipped inside and met with paper. It was a programme, curled with age, for a choral concert at St Andrew's Hall in Norwich in March 1963. On the front cover, the name Angela Beaumont leaped out at me. Feverishly I turned the pages until I came to the biographies of the soloists. And there was her picture, the same one now in my bedroom. I sat for a moment, deep in thought. My mother was a singer. My father had never told me. Or had he, and I hadn't taken it in? I remembered once he'd said my musical talent wasn't from his side of the family, but had he actually said it had come from my mother?

I read the biography.

Angela Beaumont (contralto) was a Foundation Scholar at the Royal College of Music, where she studied with Nerys Sitwell and gained several awards, including the College Song Recital Prize and a grant from the Princess Isabella Trust. She has performed extensively in oratorio and recital throughout the British Isles . . . There followed a long list of the choirs she had sung with, notable performances she'd made and the recordings she had been a part of. It was an impressive list for a woman who must still have been only twenty-eight or twenty-nine, yet to approach the height of her career.

She never reached it.

I read the programme more closely. It included the Bach *Magnificat*, some Handel and Haydn. I imagined her, bright-eyed with the excitement of performing, leaving the stage to tremendous applause, packing up her make-up, brushing her hair, slipping the programme into her case before rushing off to the post-performance party or just to catch the train back to London and Dad.

How had Dad fitted into her life? Good old faithful Dad, back at home in his shop making beautiful things with his hands. Where on earth had they met, and what had drawn them to each other? My mother: lovely, vibrant. Dad? Well, I'd seen photographs of him as a young man in his graduate's robes, or posing by a gargoyle at Notre Dame, on a tour of French cathedrals in the late 1950s: tall, serious, shy, handsome in a sensitive, cultured way. Perhaps now that Dad was so ill – dying – I would never know. The time had come to try to find out.

Dad's document case lay on the floor beside me. With no more than a gentle protesting squeak of conscience I opened it and pulled out the folders one by one. There was his Will, which I scanned quickly. It left everything to me bar a generous sum to Zac. No less than Zac deserved. I was glad. The Living Will and Power of Attorney I knew about. I replaced these and picked up the next folder. It contained Dad's driving licence and his passport, long expired now; a sheaf of papers on health-related matters, financial documents, share certificates and details of savings accounts. His talent for administration he'd applied to his personal life. All documentation relating to the business he must have kept elsewhere. I found his marriage certificate – and here for the first time I read the names of my maternal grandparents, John and Lily Beaumont; John described as a clerk. There was a history here I could discover.

I pulled out the remaining folders greedily, flipping through my old school reports and swimming certificates, the baptism certificate signed by some past rector of St Martin's. All these I put to one side – they were mine, after all. And now there was only one folder left. I took it out, disappointed at its thinness. When I opened it, a number of newspaper cuttings floated to the floor. I picked one up. It was an obituary of my mother from the *Daily Telegraph*. I started to read it but my mind was so full I couldn't take in any of it and had to start again. The information in it was familiar from the concert programme. It praised the richness and power of her voice and said she'd died in hospital after a road accident. Another, from _The Times_, compared her voice to Kathleen Ferrier's, and others, from music publications, were almost as fulsome. There was also one in German from which the words _wunderbar Alt_ – wonderful contralto – rose from the first line, though my language skills weren't up to more than that. The sound of a woman singing played in my head, and I remembered my dream on the night of the fire. A coincidence, it must be.

I laid the fragile papers carefully back in the folder, replacing it in the document case, then checked that I'd looked at everything. I had.

But now I'd been fed a few crumbs I was hungry. I had to know whether there was anything else. My previous scruples about respecting Dad's privacy were in shreds. Scanning the shelves, I took down a couple of box-files from amidst the art books, the novels by forgotten writers, and began to search. For what, I wasn't sure; just anything about my mother.

Dad seemed to have kept everything – except what I was looking for. In one file were mementoes from his time at art college – scribbled notes from friends about meeting for tea, flyers for exhibitions, a rent book, little drawings on scraps of paper. Several battered photo albums I'd been allowed to flick through before, charted his childhood in sepia. There he was, aged about three, holding Granny's hand, both wearing wool coats buttoned up to the chin. Here was Grandad in overalls, next to a newly made arched window in the workshop. Onward. There were other people, unknown to me – friends or relatives, perhaps. _Gerry and Cynthia_ one 1960s' wedding photo was labelled, the plump bride dimple-kneed in her short dress. _Great Aunt Polly/Cuckmere Haven_ showed a perky old lady with a fox terrier on a leash, the white chalk Seven Sisters cliffs in the background.

I moved on, glancing through Dad's stamp album, illustrated school projects, a box of certificates, including his stained-glass qualifications. In another box was a portrait of Dad as a young man, smiling self-consciously for the camera through the soft studio filter. He seemed so vulnerable, so untouched by suffering that I couldn't help wanting always to picture him like this rather than as the old man who lay paralysed, ravaged by the marks of time and illness.

Finally my energy gave out. I'd found out very little about my mother and a great deal about my father instead. Perhaps that was how it should be, I thought, suddenly ashamed.

Just then, a van bearing the logo of our insurance company pulled up outside. Two men got out and came into the shop below, where I could hear them moving things around and talking. Slotting the final box back in its place on the shelf, I went downstairs.

Chapter 34

We are never so lost our angels cannot find us.

Stefanie Powers in *Angels – Beyond the Light*

Later, Jeremy helped me lug bags and boxes across the Square to the vicarage and we piled them upstairs in one of the spare bedrooms. After a bite of lunch I returned to the workshop, where I'd agreed to meet Zac. Together we moved Raphael to a locked garage then went for coffee.

It was a quiet patch in the café and, since it was Anita's afternoon off and the young girl who served us was busy chatting to her boyfriend on the phone, we had the place to ourselves.

Zac looked tired and worn, as though he hadn't slept. The fire had been a tremendous shock for him, worse than for me perhaps, because my livelihood didn't depend on it like his did, and I hadn't been going there every day for twelve years.

'You'll carry on getting paid, of course,' I said, secretly hoping the finances would stand it, 'until we work out what's happening. How long it'll all take to redecorate and so on.'

He looked hard at me. 'You definitely want to keep it all going?'

I'd spent the small hours thinking about this, and when I

woke this morning I had felt certain. 'Yes,' I said firmly. 'Even though Dad won't come back.' We had to be honest about this now. 'I want to run the business, with you as manager if I'm away.'

I watched his face and was glad to see some of the tension drain from it.

I touched his hand. 'I've got to go back to the music for a bit, Zac. I hope I won't need to be too much abroad, because of Dad, but it's difficult to promise. I have to take what's given me, you see.' Learning that my mother was a musician had somehow strengthened my resolve. My music was a part of me and I didn't want to ever let it go.

'But Fran, do you think I could carry on using the workshop now, I mean? Keep the business ticking over? It would be important for custom.'

'I'm not sure it would be very nice,' I demurred. 'And it might be dangerous. Anyway, at some point you'd be in the way of the workmen.'

'There's another thing I wanted to ask you,' he said, leaning forward. 'If you were refurbishing, there are things we could do – to modernise. I'm sure all the electrical work and stuff will have to conform to regulations anyway, but we could bring everything up to date. Get new equipment.'

I felt suddenly nostalgic for our little bow-windowed shop with its worn wooden fittings and tiled porch. 'I suppose so, Zac, but I loved it as it was.'

'We could keep that look, Fran, but have a modern workshop, with great lighting.'

I knew he was right. Instead of seeing it as a tragedy, we could view this as an opportunity. But I wasn't ready for that yet. 'Let's talk about it more,' I said, 'once we hear back from the insurance company.'

It was hard to escape the feeling that, just when I'd been remaking my life, getting used to managing the shop, putting down roots, it was all being taken away from me. Well, I'd fight for it. I'd get it back. *Minster Glass* was Dad's. And I would make it mine, too.

While we were finishing our coffee, the door behind the counter opened and a man came in. I watched him as he greeted the waitress, who paused long enough in her conversation to take his order. He was slim and neat, slightly round-shouldered, with an unremarkable face and short gingery hair. He pulled his wallet out of his jeans but the waitress waved him away and started to grill bacon, the phone still clamped to her ear.

The man turned round and I realised I knew him. Our eyes met and recognition dawned in his.

'Hello, didn't we . . .?' he said.

'You were there the other night,' I interrupted, getting up.

'The fire. I've been to look. It's terrible. Are you all right now?' He came nearer and peered at me anxiously.

'I'm fine. Zac, this is—'

'Larry. Larry Finnegan. I live upstairs here.' So this was the mysterious lodger Anita had sometimes mentioned. No angel at all. I burst out laughing, imagining Amber's disappointed face.

'What's so funny?' he asked, so I explained.

'Me, an angel? Now my ma back in Killarney would think that a miracle. No, I'm no angel. Off to work, I was, and saw the place ablaze, and you sitting there like you'd fallen out of the sky.'

'I suppose I had, in a way.'

The girl, still talking, held up a plate with his sandwich on it and he went and fetched it to our table.

'Terrible about the shop,' he said to both of us. 'I'm so sorry for you.'

'Lucky you weren't burned in your bed, Larry.'

'Lucky I wasn't even in it. Sorry I had to run off after. I would have been late for work and you seemed in good hands.'

'You work nights?'

'On the reception desk at the Hyde Park Hotel. But I'm starting a management course soon, so I won't be a night owl much longer.' There was something gentle, easy and charming about him.

'So this girl who believes in angels . . .' he said.

'Do you know her? She works in the shop.'

'Would that be the lovely dark one?'

'The *other* lovely dark one,' said Zac, smiling.

'Yes, that's Amber,' I said, frowning at Zac.

'We've never been introduced, but she's a fine-looking girl,' Larry said solemnly. 'And my ma would approve of the angels.'

'I'll send Amber in with your coat then, if you'll tell me when's a good time,' I said, and his friendly face creased up with mirth.

'You do that,' he said.

The vicar and his wife couldn't have been kinder. Sarah Quentin had clearly been brought up with the idea that good food cured heartache, for tonight there were huge helpings of steak and kidney pie, and a crumble made with apples from the vicarage's solitary fruit tree. When I told them about Larry, the vicar was highly amused.

'He makes me think of our patronal St Martin, giving his coat to a beggar, don't you think so, Sarah?'

'Are you calling me a beggar?' I asked. 'Well, I suppose I'm homeless, for the moment at least.'

After supper Jeremy slipped his napkin into its ring and said, 'I'm taking a service at eight. A memorial service for All Souls

Day, when we remember the dead. The singing's rather lovely. Perhaps you'd like to come, Fran?'

So I went and sat at the back and indeed, the service was beautiful, with Ben's little Sunday choir singing excerpts from Fauré's *Requiem* between the readings. I found it hard to concentrate though, thinking over everything that had happened and all that I'd discovered about my mother. I vowed to speak to Jeremy about that.

'How are you?' Ben asked me afterwards, coming up with his arms full of robes and hymnbooks, his brow furrowed with concern. It gave me a lump in my throat just to look at him.

'Still in shock, I think. Thanks so much for helping me.'

'Not at all. I wish I could do more.'

So do I, I wanted to say. We both looked at the floor and shuffled our feet.

'Thank you again, Ben, that was very moving,' said Jeremy, emerging from the vestry. 'Now, Fran, I wanted to show you exactly where I thought the angel could go.'

He told Ben he'd lock up, then led me into the Lady Chapel. The coloured glass was dark and lifeless without sunlight streaming through it. He showed me the ugly old cupboard that had been built in front of the third window. 'We can have this taken out, you see. Perhaps re-site it on the other side of this wall, if anyone insists. Then, Bob's your uncle, we can hang the angel in front of this window.'

The window he indicated was, as far as I could tell, of exactly the same dimensions as the one the angel had fallen out of.

'I know it's a silly thing to ask now, but do you think that the colours will go well with the Memorial window?' I wondered.

'We'll have to look at it again in daylight,' mused Jeremy. 'Bring Raphael in here and put them side by side.'

'It had better work out,' I said. 'Zac will kill me otherwise.'

'I'm positive it will,' said Jeremy, laughing.

The church was empty now. Even Ben had gone.

'Jeremy . . .' I faltered.

At the same time, he said 'Fran . . .' He looked at me enquiringly. 'You first,' he prompted.

'I found something today. I need to ask you – it's about my mother.'

'Of course. Let's sit down here, shall we?'

'I found some papers in the flat. A programme for a concert my mother was in and some obituaries of her. I hadn't even realised that she was a musician.'

'A very fine contralto, I believe,' he said. He looked troubled, I thought, as though mentally wrestling with something. In the quiet darkness, though her features were hidden, I became aware of Mary in the window; sensed her calm joy.

'I need to know more about her, Jeremy.'

Finally, he seemed to decide.

'Since our previous conversation on the subject of your mother,' he began, 'I have thought deeply about the matter. I have considered your father and what he would want. In the end, I went to see him last week and sat with him and asked his permission to give you a letter he wrote, and which he meant you to have in the event of his death. I cannot honestly say that he heard me and understood, and I certainly can't say that he assented, but I felt a kind of peace after that. I know, because he told me a few months ago that he intended to pluck up the courage to talk to you, so I do believe that I am doing as he would have wanted.'

'A letter. You never mentioned that before.'

'No. Perhaps I should have done, but I wasn't sure until recently that he would wish it. Let me explain. Back in May, your father came to see me in a troubled state of mind. He said that he had something on his conscience that he wanted to confide in me and which he needed my advice about. I think the talking itself, handing the burden of his knowledge over to another human being, helped him immensely. He felt guilty, you see; a deep guilt that froze him up inside. Those are the words he used, I remember – "frozen up inside". He said he felt he had wasted his life because of this.

'It took some perseverance on my part to make him say more. As you know, he is a very private man and uncomfortable with the language of emotions. I think he felt particularly regretful about you – that he had never given you enough of himself. The past was always with him, you see. He could never allow himself to move on, to concentrate on the things that matter in the here and now. Especially you.'

'Oh Dad!' I cried out. 'Jeremy, why did it take him so long to see this?'

'It's very sad, isn't it? I tried to reassure him about his fathering, Fran. Bringing up children is hard, very hard, and there are many things I regret doing or not doing with regard to my own girls. But I had my wonderful Sarah, where he had no one to help him bring you up, my dear. And, if you don't mind me saying so, I look at you and think, Well, he did a pretty good job.'

My smile must have been mournful, for Jeremy patted my arm in a reassuring fashion before going on.

'Before I give you the letter, I'd like to explain something of your father's frame of mind when he wrote it. It might help you understand him better.'

I nodded, so he continued.

'Your father referred frequently to some secret matter which I discerned to be at the heart of his trouble. He questioned me persistently about what sins I felt might be unforgivable. I tried to explain that there is no sin God would not forgive the truly repentant sinner. But he could not accept this, said that surely saying sorry was not enough, that one must somehow earn forgiveness by a sort of spiritual hard labour. And that it was all far too late anyway.'

Here, Jeremy shook his head. 'Of course, I told him that true repentance meant turning away from his old state of mind and being willing to be reborn in the Spirit, that following the Way of the Cross was no easy option. I urged him first towards confession, when he was ready, as that was the first stage: to acknowledge and understand what one had done wrong, to let the dead weight of it fall away. And finally, one day, he began to take this step. He told me about your mother and the circumstances of her death.'

Jeremy seemed to run out of breath here, and closed his eyes as though to recover strength. I waited, a perverse part of me not wanting him to go on. *My mother's death.* All I knew was that she had died in hospital after a road accident. Suppose whatever it was I was about to learn changed everything unbearably. I almost got up and walked out.

As though sensing this, Jeremy opened his eyes and said to me, 'She was beautiful, your mother, heart-stoppingly beautiful. He showed me a photograph once . . .'

'I know,' I said icily, for it still rankled that Dad had never shown me.

'Yes,' he said, his eyes steady, meeting mine, 'of course you do. Sarah is right. You do look very much like your mother in that picture.'

'Do you think that was part of the problem?' I said, it occurring to me for the first time. 'That I reminded him too much of her?'

'There might be an element of that, yes, but more importantly, he feared that you wouldn't forgive him for what he'd done, which was to take your mother away from you.'

'What do you mean?'

'He felt responsible for her death, Fran.'

Now I was almost sick with fear, but I couldn't take the uncertainty any more. 'Jeremy,' I said, 'where is the letter? I must have it.'

'Strangely enough, Fran, I have it with me.' He drew an envelope out of his inside pocket and passed it to me.

Frances Morrison, it said on the front. *To be opened in the event of her father's death.*

With the smallest of hesitations, I opened the envelope and unfolded the thick wad of paper I found inside. It was dated 1st July 1993, four months earlier.

> *My dear Fran,*
> *If you are reading this letter, it is because I have failed finally and for ever in my duty to tell you things that you have a right to know. As I write this, I pray you never have to read these words; that instead I will have found the opportunity and the courage to say them to you face to face and can destroy this letter. But I still fear to tell you in person, my dear daughter, because I fear to lose whatever love you have left for me. I fear to lose your respect. I fear rejection. And I fear all these things precisely because I love you so much. You might not believe this, coming from your dry, grumpy old dad, but it's true. From the very first moment I held you in my arms, I wanted to protect you from all harm, to give you everything a father should. I could not predict that I would fail you so badly and so soon.*

For a moment the words were a blur of tears and I had to stop reading. Dad was finally saying all the things I needed to hear. 'Jeremy,' I said shakily, holding out the letter, 'can you read it to me, please. I can't seem to . . .'

'Of course.' He took the letter, angled it so that it caught the light, and after he found his place, read aloud in his clear, expressive voice.

'"I'm proud of you, Fran. Despite my mismanagement you've grown up beautiful and talented and independent. I know we've drifted apart and bitterly regret my stupidity, my lies and evasions. I miss you and long for you to come home. When we speak on the phone, why can I never manage to forget my pride and ask you to visit? Pride and guilt and grief have imprisoned me for too long. Jeremy has made me see this. But maybe it's all too late. All I can do now is to tell you the truth, the truth I should have told you years ago, and to beg your forgiveness.

'"I will start by telling you how I met your mother. It was at a Christmas concert at a church in North London. She sang that old German carol *"Es ist ein Ros entsprungen"* with such deep emotion that I was entranced. She was particularly beautiful that night. She wore a long black dress, shot through with crimson that matched her lips. Her hair was pinned up on her head and sparkled with jewels.

'"After the concert the singers mingled with the audience for mulled wine and mince pies. Angela stood among a group of her friends, joining in their conversation, but looking a little tired. The musician friend I'd come with caught me staring at her and offered to introduce us. She seemed even lovelier close to and had such a beautiful smile. I managed to produce some vaguely intelligent comment about the music and found her so easy to talk to, so confiding. We conversed for some time, about Bach and about her career. I discerned from one or two passing comments that she wasn't entirely at home in this cultured, well-heeled crowd. Her father worked as a clerk for Suffolk County Council and securing her training had been a real struggle. She aroused in me both protectiveness and admiration. Later, when I left, I found her on the steps of the church looking lost. I hailed a taxi for her, but we ended up sharing it, since Westminster was only a step beyond Pimlico where she had a room in someone's house.

"'By the time I stepped out of the taxi at *Minster Glass* I had her phone number carefully written on the concert programme in my breast pocket.

"'We began to meet regularly. Angela's training was based in London at this time and I went to hear her whenever she performed. At other times, we visited art exhibitions together, or the opera. I tried to share with her my love of church architecture, art and stained glass.

"'Before long, I found myself, for the first and only time in my life, deeply in love. And I could hardly believe my luck when she told me she felt the same way.

"'Our courtship was the most wonderful time – full of art and music and the excitement of discovering each other. We were a couple of innocents. We didn't think about the hows and wheres of the future, just the why: that we wanted to be together. She was a very passionate person – quite impulsive and vital. She also had a fragile side that showed itself in lapses in confidence, and I was glad to be there to help her. I tried to be strong and reassuring; was proud that she seemed to lean on me.

"'We got married the Christmas after we met, quietly at her parents' church in Ipswich, with her younger sister as bridesmaid. My parents both being dead, there was only my father's Aunt Polly there for me, and the musician friend who'd introduced us acting as best man. We moved into the flat above *Minster Glass*.

'"At first, we were terribly happy together. I worked in the shop all day while she went off to rehearse. In the evenings I would go to hear her sing. She had a voice like an angel. Angie, my angel. Once she gave me a tie-pin of an angel; lapis lazuli set in gold. I have it still . . ."'

'So that's where it came from,' I burst out. I rummaged in my handbag for the little brooch I'd rescued from the workshop floor.

'That's it,' Jeremy said, taking it from me, holding it so it gleamed in the candlelight. 'He carried it with him always.'

He passed it back to me and took up the letter once more.

'"Over the next couple of years, Angie's career began to take off. She was invited to perform all around the country and this, of course, Fran, was still a time when wives were expected to put their husbands before professional duties. I did my best to be encouraging. When work allowed I would travel with her, but that couldn't be often. And sometimes she was invited abroad and I didn't go at all.

'"Two years passed and the strains began to show. She seemed to be away so much. I could have stood her absences; it was her attitude when she came back that hurt me more. I could see that she was changing. She seemed less content with our life together. The criticisms started. The flat was difficult to make nice. Couldn't we move? she asked. But actually she didn't put much effort into making it nice. She always said she was bored by housework and cooking. She wanted to go out and eat in restaurants and have fun, which I didn't enjoy particularly, and couldn't afford, and then I felt belittled when she said she'd pay. She told me we needed to move somewhere smarter where she could invite people back. I wasn't comfortable with that idea. Her musical friends could be quite clique-ey and I often felt left out.

'"Of course, in the end I wished that I'd gone along with her desire to move, even if it had meant scrimping and saving, but which of us can see into the future? At the time it seemed as though she wasn't just criticising the flat but me as well, and so I held out."'

'Maybe that's not how she meant it though,' I couldn't help interrupting. 'Perhaps she just wanted him to share the camaraderie of this exciting life she had.' This letter was, of course, all from Dad's side and I felt some need to stand up for my mother. 'Sorry,' I said. 'Do go on.'

'"And then",' Jeremy read, '"Angela found that she was pregnant. We were stunned, having discussed the matter of starting a family and decided to put it off for a few years.

'"Your mother was very anxious all the way through her pregnancy. She was worried about how a baby would affect her work, for she could hardly travel so much once she had you. But it wasn't just that. She was affected psychologically. She had scares about her health, didn't sleep well and became convinced that people were breaking into the flat as we lay in our bed. But despite all these anxieties, we obviously hoped that our relationship would be closer when you were born, that you would draw us together again".

'That's a great responsibility for a small baby, saving its parents' marriage,' Jeremy said with a sigh. He read on.

'"For a while, after your arrival, everything was blissful. You were a quiet baby, who slept through the night almost at once. Her friends used to remark on how easy you were. After a few months, with the help of a part-time nanny, your mother was able to resume her singing in London. And she found she enjoyed looking after a baby. In fact, we were both absolutely besotted with you".'

Tears slipped down my face, and when Jeremy looked up and

saw them he fell into silence. One of the candles on the altar flickered and died with a breath of smoke. He looked at his watch and slowly folded the letter. 'Come on,' he said gently, 'we'd better go back. Sarah will be sending out search-parties. Shall we read more later? Or tomorrow even?'

'Tomorrow,' I said. 'I'm exhausted.' Then: 'Thank you,' I told him, as he locked up. I felt immensely grateful to him for being there with me.

That night I slept badly, thoughts about Dad's letter rushing like crazy round my head. In the morning, I got out everything about my mother that I'd rescued from the flat and looked at it with new eyes. Here was her photograph, still tucked into the Burne-Jones book she gave Dad. This must have been how she looked round about the time that they met, her eyes filled with life and hope.

I took the photograph and the concert programme with me when I went with Zac to see Dad that afternoon. Even if Dad couldn't see the picture or hear what I had to tell him, it helped me to talk to Zac about my mother in Dad's presence. Who knew what Dad might absorb from our conversation. Zac didn't say much, just, 'She's very lovely,' when I showed him the portrait.

That evening after dinner, Jeremy and I repaired to the lumpy armchairs in his study. He messed about getting the gas fire working, cursing it in a quite unChristian fashion. Finally, satisfied, he retrieved Dad's letter from his desk drawer and settled down in his chair.

'Are you sure you're up to this?' he asked me.

'I need to know,' I replied.

He began to read again.

'"When you were one year old, your mother left you behind

in order to travel to Germany for a series of concerts. Her own mother came to stay to help out as I had to work and, anyway, I didn't feel confident about the care of a baby. These days, young chaps change nappies at the drop of a hat. I'd never changed a nappy in my life.

'"She returned a week later and it was instantly clear that something about her was different. Some door was closed against me. She still looked after you tenderly, but with me she seemed distracted. I knew, with a sense of panic, that we were growing further and further apart, but I had no idea what to do about it. My resentment grew and festered.

'"Every time she went on tour she would leave you with me, no longer encouraging me to accompany her. In fact, she told me it was bad for you to be carted around like a bag of shopping and that, although she missed you, it was better that you stayed at home with me. When your grandmother couldn't come I depended on the nanny but, more and more, I would find myself in sole charge and was surprised to find that I enjoyed looking after you.

'"This went on until after your second birthday and then came June the twenty-third, that awful night in 1965. I've been over and over it so many times it's difficult to remember exactly what happened, but I'll do my best. Angela arrived home in the early hours of the morning, and woke me in terrible distress. She wouldn't tell me what was wrong and we quarrelled. Eventually, it all came out. She had been having an affair with another musician – a young English tenor whom she'd met on the Berlin tour. She was deeply in love with him, she told me. She looked white and exhausted, but I had no interest in her pain. I was incandescent with rage, but determined not to show it. I told her to go. She came out with some story that the affair was over, that she had come back, wanted to mend things. But

I wouldn't hear her. I was too angry, didn't want to know. She had spoiled everything for ever. I had adored her, had given her all of myself, but she had thrown it all away. I couldn't bear to look at her".'

I cried out then, and Jeremy stopped reading. 'That's so like Dad,' I whispered. I remembered the few times I had seen my father really angry with me, how cold his anger could be, how he would withdraw from me for days until I was frantic with grief, and then he'd suddenly relent. Perhaps that's how he ended up with so few friends. If he gave his loyalty he expected loyalty and obedience in return. Like King Cophetua, whose image he had ripped from my wall, he had adored his beggar maid, and she had spurned him. She was given no second chance.

'Go on,' I told Jeremy gently. He found his place on the page.

'"I left the room, returning a moment or two later with you in my arms. I wanted to hurt Angela, show her what she was losing. I told her to say goodbye to you and leave. I said I would sue for divorce and for custody of you. And, since she had spent so much time away from home, I felt in justice it would be granted to me.

'"Angela gave a great cry of despair and tried to take you from me, but I pushed her off. She cried that she had nowhere to go, so I told her roughly to go to her lover. It was then she impressed upon me that this option was no longer open to her. 'Go home to your parents then,' I said wildly, and pulling her suitcase from the top of the wardrobe I threw it to her. I watched her pack a few clothes, then pick up her handbag and her vanity case. She cried goodbye to you – an anguished goodbye that I still hear in my dreams – and went downstairs.

'"It is useless to speculate how the situation might have been redeemed, had what happened next not taken place. Don't think

I haven't been tortured by such speculations for the rest of my life. Maybe, once we'd both calmed down, we would have found some way forward. But alas, we were never given the chance.

'"I walked with you over to the window. The scene that unfolded there is forever imprinted on my memory. I saw her step out into the road and turn to look up at the window, with an expression of desolation that haunts me still. Desolation turned to terror as a car, full of partygoers, accelerated round the corner and knocked her down. We rushed down to the street but there was nothing I could do. She died in hospital later that night".'

Jeremy stopped. I stared at the opposite wall, playing it all out in my mind. *I had been there* – I had heard them quarrel – but the memory of it was, thankfully, lost to me. I had been with my father when he ran down to the street, when the ambulance came, when they'd taken her away, my mother. I imagined myself crying, screaming for her, understanding that something had gone terribly wrong but not knowing what. But I couldn't remember a thing about that night. I could only remember the way she used to hold me close; the pattern of a dress – the scent of her.

'Are you all right, my dear?' Jeremy asked quietly.

I nodded mechanically. Then after a moment I said, 'He killed her – that's what he thought, didn't he? That he killed her.'

'"That is the burden that I have carried all these years",' Jeremy read on. '"That my anger and callousness contributed to her death. I robbed you of your mother, Fran, and I can never forgive myself. I have always been afraid to tell you about her, not only because it's so painful for me, but because I feared to lose you, too. I thought you would hate me if you learned that I caused her death. If you grew up in innocence of her, I believed that you wouldn't miss her; that you would be happy. Lately

I've come to see that I was wrong. I regret the deep silence between us, the gulf I long to cross. I pray for the courage to cross it before it is too late. I remain, despite everything, Your loving father, Edward".'

Jeremy's voice ceased. We both sat for a long while without speaking.

My father had caused the death of Angela, his beautiful angel. I remembered the angel in the shop window, now a mess of smashed glass and twisted lead. It had been made in memory of her, my mother. I suddenly knew this for sure. *Each man kills the thing he loves.* That was Oscar Wilde, wasn't it? My thoughts were rambling now.

'Did you know everything he'd written, Jeremy?' I asked.

'He told me most of it, yes,' Jeremy replied.

'Do you believe his version of events? That he was guilty?'

'The important thing is that *he* still considered himself guilty, years after the event. Of course, the coroner would have looked at the matter more objectively. A woman walked into the road without looking and was knocked down by a car, driven by a drunk, which was undoubtedly going too fast. Put like that, your father deserves no blame. The driver of the car apparently spent a year of his three-year sentence in prison. Your father spent a lifetime in hell. It destroyed his relationship with your mother's family. He couldn't bear to see their suffering, so in the end it was easiest not to see them at all.'

I'd lost them, too. I remembered my argument with Dad over my grandmother's legacy – that when she died he hadn't even told me. I had no memory of my mother's parents at all.

I ran my fingers along the faded chintz of the chair's arm and pulled at a loose thread.

'What did you say to him?' I asked. I didn't know what to feel. Was I angry with my father, or sorry for him? The course of my life was decided by the events of that night so long ago, and yet I felt emotionally detached from the whole business. My father had taken the blame. He'd done his time. Now he was an old man lying in a coma. Ready for release.

'I asked him many questions about his version of events,' Jeremy continued. 'It was important that he work it all out for himself – I always feel that with people. He seemed relieved that he had told someone. It's an old cliché, isn't it, to "get something off one's chest"? But that's what it can feel like, that something heavy has been weighing down on one, like the dead albatross around the Ancient Mariner's neck, and then – one hack of the knife, so to speak, and it's gone, you're free.

'He gradually came to see that the situation was more complex than he had allowed it to be; that your mother had to share something of the guilt. It didn't help that soon after her death he had a letter from Angela's lover, a man who grieved but who clearly wished to shift any blame onto your father. He explained how the end of their relationship had come about: that he had requested she leave her husband and child and come to him and she had refused. This man implied that Angela had been too frightened of your father to leave him. In his letter he twisted everything, making Edward appear a kind of ogre. And Edward, I'm afraid, allowed himself to be swayed by this impression, believing that by taking all these accusations upon himself he was enduring the punishment he deserved.'

'But he wasn't an ogre, was he? From what you say it doesn't sound as if he deserved any of this.'

'Look into your heart, Fran,' Jeremy said quietly. 'What kind of man do you believe your father to be?'

It didn't take long to decide my answer. 'Like most of the rest of us. Basically a good person.' Dad was never an easy man. Sometimes he was moody. He was someone who found it hard to forgive and who feared he could not be forgiven in return. I remembered his gentleness with me; yet he could on occasions be irritable, strict – even fierce. But an ogre? I was never frightened of him. He was never violent.

'That's what I think, too,' said Jeremy. 'I'm sure of it, in fact. And I'm certain that he was coming to realise it. But he was only at the beginning of a long spiritual journey when he was struck down. Now we must trust that God in His great mercy will help him complete that journey.'

I longed to be where I might weep for that two-year-old girl who, long ago, lost her beautiful mother, and whose father was cast into a prison of his own making.

But there was one question to which I had as yet no answer. I told Jeremy about my dream on the night of the fire; the woman's lovely singing and the urgent voice that woke me.

'Do you believe it could have been more than a dream?'

'There are many instances in the Bible where angels spoke to people in dreams. Why shouldn't this still happen today?'

I experienced a rush of relief that Jeremy believed me.

'I'd like to think of that as the explanation,' I told him. 'Nothing else makes sense.'

Chapter 35

If some people really see angels where others see only empty space, let them paint the angels: only let not anybody else think they can paint an angel, too.

John Ruskin

LAURA'S STORY

It was September and the windows had been finished two months before, but in the general atmosphere of unrest, Mr Bond was uncertain about whether to continue with their installation. Mrs Brownlow was beside herself with distress. The benefactress's nephew was pragmatic. Mr Brownlow was pulled all ways.

'It's not as though the windows won't be installed at some point.' Pulling on her hat and gloves in the hall, Laura heard her father's voice drift from the morning room. 'Bond suggests we delay, given the effect they might have on certain members of the parish.'

'But I thought you said we shouldn't give in to these people.' She had to strain to hear her mother's gentle tones.

'Not give in, dearest, no. But remember what the Bishop advised: we should continue to assist the police to find the culprits, but not go out of our way to provoke further discontent.'

'But James, we've paid for the angel window ourselves and the other is decreed by a Will. It's not as though these people can argue that we've used church money to take bread out of others' mouths. All can use the church and have the benefit of these beautiful windows.'

'I agree with you heartily, Dora. However, these persons don't see the matter in such terms. There is a risk that they might seek to destroy the stained glass, and what then? All our efforts will have been wasted. I am the last person to want to hide our light under a bushel, but I'm bound to listen to the Bishop's advice – which is also Mr Bond's.'

Laura had to move aside hastily as her father emerged from the drawing room. He muttered an apology to her and retreated to his study. That, she knew, would be the last they saw of him until luncheon. She peeped around the door of the morning room to see her mother bent over her writing desk.

'Mama, do you need Polly this morning?'

Her mother looked up. 'Ah, Laura, I thought you'd gone for your walk. I'm glad you're still here, dear, there's a message come from . . .' she consulted a sheet of thin, yellow paper '. . . a Mr Murray – a neighbour of our Miss Badcoe. It seems Miss Badcoe has taken to her bed "with her chest", the man says, and is asking for me. Since I've a meeting with the Missionary Committee this morning I wondered if you'd go. By all means, take Polly. Ask Cook to pack you a basket.'

Laura had meant to walk across Vauxhall Bridge Road to Pimlico, to Mr Russell's address in Lupus Street; she was most put out by her mother's request. But she could hardly refuse, not least because she'd have to reveal the true nature of her outing.

She cheered up on reading the address that her mother passed her, realising that it wasn't too far out of her way. Very well, she would call on the elderly lady first, then continue on to Philip's. His invitation said there was someone he wanted her to meet. She hoped she wouldn't miss whoever it was.

Goose Lane was a mews running off Greycoat Street on the other side of the church, in the direction of Westminster Abbey. Laura had often noticed its name, painted in wobbly capitals on the wall of the corner building, but she'd never been down it before. It was muddy, gloomy and silent, the tall terraced houses blocking out sunlight.

Laura and Polly had to rap on the knocker of number 4 several times before they heard slow footsteps on the stairs and a stooped old man peeped around the door.

'Mr Murray?' enquired Laura. Relief crossed the man's creased face as she introduced herself.

'Mind the 'ole,' he said in a reedy voice as he beckoned them upstairs, and they swung their skirts around a confused area of the hall floor where the boards had split and someone had made a cack-handed job of fixing it. They trudged up seemingly endless wooden stairs, Mr Murray stopping several times to take his breath. Then they stopped at a door on the second landing. Mr Murray rapped twice and on hearing a groan from within, turned the handle. He showed the ladies into the room and withdrew, shutting the door behind him.

Inside was more bare wooden floor. The smell of damp clothes and naphthalene could not quite disguise that of unwashed human body. On a single bedstead to one side of the room near the fireplace, a frail figure huddled under a heap of blankets and coats, coughing horribly in between rasping breaths.

'Miss Badcoe, it's Laura Brownlow. Mama sent me . . . I'm so sorry you're ill . . .' Laura faltered as she met Miss Badcoe's desperate expression. The Miss Badcoe she knew from church was straight-backed, formal, neatly turned out, if forty years behind the fashion. Her boots were always polished, her gloves clean, her bonnet standing to attention along with the rest of her.

If Laura had ever given the woman a second thought – which, she had to confess, she probably hadn't – she would have imagined her living anywhere but here, in this bare room. It wasn't quite a hovel, but . . . Laura looked round the room while Polly helped the old lady sit up and began to rearrange the bedclothes for her, trying to plump up the thin, lumpy pillows.

The grate was full of cold ashes, the coal scuttle empty. There was at least a basin with a cold water tap, Laura noted. It stood by the only window, the curtains of which sagged half-open to reveal, through sooty glass, the grim back view of an edifice identical to this one.

'Shall I go to buy coal, miss?' Polly was asking her.

Laura gave her some money for coal, milk and soap, then asked Miss Badcoe which room Mr Murray inhabited, intending to see if he had hot water. He proved to be next door and promised to boil some right away. 'I give her tea this morning,' he whined, 'but I can't hardly manage myself now. I ain't no damned use to a lady by any method, begging yer pardon, miss.' His eyes glittered with wicked humour. Laura, nervous of him, retreated. When, several minutes later, he hobbled in with a steaming kettle, she told him to place it by the fire and dropped a couple of coins into his hand.

Her mind whirled as she set about her tasks, brewing a pot of tea from the scrapings in a caddy, taking out the food Mrs Jorkins had given her. She poured a bowl of warm water, found a worn towel and a tiny sliver of soap by the basin, then gently washed the sick woman's face and neck, brushed her straggly ash-coloured hair. Polly returned and soon a fire crackled in the grate, though the smoke made Miss Badcoe cough. The chimney badly needed sweeping.

All the time, running through Laura's mind, were thoughts of Miss Badcoe, present at every Sunday-morning service; Miss Badcoe polishing brass, arranging flowers; Miss Badcoe, eschewing the hassocks, always kneeling direct on the stone floor to pray; Miss Badcoe, who was Mrs Fotherington's cousin – 'on her father's side', as Miss Badcoe liked to add with a sniff. Laura didn't recall the ladies ever even sitting together. She thought of Mrs Fotherington – lively, loud-voiced, with her strong views about everything and her fine house in Vincent Square. Mrs Fotherington, who had left all her money to the church and to her dear nephew (on her mother's side) Stuart Jefferies; but nothing, it seemed, to this impoverished cousin. Of course, one didn't know the background – who might have quarrelled with whom, or whether Mrs Fotherington had ever known the true circumstances of her father's sister's daughter, but even so, there was injustice here, Laura couldn't help thinking.

She reached for one of the line of grimy storage tins, in search of sugar for the tea. *Salt*, *Sago*, *Sugar* the labels read in careful spindly letters, the capital Ss as ornate as little harps. There was something about those ornate Ss that bothered her. She'd seen them before . . . in a letter! A letter that she'd picked up from her father's desk. S for Scarlet. *Scarlet woman*.

Suddenly, revelation dawned. Miss Badcoe was the secret letter-writer. Her mother's worn face flashed into her mind, she saw dull defeat in her father's eyes. For one wild second, she was so angry she felt like tipping the tea into Miss Badcoe's lap. Then her vision cleared and she forced herself to focus with pity once more on this ailing bag of bones. Here was an elderly woman who had no one who loved her, no one *to* love; she would die unnoticed and unmourned unless she, Laura Brownlow, did something about it.

She knelt down by the bed and helped Miss Badcoe sip her tea. Behind her, Polly waited for the fire to establish itself and hung a can of broth to warm. Laura sent her out to return the kettle to Mr Murray. When the door closed she said, 'Miss Badcoe, it's you, isn't it, who writes those letters to my father.'

The sick woman became as still as an old gnarled tree; her mouth set rigid like a knothole in the bark. She said nothing, only stared into the distance. Laura took the cup from her unresisting hands.

'Miss Badcoe, I know it's you, and I'm going to tell my father. He'll tell Mr Bond and soon everybody will know.'

She waited, watching Miss Badcoe consider all this. Finally the woman crumpled and wept.

'Whatever's the matter?' asked Polly, coming back into the room. Seeing Laura's stern look she made to withdraw again, but Laura called out to her to go and fetch a doctor.

'Miss Badcoe, why did you do it?' Laura hissed. 'Do you know what misery you've caused?'

In between tears and coughing fits, the old lady confessed.

For years and years, Ivy Badcoe had done her duty in life. She'd nursed her parents as they aged, sickened and died, losing all chance of marriage and having a family of her own. Her father had mismanaged his money and Ivy was left with practically nothing except her pride. Sunday after Sunday she had attended divine service, kept up appearances, placed her mite in the collection, done her duty in various ways. Yet, somehow, she was never noticed, never cared for; her stiff pride, her formal manners, kept everyone at a distance. She was one of those for whom society seemed to have no role but to assist others; she herself was not deemed to have a right to anything – not love, companionship or attention. She had watched the parish poor receive charity – indeed, she had contributed herself where she could, never thinking that she should ask for help in return. Oh no, her parents would have turned in their grave.

She must have watched with some puzzlement as the Reverend Brownlow bestowed riches upon the church: beautiful new altar linen, with different sets for all the church seasons; the gold candlesticks; a jewel-encrusted processional cross. Her eyes were dazzled by all this beauty, she told Laura, but as the years passed and her limbs ached more and her breath grew shorter, she became frightened and her resentment grew. When Sarah Fotherington died and left part of her wealth to make a window, leaving nothing for her impoverished Cousin Ivy, something broke in Miss Badcoe's heart.

When Laura questioned her, she insisted that she had nothing to do with the violence to church property – nay, she abhorred it – but the vandalism inspired a way in which she could safely express her feelings. In anonymous letters she could pour out her hatred and frustration without anyone knowing who it was. But now everyone would know, she finished sadly, and she might as well be dead.

'Oh really, it's not that bad,' said Laura softly, thinking that this woman had clearly suffered enough. 'When Polly returns, I shall have to go, but please do not worry. I must tell my parents, but I will urge them to keep your secret. I know they will offer you nothing but pity. However, you must swear to write one more letter and one only: a letter of apology to my father. In it, I want you to ask for one thing.'

She studied the fearful rheumy eyes fixed on her.

'You must ask them for a place in one of the almshouses. We cannot allow you to live here any longer.'

Miss Badcoe lay still for a moment thinking. Then she said quietly, 'I will do what you suggest.'

*

Polly returned with only the promise of the doctor, but agreed to wait with Miss Badcoe until he came. Laura pressed the sick woman's hand in hers and left, taking care down the steep staircase despite her haste. She hardly noticed her surroundings in her anxiety to get to her assignation in good time. She was certain that her charitable solution to the problem of Miss Badcoe would appeal to her parents. They would be glad that the writer of poisonous letters was found out; would be horrified at the thought that a vulnerable and otherwise respectable old lady be humiliated. Whether she could secure the poor woman a much-coveted place in one of the almshouses was another matter, but she would ask her father to influence the commissioners.

She had been expected at Russell's house in Lupus Street at ten. Instead it was gone eleven-thirty when she arrived, out of breath and dizzy with hunger. She wished she hadn't told Polly that her parents shouldn't delay luncheon.

A skinny girl in a nurse's uniform admitted her at the street door and led her into a large, airy drawing room. Laura realised that the girl was nursemaid to Philip's son, and that the mysterious guest was the young boy himself. He knelt on the floor, his dark head close to Philip's red-gold one, both absorbed in sketching lions and tigers on a large pad of paper. The nursemaid said something about preparing the boy's luncheon and withdrew.

'Laura,' said Philip, rising stiffly and coming to take her hands.

'I'm so sorry I'm late,' she said. 'I couldn't send a message.' She explained about Miss Badcoe's sickness.

'You're here, that's what's important. Laura, this is my son, John.'

'Hello,' said Laura, studying the boy's smooth olive skin, his large black eyes and perfectly moulded lips. So, she thought with a jolt, he favours his mother rather than his father.

He met her gaze solemnly, telling her, 'My papa's going to draw a nellyphant. Aren't you, Papa?' His voice was low, the words carefully pronounced, and yet there was a suppressed anxiety in his manner that made her say reassuringly, 'Of course he will. Philip, we'd both like you to draw an elephant.'

When a comic-looking pachyderm with raging tusks and bulging eyes had been duly made to gallop across the page, the nurse fetched the boy to the kitchen to eat bread and butter. After that he was to rest before their proposed outing.

'He's quietly behaved today,' Philip whispered, lighting a pipe, which Laura had never seen him do before. 'Sometimes he won't settle. I think he's taken to you.'

'Oh, do you think so?' She felt unconscionably pleased.

'I do. Now, I've promised to show him the trains at Victoria Station, then we're to see the Queen's horses at the Royal Mews. After that, the girl returns him to his mama in Eaton Square. Will you accompany us?'

Laura readily acceded, thinking how much he had changed since that day in the studio. He seemed solicitous of her now; anxious to please.

They ate cold meat pie while John slept, then, at half-past one, they sallied forth with the boy between them, the girl, Kitty, hurrying behind.

Laura was touched to see how well they were together, father and son, as they watched the trains draw in or leave the station. Philip even found a willing driver with time to take the boy into his cab and show him the controls.

At first, when it was time to move on, John complained, but his nurse insisted, and he held his father's hand, chattering happily enough, as they walked up Buckingham Palace Road towards the Royal Mews where Queen Victoria's coaches and horses were kept.

On the other side of the busy street a hackney carriage stopped to let passengers alight. A dandified gentleman with top hat and cane could be seen paying the driver. There was a lady behind him; her face was for the moment hidden as she smoothed the folds of her dress. Then she looked up. Laura drew a sharp breath.

The boy followed the direction of her gaze. 'Mama!' he shrieked, and threw off his father's hand, dashing into the road.

'John!' Philip leaped in immediate pursuit.

Another carriage jangled up at a lick, overtaking the first; the snort of the horses like an urgent warning. Too late.

'John, get back!' screeched Marie, dodging out in front of the hackney.

Philip grabbed his son from the path of the flailing hooves. Marie tumbled under them. Laura would never forget her scream; long, high-pitched, animal, as the wheels ran over her.

That scream rang through her dreams for weeks, months, so that she woke in the early hours, shaking and sweating. Then she'd lie awake going over and over what had happened, wishing she could have done something. They should have anticipated John's excitement, known that he was tired and a little anxious about being away from his mother. If only they'd recognised Marie another second before John did. In one tiny, fatal moment of distraction they'd failed this little boy, robbed him of his mother. Philip was forever stripped of hope, Marie's parents had lost their beautiful daughter. So many people were suffering.

Despair dragged her down. It seemed that all her recent sadnesses, her uncertainties, had been but waiting for this final blow.

She wrote one short broken sentence to Philip – *I feel so wretched for you both. My prayers are all for you . . .* but heard nothing in return, though she watched the arrival of every post.

The funeral came and went. Harriet read her the account from the newspaper. It had taken place in the fashionable St George's Hanover Square, where Marie and Philip were married. The list of mourners included many famous names: Edward Burne-Jones, William Morris, John Ruskin, Alma Tadema, even the poet Swinburne winkled out of his lair for the spectacle.

Laura told her parents about the accident. Of course she had to, since she was eventually escorted home, silent and white-faced in a cab by a police officer, to collapse weeping into her mother's arms. But it was in Harriet that she confided her deepest feelings of guilt, which, as time passed and she had room to think, came to encompass not only her belief that she was somehow responsible for the accident by being there when she shouldn't – but that her calumny had begun when she'd allowed her friendship with Philip to wander beyond the boundaries of propriety and good sense.

In the journal, Fran read Laura's outpourings of anguish and found herself weeping with her. *By this scandal, I have deeply hurt everyone whom I love*, Laura had written, *slashed at the tender threads that bind us to one another.*

Although they never chided her, she could tell that her parents were disappointed. At church on Sunday it was apparent that the tragic event had become the latest gossip at firesides and dining-tables around the parish. Few of the women would meet Laura's eye, and the men glanced at her curiously. No one actually said anything, but as she knelt to pray she felt all eyes on her.

She took no comfort even from the letter that arrived from Miss Badcoe, and which her father had passed round the breakfast-table the day before, confessing to her calumnies and craving mercy.

It has taken the intervention of your daughter to make me see how I might have been mistaken in my complaints. I respectfully ask for your understanding and your forgiveness. I deserve no more, except, I beg you, for your discretion. Even now, the stiff old lady was too proud to ask for practical help, so Laura explained on Miss Badcoe's behalf. Mr Brownlow merely nodded, walked slowly away to his study without a word and shut the door.

His wife expressed her feelings more strongly. 'I cannot believe that a lady would know, let alone employ such language as she has done.'

'She's elderly and lonely . . . and perhaps a little mad, Mama,' Laura said gently. 'She deserves our pity.'

'Indeed.' Her mother sighed and capitulated as Laura knew she would. 'But I shall never be able to consider her in the same way again. And does this explain all the damage? No, it doesn't. Whatever shall become of us all?'

They didn't have to wait long for the rest of the mystery to be solved. Three nights later, on the Festival of St Michael and All Angels, one Alfred Cooper was apprehended, drunk and insensible, in the porch of the church. Two more windows had been broken, said the policeman who visited the rectory the following morning, and the man's pockets were found to be full of stones. He'd confessed, giving the names of other villains he'd ensnared.

Later that morning, a carriage and pair, briskly driven, rolled up outside the house and Harriet climbed out. There was no sign of baby Arthur. Instead, she was dragging a clearly reluctant Ida by the arm.

'Ida, tell my parents what you told me, you wretched girl,' she ordered, pulling off her gloves and settling back in her chair. Mr and Mrs Brownlow exchanged glances. Laura stood quietly by the window.

'What is it, Ida?' said Mr Brownlow, more gently, and gradually the white-faced maid stumbled out her story.

'I've done nothing wrong, sir. I was pulled all ways. I didn't know what was right.'

'It's that man they've arrested,' Harriet said. 'Her father. Ida, go on, tell them properly. I caught you last evening, didn't I? Giving him food. Which she'd stolen from my kitchen.'

'I'm sorry, madam, I've told you I'm sorry,' squeaked Ida. Humped up in misery, she was close to tears.

'Now now, my dear, you're with friends here,' said Mrs Brownlow. 'There's nothing you can't tell us.'

Little by little, they extracted from her the whole story.

'He threatened me. Told me I must save my brothers and sisters from the orphanage and get the family together again or I'd burn in hell.' Alfred Cooper resented the Brownlows, that much was obvious.

A police officer was called to speak to Ida.

At luncheon, Mr Brownlow told his wife and Laura, 'The police say that Cooper ranted about how Mrs Brownlow killed Molly and the baby and took his children away.'

'What rubbish!' cried Mrs Brownlow, spreading her napkin on her lap. 'The man's too dissolute and intemperate to provide for his wife and children, and then he blames other people for the family's misfortune. Nay, blames the whole parish, it seems. Well, now the man will be transported no doubt and it'll be an end to the matter.'

Laura picked at a thread on the tablecloth and remembered that foul hovel where the Coopers had lived. Just as she understood Miss Badcoe, now she wondered whether Mr Cooper had a story of his own. Yes, it could not be denied, he had failed his family. He had been threatening and violent, and that could not be excused. But what kind of upbringing had Alfred Cooper endured? What had made him the man he was?

'What's going to happen to Ida?' she asked as she spooned her soup.

'Harriet's very angry about the theft of the food,' said her father. 'George wants her to dismiss the girl. Such a crime cannot be seen to be condoned. However, I have written urging him to reconsider the matter. Is a young girl with a soft heart to be condemned for obeying her father? Surely not. I've suggested that they give her some other punishment, but not throw her out on the streets without a reference. I hope George will see the way of mercy.'

'I hope so, too,' said Laura, sighing. 'Some good should come of all this misery.' What good could ever come out of her own terribly calumny, she could not for the moment conceive.

And it was while she pondered this that, for the third time, Anthony Bond proposed marriage. Mindful of her family's happiness and won over by his persistence, she promised him an answer at Christmas.

In mid-October, as the leaves on the trees in the Square began to fall, a letter arrived from Philip.

It is a month since our terrible loss and only now have I returned to my senses. I must see you, Laura.

But she was resolved now. She wrote to him saying that it was best for both of them if they didn't meet.

Chapter 36

It is not uncommon for angels to appear when people are on the edge of death.

Gary Kinnaman, *Angels Dark and Light*

After reading my father's letter, I started visiting the hospital every day. Now that I knew Dad's story and understood how he had always felt about me, I wanted to spend as much time with him as possible, in an effort somehow to bridge that gulf of silence between us of which he spoke. I told him how Jeremy had shown me the letter, that I wished that he hadn't hidden so much from me, that I was glad I knew it all now.

My feelings were, in truth, confused. Part of me was very angry with him, and the more I dwelled on it, the more I resented the way he'd ruled my whole life, blighting my childhood with his secrets and his guilt. But he was a vulnerable old man now, long in the dying, and it seemed inappropriate to burden him with my anger. I became quickly frustrated, too, that here we were with the truth finally naked between us, but unable to communicate to one another all our thoughts and feelings about it. We'd lost the opportunity to mend the wounds of the past, to fill the silences. In the end I could only whisper broken words of reassurance to him as he lay unconscious, telling him that I loved him and forgave him everything. Jeremy said that it was all that was required and I took him at his word. What else could I do?

Zac sometimes came with me. I showed him Dad's letter a couple of days after Jeremy gave it to me. We sat in the Quentins' kitchen as he read it, under the baleful gaze of Lucifer the cat. When he passed it back, his face was troubled. 'I never suspected any of that,' he said. 'Your father gave nothing away about himself.'

'I'm so glad he found Jeremy to talk to,' I replied, realising that Dad had almost left it too late.

We were with Dad when he died, Zac and I. A Sister from the hospice called me at the vicarage one Friday morning in the second week of November to say that he was fading. I rang Zac to tell him I was on my way to Dulwich.

We were there all day, and in that terrible time of waiting, phrases from *The Dream of Gerontius* flowed through my mind continuously. Dad probably wouldn't be conscious that he was dying. But then, who really knew? Perhaps that important part of him, his spirit, was aware of moving forward into light and freedom. Perhaps he could feel our presence or perhaps he had already left us, was in the arms of a great angel who would bear him forth into eternity.

As dusk fell outside, a flock of geese rose above the trees with a great whir of wings, crying mournfully to one another, off on their journey south. When I turned to look at Dad once more, I saw that he, too, had gone.

Sitting next to me, Zac reached out and covered my hand with his. I leaned into him and wept.

On Monday at choir we had sung the section about the moment of Gerontius' death, when the priest and his assistants cry, 'Go forth upon thy journey . . . Go in the name of Angels and

Archangels.' I could hear the chorus running through my mind now as I looked at Dad's still face. We speak of the dead being 'at peace'. But what if Dad was, like Gerontius, on a great dramatic journey beyond death? Maybe he wasn't ready for peace yet, but I prayed that he would get there.

Later, I spoke to Jeremy about this. He seemed to think the same as me. 'Do you think he'll see my mother again?' I asked him.

'Oh yes, I believe he will.'

'They'll have a lot to talk about.'

'Yes, indeed.'

'I imagine they'll be quite cross with each other at first.'

Jeremy smiled. 'Yes, but this time I expect they'll hang on in there and work it out.'

There was only a handful of us at the crematorium the following Wednesday: me, Zac, Sarah, Anita, Mr Broadbent the bookseller and a clerk from Dad's solicitor's office. Jo couldn't come and the organist wasn't Ben, who had a heavy teaching schedule that day. Yet, despite our small party and the anonymous surroundings, Jeremy managed to make the service special and his sincere sorrow at the loss of a friend warmed us all.

'Go on thy course, and may thy place today be found in peace,' he said, as the curtains closed around the coffin.

Afterwards, we gathered outside shivering in the cold and stared at our stiff flower arrangements lying on the grass. There was only one that was unexpected. It was a simple bunch of chrysanthemums from Amber. When I read her tender note, my eyes swam with tears. It said, *May your angel carry you safely home.*

Chapter 37

Now and then when the room was otherwise lightless
A misty gray figure would appear to be seated on this bench in
the alcove
It was the tender and melancholy figure of an angel.

Tennessee Williams, *One Arm and Other Stories*

In the confused days after Dad's death, Zac and I saw each other frequently. There was an enormous amount of paperwork to get through, which he helped me do, and if a day went past without us meeting he would ring to see if I was all right.

Then one day near the end of November, he didn't ring and I missed him. I remembered that when we'd met up the day before to go through some financial matters, he'd seemed pale and distant, so now I picked up the phone and dialled his number. It rang for a long time, then there came the sound of the handset being dropped and a muffled curse, before a hoarse voice stammered, 'H-hello?'

'Zac? Zac, it's me.'

'Wait a moment. Ouch.' There was a shuffling.

'Have I rung at a bad time?'

'I was asleep. Sorry, couldn't get out of bed. Flu or something.'

I rang him again in the early afternoon after my orchestral rehearsal, and he sounded worse.

'I'm coming round,' I said, and ignoring his protests, made him give me his address. How funny that I'd never visited his home before, I thought, as I whizzed round the express super-market for some emergency supplies.

The name Burberry Mansions evokes an image of gracious Edwardian apartments like Jo's parents' place, but Zac's home turned out to be in a shabby block on a Lambeth estate. I took the creaking lift to the seventh floor, knocked on the door of Flat 72 and waited for what seemed like minutes on the draughty concrete landing.

Eventually Zac opened the door. He looked terrible, with hair like a bird's nest, his pale face blotchy, his eyes unnaturally bright. The place smelled stale and felt overheated. I followed him into a living room.

It took me a while to register what I was seeing. We were bathed in a veritable rainbow of light. Coloured glass hung against most of the windows. There was a panel of stunning roundels, blues and greens, all linked in a continuous pattern. In another, etched water nymphs swam across a dreamy river of brown and amber, where blue fish flashed; out of a leaded round pane hung from the ceiling, turning slowly, the silver outline of a stag appearing to step out of misty blue. I moved over to study a huge mirror above the mantelshelf bordered by a swirling abstract of ruby, gold and white glass, like desert sand, where little gold lizards and snakes played.

'*Dreamtime*, that one's called,' Zac said, coughing horribly.

'It's . . . incredible. Zac – you're shivering. Get back to bed at once.' He stumbled slightly, so I helped him into the bedroom, which was dark, for the curtains were drawn across the windows.

'Oh, don't look at anything,' he said, almost falling into the bed. 'It's a pit.' Then he groaned as I ignored him and pulled a curtain back slightly, so I could see the room.

He was right about it being a pit. Discarded clothes lay everywhere, the bed linen needed changing, and dirty crockery was piled on the bedside table and the floor.

'Right,' I said, a little uncertainly. The role of nurse was not coming naturally to me. Zac helped by being surprisingly biddable. I led him to the shower, hoping he wouldn't collapse in there whilst I changed the bedclothes, found him a clean pair of pyjamas and located some paracetamol. Some kind of flu seemed the mostly likely diagnosis, so I gave him some tablets with a glass of water and tucked him up in bed before turning my attention to the kitchen.

After washing up, I tried without much success to get him to eat mushroom soup with some bread and butter. Then, while he slept, I aired the rooms and tidied up, and ran a load of laundry through the washer-drier. He was still asleep when I left, so I propped up a note by his bedside promising to ring him in the morning.

I visited every day until he was over the worst. On the second day I rang Zac's doctor who said it definitely sounded like a serious bout of flu and offered nursing advice. For the first few days Zac mostly slept. When awake, he was dopey and rambling in his speech, but he let me help him change his pyjamas and comb his hair. He told me where to find his spare door key so I could let myself in.

On the third day I met a North African woman with several small children on the landing outside the flat, who asked after him anxiously and offered to call in during the evening. The following morning I found she'd left a delicious-looking stew in the fridge and I tried some of that on him, but he couldn't keep much down, so I ate it. It was miserable seeing him like this; to see the man on whom I'd leaned so much these last few weeks, who was normally so dignified, so self-reliant, forced to put himself completely into the hands of another person.

I was relieved to realise that he wasn't isolated. Apart from Etha next door there were phone calls from friends. Amber came with me once and on another occasion, when I appeared in the early evening and slotted my key in Zac's door, a youngish man with thinning blond hair opened it and introduced himself as David.

'You're from the other stained-glass studio, aren't you?' I said, remembering the name. 'I'm glad to meet you at last.'

We sat on the living-room sofa and talked in whispers for fear of waking Zac; gazing all the while at the wonderful vista of the London sky, stretched out before us, between the bits of stained glass. We could see all the way to the tower of Big Ben, peeping above the high-rise blocks, and, beyond it, the gothic pinnacles of the Houses of Parliament.

David told me how he'd got to know Zac; that Zac had come one day asking for some help with a commission for which my father didn't have the right equipment. They'd become firm friends and Zac often spent time with David and his wife and children. Janie, David's wife, was a flautist with the Philharmonic.

'Zac's a really talented guy,' whispered David, as we looked around the room at all the beautiful glass.

'I know,' I said. I started to tell him about Raphael, then remembered that he knew it already because Zac had gone to him for materials.

I wondered if David knew Zac's background – about his daughter – but didn't like to ask in case he didn't.

Best of all, he volunteered to come and help us with the new designs for *Minster Glass* and I leaped at his offer.

'And you must come to lunch one Sunday when Zac is better,' he said. 'Janie would love to meet you.'

It wasn't until the sixth day that Zac's temperature returned to normal, and another couple of days until he was strong enough to sit up in bed in his dressing-gown. He was sad and lifeless, his head full of cold, which he said made him half-deaf and stupid. He was still too weak to do anything much, not even to read. As time passed he grew stronger, but a sadness settled over him that didn't seem to lift.

'It's the flu, Zac. It takes it out of you.'

'S'pose so,' he said, sighing, but I wondered whether it was more than that.

By the end of the week it had become a ritual, travelling down on the bus to see him every day. I had been recruited to an orchestra, one of whose regular brass players had broken his arm, so there were rehearsals most days and I would come down to see Zac in the late afternoon as it began to get dark.

Once, when I arrived, he had been trying to draw in a sketch-book but when I showed interest, he chucked book and pencil down on the coffee-table beside a pot of early hyacinths Janie had brought him.

'I can't concentrate on anything,' he complained, yawning and stretching, but then he smiled and I realised with an odd pang that he was getting better. Soon I wouldn't need to come. I felt suddenly bereft.

To hide my mood I moved into the kitchen and started putting away the food I'd brought. Through the window I watched a seagull floating, motionless, as though faith alone held it suspended midair. I was reminded of myself. There had been so much change I lacked any sense of direction.

'How's the shop going?' Zac asked when I brought him tea. He moved so I could sit on the sofa beside him. It was natural now to lean against him as I had leaned against Ben on the night the window got broken. Friends, at ease with one another; though Zac had never indicated more.

'The work's starting after Christmas,' I told him.

I liked being with him. His early awkwardness, when we were still acquaintances, I knew now to be shyness, with a good dose of concern for my father thrown in.

'You were right about me and Dad,' I said, a little sadly. 'I wasn't around for him enough, was I? You must have thought I didn't care.'

'He did know you loved him though,' Zac said, squeezing my arm. 'And it was difficult for you. He wouldn't let anyone get close, would he?' He sneezed suddenly and grabbed at some tissues. 'I still feel dreadful,' he sighed.

He looked awful, it was true. His nose was swollen, his skin as grey as dishwater, his hair greasy and dull.

'But you'll feel a lot better soon, I'm sure,' I promised him. 'Right – I've got to go, I'm afraid. A big rehearsal this evening. The concert's tomorrow night, so I won't be able to come.'

'I'll miss you,' said Zac, 'but I've decided – I've been here ten days now and I'm getting out of this flat tomorrow if I have to crawl. And Fran,' he hauled himself up and came to see me out, 'as soon as I'm up to it, I'm taking you out to dinner. Will you come?'

'Of course,' I said. I would have hugged him, but just at that moment he sneezed again.

The lift, for once, came right away and before I could get out at the bottom a fearsome-looking bunch of teenagers crowded in, so I had to shove my way through. Instinctively checking my handbag after this experience, I realised I'd still got Zac's key. Damn. Well, I wasn't going back up now. And I rather liked the idea of keeping it.

Chapter 38

Oh speak again, bright angel, for thou art
As glorious to this night, being o'er my head
As is a winged messenger of heaven.

William Shakespeare, *Romeo and Juliet*

'The faculty's come for our window,' cried Jeremy on the last Saturday of November, as he hung up his coat and came to join Sarah and me at the kitchen table. He'd been down to the parish office to sort out a few things and had opened a letter from the Bishop's office.

Several officials had visited the church on different occasions to inspect Raphael, now propped up in the chapel, and the light against which it was proposed he be hung. Finally Jeremy had been given approval to dismantle the Victorian cupboard and move it, and to install Raphael.

'We'll just keep the existing plain glass,' Jeremy said, stirring saccharine into his coffee. 'So, Fran my dear, I'll contact the carpenter about the cupboard, then perhaps you and Zac would like to organise the ironwork for the window.'

Zac, now restored to health, and David and some men from the ironworks hung Raphael one morning towards the end of November, with the vicar, his churchwarden and me watching and making ourselves useful where we could. There was a hair-raising moment when we thought one of the measurements was wrong, but eventually all was made perfect. The bronze frame was welded to the wall in such a way that Raphael's panel could be easily removed if need be. A final polish and we all stood back to look.

The effect was breathtaking. In the cold light of our northern winter, the window glowed gently. The angel floated above us, blessing us with a raised hand as he looked down on us all.

'I'm so glad we've got him in good time for Christmas,' said the vicar, beaming.

'And for the *Gerontius* next week,' I remembered. Our concert would be on the following Sunday evening.

'People will have to come into the Lady Chapel especially to see, of course.'

'We'll know he's here. And you can keep the chapel door open,' I added.

There was a dedication service for the window scheduled for the evening of 13 December. 'St Lucy's Day,' the vicar said. 'A festival of light. Most appropriate.'

Life being so busy, I hadn't read Laura's diary for some time. But that evening, my mind full of Raphael, I extracted it from the pile of books I'd brought with me. There were only a few pages left to read. Raphael was finished and my journey with Laura nearly over. I'd miss them both.

It was a surprise to see that our date for the blessing of the window was exactly the same as the original dedication, albeit more than a century later.

Chapter 39

Lead me to the land of angels

Carmina Gadelica

LAURA'S STORY

On a Wednesday at the beginning of December 1880, Philip Russell brought some men from *Minster Glass* to install the two windows. Laura, who had not heard from Philip since her rebuffing reply to his letter in October, deliberately avoided visiting the church that day. But she knew she could not refuse to attend the dedication service on the following Sunday, St Lucy's Day. After all, one of the windows was in memory of Caroline, and many of the Brownlows' friends and family would be there.

The day after the men had been, however, she slipped into the church to see the windows by herself before morning prayer. How much more beautiful and alive they were, she thought, now they were in place than when propped up in the workshop. They seemed to float above her in the gloomy chapel. It was as though they had spirits; she could almost feel their presence. But she dismissed the idea. Even her father, with his love of the mystical, wouldn't approve of such nonsense.

It was the faces, above all, that fascinated her. She had been studying Mary's joyous gaze, her adoration reflected in the little boy's expression, for some minutes before it dawned on her how familiar they were. She hadn't noticed it before. Mary was Laura's mother. She'd seen that look on her face as she dandled Arthur on her lap, and although the Holy Child looked a little older than Arthur, and Arthur's features had certainly changed over the last few months, there was something about the tilt of his nose, the shape of his head that made her think Arthur had been in Philip's mind when he imagined the Christ Child.

And the angel. Only the eyes might have been Caroline's, she thought – large, heavy-lashed, languid – but this angel was more solid, squarer-faced than Caroline had ever been. Nor was the angel like Marie – she had been a dark exotic beauty. Well, Philip must have plenty of other model faces to choose from; half the women visiting the Grosvenor Gallery probably.

As she sat there looking and thinking about Caroline, a sense of peace crept over her. The angel seemed to glow brighter, warming her. Surely she wasn't imagining it? It gave her an odd feeling. Like being blessed by a very holy and awe-inspiring person.

On the afternoon of St Lucy's Day, Laura went to the church full of trepidation, knowing that she would see Philip.

Her first impression on entering the building with her mother and Mr Bond was that, far from the bright-coloured clothes such an occasion surely demanded, the back rows of pews were full of elderly men dressed in black: friends and associates of the late Mr and Mrs Fotherington, she supposed. One way or another, the church was full. Candles flickered on every window-ledge for the church interior was cast in wintry gloom.

For the actual moment of dedication all were asked to move to the Lady Chapel, as Laura's father invoked words of blessing. From every part of the crowd came little gasps of admiration as people took in the lovely serene faces of Mary and the Christ Child above the altar, the grave authority of Raphael, hand lifted in blessing, glowing in the weak and misty light.

As the congregation crowded in and around the chapel, straining to see the windows, Laura waited politely at the back. It was there she caught sight of Philip, standing at a distance, leaning against the wall of the chapel. Catching her looking at him, he smiled very sweetly.

The candlelight reflected in his eyes, highlighting his red-gold hair, warming his pale skin, giving him the aura of an angel. An angel in a frockcoat and white wing collar. Then his face dissolved in the fog of her tears and she had to look away.

Afterwards there were so many people she had to speak to – cousins who had known Caroline, friends of her parents, old schoolfriends of the Brownlow sisters. Eventually Mr Bond came to say goodbye, having need to return to his office. Laura was speaking to Mrs Fotherington's nephew, Mr Jefferies, a man of strong opinions, forcefully expressed, and his quietly spoken daughter, Prudence. She was glad to have Anthony Bond's assistance with Mr Jefferies so that she could encourage Prudence to talk.

'A most excellent man, your father, Miss Brownlow,' Mr Jefferies pronounced. 'My late aunt always spoke well of him. And our business with the window has been conducted quite satisfactorily. You will find we worship here more frequently.'

'We should be delighted to see you both,' Anthony assured him.

'We usually attend St Mary's,' gentle Prudence whispered to Laura, 'but I'm afraid Papa has taken exception to the new vicar.'

'Ruins a man's appetite for his dinner with his damn liberal views,' Jefferies grumbled. 'I won't be lectured on how to spend my hard-earned income.'

'Oh Papa,' Prudence breathed. She patted his arm. 'You do your Christian duty. Don't listen to him,' she appealed to her audience. 'My father's the kindest, most generous of men.'

'I am sure you are right, Miss Jefferies,' Anthony said gravely, but with a twinkle in his eye.

'What should I do without her?' Jefferies said, his expression tender. 'Since my wife died, three years past, she has been my comfort and my strength.'

Prudence blushed becomingly. 'It is an easy duty.'

'Womanly virtues indeed,' said Anthony. And he smiled so warmly upon Miss Jefferies that for one tiny moment Laura felt a stab of jealousy.

Later, she watched him take his leave, stopping to bow stiffly to a gaggle of giggling girls by the door. He was over-serious to the point of dullness, but her affection for him was building. Day by day his good qualities presented themselves to her. She knew how loyal he'd been to her father during his darkest moments; how hard he worked; how solicitous he was of her needs and interests. *Sesame and Lilies* was only the first of John Ruskin's works that he gave her. She still hadn't felt confident of showing him her writing, fearing her wayward women and the challenges they presented to his masculine view of the world might disturb him. Neither had she dared send one to the publisher of the magazine Philip suggested. Her family needed less public interest at the moment, not more.

What she didn't like to admit was that, now Anthony had gone she felt, well, less constrained. The Jefferies moved on to speak to George and Harriet, and for a short while she was alone. Out of the corner of her eye she watched Philip, surrounded by admirers, the men shaking his hand enthusiastically, the women confiding.

'Miss Brownlow. I'm glad to have found you.' Her thoughts

were interrupted by Miss Badcoe, now recovered from her illness and as severe as ever. With no word of thanks for Laura's
interventions on her behalf, the woman was breathtakingly
unbending. Once or twice, as she endured Miss Badcoe's rambling complaints about a neighbour at the almshouse who had
offended her finer sensibilities with clumsy overtures of friendship, Laura glanced right at Philip and their eyes met. The
second time he looked at her, he seemed to have worked his way
closer, and she forced herself to hold his gaze and smile a little.

'Miss Brownlow?' Her attention was riveted again on Miss
Badcoe. 'You're looking peaky, girl. Maybe that colour is wrong
for you.' The woman took her breath away.

'Miss Badcoe, I assure you that I am quite well. Many people
compliment me that this gold suits me exactly. Not all of us can
look comely in black.'

'Well, really, Miss Brownlow. I meant no offence.'

'And yet you frequently do offend. Miss Badcoe, I hope you
will be happy in your new lodgings and learn to like your neighbour. Good afternoon.' And before Miss Badcoe could draw
breath, Laura swept away.

Philip worked his way nearer and nearer to Laura until, as
the crowd began to thin, they found themselves standing
together. Now she saw the signs of grief etched in his face; the
tired pouches under his eyes; the angles in his face that were
sharper now, and she was moved. He took her hand and held it
in both of his.

'Miss Brownlow,' he said. 'Laura. At last. How are you?' His
eyes raked her face, studying her, she felt, more searchingly than
ever before. It was as though he were trying to commit her features to heart.

'Mr Russell, it's been a splendid occasion,' Laura's mother
broke in, appearing suddenly at her side. Philip released Laura's

hand. The spell was broken. 'We are entirely happy with our window. It means so much to us.' As she spoke, Laura's mama grasped her daughter's arm proprietorially.

'Indeed,' Laura murmured. She knew her mother meant only to protect her. How silly she had been, to yearn still to speak with Philip. Now they wouldn't ever be alone together again. He'd go on his way and their paths would never again need to cross. Maybe she'd glimpse him on the other side of the Square, visiting *Minster Glass*. But that would be all.

Her mother was enquiring after his father's health. She looked a little happier these days, Laura thought. The troubled atmosphere in the church had lifted, too. People still spoke about the disturbances. Many now confessed shame at the divisions the matter had caused in the congregation, with neighbour suspecting neighbour, the poor resenting the rich, the rich condemning the poor out of hand. A few weeks before, the Bishop had visited to rededicate the church and its altars and to pray for unity and the mission of the parish. Slowly, life was returning to normal.

Her father's spirits, too, had improved notably after word arrived from her brother Tom. He had found work as a schoolteacher in New York. It was in one of the poorer areas of the city and he wasn't earning much, but he was strong in his belief that he was contributing to the well-being of his fellow men. He had recently become engaged, he wrote, to the daughter of one of his teaching colleagues. He asked for his parents' blessing. Laura's father immediately arranged for money to be sent towards their expenses and expressed regret that they wouldn't be able to attend the wedding.

'Yes, we have much to thank God for,' her mother was telling Philip. 'My son Tom is doing well in America, settled and happy now. Our little grandson Arthur is a lusty child and we have hopes of another happy event at Christmas. Don't we, Laura?' she said, her calm eyes fixed steadily on her daughter's. 'I think you know Anthony Bond, my husband's churchwarden?'

'Mama.' Laura breathed in sharply. The matter of her impending engagement was not public knowledge.

Philip, looking from Mrs Brownlow's triumphant expression to Laura's embarrassed one, needed no further explanation. He said, 'I will look forward to hearing more of that.' There was a short frozen silence during which Laura wished the ground would swallow her. But her mother was pulling her away.

'Now Laura, we must speak to Cousin Clarice. She hardly knows anyone and she's so deaf now, poor soul, it must be very lonely. Goodbye, Mr Russell.'

'Goodbye,' Laura whispered to him. Philip's expression was strange – as though he'd realised he'd forgotten something desperately important.

The following day she received a letter from him.

Dear Laura, it said. *It's no good, I've lain unvisited by sleep. I must speak with you alone on an urgent matter. Where can I meet you? Name a place, anywhere, anytime. Laura, do this for my sake. Yours, Philip.*

Her first thought was that she should refuse his request. Her second was that she would see him alone one last time. Her third was a question: where could they meet that was private yet seemly?

Dear Philip, she wrote back. *I will meet you in the church porch at three.*

She slipped out of the house while her mother was resting, her feet sure of their way through the hushed semi-darkness.

As the pillars of the church porch reared up through the

foggy gloom she suddenly regretted coming without Polly. Would he be there? Who else might be lurking? But there was only the tall shadowy figure of Philip. He reached out his hand and pulled her into the porch. 'The door's locked,' he said, his voice warm in her ear.

'We always keep it so now.' She pressed a large key into his hand. As the door swung open and the pungent smell of incense floated around them, she was reminded of that very first afternoon, so many months ago, when he'd first surprised her by materialising like a stone saint stepping down from his niche.

The door clicked shut behind them and they moved together through the echoey stillness. In the Lady Chapel, two fat candles burned. The vandalised wooden statue of Mary had been relegated to a side table now, the mend clear on her poor broken neck. The figures in the windows were eerie glowing presences today. Philip studied them for a moment, seemingly in a reverie.

'Forgive me, I haven't seen them in this light before. It's strange to think they came into being under my hand. They appear to have achieved a life of their own quite apart from anything I've done. It's as though God has breathed life into the glass, if that's not a blasphemy.'

'I think I see your meaning. Remember what you said about the ancient belief that God's glory cascades through translucent objects in the form of light?'

They were silent. Laura waited quietly for him to speak his purpose.

Eventually he turned to face her, took both of her hands in his.

'Are you to marry Mr Bond?'

He spoke so passionately, she was struck. She snatched her hands away.

'That is a private matter. But as Mama intimated, I am to give him my answer at Christmas.'

'Laura. Don't. Please. I can't bear . . . He's not right . . .'

'It isn't your business whom I marry, Mr Russell.'

'Do you love him?'

'Now you do overstep all boundaries. I am very fond of him.'

'Fond? What basis is that for a marriage?'

Anger flared in her. 'It's a more solid one than passionate adoration, I would say, from your experience.'

'Yes, I suppose I deserved that,' Philip muttered, pushing a hand roughly through his hair. 'I'm going about this wrongly. I . . . I'm confused.'

'Confused?'

'You once told me I should forget my wife,' he said.

The clatter of hooves sounded in her head, that eerie scream of pain going on for ever and ever. Laura closed her eyes to shut out the picture of Marie falling.

'It was a callous thing to say,' she murmured. 'I didn't know what would come to pass.'

'I will learn to do it,' he said calmly. 'I know I must, in order to get on with my life. I *must* forget her.'

'But what of John?'

'John lives mostly with his grandparents now. It's easier that way. I see him often. His grandmother's teaching him Italian, you know. There's a *palazzo* he'll inherit one day, near Verona. He's growing away from me, I fear.'

'But he's still your son – a little boy missing his mother. He must need you.'

'Yes, he does miss her, but there's nothing I can do to stop that. Nothing. Yet, though it's a dreadful thing to say, her death has freed me. I can see light in the darkness sometimes now. It's a long way ahead, that light. But at least I know it's there.'

'I'm glad,' she said softly.

'And there lies the heart of the matter, Laura. I need you with me. I didn't know it until yesterday when I saw you again. You can't marry Anthony Bond. Please don't.'

'Philip, too much has changed. He loves me. He's a good man and it pleases my parents I marry him.'

'But you, you're only fond of him. You don't speak of love.'

'There are many kinds of love.'

'Could you not find a kind with which to . . . love me?'

'Philip . . .' Every word he said now was a blow, smashing up the carapace she'd built around herself since Marie's death. And yet he had not told her the most important thing of all. He had not said that he loved her.

'What would I be to you,' she said, 'after Marie? What could I possibly be? A companion. A mere shadow of a love.'

'No, no,' he said, alarm spreading across his face. At that moment, the fog outside must have momentarily cleared because the light from the angel window grew brighter; it poured in a golden pool on the tiles.

And now she felt strong, brave and merciless. 'I want no competitor where I choose to love. There must be only me.'

She stepped into the pool of golden light, so it cascaded down over her body like a gentle fire sent straight from God and felt Raphael's healing warmth stream through her.

He stared at this transformation. Laura was bathed in light, transfigured by it, and at last the scales fell from his eyes. He breathed, 'Laura. My darling.'

And as she stood there, strong and golden and beautiful, she knew that the power to decide was hers.

*

And now I came to the final page of Laura's journal.

And so, Caroline, he will be mine and I will be his. Today Philip spoke to Papa and the house is in uproar. Mama played

Beethoven thunderously all afternoon and has now retired to bed exhausted. Harriet has sent me two angry letters full of words underlined, and Mrs Jorkins shakes her head and bites her lip. Worst of all was my meeting with Anthony this evening.

I have hurt him badly. Desperately. He is without fault in all this. In taking what we want in life we destroy. It's that which makes Mama so angry, I think – my wilfulness, my selfishness. Perhaps she's right. But perhaps, too, it is easier to do good to others if we are happy? Anthony may meet a woman who would love him as he deserves. Caroline, I sincerely hope that this comes to pass. If you were here with me, I wonder if you would take my part? But you are not. I think your window has changed everything for me. I will always remember you, Caroline. The memories will always be tender. But now, as I once advised Philip, we must move into the future and leave you in God's hands. Goodbye, my darling sister.

There was no more. Just several blank pages.

So Laura married her Philip. And now I understood why I'd found the journal amongst the archives of *Minster Glass*. Philip had taken over the business from Reuben Ashe and Laura had married him. Which meant . . . what did it mean? How had the firm passed down our family through the years? Maybe Philip was a several times great-grandfather and Laura a grand-mother? Not if Philip and Marie's son John inherited the business. How could I find out?

I was glad for Laura, though sorry for poor Anthony. He had been faithful, and dogged and dutiful but that, in the end, had not won the day. I wondered what had happened to him. Perhaps he courted the gentle Prudence Jefferies, found a wife well suited to his needs? I hoped so.

Chapter 40

Every man contemplates an angel in his future self.

Ralph Waldo Emerson

Quite how we all crammed ourselves into the front of the church on the Sunday of the concert and still left enough room for the orchestra, I don't know, but Dominic and Michael somehow organised it.

Choral dress rehearsals are always dire, not least because they take place in a new venue with strange acoustics and no one sits in the same order as previous practices. The strongest singers, who always sit at the front week by week, for some reason now disappear to the back, and people like me and Jo, who enjoy skulking at the back, find themselves marooned in the front row, exposed and disorientated, with the violinists' elbows almost in their faces.

Ben looked harassed, as well he might. The previous Monday's practice had been ragged. Most people now knew their parts, but not well enough to lift their heads from their music.

Today, with the orchestra and the soloists present, he had at least to control his temper. He and Val had done well. Not only did we have Julian Wright as a marvellously tortured

Gerontius, but a delightful mezzo soprano played his Guardian Angel and a rich bass-baritone was the Angel of the Agony. The programme notes revealed stunning CVs for both. How Ben and Val had won their services for this amateur concert, I couldn't guess.

At the end of the afternoon Val reminded us about our dress for the performance – black and white – as well as to bring food for the cast party in the hall afterwards. Wine would be provided. We packed ourselves up, chattering, and I said goodbye to Jo, noticing with a stab of satisfaction that she left with Dominic. But my attention was really on Ben. He was grimmer than I'd ever seen him. I waited outside the door and caught his arm as he came through.

'Oh hi,' he said, a smile flickering across his lips. 'How are you?' He took my hand and gave me one of his soul-searching looks.

'I'm fine,' I told him, gently disengaging my hand, 'but you don't look happy. Were we truly awful?'

'No. Well, I get nervous. I'm sure we'll be all right on the night, as they say.'

'That's only two hours' time,' I reminded him. 'Anyway, I must go. And you – you should rest.'

'I'll be better after I've had something to eat. Fran – you will be at the party afterwards, won't you?'

'Of course,' I said, and cursed my voice for wobbling.

'I'll see you later, then,' he said, and I felt that familiar tug inside. Was it beginning all over again?

It might have been only an amateur choral society performance, but it was the most wonderful concert I'd ever taken part in.

Being the penitential season of Advent there were no flowers to brighten the church. But rows of candles glowed on every windowsill, and on the huge Christmas tree at the back, and the kindest of electric ceiling lights softened the white of our shirts, investing the scene with all the nostalgia of a Victorian Christmas. Our audience seemed mesmerised, too; hushed, looking around them as they squeezed into every remaining space and sat waiting for us to begin. Near the front sat Jeremy and his wife, behind them, with a friend from the hostel, was Amber and, finally – was that him? Yes. There, right at the last moment, I was relieved to see Zac slip in and make his way along a pew full of people to what must be the last empty square inch in the church.

Then the orchestra entered to applause, followed by the leader of the orchestra – Nina, in another of her medieval dresses, this one low-cut – then by the soloists, the mezzo gorgeous in glittering midnight blue, the men crisp in tails. But they were all shadows next to Ben. Even I was amazed as he hurried into his place, centre stage, and bowed theatrically, his blond hair a glorious cascade over his high white collar; a cummerbund, the same colour as the mezzo's dress, hugging his slim hips.

The strings came in first. The brave notes of the cellos soared warm and beautiful into the vast space above our heads.

As we sang I knew we were but a small part of a great drama unfolding; the most important drama of all, the story of life and death, the journey of a soul. For, though we belong to one another, sing and laugh and cry and fight together, in the end we have to make that final journey into the dark alone. Gerontius showed us the way, leaving his grieving friends, but then his angel bore him, supported him, led him safely among the devils by the judgement court, sponsoring his journey on through repentance to salvation and the promise of eternal joy.

I thought of my father throughout – how could I not? I had privately dedicated my singing to his memory, willing him, too, to find freedom from guilt and happiness; maybe to find my mother again, as they had first known and loved each other. I remembered, too, the dream I'd had the night of the fire. I wondered if it really had been her singing I'd heard; whether she was the angel who had called my name.

During the interval I looked for Zac, but he must have been swept up in the crowd who were pressing their way into the hall for drinks. So I took my bottle of water and went to visit our angel window. Tonight Raphael was blank and lifeless in the darkness. But I knew he was there, and would leap to life again with the dawn.

I became aware of someone behind me and turned. It was Michael, watching me from the doorway, a shining glass of red wine in one hand.

'I don't know about you, but I'd say it's going fantastically well,' he said, eyes gleaming in the light of the candles on the altar. 'That Wright fellow is simply marvellous.'

'I think so, too. Ben should be pleased. Have you spoken to him?'

'No,' was all he said to that, then, 'Wonderful job you did with him,' nodding towards the angel. 'I had a good look this afternoon before the rehearsal. It entirely complements the other lights in here. I congratulate you.'

'Thanks,' I said. 'It's very special to me, this window.'

'Yes, of course, your father,' he acknowledged. I could detect sympathy beneath the formal tone.

'My father, yes, but so much else that's happened in these last few months. It's proved to be quite a turning point for me in a number of ways.'

'How are matters proceeding with the shop?'

'Fine, thanks. The builders are coming in straight after Christmas. I think they'll be finished sometime in February. Then we can have a grand reopening.'

'Michael, there you are. It's about to start again, so I'll see you afterwards.' It was Nina, slipping her hand under his arm, dropping a light kiss on his cheek. He leaned into her for a moment, his stern features softened. She smiled up at me as she left and I thought she seemed sad.

'As you can see, she and I are making another go of it,' Michael said. 'It shook Ben up when you left. I made him realise that he'd hurt Nina as well by his behaviour. He had the decency to apologise to her.'

'Are they still playing together?'

'Only until their next performance, which is after Christmas. It's not easy for any of us though.'

'I can imagine,' I said soberly, thinking that their best bet would be to see less of Ben altogether. 'I hope everything works out for you, Michael.'

'Thanks,' he said, but he sounded unsure. We went to take our seats once more.

Ben seemed much more relaxed during the second half, even smiling during our 'Praise to the Holiest in the Height', which dovetailed more or less perfectly with the orchestra's efforts. As we distant voices on earth begged, 'Be merciful, be gracious, spare him, Lord,' I thought of the angel holding my father in his 'most loving arms', dipping him into the Lake of Penitence, sending him on to the next part of his journey.

The final Amens faded away into silence. Ben stood quietly, head bowed, and the applause began. It rose in a huge wave of sound. People stood in the pews and clapped and cheered. We clapped the soloists and Ben until our hands were sore; the orchestra and the choir were made to rise and sit, rise and sit, until finally we were allowed to go.

As people began to pack up and leave, I watched Jeremy go up and clasp Ben's hand. 'Well done!' I heard him say. 'Superb. The best concert we've had here.' Ben's friends and colleagues began to cluster round.

I turned to Jo. 'It was wonderful, wasn't it?' she said. 'I so enjoyed it. I didn't expect to, you know, I felt I'd missed so many rehearsals. Here, give me your score. I'll give it to Dom for you, shall I? Gina,' she said, addressing the woman behind, 'I'll take yours if you like.' And she was off collecting up the music – happy, chattering, as she used to be. I hoped everything would be all right. Jeremy had told me last night that the grant application for the hostel would have to go through the whole process again. He'd been assured that it was likely to be successful, but that everything had to be seen to be above board this time. Still, it meant the developments were delayed for another year and they might even have to reapply for planning permission.

'I wish she hadn't resigned,' Jeremy had said the week before. 'I'm a great believer in seeing things through. Jo's an excellent social worker – just the kind of person we want in the job.'

'She's got a couple of interviews lined up,' I was able to tell him. 'She'll be all right.'

Now, I watched her weave her way through the music stands to the front pew, where she started to help Dominic pack the scores into boxes. His long scarf trailed in the way so she stopped to coil it round his neck. Maybe they were still just friends – that's what she'd told me, anyway – but the manner in which he crouched, looking up at her as she tucked the fringe in neatly, that fond look on her face, suggested their friendship was developing into something new. Good old Dominic. I was certain Mrs Pryde would approve.

I passed my chair to one of Michael's team of helpers and was shaking out my coat when someone said, 'Fran.'

'Hello?' I swung round. 'Zac.' After the briefest of hesitations we hugged.

'Fan-blooming-tastic, you were,' he said. 'Never heard the piece before but it sure blows you away.'

'Thanks.' I laughed, suddenly very happy.

'So,' he said, and now he seemed hesitant again, 'I was wondering if you . . .'

'Fran, there you are.' Ben was rushing up to me, elated, throwing his arm round me, muttering a quick, 'Sorry to interrupt, old man,' to Zac before sweeping me away. I glanced behind me, trying to telegraph mock-alarm to Zac. He looked furious, but Ben had me firmly and was guiding me towards the door.

'Now you're coming to the party, aren't you?' he insisted. 'There are some people I want you to meet. A guy who's currently directing the Philharmonic, and his wife, she's something high up at the Opera House.' It was as though none of the bad stuff had happened. He was winding me up in that charm of his, that irresistible glamour. I was aware of his warm, strong hand, squeezing my arm through the silk of my blouse; I breathed in his delicious incensy smell. We moved towards the door. I glimpsed the lights of the hall and choir members peeling plastic film off plates of food.

Ben rattled on. 'This man you're going to meet. He's invited me to play the organ in . . .'

At the threshold of the church I hovered, experiencing a bolt of déjà vu. It had only been three months ago that I'd stood here waiting for Zac to finish in the chapel, watching the choir gather, saw Jo again, a moment later met Ben for the first time. I'd been waiting for Zac . . .

Despite Ben's restraining arm I turned, looked back into the church. Zac was standing there, arms crossed over his greatcoat, his normally shaggy hair tamed tonight, watching us with a furrowed expression, an air of magnificent loneliness about him.

'Come on, Fran,' Ben said, forging ahead, dragging me on. But it was all wrong. I knew that now. He held no enchantment for me any more.

'Ben,' I said, pulling away. 'I'm sorry. I'm not coming to the party. Not yet, anyway.'

'What?' he said, then he too noticed Zac. 'Oh,' he said, surprised. Then, 'I'll see you in a moment.' And he swaggered on into the hall on a sea of adulation.

I walked slowly back into the church. 'Sorry about that,' I told Zac, feeling suddenly shy. 'Ben doesn't easily take no for an answer.' Zac's stony look melted into a smile. He unfolded his arms in a gesture of release.

'It's taken you this long to see that?' he said.

I laughed, my confidence sweeping back. 'So where shall we go?'

'Thought you'd never ask,' he said. 'I promised you dinner. Ten o'clock's a bit late, but I need to talk to you about something.'

'Oh, OK.' How mysterious. 'I know a good tapas bar,' I said, remembering the place Jo had taken me. 'Then we needn't order a full meal.'

'Sounds great. Shall we go?' he said, helping me on with my coat.

'Should I have changed out of this outfit?' I asked, looking down at my long black skirt.

'Nah, you look great as you are.' And he meant it.

He waited while I checked my purse was still in my coat pocket then we hurried without a glance at the party, out into the frosty night.

Chapter 41

I saw Gabriel, like a maiden, or like the moon amongst the stars. His hair was like a woman's falling in long tresses ... He is the most beautiful of angels ... His face is like a red rose.

Ruzbehan Baqli

The roads were silent. We moved arm-in-arm, quiet as wraiths, slipping through pools of yellow lamplight, or striped by shadows of black railings, like prison bars, thrown by shafts of light from windows. Where people had forgotten to draw their curtains, tableaux of bookshelves and Christmas trees and flickering television screens could be glimpsed. Other lives, other worlds. We turned into a street where the old buildings lay dark and cold, sunk in their secrets. For a moment the mist separating past and present seemed so thin that I wouldn't have been surprised to see Laura hurrying ahead of us.

Opening the door to the tapas bar we walked firmly into the present: steamy, loud with a flamenco guitar and chatter. A couple were vacating a candlelit table in a corner behind a partition, and we took it, ordering food and drink before the waiter who came to clear had time to escape. He brought us the wine straight away.

We talked about the concert, joked about life behind the scenes at the vicarage. That morning, Jeremy had lost his spectacles and conducted an irritable hunt before his wife found them in the obvious place where he'd left them.

'Don't you feel you're on your best behaviour all the time there?' Zac asked, pouring us each more wine from the bottle. Through the candlelight he was rather Spanish-looking himself, with his black hair, dark, glittering eyes and five o'clock shadow.

'I did at first,' I said, 'but not now. They're very relaxed, really, and we're used to each other, so it's just the usual family rituals.' Family rituals. Dad and I used to have our own. Now he'd gone the memories were flooding back. Every day I could think of more good things about the past; remember our special Sunday breakfasts when I was small, walks by the river holding his hand, visits to churches where he explained the wonderful stained glass. The memories were tender, and precious, too.

'Jeremy and Sarah miss their daughters and having me with them helps,' I told Zac. 'I think fussing over me takes Sarah's mind off her worries about Miranda.'

'She's the younger one, is that right?'

'Yes, she suffers from anorexia. It's very difficult for her parents to know how to help – she keeps them at arm's length.'

'That's hard,' he said.

'Jo asked me to go and live with her again,' I told him, 'but I said no.'

'Wouldn't you feel more at home with her?' he asked.

'Funnily enough, no. Jo's place still feels like her parents' home. Anyway, I don't want to play gooseberry to her and Dominic.'

He smiled and I thought he looked distracted.

'What is it?' I asked, feeling that at last all barriers were down between us. He held his finger close to the candle flame, considering, and after a moment seemed to come to a decision of some sort.

'Fran,' he said. He couldn't look at me. 'I must tell you. I'm going away.'

'Away? What do you mean?' I was confused.

'It was while I was ill. I had time to think – about Olivia. I need to go and look for her, Fran.'

I tried to keep up. 'But you said you wouldn't ever go . . .'

'. . . where I wasn't wanted. Aye, I did. But it was something Amber said. She's a wise one, that girl. She asked me if I was at peace about it – not seeing Olivia, that is. And I said no, of course not. It torments me. And she said . . . she said I should forget my pride, go on the journey, trust and see what happened. That if you love someone, you have to work for them. Although there's a point where you have to stand back and wait, I needed to try my best first.'

'Oh,' I said, faintly. 'But where will you look? I thought she'd moved. How long will you be gone?'

'I'm going to start at the last address I had for them. I don't know how long I'll be, but I've a flight booked this week. Friday, in fact. The prices rise after that, it being the Christmas holidays. I had to decide quickly.'

'Friday,' I repeated, dully. 'But Zac, it's all so sudden.' So many questions formed in my mind, I didn't know which one to ask first, and a feeling of panic was rising.

'I need a break, Fran. To get away from everything. And I can't ask you to hold the job open. It wouldn't be fair on you. And perhaps I ought to try something new anyway. It's been a tough time.'

'I couldn't have got through it without you, Zac.' Tears were welling up now. I averted my face, not daring to let him see them. 'I don't want you to go. It's awful.'

'It's not awful, Fran. I'm really happy about it. I'm going to look for Olivia. Of course I won't turn up on the doorstep unannounced or anything. I'll find out where she is and then try to speak to Shona, get her to let me meet Olivia.'

'What happens if she won't let you?' I said, bravely looking straight at him now. I wouldn't cry. I wouldn't.

He took a slow sip of his wine, staring into the candle flame as though there were pictures in it only he could see. 'I don't know,' he said at last, unhappily. 'But at least I'll have tried. Better than sitting on my backside here, pining, isn't it?'

'When will you come back?'

'I don't know. The visa's for three months. I'm keeping up the flat for the moment, but putting my stuff into storage in case. David's looking after the glass for me. If I found a job out there, got permission to stay . . . well, maybe I'd do that. I don't know. I don't expect it would be that easy. I'll play it by ear.'

He would be gone, out of my life. I might never see him again. I hardly knew where I was, couldn't stop the tears now. I tried to look away, but he reached out his hand and touched my cheek.

'Hey,' he said really gently. 'You're crying. What's the matter? It's not the end of the world, you know.'

'Yes, it is,' I choked. The tears were coming thick and fast now. 'You can't go. Not now.' I grabbed a paper napkin and blew my nose.

'You silly girl. You'll be all right without me. You'll have Amber to help in the shop. And it shouldn't be too difficult finding someone to replace me.'

'It's not that. It's that I'll miss *you*, Zac.'

He sat there, taking in my stricken face. I watched him work it out and it was like the glimmer of a light dawning.

'You will miss me? Really? But you'll have Ben, won't you?' The expression in his eyes was unreadable.

'No, Zac, I won't have Ben. It's never really been Ben. Well, I thought it was for a bit but then I realised I was wrong.' Whatever I had felt for him was gone now. I'd been looking through a glass darkly, but now I could see the truth beyond. 'I didn't know it till just now, in the church. It's like . . . oh, I'm not putting this very well, Zac.'

He gazed at me across the table, frowning. I tried very hard to smile but my mouth wouldn't do it properly. Now I'd made a proper fool of myself.

'You don't want me to go?' he said quietly. 'You really don't?'

'I want you to find Olivia – it would be selfish of me not to. But I don't want you to go away. Or rather, I want you to come back. Very soon. I need you. I don't mean at the shop. Well, I do, of course. But it's for me. *I* need you.'

Zac stared at me for some time without speaking, a whole pantomime of emotions playing across his face. Finally he smiled, a crazy lopsided smile that became a laugh. His eyes sparkled, and now I knew that everything was all right. He reached for my hand, and we sat there holding hands, smiling stupidly at one another.

And then the waiter arrived with platters of food and merry small talk and we ate without speaking much, but still with plenty of looking at each other. Once he reached across and stroked my face. I grabbed his hand and put it to my lips, gave his finger the tenderest of little bites, which made him narrow his eyes. I held his big cool hand against my hot cheek and closed my eyes. I felt safe, protected.

'Dessert? *Café*?' asked the waiter when he withdrew the empty platters. Despite everything, we'd been ravenous.

Zac raised his eyebrows in question. 'No,' I said hastily. 'Thank you.'

I let Zac pay the bill and help me on with my coat and then once again we were out on the street. But this time, Zac's arm was round me, keeping me warm and safe. I wasn't alone any more.

Round the corner, out of sight of any passers-by, he drew me into the dark porch of some office block and we kissed. They were long, desperate kisses that left me dizzy and hungry for more. I knew the feel of his hair now, thick and springy, the roughness of his jaw, the gleam of his eyes, his skin ghostly pale in the darkness. I've no idea how much time passed. We didn't want to stop. When we came up, gasping for air, he wrapped me tightly inside his coat and I felt warm against the cold. Even so, I shivered.

'What shall we do now?' he whispered. 'No good going back to mine, it's all packed up. I'm sleeping on my own sofa.'

It was nearly midnight – too late to take him back to the vicarage. But we didn't want to say goodbye, not yet.

'I know,' I said.

The flat above *Minster Glass* was as cold inside as it was outside, the electricity being off, but we were providing our own warmth. It seemed right somehow making it a place of love again, snuggled up together in some blankets on the sofa, trying to ignore the smell of damp and smoke.

I felt so safe in his arms, as though I'd come home, really home, and I couldn't help but weep a little with happiness, as well as the thought that he was going away.

'Don't cry,' he whispered, kissing me again. After a moment he muttered in my ear, 'I love you.'

'I love you, too,' I replied wonderingly, and sat back to look at his face, strange and slightly sinister in the light from the street. I stroked his bristly cheek.

'I've loved you such a long time, Fran.'

'How long?' I asked, though I knew now. So many things

were starting to make sense. Zac's surliness. His deep misery. I'd put everything down to Dad or Olivia, but it hadn't just been them.

'Oh, only since you walked back through that door in September,' he said. 'Sad, eh?'

'Oh, Zac.'

'Yes, but you didn't notice me, did you? Not really.'

Why had I not seen it? Why do we never see these things? Because we're looking somewhere else, for something else, that's why. When what matters is right there in front of us.

'I didn't know for sure then,' he went on. 'Frankly, you got on my wick. I wanted you. I wasn't sure I liked you though. You seemed selfish.'

Selfish. Three months ago I'd have resented that. Now, it still hurt, but I saw why he might have got that impression of me. I had been closed up inside, like an unripe nut. 'You're a dark horse, Zac McDuff,' I told him. 'And you're horrible. Not liking me indeed.'

He threw back his head and laughed then, his eyes flashing in the golden light.

'But all that time I was with Ben . . .' I remembered. That must have hurt so much.

'I couldn't believe you didn't see through the guy,' Zac said savagely. 'He's got "flake" written all over him.'

I thought about that. Poor old Ben. Yes, he was 'poor old Ben' because, for all the ways in which he used people, he couldn't see himself clearly. He was blinded by the flame of ambition that fascinated him and, in the end, burned him. Still, it must have been hard for Zac to watch me with him, feeling unable to say or do anything. Certainly, I'd have put him in his place if he'd tried.

Amazingly, despite the cold, we fell asleep together until the sun rose next morning and hunger for food drove us out. We parted, promising to meet that evening. I sneaked back to the vicarage, let myself in and crept straight up the stairs, though I could hear Sarah clattering about in the kitchen. Only Lucifer, sitting by the radiator, saw me. He paused in his washing, with one leg in the air, his eyes gleaming accusingly. He was used to me now, but I couldn't say he approved of me. Jeremy and Sarah said nothing about my absence. But then perhaps they didn't know I hadn't been to bed.

We spent every hour we could together over the next few days, though what with rehearsals for a concert I was to play in at the Wigmore Hall during Christmas week and Zac needing to sort out final arrangements for his trip, the hours didn't add up to much.

'I'll be gone for just as long as it takes,' he said, stroking my hair. It was the Tuesday afternoon and we were sitting on a bench in St James's Park, the same bench where I'd seen Michael all those weeks ago. 'Then I'll be back. I promise.'

I opened my mouth to complain, then saw his face. He was holding back deep emotion and I knew I must say nothing. Although this was difficult for me, it was far more difficult for him. He was going alone on a journey into the unknown, and I needed to support him. I hugged him without speaking, and he held onto me so hard it hurt.

On his last night, Zac came to supper at the vicarage. Jo came too, with Dominic in tow. Although nothing was actually said, it had become obvious to me that my new surrogate parents had grown fond of Zac during the previous few months. When I explained somewhat shyly about the shift in our relationship, Sarah, with great tact, immediately took him under her wing as well, offering the address of some friends of theirs who lived in

Melbourne, who might offer him hospitality. She also mended a tear in his elderly jacket, a task that was utterly beyond me, let alone Zac.

Both Jo and Dominic had, in their different ways, changed. Jo seemed happier. In fact, she was almost back to the Jo I'd known at school, though there was something, a slight wariness, there now. Dominic seemed less anxious. He was back at work and life was less stressful now that his mother was in a home. Jo, being in between jobs, was to spend some time down in Horsham helping his sister Maggie clear out the family home as Maggie tired easily at this stage in her pregnancy.

'What are we doing at choir next term?' I asked Dominic at one point.

'The *Messiah*,' he replied. 'It always brings in the crowds and the music's easy to get hold of. I've been looking through everybody's questionnaires, by the way.'

'And?'

'Mixed bag,' he said. 'Ben will feel on the one hand encouraged – everyone appreciates his talent as a conductor – and on the other hand disappointed. Most want to aim for high standards. There are some who definitely share his vision, wanting to expand. But there are far more, I'm afraid, who think we should keep things pretty much as they are. Several grumble that the subscriptions are already too high.'

'Rather what I expected,' said the vicar, who had been steadily making his way through his roast lamb. 'I just hope Ben won't be demotivated. He's an excellent organist. We're damn lucky to have him.'

'Will you go to choir next term?' Zac asked me in a quiet moment, after Jo and Dominic had gone.

I considered the question. I wanted to. I'd enjoyed the singing and the camaraderie. 'Would you mind?' I asked Zac.

I watched the emotions struggle in his face. It wasn't easy for him to think of me seeing Ben, even in the distance up on his plinth. 'You'd do what you want to anyway,' he said finally, smiling. 'But for what it's worth, no, I don't mind.' He was saying, *I trust you*. I loved him for that.

'I might not have time, anyway, what with orchestral commitments and dealing with the shop. I'll try to though. I love the *Messiah*.' I knew it backwards. Maybe it wouldn't matter if I only went to some of the rehearsals.

The next morning, though the vicar had offered to drive us, Zac and I took a taxi through the early-morning darkness to the airport. It was the hardest thing in the world to watch him reach the front of the queue at the security gate, turn and wave one last time, and walk away into the crowds of the departure lounge.

Christmas was a tough time. No Dad, no Zac, no home. It was hard for the Quentins, too. They'd hoped for both their daughters to visit, but on Christmas Eve, shortly before Fenella and her fiancé arrived, a telephone call came from Miranda. She wasn't coming. Jeremy and I sat at the kitchen table, he with his head in his hands, listening as Sarah begged and pleaded with her, offered for Jeremy to go to Bristol to fetch her, but she refused. Perhaps they could come and see her at New Year, Miranda said, but we all felt she was fobbing them off. After the call ended, Sarah cried and Jeremy comforted her. I glanced at the photograph of Miranda on the dresser, a happy, engaging child in school uniform; no hint there of the anxieties of anorexia to come.

I wondered how Zac was getting on, finding Olivia. At first

we communicated regularly. Phone calls from Melbourne came, sometimes at odd hours of the night, when he sounded miserable and alone. Once, after he'd spent the evening with the Quentins' friends, he sounded more cheerful.

It took a week for him to locate Shona and Olivia, and another week to be allowed to speak to Shona. It turned out that she hadn't lived at her parents' address, where he'd been sending his cards, for many years. The elderly neighbour who told him this didn't know where she had gone, but informed him that she was married. Shona's father had, he said, died two years before, and the widow had moved the previous Christmas to a smaller house on the other side of the city. Too soon for her address to appear in phone books, Zac discovered when he went looking for E. Donaldsons. So he tried phoning other Donaldsons on the list and finally, just before Christmas, he'd tracked down Shona's uncle, given him his number at the little hotel where he was staying, and waited.

Down the phone late on Christmas Eve, Zac veered between sounding nervous and glum. He was to spend the following day with the Quentins' friends, I was relieved to hear. But I thought about him all of Christmas Day.

A week passed while the Donaldson clan consulted one another, then Zac returned to his lodgings one evening to find that Shona had called.

Zac rang me at the vicarage just after Christmas with the news that he'd seen Olivia. I couldn't make much sense of him, he was so overwhelmed, but I gathered some facts. Shona was married to a man who already had children of his own. It had been sensible to explain to Olivia as she grew up that she had a father in Britain, but that her mother wasn't able to see him any more.

'She didn't try, Fran, that's what's so hurtful,' he said. 'She could have been in touch but decided not to. It was tidier that way.'

'But she let you see your daughter today.'

'Her mother persuaded her that it would be best for Olivia. That, otherwise, Olivia might one day find out how much I had wanted to see her and would never be able to forgive her mother. Shona didn't want me to go to the house so the three of us met at a café for lunch. It was strange, so strange, seeing my daughter for the first time. Since she was a tiny baby, I mean. She's still very like Shona, but the way she moves – you'll laugh, but it reminds me of my mam. And yet they never met. How do our genes do that?'

'No idea.' I laughed. 'What's she like? As a person, I mean.'

'Quite poised and serious. She listens to you very carefully. I felt like . . . I don't know, a stranger she was being polite to. But I think she was pleased to see me. Shona's very protective of her, but I'm allowed to see her again in a couple of days. I didn't know where you take a child, but Shona's suggested roller-skating. Let's hope I can remember how to do it.'

I laughed at the thought of Zac stumbling around on skates. 'Don't kill yourself,' I said, 'for heaven's sake. I need you back in one piece.'

'You'll get me back,' he replied softly. 'But I think my heart will be in two pieces, one half here with my daughter.'

I'd thought long and hard about that. Some women might have minded, but I knew what it was like to grow up without one parent. I was proud of Zac and what he was doing, and would support him every inch of the way.

I just wanted him to come home.

Jeremy and Sarah did go down to stay with their younger daughter at New Year, leaving me alone in the house. It proved a useful time. The builders were due to start work on *Minster Glass* on the first Monday of the New Year, and I still had things to sort out.

It was strange going upstairs into Dad's attic after so long. Everything was just as I'd left it – the manuscript for his history on the desk, heaps of files and rolls of paper strewn around. I knew I had to tidy up.

The surprise came when I pulled open the desk drawers in a search for new elastic bands; the ones on some of the rolls kept breaking because they'd dried out. One drawer was stacked full of little engagement diaries, from the 1920s and 1930s, I saw. No time to look at those now. In another was a cache of picture postcards depicting stained-glass windows from around the world. Now which of my family had 'Jim' been, the person who'd sent them?

There was a ball of elastic bands in the bottom drawer, and there, too, I found a cardboard tube with a roll of paper inside. It was a family tree, meticulously written out in Dad's distinctive handwriting. I opened it out flat on the desk, and there we all were, Ashes and Russells and Morrisons staggering down through 130 years of history. And it was as I had hoped. Laura, married to Philip, was my great-great-great-grandmother. Her son Samuel, born in 1882, had married Reuben Ashe's granddaughter, so Reuben was my ancestor, too.

Dad had underscored the names of anyone who had actually owned *Minster Glass* and Samuel was one of them. Philip and Marie's son John was not. In brackets next to his name, Dad had written *Joined maternal grandfather's shipping business*. Maybe John had inherited that *palazzo* in Verona, too.

Laura had given birth to five children. All of them had survived to reach maturity, I was glad to see, but a different mortality was to strike their generation. Her third son died in

1915, aged thirty. It was impossible to tell from the simple chart how he died, but easy to believe it was at the front in France or Belgium.

I gazed around the attic, wondering what other secrets were hidden here. Maybe there'd be a photograph of Laura somewhere; if not with the business archives, somewhere else, downstairs. When I had more time, I'd search. And maybe one day I'd carry on writing Dad's history of *Minster Glass*. I felt that's what he would have wanted.

Chapter 42

'Hold it up higher. Higher. There now, don't move while I look.'

Amber marched outside and posed, head to one side, hands on hips, to make her judgement. A lifting gesture with her hands and Anita's lodger Larry, teetering on a chair, raised the new angel another six inches on its chain. Amber frowned and signed again. Down half an inch, the angel swaying dangerously, and she nodded enthusiastically. He slipped the link over the hook above the window and stepped down with obvious relief.

'She's a hard woman to please, that Amber,' he moaned, rubbing his aching arms.

'Don't think you've finished yet, Larry. When you've recovered there's the champagne to unpack,' I told him, smiling, and left him hefting bottles onto the table next to the glasses whilst I went outside to join Amber.

We contemplated the new angel with satisfaction. Amber had made her entirely by herself. In colour and design, as we had both agreed we wanted, she was similar to the one destroyed in the fire. But, of course, under Amber's hands she had come out slightly differently. She looked younger, this angel, and more feisty than Dad's 1970s' version.

'She's beautiful,' I told Amber. And now that she was in place, the shop was truly ready. I checked my watch. 'Only half an hour till people start arriving.'

'I'll help Anita bring the sandwiches,' Amber said. I watched her vanish into the café, thinking how assured she had grown over the previous couple of months. It was the beginning of February and she had been enrolled on a local college course for a month, spending much of her time on her special project, this angel. Her relationship with Larry was gentle, slow-flowering, but they were natural together, as happy as sandboys. Larry had recently begun his training in hotel management. I wondered what Mrs Finnegan back in County Kerry would think of a half-Egyptian girl for her beloved youngest, and crossed my fingers that Amber's guileless charm – and her love of angels – would make everything all right.

I gave the window one more glance then went back into the shop to help Larry.

'It'll be a squash in here,' I told him as he polished glasses with a professional flourish. 'But we can always spill over into the workshop.'

'Or out the door,' he agreed. 'It's such a lovely day for a party.'

And it was. A beautiful, unseasonably warm Saturday. There had been frost on the garden when I'd gone out first thing, but this had quickly melted, leaving dew sparkling on the branches and shrubs. Now even that had evaporated and everything looked fresh.

The party for the reopening of *Minster Glass* was Amber's idea, too. The builders had worked incredibly hard over the last five weeks, making good the structure, rewiring and decorating the whole of the ground floor, restoring the floorboards and fittings. Instead of the old musty whiff, the air was redolent with woodstain and fresh paint. The shelves were packed with new glass, the ceiling dotted with coloured lampshades, the walls sparkling with mirrors and glass picture frames. Like Amber's angel, everything had been restored to look like the vanished old, but couldn't stop itself looking new. I could live with that.

I was delighted with it all, especially the new lighting, and I hoped that Zac, when he came home, would be pleased with the workshop, with its smart shelving, state-of-the-art work-tables and machines. *If he comes home*, a little voice said inside me.

Late on New Year's Day, he'd phoned to say that he'd decided to go travelling. 'It seems crazy not to, now I'm here,' he said, and although I was disappointed I tried not to let him know it. There was something different in his voice, a lightness I'd not heard before. He'd seen Olivia two or three times more over the holiday, he told me, and then, on the spur of the moment, he'd bought a plane ticket to Sydney.

A week later, a postcard of the harbour arrived, marked with a tiny cross on the skyline: *My hostel here.* A week after that a picture of Ayers Rock at sunset slipped onto the Quentins' doormat. Finally, last week, a fleet of brightly coloured fish announced that he'd reached the Barrier Reef. Scrawled on the back was, *You won't believe the amazing things I've seen. The landscape's spectacular, the blue of the sea like light through opalescent glass. See ya, Zac xxx.*

I propped it up on the bookshelf next to the others, picked them up one by one and studied them. There was no mention of coming home. He hadn't phoned for a couple of weeks, apart from leaving a message several evenings before, when we were all out. It said something about being 'on the hoof' and that he'd ring again. He hadn't. I had no address for him except the

Quentins' friends in Melbourne. In the end I got fed up with wondering and wrote to them enclosing a letter for Zac. It was a newsy letter; I hoped the light tone would disguise how much I'd agonised over it. I reminded him how beautiful London was in the pale January light, told him I'd been asked to play the Vaughan Williams Tuba Concerto at a music festival in Birmingham the following month, that his friend David sent his best. Oh, and that the shop was nearly finished, and there was already a backlog of orders building. It didn't feel right to plead with him to return. He needed space. But I prayed that thoughts of life going on here without him would make him want to come home.

I passed the letter across the post office counter and turned to leave. Suddenly I wished that I'd been warmer, that I'd begged him to get in touch, to come home. But it was all too late. I could only wait and see.

Now I opened the shop door to let Anita and Amber in with their trays of little sandwiches, then helped them lay everything on the counter next to the stack of paper plates and serviettes.

'I'm so glad you'll open again, dear,' said Anita, brushing away my thanks. 'It's bad for business having a burned-out shop next door. This'll be good for all of us. Oh, I don't know how you can stand all these mirrors. I wouldn't be able to get away from myself.'

I laughed.

'They make it ever so sparkly and bright,' said Amber, spinning round the room in a little dance.

'Amber . . .'

'Careful of the GLASSES,' Larry yelled, just in time.

'Look – guests!' I said, spotting Jo and Dominic walking down the pavement towards us, hand-in-hand. 'And there are the Quentins.' Jeremy was cradling a vast bouquet.

'Don't worry, I'm always careful with the corks,' Larry said, catching my anxious eye as he twisted the wire off a champagne bottle.

Soon the shop was full of people. Zac's friends David and Janie brought their children, who soon went off to play in the garden. Ra came from the hostel. Everything had settled down there now. Cassie and Lisa had both been charged with offences to property and bailed. They had been sent to other accommodation. The vicar's wife had visited them once or twice. Though accused of the worse offence, Cassie was so obviously remorseful there was a good chance that her crime would be seen for what it was – a thoughtless prank that had gone badly wrong. Lisa, though, was a harder case, had reacted aggressively to attempts to help her. 'But she's exactly the wrong kind of person to send to prison,' Sarah sighed, and I had to agree.

'Amber is so happy now,' Ra whispered to me, sipping Buck's fizz. 'The change in the girl is astonishing.'

'She's easy to help,' I said.

'And lucky to find someone like you to give her a chance. That's all some of these youngsters need.' I smiled. Ra couldn't have been more than thirty himself, but with his round wire glasses and earnest expression he seemed fatherly.

'Fran, how are you? This is all simply marvellous.' Mrs Armitage sailed up in a cloud of scent, her husband close behind. 'I've been showing the children's panels to all my friends, you know. You mustn't be surprised if you get a few orders.'

'Well, thank you,' I said. 'Amber will be delighted to hear that.'

Michael and Nina arrived shortly afterwards. 'Sorry we're late. Nina had a rehearsal,' said Michael, shaking my hand. 'She's started work with a new pianist,' he whispered confidentially, as Nina fetched them drinks. 'Have you heard? About Ben, I mean.'

'What?' I looked around for Ben. After um-ing and ah-ing I'd decided to invite him, but there was no sign of him.

Before Michael could reply, we were interrupted. 'An excellent party, Miss Morrison. The champagne's superb.' It was the bookseller, his wild hair carefully combed down for the occasion. He introduced himself to Michael and soon they were talking hammer and tongs about first editions of James Joyce, and I went over to speak to Jeremy, who was studying one of the lamps in the window. 'Sarah has been admiring this lovely thing,' he said, 'and I was wondering whether it was a hint for me to buy it for her. Do you think she means it?'

'I think it would look beautiful in your living room,' I said, my mind working quickly. 'But I want to make you both a present of it. To say thank you.'

'Oh, there's no need to do that,' he said, looking embarrassed.

'If Sarah really does like it, then I insist.' I smiled, turning as Sarah came to join us. Jeremy explained and Sarah looked as excited as a small child.

'Thank you so much. That's so kind of you. But you know dear, we've loved having you.'

'And I've loved being with you both. Now I've lost Dad, it's like having another family.'

'I know,' said Sarah, hugging me, 'and that's how we feel about you, isn't it, Jeremy? I'm so glad the shop looks so lovely and it'll be wonderful to sort out your flat. Was it next week they were going to make a start?'

'Yes, so I won't be taking up space in your house that much longer.'

'Take as long as you need to. You know that.'

'Thank you.'

Jeremy cleared his throat. 'I had a strange letter from Ben earlier. It's . . . well, it's a letter of resignation.'

'Oh!' This must be the news Michael had meant. I felt suddenly strange. 'Why?'

'He's been offered some amazing job in the States, conducting a new orchestra. Boston, I think his letter said. It starts at Easter.'

'Boston? Really?' I couldn't believe it. Not that he wasn't talented, but he wasn't known as a conductor. How an earth had he blagged his way into that?

Michael appeared and explained. 'This chap from the Phil came to the concert and was impressed by Ben, apparently. He thought of him when an American colleague mentioned that they were recruiting. Put in a word for him. It's connected with some college there, so he gets his accommodation thrown in.' Michael laughed. 'Always falls on his feet, does Ben.'

Lucky Ben. Once again, then, he was flitting on to the next opportunity, not ever really having to face the mess he left behind; going on undoubtedly to create more havoc. Part of me was glad. It wasn't easy having him living across the Square, a constant reminder of my foolishness. And maybe with him abroad, Michael and Nina would have more of a chance together.

'It's a nuisance for the choir,' I said.

'Yes, and the church. Still, they've got a couple of months to sort it out, and there are always people around who can fill in for a bit.'

I moved on to talk to David, who hadn't heard from Zac either; then, feeling slightly depressed, I introduced myself to a woman on her own who turned out to be a friend of one of our best customers. She hinted at the possibility of a big commission for some luxury flats she and her husband were designing out of a deconsecrated chapel. 'The old glass is poor quality and a new design will make a splendid centrepiece to the common staircase,' she said.

'It sounds right up our street,' I told her firmly. 'I'll be in touch.'

Quite who'd design it without Zac here, I didn't know. But I couldn't turn business away. Perhaps David would do it as a freelance job.

It was well after three before everybody left. Then there was just Jo and Dominic, Amber and myself clearing away. Larry had to go to work and Anita had returned next door. Finally there was just me, locking up the shop.

I stood there on the pavement, in my coat and beret, looking up at *Minster Glass* just as I had done a few months ago, on my return to London. How much had changed in that short time.

I'd lost my father and found my mother. I'd helped recreate a beautiful window and, in the course of it, discovered a whole story from the past about people who belonged to me and about this shop that was now mine. Whatever happened – whether Zac came home or not – I'd found my place in the world.

It was late afternoon of the following Tuesday, and I was in the living room of my flat piling papers and books into boxes in preparation for its decoration. The men had started with my bedroom, moving most of the furniture into Dad's room. I'd just found an ancient address book of Dad's and, following up a hunch, had turned to B for Beaumont. In my mother's rounded handwriting, familiar from her inscription in the Edward Burne-Jones book, was written *John and Lily Beaumont*, followed by an address in Suffolk. My grandparents were dead, of course, and someone else would live there now. What was more useful was the name underneath, Gillian Beaumont. Dad's letter had mentioned my mother having a sister. The address, a hospital nurses' home, would be out of date, and if she'd married she'd have a different name. But maybe, just maybe, if I wanted to at some point, I could try to find out what had happened to her. It was an exciting thought, that I might have an aunt somewhere, even cousins.

While I was thinking about this I looked idly out of the window. The sun had disappeared now and the February afternoon was settling down into gloomy twilight. The bare trees shivered in a slight wind. There were two or three people crossing the garden. A woman in black high heels with a briefcase, her head held high; a shabby old man in a duffel coat limping along and, in the distance, a tall figure trudging under the weight of a rucksack.

My eye was drawn to the backpacker. He had untidy black hair and a beard, I saw as he came closer, and although he seemed dragged down by the weight of his burden he was walking quickly, eagerly. There was something about his gait that reminded me of Zac. But then, so many things reminded me of Zac. I watched him a moment longer and all the time a suspicion grew inside me until it became a certainty: it *was* Zac.

I'm not sure how I got down those stairs and out of the shop. Perhaps, like the angels in heaven, I flew. All I know is that I was on the pavement and it was Zac and he stopped and we stared at each other from opposite sides of the road, and then he shrugged off his backpack and held out his arms and I was nipping between the hooting cars and into his arms.

'So when did your plane land and why didn't you tell me you were coming?' I asked, breaking away from our embrace to look at him. He'd changed, there was no doubt about it. It wasn't just the hair and the beard and the fact that his pale skin was burned by the sun, there was something different about his expression. His face was more open. He looked free and happy.

'Hang on,' he said. 'Give me a moment to breathe. I'm trying to take all this in.' We were back in the shop now and I was amused when he started looking around at everything, literally open-mouthed.

'Why didn't you say you were coming?' I couldn't help asking. 'I'd have gone to meet you.'

'I wanted to surprise you,' he called over his shoulder.

'You certainly did that.' *Why didn't you write for so long?* I wanted to say. *Or phone?* But something made me hold back. The old nervousness and fear.

'Sorry. He-ey, look at this! Wow!' He'd pushed open the door to the workshop now and I followed in after him. He went straight across to the sparkling new kiln and started opening all the little doors, pulling out the trays, then turned the new ceiling lights on and off. 'This is amazing.'

'There's an etching tool arriving, too,' I gabbled, 'and you should say if there's anything else you need. That is—' I stopped, remembering that I didn't even know what his plans were. He might not want to come back and work here at all.

'What were you saying?' he prompted, coming over and taking me in his arms once more. It was a while before I could answer.

'Zac,' I said, pushing him gently away. Then giving him my sternest look, I said, 'The best thing to do right now is surely to go up and open a bottle.'

'I'm sorry I wasn't in touch much after Melbourne,' he said, taking a gulp of his wine. We were sitting amidst the mess in the living room now, both of us on the sofa, not quite touching. 'I had a sort of crisis, I suppose. It was great seeing Olivia, really great, and I got on quite well with Shona, considering everything. You know, she's thinking about bringing Olivia over, maybe next year if she can get the time off work. So I'll see her then, show her around London. Maybe I could take her up to Glasgow to meet Dad.'

'That's good.'

'After a week or two in Melbourne I got quite depressed. OK, there was a weight lifted off my shoulders. I'd done what I'd come to do – and then I didn't know what to do next. It was the Quentins' friends who helped me. They suggested I go off and see the country, and that turned out to be the best idea. But it was weird too, being on my own. I was so busy looking after myself, talking to people I met and seeing everything, I didn't think much about here. Well, that sounds bad. I did think of you, a lot, but in a peaceful way. I had to sort myself out.'

'And did you?' I needed to know.

'I think I did, yes.'

I studied his dear face, noticed again that he seemed happier, more relaxed, and said, 'You know, I think you have too.' I leaned forward and took his glass from him and we kissed, this time passionately.

We had so much to discuss but, just for the moment, nothing else in the world mattered except that we were together.

*

4 June 2003

When I finally lay down my pen I see it's dark outside. I sit alone in the pool of light from Dad's old desk lamp. Even the ghosts have left me now, their whispers dying away to silence. My story is finished.

Downstairs, Zac will be sorting through paperwork for tomorrow's tasks and listening out for little Teddy, asleep in the front bedroom. He's five now, Teddy, our light and our joy, a mischievous little angel with his father's dark curls.

Sometimes I like to sit quietly and watch him sleep.

And sometimes I wonder what happened to another little boy – a boy with no mother – who grew to manhood more than a hundred years ago.

Coda

April 1881

'He still won't speak.'

'Poor mite. Shall I go and say goodnight?'

'You can try. You'll get nothing out of him.'

'He's still so small, Philip.' Only five, only a year older than Ned had been.

'He's old enough to speak when he's spoken to.'

'He's endured so much.'

'You try then.' Philip settled in a seat by the fire and started to read his book. Laura closed the drawing-room door quietly behind her, hesitating, her fingers still on the handle, listening. Upstairs there was silence. In the hall the great clock tocked away the seconds. The sunset crawled across the floor.

'*Help me,*' she breathed.

She climbed the stairs, pushed open the door to John's room.

Lying in the half-darkness he lifted his head. But when he saw her he turned onto his front and wriggled down under the bedclothes until just the crown of his dark head was visible.

'John,' she whispered. He didn't move. She crossed the room and sat herself on the edge of his bed. 'John, dear.' He shifted slightly. What should she do now?

It was the first night that he'd stayed with them; the third night since their return from honeymoon, an ecstatically happy three-week tour of Italy. She'd wandered through churches and galleries, looking and looking at everything while Philip sketched and painted. And now they were home and real married life had begun. But already they'd struck a rock, and that rock was her stepson's unhappiness.

She'd not seen much of John alone before the wedding. He'd always been in the company of his rather formidable grandparents, usually in the drawing room of their house in Eaton Square. John would be ushered in by his nanny in his best clothes; expected to shake hands with his father and bow to Laura. A pall of grief hung over proceedings. The boy was cowed.

But now, although his principal residence was for the moment to remain Eaton Square, he was expected to come and stay in Lupus Street often, or rather in the new house they would be seeking soon.

'John,' she tried again now. 'Your father is vexed that you won't speak to us. Tell me what's wrong, please. I want to help you.'

Still nothing. Was that a little sigh, or was he weeping? She reached out her hand and gently stroked his hair, finding it soft, hot and damp. He jerked his head away.

'John,' she said, slightly sterner now. Then, more gently, 'What's the matter?'

A sob. He was crying then.

'Oh darling,' she whispered, helpless, 'don't cry, don't cry, everything's all right.' Again she stroked his hair and this time he didn't pull away, so she bent across him, tried to cuddle his small huddled form. 'What's the matter?' she whispered again.

He muttered something.

'What did you say, dear?'

'I want my mama. I want her.'

His trembling tones pierced her heart. 'Oh John, I'm so sorry.'

'I want my mama. Mama.' And now he was crying in earnest into the mattress and what could she do but peel back the blankets and scoop him up into her arms. 'My mama, my mama, my mama. I want my mama.' He burrowed into her and she held him tightly, rocking him, soothing him with words that came instinctively, words of comfort and love.

'I'll be your mama, little one,' she told him. 'I'll be your mama.'

'You can't be my mama,' he sobbed. 'My mama's with the angels and they won't let her go. I hate them, I hate the angels.'

'The angels are looking after her, darling,' she said. What on earth had his grandparents told him? 'And she's having a lovely time. She's watching you, you know, looking out for her little boy, wanting him to be good. And . . .' Laura was feeling desperate now '. . . she wants me to help look after you, I know she does.'

The boy sobbed once or twice more then lay trembling and hot in her arms, like a small wounded animal. She stroked his hair and rocked him for what felt like hours. Then, as his eyelids began to close, she laid him in the bed and pulled the clothes up around him. His eyes fluttered open for a moment, bright in the gloom. He yawned suddenly and said sleepily, 'Are you an angel, too?'

For a second she didn't understand what he meant. Then she grasped it. She would look after him like the angels looked after his mother. Yes, she liked that idea. She would guard him as long as he needed her.

'Yes,' she said. 'I'll be your angel.'

His long-fringed eyes closed now and he sighed. She kissed him gently and sat by his side until the room sank into darkness.